T
CRIC]
WHO'S WHO
2006

Foreword by
ANDREW STRAUSS

Edited by
CHRIS MARSHALL

Statistics by
RICHARD LOCKWOOD

Photographs by
GETTY IMAGES

This edition first published in the UK in 2006 by Green Umbrella Publishing

© Green Umbrella Publishing 2006
www.greenumbrella.co.uk

Publishers: Jules Gammond, Tim Exell and Vanessa Gardner

ISBN: 1905009399

Editor (for Green Umbrella Publishing): Kirsty Ennever
Picture research: Ellie Charleston
Quiz compiled by Peter Brierley
Cover design by Newleaf Design
Printed and bound in Italy

ACKNOWLEDGEMENTS

Cover photographs by Getty Images, 101 Bayham Street, London, NW1 0AG

The publishers would also like to thank the county clubs, the players
and their families for their assistance in helping to assemble
the information and photographs in this book.

Extra information has also been gathered from the pages of *The Wisden Cricketer*,
The Times, *The Sunday Times*, Cricinfo.com and CricketArchive.com

Thanks also to the following for providing additional photographs:
Bill Smith, Sam Bowles/Bowles Associates, Cambridge University CCE, Cricinfo,
Derby Evening Telegraph, Derbyshire CCC, Empics, Essex CCC, Gerard Farrell,
Glamorgan CCC, John Dawson Cricket Images, Kent Messenger Group, Kieran
Galvin (07866 733258, www.photoboxgallery.com/liveactionsport), Mikal
Ludlow/Gloucestershire Echo, Neville Chadwick Photography, Oxford University
Sports Federation, Pete Norton Photography, Richmond CC/Chris Goldie, Roger
Wootton, Sarah Williams, Scarborough Evening News, Shropshire Star, South
Australian Cricket Association, Solent News and Photo Agency, Somerset CCC,
Sussex CCC, SWpix, Vic Isaacs, Worcestershire CCC, www.durhamccc.co.uk

CONTENTS

SUPPORT CRICKET'S OFFICIAL CHARITY

Since 1950 The Lord's Taverners has given away more than £38 million in grant aid. In 2005 we gave away over 1,000 cricket equipment bags to clubs and schools and funded the installation of non-turf pitches, coaching projects and youth competitions across the UK.

Andrew 'Freddie' Flintoff - President of The Young Lord's Taverners presenting the 750th minibus

We also fund specialised sports and recreational equipment, including minibuses and sports wheelchairs, for youngsters with special needs.

Help us give young people in your area a sporting chance. Visit our website or call free on 0800 279 3520 to find out how we can help and how you can help us!

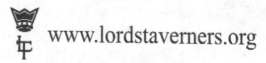
www.lordstaverners.org

FOREWORD
by Andrew Strauss

What a summer 2005 was! A vibrant domestic campaign and the battle for the Ashes captured the public's imagination, with our game enjoying unprecedented media coverage, raising the profile of cricket both in this country and beyond. Our titanic battles with Australia proved that athletes can engage in fiercely competitive, high-pressure sport, within the spirit of the game and with a smile on our faces. But can  cricket build on this new-found popularity? The football World Cup will cast a shadow over the coverage of competing sports this summer, but cricket shouldn't worry, with the exciting Pakistan and Sri Lanka teams visiting our shores. Both these sides defeated us in their backyards last time around and we are desperate to put the record straight. And then there's the small matter of the Ashes to defend, followed by the Cricket World Cup, hosted by the West Indies. Watch this space …

The one-day domestic season has undergone a restructure for 2006. The 50-over Cheltenham & Gloucester Trophy will take place over the first half of the season, with the 18 First-Class Counties being divided into two conferences, north and south. The winner of the northern conference will play the winner of the southern conference in the final at Lord's in August. A new 40-over league will be contested in the second half of the season, with the seventh-placed side in Division One playing off against the third-placed team in Division Two to decide the final place in Division One for the following season. The ever-popular Twenty20 Cup will be played in between these competitions and is sure to be a huge draw. In the four-day game, the Liverpool Victoria brand have taken over from their Frizzell affinity brand to sponsor the County Championship, and 2006 will see just two sides being promoted from Division Two and relegated from Division One instead of the three of previous years. These innovative changes to the structure of the game will challenge us, as cricketers, to produce an even more skilful and exciting product. And that can only be good for English cricket.

Our game really is thriving at all levels. The ECB have launched the brilliant Chance to Shine initiative at grass-roots, the Twenty20 Cup, as mentioned earlier, is the most exciting new competition since Kerry Packer got involved in cricket, and there is a fantastic new broadcasting deal with Sky that will undoubtedly raise the media bar through to 2009. Behind the scenes the PCA, with strong support from the ECB, continues to expand its impressive player services, especially the vital education programme which ensures that cricketers have real options for second careers. We, the players, are more involved than ever through the PCA as genuine stakeholders, and optimism abounds because we know the game is in good health.

So I urge you to enjoy the 2006 season – I'm sure it's going to be a cracker! Become involved in your county, at your club, playing, watching and, throughout, relishing your part in our great game. Thank you for your support.

Andrew Strauss
January 2006

Editor's Notes

The cricketers listed in this volume include all those who played 1st XI cricket for a first-class county at least once last season, in first-class cricket and the major domestic one-day competitions, and all those registered (at the time of going to press at the beginning of March) to play for the 18 first-class counties in 2006. The umpires' section contains the officials making up the first-class list for 2006. All players' statistics are complete to the end of the last English season (the Stop press section for individual players notes subsequent highlights) and cover first-class fixtures and the domestic one-day competitions. They do not include other matches such as limited-overs games against touring sides; neither do such matches qualify as a county debut for the purposes of this book. Test and ODI tallies for umpires are up to and including 5 March 2006.

This year sees the introduction of a new category – Player website – to enable players to publish their website details, and cricket followers to find out more about a particular player online. Meanwhile, to conserve space, I have discontinued many of the statistical extracts previously given in each player's entry (1st-Class 50s, 1st-Class 100s etc), although I have kept tallies of multiple 100s for players and one-day 100s and one-day five-wicket innings for umpires who are former players, since these cannot be found in the statistics tables. Numbers of 100s given in these tables include all multiples (200s, 300s etc). Statistics for 2005 are not given for players whose appearances in first-class cricket or one-day competitions that season were only for teams other than a county – e.g. universities (excluding international cricketers on tours to England). These appearances are, however, reflected in their career statistics and reference is made in the Extras section to the team for which they played.

Figures about 1000 runs, 50 wickets and 50 dismissals in a season refer to matches in England only. The figures for batting and bowling averages refer to the full first-class English list for 2005, followed in brackets by the 2004 figures. Inclusion in the batting averages depends on a minimum of six completed innings and an average of at least 10.00; a bowler has to have taken at least ten wickets and bowled in a minimum of six innings. Season strike rates for bowlers are allocated according to the same criteria, although any player who has taken a first-class wicket is given a career strike rate. 'Strike rate' refers to a bowler's record of balls bowled per wicket taken.

In the section on Overseas tours, the layout 'England to Pakistan 2005-06 (one-day series)', for example, indicates that a player was selected for only the one-day portion of the tour; the layout 'England to Zimbabwe (one-day series) 2004-05', on the other hand, indicates that the tour consisted of a one-day series only.

The following abbreviations apply: ODI means One-Day International; * means not out. In statistics tables All First means all first-class matches, including figures for Test matches, which are also extracted and listed separately; 1-Day Int – One-Day Internationals; C&G – C&G Trophy (including NatWest); tsL – totesport League (including previous one-day and Sunday leagues); Twenty20 – Twenty20 Cup.

Please note that Worcestershire ceased awarding caps in 2001 and now present 'colours' to each player who appears for the county in the Championship; in addition, beginning in 2004 Gloucestershire have awarded caps to players on making their first first-class appearance for the county.

A book of this complexity and detail has to be prepared several months in advance of the cricket season, and occasionally there are recent changes in a player's circumstances or the structure of the game which cannot be included in time. Many examples of facts, statistics and even opinions which can quickly become outdated in the period between the compilation of the book and its publication, months later, will spring to the reader's mind, and I ask him or her to make the necessary commonsense allowance and adjustments.

Since the last edition, *The Cricketers' Who's Who* has undergone a change of ownership, having joined the Green Umbrella list. As a consequence the project is no longer under the long-time guiding hand of Adrian Stephenson, who previously published the book under the Queen Anne Press imprint and who personally did so much to nurse each edition into print. I would like to thank Adrian for his continued advice and support during the production of this first edition with Green Umbrella Publishing.

Chris Marshall, March 2006

THE PLAYERS

KOLPAK

If a cricketer is a national of a country that has an Association Agreement with the EU (such as South Africa or Zimbabwe) and also has a valid UK work permit, he enjoys the same right to work within the EU as an EU citizen and may be eligible to play county cricket as a domestic (that is, non-overseas) player. Cricketers playing in England under this system are commonly referred to as Kolpak players, after the Kolpak ruling, a judgement in the European Court of Justice that found in favour of Maros Kolpak, a Slovakian handball goalkeeper who challenged his status as a non-EU player in Germany.

ONE-DAY INTERNATIONALS

January 5, 2006, was the 35th anniversary of the first One-Day International, which was contested by Australia and England at the MCG in 1971. Throughout the book there are 100 quiz questions relating to ODIs. Facts and figures are up to February 21, 2006.

PCA Calendar of Events 2006

Date		Event	Venue
April	24th	PCA Annual Conference – "Building Partnerships"	Brit Oval
May	17th	Regus Golf Tour	Brockett Hall
June	13th	PCA Masters v Sri Lanka – Twenty20	Arundel Cricket Ground
	15th	PCA Masters v Hampshire XI – Twenty20	The Rosebowl
	21st	Regus Golf Tour	Copt Heath
	26th	PCA Masters v Yorkshire XI	Sheffield
	27th	Regus Golf Tour	Mere
July	3rd	PCA Charity Golf Day	Little Aston
	6th	Regus Golf Tour	Worplesdon
	11th	Marriott Summer of Cricket Dinner	Marriott Regents Park
	13th	Lord's Test Match Breakfast and Match tickets	Marriott Regents Park/Lord's
	23rd	PCA Masters v Barton Under Needwood CC	Barton Under Needwood
	30th	PCA Masters v Frinton	Frinton CC
August	3rd	PCA Masters v Rensburg	High Town CCC
	17th	Oval Test Match Breakfast and Match hospitality	Marriott County Hall
	18th	Oval Test Match Breakfast and Match hospitality	Marriott County Hall
	28th	PCA Masters v Gloucestershire XI – Twenty20	Gloucestershire CCC - Bristol
September	6th	Getty's Garden Party 6 a side cricket	Sir JP Getty's Estate
	7th	Getty's Garden Party 6 a side cricket	Sir JP Getty's Estate
	25th	PCA Awards Evening	Royal Albert Hall
	TBA	International 20/20	Leicestershire CCC
October	12th-15th	Regus Golf Tour Finale	Europe- venue TBA
	26th	JLT John Inverdale Dinner - Grange City Hotel	London
November	TBA	PCA Masters v Bridgetown	Barbados

For further information about the above events
or to arrange a bespoke event for your company
please contact Fiona Holdsworth call 0207 544 8668
or e-mail fiona@pcaml.co.uk

PROFESSIONAL CRICKETERS' ASSOCIATION

ACKERMAN, H. D.   Leicestershire

Name: <u>Hylton</u> Deon Ackerman
Role: Right-hand bat, right-arm
medium bowler
Born: 14 February 1973, Cape Town, South
Africa
County debut: 2005
County cap: 2005
Test debut: 1997-98
1000 runs in a season: 1
1st-Class 200s: 1
Place in batting averages: 79th av. 38.51
Family links with cricket: Father (H. M.
Ackerman) played first-class cricket in South
Africa (1963-64 – 1981-82) and also for
Northamptonshire
Overseas tours: South Africa U24 to Sri
Lanka 1995; Western Province to Australia
1995-96, to Zimbabwe 1996-97; South Africa
A to England 1996, to Sri Lanka 1998, to Zimbabwe (one-day series) 2004; South
Africa to Zimbabwe 2001-02
Overseas teams played for: Western Province 1993-94 – 2002-03; Gauteng 2003-04;
Lions 2004-05
Extras: Scored maiden first-class double century (202*) v Northerns at Centurion in
the SuperSport Series 1997-98, in the process breaking Barry Richards's record for the
most first-class runs by a South African in a domestic season (ended 1997-98 with
1373 at 50.85). Scored century (145) for South Africa A v Sri Lanka A at Matara 1998,
winning Man of the Match award. Man of the SuperSport Series 2000-01. His other
domestic awards include Man of the Match v Griqualand West at Kimberley (81) and
v KwaZulu-Natal at Durban (86*), both in the Standard Bank Cup 2003-04. Captain of
Leicestershire 2005. Is not considered an overseas player
Best batting: 202* Western Province v Northerns, Centurion 1997-98

2005 Season

	M	Inns	NO	Runs	HS	Avge	100s	50s	Ct	St	O	M	Runs	Wkts	Avge	Best	5wI	10wM
Test																		
All First	17	29	2	1040	125	38.51	2	7	9	-								
1-Day Int																		
C & G	2	2	0	7	4	3.50	-	-	1	-								
tsL	17	17	1	528	114*	33.00	1	2	7	-								
Twenty20	9	9	1	288	79*	36.00	-	2	4	-								

Career Performances

	M	Inns	NO	Runs	HS	Avge	100s	50s	Ct	St	Balls	Runs	Wkts	Avge	Best	5wl	10wM
Test	4	8	0	161	57	20.12	-	1	1	-							
All First	135	221	22	8432	202 *	42.37	22	47	102	-	90	54	0	-	-	-	-
1-Day Int																	
C & G	2	2	0	7	4	3.50	-	-	1	-							
tsL	17	17	1	528	114 *	33.00	1	2	7	-							
Twenty20	9	9	1	288	79 *	36.00	-	2	4	-							

ADAMS, A. R. Essex

Name: <u>André</u> Ryan Adams
Role: Right-hand bat, right-arm
fast-medium bowler
Born: 17 July 1975, Auckland, New Zealand
Height: 5ft 11in **Weight:** 14st 7lbs
Nickname: Dre, Doctor
County debut: 2004
County cap: 2004
Test debut: 2001-02
Place in batting averages: 115th av. 33.90
(2004 184th av. 24.50)
Place in bowling averages: 84th av. 33.83
(2004 17th av. 24.39)
Strike rate: 65.25 (career 50.35)
Parents: Felise du Chateau and Keith Adams
Wife and date of marriage: Ardene,
5 April 2003

Children: Danté, 24 February 2004
Family links with cricket: 'Parents West Indian!'
Education: West Lake Boys, Auckland
Off-season: Playing for Auckland
Overseas tours: New Zealand to Sharjah (ARY Gold Cup) 2000-01, to Australia
2001-02 (VB Series), to Sharjah (Sharjah Cup) 2001-02, to Pakistan 2002, to Africa
(World Cup) 2002-03, to Sri Lanka 2003 (Bank Alfalah Cup), to England (NatWest
Series) 2004, to Bangladesh 2004-05 (one-day series), to Zimbabwe 2005-06
(Videocon Tri-Series), to South Africa (one-day series) 2005-06
Overseas teams played for: Takapuna, Auckland; Auckland 1997-98 –
Career highlights to date: 'Test victory against England in final game (Auckland) in
2002, my Test debut'
Cricket moments to forget: 'Losing to India in 2003 World Cup'
Cricket superstitions: 'None'

Cricketers particularly admired: Viv Richards, Michael Holding
Young players to look out for: Alastair Cook, Will Jefferson, Ravi Bopara, Rob Nicol (Auckland)
Other sports followed: Rugby (Auckland Blues, All Blacks)
Favourite band: Ryan Edwards
Relaxations: Xbox
Extras: Member of New Zealand team to 1998 Indoor Cricket World Cup. Leading wicket-taker in 1999-2000 Shell Cup one-day competition (28; av. 13.50). His ODI match awards include Man of the Match v India at Queenstown 2002-03 (5-22) and v West Indies at Port Elizabeth in the 2002-03 World Cup (35*/4-44). An overseas player with Essex July to September 2004 (deputising first for Danish Kaneria, then for Scott Brant) and in 2005; has returned for 2006. Scored maiden first-class century (91-ball 124) v Leicestershire at Leicester 2004 in his first Championship innings and batting at No. 9. Made Twenty20 international debut v Australia at Auckland 2004-05. Took Championship hat-trick (Burns, Jayasuriya, Hildreth) v Somerset at Taunton 2005
Best batting: 124 Essex v Leicestershire, Leicester 2004
Best bowling: 6-25 Auckland v Wellington, Auckland 2004-05

2005 Season

	M	Inns	NO	Runs	HS	Avge	100s	50s	Ct	St	O	M	Runs	Wkts	Avge	Best	5wI	10wM
Test																		
All First	12	12	1	373	103	33.90	1	-	14	-	391.3	111	1218	36	33.83	5-60	1	-
1-Day Int																		
C & G	1	0	0	0	0	-	-	-	-	-	8	2	17	3	5.66	3-17	-	
tsL	10	5	0	70	46	14.00	-	-	5	-	74.1	6	387	10	38.70	3-67	-	
Twenty20	7	5	1	47	25	11.75	-	-	1	-	19.1	0	142	6	23.66	2-12	-	

Career Performances

	M	Inns	NO	Runs	HS	Avge	100s	50s	Ct	St	Balls	Runs	Wkts	Avge	Best	5wI	10wM
Test	1	2	0	18	11	9.00	-	-	1	-	190	105	6	17.50	3-44	-	-
All First	54	70	2	1570	124	23.08	2	8	37	-	10122	4978	201	24.76	6-25	8	1
1-Day Int	35	28	9	348	45	18.31	-	-	4	-	1597	1387	49	28.30	5-22	1	
C & G	3	2	0	55	46	27.50	-	-	2	-	168	115	7	16.42	3-17	-	
tsL	16	7	0	98	46	14.00	-	-	7	-	589	533	12	44.41	3-67	-	
Twenty20	8	6	1	54	25	10.80	-	-	1	-	133	175	8	21.87	2-12	-	

1. Which England batsman scored the first two centuries in ODIs?

ADAMS, C. J.   Sussex

Name: Christopher (<u>Chris</u>) John Adams
Role: Right-hand bat, right-arm medium
bowler, slip fielder, county captain
Born: 6 May 1970, Whitwell, Derbyshire
Height: 6ft **Weight:** 13st 7lbs
Nickname: Grizzly, Grizwold
County debut: 1988 (Derbyshire),
1998 (Sussex)
County cap: 1992 (Derbyshire),
1998 (Sussex)
Benefit: 2003 (Sussex)
Test debut: 1999-2000
1000 runs in a season: 7
1st-Class 200s: 4
Place in batting averages: 64th av. 42.40
(2004 47th av. 47.76)
Strike rate: (career 79.19)
Parents: John and Eluned (Lyn)
Wife and date of marriage: Samantha Claire, 26 September 1992
Children: Georgia Louise, 4 October 1993; Sophie Victoria, 13 October 1998
Family links with cricket: Brother David played 2nd XI cricket for Derbyshire and
Gloucestershire. Father played for Yorkshire Schools and uncle played for Essex 2nd XI
Education: Chesterfield Boys Grammar School; Repton School
Qualifications: 6 O-levels, NCA coaching awards, Executive Development Certificate
in Coaching and Management Skills
Overseas tours: Repton School to Barbados 1987; England NCA North to Northern
Ireland 1987; England XI to New Zealand (Cricket Max) 1997; England to South Africa
and Zimbabwe 1999-2000; Sussex to Grenada 2001, 2002; Blade to Barbados 2001
Overseas teams played for: Takapuna, New Zealand 1987-88; Te Puke, New Zealand
1989-90; Primrose, Cape Town, South Africa 1991-92; Canberra Comets, Australia
1998-99; University of NSW, Australia 2000-01
Career highlights to date: 'Lifting the County Championship trophy [in 2003] for the
first time in Sussex's history'
Cricket moments to forget: 'The death of Umer Rashid in Grenada [2002]'
Cricketers particularly admired: Ian Botham
Other sports played: Golf, football, 'dabbled a bit with ice hockey'
Other sports followed: Football ('Arsenal!')
Favourite band: Spandau Ballet, Duran Duran
Relaxations: 'Family time'
Extras: Represented English Schools U15 and U19, MCC Schools U19 and, in 1989,
England YC. Took two catches as 12th man for England v India at Old Trafford in

1990. Set Derbyshire record for the highest score in the Sunday League (141*) v Kent at Chesterfield 1992. Set record for the highest score by a Derbyshire No. 3, 239 v Hampshire at Southampton 1996. Sussex Player of the Year 1998 and 1999. Set individual one-day record score for Sussex of 163 (off 107 balls) v Middlesex in the National League at Arundel 1999. Sussex 1st XI Fielder of the Season 2000. BBC South Cricketer of the Year 2001. One of *Wisden*'s Five Cricketers of the Year 2004. Scored 200 v Northamptonshire at Hove 2004, in the process becoming the third batsman (after Mark Ramprakash and Carl Hooper) to score a century against all 18 counties. Captain of Sussex since 1998

Best batting: 239 Derbyshire v Hampshire, Southampton 1996
Best bowling: 4-28 Sussex v Durham, Riverside 2001

2005 Season

	M	Inns	NO	Runs	HS	Avge	100s	50s	Ct	St	O	M	Runs	Wkts	Avge	Best	5wI	10wM
Test																		
All First	17	27	2	1060	120 *	42.40	1	9	23	-	6	0	21	0	-	-	-	-
1-Day Int																		
C & G	3	3	1	79	48	39.50	-	-	2	-								
tsL	16	16	4	592	110 *	49.33	1	3	3	-								
Twenty20	8	5	1	121	44	30.25	-	-	1	-								

Career Performances

	M	Inns	NO	Runs	HS	Avge	100s	50s	Ct	St	Balls	Runs	Wkts	Avge	Best	5wI	10wM
Test	5	8	0	104	31	13.00	-	-	6	-	120	59	1	59.00	1-42	-	-
All First	290	474	35	16813	239	38.29	42	81	336	-	3247	1911	41	46.60	4-28	-	-
1-Day Int	5	4	0	71	42	17.75	-	-	3	-							
C & G	33	32	8	1461	129 *	60.87	4	10	13	-	114	91	1	91.00	1-15	-	
tsL	231	222	38	7349	163	39.94	12	46	115	-	887	817	27	30.25	5-16	1	
Twenty20	17	14	3	340	44	30.90	-	-	5	-							

2. Which former Varsity captain became the first England bowler to take five wickets twice in ODIs?

ADAMS, J. H. K. Hampshire

Name: <u>James</u> Henry Kenneth Adams
Role: Left-hand bat, left-arm medium bowler
Born: 23 September 1980, Winchester
Height: 6ft 1in **Weight:** 14st
Nickname: Jimmy, Bison, Nugget
County debut: 2002
Place in batting averages: 190th av. 23.84
(2004 143rd av. 30.05)
Strike rate: (career 63.00)
Parents: Jenny and Mike
Marital status: Single
Family links with cricket: 'Dad played a bit
for Kent Schoolboys. Brothers Ben and Tom,
Hampshire age groups'
Education: Sherborne School;
Loughborough University
Qualifications: 9 GCSEs, 3 A-levels, Level 1
coaching

Overseas tours: England U19 to Sri Lanka (U19 World Cup) 1999-2000; West of
England to West Indies 1995; Sherborne School to Pakistan
Overseas teams played for: Woodville, Adelaide 1999-2000; Melville, Perth 2000-01
Career highlights to date: 'County debut. First first-class 100 v Somerset for
Loughborough'
Cricket moments to forget: 'Kidderminster, June 2000'
Cricketers particularly admired: 'M. Parker, R. Smith, B. Lara …'
Young players to look out for: 'J. Francis, J. Tomlinson, K. Latouf, C. Benham …'
Other sports played: Hockey (Dorset age group when 14); 'fair interest in most
sports'
Other sports followed: Football (Aston Villa); 'follow most ball sports'
Favourite band: Led Zeppelin, The Who, Blind Melon
Relaxations: Music, PlayStation, 'kick about with mates'
Extras: Played in U15 World Cup 1996. Hampshire Young Player of the Year 1998.
Represented England U19 2000. Played for Loughborough University CCE 2002-04
(captain 2003), scoring a century in each innings (103/113) v Kent at Canterbury 2002.
Represented British Universities 2002-04 (captain 2003)
Best batting: 107 LUCCE v Somerset, Taunton 2003
Best bowling: 2-16 Hampshire v Durham, Riverside 2004

2005 Season

	M	Inns	NO	Runs	HS	Avge	100s	50s	Ct	St	O	M	Runs	Wkts	Avge	Best	5wI	10wM
Test																		
All First	8	13	0	310	71	23.84	-	3	8	-	6	1	26	0	-		-	-
1-Day Int																		
C & G																			
tsL	1	1	0	0	0	0.00	-	-	-	-								
Twenty20	7	3	2	33	17 *	33.00	-	-	1	-	1	0	7	0	-		-	-

Career Performances

	M	Inns	NO	Runs	HS	Avge	100s	50s	Ct	St	Balls	Runs	Wkts	Avge	Best	5wI	10wM
Test																	
All First	36	64	5	1570	107	26.61	1	8	19	-	378	249	6	41.50	2-16	-	-
1-Day Int																	
C & G																		
tsL	7	7	0	102	40	14.57	-	-	4	-	1	6	0	-		-	-
Twenty20	7	3	2	33	17 *	33.00	-	-	1	-	6	7	0	-		-	-

ADSHEAD, S. J. Gloucestershire

Name: Stephen John Adshead
Role: Right-hand bat, wicket-keeper
Born: 29 January 1980, Worcester
Height: 5ft 8in **Weight:** 13st
Nickname: Adders, Top Shelf
County debut: 2000 (Leicestershire), 2003 (Worcestershire), 2004 (Gloucestershire)
County cap: 2003 (Worcestershire colours), 2004 (Gloucestershire)
Place in batting averages: 140th av. 30.66 (2004 87th av. 38.06)
Parents: David and Julie
Wife's name: Becky
Family links with cricket: Father and brother play club cricket in Worcester; mother keen spectator
Education: Brideley Moor HS, Redditch
Qualifications: 9 GCSEs, 3 A-levels, ECB Level 2 coaching
Career outside cricket: Coaching
Overseas tours: Leicestershire to Potchefstroom, South Africa 2001
Overseas teams played for: Fish Hoek, Cape Town 1998-99; Witwatersrand Technical, Johannesburg 1999-2000; Central Hawke's Bay, New Zealand 2000-01

Career highlights to date: 'Winning C&G final at Lord's 2004'
Cricket moments to forget: 'The whole 2002 season was a fairly miserable one'
Cricket superstitions: 'None'
Cricketers particularly admired: Alec Stewart, Steve Waugh
Young players to look out for: Steve Davies (Worcestershire)
Favourite band: U2
Relaxations: 'Spending as much time as possible with my wife Becky; gym, eating'
Extras: Scored 187-minute 57* to help save match v Lancashire at Cheltenham 2004
Best batting: 148* Gloucestershire v Surrey, The Oval 2005

2005 Season

	M	Inns	NO	Runs	HS	Avge	100s	50s	Ct	St	O	M	Runs	Wkts	Avge	Best	5wI	10wM
Test																		
All First	18	33	3	920	148 *	30.66	1	5	40	6								
1-Day Int																		
C & G	2	2	0	13	12	6.50	-	-	2	-								
tsL	10	10	0	200	52	20.00	-	1	13	3								
Twenty20	8	4	0	39	17	9.75	-	-	2	4								

Career Performances

	M	Inns	NO	Runs	HS	Avge	100s	50s	Ct	St	Balls	Runs	Wkts	Avge	Best	5wI	10wM
Test																	
All First	36	61	11	1631	148 *	32.62	1	10	86	10							
1-Day Int																	
C & G	11	9	2	185	77 *	26.42	-	1	15	6							
tsL	25	23	2	333	52	15.85	-	1	31	9							
Twenty20	15	10	2	142	81	17.75	-	1	5	7							

AFZAAL, U.   Northamptonshire

Name: Usman Afzaal
Role: Left-hand bat, slow left-arm bowler
Born: 9 June 1977, Rawalpindi, Pakistan
Height: 6ft **Weight:** 12st 7lbs
Nickname: Saeed, Gulfraz, Usy Bhai, Trevor
County debut: 1995 (Nottinghamshire), 2004 (Northamptonshire)
County cap: 2000 (Nottinghamshire), 2005 (Northamptonshire)
Test debut: 2001
1000 runs in a season: 5
Place in batting averages: 46th av. 47.48 (2004 14th av. 59.34)
Strike rate: (career 95.04)
Parents: Firdous and Shafi Mahmood
Marital status: Single

Family links with cricket: Older brother Kamran played for NAYC and for Nottinghamshire U15-U19 ('top player'); younger brother Aqib played for Notts and England U15; 'Uncle Mac and Uncle Raja great players'
Education: Manvers Pierrepont School; South Notts College
Qualifications: Coaching certificates
Career outside cricket: Printing company
Overseas tours: Nottinghamshire to South Africa; England U19 to West Indies 1994-95, to Zimbabwe 1995-96; 'the great ZRK tour to Lahore, Pakistan' 2000; England A to West Indies 2000-01; England to India and New Zealand 2001-02
Overseas teams played for: Victoria Park, Perth
Career highlights to date: 'Playing for England in the Ashes'
Cricket moments to forget: 'Every time I get out'
Cricketers particularly admired: David Gower, Saeed Anwar, Ian Botham, Clive Rice, Uncle Raja and Uncle Mac
Young players to look out for: Bilal Shafayat, Aqib Afzaal, Nadeem Malik
Other sports played: Indoor football
Other sports followed: Football ('a bit of Man U')
Relaxations: 'Praying; spending time with friends and family; listening to Indian music'
Extras: Played for England U15 and U17. Won Denis Compton Award 1996. Took wicket (Adam Gilchrist) with third ball in Test cricket v Australia at The Oval 2001. C&G Man of the Match award for his 3-8 (from four overs) and 64* v Ireland at Clontarf 2002
Best batting: 168* Northamptonshire v Essex, Northampton 2005
Best bowling: 4-101 Nottinghamshire v Gloucestershire, Trent Bridge 1998

2005 Season

	M	Inns	NO	Runs	HS	Avge	100s	50s	Ct	St	O	M	Runs	Wkts	Avge	Best	5wl	10wM
Test																		
All First	17	28	3	1187	168 *	47.48	5	1	9	-	23	5	94	1	94.00	1-10	-	-
1-Day Int																		
C & G	3	3	1	139	75	69.50	-	2	-	-								
tsL	16	15	2	610	122 *	46.92	2	2	4	-								
Twenty20	7	7	2	163	46	32.60	-	-	3	-	1	0	6	0	-	-	-	

Career Performances

	M	Inns	NO	Runs	HS	Avge	100s	50s	Ct	St	Balls	Runs	Wkts	Avge	Best	5wI	10wM
Test	3	6	1	83	54	16.60	-	1	-	-	54	49	1	49.00	1-49	-	-
All First	163	282	28	9244	168 *	36.39	22	45	81	-	6748	3637	71	51.22	4-101	-	-
1-Day Int																	
C & G	16	14	3	494	75	44.90	-	4	2	-	162	102	8	12.75	3-4	-	
tsL	96	88	12	2733	122 *	35.96	3	19	28	-	633	627	24	26.12	3-48	-	
Twenty20	16	15	3	219	46	18.25	-	-	4	-	24	33	0	-	-	-	

AHMED, J. S. Essex

Name: Jahid Sheikh Ahmed
Role: Right-hand bat, right-arm
fast-medium bowler
Born: 20 February 1986, Chelmsford
Height: 5ft 11in **Weight:** 10st 8lbs
County debut: 2005
Strike rate: (career 162.00)
Parents: Sheikh Faruque Ahmed and
Shaheda Ahmed Chowdhury
Marital status: Single
Education: St Peters High School;
University of East London
Off-season: 'University work and training'
Overseas tours: Essex to South Africa 2006
Career highlights to date: 'Making my
debut for the local first team (Burham Sport)
and returning figures of 12-5-32-8. Match
figures of 28.3-2-127-10 for Essex 2nd XI v
Hampshire 2nd XI 2005'
Cricket moments to forget: 'Dropping Matthew Hayden on my debut – he went on to
score 150 retired'
Cricketers particularly admired: Brett Lee, Wasim Akram, Brian Lara,
Sachin Tendulkar
Young players to look out for: Alastair Cook
Other sports played: Cross country ('made it to Essex trial')
Other sports followed: Football (Arsenal)
Favourite band: G-Unit
Relaxations: 'Music (R&B and rap); going clubbing; other sports; TV; games'
Extras: Essex Academy 2004. Community award from Bangladeshi channel,
presented by the High Commissioner
Best batting: 14* Essex v Worcestershire, Worcester 2005
Best bowling: 1-90 Essex v Worcestershire, Worcester 2005

2005 Season

	M	Inns	NO	Runs	HS	Avge	100s	50s	Ct	St	O	M	Runs	Wkts	Avge	Best	5wI	10wM
Test																		
All First	1	1	1	14	14 *	-	-	-	-	-	27	4	141	1	141.00	1-90	-	-
1-Day Int																		
C & G																		
tsL																		
Twenty20																		

Career Performances

	M	Inns	NO	Runs	HS	Avge	100s	50s	Ct	St	Balls	Runs	Wkts	Avge	Best	5wI	10wM
Test																	
All First	1	1	1	14	14 *	-	-	-	-	-	162	141	1	141.00	1-90	-	-
1-Day Int																	
C & G																	
tsL																	
Twenty20																	

ALI, K. — Worcestershire

Name: Kabir Ali
Role: Right-hand bat, right-arm medium-fast bowler
Born: 24 November 1980, Birmingham
Height: 6ft **Weight:** 12st 7lbs
Nickname: Kabby, Taxi
County debut: 1999
County colours: 2002
Test debut: 2003
50 wickets in a season: 3
Place in batting averages: 217th av. 20.50 (2004 262nd av. 11.62)
Place in bowling averages: 70th av. 30.94 (2004 63rd av. 32.10)
Strike rate: 44.33 (career 45.66)
Parents: Shabir Ali and M. Begum
Marital status: Single
Family links with cricket: Father played club cricket. Cousin Kadeer plays for Gloucestershire. Cousin Moeen plays for Warwickshire
Education: Moseley School; Wolverhampton University
Qualifications: GNVQ Leisure and Tourism, coaching

Overseas tours: Warwickshire U19 to Cape Town 1998; ECB National Academy to Australia and Sri Lanka 2002-03; England to Australia 2002-03 (VB Series), to South Africa 2004-05 (one-day series), to Pakistan 2005-06 (one-day series), to India 2005-06 (one-day series); England VI to Hong Kong 2003, 2004, 2005; England A to West Indies 2005-06

Overseas teams played for: Midland-Guildford, Perth

Career highlights to date: 'Playing for England'

Cricketers particularly admired: Wasim Akram, Glenn McGrath

Young players to look out for: Moeen Ali, Omer Ali, Aatif Ali

Other sports played: Football, snooker

Other sports followed: Football, snooker

Relaxations: 'Playing snooker and spending time with family and friends'

Extras: Warwickshire Youth Young Player of the Year award. Represented England U19. NBC Denis Compton Award for the most promising young Worcestershire player 2000. Junior Royals Player of the Year 2001. Worcestershire Player of the Year 2002. PCA Young Player of the Year 2002, 2003. Made Test debut in the fourth Test v South Africa at Headingley 2003, taking a wicket (Neil McKenzie) with his fifth ball. Worcestershire Young Player of the Year 2003. Don Kenyon Award 2003. Player of the Final in the Hong Kong Sixes 2004

Best batting: 84* Worcestershire v Durham, Stockton 2003

Best bowling: 8-53 Worcestershire v Yorkshire, Scarborough 2003

2005 Season

	M	Inns	NO	Runs	HS	Avge	100s	50s	Ct	St	O	M	Runs	Wkts	Avge	Best	5wl	10wM
Test																		
All First	13	18	2	328	57	20.50	-	2	9	-	376.5	59	1578	51	30.94	4-70	-	-
1-Day Int																		
C & G	2	1	0	67	67	67.00	-	1	-	-	17	1	80	1	80.00	1-16	-	
tsL	11	8	2	53	18	8.83	-	-	2	-	88.3	9	492	21	23.42	3-42	-	
Twenty20	3	3	0	33	16	11.00	-	-	2	-	11	0	89	4	22.25	2-32	-	

Career Performances

	M	Inns	NO	Runs	HS	Avge	100s	50s	Ct	St	Balls	Runs	Wkts	Avge	Best	5wl	10wM
Test	1	2	0	10	9	5.00	-	-	-	-	216	136	5	27.20	3-80	-	-
All First	69	93	17	1506	84 *	19.81	-	7	21	-	11716	7120	256	27.81	8-53	10	2
1-Day Int	8	4	1	52	25	17.33	-	-	1	-	375	340	13	26.15	3-44	-	
C & G	19	11	4	152	67	21.71	-	1	3	-	854	652	20	32.60	4-2	-	
tsL	64	39	10	388	92	13.37	-	1	11	-	2595	2239	101	22.16	5-36	1	
Twenty20	7	6	1	85	49	17.00	-	-	4	-	156	197	7	28.14	2-25	-	

Name: Kadeer Ali
Role: Right-hand bat, right-arm
medium-fast bowler
Born: 7 March 1983, Birmingham
Height: 6ft 2in **Weight:** 13st
Nickname: Kaddy
County debut: 2000 (Worcestershire),
2005 (Gloucestershire)
County cap: 2002 (Worcestershire colours),
2005 (Gloucestershire)
Place in batting averages: 208th av. 21.47
(2004 206th av. 21.60)
Strike rate: (career 124.00)
Parents: Munir Ali and Maqsood Begum
Marital status: Single
Family links with cricket: 'Brother Moeen
plays for Warwickshire CCC and England
U19; cousin Kabir Ali plays for
Worcestershire; younger brother Omar Ali plays for Warwickshire U17'
Education: Handsworth Grammar; Moseley Sixth Form College
Qualifications: 5 GCSEs, Level 1 coach
Overseas tours: England U19 to India 2000-01, to Australia and (U19 World Cup)
New Zealand 2001-02; England A to Malaysia and India 2003-04
Overseas teams played for: WA University, Perth 2002-03
Career highlights to date: 'Being in the national academy. Really enjoyed it'
Cricket moments to forget: 'First-class debut – got a pair against Glamorgan'
Cricket superstitions: 'None'
Cricketers particularly admired: Rahul Dravid, Graeme Hick
Young players to look out for: Moeen Ali ('brother')
Other sports played: Snooker
Other sports followed: Football (Birmingham City FC)
Relaxations: 'Just chilling, spending time with mates, music, movies'
Extras: Young Player awards at Warwickshire CCC. Represented England U19 2000-
02. NBC Denis Compton Award for the most promising young Worcestershire player
2001, 2002. Represented ECB National Academy v England XI at Perth 2002-03,
scoring a century (100). ECB National Academy 2003-04. Became first player to hit a
ball over the Basil D'Oliveira Stand at Worcester, v New Zealanders 2004
Opinions on cricket: 'Twenty20 is the way forward.'
Best batting: 99 Worcestershire v Yorkshire, Worcester 2003
Best bowling: 1-4 Gloucestershire v Glamorgan, Bristol 2005

2005 Season

	M	Inns	NO	Runs	HS	Avge	100s	50s	Ct	St	O	M	Runs	Wkts	Avge	Best	5wl	10wM
Test																		
All First	13	25	2	494	66	21.47	-	4	8	-	24	4	69	2	34.50	1-4	-	-
1-Day Int																		
C & G																		
tsL	5	5	0	108	56	21.60	-	1	1	-	4	0	20	0	-	-	-	-
Twenty20																		

Career Performances

	M	Inns	NO	Runs	HS	Avge	100s	50s	Ct	St	Balls	Runs	Wkts	Avge	Best	5wl	10wM
Test																	
All First	38	68	3	1304	99	20.06	-	9	18	-	372	232	3	77.33	1-4	-	-
1-Day Int																	
C & G	4	4	0	140	66	35.00	-	1	-	-	27	25	1	25.00	1-4	-	
tsL	15	15	1	357	57	25.50	-	4	1	-	24	20	0	-	-	-	
Twenty20	5	5	0	122	53	24.40	-	1	2	-							

ALI, M. M.   Warwickshire

Name: <u>Moeen</u> Munir Ali
Role: Left-hand bat, right-arm
off-spin bowler; 'batter who bowls'
Born: 18 June 1987, Birmingham
Height: 6ft **Weight:** 10st 7lbs
Nickname: Moe, Eddy, Bart, Elvis
County debut: 2005
Parents: Munir Ali and Maqsood Begum
Marital status: Single
Family links with cricket: Father is a cricket
coach; cousin Kabir Ali plays for
Worcestershire and England; brother Kadeer
Ali plays for Gloucestershire; younger
brother Omar plays youth cricket
Education: Moseley School
Qualifications: GCSEs and Leisure and
Tourism
Career outside cricket: Student
Overseas tours: 'Streets to Arena' to Pakistan 2002; England U19 to India 2004-05,
to Bangladesh 2005-06, to Sri Lanka (U19 World Cup) 2005-06
Career highlights to date: 'Becoming one of the youngest professional cricketers at
15 years old. Hitting 195* in 20 overs'

Cricket moments to forget: 'None'
Cricket superstitions: 'None'
Cricketers particularly admired: Nick Knight, Sanath Jayasuriya, Saeed Anwar, Wasim Akram, Kabir Ali, Kadeer Ali, Mohammed Sheikh
Young players to look out for: Omar Munir Ali, Atif Ali, Behram Ali
Other sports played: Football
Other sports followed: Football (Birmingham City)
Favourite band: B21
Relaxations: 'Playing snooker at Premier in Balsall Heath and listening to music (chilling out)'
Extras: Represented England U15 2002. Has won five Warwickshire youth awards since age of 11. Represented England U19 2004, 2005
Best batting: 57 Warwickshire v CUCCE, Fenner's 2005

2005 Season

	M	Inns	NO	Runs	HS	Avge	100s	50s	Ct	St	O	M	Runs	Wkts	Avge	Best	5wl	10wM
Test																		
All First	1	1	0	57	57	57.00	-	1	2	-	2	0	15	0	-		-	-
1-Day Int																		
C & G																			
tsL																			
Twenty20																			

Career Performances

	M	Inns	NO	Runs	HS	Avge	100s	50s	Ct	St	Balls	Runs	Wkts	Avge	Best	5wl	10wM
Test																	
All First	1	1	0	57	57	57.00	-	1	2	-	12	15	0	-		-	-
1-Day Int																	
C & G																		
tsL																		
Twenty20																		

3. Which India batsman shares in record partnerships for each of the first three wickets in ODIs?

ALLENBY, J. Leicestershire

Name: James (Jim) Allenby
Role: Right-hand bat, right-arm
medium bowler
Born: 12 September 1982, Perth, Australia
Height: 6ft **Weight:** 13st 8lbs
County debut: 2005 (one-day)
Parents: Michael and Julie
Marital status: Single
Family links with cricket: 'Great-
grandfather played at Yorkshire/Hampshire'
Education: Christ Church Grammar School,
Perth
Qualifications: Level 1 coach
Off-season: 'Club cricket in Perth'
Overseas teams played for: Claremont-
Nedlands CC, Perth 1993 –
Career highlights to date: 'Twenty20 finals
day at The Oval 2005'
Cricket superstitions: 'Put gear on same way each time I bat'
Cricketers particularly admired: Dean Jones
Young players to look out for: David Brown, Stewart Walters
Other sports followed: Football (Leeds United)
Favourite band: Powderfinger
Relaxations: 'Playing golf, swimming/surfing at beach'
Extras: Recorded highest individual score for Western Australia in U19 cricket (180)
v Northern Territory 2000-01. Played for Durham Board XI in the 2003 C&G. Set new
record for highest individual score in the Durham County League (266*) playing for
Brandon 2005. Is not considered an overseas player
Opinions on cricket: 'Seems to be getting more and more popular with last year's
Ashes being such a success. Twenty20 has made the game more watchable for
everyone.'

2005 Season

	M	Inns	NO	Runs	HS	Avge	100s	50s	Ct	St	O	M	Runs	Wkts	Avge	Best	5wI	10wM
Test																		
All First																		
1-Day Int																		
C & G																		
tsL	1	1	1	7	7*	-	-	-	-	-	-							
Twenty20	3	2	0	25	17	12.50	-	-	1	-								

Career Performances

	M	Inns	NO	Runs	HS	Avge	100s	50s	Ct	St	Balls	Runs	Wkts	Avge	Best	5wI	10wM
Test																	
All First																	
1-Day Int																	
C & G	1	1	0	4	4	4.00	-	-	-	-							
tsL	1	1	1	7	7*	-	-	-	-	-							
Twenty20	3	2	0	25	17	12.50	-	-	1	-							

ALLEYNE, D. Nottinghamshire

Name: David Alleyne
Role: Right-hand bat, wicket-keeper
Born: 17 April 1976, York
Height: 5ft 11in **Weight:** 13st 7lbs
Nickname: Bones, Gears
County debut: 1999 (one-day, Middlesex),
2001 (first-class, Middlesex), 2004
(Nottinghamshire)
Parents: Darcy and Jo
Marital status: Engaged to Dawn
Family links with cricket: Father played for
local club Northampton Exiles
Education: Enfield Grammar; Hertford
Regional College, Ware; City and Islington
College

Qualifications: 6 GCSEs, City and Guilds,
BTEC Diploma in Leisure Studies, Level 3
coaching award
Career outside cricket: Coaching; teaching
Overseas tours: Middlesex to Johannesburg 2000-01
Overseas teams played for: Stratford, New Zealand; Inglewood, New Zealand
1997-98; Sturt, Adelaide 1999-2000; Midland-Guildford, Perth 2000-01; Karori CC,
Wellington, New Zealand 2001-02
Cricketers particularly admired: Viv Richards, Desmond Haynes, Carl Hooper,
Jack Russell, Alec Stewart, Keith Piper
Other sports played: Judo, football (Middlesex U15, U16; Enfield Borough U16)
Other sports followed: Football (Liverpool FC)
Relaxations: 'Relaxing with Dawn and family'
Extras: Represented Middlesex U11 to U17. London Cricket College (three years).
Middlesex 2nd XI Player of the Year 1999, 2000, 2002
Best batting: 49* Middlesex v Derbyshire, Derby 2002

2005 Season

	M	Inns	NO	Runs	HS	Avge	100s	50s	Ct	St	O	M	Runs	Wkts	Avge	Best	5wI	10wM
Test																		
All First	1	2	0	46	40	23.00	-	-	5	-								
1-Day Int																		
C & G																		
tsL	2	1	0	3	3	3.00	-	-	-	-								
Twenty20	3	2	2	25	24 *	-	-	-	1	-								

Career Performances

	M	Inns	NO	Runs	HS	Avge	100s	50s	Ct	St	Balls	Runs	Wkts	Avge	Best	5wI	10wM
Test																	
All First	10	13	3	306	49 *	30.60	-	-	28	-							
1-Day Int																	
C & G	5	5	0	30	19	6.00	-	-	3	-							
tsL	27	21	2	229	58	12.05	-	1	19	6							
Twenty20	8	4	3	36	24 *	36.00	-	-	4	-							

ALLEYNE, M. W. Gloucestershire

Name: <u>Mark</u> Wayne Alleyne
Role: Right-hand bat, right-arm medium bowler, occasional wicket-keeper
Born: 23 May 1968, Tottenham, London
Height: 5ft 10in **Weight:** 14st
Nickname: Boo-Boo
County debut: 1986
County cap: 1990
Benefit: 1999
1000 runs in a season: 6
50 wickets in a season: 1
1st-Class 200s: 1
Place in bowling averages: (2004 5th av. 20.63)
Strike rate: (career 64.44)
Parents: Euclid (deceased) and Hyacinth
Wife and date of marriage: Louise Maria, 9 October 1998
Children: Jasper, 6 April 2004
Family links with cricket: Brother played for Gloucestershire 2nd XI and Middlesex YC. Father played club cricket in Barbados and England
Education: Harrison College, Barbados; Cardinal Pole School, East London

Qualifications: 6 O-levels, NCA Senior Coaching Award, volleyball coaching certificate

Overseas tours: England YC to Sri Lanka 1986-87, to Australia (U19 World Cup) 1987-88; England XI to New Zealand (Cricket Max) 1997; England A to Bangladesh and New Zealand 1999-2000 (c), to West Indies 2000-01 (c); England to Australia 1998-99 (CUB Series), to South Africa and Zimbabwe 1999-2000 (one-day series), to Kenya (ICC Knockout Trophy) 2000-01, to Pakistan and Sri Lanka 2000-01 (one-day series)

Career highlights to date: '1) England debut in Brisbane 2) England Man of the Match in East London, South Africa 3) Each one of our five consecutive trophies'

Cricket moments to forget: 'Missing promotion in the Championship and being relegated in the Norwich Union League in the same week [2001]'

Cricketers particularly admired: Gordon Greenidge, Viv Richards, Jack Russell, Steve Waugh

Other sports played: Basketball, football

Other sports followed: 'Still follow Tottenham religiously but support our local football and rugby teams'

Relaxations: 'Sport crazy but also an avid gardener. Keen historian'

Extras: Graduate of Haringey Cricket College. Cricket Select Sunday League Player of the Year 1992. Leading all-rounder in the single-division four-day era of the County Championship with 6409 runs (av. 32.53) and 216 wickets (av. 31.18) 1993-99. Captain of Gloucestershire's one-day double-winning side (NatWest and B&H Super Cup) 1999 and of treble-winning side (NatWest, B&H and Norwich Union National League) 2000. Man of the Match in ODI v South Africa at East London February 2000 (53, 3-55 and a catch to dismiss Jonty Rhodes). One of *Wisden*'s Five Cricketers of the Year 2001. Honorary fellowship from University of Gloucestershire, October 2001. Gloucestershire captain 1997-2003; Gloucestershire player/coach, club and one-day captain 2004-05. Awarded MBE in the New Year Honours 2004. Retired at the end of the 2005 season but registration retained; is Gloucestershire head coach

Best batting: 256 Gloucestershire v Northamptonshire, Northampton 1990

Best bowling: 6-49 Gloucestershire v Middlesex, Lord's 2000

2005 Season

	M	Inns	NO	Runs	HS	Avge	100s	50s	Ct	St	O	M	Runs	Wkts	Avge	Best	5wI	10wM
Test																		
All First	1	2	0	67	51	33.50	-	1	-	-	24	3	84	1	84.00	1-84	-	-
1-Day Int																		
C & G																		
tsL	14	11	3	133	26	16.62	-	-	5	-	66	0	303	8	37.87	2-15	-	
Twenty20	8	4	1	85	35	28.33	-	-	1	-	24.3	0	171	4	42.75	2-41	-	

Career Performances

	M	Inns	NO	Runs	HS	Avge	100s	50s	Ct	St	Balls	Runs	Wkts	Avge	Best	5wI	10wM
Test																	
All First	328	537	52	14943	256	30.81	22	72	273	3	26743	13659	415	32.91	6-49	9	-
1-Day Int	10	8	1	151	53	21.57	-	1	3	-	366	280	10	28.00	3-27	-	
C & G	52	40	7	671	73	20.33	-	1	16	-	2260	1437	61	23.55	5-30	1	
tsL	285	259	57	5663	134 *	28.03	3	23	115	-	9841	7926	257	30.84	5-28	1	
Twenty20	18	10	5	159	35	31.80	-	-	7	-	333	423	10	42.30	2-33	-	

AMBROSE, T. R. Warwickshire

Name: Timothy (Tim) Raymond Ambrose
Role: Right-hand bat, wicket-keeper
Born: 1 December 1982, Newcastle,
New South Wales, Australia
Height: 5ft 7in
Nickname: Shambrose, Freak, Mole
County debut: 2001 (Sussex)
County cap: 2003 (Sussex)
Place in batting averages: 167th av. 27.11
(2004 238th av. 17.13)
Parents: Raymond and Sally
Marital status: Single
Family links with cricket: 'Cousin played
Sydney first grade; father is captain of local
grade D4 team'
Education: Merewether Selective High,
NSW
Career outside cricket: Greenkeeping
Overseas tours: Sussex to Grenada 2001, 2002
Overseas teams played for: Wallsend, NSW 2000; Nelson Bay, NSW 2001;
Newcastle, NSW 2002
Career highlights to date: 'Winning the Championship 2003. Maiden first-class
century, 149 v Yorkshire'
Cricketers particularly admired: Alec Stewart, Ian Healy, Steve Waugh,
Mushtaq Ahmed
Young players to look out for: Andrew Hodd, Matt Prior, Luke Wright
Other sports played: Football, squash, golf, rugby league, rugby union, AFL,
'I'll have a go at anything'
Other sports followed: Rugby league (Newcastle Knights), Australian Rules (Sydney
Swans), football (Tottenham Hotspur)
Favourite band: Jeff Buckley, Ben Harper, Jack Johnson

Relaxations: Guitar, music
Extras: Captained Newcastle (NSW) U16 1999 Bradman Cup winning side. Played for New South Wales U17. Won NSW Junior Cricketer of the Year three years running. C&G Man of the Match award for his 95 v Buckinghamshire at Beaconsfield 2002. Left Sussex at the end of the 2005 season and has joined Warwickshire for 2006. Holds a British passport and is not considered an overseas player
Best batting: 149 Sussex v Yorkshire, Headingley 2002

2005 Season

	M	Inns	NO	Runs	HS	Avge	100s	50s	Ct	St	O	M	Runs	Wkts	Avge	Best	5wI	10wM
Test																		
All First	7	10	1	244	78	27.11	-	1	14	2								
1-Day Int																		
C & G																		
tsL	5	5	2	52	22	17.33	-	-	5	-								
Twenty20	5	2	0	15	14	7.50	-	-	3	1								

Career Performances

	M	Inns	NO	Runs	HS	Avge	100s	50s	Ct	St	Balls	Runs	Wkts	Avge	Best	5wI	10wM
Test																	
All First	47	76	5	2322	149	32.70	2	15	76	10	6	1	0	-	-	-	-
1-Day Int																	
C & G	6	6	0	173	95	28.83	-	1	4	-							
tsL	37	34	3	621	87	20.03	-	1	40	5							
Twenty20	10	7	2	123	54 *	24.60	-	1	8	4							

4. Who in 1985 became the first player to complete the double of 1000 runs and 100 wickets in ODIs?

ANDERSON, J. M.   Lancashire

Name: <u>James</u> Michael Anderson
Role: Left-hand bat, right-arm
fast-medium bowler
Born: 30 July 1982, Burnley
Height: 6ft 2in **Weight:** 13st
Nickname: Jimmy
County debut: 2001 (one-day),
2002 (first-class)
County cap: 2003
Test debut: 2003
50 wickets in a season: 2
Place in batting averages: 278th av. 10.35
Place in bowling averages: 60th av. 30.21
(2004 11th av. 22.80)
Strike rate: 51.26 (career 46.23)
Parents: Michael and Catherine
Wife and date of marriage: Daniella,
February 2006
Family links with cricket: Father and uncle played for Burnley
Education: St Theodore's RC High School; St Theodore's RC Sixth Form Centre –
both Burnley
Qualifications: 10 GCSEs, 1 A-level, 1 GNVQ, Level 2 coaching award
Off-season: Touring with England
Overseas tours: Lancashire to Cape Town 2002; ECB National Academy to Australia
2002-03; England to Australia 2002-03 (VB Series), to Africa (World Cup) 2002-03,
to Bangladesh and Sri Lanka 2003-04, to West Indies 2003-04, to Zimbabwe (one-day
series) 2004-05, to South Africa 2004-05, to Pakistan 2005-06, to India 2005-06;
England A to West Indies 2005-06
Career highlights to date: 'Receiving Lancs cap. Playing for England'
Cricket moments to forget: 'England v Australia – 2003 World Cup'
Cricketers particularly admired: Darren Gough, Nasser Hussain, Peter Martin
Young players to look out for: Jonathan Clare, David Brown
Other sports played: Golf (12 handicap), football
Other sports followed: Football (Arsenal FC), rugby league, darts
Favourite band: Oasis, U2
Relaxations: 'Watching TV, playing PlayStation, music'
Extras: Represented England U19 2001. Took 50 first-class wickets in his first full
season 2002. NBC Denis Compton Award for the most promising young Lancashire
player 2002. Won two Man of the Match awards in the 2002-03 World Cup. Took hat-
trick (Robinson, Hussain, Jefferson) v Essex at Old Trafford 2003. Recorded a five-
wicket innings return (5-73) on Test debut in the first Test v Zimbabwe at Lord's 2003.

Became the first England bowler to take an ODI hat-trick (Abdul Razzaq, Shoaib Akhtar, Mohammad Sami) v Pakistan at The Oval in the NatWest Challenge 2003. Cricket Writers' Club Young Player of the Year 2003
Best batting: 37* Lancashire v Durham, Old Trafford 2005
Best bowling: 6-23 Lancashire v Hampshire, West End 2002
Stop press: Man of the Match in the fifth ODI v Pakistan at Rawalpindi 2005-06 (4-48). Called up as a replacement to the England Test tour to India 2005-06, having already been selected for the one-day section

2005 Season

	M	Inns	NO	Runs	HS	Avge	100s	50s	Ct	St	O	M	Runs	Wkts	Avge	Best	5wI	10wM
Test																		
All First	16	19	5	145	37 *	10.35	-	-	8	-	512.4	99	1813	60	30.21	5-79	1	-
1-Day Int																		
C & G	4	2	1	3	2 *	3.00	-	-	-	-	32.3	3	142	4	35.50	2-12	-	
tsL	15	9	7	54	13 *	27.00	-	-	2	-	111	11	452	23	19.65	3-12	-	
Twenty20	10	2	1	21	16	21.00	-	-	2	-	34.4	0	307	10	30.70	2-25	-	

Career Performances

	M	Inns	NO	Runs	HS	Avge	100s	50s	Ct	St	Balls	Runs	Wkts	Avge	Best	5wI	10wM
Test	12	16	12	68	21 *	17.00	-	-	4	-	2034	1274	35	36.40	5-73	2	-
All First	50	59	30	289	37 *	9.96	-	-	18	-	8643	5072	184	27.56	6-23	8	1
1-Day Int	39	13	5	41	11	5.12	-	-	8	-	1903	1504	59	25.49	4-25	-	
C & G	11	5	4	15	7 *	15.00	-	-	2	-	579	430	15	28.66	3-14	-	
tsL	24	12	9	65	13 *	21.66	-	-	3	-	1069	770	41	18.78	3-12	-	
Twenty20	13	3	2	21	16	21.00	-	-	2	-	268	380	12	31.66	2-25	-	

5. What is the highest number of catches held in an ODI by a non-wicket-keeper?

ANDREW, G. M.   Somerset

Name: <u>Gareth</u> Mark Andrew
Role: Left-hand bat, right-arm
medium-fast bowler
Born: 27 December 1983, Yeovil
Height: 6ft **Weight:** 14st
Nickname: Gaz, Brad, Sobers
County debut: 2003
Place in bowling averages: 127th av. 45.45
Strike rate: 57.18 (career 47.75)
Parents: Peter and Susan
Marital status: Single
Family links with cricket: 'Dad and younger
brother are club cricketers'
Education: Ansford Community School;
Richard Huish College, Taunton
Qualifications: 10 GCSEs, 3 A-levels,
Level 1 coach
Career outside cricket: 'Open University
studying business'

Off-season: 'Adelaide Academy (Athletes 1)'
Overseas tours: West of England U15 to West Indies 1999; England U17 to Australia
2001; Somerset Academy to Western Australia 2002; Aus Academy to Perth 2003
Overseas teams played for: Swanbourne CC, Perth 2002-03
Career highlights to date: '4-48 against Scotland in totesport League [2004]'
Cricket moments to forget: 'Whenever bowling in the Twenty20'
Cricket superstitions: 'Always put my boots on the right feet'
Cricketers particularly admired: Ian Botham, Andrew Flintoff, Chris Cairns
Young players to look out for: Jack Cooper, Nick Gibbens, Simon Ruddick,
Chaz Thomas
Other sports played: Football (Bruton Town FC, Yeovil District U11-U16, Castle
Cary AFC)
Other sports followed: Football (Yeovil Town, Man Utd)
Injuries: Out for six weeks with a bone spur in the left ankle
Favourite band: 'Too many to mention'
Relaxations: 'Going home; chilling in Esporta; people-watching from Starbucks with
the boys'
Extras: Represented England U19 v South Africa U19 2003
Best batting: 44 Somerset v Sri Lanka A, Taunton 2004
Best bowling: 4-63 Somerset v Sri Lanka A, Taunton 2004

2005 Season

	M	Inns	NO	Runs	HS	Avge	100s	50s	Ct	St	O	M	Runs	Wkts	Avge	Best	5wI	10wM
Test																		
All First	5	6	1	68	32	13.60	-	-	1	-	104.5	14	500	11	45.45	4-134	-	-
1-Day Int																		
C & G																		
tsL	8	3	1	20	16	10.00	-	-	3	-	49.4	3	329	10	32.90	3-48	-	
Twenty20	9	3	1	29	12	14.50	-	-	5	-	24	0	182	13	14.00	4-22	-	

Career Performances

	M	Inns	NO	Runs	HS	Avge	100s	50s	Ct	St	Balls	Runs	Wkts	Avge	Best	5wI	10wM
Test																	
All First	11	14	1	163	44	12.53	-	-	5	-	1337	989	28	35.32	4-63	-	-
1-Day Int																	
C & G	2	1	0	1	1	1.00	-	-	1	-	53	35	0	-		-	-
tsL	26	15	3	111	23	9.25	-	-	9	-	823	865	31	27.90	4-48	-	
Twenty20	17	8	2	40	12	6.66	-	-	5	-	261	363	17	21.35	4-22	-	

ANYON, J. E.   Warwickshire

Name: James Edward Anyon
Role: Left-hand bat, right-arm
fast-medium bowler
Born: 5 May 1983, Lancaster
Height: 6ft 2in **Weight:** 13st 7lbs
Nickname: Jimmy
County debut: 2005
Place in bowling averages: 88th av. 35.41
Strike rate: 52.50 (career 66.31)
Parents: Peter and Christine
Marital status: Single
Family links with cricket: 'Dad used to
play village cricket'
Education: Garstang High School; Preston
College; Loughborough University
Qualifications: GCSEs, 3 A-levels,
BSc Sports Science with Management,
Level 1 coaching
Overseas teams played for: Claremont-Nedlands, Perth 2004-05
Career highlights to date: 'Bowling at Brian Lara'
Cricket moments to forget: 'Losing UCCE final 2004'
Cricketers particularly admired: Glenn McGrath, Michael Atherton

Young players to look out for: Moeen Ali
Other sports played: Football, golf
Other sports followed: Football (Man Utd, Preston North End)
Favourite band: Nuse
Relaxations: 'Playing football; socialising with mates; spending time with girlfriend'
Extras: Young Player of the Year awards at Preston CC. Bowler of the Year award at Farsley CC (Bradford League) 2004. Played for Loughborough University CCE 2003, 2004. Took Twenty20 hat-trick (Durston, Andrew, Caddick) v Somerset at Edgbaston 2005
Opinions on cricket: 'Too many non-England-qualified players.'
Best batting: 21 LUCCE v Leicestershire, Leicester 2003
Best bowling: 4-33 Warwickshire v Sussex, Edgbaston 2005

2005 Season

	M	Inns	NO	Runs	HS	Avge	100s	50s	Ct	St	O	M	Runs	Wkts	Avge	Best	5wI	10wM
Test																		
All First	6	11	7	29	10	7.25	-	-	3	-	105	15	425	12	35.41	4-33	-	-
1-Day Int																		
C & G	2	0	0	0	0	-	-	-	1	-	16	1	68	2	34.00	2-36	-	
tsL	12	1	0	0	0	0.00	-	-	1	-	74	1	372	8	46.50	3-44	-	
Twenty20	7	2	2	15	8 *	-	-	-	2	-	16.3	0	125	9	13.88	3-6	-	

Career Performances

	M	Inns	NO	Runs	HS	Avge	100s	50s	Ct	St	Balls	Runs	Wkts	Avge	Best	5wI	10wM
Test																	
All First	11	15	8	52	21	7.42	-	-	5	-	1260	919	19	48.36	4-33	-	-
1-Day Int																	
C & G	3	1	0	0	0	0.00	-	-	2	-	138	114	3	38.00	2-36	-	
tsL	12	1	0	0	0	0.00	-	-	1	-	444	372	8	46.50	3-44	-	
Twenty20	7	2	2	15	8 *	-	-	-	2	-	99	125	9	13.88	3-6	-	

ASTLE, N. J.   Durham

Name: <u>Nathan</u> John Astle
Role: Right-hand bat, right-arm medium bowler
Born: 15 September 1971, Christchurch, New Zealand
Height: 5ft 10in
County debut: Nottinghamshire (1997), Durham (2005)
Test debut: 1995-96
1st-Class 200s: 2
Place in batting averages: 112th av. 34.12
Strike rate: (career 91.55)

Overseas tours: New Zealand to India 1995-96 (one-day series), to India and Pakistan (World Cup) 1995-96, to West Indies 1995-96, to Pakistan 1996-97, to Zimbabwe 1997-98, to Australia 1997-98, to Sri Lanka 1998, to Malaysia (Commonwealth Games) 1998-99, to Bangladesh (Wills International Cup) 1998-99, to UK, Ireland and Holland (World Cup) 1999, to England 1999, to India 1999-2000, to Zimbabwe 2000-01, to Kenya (ICC Knockout Trophy) 2000-01, to South Africa 2000-01, to Australia 2001-02, to West Indies 2002, to Sri Lanka (ICC Champions Trophy) 2002-03, to Africa (World Cup) 2002-03, to India 2003-04, to England 2004, to England (ICC Champions Trophy) 2004, to Bangladesh 2004-05, to Australia 2004-05, to Zimbabwe 2005-06, plus other one-day series 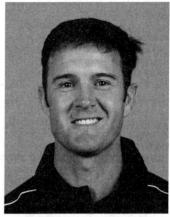 and tournaments in Sri Lanka, India, Sharjah, Singapore, Pakistan and South Africa

Overseas teams played for: Canterbury 1991-92 –

Extras: Represented New Zealand U19 1990-91. One of *New Zealand Cricket Almanack*'s two Players of the Year 1995, 1996, 2002. Holds record for the fastest 200 in Tests in terms of balls received (153), scored in the first Test v England at Christchurch 2001-02 (ended up with 222). Has won numerous domestic and international awards, including Man of the [ODI] Series v Zimbabwe 1997-98 and Man of the Match in the final of the Videocon TriSeries 2005-06 v India at Harare (115*). Overseas player with Nottinghamshire 1997; an overseas player with Durham in 2005 as a locum for Mike Hussey

Best batting: 223 New Zealanders v Queensland, Brisbane 2001-02

Best bowling: 6-22 Canterbury v Otago, Christchurch 1996-97

Stop press: Made Twenty20 international debut v South Africa at Johannesburg 2005-06

2005 Season

	M	Inns	NO	Runs	HS	Avge	100s	50s	Ct	St	O	M	Runs	Wkts	Avge	Best	5wl	10wM
Test																		
All First	5	8	0	273	65	34.12	-	3	3	-	52.4	17	117	3	39.00	3-20	-	-
1-Day Int																		
C & G																		
tsL	4	4	0	25	16	6.25	-	-	-	-	21.5	1	86	4	21.50	2-21	-	
Twenty20	7	7	0	179	64	25.57	-	2	3	-	20	0	136	6	22.66	2-14	-	

Career Performances

	M	Inns	NO	Runs	HS	Avge	100s	50s	Ct	St	Balls	Runs	Wkts	Avge	Best	5wI	10wM
Test	73	124	10	4386	222	38.47	11	21	67	-	5310	2016	46	43.82	3-27	-	-
All First	151	240	22	8449	223	38.75	19	43	123	-	12269	4430	134	33.05	6-22	2	-
1-Day Int	196	192	12	6354	145 *	35.30	15	37	74	-	4599	3580	95	37.68	4-43	-	
C & G	3	2	0	83	56	41.50	-	1	-	-	162	61	4	15.25	3-20	-	
tsL	10	10	0	217	75	21.70	-	2	3	-	365	289	13	22.23	3-22	-	
Twenty20	7	7	0	179	64	25.57	-	2	3	-	120	136	6	22.66	2-14	-	

AVERIS, J. M. M. Gloucestershire

Name: James Maxwell Michael Averis
Role: Right-hand bat, right-arm
fast-medium bowler
Born: 28 May 1974, Bristol
Height: 5ft 11in **Weight:** 13st 7lbs
Nickname: Avo, Fish, Goat
County debut: 1994 (one-day),
1997 (first-class)
County cap: 2001
Place in batting averages: 265th av. 12.93
(2004 208th av. 21.42)
Place in bowling averages: 117th av. 43.25
(2004 116th av. 39.25)
Strike rate: 70.80 (career 71.65)
Parents: Mike and Carol
Wife and date of marriage: Anna,
26 October 2002
Family links with cricket: 'Father and
grandfather played and have lots of advice'
Education: Bristol Cathedral School; Portsmouth University; St Cross College,
Oxford University
Qualifications: 10 GCSEs, 3 A-levels, BSc (Hons) Geographical Science, Diploma in
Social Studies (Oxon), FPC I and II
Overseas tours: Bristol Schools to Australia 1990-91; Gloucestershire to Zimbabwe
1997, to South Africa 1999, to Cape Town 2000, to Kimberley 2001, to Stellenbosch
2002; Bristol RFC to South Africa 1996; Oxford University RFC to Japan and
Australia 1997
Overseas teams played for: Union CC, Port Elizabeth, South Africa; Kraifontaine,
Boland, South Africa 2001
Career highlights to date: 'Winning treble in 2000'
Cricket moments to forget: 'Dropping the biggest dolly in 2000 NatWest final'

Cricket superstitions: 'Must eat on way to ground. Always use same toilet'
Cricketers particularly admired: Viv Richards, Malcolm Marshall, Ian Botham
Other sports played: Football (Bristol North West), rugby (played for Bristol RFC, captain of South West U21 1995, Oxford Blue 1996)
Other sports followed: Rugby (Bristol RFC), football (Liverpool FC)
Relaxations: 'Reading, surfing, eating out'
Extras: Double Oxford Blue in 1996-97. Played in every one-day game in Gloucestershire's treble-winning season 2000. Gloucestershire Player of the Year 2001. Had figures of 4-23 in the C&G final v Worcestershire at Lord's 2004, including hat-trick (Leatherdale, G. Batty, Hall) with the last ball of his ninth over and the first two balls of his tenth
Best batting: 48* Gloucestershire v Surrey, The Oval 2004
Best bowling: 6-32 Gloucestershire v Northamptonshire, Bristol 2004

2005 Season

	M	Inns	NO	Runs	HS	Avge	100s	50s	Ct	St	O	M	Runs	Wkts	Avge	Best	5wI	10wM
Test																		
All First	10	16	1	194	33	12.93	-	-	2	-	236	50	865	20	43.25	3-11	-	-
1-Day Int																		
C & G	2	1	1	0	0*	-	-	-	-	-	15	2	55	2	27.50	2-24	-	
tsL	12	8	4	50	16*	12.50	-	-	-	-	85	9	424	14	30.28	4-40	-	
Twenty20	1	1	0	2	2	2.00	-	-	-	-	2	0	31	0	-	-	-	-

Career Performances

	M	Inns	NO	Runs	HS	Avge	100s	50s	Ct	St	Balls	Runs	Wkts	Avge	Best	5wI	10wM
Test																	
All First	66	86	17	856	48*	12.40	-	-	14	-	10461	6273	146	42.96	6-32	5	-
1-Day Int																	
C & G	19	7	6	33	12*	33.00	-	-	2	-	919	647	35	18.48	6-23	1	
tsL	92	51	24	252	23*	9.33	-	-	11	-	4113	3324	133	24.99	5-20	3	
Twenty20	8	2	0	6	4	3.00	-	-	3	-	138	201	12	16.75	3-7	-	

6. Who has conceded the most runs in his full quota
of overs – at the time 12 overs – in ODIs?

AZHAR MAHMOOD   Surrey

Name: Azhar Mahmood Sagar
Role: Right-hand bat, right-arm
fast-medium bowler; all-rounder
Born: 28 February 1975, Rawalpindi,
Pakistan
Height: 6ft **Weight:** 13st 5lbs
Nickname: Aju
County debut: 2002
County cap: 2004
Test debut: 1997-98
1st-Class 200s: 1
Place in batting averages: 25th av. 52.90
(2004 142nd av. 30.36)
Place in bowling averages: 85th av. 34.00
(2004 47th av. 29.94)
Strike rate: 52.46 (career 48.82)
Parents: Mohammed Aslam Sagar and
Nusrat Perveen

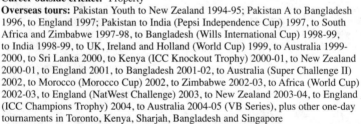

Wife and date of marriage: Ebba Azhar, 13 April 2003
Education: FG No. 1 High School, Islamabad
Qualifications: 'A-level equivalent'
Career outside cricket: 'Property'
Overseas tours: Pakistan Youth to New Zealand 1994-95; Pakistan A to Bangladesh 1996, to England 1997; Pakistan to India (Pepsi Independence Cup) 1997, to South Africa and Zimbabwe 1997-98, to Bangladesh (Wills International Cup) 1998-99, to India 1998-99, to UK, Ireland and Holland (World Cup) 1999, to Australia 1999-2000, to Sri Lanka 2000, to Kenya (ICC Knockout Trophy) 2000-01, to New Zealand 2000-01, to England 2001, to Bangladesh 2001-02, to Australia (Super Challenge II) 2002, to Morocco (Morocco Cup) 2002, to Zimbabwe 2002-03, to Africa (World Cup) 2002-03, to England (NatWest Challenge) 2003, to New Zealand 2003-04, to England (ICC Champions Trophy) 2004, to Australia 2004-05 (VB Series), plus other one-day tournaments in Toronto, Kenya, Sharjah, Bangladesh and Singapore
Overseas teams played for: Islamabad; United Bank; Rawalpindi; Pakistan International Airlines
Career highlights to date: 'First Test match (debut) against South Africa in 1997 in Pakistan (Rawalpindi). I scored 128* in the first innings and 50* in the second, plus two wickets – Man of the Match'
Cricket moments to forget: 'World Cup 1999 – final against Australia (which we lost)'
Cricket superstitions: 'None'
Cricketers particularly admired: Imran Khan, Wasim Akram, Steve Waugh

Young players to look out for: Bilal Asad, Rikki Clarke
Other sports played: Snooker, basketball, kite flying
Other sports followed: Football (Man U)
Relaxations: 'Listening to music, training, spending time with my family'
Extras: Scored 128* and 50* on Test debut in the first Test v South Africa at Rawalpindi 1997-98; during first innings shared with Mushtaq Ahmed (59) in a stand of 151, equalling the world tenth-wicket record in Tests. Scored century (136) in the first Test v South Africa at Johannesburg 1997-98, becoming the first Pakistan player to score a Test century in South Africa and achieving feat of scoring a century on Test debuts home and away. Took 6-18 v West Indies in the Coca-Cola Champions Trophy in Sharjah 1999-2000 and 5-28 v Sri Lanka in the final of the same competition, winning the Man of the Match award on both occasions. An overseas player with Surrey at the start of the 2002 season (pending the arrival of Saqlain Mushtaq) and since 2003
Best batting: 204* Surrey v Middlesex, The Oval 2005
Best bowling: 8-61 Surrey v Lancashire, The Oval 2002

2005 Season

	M	Inns	NO	Runs	HS	Avge	100s	50s	Ct	St	O	M	Runs	Wkts	Avge	Best	5wI	10wM
Test																		
All First	9	13	2	582	204 *	52.90	1	2	10	-	227.2	44	884	26	34.00	5-72	1	-
1-Day Int																		
C & G	1	1	0	4	4	4.00	-	-	-	-	9	1	61	1	61.00	1-61	-	
tsL	6	5	2	72	22 *	24.00	-	-	1	-	52	4	232	9	25.77	3-20	-	
Twenty20	7	7	3	188	40 *	47.00	-	-	-	-	20	0	141	7	20.14	2-3	-	

Career Performances

	M	Inns	NO	Runs	HS	Avge	100s	50s	Ct	St	Balls	Runs	Wkts	Avge	Best	5wI	10wM
Test	21	34	4	900	136	30.00	3	1	14	-	3015	1402	39	35.94	4-50	-	-
All First	119	185	22	4966	204 *	30.46	5	27	98	-	20114	10505	412	25.49	8-61	15	3
1-Day Int	139	107	25	1492	67	18.19	-	3	37	-	6148	4740	122	38.85	6-18	3	
C & G	5	5	0	53	20	10.60	-	-	2	-	266	233	9	25.88	4-49	-	
tsL	29	25	6	536	98	28.21	-	4	7	-	1288	1007	43	23.41	6-37	2	
Twenty20	15	14	4	337	57 *	33.70	-	1	3	-	294	337	21	16.04	4-20	-	

BAKER, T. M.   Northamptonshire

Name: <u>Thomas</u> Michael Baker
Role: Right-hand bat, right-arm
fast-medium bowler
Born: 6 July 1981, Dewsbury, West
Yorkshire
Height: 6ft 5in   **Weight:** 12st 8lbs
Nickname: Tosh
County debut: 2001 (one-day, Yorkshire),
2005 (Northamptonshire; *see Extras*)
Strike rate: (career 78.00)
Parents: Carol and Mike
Marital status: Single
Family links with cricket: Grandfather
played for Keighley. Brother James played at
Spen Victoria
Education: Whitcliffe Mount School
Qualifications: NCA Level 1 coaching,
BTEC Sports Science, GNVQ Leisure
and Tourism

Overseas tours: Yorkshire to Cape Town 2001; Northamptonshire to Grenada 2002
Overseas teams played for: Edgemead CC, Cape Town 2000-01
Cricketers particularly admired: Allan Donald, Jacques Kallis
Other sports played: Golf, football, 'anything'
Other sports followed: Football (Leeds United)
Extras: Yorkshire CCC Most Promising Young Cricketer. Took wicket (Steve
Stubbings) with the first legitimate ball of his career (the first delivery was a wide) v
Derbyshire in the B&H at Headingley 2001. Played for Northants v Sri Lankans in a
one-day fixture at Northampton 2002. Played one first-class match as a trialist for
Northamptonshire 2005; not re-engaged for 2006
Best bowling: 1-55 Northamptonshire v Leicestershire, Leicester 2005

2005 Season

	M	Inns	NO	Runs	HS	Avge	100s	50s	Ct	St	O	M	Runs	Wkts	Avge	Best	5wI	10wM
Test																		
All First	1	1	0	0	0	0.00	-	-	1	-	13	2	55	1	55.00	1-55	-	-
1-Day Int																		
C & G																			
tsL																			
Twenty20																			

Career Performances

	M	Inns	NO	Runs	HS	Avge	100s	50s	Ct	St	Balls	Runs	Wkts	Avge	Best	5wI	10wM
Test																	
All First	1	1	0	0	0	0.00	-	-	1	-	78	55	1	55.00	1-55	-	-
1-Day Int																	
C & G	1	1	0	63	63	63.00	-	1	-	-	60	49	1	49.00	1-49	-	
tsL	1	0	0	0	0	-	-	-	1	-	30	22	1	22.00	1-22	-	
Twenty20																	

BALCOMBE, D. J. Hampshire

Name: David John Balcombe
Role: Right-hand bat, right-arm
fast-medium bowler
Born: 24 December 1984, City of London
Height: 6ft 4in
Nickname: Balcs
County debut: No first-team appearance
Strike rate: (career 69.12)
Parents: Peter and Elizabeth
Marital status: Single
Education: St John's School, Leatherhead;
Durham University
Qualifications: 9 GCSEs, 3 A-levels, Level 1
coaching award
Career outside cricket: Student and
coaching
Off-season: 'Working on fitness; studying for
degree at Durham; going out to Perth over
Christmas/New Year to work on game'
Overseas tours: Surrey Academy to Perth 2004; MCC A to Canada 2005
Overseas teams played for: Midland-Guildford CC, Western Australia 2003-04
Career highlights to date: 'Taking maiden first-class five-wicket return against
Durham'
Cricket superstitions: 'Any left-sided equipment has to go on first – eg left boot,
left pad'
Cricketers particularly admired: Martin Bicknell
Young players to look out for: Will Smith, Mark Phythian, Richard Morris
Other sports played: 'A small amount of golf, badly!'
Other sports followed: Rugby, golf, football
Favourite band: Green Day, Jack Johnson
Relaxations: 'Socialising, PlayStation, sleeping!'

Extras: Played for Durham UCCE 2005 (received cap for five-wicket innings in a first-class game)

Opinions on cricket: 'I think the Twenty20 competition has really improved the range of shots in the longer form of the game, making it more exciting to watch and play, especially now it's being played internationally. It also allows players to cope far better with the pressures of playing in front of large crowds.'

Best batting: 73 DUCCE v Leicestershire, Leicester 2005
Best bowling: 5-112 DUCCE v Durham, Durham 2005

2005 Season (did not make any first-class or one-day appearances for his county)

Career Performances

	M	Inns	NO	Runs	HS	Avge	100s	50s	Ct	St	Balls	Runs	Wkts	Avge	Best	5wI	10wM
Test																	
All First	3	3	0	89	73	29.66	-	1	1	-	553	391	8	48.87	5-112	1	-
1-Day Int																	
C & G																		
tsL																		
Twenty20																		

BALL, M. C. J. Gloucestershire

Name: <u>Martyn</u> Charles John Ball
Role: Right-hand bat, off-spin bowler, slip fielder
Born: 26 April 1970, Bristol
Height: 5ft 9in **Weight:** 12st 10lbs
Nickname: Benny, Barfo
County debut: 1988
County cap: 1996
Benefit: 2002
Place in batting averages: (2004 170th av. 25.83)
Place in bowling averages: (2004 151st av. 55.36)
Strike rate: (career 80.65)
Parents: Kenneth Charles and Pamela Wendy
Wife and date of marriage: Mona, 28 September 1991
Children: Kristina, 9 May 1990; Alexandra, 2 August 1993; Harrison, 5 June 1997
Education: King Edmund Secondary School, Yate; Bath College of Further Education

Qualifications: 6 O-levels, 2 A-levels, advanced cricket coach
Overseas tours: Gloucestershire to Namibia 1991, to Kenya 1992, to Sri Lanka 1993, to Zimbabwe 1996, 1997, to South Africa 1999; MCC to New Zealand 1998-99; England to India 2001-02
Overseas teams played for: North Melbourne, Australia 1988-89; Old Hararians, Zimbabwe 1990-91
Cricketers particularly admired: Ian Botham, Vic Marks, John Emburey, Jack Russell
Other sports played: Rugby, football (both to county schoolboys level), 'enjoy golf and skiing'
Other sports followed: 'All sport – massive Man City fan'
Relaxations: 'Spending some quality time at home with family'
Extras: Represented county schools. Played for Young England 1989. Produced best match bowling figures for the Britannic County Championship 1993 season – 14-169 against Somerset at Taunton. Called up for England Test tour of India 2001-02 after withdrawal of Robert Croft
Best batting: 75 Gloucestershire v Somerset, Taunton 2003
Best bowling: 8-46 Gloucestershire v Somerset, Taunton 1993

2005 Season

	M	Inns	NO	Runs	HS	Avge	100s	50s	Ct	St	O	M	Runs	Wkts	Avge	Best	5wl	10wM
Test																		
All First	3	6	0	10	7	1.66	-	-	5	-	149	38	400	6	66.66	3-99	-	-
1-Day Int																		
C & G	2	2	1	23	12 *	23.00	-	-	1	-	19	1	75	2	37.50	2-27	-	
tsL	13	10	5	80	22	16.00	-	-	3	-	83.3	5	333	15	22.20	3-44	-	
Twenty20	8	3	0	35	21	11.66	-	-	3	-	21	0	175	8	21.87	3-24	-	

Career Performances

	M	Inns	NO	Runs	HS	Avge	100s	50s	Ct	St	Balls	Runs	Wkts	Avge	Best	5wl	10wM
Test																	
All First	183	280	53	4418	75	19.46	-	15	215	-	29196	13749	362	37.98	8-46	12	1
1-Day Int																	
C & G	38	23	9	244	33 *	17.42	-	-	30	-	1855	1262	44	28.68	3-39	-	
tsL	185	131	49	1099	45	13.40	-	-	70	-	6903	5536	179	30.92	5-33	2	
Twenty20	18	7	2	56	21	11.20	-	-	10	-	348	421	18	23.38	3-24	-	

BANDARA, C. M.   Gloucestershire

Name: Charitha <u>Malinga</u> Bandara
Role: Right-hand bat, leg-break bowler
Born: 31 December 1979, Kalutara,
Sri Lanka
Nickname: Billy
County debut: 2005
County cap: 2005
Test debut: 1998
Place in batting averages: 261st av. 13.85
Place in bowling averages: 19th av. 24.15
Strike rate: 47.02 (career 48.51)
Overseas tours: Sri Lanka U19 to South
Africa (U19 World Cup) 1997-98, to India
1998-99; Sri Lanka A to England 1999; Sri
Lanka to India 2005-06
Overseas teams played for: Kalutara Town
1996-97; Nondescripts 1998-99 – 2002-03;
Tamil Union C&AC 2003-04; Galle 2004-05;
Ragama 2005-06 –
Extras: Has represented Sri Lanka A against numerous touring sides; took 11-126
(8-49/3-77) for Sri Lanka A v England A at Colombo 2005. Was an overseas player
with Gloucestershire during the 2005 season as locum for Upul Chandana
Best batting: 79 Sri Lanka A v Pakistan A, Dambulla 2004-05
Best bowling: 8-49 Sri Lanka A v England A, Colombo 2004-05
Stop press: Made ODI debut v New Zealand at Wellington 2005-06

2005 Season

	M	Inns	NO	Runs	HS	Avge	100s	50s	Ct	St	O	M	Runs	Wkts	Avge	Best	5wI	10wM
Test																		
All First	8	14	0	194	70	13.85	-	1	6	-	352.4	69	1087	45	24.15	5-45	2	-
1-Day Int																		
C & G																			
tsL	5	4	1	79	36	26.33	-	-	2	-	39.4	2	185	7	26.42	2-28	-	
Twenty20																		

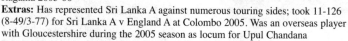

Career Performances

	M	Inns	NO	Runs	HS	Avge	100s	50s	Ct	St	Balls	Runs	Wkts	Avge	Best	5wI	10wM
Test	1	2	1	0	0 *	0.00	-	-	1	-	126	79	0	-	-	-	-
All First	89	121	26	1733	79	18.24	-	8	56	-	11304	5837	233	25.05	8-49	9	2
1-Day Int																	
C & G																	
tsL	5	4	1	79	36	26.33	-	-	2	-	238	185	7	26.42	2-28	-	
Twenty20																	

BARRICK, D. J.   Durham

Name: <u>David</u> James Barrick
Role: Right-hand bat, leg-spin bowler;
all-rounder
Born: 4 January 1984, Pontefract, Yorkshire
Height: 5ft 8in **Weight:** 11st 7lbs
Nickname: Baz
County debut: No first-team appearance
(*see Extras*)
Parents: Janet and Dave
Marital status: Single
Education: Malet Lambert School;
Wilberforce College
Qualifications: 10 GCSEs, 3 A-levels,
Levels 1 and 2 cricket coaching
Career outside cricket: Factory worker
Off-season: 'Part-time work (factory)'
Overseas tours: England U17 to Australia
2001; Durham to Dubai 2005
Overseas teams played for: Adelaide Buffalos CC 2002; Bulleen Bulls CC,
Melbourne 2003-04
Career highlights to date: 'Playing for England U17'
Cricket moments to forget: 'Involved in run-out, missed ball, broke finger, whilst
doing 12th man – right laugh!'
Cricket superstitions: 'None'
Cricketers particularly admired: Ricky Ponting, Shane Warne, Herschelle Gibbs
Young players to look out for: Chris Grey
Other sports played: Golf, football
Other sports followed: Football (Sheffield Wednesday)
Favourite band: Linkin Park
Relaxations: 'Music, watching sport and films, eating out, and the gym?!'
Extras: Played for Durham v Bangladesh A in a one-day fixture at Riverside 2005 but
has yet to appear for the county in first-class cricket or one-day competition

Opinions on cricket: 'More technical – looked at in greater detail these days. The game's faster. More professional. Not enough publicity compared to football.'

BASSANO, C. W. G. Derbyshire

Name: <u>Christopher</u> Warwick Godfrey Bassano
Role: Right-hand bat, leg-spin bowler
Born: 11 September 1975, East London, South Africa
Height: 6ft 2in **Weight:** 13st 7lbs
Nickname: Bass, Bassy
County debut: 2001
County cap: 2002
1000 runs in a season: 1
Place in batting averages: 142nd av. 30.64 (2004 69th av. 42.84)
Parents: Brian and Allison
Marital status: Single
Family links with cricket: 'Father played throughout his life, was a radio commentator, provincial manager, and held development positions in South Africa; also wrote books on cricket etc.'

Education: Grey School, Port Elizabeth; Launceston Church Grammar School, Tasmania; University of Tasmania, Hobart
Qualifications: Bachelor of Applied Science (Horticulture)
Career outside cricket: Trout fishing guide
Overseas teams played for: Launceston CC, Tasmania 1990-2002; Kingborough CC, Hobart 2003; Tasmania 2002-03
Career highlights to date: 'Being selected to play representative cricket or to play at a higher level is always a highlight'
Cricket moments to forget: 'Losing'
Cricketers particularly admired: Graeme Pollock, Steve Waugh
Other sports played: Hockey
Other sports followed: Rugby union
Favourite band: Roxette
Relaxations: Fly fishing and fly tying
Extras: Captained Eastern Province U13 1987-88. Played for Tasmania U16, U17, U19 (captain), U23 (captain), 2nd XI and 1st XI. Became the first player to score a century in each innings of his Championship debut, 186* and 106 v Gloucestershire at Derby 2001. Scored 100-ball 121 v Glamorgan at Cardiff in the C&G 2003, winning

Man of the Match award. Is diabetic. His ancestry includes a set of brothers from Venice who were musicians at the court of Henry VIII. Is not considered an overseas player. Released by Derbyshire at the end of the 2005 season

Opnions on cricket: 'The general standard of the pitches needs to improve to more closely mimic those of Test cricket. One-day pitches are particularly poor in general. There is too much cricket played. With the amount of talent we have in England, there is no reason why England can't be number one in the world for years.'

Best batting: 186* Derbyshire v Gloucestershire, Derby 2001

2005 Season

	M	Inns	NO	Runs	HS	Avge	100s	50s	Ct	St	O	M	Runs	Wkts	Avge	Best	5wI	10wM
Test																		
All First	9	14	0	429	87	30.64	-	2	4	-								
1-Day Int																		
C & G	2	2	0	63	57	31.50	-	1	1	-								
tsL	4	4	0	20	15	5.00	-	-	-	-								
Twenty20																		

Career Performances

	M	Inns	NO	Runs	HS	Avge	100s	50s	Ct	St	Balls	Runs	Wkts	Avge	Best	5wI	10wM
Test																	
All First	59	101	9	3132	186 *	34.04	5	20	34	-	12	11	0	-	-	-	-
1-Day Int																	
C & G	7	7	0	346	121	49.42	2	1	1	-							
tsL	54	53	5	1320	126 *	27.50	3	6	11	-							
Twenty20	9	7	0	119	43	17.00	-	-	3	-							

7. Which West Indies player has the best bowling figures by a debutant in ODIs?

BATTY, G. J.   Worcestershire

Name: <u>Gareth</u> Jon Batty
Role: Right-hand bat, off-spin bowler,
county vice-captain
Born: 13 October 1977, Bradford, Yorkshire
Height: 5ft 11in **Weight:** 12st 4lbs
Nickname: Batts, Boris, Stuta
County debut: 1997 (Yorkshire), 1998 (one-
day, Surrey), 1999 (first-class, Surrey),
2002 (Worcestershire)
County colours: 2002 (Worcestershire)
Test debut: 2003-04
50 wickets in a season: 2
Place in batting averages: 162nd av. 28.50
(2004 134th av. 31.33)
Place in bowling averages: 96th av. 37.57
(2004 53rd av. 30.68)
Strike rate: 72.72 (career 65.30)
Parents: David and Rosemary
Marital status: Single

Family links with cricket: Father was Yorkshire Academy coach; brother played for
Yorkshire and Somerset
Education: Bingley Grammar
Qualifications: 9 GCSEs, BTEC Art and Design, coaching certificate
Career outside cricket: 'Property'
Overseas tours: England U15 to South Africa 1993; England U19 to Zimbabwe
1995-96, to Pakistan 1996-97; ECB National Academy to Australia and Sri Lanka
2002-03; England to Bangladesh and Sri Lanka 2003-04, to West Indies 2003-04, to
Zimbabwe (one-day series) 2004-05, to South Africa 2004-05; England A to West Indies
2005-06
Overseas teams played for: Marist Newman, Australia 1999
Career highlights to date: 'Playing for England'
Cricket moments to forget: 'Every time we lose'
Cricket superstitions: 'None'
Cricketers particularly admired: Adam Hollioake 'to name but one'
Young players to look out for: Ravi Bopara, Steve Davies, Daryl Mitchell
Other sports played: Golf, rugby
Other sports followed: Rugby union (Bradford & Bingley), rugby league
(Leeds Rhinos)
Injuries: Injuries to both hands
Favourite band: Frank Sinatra
Relaxations: 'Property and spending time with family and friends'

Extras: *Daily Telegraph* Young Player of the Year 1993. Surrey Supporters' Club Most Improved Player Award and Young Player of the Year Award 2001. Surrey CCC Young Player of the Year Award 2001. ECB 2nd XI Player of the Year 2001. Leading all-rounder in the inaugural Twenty20 Cup 2003. Made Test debut in the first Test v Bangladesh at Dhaka 2003-04, taking a wicket (Alok Kapali) with his third ball. Vice-captain of Worcestershire since 2005. ECB National Academy 2005-06

Opinions on cricket: 'I think Twenty20 is great and keeps kids interested.'

Best batting: 133 Worcestershire v Surrey, The Oval 2004

Best bowling: 7-52 Worcestershire v Northamptonshire, Northampton 2004

2005 Season

	M	Inns	NO	Runs	HS	Avge	100s	50s	Ct	St	O	M	Runs	Wkts	Avge	Best	5wI	10wM
Test	2	0	0	0	0	-	-	-	1	-	15	2	44	1	44.00	1-44	-	-
All First	15	20	4	456	57	28.50	-	3	11	-	400	74	1240	33	37.57	5-87	1	-
1-Day Int																		
C & G	2	1	0	5	5	5.00	-	-	1	-	20	1	67	2	33.50	2-27	-	
tsL	11	8	2	91	44	15.16	-	-	5	-	85.1	1	445	11	40.45	3-51	-	
Twenty20	7	7	2	65	21 *	13.00	-	-	3	-	22	0	165	3	55.00	2-20	-	

Career Performances

	M	Inns	NO	Runs	HS	Avge	100s	50s	Ct	St	Balls	Runs	Wkts	Avge	Best	5wI	10wM
Test	7	8	1	144	38	20.57	-	-	3	-	1394	733	11	66.63	3-55	-	-
All First	76	116	18	2290	133	23.36	1	11	54	-	14962	7161	229	31.27	7-52	8	1
1-Day Int	6	4	1	4	3	1.33	-	-	4	-	312	253	4	63.25	2-40	-	
C & G	15	11	2	106	32 *	11.77	-	-	9	-	653	429	13	33.00	2-25	-	
tsL	76	66	16	989	83 *	19.78	-	4	25	-	2822	2215	64	34.60	4-36	-	
Twenty20	18	17	2	256	87	17.06	-	1	5	-	312	425	15	28.33	3-45	-	

8. Who were the first England opening pair to each score a century in an ODI?

BATTY, J. N.   Surrey

Name: Jonathan (Jon) Neil Batty
Role: Right-hand bat, wicket-keeper
Born: 18 April 1974, Chesterfield
Height: 5ft 10in **Weight:** 11st 6lbs
Nickname: JB
County debut: 1997
County cap: 2001
50 dismissals in a season: 3
Place in batting averages: 59th av. 43.68
(2004 116th av. 34.55)
Strike rate: (career 78.00)
Parents: Roger and Jill
Marital status: Single
Family links with cricket: Father played to a
high standard of club cricket
Education: Wheatley Park; Repton; Durham
University (St Chad's); Keble College,
Oxford
Qualifications: 10 GCSEs, 4 A-levels, BSc (Hons) in Natural Sciences, Diploma in
Social Studies (Oxon)
Overseas tours: Repton School to Holland 1991; MCC to Bangladesh 1996; Surrey to
South Africa 1997, 2001
Overseas teams played for: Mount Lawley CC, Perth 1997-2002
Career highlights to date: 'Winning three County Championships'
Cricket moments to forget: 'None!'
Cricketers particularly admired: David Gower, Alec Stewart, Jack Russell
Other sports played: Golf, squash
Other sports followed: Football (Nottingham Forest)
Relaxations: Reading, listening to music, movies
Extras: Represented Combined Universities 1994, 1995. Oxford Blue 1996. Surrey
Supporters' Club Most Improved Player 2002, 2003. BBC Radio London Listeners'
Cricketer of the Year 2003. Became second wicket-keeper (after Kent's Steve Marsh in
1991) to take eight catches in an innings (a new Surrey record) and score a century
(129) in the same match, v Kent at The Oval 2004. Captain of Surrey 2004
Best batting: 168* Surrey v Essex, Chelmsford 2003
Best bowling: 1-21 Surrey v Lancashire, Old Trafford 2000

	M	Inns	NO	Runs	HS	Avge	100s	50s	Ct	St	O	M	Runs	Wkts	Avge	Best	5wl	10wM
Test																		
All First	16	25	3	961	124	43.68	1	8	50	4								
1-Day Int																		
C & G	3	3	1	187	158 *	93.50	1	-	3	1								
tsL	17	17	1	422	82	26.37	-	2	11	3								
Twenty20	10	8	2	114	39	19.00	-	-	3	3								

Career Performances

	M	Inns	NO	Runs	HS	Avge	100s	50s	Ct	St	Balls	Runs	Wkts	Avge	Best	5wl	10wM
Test																	
All First	127	189	27	5245	168 *	32.37	10	24	334	42	78	61	1	61.00	1-21	-	-
1-Day Int																	
C & G	11	9	3	304	158 *	50.66	1	1	8	1							
tsL	109	85	15	1357	82	19.38	-	6	112	18							
Twenty20	24	20	8	217	39	18.08	-	-	15	3							

BELL, I. R.   Warwickshire

Name: <u>Ian</u> Ronald Bell
Role: Right-hand bat, right-arm medium bowler
Born: 11 April 1982, Coventry
Height: 5ft 10in **Weight:** 11st
Nickname: Belly
County debut: 1999
County cap: 2001
Test debut: 2004
1000 runs in a season: 2
1st-Class 200s: 2
Place in batting averages: 52nd av. 44.91 (2004 5th av. 68.56)
Place in bowling averages: (2004 32nd av. 27.37)
Strike rate: (career 59.58)
Parents: Terry and Barbara
Marital status: Single
Family links with cricket: Brother Keith has played for England U18
Education: Princethorpe College, Rugby
Overseas tours: Warwickshire U19 to Cape Town 1998-99; England U19 to New Zealand 1998-99, to Malaysia and (U19 World Cup) Sri Lanka 1999-2000, to India

2000-01 (c); England A to West Indies 2000-01, to Sri Lanka 2004-05 (c); ECB National Academy to Australia 2001-02, to Sri Lanka 2002-03; England to Zimbabwe (one-day series) 2004-05, to South Africa 2004-05, to Pakistan 2005-06, to India 2005-06

Overseas teams played for: University of Western Australia, Perth 2003-04

Cricket moments to forget: 'Being bowled for a duck when making county debut'

Cricketers particularly admired: Michael Atherton, Steve Waugh, Alec Stewart, Nick Knight

Young players to look out for: Keith Bell

Other sports played: Football (was at Coventry City School of Excellence), rugby, golf

Other sports followed: Football (Aston Villa), rugby union (Northampton Saints)

Relaxations: Golf, listening to music

Extras: Played for England U14, U15, U16, U17; captained England U19. NBC Denis Compton Award for the most promising young Warwickshire player 1999, 2000, 2001. Gray-Nicolls Trophy for Best Young Schools Cricketer 2000. Cricket Society's Most Promising Young Cricketer of the Year Award 2001. Recorded maiden one-day century (125) and maiden one-day five-wicket return (5-41) v Essex at Chelmsford in the NCL 2003. Scored maiden first-class double century (262*) v Sussex at Horsham 2004, in the process setting with Tony Frost (135*) a new Warwickshire record partnership for the seventh wicket (289*). Cricket Writers' Club Young Cricketer of the Year 2004. PCA Young Player of the Year award 2004. ECB National Academy 2004-05. Made ODI debut in the first ODI v Zimbabwe at Harare 2004-05, scoring 75 and winning Man of the Match award. Scored 480 first-class runs in April 2005, an English record for the month

Best batting: 262* Warwickshire v Sussex, Horsham 2004

Best bowling: 4-4 Warwickshire v Middlesex, Lord's 2004

Stop press: Appointed MBE in 2006 New Year Honours as part of 2005 Ashes-winning England team

2005 Season

	M	Inns	NO	Runs	HS	Avge	100s	50s	Ct	St	O	M	Runs	Wkts	Avge	Best	5wl	10wM
Test	7	12	2	398	162 *	39.80	1	3	8	-	7	2	20	0	-	-	-	-
All First	15	26	3	1033	231	44.91	2	6	14	-	77	16	284	6	47.33	3-64	-	-
1-Day Int																		
C & G	4	4	0	115	54	28.75	-	1	3	-	19	2	85	3	28.33	3-29	-	
tsL	9	8	0	245	137	30.62	1	1	3	-	26	0	166	4	41.50	2-28	-	
Twenty20	7	7	2	163	66 *	32.60	-	1	4	-	4	0	36	1	36.00	1-12	-	

Career Performances

	M	Inns	NO	Runs	HS	Avge	100s	50s	Ct	St	Balls	Runs	Wkts	Avge	Best	5wI	10wM
Test	8	13	2	468	162 *	42.54	1	4	10	-	42	20	0	-	-	-	-
All First	84	142	13	5553	262 *	43.04	13	28	51	-	2443	1323	41	32.26	4-4	-	-
1-Day Int	8	7	1	189	75	31.50	-	2	2	-	22	9	3	3.00	3-9	-	
C & G	14	13	1	376	68	31.33	-	4	8	-	261	188	4	47.00	3-29	-	
tsL	55	53	4	1646	137	33.59	2	12	12	-	839	759	23	33.00	5-41	1	
Twenty20	18	17	4	246	66 *	18.92	-	1	7	-	132	186	3	62.00	1-12	-	

BENHAM, C. C. Hampshire

Name: Christopher (Chris) Charles Benham
Role: Right-hand bat, right-arm
off-spin bowler
Born: 24 March 1983, Frimley, Surrey
Height: 6ft 2in **Weight:** 13st
Nickname: Benny, Beano, Benoit
County debut: 2004
Place in batting averages: 272nd av. 11.70
Parents: Frank and Sandie
Marital status: Single
Family links with cricket: 'Both older
brothers, Nick and Andy, played local
club cricket'
Education: Yateley Comprehensive School;
Yateley Sixth Form College; Loughborough
University
Qualifications: 10 GCSEs, 3 A-levels
Overseas tours: West of England U15 to
West Indies 1998
Cricketers particularly admired: Ricky Ponting, V.V.S. Laxman, Sachin Tendulkar,
Michael Vaughan
Other sports played: Football (school, district and county sides; trials with Swindon
and Crystal Palace), tennis, golf
Other sports followed: Football (Reading FC)
Favourite band: Kings of Leon
Relaxations: 'Listening to music; watching DVDs; spending time with my girlfriend;
going to the gym'
Extras: Played for ESCA U15 v Scotland. Represented England U16 v Denmark.
Played for Loughborough University CCE 2002, 2004. Represented British
Universities 2004. Scored 74 on Championship debut v Derbyshire at Derby 2004
Best batting: 74 Hampshire v Derbyshire, Derby 2004

2005 Season

	M	Inns	NO	Runs	HS	Avge	100s	50s	Ct	St	O	M	Runs	Wkts	Avge	Best	5wI	10wM
Test																		
All First	5	10	0	117	41	11.70	-	-	5	-								
1-Day Int																		
C & G																		
tsL																		
Twenty20																		

Career Performances

	M	Inns	NO	Runs	HS	Avge	100s	50s	Ct	St	Balls	Runs	Wkts	Avge	Best	5wI	10wM
Test																		
All First	9	16	1	319	74	21.26	-	1	5	-								
1-Day Int																		
C & G	1	1	0	0	0	0.00	-	-	-	-								
tsL																		
Twenty20																		

BENKENSTEIN, D. M.   Durham

Name: Dale Martin Benkenstein
Role: Right-hand bat, right-arm off-break
or medium bowler
Born: 9 June 1974, Harare, Zimbabwe
County debut: 2005
1000 runs in a season: 1
1st-Class 200s: 2
Place in batting averages: 16th av. 58.85
Place in bowling averages: 45th av. 27.75
Strike rate: 45.83 (career 71.72)
Family links with cricket: Father, Martin,
and two brothers, Brett and Boyd, played
first-class cricket
Education: Michaelhouse, KwaZulu-Natal
Overseas tours: KwaZulu-Natal to Australia
(Champions Cup) 2000-01; South Africa U24
to Sri Lanka 1995; South Africa A to Sri
Lanka 1998, to West Indies 2000; South
Africa to Malaysia (Commonwealth Games) 1998-99, to Bangladesh (Wills
International Cup) 1998-99, to New Zealand 1998-99, to Sri Lanka (ICC Champions
Trophy) 2002-03, plus one-day series and tournaments in Kenya, India and Sharjah
Overseas teams played for: Natal/KwaZulu-Natal 1992-93 – 2003-04; Dolphins
2004-05 –

Extras: Captained Natal Schools and South Africa Schools. Represented South Africa A against various touring sides. One of *South African Cricket Annual*'s five Cricketers of the Year 1997. Was captain of KwaZulu-Natal, leading the side to the double (SuperSport Series and Standard Bank Cup) in 1996-97 and 2001-02. Has won numerous domestic awards, including Man of the Match in the final of the Standard Bank Cup 2001-02 at Durban (77*). Is not considered an overseas player
Best batting: 259 KwaZulu-Natal v Northerns, Durban 2001-02
Best bowling: 4-29 Durham v Northamptonshire, Northampton 2005

2005 Season

	M	Inns	NO	Runs	HS	Avge	100s	50s	Ct	St	O	M	Runs	Wkts	Avge	Best	5wI	10wM
Test																		
All First	17	25	4	1236	162*	58.85	4	5	12	-	91.4	20	333	12	27.75	4-29	-	-
1-Day Int																		
C & G	1	1	0	29	29	29.00	-	-	-	-								
tsL	17	13	5	411	90	51.37	-	4	9	-	43	5	158	11	14.36	4-16	-	
Twenty20	7	7	2	160	53	32.00	-	1	2	-	22	0	175	11	15.90	3-10	-	

Career Performances

	M	Inns	NO	Runs	HS	Avge	100s	50s	Ct	St	Balls	Runs	Wkts	Avge	Best	5wI	10wM
Test																	
All First	130	188	21	7422	259	44.44	18	40	96	-	3658	1752	51	34.35	4-29	-	-
1-Day Int	23	20	3	306	69	18.00	-	1	3	-	65	44	4	11.00	3-5	-	
C & G	1	1	0	29	29	29.00	-	-	-	-							
tsL	17	13	5	411	90	51.37	-	4	9	-	258	158	11	14.36	4-16	-	
Twenty20	7	7	2	160	53	32.00	-	1	2	-	132	175	11	15.90	3-10	-	

---

9. Which West Indies pair put on an unbeaten
106 for the tenth wicket against England at Old Trafford
in 1984, an ODI record?

BENNING, J. G. E.   Surrey

Name: <u>James</u> Graham Edward Benning
Role: Right-hand bat, right-arm medium
bowler; batting all-rounder
Born: 4 May 1983, Mill Hill, London
Height: 5ft 11in **Weight:** 13st
Nickname: Benno
County debut: 2002 (one-day),
2003 (first-class)
Place in batting averages: 48th av. 46.42
(2004 167th av. 26.50)
Strike rate: (career 72.37)
Parents: Sandy and David
Marital status: Single
Family links with cricket: 'Dad played for
Middlesex'
Education: Caterham School
Qualifications: 12 GCSEs, 3 AS-levels
Overseas tours: Surrey YC to Barbados
1999-2000, to Sri Lanka 2002

Overseas teams played for: North Dandenong, Australia 2001-02
Career highlights to date: 'Making County Championship debut'
Cricket moments to forget: 'Dropping two catches in front of a lively crowd at
Canterbury, live on Sky'
Cricket superstitions: 'Order in which I put my kit on'
Cricketers particularly admired: Alec Stewart, Adam Hollioake
Young players to look out for: Neil Saker, Scott Newman, Ben Scott
Other sports played: Rugby, football
Other sports followed: Football (Watford)
Favourite band: 'Listen to almost all music apart from thrash metal'
Relaxations: 'Going to the gym, music, spending time around friends'
Extras: Played for England U15-U19. First recipient of Ben Hollioake Scholarship.
NBC Denis Compton Award for the most promising young Surrey player 2003
Best batting: 128 Surrey v OUCCE, The Parks 2004
Best bowling: 3-57 Surrey v Kent, Tunbridge Wells 2005

2005 Season

	M	Inns	NO	Runs	HS	Avge	100s	50s	Ct	St	O	M	Runs	Wkts	Avge	Best	5wI	10wM
Test																		
All First	4	7	0	325	124	46.42	1	3	1	-	59	3	293	6	48.83	3-57	-	-
1-Day Int																		
C & G	3	3	0	106	73	35.33	-	1	-	-	16	1	77	3	25.66	2-31	-	
tsL	17	17	0	553	72	32.52	-	4	3	-	60.1	2	371	9	41.22	3-31	-	
Twenty20	10	10	0	193	66	19.30	-	1	3	-	1	0	7	1	7.00	1-7	-	

Career Performances

	M	Inns	NO	Runs	HS	Avge	100s	50s	Ct	St	Balls	Runs	Wkts	Avge	Best	5wI	10wM
Test																	
All First	12	21	1	677	128	33.85	2	3	4	-	579	466	8	58.25	3-57	-	-
1-Day Int																	
C & G	6	6	0	176	73	29.33	-	1	1	-	114	103	4	25.75	2-31	-
tsL	29	28	0	758	72	27.07	-	6	7	-	608	660	21	31.42	4-43	-
Twenty20	20	20	0	357	66	17.85	-	1	4	-	30	43	2	21.50	1-7	-

BETTS, M. M. Middlesex

Name: Melvyn Morris Betts
Role: Right-hand bat, right-arm
fast-medium bowler
Born: 26 March 1975, Co Durham
Height: 5ft 11in **Weight:** 12st 4lbs
Nickname: Mel B, Betsy
County debut: 1993 (Durham),
2001 (Warwickshire), 2004 (Middlesex)
County cap: 1998 (Durham),
2001 (Warwickshire)
Place in batting averages: 244th av. 17.00
(2004 251st av. 14.50)
Place in bowling averages: 98th av. 38.09
(2004 132nd av. 44.38)
Strike rate: 62.50 (career 52.55)
Parents: Melvyn and Shirley
Wife and date of marriage: Angela,
3 October 1998
Children: Chloe, 16 July 1999; Megan, 14 May 2002
Family links with cricket: 'Dad played for local team Sacriston'
Education: Fyndoune Community College
Qualifications: 9 GCSEs, plus qualifications in engineering and sports and
recreational studies

Off-season: 'Spending time with family'

Overseas tours: England U19 to Sri Lanka 1993-94; England A to Zimbabwe and South Africa 1998-99; Durham CCC to South Africa 1996; MCC to Namibia and Uganda 2004-05

Career highlights to date: 'Taking 9-64 v Northamptonshire'

Cricket superstitions: 'None'

Cricketers particularly admired: David Boon

Young players to look out for: Chris Whelan

Other sports followed: Football (Newcastle United FC)

Injuries: Out for six weeks with a broken finger

Favourite band: U2

Relaxations: 'Golf and catching up with friends'

Extras: Represented England U19 1994. Took 5-22 on Championship debut for Warwickshire against his old county, Durham, at Edgbaston 2001

Opinions on cricket: 'There should be 96 overs in a day's play to make lunch and tea longer.'

Best batting: 73 Warwickshire v Lancashire, Edgbaston 2003

Best bowling: 9-64 Durham v Northamptonshire, Northampton 1997

2005 Season

	M	Inns	NO	Runs	HS	Avge	100s	50s	Ct	St	O	M	Runs	Wkts	Avge	Best	5wI	10wM
Test																		
All First	9	10	2	136	36 *	17.00	-	-	-	-	229.1	45	838	22	38.09	4-58	-	-
1-Day Int																		
C & G	1	1	0	0	0	0.00	-	-	-	-	10	1	46	3	15.33	3-46	-	
tsL	9	3	3	14	9 *	-	-	-	1	-	68	2	442	9	49.11	2-38	-	
Twenty20	7	2	0	4	4	2.00	-	-	-	-	28	0	268	5	53.60	2-51	-	

Career Performances

	M	Inns	NO	Runs	HS	Avge	100s	50s	Ct	St	Balls	Runs	Wkts	Avge	Best	5wI	10wM
Test																	
All First	115	164	37	1879	73	14.79	-	5	37	-	18028	10635	343	31.00	9-64	14	2
1-Day Int																	
C & G	11	8	1	40	14	5.71	-	-	2	-	654	488	22	22.18	4-15	-	
tsL	67	43	20	250	21	10.86	-	-	12	-	2779	2400	73	32.87	4-39	-	
Twenty20	11	3	1	17	13 *	8.50	-	-	2	-	222	347	6	57.83	2-51	-	

BICHEL, A. J.   Essex

Name: Andrew (<u>Andy</u>) John Bichel
Role: Right-hand bat, right-arm
fast-medium bowler
Born: 27 August 1970, Laidley, Queensland,
Australia
Height: 5ft 11in **Weight:** 13st 13lbs
Nickname: Bic, Andre
County debut: 2001 (Worcestershire),
2005 (Hampshire)
County cap: 2001; colours 2002 (both
Worcestershire)
Test debut: 1996-97
50 wickets in a season: 1
Place in batting averages: (2004 72nd
av. 42.17)
Place in bowling averages: 72nd av. 31.50
(2004 141st av. 46.93)
Strike rate: 51.71 (career 49.14)
Parents: Trevor and Shirley
Wife and date of marriage: Dionn, 18 April 1997
Children: Keegan, 26 October 1999; Darcy, 24 October 2002
Family links with cricket: 'Dad played local Queensland country cricket. Uncle Don
played for Queensland. Best game was against England'
Education: Laidley High; Ipswich TAFE
Qualifications: Carpentry; cricket coaching
Career outside cricket: Project management
Overseas tours: Queensland Academy to South Africa 1994; Australian Academy to
South Africa 1996; Australia A to Scotland and Ireland 1998; Australia to South Africa
1996-97, to England 1997, to New Zealand (one-day series) 1997-98, to Malaysia
(Commonwealth Games) 1998, to West Indies 1998-99, to South Africa 2001-02, to
Kenya (PSO Tri-Nation Tournament) 2002, to Sri Lanka (ICC Champions Trophy)
2002-03, to Sri Lanka and Sharjah (v Pakistan) 2002-03, to Africa (World Cup)
2002-03, to West Indies 2002-03, to India (TVS Cup) 2003-04; FICA World XI to
New Zealand 2004-05
Overseas teams played for: Queensland 1992-93 –
Career highlights to date: 'World Cup 2003'
Cricket moments to forget: 'Being sick on the field against India in India'
Cricket superstitions: 'Like my gear in its place before the game'
Cricketers particularly admired: Allan Border, Sachin Tendulkar, Glenn McGrath,
Dennis Lillee
Other sports played: Rugby league (first grade TRL); tennis (first grade LTA)

Other sports followed: Rugby league (Brisbane Broncos), AFL (Brisbane Lions)
Favourite band: U2, Cold Chisel
Relaxations: 'Beach, fishing, golf, hanging out on the islands just off Queensland coast'
Extras: Sheffield Shield Player of the Year 1996-97. Queensland Player of the Year 1998-99. An overseas player with Worcestershire 2001-02, 2004. Won the Dick Lygon Award 2001 as Worcestershire's Player of the Year; was also the Worcestershire Supporters' Association Player of the Year 2001 and the winner of the inaugural Don Kenyon Award. Man of the Match v South Africa at Sydney in the VB Series 2001-02 (5-19) and v England at Port Elizabeth in the World Cup 2002-03 (34* following 7-20, the third best bowling return in ODI history). Named Australia's State Player of the Year at the 2005 Allan Border Medal awards. Has same birthday as the late Sir Donald Bradman. Was a temporary overseas player with Hampshire during the 2005 season, replacing Craig McMillan. Scored 138 on debut for Hampshire v Gloucestershire at Cheltenham 2005, in the process sharing with Nic Pothas (139) in a new Hampshire record partnership for the eighth wicket (257). Has joined Essex as an overseas player for 2006; due to take over in mid-June from Mitchell Johnson (*see page 726*)
Best batting: 142 Worcestershire v Northamptonshire, Worcester 2004
Best bowling: 9-93 Worcestershire v Gloucestershire, Worcester 2002

2005 Season

	M	Inns	NO	Runs	HS	Avge	100s	50s	Ct	St	O	M	Runs	Wkts	Avge	Best	5wI	10wM
Test																		
All First	4	3	0	227	138	75.66	1	1	1	-	120.4	25	441	14	31.50	4-122	-	-
1-Day Int																		
C & G	2	1	0	16	16	16.00	-	-	1	-	20	1	99	4	24.75	3-57	-	
tsL	5	5	1	16	12	4.00	-	-	2	-	35	5	183	8	22.87	3-41	-	
Twenty20																		

Career Performances

	M	Inns	NO	Runs	HS	Avge	100s	50s	Ct	St	Balls	Runs	Wkts	Avge	Best	5wI	10wM
Test	19	22	1	355	71	16.90	-	1	16	-	3337	1870	58	32.24	5-60	1	-
All First	147	191	18	4237	142	24.49	6	15	77	-	29385	15514	598	25.94	9-93	29	6
1-Day Int	67	36	13	473	64	20.56	-	1	19	-	3257	2464	78	31.58	7-20	2	
C & G	12	10	2	126	38 *	15.75	-	-	2	-	595	404	24	16.83	4-17	-	
tsL	37	32	3	338	42	11.65	-	-	13	-	1631	1132	57	19.85	5-21	1	
Twenty20	6	6	3	180	58 *	60.00	-	1	5	-	126	162	8	20.25	3-36	-	

BICKNELL, D. J.　　　Nottinghamshire

Name: <u>Darren</u> John Bicknell
Role: Left-hand opening bat, occasional
slow left-arm bowler
Born: 24 June 1967, Guildford
Height: 6ft 4½in **Weight:** 14st 9lbs
Nickname: Denz, Bickers
County debut: 1987 (Surrey), 2000 (Notts)
County cap: 1990 (Surrey), 2000 (Notts)
Benefit: 1999 (Surrey)
1000 runs in a season: 9
1st-Class 200s: 2
Place in batting averages: 32nd av. 50.91
(2004 65th av. 43.20)
Strike rate: (career 54.10)
Parents: Vic and Valerie
Wife and date of marriage: Rebecca,
21 September 1992

Children: Lauren Elizabeth, 21 September
1993; Sam, 9 November 1995; Emily, 16 December 1997
Family links with cricket: Brother Martin plays for Surrey
Education: Robert Haining County Secondary; Guildford County College
of Technology
Qualifications: 8 O-levels, 2 A-levels, senior coaching award, Diploma in Golf Club
Management, 'Sage Accountancy 10-day passport to competency'
Career outside cricket: Scottish Courage brewery account manager
Overseas tours: Surrey to Sharjah 1988, 1989, to Dubai 1990, to Perth 1995;
Nottinghamshire to Johannesburg 2000, 2001, 2002; England A to Zimbabwe and
Kenya 1989-90, to Pakistan 1990-91, to Bermuda and West Indies 1991-92
Overseas teams played for: Coburg, Melbourne 1986-87
Career highlights to date: 'England A call-up. Debut for Surrey. Being capped by
Notts and Surrey. Every time I reach a hundred'
Cricket moments to forget: 'My first-ball dismissal in my debut A "Test" match v
Zimbabwe, and brother Martin getting me out twice'
Cricket superstitions: 'Try and wear same clothes if successful previously'
Cricketers particularly admired: Mark Taylor, David Gower, Angus Fraser,
Martin Bicknell
Young players to look out for: Samit Patel, Josh Mierkalns
Other sports played: Golf (11 handicap), five-a-side football
Other sports followed: Football (West Ham United, Nottingham Forest)
Favourite band: Anastacia
Relaxations: Family, golf and TV

Extras: Shared Surrey record third-wicket stand of 413 with David Ward v Kent at Canterbury in 1990. Surrey Batsman of the Year four times. Became first English cricketer to take part in more than one Championship partnership of 400-plus when he scored 180* in a first-wicket stand of 406* with Guy Welton (200*) v Warwickshire at Edgbaston 2000; the stand broke several records, including that for the highest Nottinghamshire partnership for any wicket. Was acting captain of Nottinghamshire in 2001 during the absence through injury of Jason Gallian

Opinions on cricket: 'English net facilities appalling – general. Teams should socialise more! I would like to see teams in division one being more positive in trying to win games!'

Best batting: 235* Surrey v Nottinghamshire, Trent Bridge 1994
Best bowling: 3-7 Surrey v Sussex, Guildford 1996

2005 Season

	M	Inns	NO	Runs	HS	Avge	100s	50s	Ct	St	O	M	Runs	Wkts	Avge	Best	5wI	10wM
Test																		
All First	17	27	3	1222	123	50.91	2	10	3	-	15	2	87	0	-	-	-	-
1-Day Int																		
C & G	1	1	0	3	3	3.00	-	-	-	-								
tsL	2	2	0	36	31	18.00	-	-	-	-								
Twenty20	1	1	0	10	10	10.00	-	-	-	-								

Career Performances

	M	Inns	NO	Runs	HS	Avge	100s	50s	Ct	St	Balls	Runs	Wkts	Avge	Best	5wI	10wM
Test																	
All First	306	531	43	19080	235 *	39.09	46	87	105	-	1569	1015	29	35.00	3-7	-	-
1-Day Int																	
C & G	26	26	5	942	135 *	44.85	1	5	1	-							
tsL	150	144	16	4477	125	34.97	6	31	35	-	42	45	2	22.50	1-11	-	
Twenty20	1	1	0	10	10	10.00	-	-	-	-							

BICKNELL, M. P.   Surrey

Name: <u>Martin</u> Paul Bicknell
Role: Right-hand bat, right-arm fast-medium bowler
Born: 14 January 1969, Guildford
Height: 6ft 4in **Weight:** 15st
Nickname: Bickers
County debut: 1986
County cap: 1989
Benefit: 1997; testimonial 2006
Test debut: 1993

50 wickets in a season: 11
Place in batting averages: 78th av. 38.55
(2004 160th av. 27.93)
Place in bowling averages: 62nd av. 30.37
(2004 41st av. 29.44)
Strike rate: 52.10 (career 52.03)
Parents: Vic and Val
Wife and date of marriage: Loraine,
29 September 1995
Children: Eleanor, 31 March 1995;
Charlotte, 22 July 1996
Family links with cricket: 'Brother plays,
but with no luck'
Education: Robert Haining County
Secondary
Qualifications: 2 O-levels, NCA coach
Overseas tours: England YC to Sri Lanka
1986-87, to Australia 1987-88; England A to
Zimbabwe and Kenya 1989-90, to Bermuda and West Indies 1991-92, to South Africa
1993-94; England to Australia 1990-91
Career highlights to date: 'A *Wisden* Cricketer of the Year 2001'
Cricket moments to forget: 'It's all been an experience!!'
Cricketers particularly admired: 'All honest county trundlers'
Young players to look out for: Tim Murtagh
Other sports played: Golf
Other sports followed: Football (Leeds United), golf
Relaxations: 'Playing golf, reading; spending time with my children'
Extras: Took 7-30 in National League v Glamorgan at The Oval 1999, the best
Sunday/National League return by a Surrey bowler. Had match figures of 16-119 (9-47
in the second innings) v Leicestershire at Guildford in 2000. One of *Wisden*'s Five
Cricketers of the Year 2001. Wetherell Award for the Cricket Society's leading all-
rounder in English first-class cricket 2000 and 2001. Surrey Supporters' Player of the
Year 1993, 1997, 1999, 2000, 2001. Surrey Players' Player of the Year 1997, 1998,
1999, 2000, 2001. Surrey CCC Bowler of the Season Award 2001. Took 6-42 v Kent
at The Oval 2002, in the process achieving the feat of having recorded a five-wicket
innings return against all 17 counties besides his own. His 5-128 v Kent at The Oval
2004 included his 1000th first-class wicket (Matthew Dennington)
Best batting: 141 Surrey v Essex, Chelmsford 2003
Best bowling: 9-45 Surrey v Cambridge University, The Oval 1988

2005 Season

	M	Inns	NO	Runs	HS	Avge	100s	50s	Ct	St	O	M	Runs	Wkts	Avge	Best	5wI	10wM
Test																		
All First	8	11	2	347	76	38.55	-	3	4	-	251.5	55	881	29	30.37	6-56	2	-
1-Day Int																		
C & G	2	2	1	31	20 *	31.00	-	-	2	-	20	3	50	2	25.00	1-25	-	
tsL	3	2	0	12	9	6.00	-	-	-	-	22	2	90	6	15.00	2-25	-	
Twenty20																		

Career Performances

	M	Inns	NO	Runs	HS	Avge	100s	50s	Ct	St	Balls	Runs	Wkts	Avge	Best	5wI	10wM
Test	4	7	0	45	15	6.42	-	-	2	-	1080	543	14	38.78	4-84	-	-
All First	288	352	85	6584	141	24.65	3	25	101	-	54844	26286	1054	24.93	9-45	43	4
1-Day Int	7	6	2	96	31 *	24.00	-	-	2	-	413	347	13	26.69	3-55	-	
C & G	46	23	10	263	66 *	20.23	-	1	19	-	2811	1609	62	25.95	4-35	-	
tsL	207	108	47	849	57 *	13.91	-	1	43	-	9020	6331	253	25.02	7-30	3	
Twenty20	3	2	2	11	10 *	-	-	-	1	-	66	61	4	15.25	2-11	-	

BISHOP, J. E.   Essex

Name: Justin Edward Bishop
Role: Left-hand lower middle order bat,
left-arm fast-medium opening bowler
Born: 4 January 1982, Bury St Edmunds
Height: 6ft **Weight:** 13st 8lbs
Nickname: Bish, Bash, Basher, Tractor Boy
County debut: 1999
Strike rate: (career 60.21)
Parents: Keith and Anne
Marital status: Single
Family links with cricket: Father played
for Bury St Edmunds and Suffolk
Education: County Upper School, Bury St
Edmunds; Durham University
Qualifications: GCSEs, 1 A-level (PE),
GNVQ (Advanced) Science, BA (Hons),
Level 1 coaching awards in cricket and
athletics
Overseas tours: England U19 to Malaysia and (U19 World Cup) Sri Lanka
1999-2000, to India 2000-01; British Universities to South Africa 2002, 2004
Overseas teams played for: Claremont CC, Cape Town 2004-05
Career highlights to date: 'Taking seven wickets in an U19 "One-Day International"
for England v West Indies'

Cricketers particularly admired: Mark Ilott
Other sports played: Football (Suffolk U15; John Snow College, Durham – 'uni champions 2003-04')
Other sports followed: Football (Ipswich Town FC)
Favourite band: The Thrills
Extras: Represented England U15 and U17. Took 7-42 for England U19 v Sri Lanka U19 in third 'Test' at Worcester 2000. Took 7-41 for England U19 v West Indies U19 at Chelmsford 2001, the best England U19 figures in an 'ODI'. Played for Durham University CCE 2002-04. Represented British Universities 2003 and 2004. Released by Essex at the end of the 2005 season
Best batting: 66 DUCCE v Northamptonshire, Northampton 2004
Best bowling: 5-148 Essex v Leicestershire, Chelmsford 2001

2005 Season

	M	Inns	NO	Runs	HS	Avge	100s	50s	Ct	St	O	M	Runs	Wkts	Avge	Best	5wI	10wM
Test																		
All First	1	0	0	0	0	-	-	-	2	-	16.5	3	51	2	25.50	1-19	-	-
1-Day Int																		
C & G																		
tsL																		
Twenty20																		

Career Performances

	M	Inns	NO	Runs	HS	Avge	100s	50s	Ct	St	Balls	Runs	Wkts	Avge	Best	5wI	10wM
Test																	
All First	25	33	5	433	66	15.46	-	4	7	-	3432	2248	57	39.43	5-148	1	-
1-Day Int																	
C & G	3	3	0	3	3	1.00	-	-	-	-	127	78	3	26.00	2-34	-	
tsL	20	13	6	55	16 *	7.85	-	-	4	-	701	666	23	28.95	3-33	-	
Twenty20																	

> 10. Which Australia bowler shared in a 119-run partnership with Shane Warne v South Africa at Port Elizabeth in 1993-94, an ODI record for the eighth wicket?

BLACKWELL, I. D.　　　Somerset

Name: Ian David Blackwell
Role: Left-hand middle-order bat, slow left-arm bowler, county captain
Born: 10 June 1978, Chesterfield
Height: 6ft 2in
Nickname: Le Donk, Blackdog, Donkey, Pip
County debut: 1997 (Derbyshire), 2000 (Somerset)
County cap: 2001 (Somerset)
1000 runs in a season: 2
1st-Class 200s: 1
Place in batting averages: 28th av. 52.33 (2004 11th av. 61.71)
Place in bowling averages: 143rd av. 56.03 (2004 87th av. 36.00)
Strike rate: 110.96 (career 91.44)
Parents: John and Marilyn
Marital status: Partner Beth

Family links with cricket: 'Father played a few games for Derbyshire Over 50s'
Education: Manor Secondary School; Brookfield Community School
Qualifications: 8 GCSEs, 1 A-level, Level 2 coaching award
Off-season: 'Hopefully with England to Pakistan and India'
Overseas tours: Somerset to Cape Town 2000, 2001; England VI to Hong Kong 2001; England to Sri Lanka (ICC Champions Trophy) 2002-03, to Australia 2002-03 (VB Series), to Africa (World Cup) 2002-03, to Bangladesh and Sri Lanka 2003-04 (one-day series), to West Indies 2003-04 (one-day series), to Pakistan 2005-06 (one-day series), to India 2005-06; ECB National Academy to Australia 2002-03
Overseas teams played for: Delacombe Park CC, Melbourne 1997, 1999
Career highlights to date: 'Playing for England; winning C&G Trophy 2001; winning Twenty20 2005; scoring 82 in my second ODI; scoring 247* v Derbyshire 2003; winning Sixes League 2005; winning Walter Lawrence Trophy for fastest 100'
Cricket moments to forget: 'Any of my ducks for England'
Cricket superstitions: 'Always chew gum'
Cricketers particularly admired: Ricky Ponting, Graeme Smith, Andrew Caddick, Matt Wood, Carl Gazzard, James Hildreth, 'Bestie' Durston
Young players to look out for: Callum Huggett, Jack Cooper
Other sports played: Golf (6 handicap)
Other sports followed: Football (Chesterfield FC)
Favourite band: Eminem, Jack Johnson, James Blunt
Relaxations: 'Shopping, watching films, Internet, PSP PlayStation'
Player website: www.ianblackwell.com

Extras: Played for Derbyshire from the age of eight through to the 1st XI. Became first batsman in Championship history to score two centuries (103/122) in a match batting at No. 7, v Northants at Northampton 2001. Scored 134-ball double century v Derbyshire at Taunton 2003, finishing with 247*. Returned career best innings figures of 7-90 v Glamorgan at Taunton and again v Nottinghamshire at Trent Bridge 2004. Won the Walter Lawrence Trophy 2005 (fastest first-class century of the season) for his 67-ball hundred v Derbyshire at Taunton. Won the Sky Sports Sixes League 2005 (45 sixes). Captain of Somerset since July 2005, taking over from the departing Graeme Smith

Opinions on cricket: 'I like some of the new additions to the 2006 season. The play-off is a good idea in National League. Two overseas players should mean exactly that – only long-term injuries should allow a team to replace them. Two minutes per wicket in National League should have been allowed! Stupid run penalties given as teams penalised for taking wickets and not being compensated.'

Best batting: 247* Somerset v Derbyshire, Taunton 2003
Best bowling: 7-90 Somerset v Glamorgan, Taunton 2004
                 7-90 Somerset v Nottinghamshire, Trent Bridge 2004
Stop press: Made Test debut in the first Test v India at Nagpur 2005-06

2005 Season

	M	Inns	NO	Runs	HS	Avge	100s	50s	Ct	St	O	M	Runs	Wkts	Avge	Best	5wI	10wM
Test																		
All First	17	28	4	1256	191	52.33	3	9	5	-	517.5	107	1569	28	56.03	4-86	-	-
1-Day Int																		
C & G	1	1	0	40	40	40.00	-	-	-									
tsL	18	17	2	745	134 *	49.66	2	5	4	-	131	2	659	16	41.18	5-26	1	
Twenty20	11	11	3	173	45	21.62	-	-	4	-	35	0	228	16	14.25	4-26	-	

Career Performances

	M	Inns	NO	Runs	HS	Avge	100s	50s	Ct	St	Balls	Runs	Wkts	Avge	Best	5wI	10wM
Test																	
All First	111	172	13	6232	247 *	39.19	16	29	44	-	16825	7959	184	43.25	7-90	7	-
1-Day Int	23	19	1	291	82	16.16	-	1	5	-	648	485	15	32.33	3-26	-	
C & G	19	17	2	409	86	27.26	-	2	5	-	576	436	9	48.44	2-34	-	
tsL	112	106	9	3016	134 *	31.09	3	20	26	-	3884	3249	97	33.49	5-26	1	
Twenty20	19	19	4	268	45	17.86	-	-	7	-	350	413	16	25.81	4-26	-	

BLAIN, J. A. R.   Yorkshire

Name: <u>John</u> Angus Rae Blain
Role: Right-hand bat, right-arm
fast-medium bowler
Born: 4 January 1979, Edinburgh
Height: 6ft 2in **Weight:** 13st 7lbs
Nickname: Blainy, Haggis, William, JB
County debut: 1997 (Northamptonshire),
2004 (Yorkshire)
Place in batting averages: (2004 254th
av. 13.42)
Place in bowling averages: (2004 30th
av. 26.80)
Strike rate: (career 50.53)
Parents: John and Elma
Marital status: Single
Education: Penicuik HS; Jewel and Esk
Valley College
Qualifications: 8 GCSEs, 1 A-level, HNC

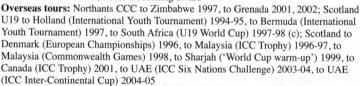

Leisure and Recreation, Level 1 coaching award
Overseas tours: Northants CCC to Zimbabwe 1997, to Grenada 2001, 2002; Scotland
U19 to Holland (International Youth Tournament) 1994-95, to Bermuda (International
Youth Tournament) 1997, to South Africa (U19 World Cup) 1997-98 (c); Scotland to
Denmark (European Championships) 1996, to Malaysia (ICC Trophy) 1996-97, to
Malaysia (Commonwealth Games) 1998, to Sharjah ('World Cup warm-up') 1999, to
Canada (ICC Trophy) 2001, to UAE (ICC Six Nations Challenge) 2003-04, to UAE
(ICC Inter-Continental Cup) 2004-05
Overseas teams played for: New Plymouth Old Boys, New Zealand 1998-99;
Taranaki Cricket Association, New Zealand 1998-99
Career highlights to date: 'World Cup 1999, England. Signing for Yorkshire CCC'
Cricket moments to forget: 'Not qualifying for the 2003 World Cup, failing to
qualify by losing the last match by six runs in Canada 2001; not qualifying for the
Champions Trophy in England 2004, losing last game to the USA in Dubai 2004'
(*USA qualified for the Champions Trophy ahead of Scotland by virtue of a net run rate
that was superior by just 0.028 runs*)
Cricket superstitions: 'Keeping a tidy kitbag'
Cricketers particularly admired: Devon Malcolm, Darren Lehmann
Young players to look out for: David Wainwright
Other sports played: Football (schoolboy forms with Hibernian FC and Falkirk FC,
making youth and reserve team appearances)
Other sports followed: Rugby
Relaxations: 'Listening to music, going out for a beer; spending time with my

girlfriend and going home to Scotland to see family; watching football, going to the gym, and sleeping!'

Extras: Has played for Scotland in first-class cricket and in the B&H and NatWest competitions; has also played for Scottish Saltires in NCL. Took 5-24 on Sunday League debut for Northamptonshire v Derbyshire at Derby 1997. Represented Scotland in the 1999 World Cup, taking 10 wickets and finishing top of the strike rate chart for the tournament. Man of the Match in the final of the ICC Inter-Continental Cup v Canada in the UAE 2004, returning match figures of 7-55 (3-27/4-28)

Opinions on cricket: 'Too many so-called British- or English-qualified imports coming into the game. County players are underestimated in world cricket. The instant success of "newcomers" to the England team shows just that.'

Best batting: 34 Northamptonshire v Surrey, Northampton 2001
Best bowling: 6-42 Northamptonshire v Kent, Canterbury 2001

2005 Season

	M	Inns	NO	Runs	HS	Avge	100s	50s	Ct	St	O	M	Runs	Wkts	Avge	Best	5wl	10wM
Test																		
All First	2	1	1	19	19 *	-	-	-	1	-	44	5	201	3	67.00	2-40	-	-
1-Day Int																		
C & G	1	1	0	6	6	6.00	-	-	-	-	9	1	34	0	-	-	-	-
tsL	6	4	1	20	11 *	6.66	-	-	-	-	37.5	1	222	7	31.71	2-40	-	
Twenty20																		

Career Performances

	M	Inns	NO	Runs	HS	Avge	100s	50s	Ct	St	Balls	Runs	Wkts	Avge	Best	5wl	10wM
Test																	
All First	33	38	16	272	34	12.36	-	-	7	-	4649	3420	92	37.17	6-42	2	-
1-Day Int	5	5	1	15	9	3.75	-	-	1	-	223	210	10	21.00	4-37	-	
C & G	4	2	0	12	6	6.00	-	-	1	-	222	145	6	24.16	2-8	-	
tsL	20	10	7	30	11 *	10.00	-	-	6	-	752	708	23	30.78	5-24	1	
Twenty20																	

11. Why was the 271st ODI, between Pakistan and India, abandoned in 1984?

BLAKEY, R. J.   Yorkshire

Name: <u>Richard</u> John Blakey
Role: Right-hand bat, wicket-keeper
Born: 15 January 1967, Huddersfield
Height: 5ft 10in **Weight:** 11st 4lbs
Nickname: Dick
County debut: 1985
County cap: 1987
Benefit: 1998
Test debut: 1992-93
1000 runs in a season: 5
50 dismissals in a season: 6
1st-Class 200s: 3
Strike rate: (career 63.00)
Parents: Brian and Pauline
Wife and date of marriage: Michelle,
28 September 1991

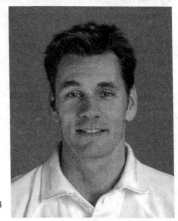

Children: Harrison Brad, 22 September 1993
Family links with cricket: Father played
local cricket
Education: Rastrick Grammar School
Qualifications: 4 O-levels, Senior NCA Coach
Overseas tours: England YC to West Indies 1984-85; Yorkshire to Barbados 1986-87,
to Cape Town 1990-91; England A to Zimbabwe and Kenya 1989-90, to Pakistan
1990-91; England to India and Sri Lanka 1992-93
Overseas teams played for: Waverley, Sydney 1985-87; Mt Waverley, Sydney
1987-88; Bionics, Zimbabwe 1989-90
Cricketers particularly admired: Martyn Moxon, Dermot Reeve, Ian Botham,
Alan Knott
Other sports followed: All
Relaxations: All sports, particularly golf and squash, eating out, drawing, photography
Extras: Yorkshire's Young Player of the Year 1989. Was awarded a citation by the
International Committee for Fair Play in 1995, the only cricketer among the 25 winners
worldwide. Vice-captain of Yorkshire 2002. Yorkshire Players' Player of the Year and
Club Player of the Year 2002
Best batting: 223* Yorkshire v Northamptonshire, Headingley 2003
Best bowling: 1-68 Yorkshire v Nottinghamshire, Sheffield 1986

Career Performances

	M	Inns	NO	Runs	HS	Avge	100s	50s	Ct	St	Balls	Runs	Wkts	Avge	Best	5wI	10wM
Test	2	4	0	7	6	1.75	-	-	2	-							
All First	348	554	87	14674	223 *	31.42	13	86	778	57	63	68	1	68.00	1-68	-	-
1-Day Int	3	2	0	25	25	12.50	-	-	2	1							
C & G	48	35	13	516	75	23.45	-	2	54	5							
tsL	249	218	52	5531	130 *	33.31	3	27	244	48							
Twenty20	7	5	1	119	32	29.75	-	-	5	1							

BOND, S. E. Gloucestershire

Name: <u>Shane</u> Edward Bond
Role: Right-hand bat, right-arm fast bowler
Born: 7 June 1975, Christchurch,
New Zealand
County debut: 2002 (Warwickshire)
Test debut: 2001-02
Strike rate: (career 49.34)
Parents: John and Judith
Wife: Tracy
Education: Papanui High School,
Christchurch
Career outside cricket: Police officer
Overseas tours: New Zealand A to India
(Buchi Babu Tournament) 2001-02; New
Zealand to Australia 2001-02, to West Indies
2002, to Sri Lanka (ICC Champions Trophy)
2002-03, to Africa (World Cup) 2002-03,
to Sri Lanka 2003, to England 2004,

to Zimbabwe 2005-06, to South Africa (one-day series) 2005-06
Overseas teams played for: Canterbury 1996-97 –
Extras: One of *New Zealand Cricket Almanack*'s two Players of the Year 2002. Was forced home from New Zealand's 2004 tour of England with a persistent back injury. Has won several international awards, including Man of the [VB] Series in Australia 2001-02 (21 wickets; av. 16.38), of the [Test] Series v West Indies 2002 and of the [Test] Series v Zimbabwe 2005-06. Warwickshire's overseas player during August 2002 as a locum for Shaun Pollock; has joined Gloucestershire as an overseas player for 2006. Attended same school in Christchurch as Andrew Caddick
Best batting: 100 Canterbury v Northern Districts, Christchurch 2004-05
Best bowling: 6-51 New Zealand v Zimbabwe, Bulawayo 2005-06

Stop press: Made Twenty20 international debut v South Africa at Johannesburg 2005-06

2005 Season (did not make any first-class or one-day appearances)

Career Performances

	M	Inns	NO	Runs	HS	Avge	100s	50s	Ct	St	Balls	Runs	Wkts	Avge	Best	5wl	10wM
Test	12	12	6	102	41*	17.00	-	-	4	-	2091	1165	56	20.80	6-51	3	1
All First	44	50	19	636	100	20.51	1	2	20	-	7402	3851	150	25.67	6-51	7	1
1-Day Int	31	14	6	127	31*	15.87	-	-	9	-	1553	1064	62	17.16	6-19	3	
C & G																	
tsL	1	0	0	0	0	-	-	-	-	-	54	32	0	-	-	-	-
Twenty20																	

BOPARA, R. S. Essex

Name: Ravinder (Ravi) Singh Bopara
Role: Right-hand top-order bat, right-arm medium bowler
Born: 4 May 1985, Newham, London
Height: 5ft 10in **Weight:** 12st
Nickname: Puppy
County debut: 2002
County cap: 2005
Place in batting averages: 95th av. 36.66 (2004 200th av. 22.28)
Place in bowling averages: 135th av. 47.95
Strike rate: 64.30 (career 74.17)
Parents: Baldish and Charanjit
Marital status: Single
Education: Brampton Manor School; Barking Abbey Sports College
Qualifications: 7 GCSEs, ECB Level 1 coaching
Overseas tours: England U19 to Australia 2002-03, to Bangladesh (U19 World Cup) 2003-04; England A to West Indies 2005-06
Career highlights to date: 'Playing against India and Pakistan overseas teams. Meeting Sachin Tendulkar; facing Shoaib Akhtar and Mohammad Sami'
Cricket moments to forget: 'I went out to bat once and didn't realise I didn't have a box on until I got hit there'
Cricketers particularly admired: Sachin Tendulkar, Viv Richards, Carl Hooper
Young players to look out for: Bilal Shafayat, 'and any players who are hungry for success'

Other sports followed: Football (Arsenal)

Favourite band: Tupac and the Outlawz

Extras: Played for Development of Excellence XI (South) v West Indies U19 2001. Represented England U19 2003 and 2004. C&G Man of the Match award v Devon at Exmouth 2005 (65*). Scored 135 v Australians in a two-day game at Chelmsford 2005. ECB National Academy 2005-06

Best batting: 105* Essex v Derbyshire, Chelmsford 2005

Best bowling: 4-93 Essex v Derbyshire, Chelmsford 2005

Stop press: Called up as a replacement to the England A tour to West Indies 2005-06

2005 Season

	M	Inns	NO	Runs	HS	Avge	100s	50s	Ct	St	O	M	Runs	Wkts	Avge	Best	5wI	10wM
Test																		
All First	17	29	5	880	105 *	36.66	1	5	7	-	214.2	26	959	20	47.95	4-93	-	-
1-Day Int																		
C & G	2	2	1	107	65 *	107.00	-	1	1	-	4	0	14	0	-		-	-
tsL	14	13	5	277	96 *	34.62	-	1	7	-	65	2	316	8	39.50	2-25	-	
Twenty20	7	5	0	68	30	13.60	-	-	2	-	14	0	124	3	41.33	1-17	-	

Career Performances

	M	Inns	NO	Runs	HS	Avge	100s	50s	Ct	St	Balls	Runs	Wkts	Avge	Best	5wI	10wM
Test																	
All First	30	51	10	1364	105 *	33.26	1	5	21	-	1706	1263	23	54.91	4-93	-	-
1-Day Int																	
C & G	4	4	1	119	65 *	39.66	-	1	2	-	48	32	2	16.00	2-18	-	
tsL	31	29	9	508	96 *	25.40	-	2	10	-	601	523	15	34.86	2-10	-	
Twenty20	17	11	1	146	30	14.60	-	-	4	-	144	204	7	29.14	3-18	-	

12. Which former Gloucestershire batsman was the first to score three consecutive ODI hundreds?

BORRINGTON, P. M.   Derbyshire

Name: <u>Paul</u> Michael Borrington
Role: Right-hand bat, right-arm off-spin
bowler, occasional wicket-keeper
Born: 24 May 1988, Nottingham
Height: 5ft 10in   **Weight:** 9st 10lbs
Nickname: Borrers, Bozza, Boz
County debut: 2005
Parents: Tony and Sheila
Marital status: Single
Family links with cricket: Father played
first-class for Derbyshire 1970-82
Education: Chellaston School; Repton
School (sixth form)
Qualifications: Taking A-levels 2006
Overseas tours: Derbyshire U15 to South
Africa 2003; England U16 to South Africa
2004; Repton to Sri Lanka 2005
Career highlights to date: 'Captaining the
Midlands to victory in the 2003 Bunbury Festival. First-class debut v Leicestershire at
the age of 17. Representing England at U15 and U17 levels'
Cricket moments to forget: 'Leaving a straight ball from Charl Willoughby on my
first-class debut against Leicestershire'
Cricketers particularly admired: Michael Vaughan
Young players to look out for: 'Current Derbyshire Academy players'
Other sports played: Football, occasional golf
Other sports followed: Football (Crewe Alexandra)
Favourite band: The Killers, Razorlight
Relaxations: 'Spending time with my friends'
Extras: NBC Denis Compton Award 2005
Opinions on cricket: 'Very impressed with the structure, organisation and coaching at
the England age-group levels. Introduction and development of county academies has
been a huge success – English cricket will reap the benefits in the next few years.'
Best batting: 28 Derbyshire v Somerset, Taunton 2005

2005 Season

	M	Inns	NO	Runs	HS	Avge	100s	50s	Ct	St	O	M	Runs	Wkts	Avge	Best	5wI	10wM
Test																		
All First	2	2	0	32	28	16.00	-	-	-	-								
1-Day Int																		
C & G																		
tsL																		
Twenty20																		

	M	Inns	NO	Runs	HS	Avge	100s	50s	Ct	St	Balls	Runs	Wkts	Avge	Best	5wl	10wM
Test																	
All First	2	2	0	32	28	16.00	-	-	-	-							
1-Day Int																	
C & G																	
tsL																	
Twenty20																	

BOTHA, A. G. Derbyshire

Name: Anthony (<u>Ant</u>) Greyvensteyn Botha
Role: Left-hand bat, slow left-arm bowler
Born: 17 November 1976, Pretoria,
South Africa
Nickname: Boats, Both, Botox
County debut: 2004
County cap: 2004
Place in batting averages: 80th av. 38.47
(2004 174th av. 25.31)
Place in bowling averages: 128th av. 45.63
(2004 88th av. 36.07)
Strike rate: 86.12 (career 71.59)
Parents: Elise and Ian
Marital status: Single
Education: Maritzburg College;
Maritzburg Technikon
Career outside cricket: 'Was sales manager
for glass company in South Africa'
Overseas tours: South Africa U19 to India 1995-96
Overseas teams played for: Natal/KwaZulu-Natal 1995-96 – 1998-99; Easterns
1999-2000 – 2002-03
Career highlights to date: 'Winning the four-day championship with Easterns 2002'
Cricket superstitions: 'None'
Cricketers particularly admired: Jonty Rhodes
Other sports played: Hockey, tennis, watersports
Other sports followed: Rugby, football
Favourite band: Barry Manilow
Relaxations: Fishing, watersports
Extras: Represented South African Schools 1995. Played for South African Academy
1997. Man of the Match v Boland at Paarl in the SuperSport Series 2000-01 and v
Eastern Province at Benoni in the Standard Bank Cup 2001-02. Scored maiden first-

class century (103) v Durham University CCE at Derby 2004, then took 5-55 in the DUCCE second innings to become the first Derbyshire player since 1937 to score a century and record a five-wicket innings return in the same first-class match. Is England-qualified

Best batting: 156* Derbyshire v Yorkshire, Derby 2005
Best bowling: 8-53 KwaZulu-Natal B v Northerns B, Centurion 1997-98

2005 Season

	M	Inns	NO	Runs	HS	Avge	100s	50s	Ct	St	O	M	Runs	Wkts	Avge	Best	5wI	10wM
Test																		
All First	17	28	7	808	156 *	38.47	1	2	7	-	473.4	109	1506	33	45.63	6-104	1	-
1-Day Int																		
C & G	2	2	1	49	34 *	49.00	-	-	2	-	20	0	84	7	12.00	4-44	-	
tsL	18	13	4	153	56 *	17.00	-	1	9	-	98.4	1	545	20	27.25	3-18	-	
Twenty20	8	7	2	80	25 *	16.00	-	-	1	-	31	0	211	9	23.44	2-16	-	

Career Performances

	M	Inns	NO	Runs	HS	Avge	100s	50s	Ct	St	Balls	Runs	Wkts	Avge	Best	5wI	10wM
Test																	
All First	72	116	19	2418	156 *	24.92	2	8	48	-	12601	5960	176	33.86	8-53	4	1
1-Day Int																	
C & G	3	3	1	53	34 *	26.50	-	-	2	-	150	112	7	16.00	4-44	-	
tsL	28	21	6	248	56 *	16.53	-	1	11	-	994	830	32	25.93	3-18	-	
Twenty20	12	10	4	101	25 *	16.83	-	-	3	-	252	288	12	24.00	2-16	-	

BOYCE, M. A. G. Leicestershire

Name: Matthew (Matt) Andrew Golding Boyce
Role: Left-hand opening bat, 'very occasional' right-arm off-spin bowler
Born: 13 August 1985, Cheltenham
Height: 5ft 10in **Weight:** 10st 12lbs
Nickname: Boycey
County debut: No first-team appearance
Parents: Anne and Andrew
Marital status: Single
Family links with cricket: 'Father played recreational cricket for over 20 years and coached youth cricket for ten years. Aunt played for Cambridge University. Brother played for Oakham School for three years in 1st XI'
Education: Oakham School; Nottingham University ('studying Management Studies and Economics')
Qualifications: 9 GCSEs, 3 A-levels
Overseas tours: Leicestershire U13 to South Africa 1998; Oakham School to South Africa 2000

Overseas teams played for: Hoppers Crossing, Melbourne 2003-04

Career highlights to date: 'Scoring first century (105) v Northants for Leics 2nd XI. Scoring 2570 runs in 2004 season for Egerton Park and Market Overton and Leics, including record score of 225 (150 balls; 30 x 4, 5 x 6) in the Rutland Championship side v Peterborough. Playing for England Development Squad v Bangladesh 2004'

Cricket moments to forget: 'Walking out to bat against Northamptonshire without a box on and facing the first over before admitting to that fact!'

Cricket superstitions: 'None'

Cricketers particularly admired: David Gower, Andrew Strauss, Brian Lara

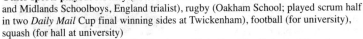

Other sports played: Hockey (Leicestershire and Midlands Schoolboys, England trialist), rugby (Oakham School; played scrum half in two *Daily Mail* Cup final winning sides at Twickenham), football (for university), squash (for hall at university)

Other sports followed: Football (Manchester United), rugby (Leicester Tigers)

Favourite band: Midtown, Queen

Relaxations: Sport – squash, gym, swimming, football, rugby; socialising, PlayStation, music

Extras: County Council Special Award for Youth Cricket. *Rutland Times* Young Cricketer of the Year. Sporting Moment of the Year (225; *see above*). Rutland League Teenage Cricketer of the Year. Leading batsman in Leicestershire League

Opinions on cricket: 'I am just starting out in the professional game, having been awarded a two-year contract with Leicestershire. I have played for the county since I was nine. I have always enjoyed success at all levels, but I am sure that the moment will come when success comes hard. However, like many counties, Leicestershire concentrate on the whole person and not just cricket in terms of training the mind as well as the body. Today's game has many support features which would have been anathema to bygone cricketers. Physios, sports psychologists, nutritionists, biomechanics are all the rage, and whilst they play an invaluable role they can't play for you. Therefore it is still a game to be played by fostering your own talent, organising yourself and perhaps not taking yourself too seriously!'

BRACKEN, N. W. — Worcestershire

Name: Nathan Wade Bracken
Role: Right-hand bat, left-arm
fast-medium bowler
Born: 12 September 1977, Penrith,
New South Wales, Australia
Height: 6ft 5in **Weight:** 14st 13lbs
County debut: 2004 (Gloucestershire)
Test debut: 2003-04
Strike rate: (career 62.76)
Education: Springwood High School, NSW
Overseas tours: New South Wales to New
Zealand 2000-01; Australia to India 2000-01
(one-day series), to England 2001, to Africa
(World Cup) 2002-03, to India (TVS Cup)
2003-04, to New Zealand (one-day series)
2005-06; Australia A to South Africa
2002-03, to Pakistan 2005-06
Overseas teams played for: New South
Wales 1998-99 –
Career highlights to date: 'Test debut and winning the World Cup'
Extras: Represented Australia U19 1995-96. Attended Commonwealth Bank
[Australian] Cricket Academy 1997. Had figures of 5-38 (including hat-trick – White,
Berry, Harwood) v Victoria at Melbourne in the ING Cup 2001-02, winning Man of
the Match award. Man of the Match v England at Adelaide in the VB Series 2002-03
(3-21). Returned innings figures of 7-4 (7-5-4-7) as New South Wales dismissed South
Australia for 29 at Sydney in the Pura Cup 2004-05. An overseas player with Gloucs
towards the end of the 2004 season; has joined Worcs as an overseas player for 2006
Best batting: 38* New South Wales v Tasmania, Hobart 2002-03
             38* New South Wales v Victoria, Melbourne 2002-03
Best bowling: 7-4 New South Wales v South Australia, Sydney 2004-05
Stop press: Made Twenty20 international debut v South Africa at Brisbane 2005-06

2005 Season (did not make any first-class or one-day appearances)

Career Performances

	M	Inns	NO	Runs	HS	Avge	100s	50s	Ct	St	Balls	Runs	Wkts	Avge	Best	5wl	10wM
Test	3	3	1	9	6 *	4.50	-	-	1	-	768	351	6	58.50	2-12	-	-
All First	50	68	25	750	38 *	17.44	-	-	13	-	9916	4225	158	26.74	7-4	7	-
1-Day Int	17	1	1	7	7 *	-	-	-	5	-	852	552	28	19.71	4-29	-	
C & G																	
tsL	2	0	0	0	0	-	-	-	-	-	108	83	4	20.75	3-37	-	
Twenty20																	

BREESE, G. R.   Durham

Name: <u>Gareth</u> Rohan Breese
Role: Right-hand bat, right-arm
off-spin bowler; all-rounder
Born: 9 January 1976, Montego Bay,
Jamaica
Height: 5ft 8in **Weight:** 13st
Nickname: Briggy
County debut: 2004
Test debut: 2002-03
Place in batting averages: 121st av. 32.50
(2004 156th av. 28.54)
Place in bowling averages: 87th av. 34.83
(2004 120th av. 41.53)
Strike rate: 64.29 (career 62.89)
Parents: Brian and Jean
Marital status: Single
Family links with cricket: Father played
league cricket in Somerset and Wales; also
played representative cricket for two parishes in Jamaica as wicket-keeper/batsman.
He is currently the cricket operations officer of the Jamaica Board
Education: Wolmer's Boys School, Kingston; University of Technology, Kingston
Qualifications: Level 2 coach, Diploma in Hotel and Resort Management
Off-season: Playing as overseas player for Jamaica
Overseas tours: West Indies U19 to Pakistan and Bangladesh 1995-96; Jamaica to
Malaysia (Commonwealth Games) 1998-99; West Indies A to England 2002; West
Indies to India 2002-03
Overseas teams played for: Jamaica 1995-96 –
Career highlights to date: 'Playing at the highest level and representing Durham over
the last two seasons'
Cricket moments to forget: 'My two Test innings'
Cricket superstitions: 'None'
Cricketers particularly admired: Jimmy Adams, Courtney Walsh, Delroy Morgan
(Jamaica), Dale Benkenstein, Gordon Muchall
Young players to look out for: Gordon Muchall, Nick Cook, Ben Harmison
Other sports played: Pool
Relaxations: 'My computer; music, shopping; hanging out with team-mates/friends'
Extras: Represented West Indies U19 1994-95. Second-highest wicket-taker in the
Busta Cup 2000-01 with 36 (av. 15.11) and in 2001-02 with 44 (av. 20.18). Captain of
Jamaica in first-class cricket 2003-04 and in one-day cricket 2004-05. Scored 165* as
Durham made 453-9 to beat Somerset at Taunton 2004. Is a British passport-holder
and is not considered an overseas player

Opinions on cricket: 'The longer format of the game, mainly at first-class level, has lost a lot of its support through possible lack of interest, so we see smaller crowds. I think we as players should do our best to play hard, exciting cricket at all times to try and force results and attract the spectator support which the game previously enjoyed.'
Best batting: 165* Durham v Somerset, Taunton 2004
Best bowling: 7-60 Jamaica v Barbados, Bridgetown 2000-01

2005 Season

	M	Inns	NO	Runs	HS	Avge	100s	50s	Ct	St	O	M	Runs	Wkts	Avge	Best	5wI	10wM
Test																		
All First	17	24	2	715	79*	32.50	-	7	16	-	332.1	61	1080	31	34.83	5-83	2	-
1-Day Int																		
C & G	1	1	0	3	3	3.00	-	-	2	-	10	2	34	2	17.00	2-34	-	
tsL	17	10	4	119	47*	19.83	-	-	10	-	91.5	2	445	16	27.81	3-30	-	
Twenty20	7	6	1	37	16*	7.40	-	-	1	-	22	0	178	7	25.42	4-21	-	

Career Performances

	M	Inns	NO	Runs	HS	Avge	100s	50s	Ct	St	Balls	Runs	Wkts	Avge	Best	5wI	10wM
Test	1	2	0	5	5	2.50	-	-	1	-	188	135	2	67.50	2-108	-	-
All First	83	129	18	3216	165*	28.97	2	24	66	-	13900	6120	221	27.69	7-60	11	3
1-Day Int																	
C & G	2	2	0	28	25	14.00	-	-	2	-	108	83	3	27.66	2-34	-	
tsL	35	23	6	359	52*	21.11	-	1	14	-	1256	983	28	35.10	3-30	-	
Twenty20	12	11	2	75	24*	8.33	-	-	4	-	252	298	14	21.28	4-14	-	

BRESNAN, T. T.   Yorkshire

Name: Timothy (Tim) Thomas Bresnan
Role: Right-hand bat, right-arm fast-medium bowler
Born: 28 February 1985, Pontefract
Height: 6ft **Weight:** 13st
Nickname: Brezy Lad, Brez
County debut: 2001 (one-day), 2003 (first-class)
Place in batting averages: 220th av. 19.94 (2004 261st av. 11.91)
Place in bowling averages: 80th av. 33.42 (2004 68th av. 32.76)
Strike rate: 58.59 (career 59.04)
Parents: Julie and Ray
Marital status: Single
Family links with cricket: 'Dad played local league cricket'
Education: Castleford High School; Pontefract New College
Qualifications: 8 GCSEs
Overseas tours: Yorkshire U16 to Cape Town 2001; England U17 to Australia 2000-01; England U19 to Australia and (U19 World Cup) New Zealand 2001-02, to Australia 2002-03, to Bangladesh (U19 World Cup) 2003-04

Career highlights to date: 'Winning [U19] "Test" series against India [2002]'
Cricket moments to forget: 'Eight ducks in a row in 2000 season, for various teams'
Cricket superstitions: 'None'
Cricketers particularly admired: Ian Botham
Young players to look out for: Joseph Sayers, Chris Gilbert, David Stiff
Other sports played: Golf, football
Other sports followed: Football (Leeds United)
Favourite band: Girls Aloud
Relaxations: Golf, PlayStation
Extras: Bunbury Festival Best All-rounder and Most Outstanding Player. Made one-day debut v Kent at Headingley 2001 aged 16 years 102 days, making him the youngest

player to represent Yorkshire since Paul Jarvis in 1981. NBC Denis Compton Award for the most promising young Yorkshire player 2002, 2003. Represented England U19 2002 and 2003
Best batting: 74 Yorkshire v Somerset, Headingley 2005
Best bowling: 5-42 Yorkshire v Worcestershire, Worcester 2005

2005 Season

	M	Inns	NO	Runs	HS	Avge	100s	50s	Ct	St	O	M	Runs	Wkts	Avge	Best	5wI	10wM
Test																		
All First	15	20	3	339	74	19.94	-	3	4	-	459	87	1571	47	33.42	5-42	1	-
1-Day Int																		
C & G	4	3	0	18	15	6.00	-	-	4	-	31.1	2	142	2	71.00	1-25	-	
tsL	15	13	2	70	17	6.36	-	-	6	-	112.4	4	615	10	61.50	4-25	-	
Twenty20	8	8	5	102	25	34.00	-	-	2	-	26	0	210	10	21.00	3-22	-	

Career Performances

	M	Inns	NO	Runs	HS	Avge	100s	50s	Ct	St	Balls	Runs	Wkts	Avge	Best	5wI	10wM
Test																	
All First	29	39	6	563	74	17.06	-	4	8	-	4192	2387	71	33.61	5-42	1	-
1-Day Int																	
C & G	11	7	1	44	15	7.33	-	-	6	-	505	384	8	48.00	2-53	-	
tsL	61	43	11	554	61	17.31	-	1	18	-	2474	2066	56	36.89	4-25	-	
Twenty20	18	14	6	209	42	26.12	-	-	7	-	374	469	20	23.45	3-22	-	

BRIDGE, G. D.   Durham

Name: <u>Graeme</u> David Bridge
Role: Right-hand bat, slow left-arm bowler
Born: 4 September 1980, Sunderland
Height: 5ft 8in **Weight:** 12st 12lbs
Nickname: Bridgey, Teet
County debut: 1999
Place in batting averages: (2004 210th
av. 21.40)
Place in bowling averages: (2004 86th
av. 35.78)
Strike rate: (career 69.94)
Parents: Anne and John
Wife and date of marriage: Leanne,
2 October 2004
Children: Olivia Molly, 13 September 2003
Family links with cricket: 'Dad and brother
played club cricket'
Education: Southmoor School, Sunderland
Qualifications: 5 GCSEs, Level 1 coaching
Career outside cricket: 'Admin, office work'
Overseas tours: England U19 to New Zealand 1998-99, to Malaysia and
(U19 World Cup) Sri Lanka 1999-2000; Durham to South Africa 2002; Durham
Academy to India
Career highlights to date: 'Making first-team debut'
Cricket moments to forget: 'Pulling up with twisted ankle on TV'
Cricket superstitions: 'Don't be late'
Cricketers particularly admired: Martin Love, David Boon
Young players to look out for: Phil Mustard, Dave Harrison, Mark Wallace
Other sports played: Football
Other sports followed: Football (Sunderland AFC 'home or away')
Favourite band: 'Anything'; Stone Roses
Relaxations: 'Horse racing (jumps)'
Extras: Played in U15 World Cup 1996. Represented England U19 1999. C&G Man
of the Match award on county one-day debut for his 3-44 v Gloucs at Bristol 2001
Best batting: 52 Durham v Leicestershire, Riverside 2004
Best bowling: 6-84 Durham v Hampshire, Riverside 2001

2005 Season

	M	Inns	NO	Runs	HS	Avge	100s	50s	Ct	St	O	M	Runs	Wkts	Avge	Best	5wI	10wM
Test																		
All First	2	3	2	37	31 *	37.00	-	-	2	-	38	7	108	4	27.00	4-54	-	-
1-Day Int																		
C & G																			
tsL	1	1	0	10	10	10.00	-	-	-	-	4	0	42	0	-	-	-	-
Twenty20																			

Career Performances

	M	Inns	NO	Runs	HS	Avge	100s	50s	Ct	St	Balls	Runs	Wkts	Avge	Best	5wI	10wM
Test																	
All First	39	64	12	918	52	17.65	-	3	20	-	6155	3060	88	34.77	6-84	1	-
1-Day Int																	
C & G	8	6	2	63	19	15.75	-	-	1	-	368	276	7	39.42	3-44	-	
tsL	33	24	8	166	24	10.37	-	-	5	-	1374	981	38	25.81	4-20	-	
Twenty20	5	3	0	19	11	6.33	-	-	1	-	113	101	7	14.42	2-16	-	

BRIGNULL, D. S. Leicestershire

Name: David (<u>Dave</u>) Stephen Brignull
Role: Right-hand bat, right-arm fast-medium bowler
Born: 27 November 1981, Forest Gate, London
Height: 6ft 4in **Weight:** 15st 10lbs
Nickname: Briggers, Brig-Dog
County debut: 2002 (one-day), 2003 (first-class)
Strike rate: (career 55.50)
Parents: Sharon Penfold and Stephen Brignull
Marital status: Single
Family links with cricket: 'Uncles on both sides of family played for Essex Schools'
Education: Lancaster Boys School; Wyggeston and Queen Elizabeth I College
Qualifications: 11 GCSEs, 3 A-levels, Level 1 coaching
Overseas tours: Leicestershire U19 to South Africa 2000-01
Overseas teams played for: Lafarge CC, Lichtenburg, South Africa 2000-01
Career highlights to date: '3-48 on Sky against Glamorgan in the National League – a game we won off the last ball'

Cricket moments to forget: 'Being hit for 26 in one over in club cricket'
Cricketers particularly admired: Robin Smith, Darren Gough
Young players to look out for: Tom New, Luke Wright
Other sports played: Rugby (Wigston RFC), volleyball (for college team that came fourth in nationals)
Other sports followed: Rugby (Leicester Tigers), football (West Ham), American football (Oakland Raiders)
Favourite band: Eminem
Relaxations: 'Music, socialising'
Extras: Represented England U17 1999. Leicestershire Youth Bowler of the Year and U19 Player of the Season 2001. Hat-trick against Derbyshire U19. Released by Leicestershire at the end of the 2005 season
Best batting: 46 Leicestershire v Middlesex, Leicester 2003
Best bowling: 3-36 Leicestershire v DUCCE, Leicester 2005

2005 Season

	M	Inns	NO	Runs	HS	Avge	100s	50s	Ct	St	O	M	Runs	Wkts	Avge	Best	5wI	10wM
Test																		
All First	1	0	0	0	0	-	-	-	-	-	13.2	4	36	3	12.00	3-36	-	-
1-Day Int																		
C & G																		
tsL	2	0	0	0	0	-	-	-	-	-	13	0	61	3	20.33	2-39	-	
Twenty20																		

Career Performances

	M	Inns	NO	Runs	HS	Avge	100s	50s	Ct	St	Balls	Runs	Wkts	Avge	Best	5wI	10wM
Test																	
All First	5	6	2	58	46	14.50	-	-	-	-	666	392	12	32.66	3-36	-	-
1-Day Int																	
C & G	3	3	1	20	9 *	10.00	-	-	3	-	154	129	4	32.25	2-35	-	
tsL	11	5	3	11	4 *	5.50	-	-	3	-	356	325	13	25.00	3-40	-	
Twenty20																	

BROAD, S. C. J.   Leicestershire

Name: Stuart Christopher John Broad
Role: Left-hand bat, right-arm medium-fast bowler; all-rounder
Born: 24 June 1986, Nottingham
Height: 6ft 5in **Weight:** 11st
Nickname: Broady
County debut: 2005
Place in batting averages: 274th av. 10.70
Place in bowling averages: 43rd av. 27.70

Strike rate: 42.83 (career 42.83)
Parents: Carole and Chris
Marital status: Single
Family links with cricket: 'Father played for
Gloucs CCC, Notts CCC and England; sister
plays for Exeter Uni Ladies 1st XI'
Education: Oakham School
Qualifications: 10 GCSEs, 3 A-levels
Overseas tours: Oakham School to South
Africa 2001; England A to West Indies
2005-06
Overseas teams played for: Hoppers
Crossing CC, Melbourne 2004-05
Cricket superstitions: 'Right pad on first;
scrape my mark three times before a new
delivery'
Cricketers particularly admired: Glenn
McGrath, Jacques Kallis, Shaun Pollock
Young players to look out for: Matthew Boyce, Paul Cook, Mark Collier
Other sports played: Hockey (Midlands age-group), golf
Other sports followed: Football (Nottingham Forest), rugby (Leicester Tigers)
Favourite band: 'Whatever's playing on the radio'
Relaxations: 'All sports, especially a round of golf; travelling'
Extras: Leicestershire Young Cricketers Batsman Award 2003. Represented England
U19 2005. ECB National Academy 2005-06
Opinions on cricket: 'Cricketers should be on 12-month contracts, and the Twenty20
should be kept a novelty and not overplayed. There should be at least eight players
eligible to play for England in each county side.'
Best batting: 31 Leicestershire v Worcestershire, Worcester 2005
Best bowling: 4-64 Leicestershire v Worcestershire, Leicester 2005
Stop press: Called up as a replacement to the England A tour to West Indies 2005-06

2005 Season

	M	Inns	NO	Runs	HS	Avge	100s	50s	Ct	St	O	M	Runs	Wkts	Avge	Best	5wI	10wM
Test																		
All First	10	12	2	107	31	10.70	-	-	1	-	214.1	37	831	30	27.70	4-64	-	-
1-Day Int																		
C & G																		
tsL	1	0	0	0	0	-	-	-	-	-	7	0	35	2	17.50	2-35	-	
Twenty20																		

Career Performances

	M	Inns	NO	Runs	HS	Avge	100s	50s	Ct	St	Balls	Runs	Wkts	Avge	Best	5wI	10wM
Test																	
All First	10	12	2	107	31	10.70	-	-	1	-	1285	831	30	27.70	4-64	-	-
1-Day Int																	
C & G																	
tsL	1	0	0	0	0	-	-	-	-	-	42	35	2	17.50	2-35	-	
Twenty20																	

BROPHY, G. L. Yorkshire

Name: <u>Gerard</u> Louis Brophy
Role: Right-hand bat, wicket-keeper
Born: 26 November 1975, Welkom, South Africa
Height: 5ft 11in **Weight:** 12st
Nickname: Scuba, Broph
County debut: 2002 (Northamptonshire)
Place in batting averages: (2004 130th av. 32.34)
Parents: Gerard and Trish
Wife and date of marriage: Alison, 3 January 2004
Education: Christian Brothers College, Boksburg; Wits Technikon (both South Africa)
Qualifications: Marketing Diploma, Level 2 coach
Overseas tours: South Africa U17 to England 1993; South African Academy to Zimbabwe 1998-99
Overseas teams played for: Gauteng 1996-97 – 1998-99; Free State 1999-2000 – 2000-01
Career highlights to date: 'Captaincy of Free State 2000-01. First dismissal [in collaboration] with Allan Donald'
Cricket moments to forget: 'Messing up a live TV interview'
Cricket superstitions: 'Right pad on first and right glove on first'
Cricketers particularly admired: Ray Jennings, Ian Healy, Allan Donald, Hansie Cronje
Other sports played: Golf, rugby
Other sports followed: Golf, rugby
Favourite band: Coldplay
Relaxations: 'Fishing, travelling, braais, scuba diving'

Extras: Captained South Africa U17. Played for Ireland in the NatWest 2000. Holds a British passport and is not considered an overseas player. Released by Northamptonshire during the 2005 season and has joined Yorkshire for 2006
Best batting: 185 South African Academy v President's XI, Harare 1999-2000

2005 Season

	M	Inns	NO	Runs	HS	Avge	100s	50s	Ct	St	O	M	Runs	Wkts	Avge	Best	5wl	10wM
Test																		
All First	3	3	1	52	52 *	26.00	-	1	6	-								
1-Day Int																		
C & G																		
tsL	3	3	0	26	11	8.66	-	-	4	-								
Twenty20																		

Career Performances

	M	Inns	NO	Runs	HS	Avge	100s	50s	Ct	St	Balls	Runs	Wkts	Avge	Best	5wl	10wM
Test																	
All First	53	86	14	2508	185	34.83	5	12	125	7	6	1	0	-	-	-	-
1-Day Int																	
C & G	4	3	0	52	24	17.33	-	-	1	1							
tsL	29	25	4	459	54	21.85	-	2	28	6							
Twenty20	6	5	2	59	18	19.66	-	-	3	1							

BROWN, A. D. Surrey

Name: <u>Alistair</u> Duncan Brown
Role: Right-hand bat, right-arm off-spin bowler, occasional wicket-keeper
Born: 11 February 1970, Beckenham
Height: 5ft 10in **Weight:** 12st 7lbs
Nickname: The Lord
County debut: 1992
County cap: 1994
Benefit: 2002
1000 runs in a season: 7
1st-Class 200s: 2
One-Day 200s: 2
Place in batting averages: 50th av. 45.61 (2004 31st av. 52.50)
Strike rate: (career 498.50)
Parents: Robert and Ann
Wife and date of marriage: Sarah, 10 October 1998

Children: Max Charles, 9 March 2001; Joe Robert, 11 March 2003
Family links with cricket: Father played for Surrey Young Amateurs in the 1950s
Education: Caterham School
Qualifications: 5 O-levels, Level II coach
Overseas tours: England VI to Singapore 1993, 1994, 1995, to Hong Kong 1997; England to Sharjah (Champions Trophy) 1997-98, to Bangladesh (Wills International Cup) 1998-99
Overseas teams played for: North Perth, Western Australia 1989-90
Career highlights to date: '118 v India at Old Trafford 1996; 203 v Hants at Guildford 1997; 268 v Glamorgan at The Oval 2002'
Cricket moments to forget: 'A great couple of days in Ireland!'
Cricket superstitions: 'Always get to the ground before 11 a.m.'
Cricketers particularly admired: Ian Botham, Viv Richards
Young players to look out for: Timothy Murtagh
Other sports played: Football, golf
Other sports followed: Football (West Ham United), rugby union (London Wasps)
Favourite band: Roachford, Snow Patrol
Relaxations: 'Golf and sleep (when the children allow)'
Extras: Man of the Match for his 118 against India in the third ODI at Old Trafford 1996. Recorded the highest-ever score in the Sunday League with 203 off 119 balls against Hampshire at Guildford in 1997 and received an individual award at the PCA dinner for that achievement. Joint winner (with Carl Hooper) of the EDS Walter Lawrence Trophy for the fastest first-class 100 of the 1998 season (72 balls v Northants at The Oval). Surrey CCC Batsman of the Season 2001. Scored 160-ball 268 out of 438-5 v Glamorgan at The Oval in the C&G 2002; it set a new record for the highest individual score in professional one-day cricket worldwide and Brown also became the first batsman to have scored two double centuries in one-day cricket. Scored 154 v Lancashire at Old Trafford 2004 to complete full set of first-class hundreds against all 17 other counties
Opinions on cricket: 'Twenty20 is here to stay and should not be tampered with too much.'
Best batting: 295* Surrey v Leicestershire, Oakham School 2000
Best bowling: 1-11 Surrey v Warwickshire, The Oval 2003

2005 Season

	M	Inns	NO	Runs	HS	Avge	100s	50s	Ct	St	O	M	Runs	Wkts	Avge	Best	5wI	10wM
Test																		
All First	16	26	5	958	152 *	45.61	3	2	19	-	5	0	14	0	-		-	-	-
1-Day Int																		
C & G	3	3	0	49	36	16.33	-	-	3	-								
tsL	17	15	1	561	108 *	40.07	1	5	10	-								
Twenty20	10	10	0	276	64	27.60	-	3	8	-								

Career Performances

	M	Inns	NO	Runs	HS	Avge	100s	50s	Ct	St	Balls	Runs	Wkts	Avge	Best	5wI	10wM
Test																	
All First	215	338	35	13164	295 *	43.44	39	53	226	1	997	518	2	259.00	1-11	-	-
1-Day Int	16	16	0	354	118	22.12	1	1	6	-	6	5	0	-	-	-	-
C & G	38	34	2	986	268	30.81	1	4	15	-	18	26	0	-	-	-	-
tsL	223	215	6	6621	203	31.67	13	31	81	-	315	320	10	32.00	3-39	-	
Twenty20	24	24	1	607	64	26.39	-	5	22	-	2	2	0	-	-	-	

BROWN, D. O.   Gloucestershire

Name: David Owen Brown
Role: Right-hand bat, right-arm medium bowler
Born: 8 December 1982, Burnley
Height: 6ft **Weight:** 13st 7lbs
Nickname: Wally, Browny
County debut: No first-team appearance
Strike rate: (career 78.00)
Parents: Peter and Valerie
Marital status: Single
Family links with cricket: 'Father played for 30 years with Burnley and Southgate. Brother Michael opens the batting for Hampshire CCC'
Education: Queen Elizabeth's Grammar School, Blackburn; Collingwood College, Durham University
Qualifications: 10 GCSEs, 4 A-levels, BA (Hons) Sport in the Community
Off-season: 'Playing for Perth CC, Western Australia'
Overseas tours: MCC B to Nepal 2003; MCC A to Canada 2005
Overseas teams played for: Claremont-Nedlands, Perth 2001-02; Perth CC 2005-06
Career highlights to date: 'Signing for Gloucestershire CCC. Playing for Durham University. Playing with Mark Dale'
Cricket moments to forget: 'First-class debut v Notts for Durham University 2003 – got golden duck and went the distance. Any time I self-destruct'
Cricket superstitions: 'None'
Cricketers particularly admired: Dale Benkenstein, Andrew Flintoff, Ricky Ponting, James Anderson
Young players to look out for: Will Smith, Ali Maiden, David Balcombe, Jonathan Clare, James Allenby, Luke Ronchi, Lee Daggett

Other sports played: Golf, football
Other sports followed: Football (Burnley FC)
Favourite band: Dire Straits, Fleetwood Mac, Eagles, 'any "cheese"'
Relaxations: 'Championship Manager; watching *The Office*, *Alan Partridge*; golf, DVDs, cinema, socialising, sleeping'
Extras: Played for Durham UCCE 2003-05. Represented British Universities 2005
Opinions on cricket: 'Too many games; not enough time for quality practice. MCC Universities a good method of providing counties with young talented cricketers. Twenty20 looks like a great format as long as authorities don't "overkill" it through too much expansion.'
Best batting: 77 DUCCE v Leicestershire, Leicester 2005
Best bowling: 2-48 DUCCE v Northamptonshire, Northampton 2004

2005 Season (did not make any first-class or one-day appearances for his county)

Career Performances

	M	Inns	NO	Runs	HS	Avge	100s	50s	Ct	St	Balls	Runs	Wkts	Avge	Best	5wl	10wM
Test																	
All First	10	16	0	442	77	27.62	-	4	7	-	780	649	10	64.90	2-48	-	-
1-Day Int																	
C & G																		
tsL																		
Twenty20																		

BROWN, D. R.   Warwickshire

Name: Douglas (<u>Dougie</u>) Robert Brown
Role: Right-hand bat, right-arm fast-medium bowler; all-rounder
Born: 29 October 1969, Stirling, Scotland
Height: 6ft 2in **Weight:** 14st 7lbs
Nickname: Hoots
County debut: 1992
County cap: 1995
Benefit: 2005
1000 runs in a season: 1
50 wickets in a season: 4
1st-Class 200s: 1
Place in batting averages: 178th av. 25.66 (2004 39th av. 50.36)
Place in bowling averages: 67th av. 30.80 (2004 65th av. 32.32)
Strike rate: 59.46 (career 54.43)
Parents: Alastair and Janette
Children: Lauren, 14 September 1998
Family links with cricket: 'Both grandads played a bit'

Education: Alloa Academy; West London Institute of Higher Education (Borough Road College)
Qualifications: 9 O-Grades, 5 Higher Grades, BEd (Hons) Physical Education, ECB Level III coach
Career outside cricket: PE teacher
Overseas tours: Scotland XI to Pakistan 1988-89; England VI to Hong Kong 1997, 2001, 2003; England A to Kenya and Sri Lanka 1997-98; England to Sharjah (Champions Trophy) 1997-98, to West Indies 1997-98 (one-day series), to Bangladesh (Wills International Cup) 1998-99; Scotland to UAE (ICC Six Nations Challenge) 2003-04, to Ireland (ICC Trophy) 2005
Overseas teams played for: Primrose, Cape Town 1992-93; Vredenburg Saldhana, Cape Town 1993-94; Eastern Suburbs, Wellington 1995-96; Wellington, New Zealand 1995-96; Namibia 2002-03
Career highlights to date: 'Playing first Lord's final v Northants 1995. England debut in Sharjah'
Cricket moments to forget: 'Phone call from David Graveney (chairman of selectors) saying you are dropped!'
Cricket superstitions: 'None'
Cricketers particularly admired: Ian Botham, Wasim Akram, Dermot Reeve 'and everyone who gives 100 per cent'
Other sports played: Golf
Other sports followed: Football (Alloa Athletic, 'and all the Midlands football teams')
Favourite band: Oasis, U2
Relaxations: 'Music, time with Lauren'
Extras: Played football at Hampden Park for Scotland U18. Has played first-class and one-day cricket for Scotland. Scored 1118 runs and took 109 wickets in all first-team county cricket 1997. Vice-captain of Warwickshire 2002-03. Warwickshire All-rounder of the Year 2002. Scored 108 v Essex at Edgbaston in the C&G 2003, winning Man of the Match award and sharing with Ashley Giles (71*) in a competition record seventh-wicket partnership (170). Scored century (108*) then returned first innings figures of 5-53 v Northamptonshire at Northampton 2004
Opinions on cricket: 'Still a great game!'
Best batting: 203 Warwickshire v Sussex, Hove 2000
Best bowling: 8-89 First-Class Counties XI v Pakistan A, Chelmsford 1997

2005 Season

	M	Inns	NO	Runs	HS	Avge	100s	50s	Ct	St	O	M	Runs	Wkts	Avge	Best	5wI	10wM
Test																		
All First	17	26	2	616	122	25.66	1	2	14	-	495.3	110	1540	50	30.80	5-128	1	-
1-Day Int																		
C & G	5	4	1	26	15	8.66	-	-	-	-	40	3	188	5	37.60	3-28	-	
tsL	16	12	6	201	48	33.50	-	-	6	-	115.5	10	521	15	34.73	3-49	-	
Twenty20	8	6	0	92	26	15.33	-	-	2	-	20	2	137	6	22.83	3-21	-	

Career Performances

	M	Inns	NO	Runs	HS	Avge	100s	50s	Ct	St	Balls	Runs	Wkts	Avge	Best	5wI	10wM
Test																	
All First	196	296	38	8083	203	31.32	10	42	124	-	28687	15159	527	28.76	8-89	20	4
1-Day Int	9	8	4	99	21	24.75	-	-	1	-	324	305	7	43.57	2-28	-	
C & G	36	31	4	658	108	24.37	1	4	9	-	1727	1218	45	27.06	5-43	1	
tsL	178	141	26	2645	82 *	23.00	-	11	45	-	6686	5290	201	26.31	4-37	-	
Twenty20	19	15	0	173	37	11.53	-	-	5	-	312	372	16	23.25	3-21	-	

BROWN, J. F. Northamptonshire

Name: Jason Fred Brown
Role: Right-hand bat, off-spin bowler
Born: 10 October 1974,
Newcastle-under-Lyme
Height: 6ft **Weight:** 13st
Nickname: Cheese, Fish, Brownie
County debut: 1996
County cap: 2000
50 wickets in a season: 3
Place in bowling averages: 51st av. 28.20
(2004 123rd av. 42.30)
Strike rate: 68.69 (career 68.32)
Parents: Peter and Cynthia
Wife and date of marriage: Sam,
26 September 1998
Children: Millie
Education: St Margaret Ward RC School,
Stoke-on-Trent
Qualifications: 9 GCSEs, Level 1 coaching qualification
Overseas tours: Kidsgrove League U18 to Australia 1990; Northants CCC to
Zimbabwe 1998, to Grenada 2000; England A to West Indies 2000-01; England
to Sri Lanka 2000-01

Overseas teams played for: North East Valley, Dunedin, New Zealand 1996-97
Cricketers particularly admired: John Emburey, Carl Hooper
Other sports played: Golf
Other sports followed: Football (Port Vale)
Relaxations: 'Reading, listening to music'
Extras: Represented Staffordshire at all junior levels, in Minor Counties, and in the NatWest 1995. Once took 10-16 in a Kidsgrove League game against Haslington U18 playing for Sandyford U18. Took 100th first-class wicket in 23rd match, v Sussex at Northampton 2000, going on to take his 50th wicket of the season in the same game, only his seventh of the summer. Took 5-27 v Somerset at Northampton in the Twenty20 2003. C&G Man of the Match award for his 5-19 v Cambridgeshire at Northampton 2004
Best batting: 38 Northamptonshire v Hampshire, Northampton 2003
Best bowling: 7-69 Northamptonshire v Durham, Riverside 2003

2005 Season

	M	Inns	NO	Runs	HS	Avge	100s	50s	Ct	St	O	M	Runs	Wkts	Avge	Best	5wI	10wM
Test																		
All First	15	16	7	47	22	5.22	-	-	1	-	629.4	184	1551	55	28.20	6-112	6	2
1-Day Int																		
C & G	2	2	1	2	2*	2.00	-	-	-	-	19	0	81	2	40.50	2-32	-	
tsL	16	4	2	12	6*	6.00	-	-	1	-	124	3	541	10	54.10	2-32	-	
Twenty20	7	0	0	0	0	-	-	-	1	-	22	0	183	5	36.60	2-21	-	

Career Performances

	M	Inns	NO	Runs	HS	Avge	100s	50s	Ct	St	Balls	Runs	Wkts	Avge	Best	5wI	10wM
Test																	
All First	90	104	46	423	38	7.29	-	-	18	-	23163	10210	339	30.11	7-69	20	5
1-Day Int																	
C & G	14	10	6	11	3	2.75	-	-	1	-	834	596	17	35.05	5-19	1	
tsL	90	30	17	77	16	5.92	-	-	23	-	4174	2917	85	34.31	4-26	-	
Twenty20	17	0	0	0	0	-	-	-	3	-	335	432	18	24.00	5-27	1	

13. Who dismissed Marsh, Yardley and Lawson
to record the first ODI hat-trick?

BROWN, K. R.   Lancashire

Name: <u>Karl</u> Robert Brown
Role: Right-hand bat, right-arm
medium bowler
Born: 17 May 1988, Bolton
Height: 5ft 10in **Weight:** 10st 11lbs
Nickname: Brownie, Charlie
County debut: No first-team appearance
Parents: Paul and Lorraine
Marital status: Single
Family links with cricket: Father has played
club cricket for over 30 years and had two
seasons as club professional at Clifton CC in
the Bolton Association
Education: Hesketh Fletcher CE, Atherton,
Lancashire
Qualifications: 8 GCSEs
Off-season: England U19 tour to Bangladesh
Overseas tours: England U16 to South
Africa 2003-04; England U19 to Bangladesh 2005-06
Career highlights to date: 'Getting a professional contract with Lancashire for 2006.
Scoring my first century for Lancs 2nd XI last season'
Cricket superstitions: 'None'
Cricketers particularly admired: Andrew Flintoff
Young players to look out for: Moeen Ali
Other sports played: 'Used to play football'; golf
Other sports followed: Football (Bolton Wanderers), golf
Favourite band/music: Floorfillers 4
Relaxations: 'Watching Bolton Wanderers FC'
Extras: Lancashire Junior Player of the Year 2004
Opinions on cricket: 'I feel that all forms of cricket will benefit from England's
Ashes success – from grass roots through to the counties.'

14. Who is the only bowler to have taken six wickets in
an ODI on more than three occasions?

BROWN, M. J.   Hampshire

Name: <u>Michael</u> James Brown
Role: Right-hand bat, 'rubbish' bowler, occasional wicket-keeper
Born: 9 February 1980, Burnley
Height: 6ft **Weight:** 11st 10lbs
Nickname: Dawson, Weasel, Yoda
County debut: 1999 (Middlesex), 2004 (Hampshire)
Place in batting averages: 195th av. 23.33 (2004 132nd av. 32.23)
Parents: Peter and Valerie
Marital status: Single

Family links with cricket: 'Father played league cricket for 30 years. Mum makes great tuna sandwiches.' Brother David played for DUCCE and is now with Gloucestershire
Education: Queen Elizabeth's Grammar School, Blackburn; Durham University
Qualifications: 10 GCSEs, 4 A-levels, 2.1 Economics/Politics
Career outside cricket: 'Property, stockbroker?'
Off-season: 'Playing for South Perth CC, Western Australia'
Overseas teams played for: Western Province CC, Cape Town 1998-99; Fremantle CC 2002-05; South Perth CC 2005-06
Career highlights to date: 'First first-class hundred v Leicestershire; C&G win; all wins'
Cricket moments to forget: 'Leaving straight balls'
Cricket superstitions: 'Always tap non-striker's end four times at end of over when at that end'
Cricketers particularly admired: Nic Pothas, Dale Benkenstein
Young players to look out for: Mitchell Marsh ('Geoff's son')
Other sports played: Football ('badly'), golf ('occasional bandit')
Other sports followed: Football (Burnley FC)
Favourite band: REM
Relaxations: 'Getting told off by my girlfriend; watching *Rainbow* with Patrick Farhart; writing down the amount of food Chris Tremlett eats'
Extras: Represented ECB U19 A v Pakistan U19 1998. Played for Durham University CCE and represented British Universities 2001, 2002. 'Was at non-striker's end as five wickets fell in one over, Middlesex 2nd XI v Glamorgan 2nd XI, July 2001'
Opinions on cricket: 'No bonus points. Outright win or first innings win – no points for a draw. Two-hour sessions. No cricket committees picking teams – leave to coach, captain etc.'
Best batting: 109* Hampshire v Glamorgan, West End 2004

2005 Season

	M	Inns	NO	Runs	HS	Avge	100s	50s	Ct	St	O	M	Runs	Wkts	Avge	Best	5wl	10wM
Test																		
All First	13	25	1	560	54	23.33	-	3	13	-								
1-Day Int																		
C & G																		
tsL																		
Twenty20																		

Career Performances

	M	Inns	NO	Runs	HS	Avge	100s	50s	Ct	St	Balls	Runs	Wkts	Avge	Best	5wl	10wM
Test																	
All First	41	72	6	1886	109 *	28.57	2	13	37	-							
1-Day Int																	
C & G																	
tsL	5	5	0	78	35	15.60	-	-	2	-							
Twenty20	3	3	0	19	14	6.33	-	-	-	-							

BROWNING, R. J.   Derbyshire

Name: <u>Richard</u> James Browning
Role: Right-hand bat, right-arm medium-fast bowler
Born: 9 October 1987, Wolverhampton
Height: 6ft 2in **Weight:** 14st 13lbs
County debut: No first-team appearance
Extras: Made 2nd XI Championship debut 2005. Selected for ECB Midlands Regional Academy Squad 2005

BRUCE, J. T. A.   Hampshire

Name: <u>James</u> Thomas Anthony Bruce
Role: Right-hand bat, right-arm
medium-fast bowler
Born: 17 December 1979, Hammersmith,
London
Height: 6ft 1in **Weight:** 13st 10lbs
Nickname: Brucey, Bula, Bear, Eugene
County debut: 2003
Place in bowling averages: 14th av. 23.14
Strike rate: 39.00 (career 62.59)
Parents: Andrew and Claire
Marital status: Single
Family links with cricket: 'All three of my
brothers have played youth cricket for
Hampshire'
Education: Eton College, Durham University
Qualifications: BA (Hons) Geography, Level
1 coaching
Overseas tours: West of England U15 to West Indies 1995; Eton College to South
Africa 1998-99; Yellowhammers to South Africa 2001-02; Durham University to
South Africa 2001
Overseas teams played for: Balmain Tigers, Sydney 2002-03; South Perth CC, Perth
2003-05
Career highlights to date: 'Making my Championship debut against Somerset.
Making my NCL debut in a day/night game on Sky v Notts at Trent Bridge [2003].
Playing in Twenty20 competition'
Cricket moments to forget: 'Having my box split in two by Mike Kasprowicz'
Cricket superstitions: 'Too many to mention'
Cricketers particularly admired: Robin Smith, Shaun Udal, Wasim Akram,
Brett Lee
Young players to look out for: Kevin Latouf, Mitchell Stokes, Edward Bruce
Other sports played: Rugby, golf
Favourite band: Powderfinger
Relaxations: 'I like spending time on the beach, watching TV and sleeping'
Extras: Played for DUCCE in 2001 and 2002. Played for Cumberland in the
C&G 2002
Best batting: 21* Hampshire v Glamorgan, West End 2003
Best bowling: 3-42 Hampshire v Glamorgan, West End 2003
                  3-42 Hampshire v Gloucestershire, Cheltenham 2005

2005 Season

	M	Inns	NO	Runs	HS	Avge	100s	50s	Ct	St	O	M	Runs	Wkts	Avge	Best	5wI	10wM
Test																		
All First	4	3	1	2	2	1.00	-	-	3	-	91	13	324	14	23.14	3-42	-	-
1-Day Int																		
C & G																		
tsL	5	2	2	16	10 *	-	-	-	1	-	35.4	2	174	4	43.50	2-35	-	
Twenty20	7	1	1	0	0 *	-	-	-	3	-	12	0	94	3	31.33	3-20	-	

Career Performances

	M	Inns	NO	Runs	HS	Avge	100s	50s	Ct	St	Balls	Runs	Wkts	Avge	Best	5wI	10wM
Test																	
All First	22	25	8	107	21 *	6.29	-	-	8	-	2826	1917	47	40.78	3-42	-	-
1-Day Int																	
C & G	1	1	0	0	0	0.00	-	-	-	-							
tsL	8	3	3	22	10 *	-	-	-	1	-	334	274	8	34.25	3-45	-	
Twenty20	13	4	1	18	12	6.00	-	-	6	-	180	235	11	21.36	3-20	-	

BRYANT, J. D. C. Derbyshire

Name: <u>James</u> Douglas Campbell Bryant
Role: Right-hand bat, right-arm
medium bowler
Born: 4 February 1976, Durban, South Africa
Height: 6ft **Weight:** 11st 10lbs
Nickname: JB
County debut: 2003 (Somerset),
2004 (Derbyshire)
1st-Class 200s: 1
Place in batting averages: 232nd av. 18.85
(2004 263rd av. 11.26)
Strike rate: (career 38.00)
Parents: Nick and Helen
Marital status: Single
Education: Maritzburg College; University
of Port Elizabeth
Qualifications: BComm (Hons) Business
Management, Level 2 coach
Career outside cricket: Entrepreneur
Overseas tours: South African Academy to Ireland and Scotland 1999; South Africa A
to West Indies 2000-01
Overseas teams played for: Eastern Province 1996-97 – 2003-04

Career highlights to date: '234* v North West and achieving South African highest first-class batting partnership – 441; and playing for South Africa A'

Other sports played: Golf, tennis, squash

Other sports followed: Rugby (Natal Sharks)

Relaxations: 'Reading, watersports, golf'

Extras: SuperSport Recruit of the Year 2000. Scored career-best 234* v North West at Potchefstroom in the SuperSport Series 2002-03, in the process sharing with Carl Bradfield (196) in a new record partnership for any wicket in South African domestic first-class cricket (441). Is a British passport-holder and is not considered an overseas player. Released by Derbyshire at the end of the 2005 season

Opinions on cricket: 'Still too many county fixtures.'

Best batting: 234* Eastern Province v North West, Potchefstroom 2002-03

Best bowling: 1-22 Eastern Province B v North West, Fochville 1998-99

2005 Season

	M	Inns	NO	Runs	HS	Avge	100s	50s	Ct	St	O	M	Runs	Wkts	Avge	Best	5wl	10wM
Test																		
All First	4	8	1	132	61	18.85	-	1	2	-								
1-Day Int																		
C & G																		
tsL	5	5	1	152	53	38.00	-	1	1	-								
Twenty20	4	3	1	84	53 *	42.00	-	1	2	-								

Career Performances

	M	Inns	NO	Runs	HS	Avge	100s	50s	Ct	St	Balls	Runs	Wkts	Avge	Best	5wl	10wM
Test																	
All First	83	150	17	4288	234 *	32.24	8	20	55	-	38	37	1	37.00	1-22	-	-
1-Day Int																	
C & G	2	1	0	9	9	9.00	-	-	-	-							
tsL	25	23	2	354	56 *	16.85	-	2	1	-							
Twenty20	9	8	2	181	53 *	30.16	-	1	4	-							

15. Which former Sussex all-rounder took 6-14 against India in Sharjah in 1985, only to finish on the losing side?

BURNS, M.   Somerset

Name: Michael Burns
Role: Right-hand bat, right-arm medium
bowler, occasional wicket-keeper
Born: 6 February 1969, Barrow-in-Furness
Height: 6ft **Weight:** 13st 7lbs
Nickname: Burner, Bunsen, George
County debut: 1991 (Warwickshire),
1997 (Somerset)
County cap: 1999 (Somerset)
Benefit: 2005 (Somerset)
1000 runs in a season: 2
1st-Class 200s: 1
Place in batting averages: 148th av. 30.25
(2004 94th av. 36.65)
Strike rate: (career 69.86)
Parents: Robert and Linda, stepfather Stan
Wife and date of marriage: Carolyn,
9 October 1994
Children: Elizabeth, 12 January 1997; Adam, 3 August 2000
Family links with cricket: 'Grandfather was a great back-garden bowler'
Education: Walney Comprehensive; Barrow College of Further Education
Qualifications: 'Few CSEs, couple of GCEs', qualified fitter at VSEL in Barrow,
coaching award
Overseas teams played for: Gill College, South Africa 1991-92; Motueka, Nelson,
New Zealand 1992-93; Alex Sports Club, Harare 1993-94; Lindisfarne, Tasmania
1999-2000
Career highlights to date: '2001 C&G final'
Cricket moments to forget: 'Losing the 1999 NatWest final to Gloucestershire'
Cricket superstitions: 'None'
Cricketers particularly admired: Marcus Trescothick
Young players to look out for: Adam Burns ('if he's no good at golf'), Arul Suppiah
Other sports played: Rugby league ('had trials for Barrow RLFC and Carlisle
RLFC'), golf
Other sports followed: Football (Liverpool FC), rugby league (Walney Central
ARLFC)
Favourite band: Eminem, Scissor Sisters, Snow Patrol
Relaxations: TV, family, cinema, Indian food
Extras: Player of the Tournament at Benson and Hedges Thailand International
Cricket Sixes in 1989. Scored 160 v Oxford Universities at Taunton on 7 April 2000,
setting new record for the earliest ever 100 in a first-class cricket season in this
country. His 221 v Yorkshire at Bath in 2001 set a new record for the highest score by

a Somerset player at the ground. C&G Man of the Match award for his 83-ball 71 in the quarter-final v Kent at Canterbury 2001. Captain of Somerset 2003-04. Released at the end of the 2005 season

Opinions on cricket: 'It is always going to be difficult finding a balance between cricketers needing more time to prepare and recover and county clubs needing to play games to generate revenue.'

Best batting: 221 Somerset v Yorkshire, Bath 2001
Best bowling: 6-54 Somerset v Leicestershire, Taunton 2001

2005 Season

	M	Inns	NO	Runs	HS	Avge	100s	50s	Ct	St	O	M	Runs	Wkts	Avge	Best	5wl	10wM
Test																		
All First	9	17	1	484	87	30.25	-	2	4	-	40.3	5	142	3	47.33	2-12	-	-
1-Day Int																		
C & G																		
tsL	8	7	0	170	107	24.28	1	-	3	-								
Twenty20																		

Career Performances

	M	Inns	NO	Runs	HS	Avge	100s	50s	Ct	St	Balls	Runs	Wkts	Avge	Best	5wl	10wM
Test																	
All First	154	248	14	7648	221	32.68	8	51	142	7	4751	2885	68	42.42	6-54	1	-
1-Day Int																	
C & G	27	26	3	698	84 *	30.34	-	5	8	-	378	337	10	33.70	2-13	-	
tsL	160	150	15	3221	115 *	23.85	3	18	83	12	1236	1216	38	32.00	4-39	-	
Twenty20	9	7	0	108	36	15.42	-	-	3	-	36	55	2	27.50	1-15	-	

16. Which Middlesbrough-born batsman recorded England's then highest individual score in ODIs when he made 142* v New Zealand at Old Trafford in 1986?

BURROWS, T. G. — Hampshire

Name: Thomas (Tom) George Burrows
Role: Right-hand middle-order bat, wicket-keeper
Born: 5 May 1985, Reading
Height: 5ft 8in **Weight:** 10st 10lbs
Nickname: T
County debut: 2005 (*see Extras*)
Parents: Anthony and Victoria
Marital status: Single
Family links with cricket: 'My father was briefly on Gloucestershire ground staff and played club cricket'
Education: Reading School
Qualifications: 12 GCSEs, 4 AS-levels, 3 A-levels, Level 1 cricket coach
Overseas tours: MCC to Namibia and Uganda 2004-05
Overseas teams played for: Melville CC, Perth 2003-04
Cricket moments to forget: 'The entire game against Somerset 2nd XI 2003'
Cricket superstitions: 'Never wear a jumper to bat'
Cricketers particularly admired: Steve Waugh, Jack Russell
Young players to look out for: David Wheeler, Kevin Latouf
Other sports played: Rugby, football
Other sports followed: Rugby (London Irish RFC), football (Chelsea FC)
Favourite band: R Kelly
Relaxations: 'Listening to music; watching rugby'
Extras: Appeared as substitute wicket-keeper for Hampshire v Yorkshire at West End 2002 but did not make full debut until 2005. Played for Berkshire in the C&G 2003
Best batting: 42 Hampshire v Kent, Canterbury 2005

2005 Season

	M	Inns	NO	Runs	HS	Avge	100s	50s	Ct	St	O	M	Runs	Wkts	Avge	Best	5wI	10wM
Test																		
All First	1	2	0	55	42	27.50	-	-	5	-								
1-Day Int																		
C & G																		
tsL																		
Twenty20	1	0	0	0	0	-	-	-	-	-								

Career Performances

	M	Inns	NO	Runs	HS	Avge	100s	50s	Ct	St	Balls	Runs	Wkts	Avge	Best	5wl	10wM
Test																	
All First	1	2	0	55	42	27.50	-	-	5	-							
1-Day Int																	
C & G	1	1	0	1	1	1.00	-	-	1	-							
tsL																	
Twenty20	1	0	0	0	0	-	-	-	-	-							

BUTCHER, M. A.   Surrey

Name: <u>Mark</u> Alan Butcher
Role: Left-hand bat, right-arm medium bowler, county captain
Born: 23 August 1972, Croydon
Height: 5ft 11in   **Weight:** 13st
Nickname: Butch, Baz
County debut: 1991
County cap: 1996
Benefit: 2005
Test debut: 1997
1000 runs in a season: 7
1st-Class 200s: 2
Place in batting averages: 101st av. 35.37
(2004 139th av. 31.00)
Strike rate: (career 61.56)
Parents: Alan and Elaine
Children: Alita, 1999
Family links with cricket: Father Alan
played for Glamorgan, Surrey and England and is now coach with Surrey; brother
Gary played for Glamorgan and Surrey; uncle Ian played for Gloucestershire and
Leicestershire; uncle Martin played for Surrey
Education: Trinity School; Archbishop Tenison's, Croydon
Qualifications: 5 O-levels, senior coaching award
Career outside cricket: Singer, guitar player
Overseas tours: England YC to New Zealand 1990-91; Surrey to Dubai 1990, 1993,
to Perth 1995; England A to Australia 1996-97; England to West Indies 1997-98, to
Australia 1998-99, to South Africa 1999-2000, to India and New Zealand 2001-02, to
Australia 2002-03, to Bangladesh and Sri Lanka 2003-04, to West Indies 2003-04, to
South Africa 2004-05
Overseas teams played for: South Melbourne, Australia 1993-94; North Perth 1994-95
Cricketers particularly admired: Ian Botham, David Gower, Viv Richards,
Larry Gomes, Graham Thorpe, Alec Stewart, Michael Holding

Other sports followed: Football (Crystal Palace)
Relaxations: Music, playing the guitar, novels, wine
Extras: Played his first game for Surrey in 1991 against his father's Glamorgan in the Refuge Assurance League at The Oval, the first-ever match of any sort between first-class counties in which a father and son have been in opposition. Captained England in third Test v New Zealand at Old Trafford 1999, deputising for the injured Nasser Hussain. Scored match-winning 173* in the fourth Test v Australia at Headingley 2001, winning Man of the Match award, and was England's Man of the Series with 456 runs (more than any other batsman on either side) at an average of 50.66. His other Test awards include England's Man of the Series v Sri Lanka 2002 and v Zimbabwe 2003. Slazenger Sheer Instinct Award 2001 for the cricketer who has impressed the most in the recent season. Captain of Surrey since 2005
Best batting: 259 Surrey v Leicestershire, Leicester 1999
Best bowling: 5-86 Surrey v Lancashire, Old Trafford 2000

2005 Season

	M	Inns	NO	Runs	HS	Avge	100s	50s	Ct	St	O	M	Runs	Wkts	Avge	Best	5wl	10wM
Test																		
All First	5	8	0	283	90	35.37	-	2	3	-	3	0	11	0	-	-	-	-
1-Day Int																		
C & G																		
tsL	5	4	1	113	46	37.66	-	-	6	-								
Twenty20																		

Career Performances

	M	Inns	NO	Runs	HS	Avge	100s	50s	Ct	St	Balls	Runs	Wkts	Avge	Best	5wl	10wM
Test	71	131	7	4288	173 *	34.58	8	23	62	-	901	541	15	36.06	4-42	-	-
All First	238	410	30	14881	259	39.16	29	82	219	-	7634	4201	124	33.87	5-86	1	-
1-Day Int																	
C & G	20	20	5	673	91	44.86	-	6	10	-	318	231	5	46.20	2-57	-	
tsL	102	88	15	1636	104	22.41	1	5	33	-	1717	1571	37	42.45	3-23	-	
Twenty20	3	3	0	148	60	49.33	-	2	-	-							

17. Who was the Devonian who played in 87 ODIs for New Zealand?

CADDICK, A. R.   Somerset

Name: <u>Andrew</u> Richard Caddick
Role: Right-hand bat, right-arm
fast-medium bowler
Born: 21 November 1968, Christchurch,
New Zealand
Height: 6ft 5in **Weight:** 14st 13lbs
Nickname: Des, Shack
County debut: 1991
County cap: 1992
Benefit: 1999
Test debut: 1993
50 wickets in a season: 9
100 wickets in a season: 1
Place in batting averages: 221st av. 19.69
(2004 216th av. 20.40)
Place in bowling averages: 46th av. 27.79
(2004 89th av. 36.17)
Strike rate: 49.24 (career 49.94)
Parents: Christopher and Audrey
Wife and date of marriage: Sarah, 27 January 1995
Children: Ashton Faye, 24 August 1998; Fraser Michael, 12 October 2001
Education: Papanui High School, Christchurch, New Zealand
Qualifications: Qualified plasterer and tiler
Career outside cricket: Plasterer and tiler
Overseas tours: New Zealand YC to Australia (U19 World Cup) 1987-88, to England
1988; England A to Australia 1992-93; England to West Indies 1993-94, to Zimbabwe
and New Zealand 1996-97, to West Indies 1997-98, to South Africa and Zimbabwe
1999-2000, to Kenya (ICC Knockout Trophy) 2000-01, to Pakistan and Sri Lanka
2000-01, to India (one-day series) and New Zealand 2001-02, to Sri Lanka (ICC
Champions Trophy) 2002-03, to Australia 2002-03, to Africa (World Cup) 2002-03
Career highlights to date: 'Bowling West Indies out at Lord's [2000] and thus getting
my name up on the board'
Cricketers particularly admired: Dennis Lillee, Richard Hadlee, Robin Smith,
Jimmy Cook
Other sports followed: 'Mostly all'
Relaxations: Golf
Extras: Whyte and Mackay Bowler of the Year 1997. Took 105 first-class wickets in
1998 season. Leading wicket-taker in the single-division four-day era of the County
Championship with 422 wickets (av. 22.48) 1993-99. Cornhill England Player of the
Year 1999-2000. Took 5-16 from 13 overs as West Indies were bowled out for 54 in
their second innings in the second Test at Lord's 2000. Took 5-14 in fourth Test v West

107

Indies at Headingley 2000, including four wickets (Jacobs, McLean, Ambrose, King) in an over. One of *Wisden*'s Five Cricketers of the Year 2001. Took 200th Test wicket (Craig McMillan) in the third Test v New Zealand at Auckland 2001-02. His international awards include England's Man of the Series v New Zealand 1999 and joint Man of the Match (with Gary Kirsten) in the third Test v South Africa at Durban 1999-2000. Retired from ODI cricket in March 2003. Took 1000th first-class wicket (Joe Sayers) v Yorkshire at Taunton 2005. Is a qualified helicopter pilot

Best batting: 92 Somerset v Worcestershire, Worcester 1995
Best bowling: 9-32 Somerset v Lancashire, Taunton 1993

2005 Season

	M	Inns	NO	Runs	HS	Avge	100s	50s	Ct	St	O	M	Runs	Wkts	Avge	Best	5wI	10wM
Test																		
All First	11	16	3	256	54	19.69	-	1	3	-	443.1	94	1501	54	27.79	6-96	4	1
1-Day Int																		
C & G	1	1	0	0	0	0.00	-	-	-	-	8	2	26	2	13.00	2-26	-	
tsL	7	3	3	18	8 *	-	-	-	2	-	44.4	3	249	8	31.12	2-12	-	
Twenty20	10	1	0	0	0	0.00	-	-	1	-	29	0	261	7	37.28	2-12	-	

Career Performances

	M	Inns	NO	Runs	HS	Avge	100s	50s	Ct	St	Balls	Runs	Wkts	Avge	Best	5wI	10wM
Test	62	95	12	861	49 *	10.37	-	-	21	-	13558	6999	234	29.91	7-46	13	1
All First	228	303	58	3616	92	14.75	-	7	78	-	50294	25823	1007	25.64	9-32	69	16
1-Day Int	54	38	18	249	36	12.45	-	-	9	-	2937	1965	69	28.47	4-19	-	
C & G	31	16	6	34	8	3.40	-	-	5	-	1832	1066	49	21.75	6-30	2	
tsL	113	46	17	335	39	11.55	-	-	17	-	4893	3629	139	26.10	4-18	-	
Twenty20	10	1	0	0	0	0.00	-	-	1	-	174	261	7	37.28	2-12	-	

CAIRNS, C. L.   Nottinghamshire

Name: Christopher (<u>Chris</u>) Lance Cairns
Role: Right-hand bat, right-arm fast-medium bowler
Born: 13 June 1970, Picton, New Zealand
Height: 6ft 2in   **Weight:** 14st
County debut: 1988
County cap: 1993
Test debut: 1989-90
1000 runs in a season: 1
50 wickets in a season: 3
Strike rate: (career 53.03)
Parents: Lance and Sue
Family links with cricket: Father played for New Zealand; uncle played first-class cricket in New Zealand

Education: Christchurch Boys' High School, New Zealand
Qualifications: Fifth and Sixth form certificates
Overseas tours: New Zealand YC to Australia (U19 World Cup) 1987-88; New Zealand Young Internationals to Zimbabwe 1988-89; New Zealand to Australia 1989-90, 1993-94, to India 1995-96, to India and Pakistan (World Cup) 1995-96, to West Indies 1995-96, to Pakistan 1996-97, to Zimbabwe 1997-98, to Australia 1997-98, to Sri Lanka 1998, to UK, Ireland and Holland (World Cup) 1999, to England 1999, to India 1999-2000, to Zimbabwe and South Africa 2000-01, to Kenya (ICC Knockout Trophy) 2000-01, to Australia 2001-02, to Africa (World Cup) 2002-03, to Pakistan (one-day series)

2003-04, to England 2004, to England (ICC Champions Trophy) 2004, to Bangladesh 2004-05 (one-day series), to Australia 2004-05 (one-day series), plus other one-day tournaments in Sharjah, India, Singapore, Sri Lanka and Zimbabwe; ICC World XI to Australia (Tsunami Relief) 2004-05
Overseas teams played for: Northern Districts 1988-89; Canterbury 1990-91 –
Cricketers particularly admired: Mick Newell, Richard Hadlee, Dennis Lillee
Extras: Won the Walter Lawrence Trophy for the fastest first-class hundred of the season 1995 (65 balls for Notts v Cambridge University at Fenner's). Cricket Society's Wetherell Award for leading all-rounder in English first-class cricket 1995. One of *New Zealand Cricket Almanack*'s two Players of the Year 1998, 1999, 2000. One of *Indian Cricket*'s five Cricketers of the Year 2000. One of *Wisden*'s Five Cricketers of the Year 2000. Had match figures of 10-100 v West Indies at Hamilton 1999-2000 to make himself and his father Lance the first father and son to have taken ten wickets in a Test match; also won Man of the Match award. His other Test and ODI awards include New Zealand's Man of the Series v England 1999 and Man of the Match for his 102* in the ICC Knockout Trophy final v India in Kenya 2000-01. An overseas player with Notts 1988-89, 1992-93, 1995-96, 2003 (one-day captain 2003); has returned for the early part of the 2006 season as a locum for Stephen Fleming. Made international Twenty20 debut v Australia at Auckland 2004-05. Retired from Test cricket in 2004 after the third Test v England at Trent Bridge; announced his retirement from all international cricket in early 2006
Best batting: 158 New Zealand v South Africa, Auckland 2003-04
Best bowling: 8-47 Nottinghamshire v Sussex, Arundel 1995
Stop press: Took 200th ODI wicket (Tillakaratne Dilshan) v Sri Lanka at Christchurch 2005-06

2005 Season (did not make any first-class or one-day appearances)

Career Performances

	M	Inns	NO	Runs	HS	Avge	100s	50s	Ct	St	Balls	Runs	Wkts	Avge	Best	5wI	10wM
Test	62	104	5	3319	158	33.52	5	22	15	-	11698	6410	218	29.40	7-27	13	1
All First	216	340	38	10679	158	35.36	13	71	79	-	34102	18278	643	28.42	8-47	30	6
1-Day Int	208	187	23	4807	115	29.31	4	25	64	-	7850	6250	195	32.05	5-42	1	
C & G	8	8	1	373	77	53.28	-	4	4	-	482	279	14	19.92	4-18	-	
tsL	74	64	16	2165	126 *	45.10	2	15	21	-	2945	2362	99	23.85	6-52	2	
Twenty20																	

CARBERRY, M. A.   Hampshire

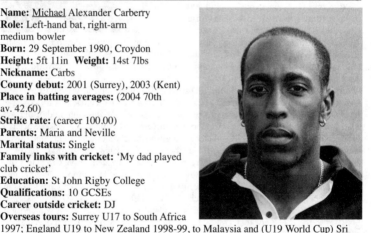

Name: <u>Michael</u> Alexander Carberry
Role: Left-hand bat, right-arm
medium bowler
Born: 29 September 1980, Croydon
Height: 5ft 11in   **Weight:** 14st 7lbs
Nickname: Carbs
County debut: 2001 (Surrey), 2003 (Kent)
Place in batting averages: (2004 70th
av. 42.60)
Strike rate: (career 100.00)
Parents: Maria and Neville
Marital status: Single
Family links with cricket: 'My dad played
club cricket'
Education: St John Rigby College
Qualifications: 10 GCSEs
Career outside cricket: DJ
Overseas tours: Surrey U17 to South Africa
1997; England U19 to New Zealand 1998-99, to Malaysia and (U19 World Cup) Sri
Lanka 1999-2000
Overseas teams played for: Portland CC, Melbourne; University CC, Perth 2005
Career highlights to date: 'Every day is a highlight'
Cricket moments to forget: 'None'
Cricketers particularly admired: Ricky Ponting, Brian Lara
Relaxations: 'Sleeping'
Extras: Scored century (126*) for ECB U18 v Pakistan U19 at Abergavenny 1998.
Represented England U19 1999, 2000. NBC Denis Compton Award for the most
promising young Surrey player 1999, 2000. Scored century (137) on Kent debut v
Cambridge UCCE at Fenner's 2003. Scored 112 as Kent scored a county record

fourth-innings 429-5 to beat Worcestershire at Canterbury 2004. Left Kent at the end of the 2005 season and has joined Hampshire for 2006
Best batting: 153* Surrey v CUCCE, Fenner's 2002
Best bowling: 1-45 Kent v Surrey, The Oval 2003

2005 Season

	M	Inns	NO	Runs	HS	Avge	100s	50s	Ct	St	O	M	Runs	Wkts	Avge	Best	5wl	10wM
Test																		
All First	1	2	0	47	47	23.50	-	-	1	-								
1-Day Int																		
C & G	3	2	0	46	41	23.00	-	-	2	-								
tsL	10	9	2	185	63	26.42	-	2	3	-								
Twenty20	7	6	3	242	59 *	80.66	-	2	2	-								

Career Performances

	M	Inns	NO	Runs	HS	Avge	100s	50s	Ct	St	Balls	Runs	Wkts	Avge	Best	5wl	10wM
Test																	
All First	35	59	6	2044	153 *	38.56	4	11	16	-	300	251	3	83.66	1-45	-	-
1-Day Int																	
C & G	8	6	0	129	51	21.50	-	1	5	-							
tsL	37	35	3	636	79	19.87	-	5	10	-	42	41	1	41.00	1-21	-	
Twenty20	17	15	5	286	59 *	28.60	-	2	6	-							

18. Who was the former policeman who kept wicket for
England in the Prudential Trophy in 1981?

CARTER, N. M.   Warwickshire

Name: <u>Neil</u> Miller Carter
Role: Left-hand bat, left-arm
fast bowler
Born: 29 January 1975, Cape Town,
South Africa
Height: 6ft 2in   **Weight:** 14st 4lbs
Nickname: Carts
County debut: 2001
County cap: 2005
Place in batting averages: 226th av. 19.45
(2004 201st av. 22.27)
Place in bowling averages: 82nd av. 33.60
(2004 134th av. 44.77)
Strike rate: 60.09 (career 64.39)
Parents: John and Heather
Marital status: Single
Education: Hottentots Holland High School;
Cape Technikon

Qualifications: Diploma in Financial Information Systems, Certified Novell Engineer,
Level 2 coaching
Career outside cricket: Computers, accounting
Overseas tours: SA Country Schools U15 to England 1992; Warwickshire to Cape
Town 2001, 2002
Overseas teams played for: Boland 1998-99 – 2003-04
Cricket moments to forget: 'Any performance under par'
Cricketers particularly admired: Jacques Kallis, Shaun Pollock, Allan Donald
Other sports played: Golf, swimming
Other sports followed: Rugby union (Stormers, Springboks), football (Sheffield
Wednesday)
Relaxations: Steam train photography ('gricing')
Extras: Won Man of the Match award in first one-day match for Warwickshire (4-21
and a 43-ball 40), in C&G v Essex at Edgbaston 2001. Swept his first ball (the last of
the game) for a match-winning four in the B&H semi-final v Lancashire at Old
Trafford 2002. Is not considered an overseas player
Best batting: 103 Warwickshire v Sussex, Hove 2002
Best bowling: 6-63 Boland v Griqualand West, Kimberley 2000-01

2005 Season

	M	Inns	NO	Runs	HS	Avge	100s	50s	Ct	St	O	M	Runs	Wkts	Avge	Best	5wI	10wM
Test																		
All First	15	23	3	389	82	19.45	-	1	7	-	410.4	83	1378	41	33.60	4-30	-	-
1-Day Int																		
C & G	5	5	0	100	32	20.00	-	-	-	-	40	4	208	14	14.85	5-66	1	
tsL	17	16	0	439	65	27.43	-	3	1	-	128	14	608	24	25.33	3-28	-	
Twenty20	9	9	0	160	40	17.77	-	-	2	-	29.5	0	222	15	14.80	5-19	1	

Career Performances

	M	Inns	NO	Runs	HS	Avge	100s	50s	Ct	St	Balls	Runs	Wkts	Avge	Best	5wI	10wM
Test																	
All First	58	76	15	1201	103	19.68	1	3	19	-	9337	5472	145	37.73	6-63	4	-
1-Day Int																	
C & G	13	11	0	256	43	23.27	-	-	3	-	651	499	24	20.79	5-66	1	
tsL	62	58	6	986	75	18.96	-	4	5	-	2700	2173	83	26.18	5-31	1	
Twenty20	22	22	0	391	47	17.77	-	-	5	-	437	510	26	19.61	5-19	1	

CHAMBERS, M. A.   Essex

Name: <u>Maurice</u> Anthony Chambers
Role: Right-hand bat, right-arm fast bowler
Born: 14 September 1987, Portland, Jamaica
Nickname: Moza
County debut: 2005
Strike rate: (career 96.00)
Parents: Melinda Fenton
Marital status: Single
Education: Homerton College of Technology; Sir George Monoux College
Career outside cricket: 'Study'
Cricket moments to forget: 'There isn't a cricketing moment that I would like to forget because I try my best to learn from my mistakes'
Cricketers particularly admired: Andrew Strauss, Stephen Harmison, Courtney Walsh, Curtly Ambrose
Other sports played: Basketball, badminton
Other sports followed: Football (Manchester United)
Extras: London Schools Cricket Association Best Bowling Award 2003. Played for MCC Young Cricketers 2004

Best batting: 2* Essex v Derbyshire, Chelmsford 2005
Best bowling: 1-73 Essex v Derbyshire, Chelmsford 2005

2005 Season

	M	Inns	NO	Runs	HS	Avge	100s	50s	Ct	St	O	M	Runs	Wkts	Avge	Best	5wI	10wM
Test																		
All First	1	1	1	2	2*	-	-	-	-	-	16	1	84	1	84.00	1-73	-	-
1-Day Int																		
C & G																		
tsL																		
Twenty20																		

Career Performances

	M	Inns	NO	Runs	HS	Avge	100s	50s	Ct	St	Balls	Runs	Wkts	Avge	Best	5wI	10wM
Test																	
All First	1	1	1	2	2*	-	-	-	-	-	96	84	1	84.00	1-73	-	-
1-Day Int																	
C & G																	
tsL																	
Twenty20																	

CHANDANA, U. D. U.　　　　Gloucestershire

Name: Umagiliya Durage Upul Chandana
Role: Right-hand bat, leg-break bowler
Born: 7 May 1972, Galle, Sri Lanka
County debut: 2005
County cap: 2005
Test debut: 1998-99
Place in batting averages: 245th av. 17.00
Place in bowling averages: 129th av. 46.25
Strike rate: 89.68 (career 50.72)
Overseas tours: Sri Lanka to Sharjah (Pepsi Austral-Asia Cup) 1993-94, to South Africa 1997-98, to England 1998, to Malaysia (Commonwealth Games) 1998, to Bangladesh (Wills International Cup) 1998-99, to UK, Ireland and Holland (World Cup) 1999, to Pakistan 1999-2000, to Kenya (ICC Knockout Trophy) 2000-01, to South Africa 2000-01, to England 2002, to Zimbabwe 2004, to Australia 2004, to England (ICC Champions Trophy) 2004, to New Zealand 2004-05, to India 2005-06 (one-day series), plus other one-day series and tournaments

in Sharjah, Singapore, West Indies, Kenya, New Zealand, Pakistan, India, Australia, Zimbabwe, Morocco and South Africa
Overseas teams played for: Tamil Union Cricket and Athletic Club 1991-92 – 2002-03; Nondescripts 2003-04 –
Extras: Represented Sri Lanka Board President's XI and Sri Lanka A against several touring sides and was captain of Sri Lanka A in series v Kenya 2001-02. Represented Sri Lanka in the Asian Test Championship 1998-99 and the ICC Champions Trophy 2002-03. Man of the Match v Bloomfield Cricket and Athletic Club in the final of the Hatna Trophy 1996-97 at Colombo (72). His international awards include Man of the Match in the second ODI v West Indies at Bridgetown 2003 (71-ball 89); in the fourth ODI v Zimbabwe at Harare 2004 (51/2-23); and in the fifth ODI v South Africa at Colombo 2004 (5-61). Was an overseas player with Gloucestershire 2005
Best batting: 194 Sri Lanka A v Kenya, Matara 2001-02
Best bowling: 7-80 Tamil Union v Bloomfield, Colombo 1998-99

2005 Season

	M	Inns	NO	Runs	HS	Avge	100s	50s	Ct	St	O	M	Runs	Wkts	Avge	Best	5wl	10wM
Test																		
All First	6	10	2	136	49 *	17.00	-	-	2	-	239.1	38	740	16	46.25	5-117	1	-
1-Day Int																		
C & G	2	2	0	6	3	3.00	-	-	1	-	19	2	76	5	15.20	4-27	-	
tsL	6	5	0	57	32	11.40	-	-	2	-	36	2	185	2	92.50	2-64	-	
Twenty20																		

Career Performances

	M	Inns	NO	Runs	HS	Avge	100s	50s	Ct	St	Balls	Runs	Wkts	Avge	Best	5wl	10wM
Test	16	24	1	616	92	26.78	-	2	7	-	2685	1535	37	41.48	6-179	3	1
All First	141	191	16	5434	194	31.05	8	29	108	-	19175	9488	378	25.10	7-80	16	1
1-Day Int	141	106	15	1570	89	17.25	-	5	77	-	5944	4602	149	30.88	5-61	1	
C & G	2	2	0	6	3	3.00	-	-	1	-	114	76	5	15.20	4-27	-	
tsL	6	5	0	57	32	11.40	-	-	2	-	216	185	2	92.50	2-64	-	
Twenty20																		

19. Who has taken the most wickets in ODIs?

CHAPPLE, G.   Lancashire

Name: Glen Chapple
Role: Right-hand bat, right-arm
medium-fast bowler
Born: 23 January 1974, Skipton, Yorkshire
Height: 6ft 2in   **Weight:** 12st 7lbs
Nickname: Chappy, Boris, Boomor, Cheeky
County debut: 1992
County cap: 1994
Benefit: 2004
50 wickets in a season: 4
Place in batting averages: 202nd av. 22.21
(2004 115th av. 34.57)
Place in bowling averages: 7th av. 21.48
(2004 113th av. 38.89)
Strike rate: 48.91 (career 56.44)
Parents: Eileen and Michael
Marital status: Single
Family links with cricket: Father played in

Lancashire League for Nelson and was a professional for Darwen and Earby
Education: West Craven High School; Nelson and Colne College
Qualifications: 8 GCSEs, 2 A-levels
Overseas tours: England U18 to Canada (International Youth Tournament) 1991;
England YC to New Zealand 1990-91; England U19 to Pakistan 1991-92, to India
1992-93; England A to India 1994-95, to Australia 1996-97; England VI to Hong Kong
2002, 2003, 2004
Cricketers particularly admired: Dennis Lillee, Robin Smith
Other sports followed: Football (Liverpool), golf
Relaxations: 'Watching films, music, socialising'
Extras: Set record for fastest century in first-class cricket (21 minutes; against
declaration bowling) v Glamorgan at Old Trafford 1993. Man of the Match in the 1996
NatWest final against Essex at Lord's for his 6-18. Lancashire Player of the Year 2002.
Called up to England squad for the third Test v South Africa at Trent Bridge 2003
Best batting: 155 Lancashire v Somerset, Old Trafford 2001
Best bowling: 6-30 Lancashire v Somerset, Blackpool 2002

2005 Season

	M	Inns	NO	Runs	HS	Avge	100s	50s	Ct	St	O	M	Runs	Wkts	Avge	Best	5wI	10wM
Test																		
All First	14	20	1	422	82	22.21	-	3	5	-	383.1	98	1010	47	21.48	5-22	2	-
1-Day Int																		
C & G	4	3	2	78	55 *	78.00	-	1	1	-	28	2	114	1	114.00	1-25	-	
tsL	8	7	1	165	71	27.50	-	1	1	-	55	3	265	11	24.09	4-23	-	
Twenty20	10	6	1	48	19	9.60	-	-	5	-	22	0	229	7	32.71	2-18	-	

Career Performances

	M	Inns	NO	Runs	HS	Avge	100s	50s	Ct	St	Balls	Runs	Wkts	Avge	Best	5wI	10wM
Test																	
All First	190	262	53	5105	155	24.42	6	22	62	-	31779	16201	563	28.77	6-30	23	1
1-Day Int																	
C & G	33	22	5	336	81 *	19.76	-	2	7	-	1688	1201	34	35.32	6-18	2	
tsL	155	84	22	1107	77 *	17.85	-	5	36	-	6285	4891	178	27.47	6-25	1	
Twenty20	21	14	3	135	55 *	12.27	-	1	8	-	354	475	21	22.61	2-13	-	

CHERRY, D. D.   Glamorgan

Name: <u>Daniel</u> David Cherry
Role: Left-hand bat, right-arm
off-cutter bowler
Born: 7 February 1980, Newport, Gwent
Height: 5ft 9in   **Weight:** 12st 8lbs
Nickname: Rhino, Banners, Kiwi, Spikesoo
County debut: 1998
1st-Class 200s: 1
Place in batting averages: 135th av. 31.03
Parents: David and Elizabeth
Marital status: Single
Family links with cricket: Father played
club cricket for Cresselly CC and now
coaches
Education: Tonbridge School, Kent;
University of Wales, Swansea
Qualifications: 10 GCSEs, 3 A-levels,
BA History, Level 2 coach
Career outside cricket: 'Criminal analysis or criminology'
Off-season: '12-month contract – training etc'
Overseas tours: Tonbridge School to Australia 1996-97; Glamorgan to Cape
Town 2002

Overseas teams played for: Doutta Stars, Melbourne 2002-03
Career highlights to date: 'Maiden first-class hundred (226 v Middlesex)'
Cricket moments to forget: 'Getting hit on the hand by a Shoaib Akhtar beamer!'
Cricket superstitions: 'None'
Cricketers particularly admired: Michael Atherton, Graham Thorpe, Steve James
Young players to look out for: James Harris, Mike O'Shea, Huw Waters
Other sports played: Rugby, rackets (Public Schools doubles champion)
Other sports followed: Rugby (Neath-Swansea Ospreys), football (Everton)
Favourite band: Super Furry Animals
Relaxations: Reading true crime books, listening to music; 'socialising with the high-quality clientele that frequents Pembrokeshire's premier nightspot – "The Sands Discotheque Deluxe"'
Extras: Played for ECB U19 XI v Pakistan U19 1998. Awarded Glamorgan 2nd XI cap 2002. Glamorgan Young Player of the Year 2005. First Glamorgan player to score a double hundred as maiden first-class century (226 v Middlesex at Southgate 2005)
Opinions on cricket: 'Brilliant to see England win the Ashes – proves that county game can produce some of the world's best players. Still worried by amount of EU/Kolpak [*see page 9*] and overseas players (some counties ended up with hardly any English-qualified players). Hope we can take advantage of the popularity of the Ashes amongst the public to revive interest for the next generation.'
Best batting: 226 Glamorgan v Middlesex, Southgate 2005

2005 Season

	M	Inns	NO	Runs	HS	Avge	100s	50s	Ct	St	O	M	Runs	Wkts	Avge	Best	5wI	10wM
Test																		
All First	14	27	0	838	226	31.03	2	1	1	-	3	1	9	0	-	-	-	-
1-Day Int																		
C & G																		
tsL	10	9	0	204	42	22.66	-	-	2	-								
Twenty20	1	1	1	43	43 *	-	-	-	-	-								

Career Performances

	M	Inns	NO	Runs	HS	Avge	100s	50s	Ct	St	Balls	Runs	Wkts	Avge	Best	5wI	10wM
Test																	
All First	24	42	1	1094	226	26.68	2	1	5	-	36	9	0	-	-	-	-
1-Day Int																	
C & G																	
tsL	12	11	0	232	42	21.09	-	-	3	-	6	9	0	-	-		
Twenty20	3	3	1	55	43 *	27.50	-	-	1	-	6	6	2	3.00	2-6	-	

CHILTON, M. J.   Lancashire

Name: <u>Mark</u> James Chilton
Role: Right-hand bat, right-arm medium bowler, county captain
Born: 2 October 1976, Sheffield
Height: 6ft 2in **Weight:** 12st 10lbs
Nickname: Dip, Chill
County debut: 1997
County cap: 2002
1000 runs in a season: 1
Place in batting averages: 99th av. 35.80 (2004 129th av. 32.36)
Strike rate: (career 147.00)
Parents: Jim and Sue
Marital status: Single
Family links with cricket: Father played local cricket
Education: Manchester Grammar School; Durham University

Qualifications: 10 GCSEs, 3 A-levels, BA (Hons) Business Economics, senior coaching award
Overseas tours: Manchester Grammar School to Barbados 1993-94, to South Africa 1995-96; Durham University to Zimbabwe 1997-98
Overseas teams played for: East Torrens, Adelaide 2000-01; North Sydney CC, Sydney 2002-03
Cricket moments to forget: 'Losing two semi-finals in last over'
Cricket superstitions: 'None'
Cricketers particularly admired: Michael Atherton, David Gower
Young players to look out for: Kyle Hogg, Steven Crook
Other sports played: Football, golf
Other sports followed: 'Interest in most sports', football (Manchester United)
Favourite band: Coldplay, Embrace
Relaxations: 'Guitar and music'
Extras: Represented England U14, U15, U17. England U15 Batsman of the Year award 1992. Played for North of England v New Zealand U19 in 1996. Played for British Universities in 1997 Benson and Hedges Cup, winning the Gold Award against Sussex (34/5-26). Captain of Lancashire since 2005
Opinions on cricket: 'We are definitely moving in the right direction, the achievements of the national side over the last couple of years reinforce that. We just need to mirror the international game as closely as possible – e.g. competitions, preparation, amount of cricket, quality of pitches etc.'
Best batting: 130 Lancashire v Yorkshire, Old Trafford 2005
Best bowling: 1-1 Lancashire v Sri Lanka A, Old Trafford 1999

2005 Season

	M	Inns	NO	Runs	HS	Avge	100s	50s	Ct	St	O	M	Runs	Wkts	Avge	Best	5wI	10wM
Test																		
All First	17	28	3	895	130	35.80	3	2	10	-	5	1	9	1	9.00	1-9	-	-
1-Day Int																		
C & G	4	4	0	68	40	17.00	-	-	-	-								
tsL	16	15	3	344	59	28.66	-	1	7	-	7	1	29	1	29.00	1-22	-	
Twenty20	10	6	2	38	12	9.50	-	-	5	-								

Career Performances

	M	Inns	NO	Runs	HS	Avge	100s	50s	Ct	St	Balls	Runs	Wkts	Avge	Best	5wI	10wM
Test																	
All First	113	184	13	5583	130	32.64	15	19	90	-	1176	599	8	74.87	1-1	-	-
1-Day Int																	
C & G	16	16	1	518	76 *	34.53	-	4	8	-	84	91	4	22.75	2-26	-	
tsL	93	86	11	2092	115	27.89	2	10	25	-	592	551	23	23.95	3-20	-	
Twenty20	18	12	5	113	23 *	16.14	-	-	7	-							

CHOPRA, V.   Essex

Name: Varun Chopra
Role: Right-hand bat, right-arm off-spin bowler
Born: 21 June 1987, Ilford, Essex
Height: 6ft 1in **Weight:** 12st
Nickname: Tidz
County debut: No first-team appearance
Parents: Chander and Surinder
Marital status: Single
Education: Ilford County HS
Qualifications: 11 GCSEs, 3 A-levels
Overseas tours: England U19 to Bangladesh 2005-06, to Sri Lanka (U19 World Cup) 2005-06; Essex to South Africa 2006
Career highlights to date: 'Captaining England U19. Joining Essex staff'
Cricket moments to forget: 'U19 World Cup semi-final [2005-06]' (*England lost to India by 234 runs, having been bowled out for 58*)
Cricket superstitions: 'Left pad on first'
Cricketers particularly admired: Sachin Tendulkar, Virender Sehwag, Shane Warne
Young players to look out for: Ravi Bopara

Other sports played: Football
Favourite band: Jagged Edge
Relaxations: 'UK grime, R&B; Pro Evolution Soccer (PS2)'
Extras: Lord's Taverners Player of the Year U13, U15, U19. Sony Sports Personality of the Year runner-up. Essex Academy. Captained England U19 2005
Opinions on cricket: 'Twenty20 has been a success and with the success of the national side more people are seeming to take an interest in the game.'
Stop press: Man of the Match v Bangladesh U19 at Colombo in the quarter-finals of the U19 World Cup 2005-06

CLARK, S. R.   Middlesex

Name: <u>Stuart</u> Rupert Clark
Role: Right-hand bat, right-arm
fast-medium bowler
Born: 28 September 1975, Sutherland,
Sydney, Australia
Height: 6ft 5½in **Weight:** 15st 9lbs
Nickname: Sarfraz
County debut: 2004
Place in bowling averages: 40th av. 27.46
(2004 6th av. 21.70)
Strike rate: 48.26 (career 63.87)
Career outside cricket: Estate agent
Overseas tours: Australia A to South Africa
2002-03, to Pakistan 2005-06; Australia to
England 2005, to New Zealand (one-day
series) 2005-06
Overseas teams played for: New South
Wales 1997-98 –

Extras: Opened the bowling for Sutherland club with Glenn McGrath. Has represented Australia A against several touring sides. New South Wales Player of the Year 2001-02 after taking 45 Pura Cup wickets (av. 23.27). Man of the Match in the ING Cup final 2002-03 v Western Australia at Perth (3-34). A temporary overseas player with Middlesex during the 2004 season, taking over from Glenn McGrath, and during the 2005 season as a locum for Scott Styris. Called up to Australia's Ashes squad 2005 as cover in the pace bowling department
Best batting: 35 New South Wales v Western Australia, Newcastle 2002-03
Best bowling: 6-84 New South Wales v Tasmania, Hobart 2002-03
Stop press: Made ODI debut v ICC World XI at Melbourne in the Super Series 2005-06. Made Twenty20 international debut v South Africa at Brisbane 2005-06

2005 Season

	M	Inns	NO	Runs	HS	Avge	100s	50s	Ct	St	O	M	Runs	Wkts	Avge	Best	5wI	10wM
Test																		
All First	4	7	3	47	17 *	11.75	-	-	1	-	120.4	22	412	15	27.46	5-61	1	-
1-Day Int																		
C & G																		
tsL	3	2	1	3	2	3.00	-	-	1	-	26	4	115	4	28.75	2-40	-	
Twenty20																		

Career Performances

	M	Inns	NO	Runs	HS	Avge	100s	50s	Ct	St	Balls	Runs	Wkts	Avge	Best	5wI	10wM
Test																	
All First	57	79	23	710	35	12.67	-	-	15	-	11817	5808	185	31.39	6-84	8	-
1-Day Int																	
C & G																	
tsL	4	2	1	3	2	3.00	-	-	1	-	201	145	5	29.00	2-40	-	
Twenty20																	

CLARKE, R.   Surrey

Name: Rikki Clarke
Role: Right-hand bat, right-arm fast-medium bowler, county vice-captain
Born: 29 September 1981, Orsett, Essex
Height: 6ft 4in **Weight:** 14st
Nickname: Clarkey, Crouchy, 50 Pence
County debut: 2001 (one-day), 2002 (first-class)
County cap: 2005
Test debut: 2003-04
Place in batting averages: 60th av. 43.11 (2004 137th av. 31.17)
Place in bowling averages: 104th av. 39.33
Strike rate: 50.72 (career 59.34)
Parents: Bob and Janet
Marital status: Single
Family links with cricket: 'Dad plays cricket for Shirenewton in the Welsh League'
Education: Broadwater; Godalming College
Qualifications: 5 GCSEs, GNVQ Leisure and Tourism
Overseas tours: Surrey U19 to Barbados; MCC Young Cricketers to Cape Town; England to Sri Lanka (ICC Champions Trophy) 2002-03, to Bangladesh and Sri Lanka

2003-04, to West Indies 2003-04; ECB National Academy to Australia and Sri Lanka 2002-03; England A to Sri Lanka 2004-05, to West Indies 2005-06

Career highlights to date: 'Making England debut in Test and one-day cricket'

Cricket moments to forget: 'Getting bowled second ball round my legs on one-day England debut'

Cricket superstitions: 'Left pad first'

Cricketers particularly admired: Andrew Flintoff, Adam Hollioake, Darren Gough

Young players to look out for: Alastair Cook, Luke Wright, Kadeer Ali, Tim Murtagh

Other sports played: Golf, snooker, football, 'any really'

Other sports followed: Football ('massive Spurs fan')

Favourite band: Usher, Mario Winans

Relaxations: 'Watching films, playing PlayStation and going to restaurants'

Extras: Named after former Tottenham Hotspur and Argentina footballer Ricky Villa. Represented England U17. Scored maiden first-class century (107*) on first-class debut v Cambridge University CCE at Fenner's 2002. NBC Denis Compton Award for the most promising young Surrey player 2002. Cricket Writers' Club Young Player of the Year 2002. Surrey Supporters' Young Player of the Year 2002. Surrey Sponsors' Young Player of the Year 2002. Made ODI debut v Pakistan at Old Trafford in the NatWest Challenge 2003, taking the wicket of Imran Nazir with his first ball in international cricket. ECB National Academy 2004-05, 2005-06. Appointed vice-captain of Surrey for 2006

Opinions on cricket: 'One overseas [player] per county.'

Best batting: 153* Surrey v Somerset, Taunton 2002

Best bowling: 4-21 Surrey v Leicestershire, Leicester 2003

2005 Season

	M	Inns	NO	Runs	HS	Avge	100s	50s	Ct	St	O	M	Runs	Wkts	Avge	Best	5wI	10wM
Test																		
All First	13	22	4	776	127 *	43.11	2	3	16	-	152.1	16	708	18	39.33	4-91	-	-
1-Day Int																		
C & G	3	3	1	106	62 *	53.00	-	1	1	-	10	1	41	2	20.50	2-41	-	
tsL	12	9	3	306	90 *	51.00	-	2	2	-	47	3	283	9	31.44	4-49	-	
Twenty20	10	10	3	190	52	27.14	-	1	7	-	17.5	1	150	10	15.00	3-11	-	

Career Performances

	M	Inns	NO	Runs	HS	Avge	100s	50s	Ct	St	Balls	Runs	Wkts	Avge	Best	5wI	10wM
Test	2	3	0	96	55	32.00	-	1	1	-	174	60	4	15.00	2-7	-	-
All First	51	84	9	2818	153 *	37.57	7	12	60	-	3976	2868	67	42.80	4-21	-	-
1-Day Int	17	10	0	99	37	9.90	-	-	11	-	404	351	10	35.10	2-28	-	
C & G	11	10	1	228	62 *	25.33	-	2	2	-	265	272	6	45.33	2-41	-	
tsL	49	45	8	1043	98 *	28.18	-	6	17	-	1244	1217	35	34.77	4-49	-	
Twenty20	17	16	4	265	52	22.08	-	1	11	-	227	292	13	22.46	3-11	-	

CLAYDON, M. E. — Yorkshire

Name: Mitchell Eric Claydon
Role: Left-hand bat, right-arm fast bowler
Born: 25 November 1982, Fairfield, Australia
Height: 6ft 4in **Weight:** 15st 9lbs
Nickname: Lips
County debut: 2005
Strike rate: (career 144.00)
Parents: Robert (Tosh) and Sue
Marital status: Single
Children: Lachlan Robert Bickhoff-Claydon, 25 February 2004
Family links with cricket: Father played for Markington CC in the Nidderdale League
Education: Westfields Sports High School, Sydney
Qualifications: Level 1 coaching
Career outside cricket: 'Real estate agent'
Off-season: 'Playing cricket in the Sydney first grade comp'
Overseas teams played for: Campbelltown-Camden Ghosts 1999-2006
Career highlights to date: 'First-class debut against Bangladesh at Headingley. Taking first first-class wicket and signing professional contract with Yorkshire'
Cricket moments to forget: 'While participating in a fielding drill consisting of high catches, misjudged the height of the ball; the next thing I knew I was lying on the physio table with an ice pack on my forehead'
Cricket superstitions: 'Must wear my gold chain that has a photo of my sister who died in 2003'
Cricketers particularly admired: Steve Waugh
Young players to look out for: Richard Pyrah, Mark Lawson
Other sports played: Rugby league, rugby union
Other sports followed: Rugby league (West Tigers), football (Leeds United)
Injuries: Out for three weeks with shin splints
Favourite band: Powderfinger
Relaxations: 'Surfing whilst home in Australia; golf'
Extras: Only player in history of Campbelltown-Camden Ghosts to have taken two first grade hat-tricks. Holds a British passport and is not considered an overseas player
Opinions on cricket: 'My opinion is all cricket should play two-hour sessions, 90 overs in a day as they do in Test cricket. Second XI cricket should play four days instead of three, and I believe Twenty20 cricket will take over.'
Best bowling: 1-27 Yorkshire v Bangladesh A, Headingley 2005

2005 Season

	M	Inns	NO	Runs	HS	Avge	100s	50s	Ct	St	O	M	Runs	Wkts	Avge	Best	5wI	10wM
Test																		
All First	1	0	0	0	0	-	-	-	-	-	24	5	92	1	92.00	1-27	-	-
1-Day Int																		
C & G																		
tsL																		
Twenty20																		

Career Performances

	M	Inns	NO	Runs	HS	Avge	100s	50s	Ct	St	Balls	Runs	Wkts	Avge	Best	5wI	10wM
Test																	
All First	1	0	0	0	0	-	-	-	-	-	144	92	1	92.00	1-27	-	-
1-Day Int																	
C & G																	
tsL																	
Twenty20																	

CLEARY, M. F.   Yorkshire

Name: <u>Mark</u> Francis Cleary
Role: Left-hand bat, right-arm
fast-medium bowler
Born: 19 July 1980, Moorabbin, Melbourne,
Australia
County debut: 2004 (Leicestershire),
2005 (Yorkshire)
County cap: 2004 (Leicestershire)
Place in batting averages: (2004 146th
av. 29.83)
Place in bowling averages: (2004 80th
av. 35.03)
Strike rate: (career 52.28)
Overseas teams played for: South Australia
2002-03 –
Extras: Has represented Australia A.
Commonwealth Bank [Australian] Cricket
Academy 2003. Man of the Match v New
South Wales at Adelaide in the ING Cup 2003-04 (74-ball 70 and 2-43). An overseas
player with Leicestershire 2004, originally as a temporary stand-in for Garnett Kruger;
a temporary overseas player with Yorkshire towards the end of the 2005 season
Best batting: 58 South Australia v Tasmania, Hobart 2003-04
Best bowling: 7-80 Leicestershire v Derbyshire, Oakham School 2004

2005 Season

	M	Inns	NO	Runs	HS	Avge	100s	50s	Ct	St	O	M	Runs	Wkts	Avge	Best	5wI	10wM
Test																		
All First	2	2	0	23	12	11.50	-	-	-	-	67	10	250	8	31.25	3-46	-	-
1-Day Int																		
C & G																		
tsL	4	3	1	50	23 *	25.00	-	-	-	-	32	4	159	2	79.50	1-33	-	
Twenty20																		

Career Performances

	M	Inns	NO	Runs	HS	Avge	100s	50s	Ct	St	Balls	Runs	Wkts	Avge	Best	5wI	10wM
Test																	
All First	30	44	10	615	58	18.08	-	1	13	-	4653	2795	89	31.40	7-80	3	-
1-Day Int																	
C & G																	
tsL	19	11	6	94	23 *	18.80	-	-	2	-	720	615	16	38.43	3-17	-	
Twenty20	7	2	2	27	24 *	-	-	-	3	-	150	199	15	13.26	3-11	-	

CLINTON, R. S.   Surrey

Name: Richard Selvey Clinton
Role: Left-hand opening bat, right-arm medium bowler
Born: 1 September 1981, Sidcup, Kent
Height: 6ft 3in **Weight:** 15st 9lbs
Nickname: Clint
County debut: 2001 (Essex), 2004 (Surrey)
Place in batting averages: 133rd av. 31.19 (2004 189th av. 24.09)
Strike rate: (career 96.50)
Parents: Cathy and Grahame
Marital status: Single
Family links with cricket: 'Father played for Surrey. Uncles, cousin and brother play high standard of club cricket in Kent Premier League'
Education: Colfes School, London; Loughborough University
Qualifications: 9 GCSEs, 3 A-levels
Overseas teams played for: Kensington CC, Adelaide; Valleys CC, Brisbane 2000-02
Cricket superstitions: 'Just a tried and tested routine'
Cricketers particularly admired: Graham Thorpe, Mark Butcher

Other sports played: Football, squash
Other sports followed: Motor racing (Formula One)
Favourite band: Aqua, The Sometime Maybes
Extras: Scored 36 and 58* on first-class debut v Surrey at Ilford 2001; scored 56 the following day on Norwich Union League debut v Durham at the same ground. Released by Essex at the end of the 2002 season. Played for Loughborough UCCE 2004, 2005. Represented British Universities 2004, 2005. Joined Surrey during the 2004 season, scoring 73 on Championship debut v Worcestershire at The Oval
Opinions on cricket: 'Too many players and counties are abusing Kolpak ruling [*see page 9*] which is denying the genuine wealth of talent at youth level the chance to progress. This will be to the detriment of the English game in the long term.'
Best batting: 107 Essex v CUCCE, Fenner's 2002
Best bowling: 2-30 Essex v Australians, Chelmsford 2001

2005 Season

	M	Inns	NO	Runs	HS	Avge	100s	50s	Ct	St	O	M	Runs	Wkts	Avge	Best	5wI	10wM
Test																		
All First	15	26	0	811	106	31.19	2	5	8	-	20.1	2	92	0	-	-	-	-
1-Day Int																		
C & G	1	1	0	5	5	5.00	-	-	-	-	3	0	16	2	8.00	2-16	-	
tsL	2	2	0	16	10	8.00	-	-	1	-	2	0	17	0	-	-	-	
Twenty20																		

Career Performances

	M	Inns	NO	Runs	HS	Avge	100s	50s	Ct	St	Balls	Runs	Wkts	Avge	Best	5wI	10wM
Test																	
All First	35	61	3	1601	107	27.60	3	9	22	-	193	152	2	76.00	2-30	-	-
1-Day Int																	
C & G	2	2	0	18	13	9.00	-	-	-	-	18	16	2	8.00	2-16	-	
tsL	14	11	3	156	56	19.50	-	1	3	-	30	42	0	-	-	-	
Twenty20																	

20. Who are the three Yorkshire-born wicket-keepers
to have played in ODIs for England?

CLOUGH, G. D.

Nottinghamshire

Name: Gareth David Clough
Role: Right-hand bat, right-arm medium bowler; all-rounder
Born: 23 May 1978, Leeds
Height: 6ft **Weight:** 12st 7lbs
Nickname: Banga, Cloughie
County debut: 1998 (Yorkshire), 2001 (Nottinghamshire)
Strike rate: (career 98.40)
Parents: David and Gillian
Wife: Fiona
Education: Pudsey Grangefield
Qualifications: 9 GCSEs, 3 A-levels, Level 1 cricket coach
Overseas tours: Yorkshire to Durban and Cape Town 1999; Nottinghamshire to Johannesburg 2001-03
Overseas teams played for: Somerset West, Cape Town 1996-97; Deepdene Bears, Melbourne 1999-2000, 2001-02
Career highlights to date: 'Making my first-class debut – Yorkshire v Glamorgan 1998, Sophia Gardens'
Cricket moments to forget: 'B&H semi-final v Surrey at The Oval 2001' (*Nottinghamshire conceded 361 runs, more than any other first-class county in B&H history, and were then dismissed for 187*)
Cricket superstitions: 'None'
Cricketers particularly admired: Steve Waugh, Ian Botham
Young players to look out for: Mark Footitt, Andrew Parkin-Coates
Other sports played: Golf, football
Other sports followed: Football (Everton FC), rugby league (Leeds Rhinos)
Favourite band: Little Me
Relaxations: 'Socialising with friends; watching films; eating good food and drinking good wine'
Extras: Topped Nottinghamshire 2nd XI bowling averages 2000 with 37 wickets at 19.05 and also scored 400 runs
Best batting: 55 Nottinghamshire v India A, Trent Bridge 2003
Best bowling: 3-69 Nottinghamshire v Gloucestershire, Trent Bridge 2001

2005 Season

	M	Inns	NO	Runs	HS	Avge	100s	50s	Ct	St	O	M	Runs	Wkts	Avge	Best	5wI	10wM
Test																		
All First	1	2	1	14	14 *	14.00	-	-	-	-	24	2	84	1	84.00	1-39	-	-
1-Day Int																		
C & G	2	1	0	22	22	22.00	-	-	2	-	15	1	63	0	-		-	-
tsL	13	8	2	59	17	9.83	-	-	3	-	60	5	292	15	19.46	3-22	-	
Twenty20	8	6	1	96	30 *	19.20	-	-	1	-	18	0	147	5	29.40	2-39	-	

Career Performances

	M	Inns	NO	Runs	HS	Avge	100s	50s	Ct	St	Balls	Runs	Wkts	Avge	Best	5wI	10wM
Test																	
All First	10	15	2	147	55	11.30	-	1	3	-	984	628	10	62.80	3-69	-	-
1-Day Int																	
C & G	7	4	1	60	27 *	20.00	-	-	4	-	318	269	4	67.25	3-47	-	
tsL	54	35	14	436	42 *	20.76	-	-	15	-	1842	1580	53	29.81	4-32	-	
Twenty20	18	14	2	190	30 *	15.83	-	-	4	-	312	412	16	25.75	2-18	-	

COETZER, K. J.   Durham

Name: <u>Kyle</u> James Coetzer
Role: Right-hand bat, right-arm medium bowler
Born: 14 April 1984, Aberdeen
Height: 5ft 11in
Nickname: Costa
County debut: 2004
Place in batting averages: (2004 212th av. 21.20)
Parents: Peter and Megan
Marital status: Single
Family links with cricket: 'All of my family plays, including two older brothers'
Education: Aberdeen Grammar School
Qualifications: Standard grades, 4 Intermediate 2s
Overseas tours: Scotland U19 to New Zealand (U19 World Cup) 2001-02, to Holland (ECC U19 Championships) 2003 (c), to Bangladesh (U19 World Cup) 2003-04 (c), to Ireland, to Denmark; Scotland to UAE (ICC Inter-Continental Cup) 2004-05, to Ireland (ICC Trophy) 2005
Overseas teams played for: Cape Town CC 2002-04; Western Cape Cricket Academy 2002-04

Cricket moments to forget: 'Being run out first ball on Scotland debut in NCL'
Cricket superstitions: 'Putting the bat in the crease when "over" is called after each over'
Cricketers particularly admired: Jacques Kallis, Allan Donald, Brian McMillan
Young players to look out for: Moneeb Iqbal, Gordon Muchall
Other sports played: Golf, basketball, football
Other sports followed: Rugby, football (Arsenal, Aberdeen)
Favourite band: Red Hot Chili Peppers
Relaxations: 'Socialising with friends'
Extras: Man of the Match (146*) v Italy in the ECC U19 Championships at Deventer 2003. Has played for Scotland in first-class and one-day cricket, including NCL 2003. Scored 67 on first-class debut, for Durham v Glamorgan at Cardiff 2004
Best batting: 133* Scotland v Kenya, Abu Dhabi 2004-05

2005 Season (did not make any first-class or one-day appearances)

Career Performances

	M	Inns	NO	Runs	HS	Avge	100s	50s	Ct	St	Balls	Runs	Wkts	Avge	Best	5wl	10wM
Test																	
All First	8	13	3	358	133 *	35.80	1	1	-	-	36	3	0	-	-	-	-
1-Day Int																	
C & G	2	2	0	40	30	20.00	-	-	2	-							
tsL	3	3	1	16	16 *	8.00	-	-	1	-							
Twenty20																	

COLLINGWOOD, P. D.   Durham

Name: Paul David Collingwood
Role: Right-hand bat, right-arm
medium bowler, county vice-captain
Born: 26 May 1976, Shotley Bridge, Tyneside
Height: 5ft 11in **Weight:** 12st
Nickname: Colly
County debut: 1995 (one-day), 1996 (first-class)
County cap: 1998
Test debut: 2003-04
1000 runs in a season: 2
Place in batting averages: 33rd av. 50.90 (2004 151st av. 29.27)
Place in bowling averages: 77th av. 32.71 (2004 107th av. 37.91)
Strike rate: 53.00 (career 79.55)
Parents: David and Janet
Marital status: Single

Family links with cricket: Father and brother play in the Tyneside Senior League for Shotley Bridge CC
Education: Blackfyne Comprehensive School; Derwentside College
Qualifications: 9 GCSEs and 2 A-levels
Overseas tours: Durham Cricket Academy to Sri Lanka 1996 (c); England VI to Hong Kong 2001, 2002; England to Zimbabwe (one-day series) 2001-02, to India and New Zealand 2001-02 (one-day series), to Australia 2002-03, to Africa (World Cup) 2002-03, to Bangladesh and Sri Lanka 2003-04, to West Indies 2003-04, to Zimbabwe (one-day series) 2004-05, to South Africa 2004-05, to Pakistan 2005-06, to India 2005-06

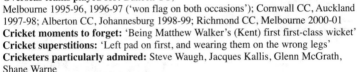

Overseas teams played for: Bulleen CC, Melbourne 1995-96, 1996-97 ('won flag on both occasions'); Cornwall CC, Auckland 1997-98; Alberton CC, Johannesburg 1998-99; Richmond CC, Melbourne 2000-01
Cricket moments to forget: 'Being Matthew Walker's (Kent) first first-class wicket'
Cricket superstitions: 'Left pad on first, and wearing them on the wrong legs'
Cricketers particularly admired: Steve Waugh, Jacques Kallis, Glenn McGrath, Shane Warne
Young players to look out for: Gordon Muchall
Other sports played: Golf (9 handicap)
Other sports followed: Football ('The Red and Whites' – Sunderland)
Extras: Took wicket (David Capel) with first ball on first-class debut against Northants, then scored 91 in Durham's first innings. Durham Player of the Year 2000. Awarded the Ron Brierley Scholarship 2000 through the ECB in conjunction with the Victorian Cricket Association, Australia; joint winner of the Jack Ryder Medal, awarded by the umpires, for his performances in Victorian Premier Cricket 2000-01. Scored 112* and took England ODI best 6-31 v Bangladesh at Trent Bridge in the NatWest Series 2005, winning Man of the Match award. His other ODI awards include Man of the Match v Sri Lanka in the VB Series at Perth 2002-03 (100) and v Zimbabwe at Edgbaston in the ICC Champions Trophy 2004 (80*). Made Twenty20 international debut v Australia at the Rose Bowl 2005. Slazenger Sheer Instinct Award 2005. Vice-captain of Durham since 2005
Best batting: 190 Durham v Sri Lankans, Riverside 2002
190 Durham v Derbyshire, Derby 2005
Best bowling: 5-52 Durham v Somerset, Stockton 2005
Stop press: Appointed MBE in 2006 New Year Honours as part of 2005 Ashes-winning England team. Scored maiden Test century (134*) in the first Test v India at Nagpur 2005-06

2005 Season

	M	Inns	NO	Runs	HS	Avge	100s	50s	Ct	St	O	M	Runs	Wkts	Avge	Best	5wI	10wM
Test	1	2	0	17	10	8.50	-	-	1	-	4	0	17	0	-	-	-	-
All First	14	25	3	1120	190	50.90	6	-	16	-	185.3	28	687	21	32.71	5-52	1	-
1-Day Int	10	7	2	230	112 *	46.00	1	1	4	-	54	1	207	11	18.81	6-31	1	
C & G	1	1	0	82	82	82.00	-	1	-	-	10	0	30	1	30.00	1-30	-	
tsL	14	14	5	289	67 *	32.11	-	2	1	-	79.5	4	358	12	29.83	3-24	-	
Twenty20																		

Career Performances

	M	Inns	NO	Runs	HS	Avge	100s	50s	Ct	St	Balls	Runs	Wkts	Avge	Best	5wI	10wM
Test	3	6	0	106	36	17.66	-	-	7	-	120	54	0	-	-	-	-
All First	119	207	14	6464	190	33.49	14	31	125	-	7622	3808	98	38.85	5-52	1	-
1-Day Int	80	70	18	1676	112 *	32.23	2	8	39	-	1707	1438	39	36.87	6-31	1	
C & G	12	11	1	344	82	34.40	-	3	1	-	306	226	5	45.20	2-7	-	
tsL	110	106	14	2842	118 *	30.89	2	18	56	-	2731	2109	69	30.56	3-20	-	
Twenty20																	

COMPTON, N. R. D.　　　　Middlesex

Name: Nicholas (Nick) Richard Denis Compton
Role: Right-hand bat, right-arm off-spin bowler; batting all-rounder
Born: 26 June 1983, Durban, South Africa
Height: 6ft 2in **Weight:** 13st 10lbs
Nickname: Compo, Ledge, Cheser
County debut: 2001 (one-day), 2004 (first-class)
Parents: Richard and Glynis
Marital status: Single
Family links with cricket: Grandfather Denis Compton played football and cricket for England
Education: Hilton College, South Africa/Harrow School; Durham University
Qualifications: 3 A-levels, ECB coach Level 1
Overseas tours: England U19 to Australia and (U19 World Cup) New Zealand 2001-02
Overseas teams played for: DHS Old Boys, Durban 1997-98; University of Western Australia, Perth 2001

Career highlights to date: '86 not out for Middlesex XI against Lancashire at Denis Compton Oval, Shenley'

Cricket moments to forget: 'Dropping three catches against Australia 2002'

Sportsmen particularly admired: Jacques Kallis, Rahul Dravid, Muhammad Ali (boxer)

Young players to look out for: Shaun Marsh (Australian), Brett Jones (Australian), Bilal Shafayat, Chris Whelan

Other sports played: Golf (6 handicap), represented Natal at junior level at tennis, football and hockey

Other sports followed: Football (Arsenal), golf, rugby union (Natal Sharks)

Relaxations: 'Chilling with a few boys on a beach; music and girls'

Extras: Played for Natal U13 and U15. Natal Academy award 1997. Middlesex U17 Batsman of the Season 1999. Middlesex U19 Player of the Season 2000. NBC Denis Compton Award for the most promising young Middlesex player 2001, 2002. Represented England U19 2002

Best batting: 56* Middlesex v CUCCE, Fenner's 2005

2005 Season

	M	Inns	NO	Runs	HS	Avge	100s	50s	Ct	St	O	M	Runs	Wkts	Avge	Best	5wI	10wM
Test																		
All First	1	2	2	95	56 *	-	-	-	1	-	-							
1-Day Int																		
C & G																		
tsL																		
Twenty20	5	2	0	22	17	11.00	-	-	4	-								

Career Performances

	M	Inns	NO	Runs	HS	Avge	100s	50s	Ct	St	Balls	Runs	Wkts	Avge	Best	5wI	10wM
Test																	
All First	5	9	4	206	56 *	41.20	-	1	3	-							
1-Day Int																	
C & G																	
tsL	15	13	4	214	86 *	23.77	-	1	2	-	30	20	0	-		-	-
Twenty20	9	5	0	27	17	5.40	-	-	6	-							

21. Who has played Test cricket, like his father, but despite more than 4000 Test runs has never played in an ODI?

COOK, A. N. Essex

Name: Alastair (<u>Ali</u>) Nathan Cook
Role: Left-hand opening bat, right-arm off-spin bowler
Born: 25 December 1984, Gloucester
Height: 6ft 2in **Weight:** 12st 10lbs
Nickname: Cooky, Chef
County debut: 2003
County cap: 2005
1000 runs in a season: 1
Place in batting averages: 27th av. 52.35 (2004 128th av. 32.63)
Strike rate: (career 42.00)
Parents: Graham and Elizabeth
Marital status: Single
Family links with cricket: 'Dad played for village side; brothers play for Maldon CC'
Education: Bedford School
Qualifications: 9 GCSEs, 3 A-levels

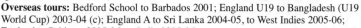

Overseas tours: Bedford School to Barbados 2001; England U19 to Bangladesh (U19 World Cup) 2003-04 (c); England A to Sri Lanka 2004-05, to West Indies 2005-06; England to Pakistan 2005-06, to India 2005-06
Cricket moments to forget: 'Running myself out first ball in U15 World Cup game against India'
Cricket superstitions: 'A few!'
Cricketers particularly admired: Graham Thorpe, Andy Flower, Graham Gooch
Young players to look out for: Ravi Bopara, James Hildreth, Mark Pettini
Other sports played: Squash, golf
Other sports followed: 'All sports'
Relaxations: 'Spending time with friends'
Extras: Played for England U15 in U15 World Cup 2000. Holds Bedford School season record and career record with 19 hundreds. Represented England U19 2003 and (as captain) 2004. Scored 69* on first-class debut v Nottinghamshire at Chelmsford 2003 and a further two half-centuries in his next two Championship matches. Had consecutive scores of 108*, 108* and 87 in the U19 World Cup 2003-04 in Bangladesh. NBC Denis Compton Award for the most promising young Essex player 2003. Scored 214 v Australians at Chelmsford in a two-day game 2005. Cricket Writers' Club Young Player of the Year and PCA Young Player of the Year awards 2005. ECB National Academy 2004-05 (part-time), 2005-06
Opinions on cricket: 'Tea should be longer.'
Best batting: 195 Essex v Northamptonshire, Northampton 2005
Best bowling: 3-13 Essex v Northamptonshire, Chelmsford 2005

Stop press: Called up as a replacement to the England tour of India 2005-06, scoring century (104*) on Test debut in the first Test at Nagpur (following 60 in first innings)

2005 Season

	M	Inns	NO	Runs	HS	Avge	100s	50s	Ct	St	O	M	Runs	Wkts	Avge	Best	5wI	10wM
Test																		
All First	17	30	2	1466	195	52.35	5	6	12	-	18	1	80	3	26.66	3-13	-	-
1-Day Int																		
C & G																		
tsL	5	5	0	234	94	46.80	-	2	2	-	3	0	10	0	-		-	-
Twenty20	1	1	0	2	2	2.00	-	-	-	-								

Career Performances

	M	Inns	NO	Runs	HS	Avge	100s	50s	Ct	St	Balls	Runs	Wkts	Avge	Best	5wI	10wM
Test																	
All First	36	64	5	2567	195	43.50	6	15	40	-	126	103	3	34.33	3-13	-	-
1-Day Int																	
C & G	3	3	0	43	27	14.33	-	-	3	-							
tsL	11	10	0	288	94	28.80	-	2	4	-	18	10	0	-		-	-
Twenty20	1	1	0	2	2	2.00	-	-	-	-							

COOK, S. J.   Kent

Name: Simon James Cook
Role: Right-hand bat, right-arm fast-medium bowler
Born: 15 January 1977, Oxford
Height: 6ft 4in **Weight:** 13st
Nickname: Cookie, Donk, Chef
County debut: 1997 (one-day, Middlesex), 1999 (first-class, Middlesex), 2005 (Kent)
County cap: 2003 (Middlesex)
Place in batting averages: 268th av. 12.06 (2004 240th av. 16.73)
Place in bowling averages: 63rd av. 30.41 (2004 52nd av. 30.62)
Strike rate: 58.12 (career 60.27)
Parents: Phil and Sue
Marital status: Single
Family links with cricket: Brothers play for Oxfordshire
Education: Matthew Arnold School
Qualifications: GCSEs, NVQ Business Administration II, Level 3 ECB coach

Career outside cricket: Coaching and property development
Overseas tours: Middlesex to South Africa 2000
Overseas teams played for: Rockingham, Perth 2001, 2002
Career highlights to date: 'Beating Australia in one-day game at Lord's; winning division two of NCL and equalling league record for wickets in a season (39)'
Cricket moments to forget: 'Being outside the circle in a one-day game when I was supposed to be in it. Danny Law was bowled, the ball went for four [off the stumps, making six no-balls in total] and he went on to win the game for Durham'
Cricket superstitions: 'None'
Cricketers particularly admired: Angus Fraser, Glenn McGrath
Young players to look out for: Billy Godleman, Eoin Morgan, Joe Denly
Other sports followed: Football (Liverpool), 'any other ball sport'
Relaxations: 'Golf, poker, property films'
Player website: www.vcamcricket.co.uk
Extras: Scored career best 93* v Nottinghamshire at Lord's 2001, helping Middlesex to avoid the follow-on, then took a wicket with the first ball of his opening spell. Equalled Adam Hollioake's record for the most wickets in a one-day league season (39) 2004
Opinions on cricket: 'I would like to see all our domestic competitions run in line with international regulations. Also lunch and tea breaks extended!'
Best batting: 93* Middlesex v Nottinghamshire, Lord's 2001
Best bowling: 8-63 Middlesex v Northamptonshire, Northampton 2002

2005 Season

	M	Inns	NO	Runs	HS	Avge	100s	50s	Ct	St	O	M	Runs	Wkts	Avge	Best	5wI	10wM
Test																		
All First	14	18	2	193	38	12.06	-	-	3	-	397.1	103	1247	41	30.41	5-44	2	-
1-Day Int																		
C & G	3	1	0	12	12	12.00	-	-	1	-	23.1	5	85	5	17.00	4-22	-	
tsL	14	8	5	91	28*	30.33	-	-	1	-	110	8	519	19	27.31	3-15	-	
Twenty20	6	4	1	39	20	13.00	-	-	2	-	20	0	171	6	28.50	2-23	-	

Career Performances

	M	Inns	NO	Runs	HS	Avge	100s	50s	Ct	St	Balls	Runs	Wkts	Avge	Best	5wI	10wM
Test																	
All First	80	105	13	1540	93*	16.73	-	3	26	-	12598	6657	209	31.85	8-63	6	-
1-Day Int																	
C & G	13	10	5	157	39*	31.40	-	-	2	-	583	422	14	30.14	4-22	-	
tsL	101	67	21	717	67*	15.58	-	2	13	-	4388	3409	130	26.22	6-37	2	
Twenty20	15	10	4	80	20	13.33	-	-	3	-	314	399	22	18.13	3-14	-	

CORK, D. G. Lancashire

Name: <u>Dominic</u> Gerald Cork
Role: Right-hand bat, right-arm
fast-medium bowler
Born: 7 August 1971, Newcastle-under-
Lyme, Staffordshire
Height: 6ft 2½in **Weight:** 14st
Nickname: Corky
County debut: 1990 (Derbyshire),
2004 (Lancashire)
County cap: 1993 (Derbyshire),
2004 (Lancashire)
Benefit: 2001 (Derbyshire)
Test debut: 1995
50 wickets in a season: 7
1st-Class 200s: 1
Place in batting averages: 129th av. 31.76
(2004 186th av. 24.27)
Place in bowling averages: 29th av. 26.00
(2004 48th av. 30.10)

Strike rate: 55.18 (career 53.26)
Parents: Gerald and Mary
Wife and date of marriage: Donna, 28 August 2000
Children: Ashleigh, 28 April 1990; Gregory, 29 September 1994
Family links with cricket: 'Father and two brothers played in the same side at Betley
CC in Staffordshire'
Education: St Joseph's College, Trent Vale, Stoke-on-Trent; Newcastle College
Qualifications: 2 O-levels, Level 2 coach
Career outside cricket: 'None at the moment, but once I retire I would like to go into
the media side'
Overseas tours: England YC to Australia 1989-90; England A to Bermuda and West
Indies 1991-92, to Australia 1992-93, to South Africa 1993-94, to India 1994-95;
England to South Africa 1995-96, to India and Pakistan (World Cup) 1995-96,
to New Zealand 1996-97, to Australia 1998-99, to Pakistan and Sri Lanka 2000-01, to
Sri Lanka (ICC Champions Trophy) 2002-03; England VI to Hong Kong 2005
Overseas teams played for: East Shirley, Christchurch, New Zealand 1990-91
Career highlights to date: 'Making my debut for England'
Cricket moments to forget: 'Every time the team loses'
Cricket superstitions: 'None'
Cricketers particularly admired: Kim Barnett, Mike Atherton, Ian Botham,
Malcolm Marshall
Other sports played: Golf, football

Other sports followed: Football (Stoke City)
Favourite band: 'Anything R&B'
Relaxations: 'Listening to music'
Extras: Scored century as nightwatchman for England Young Cricketers v Pakistan Young Cricketers at Taunton 1990. Took 8-53 before lunch on his 20th birthday, v Essex at Derby 1991. Selected for England A in 1991 – his first full season of first-class cricket. PCA Young Player of the Year 1991. Took 7-43 on Test debut against West Indies at Lord's 1995, the best innings figures by an England debutant. Took hat-trick (Richardson, Murray, Hooper) against the West Indies at Old Trafford in the fourth Test 1995. PCA Player of the Year 1995. Finished top of the Whyte and Mackay bowling ratings 1995. Cornhill England Player of the Year 1995-96. One of *Wisden*'s Five Cricketers of the Year 1996. Man of the Match in the second Test v West Indies at Lord's 2000; on his recall to the Test side he had match figures of 7-52 followed by a match-winning 33* in England's second innings. Derbyshire captain 1998-2003. Took Twenty20 hat-trick (Pietersen, Ealham, Patel) v Nottinghamshire at Old Trafford 2004
Best batting: 200* Derbyshire v Durham, Derby 2000
Best bowling: 9-43 Derbyshire v Northamptonshire, Derby 1995

2005 Season

	M	Inns	NO	Runs	HS	Avge	100s	50s	Ct	St	O	M	Runs	Wkts	Avge	Best	5wI	10wM
Test																		
All First	14	19	2	540	102 *	31.76	1	5	12	-	395.3	98	1118	43	26.00	4-27	-	-
1-Day Int																		
C & G	3	2	0	36	20	18.00	-	-	2	-	23	4	84	2	42.00	1-15	-	
tsL	13	10	0	169	44	16.90	-	-	4	-	92.3	9	383	15	25.53	4-14	-	
Twenty20	10	8	0	98	28	12.25	-	-	3	-	25	0	175	7	25.00	3-10	-	

Career Performances

	M	Inns	NO	Runs	HS	Avge	100s	50s	Ct	St	Balls	Runs	Wkts	Avge	Best	5wI	10wM
Test	37	56	8	864	59	18.00	-	3	18	-	7678	3906	131	29.81	7-43	5	
All First	250	373	48	8282	200 *	25.48	7	49	185	-	42770	21195	803	26.39	9-43	31	5
1-Day Int	32	21	3	180	31 *	10.00	-	-	6	-	1772	1368	41	33.36	3-27	-	
C & G	30	26	5	720	93	34.28	-	8	15	-	1737	1090	51	21.37	5-18	2	
tsL	152	126	13	2215	83 *	19.60	-	8	64	-	6656	4866	181	26.88	6-21	1	
Twenty20	22	19	2	204	28	12.00	-	-	4	-	288	338	13	26.00	3-9	-	

22. Who was the first person to take five wickets on his ODI debut and later became MCC's Head of Cricket?

COSKER, D. A.   Glamorgan

Name: <u>Dean</u> Andrew Cosker
Role: Right-hand bat, left-arm
spin bowler
Born: 7 January 1978, Weymouth, Dorset
Height: 5ft 11in   **Weight:** 12st 7lbs
Nickname: Lurks
County debut: 1996
County cap: 2000
Place in batting averages: 194th av. 23.38
Place in bowling averages: 137th av. 50.17
(2004 49th av. 30.17)
Strike rate: 84.78 (career 78.80)
Parents: Des and Carol
Marital status: Living with girlfriend Katie
Education: Millfield School
Qualifications: 10 GCSEs, 4 A-levels
Career outside cricket: 'Property guru'
Off-season: 'Fine-tuning my lurking skills'

Overseas tours: West of England U15 to West Indies 1993-94; Millfield School to Sri Lanka 1994-95; England U17 to Holland 1995; England U19 to Pakistan 1996-97; England A to Kenya and Sri Lanka 1997-98, to Zimbabwe and South Africa 1998-99; Glamorgan CCC to Cape Town and Jersey
Overseas teams played for: Gordon CC, Sydney 1996-97; Crusaders, Durban 2001-02
Career highlights to date: 'Every season creeping up the batting order!'
Cricket moments to forget: 'Breaking little finger whilst fielding in 2004'
Cricket superstitions: 'None that I'm willing to tell!'
Cricketers particularly admired: 'Ex-Glammy stalwarts!'
Young players to look out for: 'Academy boys at Glamorgan'
Other sports played: Golf, football
Other sports followed: 'Extreme dodgeball', football (Spurs)
Injuries: 'Continuous rat-like nibbling pain to both of my knees, which heightens extremely long days in the field!'
Favourite band: Bananarama
Relaxations: 'Mainly golf, but I do sometimes like to take scenic walks (especially over Christmas) around Snowdonia and the Cotswolds. Particularly like comedy – Alan Partridge, Peter Kay'
Extras: England U15, U17 and U19. Played for U19 TCCB Development of Excellence XI v South Africa U19 1995. Leading wicket-taker on England A tour of Zimbabwe and South Africa 1998-99 (22; av. 22.90). Third youngest Glamorgan player to receive county cap

Opinions on cricket: 'Kolpak [*see page 9*] is a disgrace to our game, ruining home-grown players' chances, just because of the greed of certain clubs.'
Best batting: 52 Glamorgan v Gloucestershire, Bristol 2005
Best bowling: 6-140 Glamorgan v Lancashire, Colwyn Bay 1998

2005 Season

	M	Inns	NO	Runs	HS	Avge	100s	50s	Ct	St	O	M	Runs	Wkts	Avge	Best	5wI	10wM
Test																		
All First	12	20	7	304	52	23.38	-	1	5	-	395.4	60	1405	28	50.17	4-57	-	-
1-Day Int																		
C & G	2	1	0	3	3	3.00	-	-	1	-	14.1	0	77	1	77.00	1-30	-	
tsL	14	4	0	11	7	2.75	-	-	7	-	101	1	491	14	35.07	3-31	-	
Twenty20	7	4	3	19	10 *	19.00	-	-	4	-	19	0	184	4	46.00	2-30	-	

Career Performances

	M	Inns	NO	Runs	HS	Avge	100s	50s	Ct	St	Balls	Runs	Wkts	Avge	Best	5wI	10wM
Test																	
All First	121	150	48	1319	52	12.93	-	1	83	-	22459	10816	285	37.95	6-140	2	-
1-Day Int																	
C & G	12	7	4	21	5	7.00	-	-	2	-	567	442	9	49.11	3-26	-	
tsL	104	45	17	224	27 *	8.00	-	-	42	-	4445	3587	111	32.31	5-54	1	
Twenty20	18	7	6	27	10 *	27.00	-	-	10	-	282	416	14	29.71	2-24	-	

COVERDALE, P. S.   Northamptonshire

Name: Paul Stephen Coverdale
Role: Right-hand bat, right-arm medium-fast bowler
Born: 24 July 1983, Harrogate
Height: 5ft 10in **Weight:** 12st 6lbs
Nickname: Covers, Flaps, Drill Sergeant, Machine
County debut: No first-team appearance
Parents: Stephen and Jane
Marital status: Single
Family links with cricket: 'Father played for Yorkshire CCC and Cambridge University and is the former Chief Executive of Northamptonshire'
Education: Wellingborough School; Loughborough University
Qualifications: 9 GCSEs, 3 A-levels, BSc (Hons) Information Management and Business Studies, Level I coach

Career outside cricket: 'Since completing university have set up a sporting memorabilia and exhibitions company (CaptureSport), specialising in creating memorabilia products for sports personalities' testimonials and benefits and for clubs'

Off-season: 'Training at Northants, running CaptureSport, and becoming involved with Ocean View Properties, a company specialising in property investment plans in southern Spain'

Overseas tours: Northamptonshire U19 to South Africa 2000

Overseas teams played for: Swanbourne, Perth 2002

Cricket moments to forget: 'Leaving a straight one first ball on a pair in a 2nd XI match a few years ago and then breaking my hand punching the dressing-room wall!'

Cricketers particularly admired: Allan Lamb, Steve Waugh, Matthew Hayden, Mike Hussey, Jacques Kallis

Players to look out for: 'David English MBE – perhaps no longer a rising star but will definitely be entertaining crowds for many years to come!'

Other sports played: 'Pub golf'

Other sports followed: Rugby union (Northampton Saints), football (Aston Villa)

Injuries: 'Broken nose from a delivery from Paul Franks that leapt and went through helmet grill'

Favourite band: Bon Jovi, Dire Straits, Whitesnake ('think the lead singer is a distant relative!')

Player website: www.capturesport.com

Extras: Played county age groups, captaining at U14, U15, U17 and U19. Represented East England Schools U18. Played for Northamptonshire Board XI in the C&G 2001, 2002 and 2003. Represented English Universities in the Home Nations Tournament 2003. Captained English Universities 2004

Opinions on cricket: 'The format of the county competitions and the pressures put on counties to hold their own as financially viable businesses force "short-termism" to occur. Counties have to be successful in the immediate and short term in order to survive. This is why staff turnover has increased rapidly and we're seeing an influx of players on short contracts from overseas, often at the expense of counties' youth systems. The counties cannot be blamed for this but it does not bode well for their future progression and long-term improvement.'

2005 Season (did not make any first-class or one-day appearances)

Career Performances

	M	Inns	NO	Runs	HS	Avge	100s	50s	Ct	St	Balls	Runs	Wkts	Avge	Best	5wI	10wM
Test																	
All First																		
1-Day Int																		
C & G	3	3	0	33	19	11.00	-	-	2	-	96	48	1	48.00	1-21	-	
tsL																		
Twenty20																		

COWAN, A. P. Essex

Name: <u>Ashley</u> Preston Cowan
Role: Right-hand bat, right-arm
fast-medium bowler, 'benefit-only
wicket-keeper'
Born: 7 May 1975, Hitchin, Hertfordshire
Height: 6ft 5in **Weight:** 15st
Nickname: Dic Dic, Wallace, Vic
County debut: 1995
County cap: 1997
Benefit: 2006
50 wickets in a season: 1
Place in bowling averages: (2004 85th
av. 35.61)
Strike rate: (career 60.58)
Parents: Jeff and Pam
Wife and date of marriage: Cath,
14 October 2001
Family links with cricket: 'Father played
village cricket. Mother made the teas'

Education: Framlingham College
Qualifications: 8 GCSEs, 3 A-levels
Overseas tours: England to West Indies 1997-98; MCC to Namibia and Uganda
2004-05
Overseas teams played for: Zingari CC, Durban 1995-97
Career highlights to date: 'Getting England blazer. Winning finals at Lord's'
Cricket moments to forget: 'Any time I get smashed around the park. Losing
[NatWest] final at Lord's 1996'
Cricketers particularly admired: Ian Botham, Allan Donald, Curtly Ambrose,
Glenn McGrath
Young players to look out for: Mark Pettini
Other sports played: Rugby (East of England U18), hockey (East of England U18,
Chelmsford), golf (single-figure handicap), squash
Other sports followed: Rugby (Saracens), golf, football ('anybody who plays
Man U')
Relaxations: Sports, sleeping, reading
Extras: Became first Essex player to take a first-class hat-trick at Castle Park,
Colchester, v Gloucestershire 1996. Took three wickets in four balls in the final over
of National League match at Southend 2000 to prevent Glamorgan scoring the six runs
needed for victory; the over also contained a run-out
Best batting: 94 Essex v Leicestershire, Leicester 1998
Best bowling: 6-47 Essex v Glamorgan, Cardiff 1999

2005 Season

	M	Inns	NO	Runs	HS	Avge	100s	50s	Ct	St	O	M	Runs	Wkts	Avge	Best	5wI	10wM
Test																		
All First	1	2	0	27	27	13.50	-	-	1	-	25	6	99	1	99.00	1-59	-	-
1-Day Int																		
C & G																		
tsL	2	1	0	14	14	14.00	-	-	-	-	12	0	77	1	77.00	1-42	-	
Twenty20																		

Career Performances

	M	Inns	NO	Runs	HS	Avge	100s	50s	Ct	St	Balls	Runs	Wkts	Avge	Best	5wI	10wM
Test																	
All First	106	158	30	2268	94	17.71	-	9	52	-	17206	9339	284	32.88	6-47	8	-
1-Day Int																	
C & G	18	12	4	67	17*	8.37	-	-	5	-	1031	690	26	26.53	4-27	-	
tsL	101	73	17	718	40*	12.82	-	-	40	-	4255	3205	121	26.48	5-14	1	
Twenty20	3	2	1	21	14*	21.00	-	-	1	-	72	88	3	29.33	2-20	-	

CRAWLEY, J. P. Hampshire

Name: <u>John</u> Paul Crawley
Role: Right-hand bat, occasional wicket-keeper
Born: 21 September 1971, Maldon, Essex
Height: 6ft 2in **Weight:** 13st 7lbs
Nickname: Creepy, Jonty, JC
County debut: 1990 (Lancashire), 2002 (Hampshire)
County cap: 1994 (Lancashire), 2002 (Hampshire)
Test debut: 1994
1000 runs in a season: 9
1st-Class 200s: 6
1st-Class 300s: 2
Place in batting averages: 49th av. 46.14 (2004 33rd av. 52.11)
Strike rate: (career 86.50)
Parents: Frank and Jean (deceased)
Marital status: Married
Family links with cricket: Father played in Manchester Association; brother Mark played for Lancashire and Nottinghamshire; brother Peter plays for Warrington CC and has played for Scottish Universities and Cambridge University; uncle was excellent fast bowler; godfather umpires in Manchester Association

Education: Manchester Grammar School; Trinity College, Cambridge;
Open University Business School
Qualifications: 10 O-levels, 2 AO-Levels, 3 A-levels, 2 S-levels, BA in History,
MA (Cantab), Professional Certificate in Management
Overseas tours: England YC to Australia 1989-90, to New Zealand 1990-91 (c);
England A to South Africa 1993-94, to West Indies 2000-01; England to Australia
1994-95, to South Africa 1995-96, to Zimbabwe and New Zealand 1996-97, to West
Indies 1997-98, to Australia 1998-99, 2002-03
Overseas teams played for: Midland-Guildford, Perth 1990
Cricketers particularly admired: Michael Atherton, Neil Fairbrother,
Graham Gooch, Alec Stewart, David Gower, Allan Donald, Ian Salisbury
Other sports followed: Football (Manchester United), golf
Relaxations: 'Playing or trying to play the guitar'
Extras: Sir John Hobbs Silver Jubilee Memorial Prize 1987. Played for England YC
1989, 1990 and (as captain) 1991; first to score 1000 runs in U19 'Tests'. Lancashire
vice-captain 1998. Topped English first-class batting averages for 1998 season (1851
runs; av. 74.04). Lancashire Player of the Year 1998. Lancashire captain 1999-2001.
Scored 272 on debut for Hampshire v Kent at Canterbury 2002, a Hampshire debut
record. Captain of Hampshire 2003
Best batting: 311* Hampshire v Nottinghamshire, West End 2005
Best bowling: 1-7 Hampshire v Surrey, The Oval 2005

2005 Season

	M	Inns	NO	Runs	HS	Avge	100s	50s	Ct	St	O	M	Runs	Wkts	Avge	Best	5wI	10wM
Test																		
All First	16	29	2	1246	311 *	46.14	3	4	14	1	2.5	0	7	1	7.00	1-7	-	-
1-Day Int																		
C & G	5	4	0	99	45	24.75	-	-	1	-								
tsL	14	14	1	466	92	35.84	-	3	8	-								
Twenty20																		

Career Performances

	M	Inns	NO	Runs	HS	Avge	100s	50s	Ct	St	Balls	Runs	Wkts	Avge	Best	5wI	10wM
Test	37	61	9	1800	156 *	34.61	4	9	29	-							
All First	303	500	50	21034	311 *	46.74	46	116	199	1	173	232	2	116.00	1-7	-	-
1-Day Int	13	12	1	235	73	21.36	-	2	1	1							
C & G	34	32	4	1045	113 *	37.32	2	5	10	-	6	4	0	-		-	-
tsL	162	158	14	4431	102	30.77	2	32	52	3							
Twenty20	10	10	1	107	23	11.88	-	-	3	-							

CROFT, R. D. B.   Glamorgan

Name: <u>Robert</u> Damien Bale Croft
Role: Right-hand bat, off-spin bowler,
county captain
Born: 25 May 1970, Morriston, Swansea
Height: 5ft 11in **Weight:** 13st 7lbs
Nickname: Crofty
County debut: 1989
County cap: 1992
Benefit: 2000
Test debut: 1996
50 wickets in a season: 7
Place in batting averages: 172nd av. 26.53
(2004 121st av. 33.90)
Place in bowling averages: 136th av. 49.62
(2004 81st av. 35.19)
Strike rate: 80.60 (career 78.56)
Parents: Malcolm and Susan
Wife: Marie

Children: Callum James Bale Croft
Family links with cricket: Father and grandfather played league cricket
Education: St John Lloyd Catholic School, Llanelli; Neath Tertiary College;
West Glamorgan Institute of Higher Education
Qualifications: 6 O-levels, OND Business Studies, HND Business Studies,
NCA senior coaching certificate
Overseas tours: England A to Bermuda and West Indies 1991-92, to South Africa
1993-94; England to Zimbabwe and New Zealand 1996-97, to West Indies 1997-98,
to Australia 1998-99, to Sharjah (Coca-Cola Cup) 1998-99, to Sri Lanka 2000-01,
to Sri Lanka 2003-04; England VI to Hong Kong 2003, 2005 (c)
Career highlights to date: 'Playing for England and winning the Championship with
Glamorgan in 1997'
Cricket moments to forget: 'None. This career is too short to forget any of it'
Cricketers particularly admired: Ian Botham, Viv Richards, Shane Warne
Young players to look out for: 'Everyone at Glamorgan'
Other sports played: 'Give anything a go'
Other sports followed: Football (Liverpool FC), rugby (Llanelli and Wales)
Interests/relaxations: 'Everything'
Extras: Captained England South to victory in International Youth Tournament 1989
and was voted Player of the Tournament. Glamorgan Young Player of the Year 1992.
Scored Test best 37* in the third Test at Old Trafford 1998, resisting for 190 minutes
to deny South Africa victory. Represented England in the 1999 World Cup. Honorary
fellow of West Glamorgan Institute of Higher Education. Scored 69-ball 119 v Surrey

at The Oval in the C&G 2002 as Glamorgan made 429 in reply to Surrey's 438-5. Glamorgan Player of the Year 2003 (jointly with Michael Kasprowicz) and 2004. Glamorgan vice-captain 2002-03; appointed captain of Glamorgan during 2003, taking over from the injured Steve James. Man of the Match in England's victory v Pakistan in the final of the Hong Kong Sixes 2003. Retired from international cricket in January 2004. Cricket Society's Wetherell Award 2004 for the leading all-rounder in English first-class cricket

Best batting: 143 Glamorgan v Somerset, Taunton 1995
Best bowling: 8-66 Glamorgan v Warwickshire, Swansea 1992

2005 Season

	M	Inns	NO	Runs	HS	Avge	100s	50s	Ct	St	O	M	Runs	Wkts	Avge	Best	5wI	10wM
Test																		
All First	17	30	2	743	90	26.53	-	3	5	-	577.4	77	2134	43	49.62	5-57	2	1
1-Day Int																		
C & G	2	2	0	76	56	38.00	-	1	-	-	17	0	56	1	56.00	1-31	-	
tsL	14	13	1	323	88	26.91	-	2	2	-	99.4	2	478	11	43.45	3-54	-	
Twenty20	7	7	2	153	62 *	30.60	-	1	3	-	23	0	217	9	24.11	2-23	-	

Career Performances

	M	Inns	NO	Runs	HS	Avge	100s	50s	Ct	St	Balls	Runs	Wkts	Avge	Best	5wI	10wM
Test	21	34	8	421	37 *	16.19	-	-	10	-	4619	1825	49	37.24	5-95	1	-
All First	317	470	85	10121	143	26.28	6	45	150	-	69212	32171	881	36.51	8-66	38	7
1-Day Int	50	36	12	344	32	14.33	-	-	11	-	2466	1743	45	38.73	3-51	-	
C & G	40	34	6	831	143	29.67	2	4	5	-	2362	1516	46	32.95	4-47	-	
tsL	214	186	30	3871	114 *	24.81	2	21	57	-	9052	6792	223	30.45	6-20	1	
Twenty20	19	16	3	303	62 *	23.30	-	2	10	-	414	573	25	22.92	3-32	-	

CROFT, S. J.   Lancashire

Name: Steven John Croft
Role: Right-hand bat, right-arm medium-fast bowler; all-rounder
Born: 11 October 1984, Blackpool
Height: 5ft 11in **Weight:** 14st
Nickname: Crofty
County debut: 2005
Parents: Elizabeth and Lawrence
Marital status: Single
Family links with cricket: Father played for local team
Education: Highfield High, Blackpool; Myerscough College
Qualifications: 10 GCSEs, First Diploma in Sports Studies, Level 2 cricket coach
Career outside cricket: Coaching
Off-season: 'Playing cricket in Australia – Melbourne'

Overseas teams played for: St Kilda, Melbourne 2005-06
Career highlights to date: 'Signing for Lancashire CCC'
Cricket moments to forget: 'Duck on 2nd XI debut'
Cricket superstitions: 'Left pad on first'
Cricketers particularly admired: Andrew Flintoff, Stuart Law, Jacques Kallis
Young players to look out for: Karl Brown, Tom Smith, Gareth Cross
Other sports played: Football ('played for Blackpool town team and trialled at Oldham FC and Wimbledon FC')
Other sports followed: Football (Newcastle)
Favourite band: Oasis, The Killers, Blink 182
Relaxations: 'Socialising with friends; music, movies, sport'
Extras: Played for Lancashire Board XI in the C&G 2003. Only third amateur to score over 1000 runs in a season in the Northern Premier League
Opinions on cricket: 'Too many Kolpak [*see page 9*] players in the game, leading to English talent not coming through. Twenty20 has been good for the game.'
Best batting: 6 Lancashire v OUCCE, The Parks 2005

2005 Season

	M	Inns	NO	Runs	HS	Avge	100s	50s	Ct	St	O	M	Runs	Wkts	Avge	Best	5wI	10wM
Test																		
All First	1	1	0	6	6	6.00	-	-	-	-	11	1	49	0	-		-	-
1-Day Int																		
C & G																		
tsL																		
Twenty20																		

Career Performances

	M	Inns	NO	Runs	HS	Avge	100s	50s	Ct	St	Balls	Runs	Wkts	Avge	Best	5wI	10wM
Test																	
All First	1	1	0	6	6	6.00	-	-	-	-	66	49	0	-		-	-
1-Day Int																	
C & G	2	2	1	11	7	11.00	-	-	-	-	48	34	1	34.00	1-27	-	
tsL																	
Twenty20																	

CROOK, A. R.   Lancashire

Name: Andrew (<u>Andy</u>) Richard Crook
Role: Right-hand bat, right-arm
off-spin bowler; all-rounder
Born: 14 October 1980, Adelaide, Australia
Height: 6ft 4in **Weight:** 14st 2lbs
Nickname: Crooky
County debut: 2004
Strike rate: (career 111.42)
Parents: Sue (mother) and Doug (stepfather);
Martyn (father)
Marital status: Single
Family links with sport: 'Brother, Steven,
ex-Lancashire, now at Northamptonshire.
Father played soccer for Australia as a
goalkeeper'
Education: Rostrevor College
Off-season: 'Travelling'

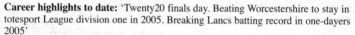

Overseas teams played for: South Australia
1998-99; Northern Districts, South Australia
Career highlights to date: 'Twenty20 finals day. Beating Worcestershire to stay in
totesport League division one in 2005. Breaking Lancs batting record in one-dayers
2005'
Cricketers particularly admired: Daniel Vettori, Adam Gilchrist, Jacques Kallis
Young players to look out for: Karl Brown
Other sports followed: Football (Blackburn Rovers)
Injuries: 'Tendonitis of left wrist and right knee!?'
Favourite band: U2, Snow Patrol, Counting Crows
Relaxations: 'Playing the guitar'
Extras: Made first-class debut for South Australia v England XI at Adelaide 1998-99.
Made new Lancashire record individual one-day score (162*), v Buckinghamshire at
Wormsley in the C&G 2005, winning Man of the Match award. Is not considered an
overseas player
Opinions on cricket: 'Twenty20 is a great game and could be the way of the future.
Anything that gets the crowds in through the gates like Twenty20 does can only be
good for the future of cricket.'
Best batting: 88 Lancashire v OUCCE, The Parks 2005
Best bowling: 3-71 Lancashire v Essex, Old Trafford 2005

2005 Season

	M	Inns	NO	Runs	HS	Avge	100s	50s	Ct	St	O	M	Runs	Wkts	Avge	Best	5wI	10wM
Test																		
All First	2	2	0	131	88	65.50	-	1	4	-	35	7	132	4	33.00	3-71	-	-
1-Day Int																		
C & G	2	2	2	168	162 *	-	1	-	1	-	3	0	14	1	14.00	1-14	-	
tsL	11	9	0	97	32	10.77	-	-	2	-	50.5	1	278	9	30.88	3-32	-	
Twenty20	10	7	3	51	15	12.75	-	-	3	-	21	0	201	7	28.71	2-25	-	

Career Performances

	M	Inns	NO	Runs	HS	Avge	100s	50s	Ct	St	Balls	Runs	Wkts	Avge	Best	5wI	10wM
Test																	
All First	5	7	0	200	88	28.57	-	1	4	-	780	509	7	72.71	3-71	-	-
1-Day Int																	
C & G	2	2	2	168	162 *	-	1	-	1	-	18	14	1	14.00	1-14	-	
tsL	11	9	0	97	32	10.77	-	-	2	-	305	278	9	30.88	3-32	-	
Twenty20	10	7	3	51	15	12.75	-	-	3	-	126	201	7	28.71	2-25	-	

CROOK, S. P.   Northamptonshire

Name: Steven Paul Crook
Role: Right-hand bat, right-arm medium-fast bowler; all-rounder
Born: 28 May 1983, Adelaide, Australia
Height: 5ft 11in **Weight:** 13st 3lbs
Nickname: Crooky, Crookster
County debut: 2003 (Lancashire), 2005 (Northamptonshire)
Strike rate: (career 90.91)
Parents: 'Dad – Martyn, mum – Sue and stepfather – Doug'
Marital status: Single
Family links with sport: 'Brother Andrew – Lancs. Dad, Martyn, played pro football'
Education: Rostrevor College
Qualifications: Matriculation
Overseas tours: Lancashire to Cape Town 2003, 2004
Overseas teams played for: Northern Districts, South Australia
Career highlights to date: 'Playing semi-final of Twenty20 2004'
Cricket moments to forget: 'Getting beaten in semi of Twenty20 2004'
Cricketers particularly admired: Andrew Flintoff, Stuart Law

Young players to look out for: Tom Smith, Steve Croft, Andy Crook
Other sports followed: Football (Tottenham Hotspur FC)
Favourite band: The Doors, The Strokes
Relaxations: 'Hanging out with mates'
Extras: Attended South Australia Cricket Academy. Represented South Australia U13-U19. Selected for Australia U19 preliminary World Cup squad 2001-02. Joined Northamptonshire towards the end of the 2005 season. Is not considered an overseas player
Opinions on cricket: 'More Twenty20!!'
Best batting: 97 Northamptonshire v Yorkshire, Northampton 2005
Best bowling: 3-54 Northamptonshire v Durham, Riverside 2005

2005 Season

	M	Inns	NO	Runs	HS	Avge	100s	50s	Ct	St	O	M	Runs	Wkts	Avge	Best	5wI	10wM
Test																		
All First	5	6	2	288	97	72.00	-	3	-	-	83.3	14	286	4	71.50	3-54	-	-
1-Day Int																		
C & G																			
tsL	3	3	1	35	21	17.50	-	-	-	-	13	0	97	2	48.50	2-47	-	
Twenty20	5	3	1	51	21	25.50	-	-	1	-	1	0	5	0	-	-	-	

Career Performances

	M	Inns	NO	Runs	HS	Avge	100s	50s	Ct	St	Balls	Runs	Wkts	Avge	Best	5wI	10wM
Test																	
All First	11	12	2	472	97	47.20	-	4	2	-	1133	750	12	62.50	3-54	-	-
1-Day Int																	
C & G																		
tsL	12	9	1	93	21	11.62	-	-	3	-	348	405	7	57.85	2-47	-	
Twenty20	11	8	1	124	27	17.71	-	-	1	-	12	22	0	-	-	-	

CROSS, G. D.   Lancashire

Name: <u>Gareth</u> David Cross
Role: Right-hand bat, wicket-keeper
Born: 20 June 1984, Bury
Height: 5ft 9in **Weight:** 11st 9lbs
Nickname: Crossy
County debut: 2005
Parents: Duncan and Margaret
Marital status: Single
Family links with cricket: 'Dad played for Prestwich. Brother Matthew plays for Monton and Weaste'
Education: Moorside High School; Eccles College

Qualifications: 9 GCSEs, GNVQ Science
Overseas teams played for: St Kilda, Melbourne 2002-04
Cricket moments to forget: 'Tim Rees top-edging the ball into my head whilst I was keeping for Salford against Bolton'
Cricket superstitions: 'Just putting batting gear on in the same order'
Cricketers particularly admired: Ian Healy, Adam Gilchrist, Graeme Rummans
Young players to look out for: Steven Croft, Steven Crook
Other sports played: Football ('had a trial for Man United when I was 13')
Other sports followed: Football (Man United)
Favourite band: Eminem, Oasis
Relaxations: 'Watching football; five-a-side football'

Extras: Manchester Association Young Player of the Year. Bolton Association Young Player of the Year 2000. ECB Premier League Young Player of the Year. Liverpool Competition Player of the Year 2004. Played for Lancashire Board XI in the C&G 2003. Made five dismissals in first innings of Championship debut v Leicestershire at Old Trafford 2005
Opinions on cricket: 'Bigger crowds because of Twenty20. More cricket in schools.'
Best batting: 22 Lancashire v Leicestershire, Old Trafford 2005

2005 Season

	M	Inns	NO	Runs	HS	Avge	100s	50s	Ct	St	O	M	Runs	Wkts	Avge	Best	5wI	10wM
Test																		
All First	2	3	0	38	22	12.66	-	-	9	2								
1-Day Int																		
C & G																		
tsL	2	2	1	13	12 *	13.00	-	-	1	3								
Twenty20																		

Career Performances

	M	Inns	NO	Runs	HS	Avge	100s	50s	Ct	St	Balls	Runs	Wkts	Avge	Best	5wI	10wM
Test																		
All First	2	3	0	38	22	12.66	-	-	9	2								
1-Day Int																		
C & G	2	2	0	23	21	11.50	-	-	4	1								
tsL	2	2	1	13	12 *	13.00	-	-	1	3								
Twenty20																		

CULLEN, D. J.   Somerset

Name: Daniel (<u>Dan</u>) James Cullen
Role: Right-hand bat, right-arm
off-spin bowler
Born: 10 April 1984, Adelaide, Australia
County debut: No first-team appearance
Strike rate: (career 59.86)
Overseas tours: Australia A to Pakistan
2005-06
Overseas teams played for: South Australia
2004-05 –
Extras: Represented Australia U19 v
England U19 2002-03. Man of the Match v
Western Australia at Perth in the Pura Cup
2004-05. Australia contract 2005-06
Best batting: 42 South Australia v Tasmania,
Hobart 2004-05
Best bowling: 5-38 South Australia v
Western Australia, Perth 2004-05
Stop press: Named Bradman Young Cricketer of the Year at the 2006 Allan Border
Medal awards

2005 Season (did not make any first-class or one-day appearances)

Career Performances

	M	Inns	NO	Runs	HS	Avge	100s	50s	Ct	St	Balls	Runs	Wkts	Avge	Best	5wl	10wM
Test																	
All First	12	21	7	221	42	15.78	-	-	5	-	2754	1441	46	31.32	5-38	2	-
1-Day Int																	
C & G																	
tsL																	
Twenty20																	

23. Who captained England in his only two ODIs at the age of 44?

CUMMINS, R. A. G.   Leicestershire

Name: <u>Ryan</u> Anthony Gilbert Cummins
Role: Right-hand lower-order bat, right-arm medium-fast bowler
Born: 14 April 1984, Sutton, Surrey
Height: 6ft 4in **Weight:** 13st 2lbs
Nickname: Yummins, Rhino
County debut: 2005
Place in bowling averages: 81st av. 33.42
Strike rate: 64.28 (career 79.50)
Parents: Tony and Sheila
Marital status: Single
Family links with cricket: 'Great-grandfather, Gilly Reay, played for Surrey. Father played county 2nd XI and sister plays county cricket for Northants'
Education: Wallington County Grammar School for Boys; Loughborough University
Qualifications: 11 GCSEs, 4 A-levels, BSc (Hons) Geography (2.2), Level 2 cricket coach, Level 1 hockey coach
Off-season: 'Training at Loughborough and Leicestershire. Coaching at the weekends'
Career highlights to date: 'Being awarded first-class contract and playing in the County Championship. Playing against the likes of Andrew Symonds, Andy and Grant Flower'
Cricket moments to forget: 'Being hit for six over the pavilion by Adam Hollioake at The Oval in 2003 for Loughborough UCCE v Surrey'
Cricketers particularly admired: Phil DeFreitas, Brian Lara, Adam Hollioake
Other sports played: 'County swimming, hockey, squash, golf, tennis'
Injuries: Out for one month with a side strain
Favourite band: Counting Crows, Jack Johnson, Otis Redding
Relaxations: 'Golf, spending time with my girlfriend and seeing mates'
Extras: Played for Loughborough UCCE 2003-05. Represented British Universities 2005
Opinions on cricket: 'The level of professionalism in the game must continue to improve, which will help to increase the standard of county cricket and also to minimise the quantity of injuries in the game today.'
Best batting: 26 LUCCE v Sussex, Hove 2005
Best bowling: 3-32 Leicestershire v Lancashire, Leicester 2005

2005 Season

	M	Inns	NO	Runs	HS	Avge	100s	50s	Ct	St	O	M	Runs	Wkts	Avge	Best	5wl	10wM
Test																		
All First	5	5	2	32	26	10.66	-	-	1	-	150	38	468	14	33.42	3-32	-	-
1-Day Int																		
C & G																		
tsL																		
Twenty20																		

Career Performances

	M	Inns	NO	Runs	HS	Avge	100s	50s	Ct	St	Balls	Runs	Wkts	Avge	Best	5wl	10wM
Test																	
All First	8	8	4	35	26	8.75	-	-	1	-	1272	825	16	51.56	3-32	-	-
1-Day Int																	
C & G																	
tsL																	
Twenty20																	

CUSDEN, S. M. J.   Kent

Name: <u>Simon</u> Mark James Cusden
Role: Right-hand lower-middle-order bat, right-arm fast-medium bowler
Born: 21 February 1985, Margate
Height: 6ft 5in **Weight:** 15st 7lbs
Nickname: Cuzzy, Big Vil, Bungle, Village, Ronnie, Freak
County debut: 2004
Place in bowling averages: (2004 54th av. 31.07)
Strike rate: (career 48.18)
Parents: Mark and Karen
Marital status: Single
Family links with cricket: 'Dad's a village legend'
Education: Simon Langton GS for Boys
Qualifications: 9 GCSEs, 4 AS-levels, 1 A-level
Overseas tours: Simon Langton GS to Barbados 2001; England U19 to Australia 2002-03; England U18 to Holland 2003
Career highlights to date: 'Wicket with my first ball for Kent'
Cricket superstitions: 'None'

Cricketers particularly admired: Allan Donald, 'Fred' Flintoff, Mark Ealham
Young players to look out for: Paul Dixey, Charlie Hemphrey, Daniel Wenham, Kevin Jones
Other sports followed: Football (Chelsea FC)
Favourite band: Foo Fighters
Relaxations: 'Spending time with mates; gym, guitar'
Extras: Part of St Lawrence and Highland Court's Kent League Premier Division winning side in first season with the club. Represented England U19 2004. Took wicket (Mal Loye) with his first ball for Kent, v Lancashire at Tunbridge Wells in the totesport League 2004. Kent Academy Scholar of the Year 2004
Opinions on cricket: 'Too many overseas [players]. Television replays for lbw and caught behind.'
Best batting: 12* Kent v Sussex, Canterbury 2004
Best bowling: 4-68 Kent v Northamptonshire, Canterbury 2004

2005 Season

	M	Inns	NO	Runs	HS	Avge	100s	50s	Ct	St	O	M	Runs	Wkts	Avge	Best	5wI	10wM
Test																		
All First	1	1	1	6	6*	-	-	-	-	-	28	1	107	3	35.66	2-50	-	-
1-Day Int																		
C & G																		
tsL																		
Twenty20																		

Career Performances

	M	Inns	NO	Runs	HS	Avge	100s	50s	Ct	St	Balls	Runs	Wkts	Avge	Best	5wI	10wM
Test																	
All First	5	7	5	28	12*	14.00	-	-	2	-	771	511	16	31.93	4-68	-	-
1-Day Int																	
C & G																	
tsL	4	2	0	4	3	2.00	-	-	-	-	126	126	2	63.00	1-29	-	
Twenty20																	

DAGGETT, L. M.   Warwickshire

Name: <u>Lee</u> Martin Daggett
Role: Right-hand bat, right-arm
fast-medium bowler
Born: 1 October 1982, Bury, Lancashire
Height: 6ft   **Weight:** 13st 7lbs
Nickname: Dags, Len, Lenny
County debut: No first-team appearance
Strike rate: (career 72.76)
Parents: Peter and Kathleen
Marital status: Single
Family links with cricket: 'Dad captained
Ramsbottom CC in the Lancashire League
and now coaches Ramsbottom CC 1st XI'
Education: Woodhey High School, Bury;
Holy Cross College, Bury; Durham
University
Qualifications: BA (Hons) Sport, Health and
Exercise (dissertation on sportsmanship,
ethics and morals in cricket)
Career outside cricket: 'Intend to qualify as a physiotherapist'
Off-season: 'Working as personal trainer. Playing out in Perth for Joondalup CC'
Overseas tours: British Universities to South Africa 2004
Overseas teams played for: Joondalup CC, Perth 2001-02, 2006
Career highlights to date: '8-94 v Durham CCC in 2004 for DUCCE'
Cricket moments to forget: 'The whole feeling and uncertainty of being a trialist'
Cricket superstitions: 'Not really'
Cricketers particularly admired: 'My father', Brett Lee, Allan Donald, Graeme
Fowler
Young players to look out for: William Rew Smith
Other sports played: Football ('used to play for Bury School of Excellence; played at
the old Wembley')
Other sports followed: Football (Manchester United), rugby (Western Force)
Injuries: Had surgery in February 2005 for a back injury but played full season
Favourite band: Ocean Colour Scene, Oasis
Relaxations: 'Cinema, running, darts, gym'
Extras: Played for Durham UCCE 2003-05. Durham University Sportsman of the
Year 2004. Represented British Universities 2005
Opinions on cricket: 'Twenty20 is the way forward. Need better structure in league
cricket in England. We could learn a lot from the structure used in Australia.'
Best batting: 7 DUCCE v Durham, Riverside 2004
Best bowling: 8-94 DUCCE v Durham, Riverside 2004

2005 Season (did not make any first-class or one-day appearances for his county)

Career Performances

	M	Inns	NO	Runs	HS	Avge	100s	50s	Ct	St	Balls	Runs	Wkts	Avge	Best	5wI	10wM
Test																	
All First	9	11	6	21	7	4.20	-	-	-	-	1237	807	17	47.47	8-94	1	-
1-Day Int																	
C & G																	
tsL																	
Twenty20																	

DAGNALL, C. E. — Leicestershire

Name: <u>Charles</u> Edward Dagnall
Role: Right-hand bat, right-arm medium-fast bowler
Born: 10 July 1976, Bury, Lancashire
Height: 6ft 3in **Weight:** '14st on a bowling day; 17st on a batting day'
Nickname: Daggers
County debut: 1999 (Warwickshire), 2002 (Leicestershire)
Place in bowling averages: (2004 61st av. 31.82)
Strike rate: (career 55.72)
Parents: Mike and Jackie
Marital status: Single
Family links with cricket: 'Dad ran town team'
Education: Bridgewater School, Worsley; UMIST
Qualifications: 9 GCSEs, 4 A-levels, BSc (Hons) Chemistry
Career outside cricket: Singer and radio presenter
Overseas tours: Warwickshire to Bloemfontein 2000, to Cape Town 2001
Overseas teams played for: Newtown and Chilwell, Geelong, Australia 1994-95; St Josephs, Geelong 1998-99
Career highlights to date: 'Winning B&H Gold Award v Worcestershire [at Worcester] in 2001'
Cricket moments to forget: 'Alan Richardson getting 91 v Hampshire'
Young players to look out for: Luke Wright
Other sports played: Golf, football, tennis, Scrabble
Other sports followed: Football (Burnley FC, 'still hate Stoke'); NFL (Tampa Bay Buccaneers)

Relaxations: 'Educating the masses about music; meeting new people; talking'
Extras: Played for Cumberland. Man of the Match in the Board XI final 1999 (Warwickshire v Essex). Topped Warwickshire 2nd XI batting averages 1998 and was third in bowling averages. Awarded Warwickshire 2nd XI cap 1999. Took a wicket with his fourth ball in first-class cricket v Oxford University at The Parks 1999. B&H Gold Award for his 21* batting at No. 11 (following 2-18) v Worcestershire at Worcester 2001. Released by Leicestershire at the end of the 2005 season
Best batting: 23* Leicestershire v Surrey, The Oval 2003
Best bowling: 6-50 Warwickshire v Derbyshire, Derby 2001

2005 Season

	M	Inns	NO	Runs	HS	Avge	100s	50s	Ct	St	O	M	Runs	Wkts	Avge	Best	5wI	10wM
Test																		
All First																		
1-Day Int																		
C & G	1	0	0	0	0	-	-	-	-	-	7	2	18	0	-		-	-
tsL	3	2	2	11	6 *	-	-	-	-	-	20	5	61	2	30.50	2-20	-	
Twenty20																		

Career Performances

	M	Inns	NO	Runs	HS	Avge	100s	50s	Ct	St	Balls	Runs	Wkts	Avge	Best	5wI	10wM
Test																	
All First	31	32	10	223	23 *	10.13	-	-	5	-	4848	2746	87	31.56	6-50	2	-
1-Day Int																	
C & G	5	4	2	32	24 *	16.00	-	-	-	-	248	146	7	20.85	3-39	-	
tsL	48	22	7	143	28	9.53	-	-	5	-	2038	1421	60	23.68	4-34	-	
Twenty20	6	1	0	2	2	2.00	-	-	1	-	120	161	6	26.83	4-22	-	

DALRYMPLE, J. W. M.   Middlesex

Name: James (Jamie) William Murray Dalrymple
Role: Right-hand bat, off-spin bowler
Born: 21 January 1981, Nairobi, Kenya
Height: 6ft **Weight:** 13st 7lbs
Nickname: JD, Pest
County debut: 2000 (one-day), 2001 (first-class)
County cap: 2004
1st-Class 200s: 2
Place in batting averages: 110th av. 34.33 (2004 77th av. 40.38)
Place in bowling averages: 108th av. 40.86 (2004 110th av. 38.67)
Strike rate: 64.86 (career 80.03)
Parents: Douglas and Patricia
Marital status: Single

Family links with cricket: 'Dad played lots of club cricket.' Brother Simon played for Oxford University in 2002 and 2004
Education: Radley College, Abingdon; St Peter's College, Oxford University
Qualifications: 10 GCSEs, 5 A-levels, degree in History
Overseas tours: Middlesex to South Africa 2000; England A to West Indies 2005-06
Cricket moments to forget: 'Middlesex v Warwickshire at Edgbaston 2003 – being part of the loss of eight wickets in a session, and the match'
Cricketers particularly admired: David Gower, Carl Hooper, Ian Botham, Mark Waugh
Other sports played: Rugby (college), hockey (university)
Other sports followed: Rugby (Northampton RUFC)
Favourite band: 'Don't have a favourite'
Relaxations: Reading, golf
Extras: Represented England U19 2000. Played for Oxford University CCE 2001 and (as captain) 2002. Represented British Universities 2001 and (as captain) 2002. Oxford Blue 2001, 2002 (captain) and 2003 (captain). Scored double century (236*) in the Varsity Match at Fenner's 2003 and took 5-49 in the Cambridge first innings. C&G Man of the Match awards v Wales Minor Counties at Lamphey (104*; second fifty in 14 balls) and v Glamorgan at Lord's (107) 2004. ECB National Academy 2005-06
Best batting: 244 Middlesex v Surrey, The Oval 2004
Best bowling: 5-49 Oxford University v Cambridge University, Fenner's 2003

2005 Season

	M	Inns	NO	Runs	HS	Avge	100s	50s	Ct	St	O	M	Runs	Wkts	Avge	Best	5wI	10wM
Test																		
All First	13	23	2	721	108	34.33	1	6	3	-	248.4	25	940	23	40.86	4-53	-	-
1-Day Int																		
C & G	2	1	0	1	1	1.00	-	-	-	-	16	4	60	3	20.00	3-24	-	
tsL	15	15	5	481	81	48.10	-	5	8	-	58	0	357	5	71.40	1-24	-	
Twenty20	9	9	3	179	39	29.83	-	-	1	-	10	0	89	4	22.25	2-26	-	

	M	Inns	NO	Runs	HS	Avge	100s	50s	Ct	St	Balls	Runs	Wkts	Avge	Best	5wI	10wM
Test																	
All First	49	83	10	2664	244	36.49	5	12	28	-	6323	3597	79	45.53	5-49	1	-
1-Day Int																	
C & G	5	4	1	232	107	77.33	2	-	3	-	198	125	6	20.83	3-24	-	
tsL	65	57	15	1151	81	27.40	-	7	26	-	1851	1581	44	35.93	4-14	-	
Twenty20	13	12	3	227	39	25.22	-	-	3	-	120	190	6	31.66	2-26	-	

DANISH KANERIA   Essex

Name: Danish Prabha Shanker Kaneria
Role: Right-hand bat, right-arm
leg-spin and googly bowler
Born: 16 December 1980, Karachi, Pakistan
Height: 6ft 1in
Nickname: Danny Boy, Dani
County debut: 2004
County cap: 2004
Test debut: 2000-01
50 wickets in a season: 1
Place in bowling averages: 79th av. 33.40
(2004 21st av. 25.53)
Strike rate: 74.00 (career 54.17)
Parents: Prabha Shanker Kaneria and Babita
P. Kaneria
Wife and date of marriage: Dharmeta
Danish Kaneria, 15 February 2004
Family links with cricket: Cousin, wicket-
keeper Anil Dalpat, played nine Tests for Pakistan 1983-84
Education: St Patrick's High School, Karachi
Off-season: Playing cricket
Overseas tours: Pakistan U19 to Sri Lanka (U19 World Cup) 1999-2000; Pakistan A
to Kenya 2000, to Sri Lanka 2001; Pakistan to Bangladesh 2001-02, to Sharjah (v
West Indies) 2001-02, to Sharjah (v Australia) 2002-03, to England (NatWest
Challenge) 2003, to New Zealand 2003-04, to Australia 2004-05, to India 2004-05, to
West Indies 2004-05, plus other one-day tournaments in Sharjah and Sri Lanka
Overseas teams played for: Pakistan National Shipping Corporation 1998-99;
Karachi Whites 1998-99, 2000-02; Pakistan Reserves 1999-2000; Habib Bank 1999-
2004-05; Karachi 2003-04; Karachi Blues 2004-05
Career highlights to date: 'Playing for Pakistan. English county cricket'
Cricket moments to forget: 'The first Test match played for Pakistan' (*2-89/0-30 in
the drawn second Test at Faisalabad 2000-01*)

Cricket superstitions: 'I kiss the ground when taking the field'
Cricketers particularly admired: Abdul Qadir, Viv Richards, Joel Garner
Other sports played: Football, table tennis
Other sports followed: Football (Brazil)
Favourite band: 'I like Indian music'
Relaxations: 'Listening to music and being with family'
Extras: Represented Pakistan U19 1998-99. The second Hindu to play in Tests for Pakistan, after his cousin Anil Dalpat. Had match figures of 12-94 (6-42/6-52) v Bangladesh at Multan in the first match of the Asian Test Championship 2001-02, winning Man of the Match award. His other international awards include Man of the [Test] Series v Bangladesh 2001-02 and Man of the Match in the second Test v Sri Lanka at Karachi 2004-05 (3-72/7-118). Returned first innings figures of 7-188 (from 49.3 overs) in the third Test v Australia at Sydney 2004-05, in the process taking his 100th Test wicket (Shane Warne). An overseas player with Essex 2004-05
Best batting: 47 Karachi Blues v Karachi Whites, Karachi 2004-05
Best bowling: 7-39 Karachi Whites v Gujranwala, Karachi 2000-01

2005 Season

	M	Inns	NO	Runs	HS	Avge	100s	50s	Ct	St	O	M	Runs	Wkts	Avge	Best	5wI	10wM
Test																		
All First	7	6	5	47	22	47.00	-	-	2	-	394.4	86	1069	32	33.40	6-74	3	1
1-Day Int																		
C & G																			
tsL	10	3	3	17	12 *	-	-	-	-	-	79	4	278	16	17.37	3-24	-	
Twenty20	7	1	0	0	0	0.00	-	-	2	-	18	0	169	4	42.25	3-27	-	

Career Performances

	M	Inns	NO	Runs	HS	Avge	100s	50s	Ct	St	Balls	Runs	Wkts	Avge	Best	5wI	10wM
Test	28	39	19	109	15	5.45	-	-	9	-	7943	3975	132	30.11	7-77	11	2
All First	85	104	53	445	47	8.72	-	-	29	-	22781	10723	421	25.47	7-39	33	5
1-Day Int	12	6	5	4	3 *	4.00	-	-	-	-	620	456	10	45.60	3-31	-	
C & G	2	1	0	2	2	2.00	-	-	-	-	120	62	5	12.40	3-30	-	
tsL	19	7	3	26	12 *	6.50	-	-	1	-	801	524	22	23.81	3-24	-	
Twenty20	7	1	0	0	0	0.00	-	-	2	-	108	169	4	42.25	3-27	-	

DAVIES, A. P.   Glamorgan

Name: <u>Andrew</u> Philip Davies
Role: Left-hand bat, right-arm
medium-fast bowler
Born: 7 November 1976, Neath
Height: 6ft **Weight:** 12st 3lbs
Nickname: Diver
County debut: 1995
Place in batting averages: 207th av. 21.50
Place in bowling averages: 138th av. 51.07
Strike rate: 77.61 (career 68.06)
Parents: Anne and Phil
Wife and date of marriage: Nerys,
1 February 2003
Children: 2
Family links with cricket: 'Brother plays
local league cricket. Dad used to play'
Education: Dwr-y-Felin, Neath; Christ
College, Brecon

Qualifications: 7 GCSEs, 1 A-level, Level 2 coach
Career outside cricket: '12-month contracts now'
Overseas tours: Wales MC to Barbados; Glamorgan to Pretoria, to Cape Town (twice)
Overseas teams played for: Marist CC, Whangarei, New Zealand 1995-96; Marist
Old Boys, Napier, New Zealand
Career highlights to date: '2 x Sunday League champions'
Cricket moments to forget: 'Surrey scoring 400 against us in 50 overs [in the C&G
2002]. We gave them a scare, though!'
Cricket superstitions: 'None'
Cricketers particularly admired: Matt Maynard, Robert Croft, Matthew Elliott
Young players to look out for: 'Some good batters but don't want to let them know'
Other sports played: 'Try to play golf'
Other sports followed: Football
Favourite band: Oasis, Stereophonics
Relaxations: 'Reading, crosswords; trying to get a pint off Crofty'
Extras: Wales U19 Player of the Year 1995. Wales Player of the Year 1996. 2nd XI
cap 1998. 2nd XI Player of the Year 1998, 1999. 1st XI Player of the Month August-
September 1998. Glamorgan's leading wicket-taker (21) in the NUL 2001
Best batting: 41* Glamorgan v Nottinghamshire, Trent Bridge 2005
Best bowling: 5-79 Glamorgan v Worcestershire, Cardiff 2002

2005 Season

	M	Inns	NO	Runs	HS	Avge	100s	50s	Ct	St	O	M	Runs	Wkts	Avge	Best	5wI	10wM
Test																		
All First	7	12	4	172	41 *	21.50	-	-	3	-	168.1	30	664	13	51.07	3-121	-	-
1-Day Int																		
C & G	2	1	0	7	7	7.00	-	-	-	-	13	0	45	3	15.00	2-30	-	
tsL	14	6	3	21	11 *	7.00	-	-	2	-	109	7	606	15	40.40	4-53	-	
Twenty20	7	5	1	16	11	4.00	-	-	2	-	25.5	1	230	8	28.75	2-32	-	

Career Performances

	M	Inns	NO	Runs	HS	Avge	100s	50s	Ct	St	Balls	Runs	Wkts	Avge	Best	5wI	10wM
Test																	
All First	30	40	8	436	41 *	13.62	-	-	7	-	3948	2456	58	42.34	5-79	1	-
1-Day Int																	
C & G	8	5	3	24	7 *	12.00	-	-	-	-	348	308	12	25.66	5-19	1	
tsL	70	29	16	116	24	8.92	-	-	10	-	2975	2515	106	23.72	5-39	1	
Twenty20	13	6	1	20	11	4.00	-	-	4	-	294	389	18	21.61	3-17	-	

DAVIES, M. A.   Durham

Name: <u>Mark</u> Anthony Davies
Role: Right-hand bat, right-arm
fast-medium bowler
Born: 4 October 1980, Stockton-on-Tees
Height: 6ft 3in **Weight:** 13st
Nickname: Davo
County debut: 1998 (one-day),
2002 (first-class)
County cap: 2005
50 wickets in a season: 1
Place in batting averages: 262nd av. 13.33
(2004 260th av. 12.22)
Place in bowling averages: 2nd av. 16.53
(2004 3rd av. 18.76)
Strike rate: 36.32 (career 45.52)
Parents: Howard and Mandy
Marital status: Single
Education: Northfield School, Billingham;
Stockton Sixth Form College
Qualifications: 5 GCSEs, NVQ Level 3 Sport and Recreation
Overseas tours: Durham to South Africa 2002
Overseas teams played for: North Kalgoorlie CC, Western Australia

Cricketers particularly admired: Glenn McGrath
Other sports played: Football, golf, boxing
Other sports followed: Football (Middlesbrough)
Relaxations: Socialising, golf
Extras: Represented England U19 2000. Attended Durham Academy. Was the first bowler to reach 50 first-class wickets in 2004
Best batting: 62 Durham v Somerset, Stockton 2005
Best bowling: 6-32 Durham v Worcestershire, Riverside 2005

2005 Season

	M	Inns	NO	Runs	HS	Avge	100s	50s	Ct	St	O	M	Runs	Wkts	Avge	Best	5wI	10wM
Test																		
All First	12	14	5	120	62	13.33	-	1	2	-	296.4	94	810	49	16.53	6-32	2	-
1-Day Int																		
C & G																		
tsL	3	2	1	1	1	1.00	-	-	-	-	14	4	42	1	42.00	1-28	-	
Twenty20																		

Career Performances

	M	Inns	NO	Runs	HS	Avge	100s	50s	Ct	St	Balls	Runs	Wkts	Avge	Best	5wI	10wM
Test																	
All First	41	63	23	478	62	11.95	-	1	7	-	6647	3199	146	21.91	6-32	7	-
1-Day Int																	
C & G	9	6	1	11	6	2.20	-	-	-	-	390	261	6	43.50	1-11	-	
tsL	50	26	10	135	31 *	8.43	-	-	9	-	2022	1399	51	27.43	4-13	-	
Twenty20	9	4	3	11	6	11.00	-	-	2	-	204	241	8	30.12	2-14	-	

DAVIES, S. M.   Worcestershire

Name: Steven (Steve) Michael Davies
Role: Left-hand bat, wicket-keeper
Born: 17 June 1986, Bromsgrove
Height: 5ft 11in **Weight:** 11st 7lbs
Nickname: Davo
County debut: 2005 (*see Extras*)
County colours: 2005
Place in batting averages: 103rd av. 34.83
Parents: Lin and Michael
Marital status: Single
Education: King Charles I School
Qualifications: 9 GCSEs, 1 A-level, 2 AS-levels
Off-season: ECB National Academy

Overseas tours: England U17 to Holland 2003; England U19 to Bangladesh (U19 World Cup) 2003-04, to India 2004-05 (c)
Career highlights to date: 'Maiden first-class century against Somerset'
Cricket superstitions: 'None'
Cricketers particularly admired: Adam Gilchrist, Chris Read
Young players to look out for: Adam Harrison, Will Gifford
Other sports played: Basketball (trials for England), golf
Other sports followed: Football (Arsenal)
Favourite band: Usher
Relaxations: 'Playing golf and basketball; socialising with friends; listening to music'
Extras: Represented England U19 2004, 2005. Played for Worcestershire v Sri Lanka

A in a limited overs fixture at Worcester 2004 but did not appear for the county in first-class cricket or one-day competition until 2005. ECB National Academy 2004-05 (part-time), 2005-06 (including visit to World Academy, India)
Opinions on cricket: 'More Twenty20 cricket.'
Best batting: 148 Worcestershire v Somerset, Worcester 2005

2005 Season

	M	Inns	NO	Runs	HS	Avge	100s	50s	Ct	St	O	M	Runs	Wkts	Avge	Best	5wl	10wM
Test																		
All First	11	19	1	627	148	34.83	1	2	11	3								
1-Day Int																		
C & G																		
tsL	7	6	2	114	43	28.50	-	-	6	3								
Twenty20																		

Career Performances

	M	Inns	NO	Runs	HS	Avge	100s	50s	Ct	St	Balls	Runs	Wkts	Avge	Best	5wl	10wM
Test																	
All First	11	19	1	627	148	34.83	1	2	11	3							
1-Day Int																	
C & G	2	1	0	13	13	13.00	-	-	-	-							
tsL	7	6	2	114	43	28.50	-	-	6	3							
Twenty20																	

DAVIS, M. J. G.   Sussex

Name: <u>Mark</u> Jeffrey Gronow Davis
Role: Right-hand bat, right-arm
off-spin bowler
Born: 10 October 1971, Port Elizabeth,
South Africa
Height: 6ft 2in **Weight:** 12st 8lbs
Nickname: Davo, Doxy, Sparky
County debut: 2001
County cap: 2002
Place in batting averages: 260th av. 14.00
(2004 247th av. 15.54)
Place in bowling averages: (2004 60th
av. 31.52)
Strike rate: (career 79.63)
Parents: Jeremy and Marilyn
Wife and date of marriage: Candice,
8 April 2000

Family links with cricket: 'Father supports
Sussex. My brothers, William and Patrick, play league cricket in Sussex'
Education: Grey High School; University of Pretoria
Qualifications: BA Psychology and English
Career outside cricket: Coach of UPE International Cricket Academy in Port
Elizabeth
Overseas tours: South Africa U24 to Sri Lanka 1995; Northern Transvaal to
Zimbabwe 1992-93, to Kenya 1994-95, 1995-96
Overseas teams played for: Northern Transvaal/Northerns 1990-91 – 1999-2000
Career highlights to date: 'Winning the County Championship [2003]. It was second
to none, unbelievable! That and my 168 v Middlesex the same season'
Cricket superstitions: 'None'
Cricketers particularly admired: 'All my team-mates', Tim May, Shane Warne
Other sports played: Golf, tennis
Other sports followed: Rugby ('support the Springboks'), football (Middlesbrough)
Favourite band: 'Very eclectic tastes – no real favourite'
Relaxations: 'Golf, music, going out with friends, watching good movies'
Extras: Represented South Africa A 1995. Captain of Northern Transvaal/Northerns
1997-2000, during which time the province won the first two trophies in its history.
Member of MCC. Scored maiden first-class century (111) v Somerset at Taunton 2002,
in the process sharing with Robin Martin-Jenkins (205*) in a record eighth-wicket
partnership for Sussex (291); the stand fell one run short of the record eighth-wicket
partnership in English first-class cricket, set in 1896. Retired at the end of the 2005
season to become club coach but registration retained. Is not considered an overseas
player

Best batting: 168 Sussex v Middlesex, Hove 2003
Best bowling: 8-37 Northerns B v North West, Potchefstroom 1994-95

2005 Season

	M	Inns	NO	Runs	HS	Avge	100s	50s	Ct	St	O	M	Runs	Wkts	Avge	Best	5wI	10wM
Test																		
All First	6	6	0	84	50	14.00	-	1	-	-	74.2	16	177	3	59.00	2-52	-	-
1-Day Int																		
C & G																		
tsL	10	7	5	51	22	25.50	-	-	-	-	62	1	273	7	39.00	2-27	-	
Twenty20	8	2	2	26	20 *	-	-	-	1	-	14	0	121	2	60.50	1-14	-	

Career Performances

	M	Inns	NO	Runs	HS	Avge	100s	50s	Ct	St	Balls	Runs	Wkts	Avge	Best	5wI	10wM
Test																	
All First	127	187	30	2941	168	18.73	2	8	67	-	18475	8368	232	36.06	8-37	5	1
1-Day Int																	
C & G	8	6	5	96	32 *	96.00	-	-	-	-	450	296	4	74.00	2-37	-	
tsL	72	48	18	537	37	17.90	-	-	13	-	3048	2334	71	32.87	4-14	-	
Twenty20	17	9	5	78	20 *	19.50	-	-	5	-	276	343	13	26.38	3-13	-	

DAWOOD, I. Yorkshire

Name: Ismail Dawood
Role: Right-hand bat, wicket-keeper
Born: 23 July 1976, Dewsbury
Height: 5ft 8in
County debut: 1994 (Northamptonshire),
1996 (Worcestershire), 1998 (Glamorgan),
2004 (Yorkshire)
Place in batting averages: 205th av. 21.73
(2004 118th av. 34.44)
Family links with cricket: Grandfather and
father played local league cricket
Education: Batley Grammar School
Qualifications: 8 GCSEs, NCA Coaching
Award
Overseas tours: Glamorgan to South Africa
1998-99; England U19 to Sri Lanka 1993-94,
to West Indies 1994-95
Overseas teams played for: Grafton,
Auckland 1992-93

Extras: Represented England U19 1994 and 1995. Scored maiden first-class century (102) v Gloucestershire at Cardiff 1999; took five catches at short leg in the same match. Conceded no byes in Lancashire's 556-6 dec. at Blackpool 1999, setting a Glamorgan record for a clean sheet. Left Glamorgan at the end of the 1999 season; played for Herefordshire 2000-04. Represented ECB XI in the Triple Crown Tournament 2001. Played for Bradford/Leeds University CCE 2003-04. Represented British Universities 2003 and 2004. Released by Yorkshire at the end of the 2005 season

Best batting: 102 Glamorgan v Gloucestershire, Cardiff 1999

2005 Season

	M	Inns	NO	Runs	HS	Avge	100s	50s	Ct	St	O	M	Runs	Wkts	Avge	Best	5wl	10wM
Test																		
All First	12	17	2	326	62*	21.73	-	2	34	1								
1-Day Int																		
C & G	4	3	0	26	23	8.66	-	-	1	1								
tsL	11	10	4	175	57	29.16	-	1	10	4								
Twenty20	8	6	2	39	15	9.75	-	-	4	2								

Career Performances

	M	Inns	NO	Runs	HS	Avge	100s	50s	Ct	St	Balls	Runs	Wkts	Avge	Best	5wl	10wM
Test																	
All First	39	61	10	1122	102	22.00	1	4	94	6							
1-Day Int																	
C & G	16	14	0	356	60	25.42	-	2	14	4							
tsL	34	29	10	354	57	18.63	-	2	30	10							
Twenty20	11	8	3	44	15	8.80	-	-	5	2							

DAWSON, R. K. J.   Yorkshire

Name: Richard Kevin James Dawson
Role: Right-hand bat, right-arm off-spin bowler
Born: 4 August 1980, Doncaster
Height: 6ft 4in **Weight:** 11st 4lbs
Nickname: Billy Dog
County debut: 2001
County cap: 2004
Test debut: 2001-02
Place in batting averages: 139th av. 30.71 (2004 183rd av. 24.52)
Place in bowling averages: 107th av. 40.66 (2004 79th av. 34.86)
Strike rate: 72.37 (career 72.45)
Parents: Kevin and Pat

Marital status: Single
Family links with cricket: Brother Gareth plays for Doncaster Town CC
Education: Batley GS; Exeter University
Qualifications: 10 GCSEs, 4 A-levels, degree in Exercise and Sports Science
Overseas tours: England U18 to Bermuda 1997; England U19 to New Zealand 1998-99; England to India and New Zealand 2001-02, to Australia 2002-03; ECB National Academy to Sri Lanka 2002-03; England A to Sri Lanka 2004-05
Cricketers particularly admired: Steve Waugh, Graeme Swann
Other sports played: Football
Other sports followed: Football (Doncaster Rovers FC)
Relaxations: Sleeping, listening to music

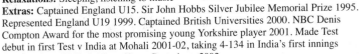

Extras: Captained England U15. Sir John Hobbs Silver Jubilee Memorial Prize 1995. Represented England U19 1999. Captained British Universities 2000. NBC Denis Compton Award for the most promising young Yorkshire player 2001. Made Test debut in first Test v India at Mohali 2001-02, taking 4-134 in India's first innings
Best batting: 87 Yorkshire v Kent, Canterbury 2002
Best bowling: 6-82 Yorkshire v Glamorgan, Scarborough 2001

2005 Season

	M	Inns	NO	Runs	HS	Avge	100s	50s	Ct	St	O	M	Runs	Wkts	Avge	Best	5wI	10wM
Test																		
All First	14	18	4	430	86	30.71	-	3	8	-	325.4	46	1098	27	40.66	4-54	-	-
1-Day Int																		
C & G	4	3	0	34	21	11.33	-	-	1	-	29.5	1	147	2	73.50	1-45	-	
tsL	13	9	3	104	27	17.33	-	-	2	-	97	3	480	17	28.23	3-28	-	
Twenty20	8	2	1	13	7	13.00	-	-	1	-	31.3	0	213	8	26.62	2-20	-	

Career Performances

	M	Inns	NO	Runs	HS	Avge	100s	50s	Ct	St	Balls	Runs	Wkts	Avge	Best	5wI	10wM
Test	7	13	3	114	19 *	11.40	-	-	3	-	1116	677	11	61.54	4-134	-	-
All First	80	119	14	2369	87	22.56	-	10	44	-	12475	6945	173	40.14	6-82	5	-
1-Day Int																	
C & G	17	7	0	52	21	7.42	-	-	4	-	746	595	12	49.58	4-34	-	
tsL	60	42	9	292	41	8.84	-	-	19	-	2221	1734	69	25.13	4-20	-	
Twenty20	13	3	1	13	7	6.50	-	-	1	-	291	355	14	25.35	2-20	-	

DEAN, K. J.   Derbyshire

Name: <u>Kevin</u> James Dean
Role: Left-hand bat, left-arm medium bowler
Born: 16 October 1975, Derby
Height: 6ft 5in **Weight:** 14st
Nickname: Deany, Red Face, The Wall, George
County debut: 1996
County cap: 1998
Benefit: 2006
50 wickets in a season: 2
Place in batting averages: (2004 221st av. 19.50)
Place in bowling averages: (2004 44th av. 29.85)
Strike rate: (career 45.10)
Parents: Ken and Dorothy
Marital status: Single
Education: Leek High School; Leek College of Further Education
Qualifications: 8 GCSEs, 1 AS-level, 3 A-levels, ECB Level 2 coaching
Career outside cricket: Working for Ladbrokes
Overseas tours: MCC to Australia 2002-03
Overseas teams played for: Sturt CC, Adelaide 1996-97
Career highlights to date: 'Can't split – 1) Hitting the winning runs against Australia for Derbyshire in 1997; 2) Getting either hat-trick'
Cricket moments to forget: 'Spending time out injured'
Cricket superstitions: 'Last person out of changing room for first session of fielding'
Cricketers particularly admired: Dominic Cork, Wasim Akram, Michael Holding
Young players to look out for: Simon Cusden, Ross Whitely
Other sports played: Football, golf, tennis, snooker
Other sports followed: Football (Derby County), horse racing
Favourite band: Stereophonics, Oasis, Pink, DJ Sammy
Extras: Achieved first-class hat-trick (E. Smith, Hooper, Llong) against Kent at Derby 1998. Took second first-class hat-trick (Habib, Kumble, Ormond) v Leicestershire at Leicester 2000. Joint leading wicket-taker in English first-class cricket 2002 (with Martin Saggers) with 83 wickets (av. 23.50). Derbyshire Player of the Year 2002 (jointly with Michael DiVenuto)
Best batting: 54* Derbyshire v Worcestershire, Derby 2002
Best bowling: 8-52 Derbyshire v Kent, Canterbury 2000

2005 Season

	M	Inns	NO	Runs	HS	Avge	100s	50s	Ct	St	O	M	Runs	Wkts	Avge	Best	5wI	10wM
Test																		
All First	4	6	1	52	12	10.40	-	-	-	-	104.5	22	319	6	53.16	3-36	-	-
1-Day Int																		
C & G	2	2	2	5	5*	-	-	-	1	-	15	0	53	0	-		-	-
tsL	7	2	2	2	1*	-	-	-	2	-	42	4	198	11	18.00	5-45	1	
Twenty20	7	1	1	3	3*	-	-	-	2	-	19	0	146	3	48.66	2-20	-	

Career Performances

	M	Inns	NO	Runs	HS	Avge	100s	50s	Ct	St	Balls	Runs	Wkts	Avge	Best	5wI	10wM
Test																	
All First	100	136	42	1111	54*	11.81	-	2	20	-	16147	9185	358	25.65	8-52	15	4
1-Day Int																	
C & G	17	7	4	17	8	5.66	-	-	7	-	912	599	28	21.39	3-6	-	
tsL	96	46	25	197	16*	9.38	-	-	16	-	4115	3186	104	30.63	5-32	2	
Twenty20	7	1	1	3	3*	-	-	-	2	-	114	146	3	48.66	2-20	-	

DE BRUYN, Z.   Worcestershire

Name: Zander de Bruyn
Role: Right-hand bat, right-arm
fast-medium bowler
Born: 5 July 1975, Johannesburg,
South Africa
County debut: 2005
County colours: 2005
Test debut: 2004-05
1st-Class 200s: 1
Place in batting averages: 134th av. 31.12
Strike rate: (career 67.60)
Education: Hoerskool Helpmekaar;
Hoerskool Randburg
Overseas tours: South Africa A to Zimbabwe
2004, to Sri Lanka 2005-06; South Africa to
India 2004-05
Overseas teams played for:
Transvaal/Gauteng 1995-96 – 2000-01;
Easterns 2002-03 – 2003-04; Titans 2004-05 –
Extras: Represented South Africa Schools. Played for Surrey Board XI in the NatWest
2000 and C&G 2001. Scored 1015 runs (av. 72.50) in the SuperSport Series 2003-04,
becoming only the second player (after Barry Richards) to record 1000 runs in a

season in the South African domestic first-class competition. Has won numerous awards, including Man of the Match v Western Province in the semi-finals of the Standard Bank Cup at Cape Town 2003-04 (5-44/29) and v Yorkshire at Headingley in the C&G 2005 (3-24/82). An overseas player with Worcestershire 2005
Best batting: 266* Easterns v Griqualand West, Kimberley 2003-04
Best bowling: 6-120 Transvaal B v Western Province B, Cape Town 1996-97

2005 Season

	M	Inns	NO	Runs	HS	Avge	100s	50s	Ct	St	O	M	Runs	Wkts	Avge	Best	5wI	10wM
Test																		
All First	11	16	0	498	161	31.12	1	2	10	-	192	27	780	8	97.50	1-13	-	-
1-Day Int																		
C & G	2	1	0	82	82	82.00	-	1	-	-	11	2	41	4	10.25	3-24	-	
tsL	9	8	1	306	62	43.71	-	4	3	-	38	1	180	2	90.00	1-25	-	
Twenty20	7	7	1	165	76 *	27.50	-	1	-	-	17	0	166	8	20.75	3-43	-	

Career Performances

	M	Inns	NO	Runs	HS	Avge	100s	50s	Ct	St	Balls	Runs	Wkts	Avge	Best	5wI	10wM
Test	3	5	1	155	83	38.75	-	1	-	-	216	92	3	30.66	2-32	-	-
All First	75	129	16	4773	266 *	42.23	11	23	47	-	6684	3834	100	38.34	6-120	1	-
1-Day Int																	
C & G	5	4	1	240	113 *	80.00	1	1	-	-	84	63	6	10.50	3-24	-	
tsL	9	8	1	306	62	43.71	-	4	3	-	228	180	2	90.00	1-25	-	
Twenty20	7	7	1	165	76 *	27.50	-	1	-	-	102	166	8	20.75	3-43	-	

DEFREITAS, P. A. J. Leicestershire

Name: Phillip Anthony Jason DeFreitas
Role: Right-hand bat, right-arm fast-medium bowler
Born: 18 February 1966, Scotts Head, Dominica
Height: 6ft **Weight:** 13st 7lbs
Nickname: Padge, Daffy, Linchy
County debut: 1985 (Leics), 1989 (Lancs), 1994 (Derbys)
County cap: 1986 (Leics), 1989 (Lancs), 1994 (Derbys)
Benefit: 2004 (Leics)
Test debut: 1986-87
50 wickets in a season: 14
Place in batting averages: (2004 192nd av. 23.17)
Place in bowling averages: 83rd av. 33.83 (2004 74th av. 34.32)
Strike rate: 55.50 (career 57.74)
Parents: Sybil and Martin
Marital status: Divorced

Children: Alexandra Elizabeth Jane,
5 August 1991
Family links with cricket: Father played in
Windward Islands. All six brothers play
Education: Willesden High School
Qualifications: 2 O-levels
Overseas tours: England YC to West Indies
1984-85; England to Australia 1986-87, to
Pakistan, Australia and New Zealand 1987-
88, to India (Nehru Cup) and West Indies
1989-90, to Australia 1990-91, to New
Zealand 1991-92, to India and Sri Lanka
1992-93, to Australia 1994-95, to South Africa
1995-96, to India and Pakistan (World Cup)
1995-96; England XI to New Zealand (Cricket
Max) 1997

Overseas teams played for: Port Adelaide,
South Australia 1985; Mosman, Sydney
1988; Boland, South Africa 1993-94, 1995-96
Cricketers particularly admired: Ian Botham, Geoff Boycott, Mike Gatting,
Viv Richards, Malcolm Marshall, David Hughes, Neil Fairbrother
Other sports followed: Football (Manchester City)
Extras: Left Leicestershire and joined Lancashire at end of 1988 season. Man of the
Match in 1990 NatWest Trophy final at Lord's (5-26). One of *Wisden*'s Five Cricketers
of the Year 1992. Man of the Tournament in the Hong Kong Sixes 1993. England
Player of the [Test] Series against New Zealand 1994. Captained Derbyshire for part of
1997 season after the departure of Dean Jones. Appeared in two World Cup finals.
Took 1000th first-class wicket (Usman Afzaal) v Notts at Trent Bridge 1999. Left
Derbyshire at end of 1999 season and rejoined Leicestershire for 2000. Took 6-65 v
Glamorgan at Cardiff 2001, in the process achieving the feat of having recorded a five-
wicket innings return against all 18 counties. Passed 10,000 runs in first-class cricket v
Somerset at Leicester 2002 to achieve the career double of 10,000 runs and 1000
wickets. Scored 103 v Sussex at Leicester 2003, following up with 5-55 in Sussex's
first innings. Captain of Leicestershire 2003 until standing down in July 2004. Retired
at the end of the 2005 season
Best batting: 123* Leicestershire v Lancashire, Leicester 2000
Best bowling: 7-21 Lancashire v Middlesex, Lord's 1989

2005 Season

	M	Inns	NO	Runs	HS	Avge	100s	50s	Ct	St	O	M	Runs	Wkts	Avge	Best	5wI	10wM
Test																		
All First	4	7	0	62	20	8.85	-	-	-	-	111	21	406	12	33.83	4-76	-	-
1-Day Int																		
C & G																		
tsL																		
Twenty20																		

Career Performances

	M	Inns	NO	Runs	HS	Avge	100s	50s	Ct	St	Balls	Runs	Wkts	Avge	Best	5wI	10wM
Test	44	68	5	934	88	14.82	-	4	14	-	9838	4700	140	33.57	7-70	4	-
All First	372	533	50	10991	123 *	22.75	10	54	127	-	72063	34809	1248	27.89	7-21	61	6
1-Day Int	103	66	23	690	67	16.04	-	1	26	-	5712	3775	115	32.82	4-35	-	
C & G	49	33	4	526	69	18.13	-	1	9	-	2937	1495	63	23.73	5-13	4	
tsL	238	184	29	2969	90	19.15	-	8	44	-	9692	7029	249	28.22	5-26	2	
Twenty20	9	8	1	54	18	7.71	-	-	-	-	138	204	8	25.50	3-39	-	

DENLY, J. L.   Kent

Name: Joseph (Joe) Liam Denly
Role: Right-hand bat,
leg-spin bowler
Born: 16 March 1986, Canterbury
Height: 6ft **Weight:** 11st 9lbs
Nickname: No Pants
County debut: 2004
Parents: Jayne and Nick
Marital status: Single
Family links with cricket: 'Dad and brother
play local cricket'
Education: Chaucer Technology School
Qualifications: 10 GCSEs, Level 1 coach
Career outside cricket: 'Football'
Off-season: 'Playing Sydney grade cricket'
Overseas tours: England U18 to Holland
2003; England U19 to India 2004-05
Overseas teams played for: Hamersley
Carine, Perth 2003; UTS Balmain Tigers, Sydney 2005-06
Career highlights to date: 'Making my first-class debut'
Cricket moments to forget: 'Golden duck on first-class debut'
Cricket superstitions: 'Left pad on first'

Cricketers particularly admired: Steve Waugh
Young players to look out for: Sam Denly
Other sports played: Football (Charlton Athletic U14, U15)
Other sports followed: Football (Arsenal)
Injuries: Out for two weeks with a broken thumb and finger
Favourite band: Westlife
Extras: Has represented England U17, U18 and U19
Opinions on cricket: 'It's great'
Best batting: 10 Kent v Gloucestershire, Maidstone 2005

2005 Season

	M	Inns	NO	Runs	HS	Avge	100s	50s	Ct	St	O	M	Runs	Wkts	Avge	Best	5wl	10wM
Test																		
All First	1	2	0	14	10	7.00	-	-	-	-								
1-Day Int																		
C & G																		
tsL	6	6	1	67	49	13.40	-	-	-	-								
Twenty20																		

Career Performances

	M	Inns	NO	Runs	HS	Avge	100s	50s	Ct	St	Balls	Runs	Wkts	Avge	Best	5wl	10wM
Test																	
All First	2	3	0	14	10	4.66	-	-	-	-							
1-Day Int																	
C & G																	
tsL	6	6	1	67	49	13.40	-	-	-	-							
Twenty20	3	1	0	4	4	4.00	-	-	2	-							

24. Which two sets of fathers and sons have played in ODIs for England?

DENNINGTON, M. J. — Kent

Name: Matthew (<u>Matt</u>) John Dennington
Role: Right-hand bat, right-arm
medium-fast bowler
Born: 16 October 1982, Durban,
South Africa
Height: 6ft 1in **Weight:** 12st 10lbs
Nickname: Denners, Denzel
County debut: 2003 (one-day),
2004 (first-class)
Place in batting averages: 198th av. 23.00
(2004 248th av. 15.42)
Strike rate: (career 58.18)
Parents: John and Yvonne
Marital status: Single
Education: Northwood Boys, Durban;
Varsity College and University of South
Africa (UNISA)
Qualifications: Matriculation

Overseas teams played for: Crusaders CC, Durban 1998-2002; KwaZulu-Natal B 2002-03
Career highlights to date: 'Taking three wickets in a Championship game against Surrey and getting 50* to save the game'
Cricket moments to forget: 'Colliding with team-mate going for a catch on the boundary and breaking my kneecap'
Cricket superstitions: 'Not a superstitious cricketer'
Cricketers particularly admired: Paddy Clift, Allan Donald
Other sports played: Golf
Other sports followed: Rugby (Natal Sharks)
Favourite band: Red Hot Chili Peppers
Relaxations: 'Going to gym; surfing and other watersports; playing golf'
Extras: Natal Schools 1999-2000. Natal Academy 2001-02. Natal B 2002
Best batting: 55 Kent v Hampshire, Canterbury 2005
Best bowling: 3-23 Kent v Bangladesh A, Canterbury 2005

2005 Season

	M	Inns	NO	Runs	HS	Avge	100s	50s	Ct	St	O	M	Runs	Wkts	Avge	Best	5wI	10wM
Test																		
All First	4	8	1	161	55	23.00	-	2	3	-	62.1	15	206	7	29.42	3-23	-	-
1-Day Int																		
C & G																		
tsL	3	1	0	17	17	17.00	-	-	-	-	17	0	107	1	107.00	1-57	-	
Twenty20	3	0	0	0	0	-	-	-	1	-	5	0	58	1	58.00	1-28	-	

Career Performances

	M	Inns	NO	Runs	HS	Avge	100s	50s	Ct	St	Balls	Runs	Wkts	Avge	Best	5wI	10wM
Test																	
All First	11	17	3	269	55	19.21	-	3	5	-	931	574	16	35.87	3-23	-	-
1-Day Int																	
C & G	2	2	0	14	13	7.00	-	-	-	-	108	98	1	98.00	1-51	-	
tsL	13	9	4	84	26 *	16.80	-	-	3	-	402	446	6	74.33	3-53	-	
Twenty20	8	3	0	22	12	7.33	-	-	2	-	144	222	9	24.66	4-28	-	

DERNBACH, J. W.　　　　　Surrey

Name: <u>Jade</u> Winston Dernbach
Role: Right-hand bat, right-arm fast bowler
Born: 3 March 1986, Johannesburg, South Africa
Height: 6ft 2in **Weight:** 13st
County debut: 2003
Strike rate: (career 73.60)
Parents: Carmen and Graeme
Marital status: Single
Education: St John the Baptist
Overseas tours: La Manga tournament, Spain 2003
Career highlights to date: 'Making my first-team debut for Surrey against India A'
Cricket moments to forget: 'Going out first ball in the ECB U17 final in 2003'
Cricketers particularly admired: Jacques Kallis, Jonty Rhodes, James Anderson, Rikki Clarke
Other sports played: Rugby (Surrey U16)
Other sports followed: Football (Arsenal)
Favourite band: Usher

Relaxations: 'Going out with friends; swimming, playing football and rugby; listening to music'

Extras: Sir Jack Hobbs Fair Play Award. Surrey U19 Player of the Year. Made first-class debut v India A at The Oval 2003 aged 17, becoming the youngest player for 30 years to play first-class cricket for Surrey. Surrey Academy 2003, 2004

Best batting: 3 Surrey v India A, The Oval 2003

Best bowling: 2-66 Surrey v Warwickshire, Edgbaston 2005

2005 Season

	M	Inns	NO	Runs	HS	Avge	100s	50s	Ct	St	O	M	Runs	Wkts	Avge	Best	5wI	10wM
Test																		
All First	3	3	2	2	1*	2.00	-	-	1	-	48.2	5	261	4	65.25	2-66	-	-
1-Day Int																		
C & G																			
tsL	7	2	0	22	21	11.00	-	-	2	-	44	1	250	10	25.00	4-36	-	
Twenty20	1	0	0	0	0	-	-	-	1	-	4	0	52	0	-	-	-	-

Career Performances

	M	Inns	NO	Runs	HS	Avge	100s	50s	Ct	St	Balls	Runs	Wkts	Avge	Best	5wI	10wM
Test																	
All First	4	4	2	5	3	2.50	-	-	1	-	368	335	5	67.00	2-66	-	-
1-Day Int																	
C & G																		
tsL	7	2	0	22	21	11.00	-	-	2	-	264	250	10	25.00	4-36	-	
Twenty20	1	0	0	0	0	-	-	-	1	-	24	52	0	-	-	-	-

25. Which Australian black belt in taekwondo has played 97 Tests but only 8 ODIs?

Name: Neil John Dexter
Role: Right-hand bat, right-arm medium
bowler; all-rounder
Born: 21 August 1984, Johannesburg,
South Africa
Height: 6ft **Weight:** 11st 4lbs
Nickname: Ted, Dex
County debut: 2005
Strike rate: (career 96.00)
Parents: John and Susan
Marital status: Single
Education: Northwood School, Durban;
UNISA (University of South Africa)
Qualifications: Matric
Overseas teams played for: Crusaders CC
2000-06
Career highlights to date: 'Scoring 79 not
out on debut v Notts during 2005 season'
Cricketers particularly admired: Kepler Wessels, Steve Waugh
Young players to look out for: Joe Denly
Other sports played: Golf, surfing, skiing
Other sports followed: Football, tennis, 'most sports'
Favourite band: Simple Plan
Extras: Played for Natal U13-19, Natal Academy and Natal A. Is not considered an
overseas player
Opinions on cricket: 'Very professional with lots of opportunities.'
Best batting : 79* Kent v Nottinghamshire, Canterbury 2005
Best bowling : 1-42 Kent v Nottinghamshire, Canterbury 2005

2005 Season

	M	Inns	NO	Runs	HS	Avge	100s	50s	Ct	St	O	M	Runs	Wkts	Avge	Best	5wI	10wM
Test																		
All First	3	6	1	176	79 *	35.20	-	2	4	-	32	3	161	2	80.50	1-42	-	-
1-Day Int																		
C & G																		
tsL	2	2	0	5	5	2.50	-	-	-	-	10	0	68	3	22.66	2-33	-	
Twenty20																		

Career Performances

	M	Inns	NO	Runs	HS	Avge	100s	50s	Ct	St	Balls	Runs	Wkts	Avge	Best	5wI	10wM
Test																	
All First	3	6	1	176	79 *	35.20	-	2	4	-	192	161	2	80.50	1-42	-	-
1-Day Int																	
C & G																		
tsL	2	2	0	5	5	2.50	-	-	-	-	60	68	3	22.66	2-33	-	
Twenty20																	

DIVENUTO, M. J. Derbyshire

Name: <u>Michael</u> James DiVenuto
Role: Left-hand bat, right-arm medium/
leg-break bowler, county vice-captain
Born: 12 December 1973, Hobart, Tasmania
Height: 5ft 11in **Weight:** 12st 12lbs
Nickname: Diva
County debut: 1999 (Sussex),
2000 (Derbyshire)
County cap: 1999 (Sussex),
2000 (Derbyshire)
1000 runs in a season: 5
1st-Class 200s: 2
Place in batting averages: 37th av. 49.70
Strike rate: (career 160.20)
Parents: Enrico and Elizabeth
Wife and date of marriage: Renae,
31 December 2003
Family links with cricket: 'Dad and older
brother Peter both played grade cricket in Tasmania.' Brother Peter also played for
Italy
Education: St Virgil's College, Hobart
Qualifications: HSC (5 x Level III subjects), Level 3 cricket coach
Off-season: Playing for Tasmania
Overseas tours: Australian Cricket Academy to India and Sri Lanka 1993, to South
Africa 1996; Australia A to Malaysia (Super 8s) 1997 (c), to Scotland and Ireland 1998
(c), to Los Angeles 1999; Australia to South Africa 1996-97 (one-day series),
to Hong Kong (Super 6s) 1997, to Malaysia (Super 8s) 1998; Tasmania to Zimbabwe
1995-96
Overseas teams played for: North Hobart CC, Tasmania; Kingborough, Tasmania;
Tasmania 1991-92 –
Career highlights to date: 'Playing for Australia. Man of the Match award v South

Africa at Johannesburg 1997. Dismissing Jamie Cox at Taunton in 1999, my first wicket in first-class cricket'

Cricket moments to forget: 'Being dismissed by Jamie Cox at Taunton in 1999, *his* first wicket in first-class cricket'

Cricketers particularly admired: David Boon, Dean Jones, Kepler Wessels, Mark and Steve Waugh

Other sports played: Australian Rules (Tasmanian U15, U16 and Sandy Bay FC)

Other sports followed: Australian Rules football (Geelong Cats)

Favourite band: U2

Relaxations: Golf, sleeping and eating

Extras: Man of the Match for his 89 in fifth ODI v South Africa at Johannesburg 1997. Scored 173* v Derbyshire Board XI at Derby in NatWest 2000, a record for Derbyshire in one-day cricket. Carried his bat for 192* v Middlesex at Lord's 2002; also scored 113 in the second innings. Derbyshire Player of the Year 2002 (jointly with Kevin Dean). First batsman to 1000 Championship runs 2003. Vice-captain of Derbyshire since 2002 (was appointed captain for 2004 but was unable to take up post due to back surgery)

Best batting: 230 Derbyshire v Northamptonshire, Derby 2002

Best bowling: 1-0 Tasmania v Queensland, Brisbane 1999-2000

2005 Season

	M	Inns	NO	Runs	HS	Avge	100s	50s	Ct	St	O	M	Runs	Wkts	Avge	Best	5wI	10wM
Test																		
All First	13	26	2	1193	203	49.70	3	5	12	-								
1-Day Int																		
C & G	2	2	0	21	18	10.50	-	-	-	-								
tsL	17	17	1	753	129 *	47.06	3	2	6	-								
Twenty20	8	8	1	204	77 *	29.14	-	2	2	-								

Career Performances

	M	Inns	NO	Runs	HS	Avge	100s	50s	Ct	St	Balls	Runs	Wkts	Avge	Best	5wI	10wM
Test																	
All First	209	371	19	15013	230	42.65	32	91	229	-	801	480	5	96.00	1-0	-	-
1-Day Int	9	9	0	241	89	26.77	-	2	1	-							
C & G	11	11	1	455	173 *	45.50	1	3	6	-							
tsL	87	86	5	3043	130	37.56	6	16	26	-	30	30	0	-	-	-	-
Twenty20	13	13	3	402	77 *	40.20	-	4	2	-	78	88	5	17.60	3-19	-	

DIXEY, P. G.   Kent

Name: <u>Paul</u> Garrod Dixey
Role: Right-hand bat, wicket-keeper
Born: 2 November 1987, Canterbury
Height: 5ft 8in **Weight:** 10st 7lbs
Nickname: Dix
County debut: 2005
Parents: James and Lindsay
Marital status: Single
Family links with cricket: 'Dad used to play
club cricket for St Lawrence and Highland
Court'
Education: King's School, Canterbury
Off-season: 'Still at school!'
Overseas tours: England U16 to South
Africa
Career highlights to date: 'First-class debut
against Bangladesh A at Canterbury'
Cricket moments to forget: 'Losing to
Western Province U17 at Fairbairn College off the last ball of a closely fought two-day
game'
Cricket superstitions: 'None'
Cricketers particularly admired: Adam Gilchrist
Young players to look out for: Alex Blake, Sam Northeast
Other sports played: Rugby (King's 1st XV), hockey (King's 1st XI)
Other sports followed: NFL, rugby (Bath)
Injuries: Out for a week with a thumb injury
Favourite band: Athlete, Feeder, Stereophonics
Relaxations: 'Skiing, fly fishing'
Extras: *Daily Telegraph* Bunbury ESCA Wicket-keeping Scholarship Award 2003;
Magic Moment Award (Bunbury 2003)
Opinions on cricket: 'Twenty20 is definitely the way to increase interest and
participation in cricket in our country.'
Best batting : 24 Kent v Bangladesh A, Canterbury 2005

2005 Season

	M	Inns	NO	Runs	HS	Avge	100s	50s	Ct	St	O	M	Runs	Wkts	Avge	Best	5wI	10wM
Test																		
All First	1	2	1	40	24	40.00	-	-	3	-								
1-Day Int																		
C & G																		
tsL																		
Twenty20																		

Career Performances

	M	Inns	NO	Runs	HS	Avge	100s	50s	Ct	St	Balls	Runs	Wkts	Avge	Best	5wI	10wM
Test																	
All First	1	2	1	40	24	40.00	-	-	3	-							
1-Day Int																	
C & G																	
tsL																	
Twenty20																	

DOSHI, N. D.   Surrey

Name: <u>Nayan</u> Dilip Doshi
Role: Right-hand bat, left-arm spin bowler
Born: 6 October 1978, Nottingham
Height: 6ft 4in
Nickname: Dosh, Troll, Turtlehead
County debut: 2004
Place in batting averages: (2004 255th av. 13.40)
Place in bowling averages: 134th av. 47.26 (2004 27th av. 26.51)
Strike rate: 76.73 (career 70.50)
Parents: Dilip and Kalindi
Marital status: Engaged
Family links with cricket: Father is former India Test and ODI spin bowler Dilip Doshi, who also played for Nottinghamshire and Warwickshire

Education: King Alfred School, London
Career outside cricket: Family business
Overseas teams played for: Saurashtra, India 2001-02 –
Career highlights to date: 'Twenty20 semi-final 2004'
Cricket moments to forget: 'Too many'
Cricketers particularly admired: Viv Richards, Sachin Tendulkar, Garfield Sobers
Favourite band: 'Like lots of them'
Relaxations: Wildlife photography
Extras: Made first-class debut for Saurashtra v Baroda at Rajkot 2001-02. Recorded maiden first-class ten-wicket match return (5-125/6-57) v Lancashire at Old Trafford 2004 and another (3-73/7-110) v Sussex at Hove in the following Championship match. Is England-qualified
Best batting: 33 Surrey v Nottinghamshire, The Oval 2005
Best bowling: 7-110 Surrey v Sussex, Hove 2004

2005 Season

	M	Inns	NO	Runs	HS	Avge	100s	50s	Ct	St	O	M	Runs	Wkts	Avge	Best	5wI	10wM
Test																		
All First	11	14	3	93	33	8.45	-	-	1	-	294.1	58	1087	23	47.26	3-58	-	-
1-Day Int																		
C & G	2	0	0	0	0	-	-	-	1	-	17	0	125	2	62.50	2-61	-	
tsL	15	6	2	62	29	15.50	-	-	2	-	117	2	594	16	37.12	2-28	-	
Twenty20	10	2	2	1	1 *	-	-	-	3	-	29	0	230	17	13.52	4-27	-	

Career Performances

	M	Inns	NO	Runs	HS	Avge	100s	50s	Ct	St	Balls	Runs	Wkts	Avge	Best	5wI	10wM
Test																	
All First	30	43	7	299	33	8.30	-	-	4	-	4935	2617	70	37.38	7-110	4	2
1-Day Int																	
C & G	3	1	0	0	0	0.00	-	-	1	-	120	137	3	45.66	2-61	-	
tsL	25	10	5	97	29	19.40	-	-	4	-	1002	853	20	42.65	2-28	-	
Twenty20	17	3	2	2	1 *	2.00	-	-	6	-	330	391	25	15.64	4-27	-	

DURSTON, W. J. — Somerset

Name: Wesley (<u>Wes</u>) John Durston
Role: Right-hand bat, right-arm off-spin bowler; all-rounder
Born: 6 October 1980, Taunton
Height: 5ft 10in **Weight:** 12st
Nickname: Ace, Pringles
County debut: 2002
Place in batting averages: 98th av. 35.88
Strike rate: (career 77.57)
Parents: Gillian and Steven
Wife and date of marriage: Christina, 4 October 2003
Children: Daisy, 4 July 2004
Family links with cricket: 'Dad and my two brothers, Dan and Greg, all play. On occasions all four played in same local team (Compton Dundon)'
Education: Millfield School; University College, Worcester
Qualifications: 10 GCSEs, 2 A-levels, BSc Sports Studies, ECB Level II cricket coaching
Career outside cricket: Coaching

Overseas tours: West of England to West Indies 1996
Career highlights to date: 'Three centuries (106, 162*, 126) in three days at Tonbridge Festival for Millfield School 1999. First-class debut v West Indies A 2002, scoring 26 and 55, and the match tied chasing 454 to win'
Cricket moments to forget: 'Scoring 0 v Kent, being lbw and breaking left big toe in NUL 2002'
Cricket superstitions: 'Right foot on and off field first. Placing my right inner glove in my pocket while I bat'
Cricketers particularly admired: Brian Lara, Graham Gooch, Muttiah Muralitharan
Young players to look out for: James Hildreth, Richard Timms, Jack Cooper
Other sports played: Hockey (Taunton Vale), football, golf
Other sports followed: Football 'passionately' (Man Utd), 'any sport that's on TV'
Relaxations: 'Spending time with wife and daughter; all sport (viewing); going to the gym'
Extras: Captained winning Lord's Taverners team v Shrewsbury School at Trent Bridge 1996. Wetherell Schools All-rounder Award 1999; scored 956 runs and took 35 wickets. Has captained Somerset 2nd XI on occasion. Scored 44-ball 55 on first-class debut at Taunton 2002 as Somerset, chasing 454 to win, tied with West Indies A
Best batting: 146* Somerset v Derbyshire, Derby 2005
Best bowling: 3-23 Somerset v Sri Lanka A, Taunton 2004

2005 Season

	M	Inns	NO	Runs	HS	Avge	100s	50s	Ct	St	O	M	Runs	Wkts	Avge	Best	5wI	10wM
Test																		
All First	7	11	2	323	146 *	35.88	1	-	5	-	92	8	449	6	74.83	2-82	-	-
1-Day Int																		
C & G																		
tsL	8	7	5	199	58 *	99.50	-	1	3	-	35	1	211	7	30.14	2-21	-	
Twenty20	11	9	4	106	32 *	21.20	-	-	4	-	5	0	43	4	10.75	3-25	-	

Career Performances

	M	Inns	NO	Runs	HS	Avge	100s	50s	Ct	St	Balls	Runs	Wkts	Avge	Best	5wI	10wM
Test																	
All First	12	20	3	538	146 *	31.64	1	1	18	-	1086	754	14	53.85	3-23	-	-
1-Day Int																	
C & G	2	2	0	75	50	37.50	-	1	-	-	84	75	2	37.50	1-32	-	
tsL	18	16	7	353	58 *	39.22	-	2	4	-	300	303	7	43.28	2-21	-	
Twenty20	16	13	4	191	34	21.22	-	-	5	-	66	108	7	15.42	3-25	-	

EALHAM, M. A.   Nottinghamshire

Name: <u>Mark</u> Alan Ealham
Role: Right-hand bat, right-arm
medium bowler; all-rounder
Born: 27 August 1969, Ashford, Kent
Height: 5ft 10in **Weight:** 14st
Nickname: Ealy, Border, Skater
County debut: 1989 (Kent),
2004 (Nottinghamshire)
County cap: 1992 (Kent),
2004 (Nottinghamshire)
Benefit: 2003 (Kent)
Test debut: 1996
1000 runs in a season: 1
50 wickets in a season: 1
Place in batting averages: 147th av. 30.25

(2004 46th av. 48.38)
Place in bowling averages: 5th av. 20.80
(2004 95th av. 36.61)
Strike rate: 41.87 (career 58.82)
Parents: Alan and Sue
Wife and date of marriage: Kirsty, 24 February 1996
Children: George, 8 March 2002
Family links with cricket: Father played for Kent
Education: Stour Valley Secondary School
Qualifications: 9 CSEs
Career outside cricket: Plumber
Overseas tours: England A to Australia 1996-97, to Kenya and Sri Lanka 1997-98;
England VI to Hong Kong 1997, 2001; England to Sharjah (Champions Trophy) 1997-
98, to Bangladesh (Wills International Cup) 1998-99, to Australia 1998-99 (CUB
Series), to Sharjah (Coca-Cola Cup) 1998-99, to South Africa and Zimbabwe 1999-
2000 (one-day series), to Kenya (ICC Knockout Trophy) 2000-01, to Pakistan and Sri
Lanka 2000-01 (one-day series)
Overseas teams played for: South Perth, Australia 1992-93; University, Perth
1993-94
Cricketers particularly admired: Ian Botham, Viv Richards, Robin Smith,
Steve Waugh, Paul Blackmore and Albert 'for his F and G'
Other sports followed: Football (Manchester United), 'and most other sports'
Relaxations: Playing golf and snooker, watching films
Extras: Set then record for fastest Sunday League century (44 balls), v Derbyshire at
Maidstone 1995. Represented England in the 1999 World Cup. Returned a then
England best ODI bowling analysis with his 5-15 v Zimbabwe at Kimberley in
January 2000; all five were lbw. Vice-captain of Kent 2001

Best batting: 153* Kent v Northamptonshire, Canterbury 2001
Best bowling: 8-36 Kent v Warwickshire, Edgbaston 1996

2005 Season

	M	Inns	NO	Runs	HS	Avge	100s	50s	Ct	St	O	M	Runs	Wkts	Avge	Best	5wI	10wM
Test																		
All First	15	19	3	484	72	30.25	-	3	5	-	390.5	90	1165	56	20.80	5-31	1	-
1-Day Int																		
C & G	2	1	0	0	0	0.00	-	-	-	-	20	6	52	6	8.66	4-28	-	
tsL	14	11	3	195	35	24.37	-	-	6	-	82.5	4	400	11	36.36	4-18	-	
Twenty20	6	6	1	103	45	20.60	-	-	1	-	24	0	174	6	29.00	2-22	-	

Career Performances

	M	Inns	NO	Runs	HS	Avge	100s	50s	Ct	St	Balls	Runs	Wkts	Avge	Best	5wI	10wM
Test	8	13	3	210	53 *	21.00	-	2	4	-	1060	488	17	28.70	4-21	-	-
All First	223	343	52	9496	153 *	32.63	10	59	114	-	29824	14250	507	28.10	8-36	20	1
1-Day Int	64	45	4	716	45	17.46	-	-	9	-	3222	2193	67	32.73	5-15	2	
C & G	33	28	7	562	58 *	26.76	-	2	8	-	1781	925	43	21.51	4-10	-	
tsL	209	176	45	3390	112	25.87	1	14	62	-	8437	6128	213	28.77	6-53	2	
Twenty20	16	16	1	287	91	19.13	-	1	1	-	358	403	14	28.78	2-22	-	

EDWARDS, N. J.   Somerset

Name: <u>Neil</u> James Edwards
Role: Left-hand bat, occasional right-arm medium bowler
Born: 14 October 1983, Truro, Cornwall
Height: 6ft 3in **Weight:** 14st
Nickname: Toastie, Shanksy
County debut: 2002
Place in batting averages: (2004 157th av. 28.26)
Strike rate: (career 131.50)
Parents: Lynn and John
Marital status: Single
Family links with cricket: 'Cousin played first-class cricket for Worcestershire'
Education: Cape Cornwall School; Richard Huish College
Qualifications: 11 GCSEs, 3 A-levels, Level 1 coach
Overseas tours: Cornwall U13 to South Africa 1997; West of England to West Indies 1999; Somerset Academy to Australia 2002; England U19 to Australia 2002-03

Career highlights to date: '160 for Somerset v Hampshire in County Championship 2003'
Cricket moments to forget: 'Duck on debut for Cornwall'
Cricket superstitions: 'Never change batting gloves when batting'
Cricketers particularly admired: Marcus Trescothick, Matthew Hayden
Other sports played: Football
Other sports followed: Football (Stoke City FC)
Favourite band: 'I listen to any music'
Relaxations: 'Spending time at home in Cornwall with girlfriend, family and friends; playing on my Xbox'
Extras: Scored 213 for Cornwall U19 v Dorset U19 at 16 years old. Scored a second innings 97 in England U19's victory over Australia U19 in the first 'Test' at Adelaide 2002-03. Represented England U19 2003. Somerset Wyverns Award for Best Performance by an Uncapped Player 2003 (160 v Hampshire)
Best batting: 160 Somerset v Hampshire, Taunton 2003
Best bowling: 1-16 Somerset v Derbyshire, Taunton 2004

2005 Season

	M	Inns	NO	Runs	HS	Avge	100s	50s	Ct	St	O	M	Runs	Wkts	Avge	Best	5wl	10wM
Test																		
All First	1	1	0	42	42	42.00	-	-	-	-								
1-Day Int																		
C & G																		
tsL																		
Twenty20																		

Career Performances

	M	Inns	NO	Runs	HS	Avge	100s	50s	Ct	St	Balls	Runs	Wkts	Avge	Best	5wl	10wM
Test																	
All First	17	31	0	997	160	32.16	1	3	13	-	263	181	2	90.50	1-16	-	-
1-Day Int																	
C & G																	
tsL																	
Twenty20	1	1	0	1	1	1.00	-	-	-	-							

ELLIOTT, M. T. G.   Glamorgan

Name: <u>Matthew</u> Thomas Gray Elliott
Role: Left-hand bat, left-arm
orthodox bowler
Born: 28 September 1971, Chelsea,
Victoria, Australia
Height: 6ft 3in **Weight:** 13st 8lbs
Nickname: Hoarse, Herb
County debut: 2000 (Glamorgan),
2002 (Yorkshire)
County cap: 2000 (Glamorgan)
Test debut: 1996-97
1000 runs in a season: 2
1st-Class 200s: 2
Place in batting averages: 23rd av. 53.28
(2004 25th av. 53.84)
Strike rate: (career 95.53)
Parents: John and Glenda
Wife and date of marriage: Megan,
11 December 1994
Children: Zachary, 22 November 1997; Samuel, 18 February 2000;
William, June 2004
Education: Kyabram Secondary College
Qualifications: VCE
Overseas tours: Young Australia (Australia A) to England and Netherlands 1995;
Australia to South Africa 1996-97, to England 1997, to West Indies 1998-99; FICA
World XI to New Zealand 2004-05
Overseas teams played for: Victoria 1992-93 – 2004-05; South Australia 2005-06 –
Career highlights to date: 'Taking the 2002 C&G Trophy through Scarborough on an
open-top bus with a police escort!'
Cricket moments to forget: 'Being dismissed by Dean Cosker at Sophia Gardens in
'97!'
Cricket superstitions: 'Always put left shoe on first'
Cricketers particularly admired: Shane Warne, Allan Border, Steve Waugh
Other sports played: Australian Rules football
Other sports followed: Australian Rules football (Collingwood FC)
Relaxations: 'Fishing; reading biographies; drinking Corona'
Extras: Scored 556 runs (av. 55.60) in the 1997 Ashes series. One of *Wisden*'s Five
Cricketers of the Year 1998. Sheffield Shield Player of the Year 1995-96 and 1998-99.
Overseas player with Glamorgan 2000 and 2004 to date. Scored 177 and shared in
county record first-wicket partnership of 374 with Stephen James v Sussex at Colwyn
Bay 2000. Victoria's one-day captain 2001-02, becoming overall skipper for the

remainder of the campaign on the retirement of Paul Reiffel during the season. Was Yorkshire's overseas player for the latter part of 2002. C&G Man of the Match award for his 128* in the final v Somerset at Lord's 2002. Pura Cup Player of the Year 2003-04 and Man of the Match in the final v Queensland at Melbourne (155/55*). *Wisden Australia*'s Pura Cup Cricketer of the Year 2003-04

Best batting: 203 Victoria v Tasmania, Melbourne 1995-96
Best bowling: 3-68 Victoria v Queensland, Melbourne 2004-05

2005 Season

	M	Inns	NO	Runs	HS	Avge	100s	50s	Ct	St	O	M	Runs	Wkts	Avge	Best	5wI	10wM
Test																		
All First	7	14	0	746	162	53.28	2	5	6	-	5	0	20	0	-	-	-	-
1-Day Int																		
C & G	2	2	1	120	100 *	120.00	1	-	-	-	6	0	34	0	-	-	-	
tsL	5	4	1	111	43	37.00	-	-	4	-	3.2	0	32	0	-	-	-	
Twenty20	7	7	1	213	52 *	35.50	-	2	2	-								

Career Performances

	M	Inns	NO	Runs	HS	Avge	100s	50s	Ct	St	Balls	Runs	Wkts	Avge	Best	5wI	10wM
Test	21	36	1	1172	199	33.48	3	4	14	-	12	4	0	-	-	-	-
All First	190	349	26	16141	203	49.97	50	76	206	-	1242	754	13	58.00	3-68	-	-
1-Day Int	1	1	0	1	1	1.00	-	-	-	-							
C & G	8	8	2	601	156	100.16	3	2	-	-	36	34	0	-	-	-	-
tsL	33	32	10	1492	115 *	67.81	4	8	15	-	50	55	0	-	-	-	-
Twenty20	9	9	1	276	52 *	34.50	-	2	3	-							

---

26. Which All Black rugby star made his return to the New Zealand ODI cricket side in 2005 after an absence of 12 years?

ERVINE, S. M.   Hampshire

Name: <u>Sean</u> Michael Ervine
Role: Left-hand bat, right-arm
medium-fast bowler
Born: 6 December 1982, Harare, Zimbabwe
Height: 6ft 2in **Weight:** 14st 8lbs
Nickname: Siuc
County debut: 2005
County cap: 2005
Test debut: 2003
Place in batting averages: 144th av. 30.40
Place in bowling averages: 75th av. 32.38
Strike rate: 53.45 (career 58.49)
Family links with cricket: Brother Craig
played for Midlands in Zimbabwe
Overseas tours: Zimbabwe U19 to Sri Lanka
(U19 World Cup) 1999-2000, to New
Zealand (U19 World Cup) 2001-02;
Zimbabwe to Bangladesh 2001-02, to Sri
Lanka 2001-02 (one-day series), to Sri Lanka (ICC Champions Trophy) 2002-03, to
England 2003, to Australia 2003-04, plus one-day tournaments in Sharjah
Overseas teams played for: Midlands, Zimbabwe 2001-02 – 2003-04; Western
Australia 2004-05
Extras: CFX [Zimbabwean] Academy 2000-01. Represented Zimbabwe in the World
Cup 2002-03. Struck 99-ball century (100) at Adelaide in the VB Series 2003-04 as
Zimbabwe fell just three runs short of India's 280-7. Man of the Match in the first Test
v Bangladesh at Harare 2003-04 (86/74). C&G Man of the Match awards in the semi-
final v Yorkshire at West End (100) and in the final v Warwickshire at Lord's (104)
2005. Holds an Irish passport and is not considered an overseas player
Best batting: 126 Midlands v Manicaland, Mutare 2002-03
Best bowling: 6-82 Midlands v Mashonaland, Kwekwe 2002-03

2005 Season

	M	Inns	NO	Runs	HS	Avge	100s	50s	Ct	St	O	M	Runs	Wkts	Avge	Best	5wI	10wM
Test																		
All First	16	28	1	821	75	30.40	-	7	8	-	374.1	79	1360	42	32.38	5-60	3	-
1-Day Int																		
C & G	5	4	1	232	104	77.33	2	-	-	-	30	1	177	7	25.28	5-50	1	
tsL	14	13	0	299	47	23.00	-	-	7	-	78	6	397	13	30.53	3-32	-	
Twenty20	7	6	0	116	46	19.33	-	-	1	-	15	0	117	8	14.62	2-13	-	

Career Performances

	M	Inns	NO	Runs	HS	Avge	100s	50s	Ct	St	Balls	Runs	Wkts	Avge	Best	5wI	10wM
Test	5	8	0	261	86	32.62	-	3	7	-	570	388	9	43.11	4-146	-	-
All First	46	76	7	2331	126	33.78	4	15	44	-	5674	3543	97	36.52	6-82	5	-
1-Day Int	42	34	7	698	100	25.85	1	2	5	-	1649	1561	41	38.07	3-29	-	
C & G	5	4	1	232	104	77.33	2	-	-	-	180	177	7	25.28	5-50	1	
tsL	14	13	0	299	47	23.00	-	-	7	-	468	397	13	30.53	3-32	-	
Twenty20	7	6	0	116	46	19.33	-	-	1	-	90	117	8	14.62	2-13	-	

EUSTACE, S. M. Warwickshire

Name: Stuart Malcolm Eustace
Role: Left-hand bat, wicket-keeper
Born: 3 May 1979, Birmingham
Height: 5ft 11in **Weight:** 12st 4lbs
Nickname: Stace
County debut: 2005
Parents: Malcolm and Jean
Marital status: Partner Sharon
Family links with cricket: 'Dad played for
Warwickshire Colts, Harborne, Moseley and
Dorridge. Brother plays for Northampton Uni
and Moseley'
Education: Bromsgrove School; Birmingham
College of Food, Tourism and Creative
Studies
Qualifications: 9 GCSEs, ECB level 2
coaching
Career outside cricket: 'Sales'
Off-season: 'Working for Livingbase'
Overseas tours: Tours with MCC YC, Moseley CC, Dunstall CC, Exmouth CC,
Devon CCC, Derbyshire CCC
Overseas teams played for: Portland Colts 1998-99; Queensland University 1999-
2000
Career highlights to date: 'Making Twenty20 debut last season after not playing for
Warwickshire for the previous six seasons'
Cricket moments to forget: 'My first innings in Twenty20 cricket'
Cricketers particularly admired: Keith Piper, Graham Thorpe, Mark Butcher,
Allan Donald
Young players to look out for: Ian Westwood, Luke Parker, Ed Newton, Ed Binham,
Vanraj Padhaal
Other sports played: Football, rugby, tennis

Other sports followed: Football (Birmingham City)
Favourite band: Take That
Relaxations: 'Spending time with my friends and partner; travelling abroad'
Extras: Warwickshire CCC U17 Player of the Year. England Schools U19. Was England U19 non-travelling reserve for World Cup 1997-98. MCC Young Cricketers 1998-99. Played for Devon and several county 2nd XIs 1997-2002. Dunstall CC Player of the Year 2004. Was on sabbatical from Pertemps People Development Group summer 2005. Released by Warwickshire at the end of the 2005 season
Opinions on cricket: 'A more professional approach should be taken from people sitting on cricket committees. It seems common practice for people sitting down at the end of a season to make decisions on an individual without actually seeing them play. Cricket is a game of opinions. However, it would be nice if people took the time to educate themselves before forming such opinions.'

2005 Season

	M	Inns	NO	Runs	HS	Avge	100s	50s	Ct	St	O	M	Runs	Wkts	Avge	Best	5wl	10wM
Test																		
All First	1	0	0	0	0	-	-	-	1	-								
1-Day Int																		
C & G																		
tsL																		
Twenty20	6	3	1	4	2 *	2.00	-	-	5	1								

Career Performances

	M	Inns	NO	Runs	HS	Avge	100s	50s	Ct	St	Balls	Runs	Wkts	Avge	Best	5wl	10wM
Test																	
All First	1	0	0	0	0	-	-	-	1	-							
1-Day Int																	
C & G																	
tsL																	
Twenty20	6	3	1	4	2 *	2.00	-	-	5	1							

27. Which Wiltshire-born all-rounder took 6-39 v India in one of his
16 ODIs before joining Somerset to see out his career?

FAISAL SHAHID Worcestershire

Name: Faisal Hassan Shahid
Role: Right-hand bat, right-arm medium bowler; all-rounder
Born: 4 March 1986, Birmingham
Height: 5ft 11in **Weight:** 12st
Nickname: Faz
County debut: No first-team appearance
Parents: Shahid Aziz and Nasim Shahid
Marital status: Single
Family links with cricket: 'Younger brother (Zain Shahid) is a promising spinner, playing for Worcester U14 and at regional level'
Education: Old Swinford Hospital School; Worcester University
Qualifications: 9 GCSEs, 3 A-levels, currently studying for Sports Science degree and for ECB Level 2 coaching badge
Career outside cricket: 'Completing ECB Level 2 coaching badge. Studying Sports Science at Worcester University'
Off-season: 'Attending the Dennis Lillee Fast Bowling Clinic in India'
Overseas tours: Streets-to-Arena to Pakistan 2002
Career highlights to date: 'Representing England at U17 and U18 levels. Winning the Birmingham premier league with Halesowen'
Cricket moments to forget: 'Falling over on the way to field my first ball in second-team cricket'
Cricketers particularly admired: Andrew Flintoff, Graeme Hick, Vikram Solanki, Wasim Akram
Young players to look out for: Zain Shahid, Steve Davies
Other sports played: Football (captained school side)
Other sports followed: Football (Liverpool)
Favourite band: D12
Relaxations: 'Listening to music; reading sports journals'
Extras: Scored first Birmingham league century aged 13. Midlands Cricketer of the Year 2002. Graduate of Worcestershire CCC Academy
Opinions on cricket: 'Hopefully the introduction of the Twenty20 format will revolutionise the game and help it attract an even larger global following. No doubt the Ashes win of last summer has increased the appeal on a national level.'

FERLEY, R. S.   Kent

Name: <u>Robert</u> Steven Ferley
Role: Right-hand bat, left-arm spin bowler
Born: 4 February 1982, Norwich
Height: 5ft 8in **Weight:** 12st 4lbs
Nickname: Mr Shaky Shake, Billy Bob,
Bob Turkey
County debut: 2003
Place in bowling averages: (2003 128th
av. 43.00)
Strike rate: (career 67.42)
Parents: Pam and Tim (divorced)
Marital status: Single
Education: King Edward VII High School;
Sutton Valence School (A-levels); Grey
College, Durham University
Qualifications: 10 GCSEs, 3 A-levels
Overseas tours: England U19 to India 2000-
01; British Universities to South Africa 2002
Cricketers particularly admired: Steve Waugh, Steve Marsh, Min Patel,
Charles Clarke
Young players to look out for: James Tredwell
Other sports played: Rugby, hockey, tennis, football
Other sports followed: Football (Liverpool)
Relaxations: 'Films, interior design, keeping fit'
Extras: Represented England U17 1999. Played for Durham University CCE 2001,
2002 and 2003. Represented British Universities 2001, 2002 and 2003. Represented
England U19 2001. Took 4-76 on Championship debut v Surrey at The Oval 2003
Best batting: 78* DUCCE v Durham, Durham 2003
Best bowling: 4-76 Kent v Surrey, The Oval 2003

2005 Season

	M	Inns	NO	Runs	HS	Avge	100s	50s	Ct	St	O	M	Runs	Wkts	Avge	Best	5wI	10wM
Test																		
All First	1	2	0	33	23	16.50	-	-	-	-	8	1	26	1	26.00	1-26	-	-
1-Day Int																		
C & G	3	1	0	1	1	1.00	-	-	-	-	25	0	100	2	50.00	1-20	-	
tsL	11	5	2	36	16*	12.00	-	-	6	-	77	0	393	12	32.75	3-36	-	
Twenty20	5	1	1	1	1*	-	-	-	2	-	14	0	131	1	131.00	1-22	-	

Career Performances

	M	Inns	NO	Runs	HS	Avge	100s	50s	Ct	St	Balls	Runs	Wkts	Avge	Best	5wl	10wM
Test																	
All First	23	31	7	466	78 *	19.41	-	2	8	-	3034	1890	45	42.00	4-76	-	-
1-Day Int																	
C & G	5	2	0	7	6	3.50	-	-	-	-	232	143	5	28.60	2-30	-	
tsL	22	14	5	192	42	21.33	-	-	10	-	988	790	26	30.38	3-36	-	
Twenty20	6	2	2	17	16 *	-	-	-	2	-	90	140	2	70.00	1-9	-	

FINN, S. T. Middlesex

Name: <u>Steven</u> Thomas Finn
Role: Right-hand bat, right-arm medium-fast bowler
Born: 4 April 1989, Watford
Height: 6ft 7in **Weight:** 13st 9lbs
Nickname: Finny
County debut: 2005
Strike rate: (career 60.00)
Parents: Diana and Terry
Marital status: Single
Family links with cricket: 'Dad played top-level club cricket'
Education: Parmiter's School, Garston, Herts
Qualifications: 11 GCSEs
Career outside cricket: 'Student – studying A-levels'
Off-season: 'Training'
Overseas tours: England U16 to South Africa 2004-05
Career highlights to date: 'First-class debut – 1 June 2005'
Cricket superstitions: 'None'
Cricketers particularly admired: Glenn McGrath
Young players to look out for: Billy Godleman, Dan Housego, Rhys Williams
Other sports played: Basketball (county), football (district)
Other sports followed: Football (Watford)
Favourite band: Coldplay
Relaxations: 'Music, PlayStation, films'
Extras: Has represented England U15, U16 and U17
Opinions on cricket: 'Happy with the numerous opportunities that are given to young players like myself.'
Best bowling: 1-16 Middlesex v CUCCE, Fenner's 2005

2005 Season

	M	Inns	NO	Runs	HS	Avge	100s	50s	Ct	St	O	M	Runs	Wkts	Avge	Best	5wI	10wM
Test																		
All First	1	0	0	0	0	-	-	-	-	-	20	6	53	2	26.50	1-16	-	-
1-Day Int																		
C & G																		
tsL																		
Twenty20																		

Career Performances

	M	Inns	NO	Runs	HS	Avge	100s	50s	Ct	St	Balls	Runs	Wkts	Avge	Best	5wI	10wM
Test																	
All First	1	0	0	0	0	-	-	-	-	-	120	53	2	26.50	1-16	-	-
1-Day Int																	
C & G																	
tsL																	
Twenty20																	

FISHER, I. D.   Gloucestershire

Name: Ian Douglas Fisher
Role: Left-hand bat, left-arm spin bowler
Born: 31 March 1976, Bradford
Height: 5ft 11in **Weight:** 13st 6lbs
Nickname: Fish, Flash, Fishy
County debut: 1995-96 (Yorkshire),
2002 (Gloucestershire)
County cap: 2004
Place in batting averages: 216th av. 20.66
(2004 225th av. 18.82)
Place in bowling averages: 123rd av. 44.68
(2004 140th av. 46.65)
Strike rate: 80.73 (career 74.84)
Parents: Geoff and Linda
Marital status: Single
Family links with cricket: Father played
club cricket
Education: Beckfoot Grammar School
Qualifications: 9 GCSEs, NCA coaching
award, sports leader's award, lifesaver (bronze), YMCA gym instructor
Overseas tours: Yorkshire to Zimbabwe 1996, to South Africa 1998, 1999, 2001,
to Perth 2000; MCC to Sri Lanka 2001

Overseas teams played for: Somerset West, Cape Town 1994-95; Petone Riverside, Wellington, New Zealand 1997-98
Career highlights to date: 'Winning the Championship with Yorkshire [2001]'
Cricket moments to forget: 'My pair'
Cricketers particularly admired: Darren Lehmann, Shane Warne
Young players to look out for: Tim Bresnan
Other sports played: Football (Westbrook)
Other sports followed: Football (Leeds United)
Relaxations: Music, movies, catching up with friends, shopping, eating out
Extras: Played England U17 and Yorkshire Schools U15, U16 and Yorkshire U19. Bowled the last first-class ball delivered at Northlands Road, Southampton, September 2000. Recorded three Championship five-wicket returns in successive innings 2003, including maiden ten-wicket match (5-30/5-93) v Durham at Bristol
Best batting: 103* Gloucestershire v Essex, Gloucester 2002
Best bowling: 5-30 Gloucestershire v Durham, Bristol 2003

2005 Season

	M	Inns	NO	Runs	HS	Avge	100s	50s	Ct	St	O	M	Runs	Wkts	Avge	Best	5wI	10wM
Test																		
All First	9	17	2	310	43	20.66	-	-	8	-	255.4	47	849	19	44.68	4-89	-	-
1-Day Int																		
C & G																		
tsL	3	3	2	12	11 *	12.00	-	-	1	-	22	1	121	3	40.33	2-46	-	
Twenty20	3	0	0	0	0	-	-	-	-	-	6	0	59	1	59.00	1-45	-	

Career Performances

	M	Inns	NO	Runs	HS	Avge	100s	50s	Ct	St	Balls	Runs	Wkts	Avge	Best	5wI	10wM
Test																	
All First	70	104	17	1962	103 *	22.55	1	7	25	-	10852	5798	145	39.98	5-30	7	1
1-Day Int																	
C & G	3	1	0	5	5	5.00	-	-	2	-	150	87	3	29.00	1-21	-	
tsL	38	23	9	112	23	8.00	-	-	9	-	1414	1046	42	24.90	3-18	-	
Twenty20	8	2	1	9	8	9.00	-	-	4	-	84	120	7	17.14	4-22	-	

28. Who made his ODI debut for Australia in 1983 but played his final ODI in 1994 for another country?

FLEMING, S. P.   Nottinghamshire

Name: <u>Stephen</u> Paul Fleming
Role: Left-hand bat, occasional right-arm
slow-medium bowler, county captain
Born: 1 April 1973, Christchurch,
New Zealand
Height: 6ft 3in
County debut: 2001 (Middlesex),
2003 (Yorkshire), 2005 (Nottinghamshire)
County cap: 2001 (Middlesex), 2005 (Notts)
Test debut: 1993-94
1000 runs in a season: 1
1st-Class 200s: 3
Place in batting averages: 13th av. 60.53
(2004 26th av. 53.55)
Education: Cashmere High School;
Christchurch College of Education
Overseas tours: New Zealand U19 to India
1991-92; New Zealand to England 1994, to

South Africa 1994-95, to India 1995-96, to India and Pakistan (World Cup) 1995-96,
to West Indies 1995-96, to Pakistan 1996-97, to Zimbabwe 1997-98 (c), to Australia
1997-98 (c), to Sri Lanka 1997-98 (c), to Bangladesh (Wills International Cup) 1998-
99 (c), to UK, Ireland and Holland (World Cup) 1999 (c), to England 1999 (c), to
India 1999-2000 (c), to Zimbabwe 2000-01 (c), to Kenya (ICC Knockout Trophy)
2000-01 (c), to South Africa 2000-01 (c), to Australia 2001-02 (c), to Pakistan 2002
(c), to West Indies 2002 (c), to Sri Lanka (ICC Champions Trophy) 2002-03 (c), to
Africa (World Cup) 2002-03 (c), to Sri Lanka 2003 (c), to India 2003-04 (c), to
England 2004 (c), to England (ICC Champions Trophy) 2004 (c), to Bangladesh 2004-
05 (c), to Australia 2004-05 (c), to Zimbabwe 2005-06 (c), to South Africa (one-day
series) 2005-06 (c), plus other one-day tournaments in Sharjah, India, Singapore and
Sri Lanka; ICC World XI to Australia (Tsunami Relief) 2004-05
Overseas teams played for: Canterbury 1991-92 – 1999-2000; Wellington 2000-01 –
Extras: Captain of New Zealand since 1996-97. Led his country to series victory in
England in 1999, which included New Zealand's first wins at Lord's and The Oval.
His Test awards include Man of the Match in the first Test v West Indies at
Bridgetown 2002 (130) and in the first Test v Pakistan at Hamilton 2003-04 (192). Has
won numerous ODI awards, including Man of the Match for his 134* v South Africa
at Johannesburg in the 2002-03 World Cup and Man of the NatWest Series in England
2004. One of *New Zealand Cricket Almanack*'s two Players of the Year 1998, 2003,
2004. Is New Zealand's most-capped Test player and highest Test run-scorer. Made
Twenty20 international debut v Australia at Auckland 2004-05. Was Middlesex
overseas player in 2001; was a Yorkshire overseas player in 2003; an overseas player
with Nottinghamshire and captain since 2005

Best batting: 274* New Zealand v Sri Lanka, Colombo 2002-03

2005 Season

	M	Inns	NO	Runs	HS	Avge	100s	50s	Ct	St	O	M	Runs	Wkts	Avge	Best	5wI	10wM
Test																		
All First	11	16	1	908	238	60.53	4	2	14	-								
1-Day Int																		
C & G	2	2	0	69	50	34.50	-	1	-	-								
tsL	11	10	1	355	102 *	39.44	1	2	9	-								
Twenty20	6	6	0	117	56	19.50	-	1	2	-								

Career Performances

	M	Inns	NO	Runs	HS	Avge	100s	50s	Ct	St	Balls	Runs	Wkts	Avge	Best	5wI	10wM
Test	96	165	10	6050	274 *	39.03	8	40	140	-							
All First	202	334	29	13079	274 *	42.88	27	76	265	-	102	129	0	-	-	-	-
1-Day Int	240	231	19	6873	134 *	32.41	6	40	114	-	29	28	1	28.00	1-8	-	
C & G	2	2	0	69	50	34.50	-	1	-	-							
tsL	28	26	2	747	139 *	31.12	2	3	14	-							
Twenty20	10	10	0	179	58	17.90	-	2	3	-							

FLINTOFF, A. Lancashire

Name: Andrew Flintoff
Role: Right-hand bat, right-arm
fast-medium bowler
Born: 6 December 1977, Preston
Height: 6ft 4in
County debut: 1995
County cap: 1998
Benefit: 2006
Test debut: 1998
Place in batting averages: 74th av. 39.06
(2004 13th av. 60.30)
Place in bowling averages: 22nd av. 25.05
(2004 18th av. 24.50)
Strike rate: 44.26 (career 66.42)
Parents: Colin and Susan
Wife and date of marriage: Rachael,
5 March 2005
Children: Holly, 6 September 2004
Family links with cricket: Brother Chris and father both play local league cricket
Education: Ribbleton Hall High School
Qualifications: 9 GCSEs

Off-season: Touring with England
Overseas tours: England Schools U15 to South Africa 1993; England U19 to West Indies 1994-95, to Zimbabwe 1995-96, to Pakistan 1996-97 (c); England A to Kenya and Sri Lanka 1997-98, to Zimbabwe and South Africa 1998-99; England to Sharjah (Coca-Cola Cup) 1998-99, to South Africa and Zimbabwe 1999-2000, to Kenya (ICC Knockout Trophy) 2000-01, to Pakistan and (one-day series) Sri Lanka 2000-01, to Zimbabwe (one-day series) 2001-02, to India and New Zealand 2001-02, to Australia 2002-03, to Africa (World Cup) 2002-03, to Bangladesh and Sri Lanka 2003-04, to West Indies 2003-04, to South Africa 2004-05, to Pakistan 2005-06, to India 2005-06; ECB National Academy to Australia 2001-02; England VI to Hong Kong 2001; ICC World XI to Australia (Super Series) 2005-06
Other sports/games played: Represented Lancashire Schools at chess
Extras: Represented England U14 to U19. Cricket Writers' Club Young Player of the Year and PCA Young Player of the Year 1998. Scored first century before lunch by a Lancashire batsman in a Roses match, v Yorkshire at Old Trafford 1999. Won the EDS Walter Lawrence Trophy 1999 (for the fastest first-class century of the season). Lancashire Player of the Year 2000. Vice-captain of Lancashire 2002. BBC North West Sports Personality of the Year 2003. One of *Wisden*'s Five Cricketers of the Year 2004. Vodafone England Cricketer of the Year 2003-04. Shared with Andrew Strauss in a record stand for any wicket for England in ODIs (226) v West Indies at Lord's in the NatWest Series 2004. Made Twenty20 international debut v Australia at the Rose Bowl 2005. His Test awards include England's Man of the Series v West Indies 2004 and v Australia 2005 plus the inaugural Compton-Miller Medal 2005 for Ashes Player of the Series. His ODI awards include Man of the NatWest Series 2003 and Man of the Series v Bangladesh 2003-04. Winner of inaugural ICC One-Day Player of the Year award 2003-04. PCA Player of the Year award 2004, 2005. ICC Player of the Year award (jointly with Jacques Kallis) 2005. BBC Sports Personality of the Year 2005
Best batting: 167 England v West Indies, Edgbaston 2004
Best bowling: 5-24 Lancashire v Hampshire, Southampton 1999
Stop press: Appointed MBE in 2006 New Year Honours as part of 2005 Ashes-winning England team. Captained England in the first Test v India at Nagpur 2005-06 in the absence of Michael Vaughan and Marcus Trescothick

2005 Season

	M	Inns	NO	Runs	HS	Avge	100s	50s	Ct	St	O	M	Runs	Wkts	Avge	Best	5wI	10wM
Test	7	10	0	402	102	40.20	1	3	4	-	230.5	37	793	33	24.03	5-78	1	-
All First	11	16	1	586	102	39.06	1	5	8	-	250.5	43	852	34	25.05	5-78	1	-
1-Day Int	10	7	0	202	87	28.85	-	1	1	-	87	6	392	14	28.00	4-29	-	
C & G	3	3	1	26	11 *	13.00	-	-	1	-	19	0	56	7	8.00	4-26	-	
tsL	3	3	0	61	40	20.33	-	-	1	-	9	1	32	1	32.00	1-32	-	
Twenty20	2	2	0	51	49	25.50	-	-	-	-	8	0	63	3	21.00	2-33	-	

Career Performances

	M	Inns	NO	Runs	HS	Avge	100s	50s	Ct	St	Balls	Runs	Wkts	Avge	Best	5wI	10wM
Test	52	82	3	2641	167	33.43	5	17	34	-	9292	4621	143	32.31	5-58	2	-
All First	141	218	15	7347	167	36.19	15	41	149	-	15211	7381	229	32.23	5-24	3	-
1-Day Int	90	78	11	2313	123	34.52	3	14	29	-	3329	2358	96	24.56	4-14	-	
C & G	27	23	5	732	135 *	40.66	1	3	17	-	888	557	26	21.42	4-26	-	
tsL	62	61	3	1439	143	24.81	1	6	18	-	1445	1075	48	22.39	4-24	-	
Twenty20	5	5	0	182	85	36.40	-	1	1	-	83	102	5	20.40	2-15	-	

FLOWER, A. Essex

Name: Andrew (<u>Andy</u>) Flower
Role: Left-hand bat, wicket-keeper,
occasional right-arm medium/off-spin bowler
Born: 28 April 1968, Cape Town,
South Africa
Height: 5ft 10in
Nickname: Petals
County debut: 2002
County cap: 2002
Test debut: 1992-93
1000 runs in a season: 4
1st-Class 200s: 3
Place in batting averages: 5th av. 71.00
(2004 67th av. 43.11)
Strike rate: (career 96.83)
Family links with cricket: Younger brother
Grant played for Zimbabwe and also plays
for Essex

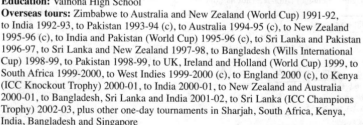

Education: Vainona High School
Overseas tours: Zimbabwe to Australia and New Zealand (World Cup) 1991-92,
to India 1992-93, to Pakistan 1993-94 (c), to Australia 1994-95 (c), to New Zealand
1995-96 (c), to India and Pakistan (World Cup) 1995-96 (c), to Sri Lanka and Pakistan
1996-97, to Sri Lanka and New Zealand 1997-98, to Bangladesh (Wills International
Cup) 1998-99, to Pakistan 1998-99, to UK, Ireland and Holland (World Cup) 1999, to
South Africa 1999-2000, to West Indies 1999-2000 (c), to England 2000 (c), to Kenya
(ICC Knockout Trophy) 2000-01, to India 2000-01, to New Zealand and Australia
2000-01, to Bangladesh, Sri Lanka and India 2001-02, to Sri Lanka (ICC Champions
Trophy) 2002-03, plus other one-day tournaments in Sharjah, South Africa, Kenya,
India, Bangladesh and Singapore
Overseas teams played for: Mashonaland 1993-94 – 2002-03; South Australia
2003-04

Other sports played: Tennis, squash; rugby, hockey (at school)
Extras: Scored century (115*) on ODI debut v Sri Lanka at New Plymouth in the 1992 World Cup. Appeared in Zimbabwe's inaugural Test, v India at Harare 1992-93. Scored 156 v Pakistan at Harare 1994-95 in Zimbabwe's first Test win, in the process sharing with Grant Flower (201*) in a record fourth-wicket stand for Zimbabwe in Tests (269). Man of the Series v India 2000-01 (232*, 183*, 70 and 55; av. 270.00). FICA International Player of the Year 2001. Scored 142 and 199* v South Africa in the first Test at Harare 2001, becoming the first wicket-keeper to score a century in each innings of a Test match and the first to go to the top of the PricewaterhouseCoopers ratings for Test batsmen. Scored 142* v England at Harare 2001-02, in the process sharing with Heath Streak in a new world record seventh-wicket partnership for ODIs (130). One of *Wisden*'s Five Cricketers of the Year 2002. Overseas player with Essex since 2002. A former captain of Zimbabwe. Retired from international cricket after the 2002-03 World Cup. Is no longer considered an overseas player
Best batting: 232* Zimbabwe v India, Nagpur 2000-01
Best bowling: 1-1 Mashonaland v Mashonaland CD, Harare South 1993-94

2005 Season

	M	Inns	NO	Runs	HS	Avge	100s	50s	Ct	St	O	M	Runs	Wkts	Avge	Best	5wI	10wM
Test																		
All First	16	25	6	1349	188	71.00	6	4	11	-								
1-Day Int																		
C & G	2	2	0	82	69	41.00	-	1	-	-								
tsL	13	13	5	307	127 *	38.37	1	-	3	-								
Twenty20	7	6	2	144	59	36.00	-	1	1	-								

Career Performances

	M	Inns	NO	Runs	HS	Avge	100s	50s	Ct	St	Balls	Runs	Wkts	Avge	Best	5wI	10wM
Test	63	112	19	4794	232 *	51.54	12	27	151	9	3	4	0	-	-	-	-
All First	206	345	63	14844	232 *	52.63	42	72	344	21	581	250	6	41.66	1-1	-	-
1-Day Int	213	208	16	6785	145	35.33	4	55	141	32	30	23	0	-	-	-	
C & G	9	8	1	470	106	67.14	1	4	4	-							
tsL	58	56	11	1738	127 *	38.62	3	11	33	6							
Twenty20	17	16	2	545	83	38.92	-	4	5	-							

29. Named after a West Indies cricketer by a famous father, who played 11 ODIs in 2004?

FLOWER, G. W.   Essex

Name: <u>Grant</u> William Flower
Role: Right-hand bat, slow left-arm bowler
Born: 20 December 1970, Harare, Zimbabwe
Height: 5ft 10in
County debut: 2002 (Leicestershire),
2005 (Essex)
County cap: 2005 (Essex)
Test debut: 1992-93
1st-Class 200s: 3
Place in batting averages: 215th av. 20.89
Strike rate: (career 77.22)
Family links with cricket: Younger brother
of Andy Flower (also plays for Essex)
Education: St George's College, Harare
Overseas tours: Zimbabwe to India 1992-93,
to Pakistan 1993-94, to Australia (one-day
series) 1994-95, to New Zealand 1995-96, to

India and Pakistan (World Cup) 1995-96, to
Sri Lanka and Pakistan 1996-97, to Sri Lanka and New Zealand 1997-98, to
Bangladesh (Wills International Cup) 1998-99, to Pakistan 1998-99, to UK, Ireland
and Holland (World Cup) 1999, to South Africa 1999-2000, to West Indies 1999-2000,
to England 2000, to Kenya (ICC Knockout Trophy) 2000-01, to India 2000-01, to New
Zealand and Australia 2000-01, to Bangladesh, Sri Lanka and India 2001-02, to Sri
Lanka (ICC Champions Trophy) 2002-03, to England 2003, to Australia 2003-04 (VB
Series), plus other one-day tournaments in Sharjah, South Africa, Kenya, India,
Bangladesh and Singapore
Overseas teams played for: Mashonaland 1994-95 – 2003-04
Extras: Appeared in Zimbabwe's inaugural Test, v India at Harare 1992-93. Scored
201* v Pakistan at Harare 1994-95 in Zimbabwe's first Test win, in the process sharing
with Andy Flower (156) in a record fourth-wicket stand for Zimbabwe in Tests (269).
Became the first player to score a hundred in each innings of a Test for Zimbabwe
(104/151) in the first Test v New Zealand at Harare 1997-98. His Test awards include
Man of the Series v New Zealand 1997-98. His ODI awards include Zimbabwe's Man
of the Series v Pakistan 1996-97, as well as Man of the Match v England at Trent
Bridge in the NatWest Series 2003 (96*) and v Australia at Adelaide in the VB Series
2003-04 (94). Was Leicestershire's overseas player during June 2002. Is no longer
considered an overseas player
Best batting: 242* Mashonaland v Matabeleland, Harare 1996-97
Best bowling: 7-31 Zimbabweans v Lahore Division, Lahore 1998-99

2005 Season

	M	Inns	NO	Runs	HS	Avge	100s	50s	Ct	St	O	M	Runs	Wkts	Avge	Best	5wl	10wM
Test																		
All First	12	19	0	397	115	20.89	1	3	5	-	131.3	32	393	9	43.66	3-112	-	-
1-Day Int																		
C & G	2	2	0	54	33	27.00	-	-	1	-	5.2	2	15	1	15.00	1-2	-	
tsL	12	12	2	466	90 *	46.60	-	5	4	-	67	0	283	17	16.64	3-21	-	
Twenty20	7	3	2	7	4	7.00	-	-	3	-	16.4	0	125	8	15.62	3-20	-	

Career Performances

	M	Inns	NO	Runs	HS	Avge	100s	50s	Ct	St	Balls	Runs	Wkts	Avge	Best	5wl	10wM
Test	67	123	6	3457	201 *	29.54	6	15	42	-	3378	1537	25	61.48	4-41	-	-
All First	161	278	22	9703	242 *	37.90	20	54	142	-	11892	5259	154	34.14	7-31	3	-
1-Day Int	219	212	18	6535	142 *	33.68	6	40	85	-	5420	4187	104	40.25	4-32	-	
C & G	4	4	0	65	33	16.25	-	-	2	-	98	48	3	16.00	2-33	-	
tsL	15	14	2	488	90 *	40.66	-	5	4	-	488	345	18	19.16	3-21	-	
Twenty20	7	3	2	7	4	7.00	-	-	3	-	100	125	8	15.62	3-20	-	

FOOTITT, M. H. A.   Nottinghamshire

Name: <u>Mark</u> Harold Alan Footitt
Role: Right-hand bat, left-arm fast bowler
Born: 25 November 1985, Nottingham
Height: 6ft 2in **Weight:** 12st 7lbs
Nickname: Footy
County debut: 2005
Strike rate: (career 43.50)
Parents: Graham and Julie
Marital status: Engaged to Kerry Ann
Pashley
Family links with cricket: 'Dad and grandad
played local cricket'
Education: Carlton le Willows School
Qualifications: 3 GCSEs, Level 1 coaching
Off-season: 'With the National Academy'
Overseas tours: Nottinghamshire to South
Africa 2006
Career highlights to date: 'Playing my first
game for Notts. Being picked for the National Academy 2006'
Cricket moments to forget: 'My first Twenty20 game'
Cricket superstitions: 'None'
Cricketers particularly admired: Brett Lee

Other sports played: Football
Other sports followed: Football (Man Utd)
Injuries: Ankle operation during 2005-06 off-season
Favourite band: The Killers
Relaxations: 'Playing on PS2 and PC; watching TV/DVDs'
Extras: Attended MRF Pace Foundation, India 2000, 2001, 2006. Played for Notts Board XI in the 2002 C&G. Represented England U19 2005. ECB National Academy 2005-06
Best batting: 19* Nottinghamshire v Hampshire, West End 2005
Best bowling: 4-45 Nottinghamshire v Glamorgan, Trent Bridge 2005

2005 Season

	M	Inns	NO	Runs	HS	Avge	100s	50s	Ct	St	O	M	Runs	Wkts	Avge	Best	5wI	10wM
Test																		
All First	2	3	1	35	19 *	17.50	-	-	1	-	43.3	6	260	6	43.33	4-45	-	-
1-Day Int																		
C & G																		
tsL																		
Twenty20	1	0	0	0	0	-	-	-	-	-	2	0	34	0	-		-	-

Career Performances

	M	Inns	NO	Runs	HS	Avge	100s	50s	Ct	St	Balls	Runs	Wkts	Avge	Best	5wI	10wM
Test																	
All First	2	3	1	35	19 *	17.50	-	-	1	-	261	260	6	43.33	4-45	-	-
1-Day Int																	
C & G	1	0	0	0	0	-	-	-	-	-	18	18	0	-		-	-
tsL																	
Twenty20	1	0	0	0	0	-	-	-	-	-	12	34	0	-		-	-

FOSTER, E. J.   Worcestershire

Name: Edward (Ed) John Foster
Role: Left-hand bat, wicket-keeper
Born: 21 January 1985, Shrewsbury
Height: 6ft 1in **Weight:** 12st
Nickname: Fos, Fossie
County debut: No first-team appearance
Parents: John and Jean
Marital status: Single
Family links with cricket: Father captained Shropshire CCC; brother Robert plays for Shropshire CCC
Education: Meole Brace Secondary; Loughborough University
Qualifications: '10½ GCSEs', 3 A-levels, 1 AS-level, ECB Level 2 coaching

Career outside cricket: Student
Off-season: University
Overseas teams played for: Claremont-Nedlands CC, Perth
Career highlights to date: 'Scoring 83 and 22* in Loughborough UCCE's victory over Worcestershire in 2005. Playing at Lord's with LUCCE in 2005'
Cricket superstitions: 'Left pad on first'
Cricketers particularly admired: Alec Stewart
Young players to look out for: Steve Davies, Jimmy Taylor, Paul Harrison, Rob Foster, Chris Murtagh
Other sports played: Football (recreational)
Other sports followed: Football (Arsenal, Shrewsbury Town)
Relaxations: TV, computer games
Extras: Worcestershire Academy 2002-03. Played for Loughborough UCCE 2005. Midland Club Cricket Conference Player of the Year 2005
Opinions on cricket: 'Keep improving the standard of first-class cricket. UCCEs provide younger players with a first or second opportunity.'
Best batting: 83 LUCCE v Worcestershire, Kidderminster 2005

2005 Season (did not make any first-class or one-day appearances for his county)

Career Performances

	M	Inns	NO	Runs	HS	Avge	100s	50s	Ct	St	Balls	Runs	Wkts	Avge	Best	5wI	10wM
Test																	
All First	1	2	1	105	83	105.00	-	1	-	-							
1-Day Int																	
C & G																	
tsL																	
Twenty20																	

30. Which former Leicestershire cricketer bowled the first ball in ODI cricket?

FOSTER, J. S.　　　　　　　　　　Essex

Name: <u>James</u> Savin Foster
Role: Right-hand bat, wicket-keeper
Born: 15 April 1980, Whipps Cross, London
Height: 6ft **Weight:** 12st
Nickname: Fozzy, Chief
County debut: 2000
County cap: 2001
Test debut: 2001-02
1000 runs in a season: 1
50 dismissals in a season: 2
1st-Class 200s: 1
Place in batting averages: 93rd av. 36.71
(2004 34th av. 51.85)
Parents: Martin and Diana
Marital status: Single
Family links with cricket: 'Dad played for
Essex Amateurs'
Education: Forest School; Durham
University

Qualifications: 10 GCSEs, 3 A-levels, hockey and cricket Level 1 coaching awards
Overseas tours: BUSA to South Africa 1999; Durham University to South Africa
1999, to Vienna (European Indoor Championships) 1999; England A to West Indies
2000-01; England to Zimbabwe (one-day series) 2001-02, to India and New Zealand
2001-02, to Australia 2002-03
Career highlights to date: 'Playing for my country'
Cricketers particularly admired: Nasser Hussain, Stuart Law, Robert Rollins,
Ian Healy, Jack Russell, Alec Stewart, Adam Gilchrist
Other sports played: Hockey (Essex U21), tennis (played for GB U14 v Sweden
U14; national training squad)
Other sports followed: Football (Wimbledon FC)
Relaxations: Socialising
Extras: Essex U17 Player of the Year 1997. Represented ECB U19 1998 and England
U19 1999. Represented BUSA 1999, 2000 and 2001. Voted Essex Cricket Society 2nd
XI Player of the Year 2000. Played for Durham University CCE 2001. NBC Denis
Compton Award for the most promising young Essex player 2001. Scored 40 in second
Test v India at Ahmedabad 2001-02, in the process sharing with Craig White in a
record seventh-wicket partnership for England in Tests in India (105). Achieved double
(1037 runs plus 51 dismissals) 2004
Best batting: 212 Essex v Leicestershire, Chelmsford 2004

2005 Season

	M	Inns	NO	Runs	HS	Avge	100s	50s	Ct	St	O	M	Runs	Wkts	Avge	Best	5wl	10wM
Test																		
All First	17	25	4	771	107 *	36.71	1	5	35	6								
1-Day Int																		
C & G	2	1	0	24	24	24.00	-	-	3	-								
tsL	15	9	2	117	38 *	16.71	-	-	15	6								
Twenty20	7	5	3	91	62 *	45.50	-	1	4	5								

Career Performances

	M	Inns	NO	Runs	HS	Avge	100s	50s	Ct	St	Balls	Runs	Wkts	Avge	Best	5wl	10wM
Test	7	12	3	226	48	25.11	-	-	17	1							
All First	89	133	17	3766	212	32.46	6	16	211	25	12	6	0	-	-	-	-
1-Day Int																	
C & G	8	6	1	115	33	23.00	-	-	16	1							
tsL	63	50	13	723	56 *	19.54	-	1	74	13							
Twenty20	16	11	3	117	62 *	14.62	-	1	7	6							

FRANCE, B. J.   Derbyshire

Name: Benjaman (<u>Ben</u>) John France
Role: Left-hand bat, right-arm seam bowler
Born: 14 May 1982, Brunei
Height: 5ft 11in **Weight:** 12st 7lbs
Nickname: Benny, Frenchy, Froggy
County debut: 2004
Place in batting averages: 254th av. 14.53
(2004 231st av. 18.00)
Strike rate: (career 120.00)
Parents: Joseph and Jackie
Marital status: Single
Family links with cricket: Brother played
Minor Counties cricket for Oxfordshire and
also played for the Combined Services
Education: Bromsgrove School; Oxford
College
Qualifications: 9 GCSEs, BTEC National
Diploma in Sports Science
Overseas teams played for: Parramatta, Sydney 2000-01
Career highlights to date: 'Making first-class debut v Notts 2004'
Cricket moments to forget: 'My first spell of bowling in first-class cricket'
Cricket superstitions: 'Magpies. Also put kit on in certain order'

Cricketers particularly admired: Stephen Waugh, Brian Lara
Other sports played: Rugby (England U18)
Other sports followed: Rugby (Leicester Tigers)
Favourite band: Blue
Relaxations: Fishing, cinema, gym
Extras: Played for Suffolk 2003 and 2004 and was second-highest run-scorer in the Minor Counties Championship 2004 (566 at 80.85, including 179* v Cambridgeshire at Mildenhall)
Opinions on cricket: 'Too many non-England-qualified players.'
Best batting: 56 Derbyshire v Leicestershire, Derby 2004
　　　　　　　 56 Derbyshire v Essex, Chelmsford 2005
Best bowling: 1-37 Derbyshire v Leicestershire, Leicester 2005

2005 Season

	M	Inns	NO	Runs	HS	Avge	100s	50s	Ct	St	O	M	Runs	Wkts	Avge	Best	5wI	10wM
Test																		
All First	7	13	0	189	56	14.53	-	1	3	-	16	3	70	1	70.00	1-37	-	-
1-Day Int																		
C & G																		
tsL	1	1	0	31	31	31.00	-	-	-	-								
Twenty20																		

Career Performances

	M	Inns	NO	Runs	HS	Avge	100s	50s	Ct	St	Balls	Runs	Wkts	Avge	Best	5wI	10wM
Test																	
All First	11	20	0	315	56	15.75	-	2	5	-	120	90	1	90.00	1-37	-	-
1-Day Int																	
C & G	1	1	0	8	8	8.00	-	-	-	-							
tsL	2	2	0	44	31	22.00	-	-	-	-							
Twenty20																	

FRANCIS, J. D.   Somerset

Name: John Daniel Francis
Role: Left-hand bat, slow left-arm bowler
Born: 13 November 1980, Bromley, Kent
Height: 5ft 11in **Weight:** 13st
Nickname: Long John, Franky, Junior
County debut: 2001 (Hampshire), 2004 (Somerset)
1000 runs in a season: 1
Place in batting averages: 68th av. 40.84 (2004 90th av. 36.93)
Strike rate: (career 66.75)
Parents: Linda and Daniel

Marital status: Single
Family links with cricket: Brother Simon played for Hampshire 1997-2001; now plays for Somerset. Father played club cricket. Grandfather played in the services
Education: King Edward VI, Southampton; Durham and Loughborough Universities
Qualifications: 10 GCSEs, 3 A-levels, BSc Sports Science, ECB Level 1 coaching award
Overseas tours: Twyford School to Barbados 1993; West of England U15 to West Indies 1995; King Edward VI, Southampton to South Africa 1998; Durham University to South Africa 2000; British Universities to South Africa 2002
Career highlights to date: 'Scoring maiden first-class century for Somerset v Yorkshire at Scarborough 2004, sharing in a partnership of 197 runs with Ricky Ponting'
Cricket moments to forget: 'Getting first ever pair, in a match v Yorkshire'
Cricket superstitions: 'Too many to say'
Cricketers particularly admired: Graham Thorpe, Adam Hollioake, Mike Hussey, Simon Francis
Young players to look out for: James Hildreth, Matt Wood, Ben Riches, Andrew Dunn
Other sports played: Hockey (England U18), golf, squash
Favourite band: David Gray
Relaxations: Drawing and painting, socialising
Extras: Hampshire Young Sportsman of the Year 1995. Sir John Hobbs Silver Jubilee Memorial Prize for outstanding U16 player of the year 1996. Leading run-scorer in U15 World Cup 1996. Played for Loughborough University CCE 2001, 2002 and 2003. NBC Denis Compton Award for the most promising young Hampshire player 2002. Represented British Universities 2002 and 2003
Best batting: 125* Somerset v Yorkshire, Headingley 2005
Best bowling: 1-1 Hampshire v Leicestershire, Leicester 2002

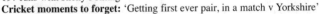

2005 Season

	M	Inns	NO	Runs	HS	Avge	100s	50s	Ct	St	O	M	Runs	Wkts	Avge	Best	5wl	10wM
Test																		
All First	17	31	5	1062	125 *	40.84	4	5	8	-								
1-Day Int																		
C & G	1	1	0	5	5	5.00	-	-	-	-								
tsL	18	16	2	465	73 *	33.21	-	3	5	-								
Twenty20	2	2	1	6	3 *	6.00	-	-	-	-								

Career Performances

	M	Inns	NO	Runs	HS	Avge	100s	50s	Ct	St	Balls	Runs	Wkts	Avge	Best	5wl	10wM
Test																	
All First	49	87	8	2507	125 *	31.73	6	14	27	-		267	155	4	38.75	1-1	-	-
1-Day Int																	
C & G	2	2	0	8	5	4.00	-	-	1	-							
tsL	58	55	9	1625	103 *	35.32	1	11	12	-							
Twenty20	7	7	3	122	31	30.50	-	-	-	-							

FRANCIS, S. R. G.   Somerset

Name: <u>Simon</u> Richard George Francis
Role: Right-hand bat, right-arm
medium-fast bowler
Born: 15 August 1978, Bromley, Kent
Height: 6ft 1in **Weight:** 14st
Nickname: Franco, Guru
County debut: 1997 (Hampshire),
2002 (Somerset)
Place in bowling averages: (2004 92nd
av. 36.39)
Strike rate: (career 62.45)
Parents: Daniel and Linda
Marital status: Single
Family links with cricket: Brother John
plays at Somerset. Father played club cricket.
Grandfather played for the Navy
Education: King Edward VI, Southampton;
Durham University
Qualifications: 9 GCSEs, 1 AS-Level, 3 A-levels, BA (Hons) Sport in the
Community, Level 1 coaching in hockey, Level III coaching in cricket
Career outside cricket: Cricket and hockey coaching
Overseas tours: England U17 to Holland (International Youth Tournament) 1995;
England U19 to Pakistan 1996-97; Durham University to Zimbabwe 1997-98;
Hampshire to Boland 2001; England A to Malaysia and India 2003-04
Overseas teams played for: Maties (Stellenbosch University), South Africa 2000;
Melville CC, Perth 2001
Cricket moments to forget: 'Whole of the B&H competition 2002'
Cricketers particularly admired: Malcolm Marshall, Richard Hadlee, Allan Donald,
Graham Dilley
Young players to look out for: John Francis
Other sports played: Golf, hockey (England U18 1995)

Relaxations: 'Films, sleeping, reading, listening to music'
Extras: Played in Durham University's BUSA Championship-winning side 1999. Took hat-trick v Loughborough UCCE at Taunton 2003. ECB National Academy 2003-04. His 8-66 v Derbyshire at Derby in the C&G 2004 is the best return by a Somerset bowler in one-day cricket
Best batting: 44 Somerset v Yorkshire, Taunton 2003
Best bowling: 5-42 Somerset v Glamorgan, Taunton 2004

2005 Season

	M	Inns	NO	Runs	HS	Avge	100s	50s	Ct	St	O	M	Runs	Wkts	Avge	Best	5wI	10wM
Test																		
All First	6	9	5	87	29	21.75	-	-	6	-	114.4	16	520	5	104.00	2-81	-	-
1-Day Int																		
C & G	1	1	1	10	10 *	-	-	-	1	-	10	2	31	3	10.33	3-31	-	
tsL	12	4	2	20	16 *	10.00	-	-	2	-	83	6	456	15	30.40	2-25	-	
Twenty20	8	2	1	1	1	1.00	-	-	1	-	21	0	221	4	55.25	2-29	-	

Career Performances

	M	Inns	NO	Runs	HS	Avge	100s	50s	Ct	St	Balls	Runs	Wkts	Avge	Best	5wI	10wM
Test																	
All First	55	72	32	424	44	10.60	-	-	17	-	8171	5284	131	40.33	5-42	3	-
1-Day Int																	
C & G	4	1	1	10	10 *	-	-	-	1	-	215	126	12	10.50	8-66	1	
tsL	55	29	14	196	33 *	13.06	-	-	12	-	2232	2036	59	34.50	4-60	-	
Twenty20	18	9	4	31	9 *	6.20	-	-	4	-	318	524	9	58.22	2-22	-	

31. Who was Ian Botham's first captain in an ODI?

FRANKS, P. J.   Nottinghamshire

Name: <u>Paul</u> John Franks
Role: Left-hand bat, right-arm
fast-medium bowler
Born: 3 February 1979, Sutton-in-Ashfield
Height: 6ft 1½in **Weight:** 13st 10lbs
Nickname: Pike, Franno, The General
County debut: 1996
County cap: 1999
50 wickets in a season: 2
Place in batting averages: (2004 88th
av. 37.29)
Place in bowling averages: (2004 46th
av. 29.93)
Strike rate: (career 55.07)
Parents: Pat and John
Marital status: Single
Family links with cricket: 'Dad was a local
league legend'
Education: Minster School, Southwell; West Notts College
Qualifications: 7 GCSEs, GNVQ (Advanced) Leisure Management, coaching Level 1
Overseas tours: England U19 to Pakistan 1996-97, to South Africa (including U19
World Cup) 1997-98; England A to Zimbabwe and South Africa 1998-99, to
Bangladesh and New Zealand 1999-2000, to West Indies 2000-01, to Sri Lanka 2004-
05; Notts CCC to South Africa 1998, 1999
Career highlights to date: 'England [one-day] debut v West Indies on home ground
in 2000'
Cricket moments to forget: 'Any time I get my poles removed or go the distance'
Cricketers particularly admired: Glenn McGrath, Mike Atherton, Allan Donald,
Phil DeFreitas
Young players to look out for: Kyle Hogg, Nadeem Malik, Bilal Shafayat, Matt Prior
Other sports played: Golf
Other sports followed: Football (Mansfield Town)
Relaxations: 'Taking it generally steady'
Extras: Took Championship hat-trick v Warwickshire at Trent Bridge 1997 (aged 18
years 163 days). Won U19 World Cup winner's medal in Johannesburg 1998. NBC
Denis Compton Award 1999. Cricket Writers' Young Player of the Year 2000. Vice-
captain of Nottinghamshire 2003-04. ECB National Academy 2004-05.
Best batting: 123* Nottinghamshire v Leicestershire, Leicester 2003
Best bowling: 7-56 Nottinghamshire v Middlesex, Lord's 2000

2005 Season

	M	Inns	NO	Runs	HS	Avge	100s	50s	Ct	St	O	M	Runs	Wkts	Avge	Best	5wl	10wM
Test																		
All First	5	6	3	195	104 *	65.00	1	-	-	-	107	17	453	9	50.33	2-37	-	-
1-Day Int																		
C & G																		
tsL	3	2	0	47	36	23.50	-	-	-	-	2.3	0	20	0	-		-	-
Twenty20	8	7	4	92	25 *	30.66	-	-	-	-								

Career Performances

	M	Inns	NO	Runs	HS	Avge	100s	50s	Ct	St	Balls	Runs	Wkts	Avge	Best	5wl	10wM
Test																	
All First	121	177	37	3781	123 *	27.00	3	17	43	-	19000	10335	345	29.95	7-56	11	-
1-Day Int	1	1	0	4	4	4.00	-	-	1	-	54	48	0	-	-	-	
C & G	15	10	4	225	84 *	37.50	-	1	4	-	726	560	23	24.34	3-7	-	
tsL	87	71	19	1074	64	20.65	-	3	14	-	3367	2780	104	26.73	6-27	2	
Twenty20	16	14	6	185	29 *	23.12	-	-	3	-	39	51	3	17.00	2-31	-	

FRIEDLANDER, M. J.   Northamptonshire

Name: Matthew James Friedlander
Role: Right-hand bat, right-arm fast-medium bowler
Born: 1 August 1979, Durban, South Africa
Height: 6ft 1in **Weight:** 13st 5lbs
Nickname: Thumper
County debut: 2005
Strike rate: (career 58.80)
Parents: Gail and Basil
Marital status: Single
Education: Hilton College; Anglia Ruskin University, Cambridge
Career outside cricket: 'Student, studying law'
Overseas teams played for: University of Stellenbosch; Boland 2003-04
Career highlights to date: '81 against Essex and 3-67 against Bangladesh'
Cricket moments to forget: 'Any injuries!'
Cricketers particularly admired: Brett Lee, Allan Donald, Kevin Pietersen
Other sports played: Hockey, golf, tennis
Other sports followed: Rugby (Natal Sharks)

Injuries: 'Calf and back niggles – a few here and there'
Favourite band: The Killers
Relaxations: 'Studies'
Extras: Made first-class debut for Boland 2003-04. Played for Cambridge UCCE 2005. Represented British Universities 2005. Played one first-class game for Northamptonshire as a trialist 2005; not re-engaged for 2006
Best batting: 81 CUCCE v Essex, Fenner's 2005
Best bowling: 3-67 Northamptonshire v Bangladeshis, Northampton 2005

2005 Season

	M	Inns	NO	Runs	HS	Avge	100s	50s	Ct	St	O	M	Runs	Wkts	Avge	Best	5wl	10wM
Test																		
All First	4	5	0	113	81	22.60	-	1	2	-	64	7	345	8	43.12	3-67	-	-
1-Day Int																		
C & G																		
tsL																		
Twenty20																		

Career Performances

	M	Inns	NO	Runs	HS	Avge	100s	50s	Ct	St	Balls	Runs	Wkts	Avge	Best	5wl	10wM
Test																	
All First	6	9	0	164	81	18.22	-	1	2	-	588	497	10	49.70	3-67	-	-
1-Day Int																	
C & G																	
tsL																	
Twenty20																	

32. Which former Kent all-rounder and international captain made ten ODI appearances, followed by three later in life as a match referee?

FRIEND, T. J. — Derbyshire

Name: <u>Travis</u> John Friend
Role: Right-hand bat, right-arm
fast-medium bowler
Born: 7 January 1981, Kwekwe, Zimbabwe
Nickname: Chunks
County debut: 2005
Test debut: 2001
Place in batting averages: 219th av. 20.00
Strike rate: (career 70.98)
Family links with cricket: Father, Ian,
played for Rhodesia B; grandfather and
great uncles also played
Education: St George's College, Harare
Overseas tours: Zimbabwe U19 to Sri Lanka
(U19 World Cup) 1999-2000; Zimbabwe to
Sharjah (Coca-Cola Champions Trophy)
2000-01, to India 2000-01, to New Zealand
2000-01, to Australia (CUB Series) 2000-01,

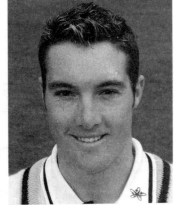

to Bangladesh 2001-02, to Sri Lanka 2001-02, to India 2001-02, to England 2003, to
Australia 2003-04 (VB Series), plus other one-day tournaments in Sharjah
Overseas teams played for: Midlands 2000-01 – 2003-04
Cricketers particularly admired: Jacques Kallis
Other sports played: Rugby (provincial age-group), golf
Extras: Represented Zimbabwe at U14 (captain), U16 and U19. Attended CFX
[Zimbabwe] Academy 2000. Represented Zimbabwe in the World Cup 2002-03. Man
of the Match in the first Test v Bangladesh at Dhaka 2001-02 (5-31/81/2-26). Man of
the [ODI] Series v Kenya 2002-03. Is not considered an overseas player. Released by
Derbyshire at the end of the 2005 season
Best batting: 183 Midlands v Manicaland, Kwekwe 2003-04
Best bowling: 5-16 Midlands v Matabeleland, Kwekwe 2003-04

2005 Season

	M	Inns	NO	Runs	HS	Avge	100s	50s	Ct	St	O	M	Runs	Wkts	Avge	Best	5wl	10wM
Test																		
All First	3	6	0	120	82	20.00	-	1	2	-								
1-Day Int																		
C & G																		
tsL	9	9	1	143	52	17.87	-	1	5	-	9	0	50	2	25.00	2-50	-	
Twenty20	4	3	0	41	24	13.66	-	-	-	-								

Career Performances

	M	Inns	NO	Runs	HS	Avge	100s	50s	Ct	St	Balls	Runs	Wkts	Avge	Best	5wI	10wM
Test	13	19	4	447	81	29.80	-	3	2	-	2000	1090	25	43.60	5-31	1	-
All First	44	66	9	1791	183	31.42	3	7	33	-	5608	3154	79	39.92	5-16	2	-
1-Day Int	51	39	5	548	91	16.11	-	3	17	-	1930	1779	37	48.08	4-55	-	
C & G																	
tsL	9	9	1	143	52	17.87	-	1	5	-	54	50	2	25.00	2-50	-	
Twenty20	4	3	0	41	24	13.66	-	-	-	-							

FROST, T. Warwickshire

Name: Tony Frost
Role: Right-hand bat, wicket-keeper
Born: 17 November 1975, Stoke-on-Trent
Height: 5ft 10in **Weight:** 10st 6lbs
County debut: 1997
County cap: 1999
50 dismissals in a season: 1
Place in batting averages: 214th av. 20.95
(2004 62nd av. 43.69)
Parents: Ivan and Christine
Marital status: Single
Family links with cricket: Father played for
Staffordshire
Education: James Brinkley High School;
Stoke-on-Trent College
Qualifications: 5 GCSEs
Overseas tours: Kidsgrove U18 to Australia
1990-91
Other sports followed: Football, golf
Extras: Represented Staffordshire at all levels from U11 to U19. Won Texaco U16
competition with Staffordshire in 1992. Played for Development of Excellence XI
U17, U18, and U19. Scored century (135*) v Sussex at Horsham 2004, in the process
setting with Ian Bell (262*) a new Warwickshire record partnership for the seventh
wicket (289*). C&G Man of the Match award in the semi-final v Lancashire at
Edgbaston 2005
Best batting: 135* Warwickshire v Sussex, Horsham 2004

2005 Season

	M	Inns	NO	Runs	HS	Avge	100s	50s	Ct	St	O	M	Runs	Wkts	Avge	Best	5wl	10wM
Test																		
All First	16	25	2	482	91	20.95	-	2	42	1								
1-Day Int																		
C & G	5	3	2	66	36 *	66.00	-	-	13	-								
tsL	13	6	2	51	25 *	12.75	-	-	10	5								
Twenty20	1	1	0	11	11	11.00	-	-	1	1								

Career Performances

	M	Inns	NO	Runs	HS	Avge	100s	50s	Ct	St	Balls	Runs	Wkts	Avge	Best	5wl	10wM
Test																		
All First	84	121	16	2747	135 *	26.16	3	12	204	16	12	15	0	-	-	-	-
1-Day Int																		
C & G	13	8	2	131	47	21.83	-	-	21	1								
tsL	55	28	11	268	25 *	15.76	-	-	44	17								
Twenty20	7	4	1	50	31	16.66	-	-	6	7								

FULTON, D. P. Kent

Name: David (<u>Dave</u>) Paul Fulton
Role: Right-hand top-order bat, left-arm spin bowler, occasional wicket-keeper
Born: 15 November 1971, Lewisham
Height: 6ft 2in **Weight:** 12st 7lbs
Nickname: Tav, Rave
County debut: 1992
County cap: 1998
Benefit: 2006
1000 runs in a season: 3
1st-Class 200s: 2
Place in batting averages: 153rd av. 29.75 (2004 75th av. 40.96)
Strike rate: (career 187.00)
Parents: John and Ann
Wife and date of marriage: Claudine Kay Tomlin, 19 December 2003

Children: Freddie Tom, 30 September 2004
Family links with cricket: Father played for village
Education: The Judd School, Tonbridge; University of Kent at Canterbury
Qualifications: 10 GCSEs, 3 A-levels, BA (Hons) Politics and International Relations, advanced cricket coach, rugby coach, gym instructor qualification

Career outside cricket: Journalist
Overseas tours: Kent SCA U17 to Singapore and New Zealand 1987-88; Kent to France 1998, to Port Elizabeth 2001
Overseas teams played for: Avendale CC, Cape Town 1993-94; Victoria CC, Cape Town 1994-95; University of WA, Perth 1995-96; Petersham-Marrickville CC, Sydney 1998-99, 1999-2000
Career highlights to date: 'Will Kendall caught and bowled Fulton (first and only first-class victim). PCA Player of the Year 2001'
Cricket moments to forget: 'Already forgotten'
Cricketers particularly admired: Gordon Greenidge, Graham Gooch, Courtney Walsh, Steve Waugh
Other sports played: Chess (England junior), table tennis ('top 10 in UK as a junior'; played for South England juniors); rugby, football, tennis, golf, squash
Other sports followed: Football (Nottingham Forest), rugby (Harlequins)
Relaxations: 'Reading, music, fitness; walking Poppy, our dog'
Player website: www.davidfulton2006.com
Extras: Was the last person to catch Viv Richards in a first-class match, in 1993. Scored double century (208*) and century (104*) v Somerset at Canterbury 2001, also taking seven catches in the match. First batsman to 1000 first-class runs in 2001 and the season's leading English batsman in terms of runs scored and average with 1892 runs (av. 75.68). Kent Batsman of the Year (Denness Award) 2001. PCA Player of the Year 2001. Captain of Kent in County Championship 2002; overall captain of Kent 2003-05
Best batting: 208* Kent v Somerset, Canterbury 2001
Best bowling: 1-37 Kent v Oxford University, Canterbury 1996

2005 Season

	M	Inns	NO	Runs	HS	Avge	100s	50s	Ct	St	O	M	Runs	Wkts	Avge	Best	5wI	10wM
Test																		
All First	16	29	1	833	110	29.75	1	5	16	-	2	0	5	0	-	-	-	-
1-Day Int																		
C & G	2	2	0	23	16	11.50	-	-	-	-								
tsL	9	7	0	189	57	27.00	-	1	1	-								
Twenty20																		

Career Performances

	M	Inns	NO	Runs	HS	Avge	100s	50s	Ct	St	Balls	Runs	Wkts	Avge	Best	5wI	10wM
Test																	
All First	185	326	19	11156	208 *	36.33	26	47	259	-	187	117	1	117.00	1-37	-	-
1-Day Int																	
C & G	20	19	1	452	78	25.11	-	3	10	-	6	9	0	-	-	-	
tsL	76	69	4	1251	82	19.24	-	3	28	-							
Twenty20	5	4	2	40	15	20.00	-	-	1	-							

GALE, A. W. Yorkshire

Name: <u>Andrew</u> William Gale
Role: Left-hand bat
Born: 28 November 1983, Dewsbury
Height: 6ft 2in **Weight:** 13st 5lbs
Nickname: Galey
County debut: 2004
Place in batting averages: (2004 264th
av. 11.14)
Parents: Denise and Alan
Marital status: 'Attached'
Family links with cricket: Grandfather keen
cricketer
Education: Heckmondwike Grammar
Qualifications: 10 GCSEs, 3 A-levels,
Level 2 cricket coaching
Overseas tours: England U17 to Australia
2001; England U19 to Australia 2002-03;
Yorkshire to Grenada 2002
Career highlights to date: '164 for Yorkshire 2nd XI v Leicestershire 2nd XI 2002.
Being on Yorkshire staff. Captaining England U19'
Cricket superstitions: 'Don't like odd numbers'
Cricketers particularly admired: Marcus Trescothick, Mark Butcher, Graeme Smith
Young players to look out for: Tim Bresnan, Joe Sayers, Chris Taylor, Richard Pyrah
Other sports played: Football, golf
Other sports followed: Football (Huddersfield Town)
Relaxations: 'Golf and listening to music; spending time with girlfriend; playing
PlayStation'
Extras: Has played for England since U15 level. Yorkshire League Young Batsman of
the Year 2002
Opinions on cricket: 'Should have just one overseas player; if we have two it could
take the places of youngsters who may have the potential to be as good as the
overseas.'
Best batting: 29 Yorkshire v Derbyshire, Headingley 2004

2005 Season

	M	Inns	NO	Runs	HS	Avge	100s	50s	Ct	St	O	M	Runs	Wkts	Avge	Best	5wl	10wM
Test																		
All First																		
1-Day Int																		
C & G																		
tsL	3	3	0	38	38	12.66	-	-	-	-								
Twenty20																		

Career Performances

	M	Inns	NO	Runs	HS	Avge	100s	50s	Ct	St	Balls	Runs	Wkts	Avge	Best	5wl	10wM
Test																	
All First	4	7	0	78	29	11.14	-	-	2	-							
1-Day Int																	
C & G	4	4	0	51	17	12.75	-	-	1	-							
tsL	12	12	1	251	70 *	22.81	-	1	5	-							
Twenty20	3	3	0	56	38	18.66	-	-	2	-							

GALLIAN, J. E. R.   Nottinghamshire

Name: <u>Jason</u> Edward Riche Gallian
Role: Right-hand bat, right-arm
medium bowler
Born: 25 June 1971, Manly, NSW, Australia
Height: 6ft **Weight:** 14st
Nickname: Gal
County debut: 1990 (Lancashire),
1998 (Nottinghamshire)
County cap: 1994 (Lancashire),
1998 (Nottinghamshire)
Benefit: 2005 (Nottinghamshire)
Test debut: 1995
1000 runs in a season: 6
1st-Class 300s: 1
Place in batting averages: 24th av. 53.04
(2004 45th av. 48.73)
Strike rate: (career 74.50)
Parents: Ray and Marilyn
Wife and date of marriage: Charlotte, 2 October 1999
Children: Tom, 12 April 2001; Harry, 8 September 2003
Family links with cricket: Father played for Stockport
Education: The Pittwater House Schools, Australia; Oxford University
Qualifications: Higher School Certificate, Diploma in Social Studies
(Keble College, Oxford)
Overseas tours: Australia U20 to West Indies 1989-90; England A to India 1994-95,
to Pakistan 1995-96, to Australia 1996-97; England to South Africa 1995-96;
Nottinghamshire to Johannesburg 2000, to South Africa 2001; MCC to UAE and
Oman 2004
Overseas teams played for: NSW U19 1988-89; NSW Colts and NSW 2nd XI
1990-91; Manly 1993-94
Career highlights to date: 'Playing Test cricket'

Cricket moments to forget: 'Breaking a finger in my first Test match'
Cricket superstitions: 'None'
Cricketers particularly admired: Desmond Haynes, Mike Gatting
Young players to look out for: Samit Patel
Other sports followed: Rugby league and union, football
Favourite band: INXS
Relaxations: Listening to music, playing golf
Extras: Represented Australia YC 1988-90 (captain v England YC 1989-90); also represented Australia U20 and U21 1991-92. Took wicket of D. A. Hagan of Oxford University with his first ball in first-class cricket 1990. Played for Oxford University and Combined Universities 1992; captained Oxford University 1993. Recorded highest individual score in history of Old Trafford with his 312 v Derbyshire in 1996. Captain of Nottinghamshire from part-way through the 1998 season to 2002 and in 2004; Nottinghamshire club captain and captain in first-class cricket 2003
Best batting: 312 Lancashire v Derbyshire, Old Trafford 1996
Best bowling: 6-115 Lancashire v Surrey, Southport 1996

2005 Season

	M	Inns	NO	Runs	HS	Avge	100s	50s	Ct	St	O	M	Runs	Wkts	Avge	Best	5wI	10wM
Test																		
All First	17	27	4	1220	199	53.04	3	5	14	-	30	4	180	0	-	-	-	-
1-Day Int																		
C & G	2	2	0	5	4	2.50	-	-	-	-								
tsL	5	5	0	74	53	14.80	-	1	-	-								
Twenty20																		

Career Performances

	M	Inns	NO	Runs	HS	Avge	100s	50s	Ct	St	Balls	Runs	Wkts	Avge	Best	5wI	10wM
Test	3	6	0	74	28	12.33	-	-	1	-	84	62	0	-	-	-	-
All First	204	350	35	12554	312	39.85	32	60	174	-	7078	4099	95	43.14	6-115	1	-
1-Day Int																	
C & G	22	22	1	564	101 *	26.85	1	4	10	-	210	164	2	82.00	1-11	-	
tsL	137	135	11	3984	130	32.12	5	24	47	-	904	888	30	29.60	2-10	-	
Twenty20	8	8	0	152	62	19.00	-	1	1	-							

33. Who is the only batsman to have scored three consecutive hundreds in both ODI and Test cricket?

GANGULY, S. C. Glamorgan

Name: <u>Sourav</u> Chandidas Ganguly
Role: Left-hand bat, right-arm
medium bowler
Born: 8 July 1972, Kolkata (Calcutta), India
Height: 5ft 11in
County debut: 2000 (Lancashire),
2005 (Glamorgan)
Test debut: 1996
1st-Class 200s: 2
Place in batting averages: 10th av. 62.57
Strike rate: (career 68.20)
Family links with cricket: Brother Snehasish
played for Bengal 1986-87 – 1996-97
Education: St Xavier's College
Overseas tours: India U19 to Bangladesh
(Beximco Asia Youth Cup) 1989-90; India to
Australia 1991-92, to England 1996, to South
Africa 1996-97, to West Indies 1996-97, to

Sri Lanka 1997, to Zimbabwe 1998-99, to Bangladesh (Wills International Cup) 1998-
99, to New Zealand 1998-99, to UK, Ireland and Holland (World Cup) 1999, to
Australia 1999-2000, to Kenya (ICC Knockout Trophy) 2000-01 (c), to Bangladesh
2000-01 (c), to Zimbabwe 2001 (c), to Sri Lanka 2001 (c), to South Africa 2001-02
(c), to West Indies 2001-02 (c), to England 2002 (c), to Sri Lanka (ICC Champions
Trophy) 2002-03 (c), to New Zealand 2002-03 (c), to Africa (World Cup) 2002-03 (c),
to Australia 2003-04 (c), to Pakistan 2003-04 (c), to England (ICC Champions Trophy)
2004 (c), to Bangladesh 2004-05 (c), to Zimbabwe 2005-06 (c), plus other one-day
tournaments in Sri Lanka, Toronto, Pakistan, Sharjah, Bangladesh, Singapore, Kenya,
Holland, England; Asian Cricket Council XI to Australia (Tsunami Relief) 2004-05 (c)
Overseas teams played for: Bengal 1989-90 –
Extras: Scored century (131) on Test debut, v England at Lord's 1996, and another
(136) in the following Test at Trent Bridge to become the third player, after Lawrence
Rowe and Alvin Kallicharran, to score a century in his first two Test innings. Was one
of *Indian Cricket*'s five Cricketers of the Year 1996. Scored 183 v Sri Lanka at
Taunton in the 1999 World Cup, sharing with Rahul Dravid in a second-wicket stand
of 318, a then ODI (and still a World Cup) record for any wicket. CEAT International
Player of the Year 2000. His many, many awards include Man of the [ODI] Series v
West Indies 2001-02 and Man of the Match in the first Test v Australia at Brisbane
2003-04 (144). Captain of India from February 2000 to October 2005. Was
Lancashire's overseas player in 2000; was an overseas player with Glamorgan in 2005
Best batting: 200* Bengal v Bihar, Kolkata 1994-95
Best bowling: 6-46 Bengal v Orissa, Kolkata 2000-01

2005 Season

	M	Inns	NO	Runs	HS	Avge	100s	50s	Ct	St	O	M	Runs	Wkts	Avge	Best	5wI	10wM
Test																		
All First	5	9	2	438	142	62.57	1	3	2	-	38	4	148	3	49.33	3-68	-	-
1-Day Int																		
C & G																		
tsL	3	3	0	77	53	25.66	-	1	-	-	12	0	65	2	32.50	1-19	-	
Twenty20	6	5	0	114	36	22.80	-	-	1	-	13	0	104	5	20.80	3-27	-	

Career Performances

	M	Inns	NO	Runs	HS	Avge	100s	50s	Ct	St	Balls	Runs	Wkts	Avge	Best	5wI	10wM
Test	84	135	12	5066	173	41.18	12	25	57	-	2360	1312	25	52.48	3-28	-	-
All First	194	302	38	11661	200*	44.17	23	69	142	-	8562	4916	125	39.32	6-46	3	-
1-Day Int	279	270	21	10123	183	40.65	22	60	96	-	4123	3470	93	37.31	5-16	2	
C & G	4	4	1	272	120*	90.66	1	2	3	-	180	123	3	41.00	3-26	-	
tsL	16	16	2	646	102	46.14	2	5	4	-	402	307	9	34.11	3-22	-	
Twenty20	6	5	0	114	36	22.80	-	-	1	-	78	104	5	20.80	3-27	-	

GAYLE, C. H. Worcestershire

Name: Christopher (<u>Chris</u>) Henry Gayle
Role: Left-hand bat, right-arm
off-spin bowler
Born: 21 September 1979, Kingston, Jamaica
County debut: 2005
County colours: 2005
Test debut: 1999-2000
1st-Class 200s: 4
1st-Class 300s: 1
Place in batting averages: 127th av. 32.00
Strike rate: (career 93.09)
Overseas tours: West Indies U19 to South
Africa (U19 World Cup) 1997-98; West
Indies A to India 1998-99, to England 2002;
West Indies to Toronto (DMC Cup) 1999, to
England 2000, to Zimbabwe and Kenya 2001,
to Sri Lanka 2001-02, to Sharjah (v Pakistan)
2001-02, to Sri Lanka (ICC Champions
Trophy) 2002-03, to India and Bangladesh
2002-03, to Africa (World Cup) 2002-03, to Zimbabwe and South Africa 2003-04, to
England 2004, to England (ICC Champions Trophy) 2004, to Australia 2005-06, plus
other one-day tournaments in Sharjah and Australia; ICC World XI to Australia
(Tsunami Relief) 2004-05, to Australia (Super Series) 2005-06

Overseas teams played for: Jamaica 1998-99 –
Extras: Scored 79-ball century (ending up with 116) in the third Test v South Africa at Cape Town 2003-04. Scored 317 in the fourth Test v South Africa at Antigua 2004-05, winning the Man of the Match award. His numerous other domestic and international awards include Man of the [ODI] Series v India 2002-03 and v Zimbabwe 2003-04. Was an overseas player with Worcestershire during the 2005 season as a locum for Zander de Bruyn
Best batting: 317 West Indies v South Africa, St John's 2004-05
Best bowling: 5-34 West Indies v England, Edgbaston 2004

2005 Season

	M	Inns	NO	Runs	HS	Avge	100s	50s	Ct	St	O	M	Runs	Wkts	Avge	Best	5wI	10wM
Test																		
All First	3	6	0	192	57	32.00	-	2	6	-	33	6	78	3	26.00	2-18	-	-
1-Day Int																		
C & G																		
tsL	5	5	1	176	53 *	44.00	-	2	1	-	21	1	95	3	31.66	2-25	-	
Twenty20																		

Career Performances

	M	Inns	NO	Runs	HS	Avge	100s	50s	Ct	St	Balls	Runs	Wkts	Avge	Best	5wI	10wM
Test	52	91	3	3466	317	39.38	7	19	60	-	3205	1374	38	36.15	5-34	2	-
All First	118	212	16	8860	317	45.20	22	43	111	-	7727	3123	83	37.62	5-34	2	-
1-Day Int	121	118	6	4362	153 *	38.94	11	23	55	-	3945	3111	100	31.11	5-46	1	
C & G																	
tsL	5	5	1	176	53 *	44.00	-	2	1	-	126	95	3	31.66	2-25	-	
Twenty20																	

GAZZARD, C. M.   Somerset

Name: <u>Carl</u> Matthew Gazzard
Role: Right-hand bat, wicket-keeper
Born: 15 April 1982, Penzance
Height: 6ft **Weight:** 13st
Nickname: Gazza, Sling Boy, Coral
County debut: 2002
Place in batting averages: 191st av. 23.75
Parents: Paul and Alison
Marital status: Single
Family links with cricket: Father and brother both played for Cornwall Schools; mother's a keen follower
Education: Mounts Bay Comprehensive; Richard Huish College, Taunton
Qualifications: 10 GCSEs, 2 A-levels, Level 1 and 2 coaching

Overseas tours: Cornwall Schools U13 to Johannesburg; West of England U15 to West Indies; Somerset Academy to Durban 1999
Overseas teams played for: Subiaco-Floreat, Perth 2000-01; Scarborough, Perth 2002-03
Career highlights to date: '157 v Derby in totesport game [2004]'
Cricket moments to forget: 'Dislocating my shoulder in Perth – kept me out for 2001 season'
Cricket superstitions: 'None'
Cricketers particularly admired: Marcus Trescothick, Graham Rose
Young players to look out for: James Hildreth
Other sports played: Football (played through the age groups for Cornwall)
Other sports followed: Football (West Ham United)
Favourite band: Red Hot Chili Peppers
Relaxations: 'Walking Stella and Elle. Following the Pilgrims with JP'
Extras: Played for England U13, U14, U15, U19. Won the Graham Kersey Award for Best Wicket-keeper at Bunbury Festival. Played for Cornwall in Minor Counties aged 16. Scored 136-ball 157 (his maiden one-day century) v Derbyshire at Derby in the totesport League 2004. Man of the Match in Twenty20 Cup semi-final v Leicestershire at The Oval 2005
Opinions on cricket: 'Great to have England performing well. Twenty20 cricket is great fun; good for everyone.'
Best batting: 74 Somerset v Worcestershire, Worcester 2005

2005 Season

	M	Inns	NO	Runs	HS	Avge	100s	50s	Ct	St	O	M	Runs	Wkts	Avge	Best	5wl	10wM
Test																		
All First	8	10	2	190	74	23.75	-	1	15	-								
1-Day Int																		
C & G																		
tsL	10	6	0	135	62	22.50	-	1	9	3								
Twenty20	11	8	2	90	29	15.00	-	-	3	4								

Career Performances

	M	Inns	NO	Runs	HS	Avge	100s	50s	Ct	St	Balls	Runs	Wkts	Avge	Best	5wl	10wM
Test																	
All First	14	20	4	427	74	26.68	-	1	26	1							
1-Day Int																	
C & G	3	3	0	35	16	11.66	-	-	4	-							
tsL	33	28	1	775	157	28.70	1	4	29	4							
Twenty20	16	13	2	195	39	17.72	-	-	6	4							

GIBSON, O. D.   Durham

Name: <u>Ottis</u> Delroy Gibson
Role: Right-hand bat, right-arm fast bowler;
all-rounder
Born: 16 March 1969, Barbados
Height: 6ft 2in **Weight:** 13st 7lbs
Nickname: Gibbo
County debut: 1994 (Glamorgan),
2004 (Leicestershire)
County cap: 2004 (Leicestershire)
Test debut: 1995
50 wickets in a season: 2
Place in batting averages: 230th av. 18.95
(2004 145th av. 30.00)
Place in bowling averages: 95th av. 37.37
(2004 14th av. 24.08)
Strike rate: 66.46 (career 51.30)
Parents: Barry and Hazel
Marital status: Single
Children: Michael James
Education: Ellerslie Secondary School, Barbados
Qualifications: 3 O-levels, Level 4 coaching certificate
Career outside cricket: Coach
Off-season: 'Relaxing'
Overseas tours: West Indies A to Sri Lanka 1996-97, to South Africa 1997-98; West
Indies to England 1995, to Australia 1995-96, to India and Pakistan (World Cup) 1995-
96, to Malaysia (Commonwealth Games) 1998-99, to South Africa 1998-99, plus one-
day tournament in Sharjah
Overseas teams played for: Barbados 1990-91 – 1997-98; Border 1992-93 –
1994-95; Griqualand West 1998-99 – 1999-2000; Gauteng 2000-01
Career highlights to date: 'Debut for West Indies'
Cricketers particularly admired: Brian Lara, Courtney Walsh

Young players to look out for: Stuart Broad
Other sports played: 'Represented school at football, basketball, volleyball. Love golf'
Other sports followed: Golf, football (Man United)
Favourite band: Oasis
Relaxations: 'Watching TV'
Extras: One of *South African Cricket Annual*'s five Cricketers of the Year 1993. Was Glamorgan overseas player 1994-96. Scored maiden first-class century (101*) from 69 balls for West Indians v Somerset at Taunton 1995, batting at No. 9. Has won numerous domestic match awards and was also Man of the Match v Australia at Brisbane in B&H World Series Cup 1995-96 (40-ball 52/2-38). Leicestershire Player of the Year 2004. Left Leicestershire at the end of the 2005 season and has joined Durham for 2006. Is UK resident and no longer considered an overseas player
Opinions on cricket: 'Championship cricket should be 90 overs per day.'
Best batting: 101* West Indians v Somerset, Taunton 1995
Best bowling: 7-55 Border v KwaZulu-Natal, Durban 1994-95

2005 Season

	M	Inns	NO	Runs	HS	Avge	100s	50s	Ct	St	O	M	Runs	Wkts	Avge	Best	5wI	10wM
Test																		
All First	15	24	4	379	91	18.95	-	2	2	-	498.3	84	1682	45	37.37	6-56	1	-
1-Day Int																		
C & G	2	2	1	25	21 *	25.00	-	-	1	-	16	2	63	4	15.75	3-22	-	
tsL	17	9	1	120	38 *	15.00	-	-	7	-	119	13	537	23	23.34	4-37	-	
Twenty20	9	7	1	66	18	11.00	-	-	4	-	34	0	248	7	35.42	2-26	-	

Career Performances

	M	Inns	NO	Runs	HS	Avge	100s	50s	Ct	St	Balls	Runs	Wkts	Avge	Best	5wI	10wM
Test	2	4	0	93	37	23.25	-	-	-	-	472	275	3	91.66	2-81	-	-
All First	149	222	30	4430	101 *	23.07	1	23	57	-	27192	15198	530	28.67	7-55	23	5
1-Day Int	15	11	1	141	52	14.10	-	1	3	-	739	621	34	18.26	5-40	2	
C & G	9	9	2	256	102 *	36.57	1	-	3	-	456	293	14	20.92	3-22	-	
tsL	62	45	12	634	47 *	19.21	-	-	19	-	2295	1747	67	26.07	4-37	-	
Twenty20	16	12	2	125	18	12.50	-	-	5	-	331	411	14	29.35	2-26	-	

34. Which current county bowler has played the same
number of Tests as his father but two more ODIs?

GIDMAN, A. P. R.   Gloucestershire

Name: Alexander (<u>Alex</u>) Peter
Richard Gidman
Role: Right-hand bat, right-arm medium
bowler, county vice-captain
Born: 22 June 1981, High Wycombe
Height: 6ft 2in **Weight:** 14st
Nickname: G, Giddo
County debut: 2001 (one-day),
2002 (first-class)
County cap: 2004
1000 runs in a season: 1
Place in batting averages: 85th av. 37.48
(2004 114th av. 34.76)
Place in bowling averages: 103rd av. 39.07
(2004 146th av. 51.68)
Strike rate: 57.30 (career 68.81)
Parents: Alistair and Jane
Marital status: Single
Family links with cricket: Brother an MCC Young Cricketer
Education: Wycliffe College
Qualifications: 6 GCSEs, 1 A-level, GNVQ Level 2 in Leisure and Tourism
Overseas tours: MCC Young Cricketers to Cape Town 1999; Gloucestershire to South
Africa; England A to Malaysia and India 2003-04 (c), to Sri Lanka 2004-05
Overseas teams played for: Albion CC, New Zealand 2001
Career highlights to date: 'Two C&G Trophy final victories. Academy captain'
Cricket moments to forget: 'C&G quarter-final loss to Kent 2002'
Cricket superstitions: 'None'
Cricketers particularly admired: Steve Waugh
Young players to look out for: Steve Snell
Other sports played: Golf
Other sports followed: Football (Wolves), rugby (Gloucester)
Favourite band: Matchbox Twenty, Train
Relaxations: 'Just chilling out; movies, golf'
Extras: Gloucestershire Young Player of the Year 2002, 2003. NBC Denis Compton
Award for the most promising young Gloucestershire player 2002, 2003. ECB
National Academy 2003-04, 2004-05. Appointed vice-captain of Glos for 2006
Opinions on cricket: 'County cricket is a great breeding ground for international
cricket. However, I don't feel that I have enough time to work on things in the season.
You can play with bad habits for long periods of time.'
Best batting: 142 Gloucestershire v Surrey, Bristol 2005
Best bowling: 4-47 Gloucestershire v Glamorgan, Cardiff 2005

2005 Season

	M	Inns	NO	Runs	HS	Avge	100s	50s	Ct	St	O	M	Runs	Wkts	Avge	Best	5wI	10wM
Test																		
All First	16	30	3	1012	142	37.48	3	4	14	-	124.1	11	508	13	39.07	4-47	-	-
1-Day Int																		
C & G	2	2	1	58	58 *	58.00	-	1	1	-	2	0	18	0	-	-	-	-
tsL	15	14	0	276	71	19.71	-	2	3	-	14	1	49	2	24.50	1-23	-	
Twenty20	8	5	0	48	17	9.60	-	-	1	-								

Career Performances

	M	Inns	NO	Runs	HS	Avge	100s	50s	Ct	St	Balls	Runs	Wkts	Avge	Best	5wI	10wM
Test																	
All First	52	90	7	2867	142	34.54	4	19	40	-	3303	2263	48	47.14	4-47	-	-
1-Day Int																	
C & G	14	13	3	238	58 *	23.80	-	1	5	-	316	260	5	52.00	2-12	-	
tsL	49	45	5	991	73	24.77	-	5	19	-	558	465	10	46.50	3-26	-	
Twenty20	14	9	1	170	61	21.25	-	1	5	-	12	25	1	25.00	1-25	-	

GIFFORD, W. M. Worcestershire

Name: William (Will) McLean Gifford
Role: Right-hand middle-order bat,
right-arm medium bowler
Born: 10 October 1985, Sutton Coldfield
Height: 5ft 11in **Weight:** 12st
Nickname: Giff
County debut: No first-team appearance
Parents: Andy and Kim
Marital status: Single
Family links with cricket: 'Dad played local
cricket. Brother plays at school'
Education: Malvern College; Loughborough
University
Qualifications: 10 GCSEs, 3 A-levels
Overseas tours: Staffordshire U16 to
Barbados 2000; Malvern College to South
Africa 2001; England U19 to India 2004-05
Career highlights to date: 'Being selected
for England U19. Offer of contract from Worcestershire'
Cricket superstitions: 'Left pad on first'
Cricketers particularly admired: Ricky Ponting, Michael Clarke, Vikram Solanki
Young players to look out for: Steve Davies, Moeen Ali, Adam Harrison

Other sports played: Hockey (Midlands U15), football, golf
Other sports followed: Football (West Brom)
Favourite band: Busted
Extras: Made 2nd XI Championship debut for Worcestershire 2003. Captained Loughborough UCCE 2005. Represented British Universities 2005
Opinions on cricket: 'Introduction of Twenty20 has been brilliant for domestic cricket.'
Best batting: 33 LUCCE v Nottinghamshire, Trent Bridge 2005

2005 Season (did not make any first-class or one-day appearances for his county)

Career Performances

	M	Inns	NO	Runs	HS	Avge	100s	50s	Ct	St	Balls	Runs	Wkts	Avge	Best	5wI	10wM
Test																	
All First	3	5	1	78	33	19.50	-	-	3	-							
1-Day Int																	
C & G																	
tsL																	
Twenty20																	

GILBERT, C. R.   *Yorkshire*

Name: Christopher (Chris) Robert Gilbert
Role: Right-hand bat, right-arm medium bowler; all-rounder
Born: 16 April 1984, Scarborough
Height: 5ft 10in **Weight:** 12st 11lbs
Nickname: Gilly
County debut: No first-team appearance
Parents: Roger and Vicky
Marital status: Single
Family links with cricket: 'Dad sports teacher and played some representative. Brother plays for Scarborough and played Yorkshire senior schools'
Education: Scarborough College
Qualifications: Level 2 coaching
Career outside cricket: Coaching
Off-season: 'Perth, Australia'
Overseas tours: England U17 to Australia

2001; England U19 to Australia and (U19 World Cup) New Zealand 2001-02
Overseas teams played for: Scarborough, Perth; Upper Valley, New Zealand
Career highlights to date: 'Gaining a contract with Yorkshire'

Cricket moments to forget: 'Getting out to my brother in the league!'
Cricket superstitions: 'None'
Cricketers particularly admired: Craig White, Darren Gough
Young players to look out for: Greg Wood, Mark Lawson
Other sports played: Hockey (England U16, U18)
Other sports followed: Premiership football and rugby
Injuries: Out for seven weeks with a side strain
Favourite band: Green Day, Arctic Monkeys, Kaiser Chiefs
Relaxations: 'Travelling'
Extras: Played for Yorkshire Board XI in the 2003 C&G
Opinions on cricket: 'Quick and energetic – good to play and watch'

2005 Season (did not make any first-class or one-day appearances)

Career Performances

	M	Inns	NO	Runs	HS	Avge	100s	50s	Ct	St	Balls	Runs	Wkts	Avge	Best	5wl	10wM
Test																	
All First																	
1-Day Int																	
C & G	1	1	0	13	13	13.00	-	-	1	-	42	33	0	-		-	-
tsL																	
Twenty20																	

35. Which wicket-keeper shares the ODI ninth-wicket
partnership record with Kapil Dev?

GILES, A. F.   Warwickshire

Name: <u>Ashley</u> Fraser Giles
Role: Right-hand bat, slow left-arm bowler
Born: 19 March 1973, Chertsey, Surrey
Height: 6ft 4in **Weight:** 15st 7lbs
Nickname: Splash, Skinny, Gilo
County debut: 1993
County cap: 1996
Benefit: 2006
Test debut: 1998
50 wickets in a season: 2
Place in batting averages: 212th av. 21.07
(2004 99th av. 36.12)
Place in bowling averages: 58th av. 30.08
(2004 31st av. 26.82)
Strike rate: 57.14 (career 68.46)
Parents: Michael and Paula
Wife and date of marriage: Stine,
9 October 1999
Children: Anders Fraser, 29 May 2000; Matilde, February 2002
Family links with cricket: Father played and brother Andrew a club cricketer at
Ripley, Surrey
Education: George Abbott County Secondary, Burpham, Guildford
Qualifications: 9 GCSEs, 2 A-levels, coaching certificate
Overseas tours: Surrey U19 to Barbados 1990-91; Warwickshire to Cape Town 1996,
1997, to Bloemfontein 1998; England A to Australia 1996-97, to Kenya and Sri Lanka
1997-98; England to Sharjah (Champions Trophy) 1997-98, to Bangladesh (Wills
International Cup) 1998-99, to Australia 1998-99 (CUB Series), to South Africa and
Zimbabwe 1999-2000 (one-day series), to Kenya (ICC Knockout Trophy) 2000-01,
to Pakistan and Sri Lanka 2000-01, to India and New Zealand 2001-02, to Sri Lanka
(ICC Champions Trophy) 2002-03, to Australia 2002-03, to Africa (World Cup) 2002-
03, to Bangladesh and Sri Lanka 2003-04, to West Indies 2003-04, to Zimbabwe (one-
day series) 2004-05, to South Africa 2004-05, to Pakistan 2005-06
Overseas teams played for: Vredenburg/Saldanha, Cape Town 1992-95; Avendale
CC, Cape Town 1995-96
Cricketers particularly admired: Dermot Reeve, Tim Munton, Dougie Brown,
Ian Botham
Other sports played: Golf (14 handicap), football
Other sports followed: Football (QPR)
Relaxations: 'Cinema, music, spending lots of time with my family'
Extras: Surrey Young Cricketer of the Year 1991. NBC Denis Compton Award for
Warwickshire 1996. Warwickshire Player of the Year 1996 and 2000. Warwickshire

Most Improved Player 1996. Cricket Society's Leading Young All-rounder 1996. Scored hundred (123*) and had five-wicket innings return (5-28) v Oxford University at The Parks 1999. Took 17 Test wickets v Pakistan 2000-01, the highest total by an England bowler in a series in Pakistan. Man of the Match in ODI v India at Delhi 2001-02 (5-57). Scored 71* v Essex at Edgbaston in the C&G 2003, sharing with Dougie Brown (108) in a competition record seventh-wicket partnership (170). Man of the Match in the first Test v West Indies at Lord's 2004 (4-129/5-81). One of *Wisden*'s Five Cricketers of the Year 2005

Best batting: 128* Warwickshire v Sussex, Hove 2000
Best bowling: 8-90 Warwickshire v Northamptonshire, Northampton 2000
Stop press: Winner of special cricket edition of *The Weakest Link*, autumn 2005. Appointed MBE in 2006 New Year Honours as part of 2005 Ashes-winning England team

2005 Season

	M	Inns	NO	Runs	HS	Avge	100s	50s	Ct	St	O	M	Runs	Wkts	Avge	Best	5wI	10wM
Test	5	10	2	155	59	19.37	-	1	5	-	160	18	578	10	57.80	3-78	-	-
All First	9	16	3	274	62	21.07	-	2	5	-	323.5	44	1023	34	30.08	6-44	3	-
1-Day Int	8	4	2	51	25*	25.50	-	-	2	-	67	2	300	3	100.00	1-28	-	
C & G	2	1	0	6	6	6.00	-	-	1	-	20	1	91	2	45.50	2-41	-	
tsL	3	1	0	5	5	5.00	-	-	2	-	27	1	104	5	20.80	3-34	-	
Twenty20																		

Career Performances

	M	Inns	NO	Runs	HS	Avge	100s	50s	Ct	St	Balls	Runs	Wkts	Avge	Best	5wI	10wM
Test	50	73	11	1278	59	20.61	-	4	30	-	11238	5297	137	38.66	5-57	5	-
All First	173	239	43	5129	128*	26.16	3	22	78	-	36284	15393	530	29.04	8-90	26	3
1-Day Int	62	35	13	385	41	17.50	-	-	22	-	2856	2069	55	37.61	5-57	1	
C & G	28	19	6	512	107	39.38	1	3	5	-	1505	1045	41	25.48	5-21	1	
tsL	93	60	14	850	61*	18.47	-	2	31	-	3570	2570	124	20.72	5-36	1	
Twenty20	2	1	1	0	0*	-	-	-	-	-	42	34	2	17.00	2-21	-	

36. Which Sri Lanka bowler had the most expensive ten-over spell in ODIs prior to Muralitharan's 0-99 against Australia this year?

GILLESPIE, J. N. Yorkshire

Name: <u>Jason</u> Neil Gillespie
Role: Right-hand bat, right-arm fast bowler
Born: 19 April 1975, Darlinghurst,
Sydney, Australia
Height: 6ft 5in
Nickname: Dizzy
County debut: No first-team appearance
Test debut: 1996-97
Place in batting averages: 182nd av. 24.83
Strike rate: (career 53.41)
Education: Cabra College, Adelaide
Overseas tours: Australia U19 to India 1993-
94; Australia A to Scotland and Ireland 1998;
Australia to Sri Lanka (Singer World Series)
1996, to South Africa 1996-97, to England
1997, to West Indies 1998-99, to Sri Lanka
1999, to Kenya (ICC Knockout Trophy)
2000-01, to India 2000-01, to England 2001,

to South Africa 2001-02, to Sri Lanka (ICC Champions Trophy) 2002-03, to Sri Lanka
and Sharjah (v Pakistan) 2002-03, to Africa (World Cup) 2002-03, to West Indies
2002-03, to Sri Lanka 2003-04, to England (ICC Champions Trophy) 2004, to India
2004-05, to New Zealand 2004-05, to England 2005, plus other one day series and
tournaments in India, Kenya, Zimbabwe, Holland and England
Overseas teams played for: South Australia 1994-95 –
Extras: Is the first known male cricketer of indigenous descent (great-grandson of a
Kamilaroi warrior) to have played Test cricket for Australia. One of *Wisden*'s Five
Cricketers of the Year 2002. Is fifth in the all-time list of Australia's Test wicket-
takers. His match awards include Man of the Match v England in the fourth Test at
Headingley 1997 (7-37/2-65) and v India at Centurion in the 2002-03 World Cup (3-13
from 10 overs). Made Twenty20 international debut v England at the Rose Bowl 2005.
Has joined Yorkshire as an overseas player for 2006
Best batting: 58 South Australia v Western Australia, Perth 1996-97
Best bowling: 8-50 South Australia v New South Wales, Sydney 2001-02

2005 Season

	M	Inns	NO	Runs	HS	Avge	100s	50s	Ct	St	O	M	Runs	Wkts	Avge	Best	5wl	10wM
Test	3	6	0	47	26	7.83	-	-	1	-	67	6	300	3	100.00	2-91	-	-
All First	5	8	2	149	53 *	24.83	-	1	1	-	110	16	445	7	63.57	2-40	-	-
1-Day Int	10	3	0	15	14	5.00	-	-	2	-	77.2	3	403	8	50.37	3-44	-	-
C & G																		
tsL																		
Twenty20																		

Career Performances

	M	Inns	NO	Runs	HS	Avge	100s	50s	Ct	St	Balls	Runs	Wkts	Avge	Best	5wI	10wM
Test	69	90	26	987	54 *	15.42	-	2	25	-	13976	6680	251	26.61	7-37	8	-
All First	118	154	39	1816	58	15.79	-	6	46	-	22648	10785	424	25.43	8-50	15	1
1-Day Int	97	39	16	289	44 *	12.56	-	-	10	-	5144	3611	142	25.42	5-22	3	
C & G																	
tsL																	
Twenty20																	

GODLEMAN, B-A.   Middlesex

Name: Billy-Ashley (<u>Billy</u>) Godleman
Role: Left-hand bat
Born: 11 February 1989, Islington, London
Height: 6ft 3in **Weight:** 13st 7lbs
County debut: 2005
Parents: Ashley Fitzgerald and Johnny Godleman
Marital status: Single
Family links with cricket: 'Dad played and coached'
Education: Islington Green School
Qualifications: 8 GCSEs
Off-season: 'Working at gym; fitness; training at county academy'
Overseas tours: England U16 to South Africa 2004-05
Career highlights to date: 'Scoring 69* on my first-class debut v Cambridge UCCE.
Three second-team 100s (v Sussex, Essex and Surrey); 820 runs, av. 64'
Cricket moments to forget: 'Drawing final league game of season against Hampstead for my club Brondesbury – had them nine down but couldn't bowl them out to win league'
Cricket superstitions: 'Check bat alignment every ball'
Cricketers particularly admired: Andy Flower, Graeme Smith
Young players to look out for: Johnny Godleman Jnr, Steven Finn, Eoin Morgan
Other sports played: Football
Other sports followed: Football (Liverpool FC), rugby union, cricket (Brondesbury)
Favourite band: Nas, 2pac, Pink Floyd, Steely Dan, Van Morrison
Relaxations: 'Music, watching football (specifically Liverpool), watching cricket'
Extras: Named best player in country U13, U14 and U15 at regional tournaments; scored 168-ball 143 for South v West at Bunbury U15 Festival at Nottingham 2004. Made 2nd XI Trophy debut for Middlesex 2003

Opinions on cricket: 'You get out what you put in.'
Best batting: 69* Middlesex v CUCCE, Fenner's 2005

2005 Season

	M	Inns	NO	Runs	HS	Avge	100s	50s	Ct	St	O	M	Runs	Wkts	Avge	Best	5wI	10wM
Test																		
All First	1	1	1	69	69*	-		-	1	-	-							
1-Day Int																		
C & G																		
tsL																		
Twenty20																		

Career Performances

	M	Inns	NO	Runs	HS	Avge	100s	50s	Ct	St	Balls	Runs	Wkts	Avge	Best	5wI	10wM
Test																	
All First	1	1	1	69	69*	-		-	1	-							
1-Day Int																	
C & G																	
tsL																	
Twenty20																	

GOLWALKAR, Y. A.   Middlesex

Name: Yogesh Ashok Golwalkar
Role: Left-hand bat, right-arm
leg-spin bowler
Born: 13 February 1980, Indore, India
County debut: 2005
Strike rate: (career 67.15)
Overseas tours: India A to Zimbabwe 2004,
to Kenya 2004
Overseas teams played for: Madhya
Pradesh 2000-01 –
Extras: Played for Essex 2nd XI 2005.
Temporary professional with Ramsbottom in
the Lancashire League 2005. A temporary
overseas player with Middlesex during the
2005 season, replacing Stuart Clark who was
called into Australia's Ashes squad
Best batting: 41* Madhya Pradesh v Orissa,
Gwalior 2000-01
Best bowling: 8-127 Madhya Pradesh v Railways, Indore 2004-05

2005 Season

	M	Inns	NO	Runs	HS	Avge	100s	50s	Ct	St	O	M	Runs	Wkts	Avge	Best	5wI	10wM
Test																		
All First	2	2	0	5	3	2.50	-	-	-	-	104.4	25	329	7	47.00	3-41	-	-
1-Day Int																		
C & G																		
tsL																		
Twenty20																		

Career Performances

	M	Inns	NO	Runs	HS	Avge	100s	50s	Ct	St	Balls	Runs	Wkts	Avge	Best	5wI	10wM
Test																		
All First	30	43	11	282	41 *	8.81	-	-	13	-	6332	3166	91	34.79	8-127	4	1
1-Day Int																		
C & G																		
tsL																		
Twenty20																		

GOODWIN, M. W. Sussex

Name: Murray William Goodwin
Role: Right-hand bat, right-arm medium/
leg-spin bowler
Born: 11 December 1972, Harare, Zimbabwe
Height: 5ft 9in **Weight:** 11st 2lbs
Nickname: Muzza, Fuzz, Goodie
County debut: 2001
County cap: 2001
Test debut: 1997-98
1000 runs in a season: 4
1st-Class 200s: 3
1st-Class 300s: 1
Place in batting averages: 18th av. 57.50
(2004 111th av. 35.00)
Strike rate: (career 99.28)
Parents: Penny and George
Wife and date of marriage: Tarsha,
13 December 1997
Children: Jayden William
Family links with cricket: 'Dad is a coach. Eldest brother played for Zimbabwe'
Education: St John's, Harare, Zimbabwe; Newtonmoore Senior High, Bunbury,
Western Australia

Qualifications: Level II coach
Career outside cricket: Coaching, commentating; business
Off-season: Playing for Western Australia
Overseas tours: Australian Cricket Academy to South Africa 1992, to Sri Lanka and India 1993; Zimbabwe to Sri Lanka and New Zealand 1997-98, to Bangladesh (Wills International Cup) 1998-99, to Pakistan 1998-99, to UK, Ireland and Holland (World Cup) 1999, to South Africa 1999-2000, to West Indies 1999-2000, to England 2000
Overseas teams played for: Excelsior, Holland 1997; Mashonaland 1997-98 – 1998-99; Western Australia 1994-95 – 1996-97, 2000-01 –
Career highlights to date: 'Becoming the highest individual scorer in Sussex's history – 335* v Leicestershire, September 2003 at Hove. Broke Duleepsinhji's record of 333 in 1930'
Cricketers particularly admired: Allan Border, Steve Waugh, Curtly Ambrose, Sachin Tendulkar
Young players to look out for: Shaun Marsh
Other sports played: Hockey (WA Country), golf, tennis
Other sports followed: 'All'
Favourite band: 'No real favourites; I have a very eclectic collection'
Relaxations: 'Socialising with friends'
Extras: Attended Australian Cricket Academy. Scored 166* v Pakistan at Bulawayo 1997-98, in the process sharing with Andy Flower (100*) in the highest partnership for Zimbabwe for any wicket in Tests (277*). His international awards include Man of the Match in ODI v Sri Lanka at Colombo 1997-98 (111) and in the second Test v England at Trent Bridge 2000 (148*). Retired from international cricket in 2000. Scored double century (203*) and century (115) v Nottinghamshire at Trent Bridge 2001. Joint Sussex Player of the Year (with Richard Montgomerie) 2001. Scored 335* v Leicestershire at Hove 2003, surpassing K. S. Duleepsinhji's 333 in 1930 to set a new record for the highest individual score for Sussex (and winning the Sussex Outstanding Performance of the Year Award 2003). Overseas player with Sussex 2001-04. Is no longer considered an overseas player
Best batting: 335* Sussex v Leicestershire, Hove 2003
Best bowling: 2-23 Zimbabweans v Lahore Division, Lahore 1998-99

2005 Season

	M	Inns	NO	Runs	HS	Avge	100s	50s	Ct	St	O	M	Runs	Wkts	Avge	Best	5wl	10wM
Test																		
All First	15	25	1	1380	158	57.50	4	7	8	-								
1-Day Int																		
C & G	3	2	0	87	59	43.50	-	1	2	-								
tsL	16	15	2	425	86 *	32.69	-	3	6	-								
Twenty20	8	4	0	56	28	14.00	-	-	-	-								

Career Performances

	M	Inns	NO	Runs	HS	Avge	100s	50s	Ct	St	Balls	Runs	Wkts	Avge	Best	5wl	10wM
Test	19	37	4	1414	166 *	42.84	3	8	10	-	119	69	0	-	-	-	-
All First	175	306	23	13433	335 *	47.46	40	58	112	-	695	357	7	51.00	2-23	-	-
1-Day Int	71	70	3	1818	112 *	27.13	2	8	20	-	248	210	4	52.50	1-12	-	
C & G	13	12	1	454	110 *	41.27	1	2	3	-	42	56	1	56.00	1-28	-	
tsL	83	81	11	2590	129 *	37.00	4	18	28	-							
Twenty20	17	12	0	148	38	12.33	-	-	3	-							

GOUDIE, G. Middlesex

Name: Gordon Goudie
Role: Right-hand bat, right-arm
medium-fast bowler
Born: 12 August 1987, Aberdeen
Height: 6ft **Weight:** 13st 12lbs
Nickname: Goudz
County debut: No first-team appearance
Parents: Morag and Gordon
Marital status: Single
Education: Bankhead Academy, Aberdeen
Qualifications: 7 Standard Grades, 4 Higher
Grades, South African Level 2 coaching
Off-season: 'Playing cricket in South Africa'
Overseas tours: Scotland U19 to Bangladesh
(U19 World Cup) 2003-04, to Sri Lanka (U19
World Cup) 2005-06
Career highlights to date: 'Playing in two
ICC U19 Cricket World Cups in Bangladesh
and Sri Lanka'

Cricket moments to forget: 'Being part of the Scotland U19 team that was bowled
out for 22 against Australia at the U19 World Cup in Bangladesh 2004'
Cricket superstitions: 'Left pad always goes on first'
Cricketers particularly admired: Andrew Flintoff, Glenn McGrath
Other sports followed: 'Any sport', football (Glasgow Rangers)
Favourite band: 'All types of music – no real favourite'
Relaxations: 'Listening to music; going out with friends for a few drinks'
Extras: Aberdeen Junior Male Sports Personality of the Year 2003. Cricket Scotland
Young Player of the Year 2004. Played for Scottish Saltires in the totesport League
2004, 2005. Made first-class debut for Scotland v Holland at Utrecht in the ICC Inter-
Continental Cup 2005. Attended ICC High Performance Winter Training Camp,
Pretoria 2005
Best batting: 12 Scotland v Holland, Utrecht 2005

Career Performances

	M	Inns	NO	Runs	HS	Avge	100s	50s	Ct	St	Balls	Runs	Wkts	Avge	Best	5wl	10wM
Test																	
All First	1	1	0	12	12	12.00	-	-	-	-							
1-Day Int																	
C & G																	
tsL	4	3	1	7	4	3.50	-	-	1	-	123	127	2	63.50	1-45	-	
Twenty20																	

GOUGH, D. Essex

Name: Darren Gough
Role: Right-hand bat, right-arm fast bowler,
county vice-captain
Born: 18 September 1970, Barnsley
Height: 5ft 11in **Weight:** 13st 9lbs
Nickname: Rhino, Dazzler
County debut: 1989 (Yorkshire),
2004 (Essex)
County cap: 1993 (Yorkshire), 2004 (Essex)
Benefit: 2001 (Yorkshire)
Test debut: 1994
50 wickets in a season: 4
Place in batting averages: 88th av. 37.00
(2004 243rd av. 16.00)
Place in bowling averages: 71st av. 31.07
(2004 10th av. 22.40)
Strike rate: 64.85 (career 51.03)
Parents: Trevor and Christine
Children: Liam James, 24 November 1994; Brennan Kyle, 9 December 1997
Education: Priory Comprehensive; Airedale and Wharfedale College (part-time)
Qualifications: 2 O-levels, 5 CSEs, BTEC Leisure, NCA coaching award
Overseas tours: England YC to Australia 1989-90; Yorkshire to Barbados 1989-90,
to South Africa 1991-92, 1992-93; England A to South Africa 1993-94; England to
Australia 1994-95, to South Africa 1995-96, to India and Pakistan (World Cup) 1995-96,
to Zimbabwe and New Zealand 1996-97, to Australia 1998-99, to Sharjah (Coca-Cola
Cup) 1998-99, to South Africa and Zimbabwe 1999-2000, to Kenya (ICC Knockout
Trophy) 2000-01, to Pakistan and Sri Lanka 2000-01, to India and New Zealand 2001-02
(one-day series), to Australia 2002-03, to West Indies 2003-04 (one-day series), to
Zimbabwe (one-day series) 2004-05, to South Africa 2004-05 (one-day series); ICC
World XI to Australia (Tsunami Relief) 2004-05

Overseas teams played for: East Shirley, Christchurch, New Zealand 1991-92
Cricketers particularly admired: Shane Warne, Steve Waugh, Ian Botham, Michael Atherton, Malcolm Marshall
Other sports played: Golf, football
Other sports followed: Football (Barnsley and Tottenham Hotspur)
Relaxations: Golf, cinema
Extras: Yorkshire Sports Personality of the Year 1994. Cornhill England Player of the Year 1994-95, 1998-99. Whyte and Mackay Bowler of the Year 1996. Took Test hat-trick (Healy, MacGill, Miller) v Australia at Sydney 1998-99. *Sheffield Star* Sports Personality of the Year. One of *Wisden*'s Five Cricketers of the Year 1999. Won Freeserve Fast Ball award 2000 for a delivery timed at 93.1 mph during the first Test v Zimbabwe at Lord's. Vodafone England Cricketer of the Year 2000-01. *GQ* Sportsman of the Year 2001. Took 200th Test wicket (Rashid Latif) v Pakistan at Lord's 2001 in his 50th Test. His international awards include England's Man of the [Test] Series v West Indies 2000 and Man of the [Test] Series v Sri Lanka 2000-01. Retired from Test cricket during the 2003 season. Granted Freedom of the City of London in March 2004. Took 200th ODI wicket (Harbhajan Singh) v India at Lord's in the NatWest Challenge 2004, becoming the first England bowler to reach the milestone. Made Twenty20 international debut v Australia at the Rose Bowl 2005. Vice-captain of Essex since 2005
Best batting: 121 Yorkshire v Warwickshire, Headingley 1996
Best bowling: 7-28 Yorkshire v Lancashire, Headingley 1995
Stop press: Winner, with Lilia Kopylova, of *Strictly Come Dancing*, December 2005

2005 Season

	M	Inns	NO	Runs	HS	Avge	100s	50s	Ct	St	O	M	Runs	Wkts	Avge	Best	5wI	10wM
Test																		
All First	10	10	2	296	93	37.00	-	2	1	-	291.5	72	839	27	31.07	5-85	1	-
1-Day Int	9	3	2	63	46 *	63.00	-	-	-	-	73.3	2	416	10	41.60	3-70	-	
C & G	2	1	0	9	9	9.00	-	-	-	-	15	1	50	3	16.66	3-18	-	
tsL	9	2	1	20	16	20.00	-	-	-	-	76.4	5	296	19	15.57	4-16	-	
Twenty20																		

Career Performances

	M	Inns	NO	Runs	HS	Avge	100s	50s	Ct	St	Balls	Runs	Wkts	Avge	Best	5wI	10wM
Test	58	86	18	855	65	12.57	-	2	13	-	11821	6503	229	28.39	6-42	9	-
All First	219	293	54	4067	121	17.01	1	17	45	-	40010	21089	784	26.89	7-28	29	3
1-Day Int	157	85	38	590	46 *	12.55	-	-	25	-	8398	6137	235	26.11	5-44	2	
C & G	32	17	1	254	46	15.87	-	-	3	-	1949	1161	64	18.14	7-27	2	
tsL	134	82	23	793	72 *	13.44	-	1	20	-	5777	4084	174	23.47	5-13	2	
Twenty20	3	3	2	35	17	35.00	-	-	-	-	66	67	3	22.33	2-29	-	

GRANT, R. N.   Glamorgan

Name: <u>Richard</u> Neil Grant
Role: Right-hand bat, right-arm
medium bowler; all-rounder
Born: 5 June 1984, Neath
Height: 5ft 10in   **Weight:** 13st 5lbs
Nickname: Granty, Pingu, Big Nose
County debut: 2004 (one-day),
2005 (first-class)
Place in batting averages: 241st av. 17.16
Parents: Kevin and Moira
Marital status: Single

Family links with cricket: 'Brother played
for MCC YCs and Glamorgan 2nd XI; Dad
played local cricket for Neath'
Education: Cefn Saeson Comprehensive,
Neath; Neath Port Talbot College
Qualifications: 6 GCSEs, NVQ Level II
Carpentry, Level II Coaching award
Career outside cricket: '12-month contract'
Off-season: 'Coaching and training'
Overseas tours: South Wales Junior League to Australia 1998; Wales U16 to Jersey
2000; Neath Port Talbot College to Goa 2001, to Malta 2002, to South Africa 2003
Overseas teams played for: Havelock North, Napier, New Zealand 2003-04
Career highlights to date: 'totesport League debut'
Cricket moments to forget: 'None, they have all been great'
Cricket superstitions: 'Left pad on first'
Cricketers particularly admired: Simon Jones ('coming back from serious injury')
Young players to look out for: Mike O'Shea, Gareth Rees
Other sports played: Golf, squash, snooker
Other sports followed: Football (Swansea City)
Favourite band: Coldplay
Relaxations: 'Spending time with girlfriend (Sam) and playing PlayStation'
Extras: Neath Port Talbot College Sportsman of the Year 2002; Neath Port Talbot
County Borough Council Sportsman of the Year 2002. Glamorgan 2nd XI Player of
the Year 2005
Opinions on cricket: 'Too many overs in a day – should be 90 overs; and shorter
lunch and longer tea – half an hour each.'
Best batting: 33 Glamorgan v Nottinghamshire, Trent Bridge 2005

2005 Season

	M	Inns	NO	Runs	HS	Avge	100s	50s	Ct	St	O	M	Runs	Wkts	Avge	Best	5wl	10wM
Test																		
All First	4	7	1	103	33	17.16	-	-	1	-	3	0	18	0	-	-	-	-
1-Day Int																		
C & G																		
tsL	12	10	2	157	29	19.62	-	-	3	-	15	0	105	1	105.00	1-18	-	
Twenty20	2	1	0	36	36	36.00	-	-	1	-	5	0	50	4	12.50	4-38	-	

Career Performances

	M	Inns	NO	Runs	HS	Avge	100s	50s	Ct	St	Balls	Runs	Wkts	Avge	Best	5wl	10wM
Test																	
All First	4	7	1	103	33	17.16	-	-	1	-	18	18	0	-	-	-	-
1-Day Int																	
C & G																	
tsL	14	12	2	183	29	18.30	-	-	3	-	138	159	2	79.50	1-18	-	
Twenty20	2	1	0	36	36	36.00	-	-	1	-	30	50	4	12.50	4-38	-	

GRAY, A. K. D.   Derbyshire

Name: Andrew (<u>Andy</u>) Kenneth
Donovan Gray
Role: Right-hand bat, right-arm
off-spin bowler
Born: 19 May 1974, Armadale,
Western Australia
Nickname: Graysie
County debut: 2001 (Yorkshire),
2005 (Derbyshire)
Place in batting averages: 154th av. 29.62
Place in bowling averages: 133rd av. 47.08
Strike rate: 87.33 (career 89.71)
Overseas teams played for: Willetton,
Western Australia
Extras: Scored maiden first-class century
(104) v Somerset at Taunton 2003. Is not
considered an overseas player
Best batting: 104 Yorkshire v Somerset,
Taunton 2003
Best bowling: 4-128 Yorkshire v Surrey, The Oval 2001

2005 Season

	M	Inns	NO	Runs	HS	Avge	100s	50s	Ct	St	O	M	Runs	Wkts	Avge	Best	5wI	10wM
Test																		
All First	8	13	5	237	77 *	29.62	-	1	9	-	174.4	28	565	12	47.08	3-56	-	-
1-Day Int																		
C & G																			
tsL	12	4	1	18	13	6.00	-	-	4	-	62.1	0	295	13	22.69	3-47	-	
Twenty20	7	2	0	2	1	1.00	-	-	1	-	26	0	176	7	25.14	2-21	-	

Career Performances

	M	Inns	NO	Runs	HS	Avge	100s	50s	Ct	St	Balls	Runs	Wkts	Avge	Best	5wI	10wM
Test																	
All First	26	39	8	886	104	28.58	1	3	25	-	3768	1924	42	45.80	4-128	-	-
1-Day Int																	
C & G	3	1	0	0	0	0.00	-	-	3	-	168	152	5	30.40	3-37	-	
tsL	36	18	7	129	30 *	11.72	-	-	9	-	1112	907	30	30.23	4-34	-	
Twenty20	15	5	0	19	13	3.80	-	-	5	-	297	387	16	24.18	3-18	-	

GREENIDGE, C. G. Gloucestershire

Name: <u>Carl</u> Gary Greenidge
Role: Right-hand bat, right-arm
fast-medium bowler
Born: 20 April 1978, Basingstoke
Height: 5ft 10in **Weight:** 12st 8lbs
Nickname: Carlos, Gs, Jackal
County debut: 1998 (one-day, Surrey),
1999 (first-class, Surrey), 2002
(Northamptonshire), 2005 (Gloucestershire)
County cap: 2005 (Gloucestershire)
50 wickets in a season: 1
Place in bowling averages: (2004 77th
av. 34.60)
Strike rate: (career 54.55)
Parents: Gordon and Anita
Marital status: Single
Family links with cricket: Father Gordon
played for Hampshire and West Indies, as did
cousin (on mother's side) Andy Roberts
Education: St Michael's, Barbados; Heathcote School, Chingford; City of
Westminster College
Qualifications: GNVQ Leisure and Tourism, NCA senior coaching award

Cricket moments to forget: 'Yorkshire v Northants, April 2003, first game of the season – easily my worst ever game' (*Northants conceded 673 runs and lost by an innings*)
Cricket superstitions: 'None'
Cricketers particularly admired: Malcolm Marshall, Michael Holding, Viv Richards
Young players to look out for: Scott Newman, Michael Carberry
Other sports played: Football ('PlayStation!')
Other sports followed: Football (Arsenal), basketball (LA Lakers)
Favourite band: Bob Marley and the Wailers
Relaxations: 'PlayStation, movies, reading, music'
Extras: Spent a year on Lord's groundstaff. Took 5-60 (8-124 the match) on Championship debut for Surrey, v Yorkshire at The Oval 1999
Best batting: 46 Northamptonshire v Derbyshire, Derby 2002
Best bowling: 6-40 Northamptonshire v Durham, Riverside 2002

2005 Season

	M	Inns	NO	Runs	HS	Avge	100s	50s	Ct	St	O	M	Runs	Wkts	Avge	Best	5wI	10wM
Test																		
All First	4	7	2	72	25	14.40	-	-	-	-	79.5	17	284	6	47.33	2-78	-	-
1-Day Int																		
C & G																		
tsL	2	1	1	2	2*	-	-	-	1	-	14	2	61	3	20.33	2-40	-	
Twenty20	8	3	2	6	5*	6.00	-	-	1	-	28	2	221	11	20.09	3-15	-	

Career Performances

	M	Inns	NO	Runs	HS	Avge	100s	50s	Ct	St	Balls	Runs	Wkts	Avge	Best	5wI	10wM
Test																	
All First	36	41	7	306	46	9.00	-	-	12	-	5619	3687	103	35.79	6-40	4	-
1-Day Int																	
C & G	3	1	0	12	12	12.00	-	-	1	-	144	160	1	160.00	1-73	-	
tsL	40	17	5	71	20	5.91	-	-	14	-	1684	1537	48	32.02	3-22	-	
Twenty20	12	4	3	8	5*	8.00	-	-	3	-	234	327	16	20.43	3-15	-	

---

37. Which bowler was the first to take five wickets for England in an ODI but failed to emulate the achievement in a 30-match Test career?

GRIFFITHS, D. A. Hampshire

Name: <u>David</u> Andrew Griffiths
Role: Left-hand bat, right-arm
fast bowler
Born: 10 September 1985, Newport,
Isle of Wight
Height: 6ft 1in **Weight:** 12st 7lbs
Nickname: Griff
County debut: No first-team appearance
Parents: Adrian Griffiths and Lizbeth Porter;
Dave Porter (stepfather); Sharon Griffiths
(stepmother)
Marital status: Girlfriend Sophia
Family links with cricket: 'Father captained
Wales. Stepfather captained Isle of Wight.
Uncles play league cricket'
Education: Sandown High School,
Isle of Wight
Qualifications: Level 1 cricket coaching

Career outside cricket: Handyman
Off-season: 'Training in UK due to stress fracture'
Overseas tours: West of England U15 to West Indies 2001; England U19 to India
2004-05
Career highlights to date: 'England U19 v Essex 2nd XI – 5-9 in seven overs,
including a hat-trick'
Cricket moments to forget: 'Not being able to play this season (2005)'
Cricket superstitions: 'At end of run-up always turn left to run in to bowl'
Cricketers particularly admired: Brian Lara, Darren Gough
Young players to look out for: Kevin Latouf, Joe Denly, Ben Harmison, Moe Ali
Other sports played: Football (Isle of Wight U11-U18), rugby (IOW)
Other sports followed: Football (Man Utd), rugby league (St Helens)
Injuries: Out for the whole of the 2005 season with a stress fracture to the lower back
Favourite band: Jack Johnson
Relaxations: Golf, skiing
Extras: Represented England U19 2004. Southern League Young Player of the Year
2004
Opinions on cricket: 'Twenty20 is awesome, bringing in younger crowds and
families who have a great enthusiasm for the game.'

GROENEWALD, T. D. Warwickshire

Name: Timothy (Tim) Duncan Groenewald
Role: Right-hand bat, right-arm fast-medium
bowler; all-rounder
Born: 10 January 1984, Pietermaritzburg,
South Africa
Height: 6ft 2in **Weight:** 14st
Nickname: TG, Groenie
County debut: No first-team appearance
Parents: Neil and Tessa
Marital status: Single
Education: Maritzburg College, Natal;
University of South Africa
Qualifications: Marketing degree ('currently
third year')
Career outside cricket: Student
Off-season: 'Club cricket in South Africa'
Overseas teams played for: Zingari CC,
Natal 1998-2006; Natal Inland 2002-05

Career highlights to date: 'Opening the bowling for Natal Dolphins with Lance
Klusener. Getting contracted to Warwickshire'
Cricket moments to forget: 'Getting out for 99 (aged 10)'
Cricket superstitions: 'None. Not superstitious'
Cricketers particularly admired: Allan Donald, Steve Waugh, Hansie Cronje
Young players to look out for: Chris Woakes
Other sports played: Hockey (Midlands U21 A 2003), tennis and golf ('socially')
Other sports followed: Rugby (Natal Sharks)
Favourite band: Green Day, Coldplay
Relaxations: 'Listening to music, watching sport, sleeping, spending time with
friends'
Extras: Leading wicket-taker at National U19 Week and represented South African
Schools Colts U19
Opinions on cricket: 'Really enjoy the shorter games such as Twenty20 – think it
does a lot for the game and brings more people to cricket. I think that there should be
more positive results in four-day cricket.'

GUY, S. M. Yorkshire

Name: <u>Simon</u> Mark Guy
Role: Right-hand bat, wicket-keeper
Born: 17 November 1978, Rotherham
Height: 5ft 7in **Weight:** 10st 7lbs
Nickname: Rat
County debut: 2000
Place in batting averages: (2004 266th
av. 10.33)
Parents: Darrell and Denise
Wife and date of marriage: Suzanne,
13 October 2001
Children: Isaac Simon, 15 January 2004
Family links with cricket: 'Father played for
Notts and Worcs 2nd XI and for Rotherham
Town CC. Brothers play local cricket for
Treeton CC'
Education: Wickersley Comprehensive
School
Qualifications: GNVQ in Leisure and Recreation, qualified cricket coach
Overseas tours: Yorkshire to South Africa 1999, 2001, to Grenada 2002
Overseas teams played for: Orange CYMS, NSW 1999-2000
Career highlights to date: 'Playing the last ever County Championship game at
Southampton [Northlands Road in 2000] and winning off the last ball with 13
Yorkshire and past Yorkshire men on the pitch at the same time'
Cricket moments to forget: 'On my debut against the Zimbabweans, smashing a door
after getting out – but I still say it was an accident'
Cricket superstitions: 'This book is not big enough'
Cricketers particularly admired: Darren Lehmann, Jack Russell
Young players to look out for: Joe Sayers
Other sports played: 'I like to play all sports', rugby (played for South Yorkshire and
Yorkshire)
Other sports followed: Rugby (Rotherham RUFC), 'Treeton Welfare CC, where all
my family play'
Relaxations: 'Playing all sports, socialising with friends, watching cartoons, and
eating a lot'
Extras: Topped Yorkshire 2nd XI batting averages 1998 (106.00). Awarded 2nd XI
cap 2000. Took five catches in an innings for first time for Yorkshire 1st XI v Surrey
at Scarborough 2000
Best batting: 42 Yorkshire v Somerset, Taunton 2000
               42 Yorkshire v Derbyshire, Derby 2005

2005 Season

	M	Inns	NO	Runs	HS	Avge	100s	50s	Ct	St	O	M	Runs	Wkts	Avge	Best	5wI	10wM
Test																		
All First	5	6	1	117	42	23.40	-	-	13	1								
1-Day Int																		
C & G																		
tsL	7	7	3	134	40	33.50	-	-	5	2								
Twenty20																		

Career Performances

	M	Inns	NO	Runs	HS	Avge	100s	50s	Ct	St	Balls	Runs	Wkts	Avge	Best	5wI	10wM
Test																		
All First	26	37	4	462	42	14.00	-	-	71	7	24	8	0	-	-	-	-
1-Day Int																		
C & G	1	0	0	0	0	-	-	-	3	-								
tsL	14	11	3	171	40	21.37	-	-	13	5								
Twenty20																		

HABIB, A. Leicestershire

Name: Aftab Habib
Role: Right-hand bat, 'very, very slow bowler'
Born: 7 February 1972, Reading
Height: 5ft 9in **Weight:** 13st
Nickname: Afie, Tabby, Inzy, Habiby
County debut: 1992 (Middlesex), 1995 (Leicestershire), 2002 (Essex)
County cap: 1998 (Leicestershire), 2002 (Essex)
Test debut: 1999
1000 runs in a season: 2
1st-Class 200s: 1
Place in batting averages: 87th av. 37.10 (2004 108th av. 35.27)
Strike rate: (career 106.00)
Parents: Tahira (deceased) and Hussain
Marital status: Single
Family links with cricket: Cousin of Zahid Sadiq (ex-Surrey and Derbyshire)
Education: Taunton School
Qualifications: 7 GCSEs, Level 2 coaching
Career outside cricket: Property management

Overseas tours: Berkshire CCC to South Africa 1996; England YC to Australia 1989-90, to New Zealand 1990-91; England A to Bangladesh and New Zealand 1999-2000, to West Indies 2000-01

Overseas teams played for: Globe Wakatu, Nelson, New Zealand 1992-93, 1996-97; Riccarton CC, Christchurch, New Zealand 1997-98; Kingborough CC, Hobart

Career highlights to date: 'Playing for England in 1999'

Cricket moments to forget: 'Losing three one-day finals and a Test match at Lord's'

Cricketers particularly admired: Sachin Tendulkar, Mark Waugh, Ricky Ponting

Young players to look out for: Ravi Bopara

Other sports played: 'Enjoy most sports', football (Reading Schools)

Other sports followed: Football (Reading FC, Liverpool), rugby (Leicester Tigers, New Zealand All Blacks)

Favourite band: Adnan Sami

Relaxations: 'Music, reading, golf, cinema'

Extras: Played for England U15-U19. Middlesex 2nd XI Seaxe Player of the Year 1992. Leicestershire 2nd XI Player of the Year 1995. Championship medals with Leicestershire in 1996 and 1998. Scored 101* for England A v New Zealand A to help save the first 'Test' at Lincoln 1999-2000. Left Essex at the end of the 2004 season and rejoined Leicestershire for 2005

Opinions on cricket: 'Not happy with the amount of Kolpak players [*see page 9*] now being signed by counties. This is not helping our own young players' development.'

Best batting: 215 Leicestershire v Worcestershire, Leicester 1996

Best bowling: 1-10 Essex v Kent, Chelmsford 2003

2005 Season

	M	Inns	NO	Runs	HS	Avge	100s	50s	Ct	St	O	M	Runs	Wkts	Avge	Best	5wl	10wM
Test																		
All First	13	21	2	705	153*	37.10	1	3	8	-								
1-Day Int																		
C & G	2	2	0	43	26	21.50	-	-	2	-								
tsL	11	11	1	241	65*	24.10	-	2	3	-								
Twenty20																		

Career Performances

	M	Inns	NO	Runs	HS	Avge	100s	50s	Ct	St	Balls	Runs	Wkts	Avge	Best	5wl	10wM
Test	2	3	0	26	19	8.66	-	-	-	-							
All First	158	240	29	8869	215	42.03	21	46	79	-	106	80	1	80.00	1-10	-	-
1-Day Int																	
C & G	21	17	3	401	67	28.64	-	2	8	-	46	40	2	20.00	2-5	-	
tsL	103	92	18	1984	99*	26.81	-	10	31	-	13	18	0	-	-	-	
Twenty20	2	2	1	26	16*	26.00	-	-	1	-							

HALL, A. J.　　　　　　　　　　　　Kent

Name: <u>Andrew</u> James Hall
Role: Right-hand bat, right-arm
fast-medium bowler; all-rounder
Born: 31 July 1975, Johannesburg,
South Africa
County debut: 2003 (Worcestershire),
2005 (Kent)
County cap: 2003 (Worcestershire colours),
2005 (Kent)
Test debut: 2001-02
Place in batting averages: 81st av. 38.42
(2004 127th av. 32.82)
Place in bowling averages: 25th av. 25.70
(2004 102nd av. 37.46)
Strike rate: 52.17 (career 55.96)
Wife: Leanie
Education: Hoërskool Alberton
Overseas tours: South Africa to Sri Lanka
(Singer Triangular Series) 2000, to Australia (Super Challenge) 2000, to Singapore
(Godrej Singapore Challenge) 2000-01, to Kenya (ICC Knockout Trophy) 2000-01,
to Bangladesh (TVS Cup) 2003, to England 2003, to Pakistan 2003-04, to India
2004-05, to West Indies 2004-05, to India (one-day series) 2005-06, to Australia
2005-06 (VB Series)
Overseas teams played for: Transvaal/Gauteng 1994-95 – 2000-01;
Easterns 2001-02 – 2003-04; Lions 2004-05 –
Extras: Played for South Africa Academy 1997. Was shot in the hand and face by a
mugger in Johannesburg in 1999 and was car-jacked in 2002. Man of the Match in tied
indoor ODI v Australia at Melbourne 2000. One of *South African Cricket Annual*'s
five Cricketers of the Year 2002. His South African domestic awards include Man of
the SuperSport Series 2002-03 and Man of the Match in the final (6-77/5-22). An
overseas player with Worcestershire 2003-04; an overseas player with Kent since
2005. Man of the Match v Lancashire in the C&G semi-final at Worcester 2003. Man
of the Match in the first Test v India at Kanpur 2004-05 (163)
Best batting: 163 South Africa v India, Kanpur 2004-05
Best bowling: 6-77 Easterns v Western Province, Benoni 2002-03
Stop press: Made Twenty20 international debut v Australia at Brisbane 2005-06

	M	Inns	NO	Runs	HS	Avge	100s	50s	Ct	St	O	M	Runs	Wkts	Avge	Best	5wI	10wM
Test																		
All First	11	16	2	538	133	38.42	1	2	9	-	347.5	71	1028	40	25.70	4-32	-	-
1-Day Int																		
C & G	1	1	0	62	62	62.00	-	1	1	-	10	0	46	1	46.00	1-46	-	
tsL	9	9	0	324	72	36.00	-	3	5	-	68.3	12	265	13	20.38	3-17	-	
Twenty20	8	8	2	161	43 *	26.83	-	-	3	-	22.2	2	201	6	33.50	2-30	-	

Career Performances

	M	Inns	NO	Runs	HS	Avge	100s	50s	Ct	St	Balls	Runs	Wkts	Avge	Best	5wI	10wM
Test	15	23	3	559	163	27.95	1	2	12	-	2191	1153	31	37.19	3-1	-	-
All First	106	156	20	4586	163	33.72	5	31	77	-	18132	8372	324	25.83	6-77	11	1
1-Day Int	50	35	7	619	81	22.10	-	2	19	-	1513	1122	39	28.76	3-29	-	
C & G	13	12	0	324	78	27.00	-	3	5	-	575	424	18	23.55	4-33	-	
tsL	28	26	5	616	72	29.33	-	4	8	-	1137	801	35	22.88	4-26	-	
Twenty20	16	16	2	263	46	18.78	-	-	3	-	319	431	16	26.93	2-17	-	

HAMILTON, G. M.   Durham

Name: <u>Gavin</u> Mark Hamilton
Role: Left-hand bat, right-arm medium-fast bowler
Born: 16 September 1974, Broxburn
Height: 6ft 3in **Weight:** 13st
Nickname: Hammy, Jock, Dits, 'anything Scottish'
County debut: 1994 (Yorkshire), 2004 (Durham)
County cap: 1998 (Yorkshire)
Test debut: 1999-2000
50 wickets in a season: 1
Place in batting averages: (2004 196th av. 22.85)
Strike rate: (career 49.38)
Parents: Gavin and Wendy
Marital status: Single
Family links with cricket: Father 'long-term fast bowler at club level' (Sidcup, Kent; West Lothian, Scotland). Brother opening bat for Sidcup CC and has opened batting for Scotland
Education: Hurstmere School, Sidcup
Qualifications: 10 GCSEs and two coaching awards

Overseas tours: England to South Africa and Zimbabwe 1999-2000; Yorkshire pre-season tours to South Africa, Zimbabwe and West Indies; Scotland to UAE (ICC Six Nations Challenge) 2003-04, to UAE (ICC Inter-Continental Cup) 2004-05, to Ireland (ICC Trophy) 2005

Overseas teams played for: Welling, Municipals, and Stellenbosch University – all South Africa; Spotswood, Melbourne

Cricketers particularly admired: Craig White, Mark Robinson, Chris Adams

Other sports played: Golf ('a lot of it'), football (Arsenal YTS)

Other sports followed: Football (Falkirk FC)

Relaxations: Listening to music and reading the paper

Extras: Took ten wickets (5-69/5-43) and scored 149 runs (79/70) v Glamorgan at Cardiff 1998. Wetherell Award for the Cricket Society's leading all-rounder in English first-class cricket 1998; Yorkshire Players' Player of the Year 1998; Yorkshire Supporters' Player of the Year 1998. Scored 217 runs (av. 54.25, including the first World Cup fifty by a Scotland batsman) in the 1999 World Cup, more than any England batsman. Played in Scotland side that won the ICC Inter-Continental Cup 2004-05, scoring century (115) in the final v Canada in Sharjah. Played six totesport League matches for Scottish Saltires on loan from Durham 2005, top-scoring with 60 against former county Yorkshire at Headingley. Retired at the end of the 2005 season

Best batting: 125 Yorkshire v Hampshire, Headingley 2000

Best bowling: 7-50 Yorkshire v Surrey, Headingley 1998

2005 Season

	M	Inns	NO	Runs	HS	Avge	100s	50s	Ct	St	O	M	Runs	Wkts	Avge	Best	5wI	10wM
Test																		
All First																		
1-Day Int																		
C & G																		
tsL	12	12	1	199	60	18.09	-	1	3	-								
Twenty20																		

Career Performances

	M	Inns	NO	Runs	HS	Avge	100s	50s	Ct	St	Balls	Runs	Wkts	Avge	Best	5wI	10wM
Test	1	2	0	0	0	0.00	-	-	-	-	90	63	0	-	-	-	-
All First	91	126	21	2779	125	26.46	2	17	32	-	12222	6368	248	25.67	7-50	9	2
1-Day Int	5	5	1	217	76	54.25	-	2	1	-	214	149	3	49.66	2-36	-	
C & G	11	9	3	148	39	24.66	-	-	3	-	504	340	19	17.89	3-27	-	
tsL	89	67	14	1111	76	20.96	-	5	15	-	2521	2101	81	25.93	5-16	2	
Twenty20	3	3	1	41	41 *	20.50	-	-	1	-							

HAMILTON-BROWN, R. J.   Surrey

Name: <u>Rory</u> James Hamilton-Brown
Role: Right-hand bat, right-arm off-spin
bowler; batting all-rounder
Born: 3 September 1987, London
('overlooking Lord's')
Height: 6ft **Weight:** 13st 6lbs
Nickname: Razza
County debut: 2005
Parents: Roger and Holly
Marital status: Single
Family links with cricket: 'Father played at
Warwickshire. Dennis Amiss is my
godfather'
Education: Millfield School
Career outside cricket: 'Still at school until
summer 2006'
Overseas tours: England U16 to South
Africa; England U19 to Bangladesh 2005-06,
to Sri Lanka (U19 World Cup) 2005-06
Cricketers particularly admired: Jacques Kallis
Young players to look out for: Tom Maynard, Kieron Powell
Other sports played: Rugby (England U16 – full back)
Favourite band: 'Any R&B'
Relaxations: 'Music, dancing, and my girlfriend when I have time'
Extras: Captained England U15. *Daily Telegraph* Bunbury Scholar (Batsman) 2003.
Broke Millfield batting record 2004 at 16. Made 2nd XI Championship debut 2004,
scoring 43 and 84 v Sussex 2nd XI at Hove
Best batting: 9 Surrey v Bangladesh A, The Oval 2005

2005 Season

	M	Inns	NO	Runs	HS	Avge	100s	50s	Ct	St	O	M	Runs	Wkts	Avge	Best	5wI	10wM
Test																		
All First	1	2	0	14	9	7.00	-	-	1	-								
1-Day Int																		
C & G																		
tsL	2	1	0	20	20	20.00	-	-	-	-								
Twenty20																		

Career Performances

	M	Inns	NO	Runs	HS	Avge	100s	50s	Ct	St	Balls	Runs	Wkts	Avge	Best	5wI	10wM
Test																	
All First	1	2	0	14	9	7.00	-	-	1	-							
1-Day Int																	
C & G																	
tsL	2	1	0	20	20	20.00	-	-	-	-							
Twenty20																	

HANCOCK, T. H. C.   Gloucestershire

Name: Timothy (<u>Tim</u>) Harold Coulter Hancock
Role: Right-hand bat, right-arm medium bowler
Born: 20 April 1972, Reading
Height: 5ft 11in   **Weight:** 12st 7lbs
Nickname: Herbie
County debut: 1991
County cap: 1998
Benefit: 2005
1000 runs in a season: 1
1st-Class 200s: 1
Place in batting averages: 238th av. 17.62 (2004 79th av. 40.08)
Strike rate: (career 67.46)
Parents: John and Jennifer
Wife and date of marriage: Rachael, 26 September 1998
Children: George, 30 January 2000; Annabel Rachael, 28 August 2001
Family links with cricket: 'Dad and brother very keen players'
Education: St Edward's, Oxford; Henley College
Qualifications: 8 GCSEs, senior coaching award
Overseas tours: Gloucestershire to Kenya 1991, to Sri Lanka 1992-93, to Zimbabwe (two visits)
Overseas teams played for: CBC Old Boys, Bloemfontein 1991-92; Wynnum Manley, Brisbane 1992-93; Harlequins, Durban 1994-95
Career highlights to date: 'Winning at Lord's ... and doing the treble in one-day competitions in 2000'
Cricket moments to forget: 'Breaking my hand in fielding practice days before the 2001 B&H final'
Cricketers particularly admired: Viv Richards, Gordon Greenidge, Ian Botham

Other sports played: Hockey (played for Oxfordshire U19), golf
Relaxations: 'Family life and a round of golf'
Extras: Vice-captain of Gloucestershire 2000-02. Man of the Match award in the NatWest quarter-final v Northamptonshire at Bristol 2000 (110). Released by Gloucestershire at the end of the 2005 season
Best batting: 220* Gloucestershire v Nottinghamshire, Trent Bridge 1998
Best bowling: 3-5 Gloucestershire v Essex, Colchester 1998

2005 Season

	M	Inns	NO	Runs	HS	Avge	100s	50s	Ct	St	O	M	Runs	Wkts	Avge	Best	5wI	10wM
Test																		
All First	5	9	1	141	41 *	17.62	-	-	11	-	7	2	31	1	31.00	1-14	-	-
1-Day Int																		
C & G	1	1	0	6	6	6.00	-	-	-	-								
tsL	1	1	0	2	2	2.00	-	-	-	-								
Twenty20																		

Career Performances

	M	Inns	NO	Runs	HS	Avge	100s	50s	Ct	St	Balls	Runs	Wkts	Avge	Best	5wI	10wM
Test																	
All First	185	322	21	8485	220 *	28.18	7	51	124	-	3171	1816	47	38.63	3-5	-	-
1-Day Int																	
C & G	22	20	0	809	135	40.45	2	5	8	-	233	178	13	13.69	6-58	1	
tsL	143	131	4	2430	82	19.13	-	10	50	-	702	659	22	29.95	3-18	-	
Twenty20	5	4	0	110	56	27.50	-	1	2	-							

HARBHAJAN SINGH   Surrey

Name: Harbhajan Singh
Role: Right-hand bat, right-arm off-spin bowler
Born: 3 July 1980, Jalandhar, Punjab
Nickname: Bhaji
County debut: 2005
Test debut: 1997-98
Place in bowling averages: 27th av. 25.85
Strike rate: 56.15 (career 56.68)
Overseas tours: India U19 to South Africa (U19 World Cup) 1997-98; India to Sharjah (Coca-Cola Cup) 1997-98, to Malaysia (Commonwealth Games) 1998-99, to Zimbabwe 1998-99, to New Zealand 1998-99, to Sri Lanka (Asian Test Championship) 1998-99, to Australia 1999-2000, to Zimbabwe 2001, to Sri Lanka 2001, to South Africa 2001-02, to West Indies 2001-02, to England 2002, to Sri Lanka (ICC Champions Trophy) 2002-03, to New Zealand 2002-03, to Africa (World Cup) 2002-03, to Australia 2003-04, to England (NatWest Challenge) 2004, to England

(ICC Champions Trophy) 2004, to
Bangladesh 2004-05, to Zimbabwe 2005-06,
to Pakistan 2005-06, plus one-day
tournaments in Sri Lanka, Los Angeles and
Bangladesh

Overseas teams played for: Punjab (India)
1997-98 –

Extras: Popularly nicknamed the
'Turbanator'. Represented India U19 1995-
96. Became the first Indian to take a Test hat-
trick (Ponting, Gilchrist, Warne), in the
second Test v Australia at Kolkata 2000-01.
Took 32 wickets (av. 17.03) in three-Test
series v Australia 2000-01 and was Man of
the Series. His other Test awards include Man
of the Series v West Indies 2002-03 (20
wickets; av. 16.75) and Man of the Match in
the second Test v South Africa at Kolkata

2004-05 (2-54/7-87). One of *Indian Cricket*'s five Cricketers of the Year 2001. An
overseas player with Surrey 2005

Best batting: 84 Punjab v Haryana, Amritsar 2000-01
           84 Surrey v Gloucestershire, Bristol 2005

Best bowling: 8-84 India v Australia, Chennai (Madras) 2000-01

2005 Season

	M	Inns	NO	Runs	HS	Avge	100s	50s	Ct	St	O	M	Runs	Wkts	Avge	Best	5wI	10wM
Test																		
All First	4	5	1	124	84	31.00	-	1	2	-	187.1	42	517	20	25.85	6-36	1	-
1-Day Int																		
C & G																		
tsL	1	1	0	1	1	1.00	-	-	1	-	9	0	59	1	59.00	1-59	-	
Twenty20	8	3	1	11	6	5.50	-	-	2	-	23	0	152	4	38.00	2-22	-	

Career Performances

	M	Inns	NO	Runs	HS	Avge	100s	50s	Ct	St	Balls	Runs	Wkts	Avge	Best	5wI	10wM
Test	47	66	12	782	66	14.48	-	2	21	-	12736	5793	205	28.25	8-84	16	3
All First	102	134	27	2006	84	18.74	-	6	49	-	24607	11458	434	26.40	8-84	27	4
1-Day Int	107	57	17	486	46	12.15	-	-	29	-	5721	3983	127	31.36	5-43	1	
C & G																	
tsL	1	1	0	1	1	1.00	-	-	1	-	54	59	1	59.00	1-59	-	
Twenty20	8	3	1	11	6	5.50	-	-	2	-	138	152	4	38.00	2-22	-	

HARDINGES, M. A.　　　　Gloucestershire

Name: <u>Mark</u> Andrew Hardinges
Role: Right-hand bat, right-arm
medium-fast bowler
Born: 5 February 1978, Gloucester
Height: 6ft 1in **Weight:** 13st 7lbs
Nickname: Dinges
County debut: 1999
County cap: 2004
Place in batting averages: 239th av. 17.56
Place in bowling averages: 54th av. 28.59
Strike rate: 48.71 (career 62.71)
Parents: David and Jean
Marital status: Single
Family links with cricket: Brother and
father played club cricket
Education: Malvern College; Bath
University

Qualifications: 10 GCSEs, 3 A-levels, BSc
(Hons) Economics and Politics
Overseas tours: Malvern College to South Africa 1996; Gloucestershire to South
Africa 1999, 2000
Overseas teams played for: Newtown and Chilwell, Geelong, Australia 1997
Career highlights to date: 'Norwich Union debut v Notts 2001 – scored 65 and set
domestic one-day seventh-wicket partnership record (164) with J. Snape. Also Lord's
final v Surrey'
Cricket moments to forget: 'Glos v Somerset [Norwich Union 2001] – bowled three
overs for 30 and was run out for 0 on Sky TV'
Cricketers particularly admired: Kim Barnett, Steve Waugh, Mark Alleyne
Other sports played: Golf, tennis (Gloucester U14), football (university first team)
Other sports followed: Football (Tottenham)
Relaxations: Golf
Extras: Represented British Universities 2000. C&G Man of the Match award for his
4-19 v Shropshire at Shrewsbury School 2002. Scored maiden one-day century (111*)
v Lancashire at Old Trafford in the totesport League 2005, in the process sharing with
Ramnaresh Sarwan (118*) in a new competition record fifth-wicket partnership (221*)
Best batting: 172 Gloucestershire v OUCCE, The Parks 2002
Best bowling: 5-51 Gloucestershire v Kent, Maidstone 2005

2005 Season

	M	Inns	NO	Runs	HS	Avge	100s	50s	Ct	St	O	M	Runs	Wkts	Avge	Best	5wI	10wM
Test																		
All First	13	25	2	404	58 *	17.56	-	1	10	-	259.5	53	915	32	28.59	5-51	1	-
1-Day Int							.											
C & G	2	2	0	42	26	21.00	-	-	2	-	14	0	57	2	28.50	2-34	-	
tsL	16	15	2	288	111 *	22.15	1	1	6	-	83.3	4	451	10	45.10	4-40	-	
Twenty20	8	5	1	103	40	25.75	-	-	2	-	18.4	0	177	9	19.66	3-18	-	

Career Performances

	M	Inns	NO	Runs	HS	Avge	100s	50s	Ct	St	Balls	Runs	Wkts	Avge	Best	5wI	10wM
Test																	
All First	24	37	4	731	172	22.15	1	2	16	-	2885	1652	46	35.91	5-51	1	-
1-Day Int																	
C & G	7	6	0	56	26	9.33	-	-	4	-	204	130	8	16.25	4-19	-	
tsL	36	33	6	482	111 *	17.85	1	2	13	-	1191	1040	24	43.33	4-40	-	
Twenty20	16	10	2	153	40	19.12	-	-	3	-	160	249	12	20.75	3-18	-	

HARMISON, B. W. Durham

Name: <u>Ben</u> William Harmison
Role: Left-hand bat, right-arm medium-fast bowler; all-rounder
Born: 9 January 1986, Ashington, Northumberland
Height: 6ft 5in **Weight:** 13st 7lbs
Nickname: Harmy
County debut: No first-team appearance (*see Extras*)
Parents: Margaret and James (Jim)
Marital status: Single
Family links with cricket: Brother Stephen plays for Durham and England. Father Jim and brother James play league cricket for Ashington CC
Education: Ashington High School
Off-season: 'Training and going to India with Durham CCC'
Overseas tours: England U19 to Bangladesh (U19 World Cup) 2003-04, to India 2004-05; Durham to India 2005
Career highlights to date: 'Representing England and getting a pro contract at Durham'

Cricket moments to forget: 'Getting a first-baller on Durham debut v Bangladesh A'
Cricket superstitions: 'Left pad first'
Cricketers particularly admired: Andrew Flintoff, Stephen Harmison
Young players to look out for: Moeen Ali, Joe Denly, 'all Durham Academy'
Other sports played: Football
Other sports followed: Football (Newcastle)
Injuries: 'Left ankle stopped me bowling threequarters of the season'
Favourite band: 'None – love R&B'
Relaxations: 'Listening to music; going to gym'
Extras: Represented England U19 2005. Played for Durham v Bangladesh A in a 50-over match at Riverside 2005 but has yet to appear for the county in first-class cricket or one-day competition
Opinions on cricket: 'Give young Englishmen more of a chance instead of looking overseas!'

HARMISON, S. J.   Durham

Name: <u>Stephen</u> James Harmison
Role: Right-hand bat, right-arm
fast bowler
Born: 23 October 1978, Ashington,
Northumberland
Height: 6ft 4in **Weight:** 14st
Nickname: Harmy
County debut: 1996
County cap: 1999
Test debut: 2002
50 wickets in a season: 3
Place in bowling averages: 6th av. 21.14
(2004 20th av. 25.42)
Strike rate: 38.46 (career 56.24)
Parents: Jimmy and Margaret
Wife and date of marriage: Hayley,
8 October 1999
Children: Emily Alice, 1 June 1999; Abbie

Family links with cricket: Brother James has played for Northumberland; brother Ben played for England U19 and is now at Durham
Education: Ashington High School
Overseas tours: England U19 to Pakistan 1996-97; England A to Zimbabwe and South Africa 1998-99; ECB National Academy to Australia 2001-02; England to Australia 2002-03, to Africa (World Cup) 2002-03, to Bangladesh 2003-04, to West Indies 2003-04, to South Africa 2004-05, to Pakistan 2005-06, to India 2005-06; ICC World XI to Australia (Super Series) 2005-06

Cricketers particularly admired: David Boon, Courtney Walsh
Other sports played: Football (played for Ashington in Northern League), golf, snooker
Other sports followed: Football (Newcastle United)
Relaxations: Spending time with family
Extras: Had match figures of 9-79 (5-35/4-44) in the first Test v Bangladesh at Dhaka 2003-04, winning Man of the Match award. Man of the [Test] Series v West Indies 2003-04 (23 wickets at 14.86, including 7-12 at Kingston) and England's Man of the [Test] Series v New Zealand 2004 (21 wickets at 22.09). Had match figures of 9-121 (6-46/3-75) in the fourth Test v West Indies at The Oval 2004 to go to the top of the PricewaterhouseCoopers ratings for Test bowlers. Became second England bowler (after James Anderson) to take an ODI hat-trick (Kaif, Balaji, Nehra), v India at Trent Bridge in the NatWest Challenge 2004. One of *Wisden*'s Five Cricketers of the Year 2005. Became first bowler to take a first-class hat-trick for Durham (Pipe, Mason, Wigley) v Worcestershire at Riverside 2005. Made Twenty20 international debut v Australia at the Rose Bowl 2005
Best batting: 42 England v South Africa, Cape Town 2004-05
Best bowling: 7-12 England v West Indies, Kingston 2003-04
Stop press: Appointed MBE in 2006 New Year Honours as part of 2005 Ashes-winning England team

2005 Season

	M	Inns	NO	Runs	HS	Avge	100s	50s	Ct	St	O	M	Runs	Wkts	Avge	Best	5wI	10wM
Test	7	8	2	60	20 *	10.00	-	-	2	-	215	28	750	27	27.77	5-38	2	-
All First	11	11	3	61	20 *	7.62	-	-	3	-	346.1	54	1142	54	21.14	6-52	4	-
1-Day Int	9	3	3	17	11 *	-	-	-	2	-	86.5	6	404	17	23.76	5-33	1	
C & G	1	1	0	1	1	1.00	-	-	-	-	10	1	45	3	15.00	3-45	-	
tsL	1	0	0	0	0	-	-	-	-	-	9	0	24	1	24.00	1-24	-	
Twenty20																		

Career Performances

	M	Inns	NO	Runs	HS	Avge	100s	50s	Ct	St	Balls	Runs	Wkts	Avge	Best	5wI	10wM
Test	35	45	13	347	42	10.84	-	-	5	-	7579	3932	138	28.49	7-12	6	-
All First	116	157	43	1038	42	9.10	-	-	21	-	22665	11660	403	28.93	7-12	13	-
1-Day Int	34	14	9	54	13 *	10.80	-	-	8	-	1802	1435	50	28.70	5-33	1	
C & G	6	5	2	5	2 *	1.66	-	-	3	-	312	229	7	32.71	3-45	-	
tsL	33	12	6	29	11 *	4.83	-	-	3	-	1516	1238	40	30.95	4-43	-	
Twenty20	1	0	0	0	0	-	-	-	-	-	24	19	1	19.00	1-19	-	

HARRIS, A. J.   Nottinghamshire

Name: <u>Andrew</u> James Harris
Role: Right-hand bat, right-arm
fast-medium bowler
Born: 26 June 1973, Ashton-under-Lyne,
Lancashire
Height: 6ft   **Weight:** 11st 9lbs
Nickname: AJ, Honest
County debut: 1994 (Derbyshire),
2000 (Nottinghamshire)
County cap: 1996 (Derbyshire),
2000 (Nottinghamshire)
50 wickets in a season: 1
Place in bowling averages: 34th av. 26.38
Strike rate: 39.83 (career 51.31)
Parents: Norman (deceased) and Joyce
Wife and date of marriage: Kate,
7 October 2000
Children: Jacob Alexander, 28 August 2002
Education: Hadfield Comprehensive School; Glossopdale Community College
Qualifications: 6 GCSEs, 1 A-level
Overseas tours: England A to Australia 1996-97
Overseas teams played for: Ginninderra West Belconnen, Australian Capital Territory
1992-93; Victoria University of Wellington CC, New Zealand 1997-98
Cricket superstitions: 'None'
Cricketers particularly admired: Merv Hughes, Allan Donald
Young players to look out for: Bilal Shafayat
Other sports played: Golf, snooker, football
Other sports followed: Football (Man City)
Relaxations: 'Good food, good wine and the odd game of golf'
Extras: Nottinghamshire Player of the Year 2002. Had the misfortune to be 'timed
out' v Durham UCCE at Trent Bridge 2003 (was suffering from groin injury)
Best batting: 41* Nottinghamshire v Northamptonshire, Northampton 2002
Best bowling: 7-54 Nottinghamshire v Northamptonshire, Trent Bridge 2002

2005 Season

	M	Inns	NO	Runs	HS	Avge	100s	50s	Ct	St	O	M	Runs	Wkts	Avge	Best	5wl	10wM
Test																		
All First	12	12	4	75	35	9.37	-	-	4	-	325.2	54	1293	49	26.38	6-76	3	-
1-Day Int																		
C & G	1	0	0	0	0	-	-	-	-	-	9.2	1	31	3	10.33	3-31	-	
tsL	7	4	3	10	4 *	10.00	-	-	-	-	49.5	4	280	13	21.53	4-41	-	
Twenty20	7	2	2	0	0 *	-	-	-	3	-	19.4	0	201	4	50.25	2-34	-	

Career Performances

	M	Inns	NO	Runs	HS	Avge	100s	50s	Ct	St	Balls	Runs	Wkts	Avge	Best	5wI	10wM
Test																	
All First	104	141	37	911	41 *	8.75	-	-	32	-	17910	10804	349	30.95	7-54	15	3
1-Day Int																	
C & G	12	5	3	21	11 *	10.50	-	-	1	-	657	433	14	30.92	3-10	-	
tsL	91	32	16	119	16 *	7.43	-	-	21	-	3874	3407	115	29.62	5-35	1	
Twenty20	13	3	2	0	0 *	0.00	-	-	4	-	202	339	9	37.66	2-30	-	

HARRISON, A. J.   Glamorgan

Name: <u>Adam</u> James Harrison
Role: Right-hand bat, right-arm
medium-fast bowler; all-rounder
Born: 30 October 1985, Newport, Gwent
Height: 6ft 2in **Weight:** 12st 13lbs
Nickname: Ads, Hazza, Ceedo
County debut: 2005
Strike rate: (career 61.00)
Parents: Stuart and Susan
Marital status: Single
Family links with cricket: 'Father played in
1970s for Glamorgan. Brother [David]
currently on staff'
Education: West Monmouth Comprehensive
School; St Albans High School
Qualifications: 10 GCSEs, 2 A-levels,
Level 1 coaching award
Off-season: 'Rehab from ankle surgery'
Overseas tours: West of England U15 to West Indies 2001; England U18 to Holland
2003; England U19 to Qatar 2003, to Bangladesh (U19 World Cup) 2003-04, to India
2004-05
Career highlights to date: 'Glamorgan debut 2005. First-class debut 2004 (MCC).
U19 World Cup 2004'
Cricket moments to forget: 'Losing semi-final of U19 World Cup 2004 against West
Indies'
Cricket superstitions: 'Left pad and boot first'
Cricketers particularly admired: Andrew Flintoff, Jacques Kallis, Steve Watkin,
Alex Wharf
Young players to look out for: Steve Davies, Will Bragg
Other sports played: Golf, squash (Wales U11-U13), football ('keeper for Football
Association of Wales 2002-03')

Other sports followed: Football (Manchester United)
Injuries: Out for two months at the end of the season with a posterior impingement (ankle spur)
Favourite band: Dire Straits
Relaxations: 'Socialising with friends; training'
Extras: BBC *Test Match Special* U15 Cricketer of the Year 2001. Sir John Hobbs Memorial Award 2001. Royal Variety Club Outstanding Newcomer Award 2002. NBC Denis Compton Award for the most promising young Glamorgan player 2003. Represented England U19 2003, 2004, 2005. Made first-class debut for MCC v Sussex at Lord's 2004. ECB National Academy 2004-05 (part-time)
Opinions on cricket: 'Too much cricket played. Tea breaks/lunch breaks 30 minutes each.'
Best batting: 34* MCC v Sussex, Lord's 2004
Best bowling: 2-65 MCC v Sussex, Lord's 2004

2005 Season

	M	Inns	NO	Runs	HS	Avge	100s	50s	Ct	St	O	M	Runs	Wkts	Avge	Best	5wI	10wM
Test																		
All First	1	1	0	0	0	0.00	-	-	-	-	15	2	54	1	54.00	1-54	-	-
1-Day Int																		
C & G																		
tsL																		
Twenty20	3	1	1	1	1 *	-	-	-	2	-	11.1	1	92	5	18.40	2-12	-	

Career Performances

	M	Inns	NO	Runs	HS	Avge	100s	50s	Ct	St	Balls	Runs	Wkts	Avge	Best	5wI	10wM
Test																	
All First	2	2	1	34	34 *	34.00	-	-	-	-	244	162	4	40.50	2-65	-	-
1-Day Int																	
C & G																	
tsL																	
Twenty20	3	1	1	1	1 *	-	-	-	2	-	67	92	5	18.40	2-12	-	

38. Which countries featured in the first ODI to result in a tie?

HARRISON, D. S.　　　Glamorgan

Name: <u>David</u> Stuart Harrison
Role: Right-hand bat, right-arm fast-medium bowler, occasional wicket-keeper; all-rounder
Born: 31 July 1981, Newport, Gwent
Height: 6ft 4½in **Weight:** 'under 15st!'
Nickname: Harry, Hazza, Roof, Butter, Des, Morehead, Desmond
County debut: 1999
50 wickets in a season: 1
Place in batting averages: 270th av. 11.77 (2004 203rd av. 21.94)
Place in bowling averages: 141st av. 53.19 (2004 35th av. 27.78)
Strike rate: 80.80 (career 60.08)
Parents: Stuart and Susan
Marital status: Single

Family links with cricket: 'Father played for Glamorgan in early 1970s. Brother Adam is currently on Glamorgan staff'
Education: West Monmouth Comprehensive, Pontypool; Usk College; 'touring with Cliff Dare!'
Qualifications: 8 GCSEs, 2 A-levels, Levels 1 and 2 coaching awards, qualified school caretaker
Career outside cricket: 'Hoping to start a part-time degree at university in September [2006]'
Off-season: 'Twelve-month contract with Glamorgan. MCC tour to Bahrain, December 2005'
Overseas tours: Gwent U15 to Cape Town 1996; Wales U16 to Jersey 1996, 1997; England U19 to Malaysia and (U19 World Cup) Sri Lanka 1999-2000; Glamorgan to Cape Town 2002; England A to Sri Lanka 2004-05; MCC to Bahrain 2005-06
Overseas teams played for: Claremont, Cape Town 2002 (one game during Glamorgan tour)
Career highlights to date: 'Glamorgan debut; winning NL at Canterbury 2002; selection for National Academy and A tour 2004-05; winning NL 2004'
Cricket moments to forget: 'Getting two pairs in two years at same ground (Rose Bowl)!'
Cricket superstitions: 'Try my best!'
Cricketers particularly admired: Mike Kasprowicz, Glenn McGrath, Shaun Pollock
Young players to look out for: 'Little brother, Cliff Dare!'
Other sports played: Squash (Wales junior squad), rugby (East Wales U11 caps), kick boxing

Other sports followed: Rugby (Newport Gwent Dragons), football (Man Utd)
Favourite band: Take That
Relaxations: 'Spending time with girlfriend; mountain walking with my dog, Jake; playing golf; Sky Plus; socialising'
Extras: Has played for Glamorgan from U12, becoming seventh youngest to play for 1st XI, aged 17. Represented England at U17, U18 and U19. Glamorgan Young Player of the Year 2003, 2004. ECB National Academy 2004-05
Opinions on cricket: 'We need more English-qualified players playing the game. Too many people playing who can't play for England.'
Best batting: 88 Glamorgan v Essex, Chelmsford 2004
Best bowling: 5-48 Glamorgan v Somerset, Swansea 2004

2005 Season

	M	Inns	NO	Runs	HS	Avge	100s	50s	Ct	St	O	M	Runs	Wkts	Avge	Best	5wI	10wM
Test																		
All First	17	29	2	318	75*	11.77	-	1	9	-	417.3	71	1649	31	53.19	5-117	1	-
1-Day Int																		
C & G	2	1	0	16	16	16.00	-	-	-	-	12	1	53	2	26.50	2-16	-	
tsL	13	7	1	62	18	10.33	-	-	2	-	99.4	11	389	21	18.52	5-33	1	
Twenty20	4	2	0	1	1	0.50	-	-	2	-	16	0	104	7	14.85	2-17	-	

Career Performances

	M	Inns	NO	Runs	HS	Avge	100s	50s	Ct	St	Balls	Runs	Wkts	Avge	Best	5wI	10wM
Test																	
All First	55	82	11	1060	88	14.92	-	3	20	-	8112	4813	135	35.65	5-48	5	-
1-Day Int																	
C & G	4	2	1	26	16	26.00	-	-	-	-	180	131	4	32.75	2-16	-	
tsL	39	24	7	207	37*	12.17	-	-	5	-	1618	1262	44	28.68	5-26	2	
Twenty20	6	3	0	5	4	1.66	-	-	2	-	126	165	8	20.62	2-17	-	

39. Only two Trinidadians have captained West Indies in ODIs. Brian Lara is one, but which former Cambridge University player was the other?

HARRISON, P. W.   Leicestershire

Name: <u>Paul</u> William Harrison
Role: Right-hand bat, wicket-keeper
Born: 22 May 1984, Cuckfield, West Sussex
Height: 6ft 2in **Weight:** 12st 12lbs
Nickname: Harry, Potter
County debut: 2005 (Warwickshire; *see Extras*)
Parents: Angela and Brian
Marital status: Single
Family links with cricket: 'Dad and uncle played league cricket in Sussex. Brother Leigh played YCs and 2nd XI at Sussex'
Education: The Forest School; College of Richard Collyer, Horsham; Loughborough University
Qualifications: 3 A-levels, 'studying for Geography and Sports Science degree', Level 1 coaching
Off-season: 'At Loughborough University or in Australia'
Overseas tours: Sussex Young Cricketers to Sri Lanka 2001, to South Africa 2003
Overseas teams played for: Tuart Hill, Perth 2002
Career highlights to date: 'Beating Worcestershire first team with Loughborough UCCE 2005'
Cricket moments to forget: 'Dropping a catch on the boundary for my club that would have got us promoted to the premier division'
Cricketers particularly admired: Mark Waugh, Alec Stewart, Adam Gilchrist
Young players to look out for: David Wainwright, Ryan Cummins
Other sports played: Football (county U18), golf (Mannings Heath; 7 handicap)
Other sports followed: Football (Arsenal, Brighton & Hove Albion)
Favourite band: Red Hot Chili Peppers
Relaxations: 'Playing Pro Evo, normally getting beaten by Chris Murtagh; listening to Danny Miller's music blaring from his room'
Extras: Sussex U19 Player of the Year. Played for Loughborough UCCE 2004, 2005. Played one first-class game for Warwickshire 2005. Played for Leicestershire v Somerset in the International Twenty20 Club Championship 2005 but has yet to appear for the county in first-class cricket or domestic one-day competition; is registered with Leicestershire for 2006
Opinions on cricket: 'Maybe ruling on Kolpaks [*see page 9*] and overseas players could be reviewed... Need to keep the youngsters interested and give them a chance if deserved now the game's status is on a high.'
Best batting: 54 LUCCE v Nottinghamshire, Trent Bridge 2005

2005 Season

	M	Inns	NO	Runs	HS	Avge	100s	50s	Ct	St	O	M	Runs	Wkts	Avge	Best	5wI	10wM
Test																		
All First	4	6	2	143	54	35.75	-	1	5	-								
1-Day Int																		
C & G																		
tsL																		
Twenty20																		

Career Performances

	M	Inns	NO	Runs	HS	Avge	100s	50s	Ct	St	Balls	Runs	Wkts	Avge	Best	5wI	10wM
Test																		
All First	7	10	3	220	54	31.42	-	1	9	-								
1-Day Int																		
C & G																		
tsL																		
Twenty20																		

HARVEY, I. J. Yorkshire

Name: <u>Ian</u> Joseph Harvey
Role: Right-hand bat, right-arm
fast-medium bowler
Born: 10 April 1972, Wonthaggi,
Victoria, Australia
Height: 5ft 9in **Weight:** 12st 8lbs
Nickname: Freak
County debut: 1999 (Gloucestershire),
2004 (Yorkshire)
County cap: 1999 (Gloucestershire),
2005 (Yorkshire)
1st-Class 200s: 1
Place in batting averages: 62nd av. 42.88
(2004 178th av. 24.81)
Place in bowling averages: 32nd av. 26.26
Strike rate: 57.70 (career 56.74)
Family links with cricket: Brothers play
club cricket in Australia
Education: Wonthaggi Technical College
Overseas tours: Australian Academy to New Zealand 1994-95; Australia to Sharjah
(Coca-Cola Cup) 1997-98, to New Zealand 1999-2000 (one-day series), to Kenya
(ICC Knockout Trophy) 2000-01, to India 2000-01 (one-day series), to England 2001

(one-day series), to South Africa 2001-02 (one-day series), to Africa (World Cup) 2002-03, to West Indies 2002-03 (one-day series), to India (TVS Cup) 2003-04, to Sri Lanka 2003-04 (one-day series), to Zimbabwe (one-day series) 2004, to Holland (Videocon Cup) 2004, to England (ICC Champions Trophy) 2004; Australia A to South Africa 2002-03; FICA World XI to New Zealand 2004-05

Overseas teams played for: Victoria 1993-94 – 2004-05; Cape Cobras 2005-06 –
Extras: The nickname 'Freak' is a reference to his brilliant fielding and was reportedly coined by Shane Warne. Attended Commonwealth Bank [Australian] Cricket Academy 1994. An overseas player with Gloucestershire 1999-2003. Man of the Match in the Carlton Series first final v West Indies at Sydney 2000-01 (47*/2-5). Won the Walter Lawrence Trophy 2001 for the season's fastest first-class hundred with his 61-ball century v Derbyshire at Bristol; also took 5-89 in Derbyshire's second innings. Has won numerous Australian and English domestic awards, including C&G Man of the Match in the final v Worcestershire at Lord's 2003 (2-37 and a 36-ball 61). Scored the first ever century in the Twenty20 (100* from 50 balls), v Warwickshire at Edgbaston 2003. An overseas player with Yorkshire 2004-05. One of *Wisden*'s Five Cricketers of the Year 2004
Best batting: 209* Yorkshire v Somerset, Headingley 2005
Best bowling: 8-101 Australia A v South Africa A, Adelaide 2002-03

2005 Season

	M	Inns	NO	Runs	HS	Avge	100s	50s	Ct	St	O	M	Runs	Wkts	Avge	Best	5wI	10wM
Test																		
All First	13	20	2	772	209 *	42.88	2	4	8	-	288.3	83	788	30	26.26	5-40	1	-
1-Day Int																		
C & G	3	3	0	131	74	43.66	-	2	1	-	27	1	138	5	27.60	3-41	-	
tsL	13	13	1	277	69	23.08	-	1	4	-	86	7	477	8	59.62	3-64	-	
Twenty20	8	8	0	316	109	39.50	1	2	3	-	26	0	204	8	25.50	2-8	-	

Career Performances

	M	Inns	NO	Runs	HS	Avge	100s	50s	Ct	St	Balls	Runs	Wkts	Avge	Best	5wI	10wM
Test																	
All First	149	246	23	7428	209 *	33.30	11	43	105	-	22982	11099	405	27.40	8-101	15	2
1-Day Int	73	51	11	715	48 *	17.87	-	-	17	-	3279	2577	85	30.31	4-16	-	
C & G	20	19	0	441	74	23.21	-	3	7	-	1056	702	41	17.12	5-23	1	
tsL	78	76	5	2020	96	28.45	-	10	21	-	3364	2473	132	18.73	5-19	4	
Twenty20	16	16	3	686	109	52.76	3	3	4	-	347	411	20	20.55	3-28	-	

HASSAN ADNAN   Derbyshire

Name: Mohammad Hassan Adnan Syed
Role: Right-hand bat, right-arm
off-spin bowler
Born: 15 May 1975, Lahore, Punjab
Height: 5ft 9in **Weight:** 12st 5lbs
Nickname: Hass
County debut: 2003
County cap: 2004
1000 runs in a season: 1
Place in batting averages: 159th av. 29.17
(2004 36th av. 51.11)
Strike rate: (career 133.00)
Parents: Hassan Adnan
Marital status: Single
Education: MAO College, Lahore
Overseas teams played for: Islamabad
1994-95, 2000-01; Gujranwala 1997-98 –
1998-99; Water and Power Development
Authority (WAPDA) 1997-98 – 2004-05

Career highlights to date: '140 v Notts at Derby; 113* v New Zealand [both 2004]'
Cricketers particularly admired: Steve Waugh
Young players to look out for: 'All players at DCCC!'
Other sports played: Badminton
Other sports followed: Badminton
Favourite music: Rock
Relaxations: Music, watching TV
Extras: Won two Man of the Match awards in the Tissot Cup domestic competition in
Pakistan. Scored century (113*) as Derbyshire beat New Zealanders in 50-over match
at Derby 2004. Scored 1000 (1247) County Championship runs in his first full season
2004. Derbyshire Supporters' Club Player of the Year 2004. Is England-qualified
Best batting: 191 Derbyshire v Somerset, Taunton 2005
Best bowling: 1-4 Derbyshire v Yorkshire, Derby 2004
             1-4 WAPDA v Allied Bank, Karachi 2004-05

2005 Season

	M	Inns	NO	Runs	HS	Avge	100s	50s	Ct	St	O	M	Runs	Wkts	Avge	Best	5wI	10wM
Test																		
All First	16	29	1	817	191	29.17	2	3	9	-	15	0	52	0	-	-	-	-
1-Day Int																		
C & G	2	2	0	9	6	4.50	-	-	-	-								
tsL	7	7	1	256	62	42.66	-	3	1	-								
Twenty20	2	1	0	26	26	26.00	-	-	-	-	2	0	18	0	-	-	-	

Career Performances

	M	Inns	NO	Runs	HS	Avge	100s	50s	Ct	St	Balls	Runs	Wkts	Avge	Best	5wI	10wM
Test																	
All First	98	163	20	5919	191	41.39	9	41	58	-	399	281	3	93.66	1-4	-	-
1-Day Int																	
C & G	3	3	0	87	78	29.00	-	1	-	-							
tsL	26	25	3	680	62	30.90	-	8	11	-	115	107	3	35.66	2-13	-	
Twenty20	6	5	0	87	32	17.40	-	-	2	-	36	49	1	49.00	1-18	-	

HAVELL, P. M. R.   Derbyshire

Name: Paul Matthew Roger Havell
Role: Left-hand bat, right-arm
fast-medium bowler
Born: 4 July 1980, Melbourne, Australia
Height: 6ft 3in **Weight:** 14st 2lbs
Nickname: Havler, Two Tone Malone,
Trigger, William Hill, Ladbrokes, Einstein
County debut: 2001 (Sussex),
2003 (Derbyshire)
Place in bowling averages: (2004 111th
av. 38.76)
Strike rate: (career 54.68)
Parents: Roger and Caroline
Marital status: Single
Family links with cricket: 'Brother Mark
played for Sussex U19 until his back had
problems'
Education: Warden Park School
Qualifications: 9 GCSEs, 1 A-level, Level 2 coach, Ambulance Driving Certificate
Overseas tours: Sussex U19 to Barbados 1997-98; Sussex to Grenada 2000-01
Overseas teams played for: East Doncaster CC, Australia 1998-99; Carlton CC,
Melbourne 2000-01; Fairfield-Liverpool, Sydney 2002-03
Career highlights to date: 'Going 10 overs without bowling a no-ball'
Cricket moments to forget: 'Bowling no-balls'
Cricket superstitions: 'Don't like being dropped'
Cricketers particularly admired: Viv Richards, David Gower, Ian Botham, David
Houghton, Karl Krikken, Mike Hendrick
Young players to look out for: 'Any from DCCC'
Extras: Sussex Young Cricketer of the Year 1995. Joined Derbyshire during 2003,
taking 4-129 on debut v South Africans at Derby. Released by Derbyshire at the end of
the 2005 season

Opinions on cricket: 'Work hard, play hard, Matthew Maynard. Keep cricket simple – it's not rocket surgery.'
Best batting: 13* Derbyshire v Yorkshire, Derby 2004
Best bowling: 4-75 Derbyshire v Durham, Riverside 2004

2005 Season

	M	Inns	NO	Runs	HS	Avge	100s	50s	Ct	St	O	M	Runs	Wkts	Avge	Best	5wI	10wM
Test																		
All First	3	5	4	10	6*	10.00	-	-	-	-	81.5	9	385	6	64.16	3-106	-	-
1-Day Int																		
C & G																			
tsL	1	0	0	0	0	-	-	-	-	-								
Twenty20																			

Career Performances

	M	Inns	NO	Runs	HS	Avge	100s	50s	Ct	St	Balls	Runs	Wkts	Avge	Best	5wI	10wM
Test																	
All First	16	21	15	52	13*	8.66	-	-	4	-	2242	1713	41	41.78	4-75	-	-
1-Day Int																	
C & G																		
tsL	6	3	0	8	4	2.66	-	-	-	-	137	116	3	38.66	3-28	-	
Twenty20	1	0	0	0	0	-	-	-	-	-	24	32	2	16.00	2-32	-	

HAYWARD, M.   Middlesex

Name: Mornantau (<u>Nantie</u>) Hayward
Role: Right-hand bat, right-arm fast bowler
Born: 6 March 1977, Uitenhage, South Africa
Height: 6ft 1in **Weight:** 13st 7lbs
County debut: 2003 (Worcestershire), 2004 (Middlesex)
County colours: 2003 (Worcestershire)
Test debut: 1999-2000
50 wickets in a season: 1
Place in bowling averages: (2004 42nd av. 29.61)
Strike rate: (career 52.89)
Parents: Maruis and Emmarencia
Wife and date of marriage: Marlize, 6 March 2004
Education: Daniel Pienaar Technical High
Overseas tours: South Africa U19 to India 1995-96; South Africa to England 1998, to India 1999-2000, to Sharjah (Coca-Cola Sharjah Cup) 1999-2000, to Sri Lanka 2000, to Australia (Super Challenge) 2000, to Australia 2001-02, to Sri Lanka 2004
Overseas teams played for: Eastern Province 1995-96 – 2003-04; Warriors 2004-05; Dolphins 2005-06 –

Cricket moments to forget: 'Tour to Sri Lanka' (*South Africa lost Test series 1-0 and ODI series 5-0 in 2004*)
Cricketers particularly admired: Allan Donald, Lance Klusener
Young players to look out for: Scott Newman
Other sports followed: Rugby (South Africa)
Relaxations: Fishing
Extras: Represented South Africa Schools 1995. Represented South Africa Academy 1997. Made Test debut in second Test v England at Port Elizabeth 1999-2000, taking 4-75 in England's first innings. Man of the Match award for his 4-31 in fifth Coca-Cola Cup match v India at Sharjah 1999-2000. One of *South African Cricket Annual*'s five Cricketers of the Year 2000. An overseas player with Worcestershire 2003, taking 5-70 (9-165 in match) on Championship debut v Hampshire at Worcester; an overseas player with Middlesex 2004-05
Best batting: 55* Eastern Province v Boland, Port Elizabeth 1997-98
Best bowling: 6-31 Eastern Province v Easterns, Port Elizabeth 1999-2000

2005 Season

	M	Inns	NO	Runs	HS	Avge	100s	50s	Ct	St	O	M	Runs	Wkts	Avge	Best	5wI	10wM
Test																		
All First	4	5	3	20	12*	10.00	-	-	1	-	94	9	380	8	47.50	2-23	-	-
1-Day Int																		
C & G																		
tsL	2	1	1	6	6*	-	-	-	1	-	13.3	0	54	4	13.50	3-33	-	
Twenty20																		

Career Performances

	M	Inns	NO	Runs	HS	Avge	100s	50s	Ct	St	Balls	Runs	Wkts	Avge	Best	5wI	10wM
Test	16	17	7	66	14	6.60	-	-	4	-	2821	1609	54	29.79	5-56	1	-
All First	114	129	47	926	55*	11.29	-	1	32	-	20524	11082	388	28.56	6-31	9	2
1-Day Int	21	5	1	12	4	3.00	-	-	4	-	993	858	21	40.85	4-31	-	
C & G	7	1	0	4	4	4.00	-	-	2	-	330	256	14	18.28	5-49	1	
tsL	20	5	4	20	11	20.00	-	-	2	-	802	651	28	23.25	4-21	-	
Twenty20	3	1	0	2	2	2.00	-	-	-	-	62	86	3	28.66	3-21	-	

HEATHER, S. A.

Sussex

Name: Sean Andrew Heather
Role: Right-hand bat, right-arm medium bowler
Born: 5 February 1982, Chichester
Height: 6ft **Weight:** 12st
Nickname: Seany, Badger, Road Kill, Lucky
County debut: 2005
Parents: Andrew and Carole
Marital status: Single
Education: Chichester High School for Boys; Chichester High School Sixth Form College
Qualifications: 4 GCSEs, Advanced GNVQ Leisure and Tourism
Career outside cricket: Computer analyst for West Sussex County Council
Off-season: Playing cricket in New Zealand
Overseas teams played for: Swanbourne, Perth 2000-01; Sydenham, Christchurch 2005
Career highlights to date: 'Breaking the Sussex Premier League's run-scoring record in 2004, scoring 1086 runs in the season'
Cricketers particularly admired: Darren Gough, James Kirtley
Young players to look out for: Luke Wright
Other sports played: Golf, football
Other sports followed: Football (Liverpool FC)
Injuries: Out during March/April 2005 with a side strain
Favourite band: Queen
Relaxations: Playing snooker
Extras: *Wisden* Cockspur Club Cricketer of the Year 2004
Best batting: 7 Sussex v Bangladeshis, Hove 2005

2005 Season

	M	Inns	NO	Runs	HS	Avge	100s	50s	Ct	St	O	M	Runs	Wkts	Avge	Best	5wI	10wM
Test																		
All First	1	1	0	7	7	7.00	-	-	-	-								
1-Day Int																		
C & G																		
tsL																		
Twenty20																		

	M	Inns	NO	Runs	HS	Avge	100s	50s	Ct	St	Balls	Runs	Wkts	Avge	Best	5wI	10wM
Test																	
All First	1	1	0	7	7	7.00	-	-	-	-							
1-Day Int																	
C & G																	
tsL																	
Twenty20																	

HEGG, W. K.   Lancashire

Name: Warren Kevin Hegg
Role: Right-hand bat, wicket-keeper
Born: 23 February 1968, Manchester
Height: 5ft 9in   **Weight:** 12st 10lbs
Nickname: Chucky
County debut: 1986
County cap: 1989
Benefit: 1999 (£178,000)
Test debut: 1998-99
50 dismissals in a season: 6
Place in batting averages: 118th av. 33.46
(2004 149th av. 29.42)
Parents: Kevin (deceased) and Glenda
Wife and date of marriage: Joanne,
29 October 1994
Children: Chloe Louise, 13 November 1998
Family links with cricket: Brother Martin
local league cricketer
Education: Unsworth High School; Stand College, Whitefield
Qualifications: 5 O-levels, 7 CSEs, qualified coach
Overseas tours: NCA North U19 to Bermuda 1985; England YC to Sri Lanka
1986-87, to Australia (U19 World Cup) 1987-88; England A to Pakistan and Sri Lanka
1990-91, to Australia 1996-97; England to Australia 1998-99, to India and New
Zealand 2001-02
Overseas teams played for: Sheffield, Tasmania 1988-90, 1992-93
Cricketers particularly admired: Ian Botham, Alan Knott, Bob Taylor,
Gehan Mendis, Ian Healy
Other sports played: Football (Old Standians)
Other sports followed: Rugby league (Salford City Reds), football (Man United)
Relaxations: 'Golf, golf, golf'
Extras: Became youngest player for 30 years to score a century for Lancashire with

his 130 v Northamptonshire at Northampton in 1987 aged 19 (in his fourth first-class game). Took 11 catches in match v Derbyshire at Chesterfield 1989, equalling world first-class record. Wombwell Cricket Lovers' Society joint Wicket-keeper of the Year 1993. Vice-captain of Lancashire 1999 and 2001. Lancashire Player of the Year 2001. Lancashire captain 2002-04, the first wicket-keeper to hold the post in an official capacity. Retired at the end of the 2005 season

Best batting: 134 Lancashire v Leicestershire, Old Trafford 1996

2005 Season

	M	Inns	NO	Runs	HS	Avge	100s	50s	Ct	St	O	M	Runs	Wkts	Avge	Best	5wI	10wM
Test																		
All First	15	21	6	502	77 *	33.46	-	3	41	5								
1-Day Int																		
C & G	4	2	0	3	3	1.50	-	-	6	2								
tsL	14	11	4	103	33 *	14.71	-	-	13	2								
Twenty20	10	5	2	19	11 *	6.33	-	-	5	2								

Career Performances

	M	Inns	NO	Runs	HS	Avge	100s	50s	Ct	St	Balls	Runs	Wkts	Avge	Best	5wI	10wM
Test	2	4	0	30	15	7.50	-	-	8	-							
All First	348	504	99	11302	134	27.90	7	55	857	94	6	7	0	-	-	-	-
1-Day Int																	
C & G	54	30	2	434	60	15.50	-	1	67	9							
tsL	264	165	59	2118	54	19.98	-	2	279	44							
Twenty20	20	13	4	104	45	11.55	-	-	10	9							

HEMP, D. L.   Glamorgan

Name: <u>David</u> Lloyd Hemp
Role: Left-hand bat
Born: 15 November 1970, Hamilton, Bermuda
Height: 6ft 1in   **Weight:** 12st 7lbs
Nickname: Hempy, Mad Dog, Scraps
County debut: 1991 (Glamorgan), 1997 (Warwickshire)
County cap: 1994 (Glamorgan), 1997 (Warwickshire)
1000 runs in a season: 5
Place in batting averages: 58th av. 44.16 (2004 59th av. 44.80)
Strike rate: (career 60.70)
Parents: Clive and Elisabeth
Wife and date of marriage: Angela, 16 March 1996
Children: Cameron, January 2002
Family links with cricket: Father and brother both played for Swansea CC
Education: Olchfa Comprehensive School; Millfield School; Birmingham University

Qualifications: 5 O-levels, 2 A-levels, MBA, Level III coaching award
Career outside cricket: PR/marketing; coaching
Off-season: 'Spending four months working with the Bermuda Cricket Board'
Overseas tours: Welsh Cricket Association U18 to Barbados 1986; Welsh Schools U19 to Australia 1987-88; Glamorgan to Trinidad 1990; South Wales Cricket Association to New Zealand and Australia 1991-92; England A to India 1994-95
Overseas teams played for: Crusaders, Durban 1992-98
Career highlights to date: '99* England A v India A, Calcutta "Test" match 1994-95'
Cricket moments to forget: 'None'
Cricket superstitions: 'None'
Cricketers particularly admired: David Gower, Viv Richards
Young players to look out for: Moeen Ali, Graham Wagg
Other sports played: Football, golf
Other sports followed: Football (Swansea City, West Ham United)
Favourite band: Manic Street Preachers, Stereophonics
Relaxations: Golf, reading
Extras: In 1989 scored 104* and 101* for Welsh Schools U19 v Scottish Schools U19 and 120 and 102* v Irish Schools U19. Scored 258* for Wales v MCC 1991. Scored two 100s (138/114*) v Hampshire at Southampton 1997. Vice-captain of Warwickshire 2001. Left Warwickshire in the 2001-02 off-season and rejoined Glamorgan for 2002. Scored 88-ball 102 v Surrey at The Oval in the C&G 2002 as Glamorgan made 429 in reply to Surrey's 438-5. Won Glamorgan's Byron Denning Award 2004. Glamorgan Player of the Year 2005. Glamorgan senior pro
Best batting: 186* Warwickshire v Worcestershire, Edgbaston 2001
Best bowling: 3-23 Glamorgan v South Africa A, Cardiff 1996

2005 Season

	M	Inns	NO	Runs	HS	Avge	100s	50s	Ct	St	O	M	Runs	Wkts	Avge	Best	5wI	10wM
Test																		
All First	16	32	1	1369	171 *	44.16	3	8	9	-								
1-Day Int																		
C & G	2	2	0	57	37	28.50	-	-	-	-								
tsL	14	12	5	400	84 *	57.14	-	4	4	-								
Twenty20	7	6	0	85	40	14.16	-	-	3	-								

Career Performances

	M	Inns	NO	Runs	HS	Avge	100s	50s	Ct	St	Balls	Runs	Wkts	Avge	Best	5wl	10wM
Test																	
All First	218	370	34	12066	186 *	35.91	22	69	142	-	1032	778	17	45.76	3-23	-	-
1-Day Int																	
C & G	28	27	3	997	112	41.54	4	3	6	-	48	43	1	43.00	1-40	-	
tsL	165	140	23	2795	84 *	23.88	-	14	68	-	86	97	6	16.16	3-11	-	
Twenty20	19	18	2	377	74	23.56	-	1	10	-							

HENDERSON, C. W.   Leicestershire

Name: <u>Claude</u> William Henderson
Role: Right-hand bat, left-arm spin bowler
Born: 14 June 1972, Worcester, South Africa
Height: 6ft 2in **Weight:** 14st
Nickname: Hendo, Hendy
County debut: 2004
County cap: 2004
Test debut: 2001-02
Place in batting averages: 188th av. 24.29
(2004 241st av. 16.38)
Place in bowling averages: 116th av. 42.90
(2004 83rd av. 35.20)
Strike rate: 97.69 (career 73.28)
Parents: Henry and Susan
Wife and date of marriage: Nicci,
29 March 2003
Family links with cricket: Brother James an
opening batsman for Free State; father played
league cricket and for Boland B
Education: Worcester High School
Qualifications: 2 A-levels, Level 2 coaching
Overseas tours: South Africa A to Sri Lanka 1998; South Africa to Zimbabwe 2001-02, to Australia 2001-02
Overseas teams played for: Boland 1990-91 – 1997-98; Western Province 1998-99-2003-04
Career highlights to date: 'Playing for South Africa against Australia at Adelaide 2001-02 (seven wickets in the match)'
Cricket moments to forget: 'Losing to Devon in the C&G Trophy [2004]'
Cricketers particularly admired: Jacques Kallis, Shane Warne
Other sports played: Golf, fishing
Other sports followed: Rugby (South Africa, Western Province, Leicester Tigers)

Favourite band: U2

Relaxations: 'Sightseeing, cinema; spending time with family and friends'

Extras: Has won several match awards in South African domestic cricket. Scored fifty (63) and recorded five-wicket innings return (5-28) on Championship debut for Leicestershire v Glamorgan at Leicester 2004; recorded a further five-wicket return (5-24) on one-day debut v Yorkshire at Headingley in the totesport League 2004. Is not considered an overseas player

Best batting: 71 Western Province v KwaZulu-Natal, Cape Town 2003-04

Best bowling: 7-57 Boland v Eastern Province, Paarl 1994-95

2005 Season

	M	Inns	NO	Runs	HS	Avge	100s	50s	Ct	St	O	M	Runs	Wkts	Avge	Best	5wI	10wM
Test																		
All First	15	21	4	413	55	24.29	-	2	6	-	537.2	121	1416	33	42.90	5-63	1	-
1-Day Int																		
C & G	2	2	1	27	14 *	27.00	-	-	1	-	11.1	0	60	3	20.00	2-46	-	
tsL	15	8	2	49	19 *	8.16	-	-	3	-	92.1	6	389	13	29.92	3-25	-	
Twenty20	9	4	1	15	9 *	5.00	-	-	1	-	16.1	0	123	4	30.75	2-24	-	

Career Performances

	M	Inns	NO	Runs	HS	Avge	100s	50s	Ct	St	Balls	Runs	Wkts	Avge	Best	5wI	10wM
Test	7	7	0	65	30	9.28	-	-	2	-	1962	929	22	42.22	4-116	-	-
All First	146	196	48	2487	71	16.80	-	7	56	-	37155	15448	507	30.46	7-57	16	-
1-Day Int	4	0	0	0	0	-	-	-	-	-	217	132	7	18.85	4-17	-	
C & G	6	4	1	61	32	20.33	-	-	3	-	307	170	10	17.00	2-8	-	
tsL	33	18	6	113	27	9.41	-	-	3	-	1208	862	41	21.02	5-24	1	
Twenty20	16	7	2	19	9 *	3.80	-	-	4	-	217	261	13	20.07	3-26	-	

40. Which three wicket-keepers have captained Pakistan in ODIs?

HICK, G. A.   Worcestershire

Name: <u>Graeme</u> Ashley Hick
Role: Right-hand bat, off-spin bowler
Born: 23 May 1966, Harare, Zimbabwe
Height: 6ft 3in **Weight:** 14st 4lbs
Nickname: Hicky, Ash
County debut: 1984
County cap: 1986; colours 2002
Benefit: 1999; testimonial 2006
Test debut: 1991
1000 runs in a season: 18
1st-Class 200s: 13
1st-Class 300s: 2
1st-Class 400s: 1
Place in batting averages: 107th av. 34.51
(2004 9th av. 63.56)
Strike rate: (career 90.03)
Parents: John and Eve
Wife and date of marriage: Jackie,
5 October 1991
Children: Lauren Amy, 12 September 1992; Jordan Ashley, 5 September 1995
Family links with cricket: Father has served on Zimbabwe Cricket Union Board of
Control and played representative cricket in Zimbabwe
Education: Prince Edward Boys' High School, Zimbabwe
Qualifications: 4 O-levels, NCA coaching award
Overseas tours: Zimbabwe to England (World Cup) 1983, to Sri Lanka 1983-84, to
England 1985; England to Australia and New Zealand (World Cup) 1991-92, to India
and Sri Lanka 1992-93, to West Indies 1993-94, to Australia 1994-95, to South Africa
1995-96, to India and Pakistan (World Cup) 1995-96, to Sharjah (Akai Singer
Champions Trophy) 1997-98, to West Indies 1997-98 (one-day series), to Bangladesh
(Wills International Cup) 1998-99, to Australia 1998-99, to Sharjah (Coca-Cola Cup)
1998-99, to South Africa and Zimbabwe 1999-2000 (one-day series), to Kenya (ICC
Knockout Trophy) 2000-01, to Pakistan and Sri Lanka 2000-01; FICA World XI to
New Zealand 2004-05
Overseas teams played for: Old Hararians, Zimbabwe 1982-90; Northern Districts,
New Zealand 1987-89; Queensland 1990-91; Auckland 1997-98
Cricketers particularly admired: Steve Waugh, Glenn McGrath
Other sports played: Golf ('relaxation'), hockey (played for Zimbabwe)
Other sports followed: Football (Liverpool FC), golf, tennis, squash, hockey
Extras: One of *Wisden*'s Five Cricketers of the Year 1987. In 1988 he made 405* v
Somerset at Taunton and scored 1000 first-class runs by the end of May. Qualified to
play for England 1991. Scored hundredth first-class 100 (132) v Sussex at Worcester

1998; at the age of 32, he became the second youngest player after Wally Hammond to score one hundred 100s. Won ODI Man of the Match awards v Zimbabwe, the country of his birth, for his match-winning 87* at Bulawayo and his 80 and 5-33 at Harare, February 2000. Scored 200* v Durham at Riverside 2001, in the process achieving the feat of having recorded centuries against each of the other 17 counties, both home and away. Captain of Worcestershire 2000-02. Became leading run-scorer in the history of the one-day league, v Middlesex at Lord's 2005. Took eight catches in match v Essex at Chelmsford 2005, equalling the Worcestershire record. Scored 128th career first-class century v Essex at Worcester 2005 to draw level with Graham Gooch in ninth spot on the all-time first-class century-makers' list

Best batting: 405* Worcestershire v Somerset, Taunton 1988
Best bowling: 5-18 Worcestershire v Leicestershire, Worcester 1995

2005 Season

	M	Inns	NO	Runs	HS	Avge	100s	50s	Ct	St	O	M	Runs	Wkts	Avge	Best	5wI	10wM
Test																		
All First	16	29	2	932	176	34.51	2	5	36	-								
1-Day Int																		
C & G	2	1	0	22	22	22.00	-	-	1	-								
tsL	15	14	1	279	52	21.46	-	1	3	-								
Twenty20	7	7	0	239	87	34.14	-	3	3	-								

Career Performances

	M	Inns	NO	Runs	HS	Avge	100s	50s	Ct	St	Balls	Runs	Wkts	Avge	Best	5wI	10wM
Test	65	114	6	3383	178	31.32	6	18	90	-	3057	1306	23	56.78	4-126	-	-
All First	486	806	78	38437	405 *	52.79	128	147	633	-	20889	10308	232	44.43	5-18	5	1
1-Day Int	120	118	15	3846	126 *	37.33	5	27	64	-	1236	1026	30	34.20	5-33	1	
C & G	57	55	8	2359	172 *	50.19	7	10	28	-	1283	817	24	34.04	4-54	-	
tsL	274	262	39	9243	141 *	41.44	15	64	88	-	2954	2564	88	29.13	4-21	-	
Twenty20	13	13	1	438	116 *	36.50	1	4	6	-							

41. Which veteran of 52 ODIs as an umpire
played for Derbyshire 1973-75?

HILDRETH, J. C.　　　　　　　　　Somerset

Name: <u>James</u> Charles Hildreth
Role: Right-hand bat, right-arm medium
bowler; all-rounder
Born: 9 September 1984, Milton Keynes
Height: 5ft 10in **Weight:** 12st
Nickname: Hildy, Hildz
County debut: 2003
Place in batting averages: 86th av. 37.48
(2004 71st av. 42.22)
Strike rate: (career 96.00)
Parents: David and Judy
Marital status: Single
Family links with cricket: 'Dad played
county league cricket in Kent and Northants'
Education: Millfield School
Qualifications: 10 GCSEs, 3 A-levels, ECB
Level 1 coaching
Overseas tours: 'West' to West Indies 1999,
2000; Millfield to Sri Lanka 2001; England U19 to Bangladesh (U19 World Cup)
2003-04
Career highlights to date: 'Maiden first-class hundred [101] v Durham 2004; 210 for
England U19 v Bangladesh U19 2004; first-class hundred [108] v Notts 2004'
Cricket moments to forget: 'Being bowled first ball by Shoaib Akhtar'
Cricket superstitions: 'Left pad before right when getting padded up'
Other sports played: Hockey (West of England), squash (South of England), tennis
(South of England), football (England Independent Schools, Luton Town), rugby
(Millfield)
Other sports followed: Football (Charlton Athletic)
Favourite band: Jack Johnson
Relaxations: Travelling, snowboarding, music
Extras: NBC Denis Compton Award for the most promising young Somerset player
2003. Scored maiden first-class century (101) plus 72 in the second innings v Durham
at Taunton 2004 in his second Championship match. Represented England U19 v
Bangladesh U19 2004, scoring 210 in second 'Test' at Taunton. Cricket Society's Most
Promising Young Cricketer of the Year 2004. ECB National Academy 2004-05 (part-
time)
Best batting: 125* Somerset v Essex, Colchester 2005
Best bowling: 2-39 Somerset v Hampshire, Taunton 2004

2005 Season

	M	Inns	NO	Runs	HS	Avge	100s	50s	Ct	St	O	M	Runs	Wkts	Avge	Best	5wI	10wM
Test																		
All First	16	29	4	937	125 *	37.48	2	6	15	-	15	0	73	0	-		-	-
1-Day Int																		
C & G	1	1	0	1	1	1.00	-	-	1	-								
tsL	18	17	5	427	75 *	35.58	-	2	4	-	2	0	11	0	-		-	-
Twenty20	11	11	1	203	71	20.30	-	1	3	-	18.4	0	148	10	14.80	3-24	-	

Career Performances

	M	Inns	NO	Runs	HS	Avge	100s	50s	Ct	St	Balls	Runs	Wkts	Avge	Best	5wI	10wM
Test																	
All First	30	51	6	1706	125 *	37.91	4	11	27	-	192	149	2	74.50	2-39	-	-
1-Day Int																	
C & G	2	2	0	5	4	2.50	-	-	2	-	36	44	1	44.00	1-44	-	
tsL	41	39	7	931	85	29.09	-	4	13	-	18	17	0	-		-	-
Twenty20	16	16	1	348	71	23.20	-	3	4	-	112	148	10	14.80	3-24	-	

HODD, A. J.   Sussex

Name: Andrew John Hodd
Role: Right-hand bat, wicket-keeper
Born: 12 January 1984, Chichester
Height: 5ft 9½in **Weight:** 11st 8lbs
Nickname: Hoddy
County debut: 2003 (Sussex; *see Extras*),
2005 (Surrey)
Parents: Karen and Adrian
Marital status: Single
Family links with cricket: 'Long line of
enthusiastic club cricketers'
Education: Bexhill High School; Bexhill
College; 'short stint at Loughborough Uni'
Qualifications: 9 GCSEs, 4 A-levels, Level 1
coach
Career outside cricket: Coaching
Off-season: 'At home working hard on my
game!'
Overseas tours: South of England U14 to West Indies 1998; Sussex Academy to Cape
Town 1999, to Sri Lanka 2001; England U17 to Australia 2000-01; England U19 to
Australia 2002-03
Career highlights to date: 'Achieving a contract with Sussex'

Cricket moments to forget: '"And we forget because we must" – Matthew Arnold, or was it Geoff Arnold?'
Cricket superstitions: 'Too many! Must drink coffee the morning of a game'
Cricketers particularly admired: David Hussey, Matt Prior
Young players to look out for: Luke Wright, Ollie Rayner, Ben Brown
Other sports played: Golf, football, boxing
Other sports followed: Football (Brighton & Hove Albion)
Injuries: Out for two weeks with a subluxed right shoulder
Favourite band: Hard-Fi
Relaxations: 'Cinema, DVDs, gym, going out'
Extras: Played for England U14, U15, U17 and U19. Graham Kersey Trophy, Bunbury 1999. Several junior Player of the Year awards at Sussex. Sussex County League Young Player of the Year 2002. Played for Sussex v West Indies A in a limited overs fixture at Hove 2002 but did not appear for the county in first-class cricket or one-day competition until 2003. Sussex 2nd XI Player of the Year 2003. Joined Surrey for 2004, leaving at the end of the 2005 season to rejoin Sussex for 2006
Opinions on cricket: 'Winning the Ashes must mean that many things about the game in this country are right. I hope the game can build on this success in a positive way.'
Best batting: 57* Surrey v Bangladesh A, The Oval 2005

2005 Season

	M	Inns	NO	Runs	HS	Avge	100s	50s	Ct	St	O	M	Runs	Wkts	Avge	Best	5wl	10wM
Test																		
All First	1	2	2	112	57 *	-		-	2	1	-							
1-Day Int																		
C & G																		
tsL	1	1	0	9	9	9.00	-	-	-	-								
Twenty20	1	0	0	0	0	-	-	-	-	-								

Career Performances

	M	Inns	NO	Runs	HS	Avge	100s	50s	Ct	St	Balls	Runs	Wkts	Avge	Best	5wl	10wM
Test																	
All First	2	2	2	112	57 *	-		-	2	3	-						
1-Day Int																	
C & G	1	1	0	1	1	1.00	-		-	1	-						
tsL	1	1	0	9	9	9.00	-		-	-	-						
Twenty20	1	0	0	0	0	-	-		-	-	-						

HODGE, B. J.   Lancashire

Name: Bradley (<u>Brad</u>) John Hodge
Role: Right-hand bat, right-arm
off-spin bowler
Born: 29 December 1974, Sandringham,
Melbourne, Australia
Height: 5ft 7½in **Weight:** 12st 8lbs
Nickname: Bunk
County debut: 2002 (Durham), 2003
(Leicestershire), 2005 (Lancashire)
County cap: 2003 (Leicestershire)
1000 runs in a season: 2
1st-Class 200s: 6
1st-Class 300s: 1
Place in batting averages: 122nd av. 32.50
(2004 10th av. 61.92)
Place in bowling averages: (2004 93rd
av. 36.50)
Strike rate: (career 73.32)
Parents: John and Val
Wife: Megan

Education: St Bede's College, Mentone; Deakin University
Overseas tours: Australia U19 to New Zealand 1992-93; Commonwealth Bank
[Australian] Cricket Academy to Zimbabwe 1998-99; Australia A to Los Angeles
(Moov America Challenge) 1999, to Pakistan 2005-06; Australia to India 2004-05, to
New Zealand 2004-05, to England 2005, to New Zealand (one-day series) 2005-06
Overseas teams played for: Victoria 1993-94 –
Cricketers particularly admired: Allan Border, Dennis Lillee, Dean Jones,
Sachin Tendulkar
Other sports played/followed: Australian Rules football (Melbourne), golf, tennis,
soccer, skiing
Extras: Attended Commonwealth Bank [Australian] Cricket Academy 1993. Leading
run-scorer for Victoria in the Sheffield Shield in his first season (1993-94) with 903
runs (av. 50.16). Victoria's Pura Cup Player of the Year 2000-01 and 2001-02; winner
of the national Pura Cup Player of the Season Award 2001-02 (jointly with Jimmy
Maher of Queensland). Was Durham's overseas player 2002 from late July; an
overseas player with Leicestershire 2003-04. Scored 202* v Loughborough UCCE at
Leicester 2003, in the process sharing with Darren Maddy (229*) in a record
partnership for any wicket for Leicestershire (436*). His 302* v Nottinghamshire at
Trent Bridge 2003 is the highest individual first-class score by a Leicestershire player.
ING Cup Player of the Year 2003-04. Man of the Match in the Twenty20 Cup final at
Edgbaston 2004 for his 53-ball 77*. Appointed vice-captain of Leicestershire for 2004;

assumed the captaincy in July on the resignation of Phillip DeFreitas. An overseas player with Lancashire since 2005

Best batting: 302* Leicestershire v Nottinghamshire, Trent Bridge 2003
Best bowling: 4-17 Australia A v West Indians, Hobart 2000-01
Stop press: Made Test debut in the second Test v West Indies at Hobart 2005-06 and ODI debut v New Zealand in Auckland 2005-06. Man of the Match in the first Test v South Africa at Perth 2005-06 (41/203*)

2005 Season

	M	Inns	NO	Runs	HS	Avge	100s	50s	Ct	St	O	M	Runs	Wkts	Avge	Best	5wI	10wM
Test																		
All First	8	13	1	390	110 *	32.50	1	1	7	-	17	3	35	1	35.00	1-14	-	-
1-Day Int																		
C & G	1	1	0	82	82	82.00	-	1	-	-								
tsL	4	4	0	46	27	11.50	-	-	-	-								
Twenty20	6	6	2	330	90 *	82.50	-	3	4	-	19	0	137	13	10.53	4-17	-	

Career Performances

	M	Inns	NO	Runs	HS	Avge	100s	50s	Ct	St	Balls	Runs	Wkts	Avge	Best	5wI	10wM
Test																	
All First	164	292	26	12400	302 *	46.61	37	46	92	-	4515	2581	62	41.62	4-17	-	-
1-Day Int																	
C & G	5	5	0	107	82	21.40	-	1	3	-	30	22	0	-	-	-	-
tsL	40	38	3	1170	154 *	33.42	2	4	17	-	558	472	12	39.33	3-34	-	
Twenty20	19	19	3	854	97	53.37	-	8	11	-	222	265	19	13.94	4-17	-	

HODGKINSON, R.   Nottinghamshire

Name: Richard Hodgkinson
Role: Right-hand bat, right-arm fast bowler
Born: 9 December 1983, Sutton-in-Ashfield
Height: 6ft 4in **Weight:** 14st
Nickname: Hodgy
County debut: 2005 (one-day)
Parents: Neil and Pam
Marital status: Single
Education: Kirkby Centre; West Notts College
Qualifications: 9 GCSEs, BTEC First Diploma in Sports Science, Level 1 coach
Career outside cricket: Assistant greenkeeper at Oakland Park GC, Bucks
Off-season: 'Working; training for coming season'
Overseas tours: Nottinghamshire to Johannesburg 2003
Overseas teams played for: Mildura Settlers and Claremont-Nedlands (both Australia) 2000

Career highlights to date: 'Making first-team debut against Worcestershire on Sky Sports, taking 1-42 from eight overs'
Cricket moments to forget: 'Being bowled first ball by Chaminda Vaas in the same game'
Cricketers particularly admired: Ryan Sidebottom, Paul Franks
Other sports played: Football (had trials for Nottingham Forest and Mansfield Town), golf
Other sports followed: Football (Mansfield Town)
Injuries: Out for the first half of the season with a spur on the left ankle
Favourite band: Foo Fighters, Keane, Notorious BIG
Relaxations: 'Swimming, gym, reading, listening to music, walking the dogs'

Extras: Played for Nottinghamshire Board XI in the 2002 C&G. Attended Dennis Lillee's fast-bowling clinic in Chennai (Madras) 2004, 2005. Left Nottinghamshire at the end of the 2005 season
Opinions on cricket: 'Too much cricket. Not enough breaks in the season; more time to rest.'

2005 Season

	M	Inns	NO	Runs	HS	Avge	100s	50s	Ct	St	O	M	Runs	Wkts	Avge	Best	5wI	10wM
Test																		
All First																		
1-Day Int																		
C & G																		
tsL	1	1	0	0	0	0.00	-	-	1	-	8	0	42	1	42.00	1-42	-	
Twenty20																		

Career Performances

	M	Inns	NO	Runs	HS	Avge	100s	50s	Ct	St	Balls	Runs	Wkts	Avge	Best	5wI	10wM
Test																	
All First																	
1-Day Int																	
C & G	1	0	0	0	0	-	-	-	-	-	48	36	2	18.00	2-36	-	
tsL	1	1	0	0	0	0.00	-	-	1	-	48	42	1	42.00	1-42	-	
Twenty20																	

HODNETT, G. P. Gloucestershire

Name: <u>Grant</u> Phillip Hodnett
Role: Right-hand top-order bat, right-arm
leg-spin bowler, occasional wicket-keeper
Born: 17 August 1982, Johannesburg,
South Africa
Height: 6ft 4in **Weight:** 14st
Nickname: Hodders, Hoddy
County debut: 2005
County cap: 2005
Parents: Phillip and Julia
Marital status: Single
Family links with cricket: 'Brother Kyle is
on the MCC YC staff'
Education: Northwood High School, Durban
Qualifications: Matriculation, ECB Level 1
coach, GFA Fitness Instructor
Career outside cricket: 'Personal trainer;
cricket coach; sports nutrition sales'
Overseas tours: Gloucestershire to South Africa 2006
Overseas teams played for: Durban Collegians 2005-06
Career highlights to date: 'First-class and Championship debut against Warwickshire
at Edgbaston 2005'
Cricket moments to forget: 'I've forgotten it already'
Cricket superstitions: 'None'
Cricketers particularly admired: Hansie Cronje, Jonty Rhodes, Steve Waugh,
Andrew Flintoff, Michael Atherton
Young players to look out for: Kyle Hodnett, Neil Dexter, Steve Snell
Other sports played: Golf, squash, bodyboarding, football, rugby
Other sports followed: Rugby union (England), football (Newcastle United)
Injuries: Out for six weeks with a fractured right hand
Favourite band: Blink-182
Relaxations: 'Going to gym; swimming; reading sports magazines'
Extras: Represented KwaZulu-Natal Schools. West of England Premier League
Batsman of the Year 2004. Is not considered an overseas player
Opinions on cricket: 'I am in favour of the more traditional game of cricket, although
I can understand the need to bring the game to the people – i.e. Twenty20 – from an
entertainment and financial point of view.'
Best batting: 49 Gloucestershire v Warwickshire, Edgbaston 2005

2005 Season

	M	Inns	NO	Runs	HS	Avge	100s	50s	Ct	St	O	M	Runs	Wkts	Avge	Best	5wl	10wM
Test																		
All First	1	2	0	59	49	29.50	-	-	1	-								
1-Day Int																		
C & G																		
tsL																		
Twenty20																		

Career Performances

	M	Inns	NO	Runs	HS	Avge	100s	50s	Ct	St	Balls	Runs	Wkts	Avge	Best	5wl	10wM
Test																		
All First	1	2	0	59	49	29.50	-	-	1	-								
1-Day Int																		
C & G																		
tsL																		
Twenty20																		

HOGG, K. W. Lancashire

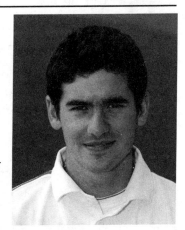

Name: Kyle William Hogg
Role: Left-hand bat, right-arm
fast-medium bowler; all-rounder
Born: 2 July 1983, Birmingham
Height: 6ft 4in **Weight:** 13st
Nickname: Boss, Hoggy
County debut: 2001
Place in batting averages: (2004 267th
av. 10.28)
Strike rate: (career 65.89)
Parents: Sharon and William
Marital status: Single
Family links with cricket: Father played for
Lancashire and Warwickshire; grandfather
Sonny Ramadhin played for Lancashire and
West Indies
Education: Saddleworth High School
Qualifications: GCSEs
Off-season: 'Training (12-month contract)'
Overseas tours: England U19 to India 2000-01, to Australia and (U19 World Cup)
New Zealand 2001-02; Lancashire to South Africa, to Grenada; ECB National
Academy to Australia and Sri Lanka 2002-03

Cricket moments to forget: '[B&H 2002] semi-final v Warwickshire'
Cricket superstitions: 'None'
Cricketers particularly admired: Andrew Flintoff, David Byas, Stuart Law, Carl Hooper
Other sports played: Football
Other sports followed: Football (Man Utd)
Favourite band: Stone Roses, Red Hot Chili Peppers, Bob Marley
Relaxations: 'Relaxing with friends'
Extras: Represented England U19 2001, 2002. NBC Denis Compton Award for the most promising young Lancashire player 2001. Recorded maiden first-class five-wicket return (5-48) on Championship debut v Leicestershire at Old Trafford 2002. Included in provisional England squad of 30 for the 2002-03 World Cup
Best batting: 53 Lancashire v Nottinghamshire, Trent Bridge 2003
Best bowling: 5-48 Lancashire v Leicestershire, Old Trafford 2002

2005 Season

	M	Inns	NO	Runs	HS	Avge	100s	50s	Ct	St	O	M	Runs	Wkts	Avge	Best	5wl	10wM
Test																		
All First	2	4	0	18	9	4.50	-	-	2	-	34.2	9	113	3	37.66	2-40	-	-
1-Day Int																		
C & G	1	0	0	0	0	-	-	-	-	-								
tsL	11	10	3	182	41 *	26.00	-	-	3	-	49	3	286	8	35.75	3-65	-	
Twenty20																		

Career Performances

	M	Inns	NO	Runs	HS	Avge	100s	50s	Ct	St	Balls	Runs	Wkts	Avge	Best	5wl	10wM
Test																	
All First	21	29	1	448	53	16.00	-	3	10	-	2570	1509	39	38.69	5-48	1	-
1-Day Int																	
C & G	6	4	2	9	8	4.50	-	-	-	-	210	168	3	56.00	2-27	-	
tsL	48	29	9	412	41 *	20.60	-	-	10	-	1639	1400	48	29.16	4-20	-	
Twenty20	2	2	0	9	7	4.50	-	-	-	-	25	47	1	47.00	1-16	-	

42. Who are the three pairs of brothers to have captained their countries in ODIs?

HOGGARD, M. J.   Yorkshire

Name: <u>Matthew</u> James Hoggard
Role: Right-hand bat, right-arm
fast-medium bowler
Born: 31 December 1976, Leeds
Height: 6ft 2in **Weight:** 14st
Nickname: Oggie
County debut: 1996
County cap: 2000
Test debut: 2000
50 wickets in a season: 2
Place in batting averages: 267th av. 12.38
(2004 228th av. 18.38)
Place in bowling averages: 44th av. 27.72
(2004 66th av. 32.38)
Strike rate: 48.14 (career 52.67)
Parents: Margaret and John
Wife and date of marriage: Sarah,
2 October 2004

Family links with cricket: 'Dad is a cricket badger'
Education: Pudsey Grangefield
Qualifications: GCSEs and A-levels
Off-season: Touring with England
Overseas tours: Yorkshire CCC to South Africa; England U19 to Zimbabwe 1995-96;
England to Kenya (ICC Knockout Trophy) 2000-01, to Pakistan and Sri Lanka
2000-01, to Zimbabwe (one-day series) 2001-02, to India and New Zealand 2001-02,
to Sri Lanka (ICC Champions Trophy) 2002-03, to Australia 2002-03, to Africa (World
Cup) 2002-03, to Bangladesh and Sri Lanka 2003-04, to West Indies 2003-04, to South
Africa 2004-05, to Pakistan 2005-06, to India 2005-06
Overseas teams played for: Pirates, Johannesburg 1995-97; Free State 1998-2000
Cricketers particularly admired: Allan Donald, Courtney Walsh
Young players to look out for: Joe Sayers, Michael Lumb, Tim Bresnan
Other sports played: Rugby
Other sports followed: Rugby league (Leeds Rhinos)
Relaxations: Dog walking
Extras: Was top wicket-taker in the 2000 National League competition with 37
wickets at 12.37. PCA Young Player of the Year 2000. Took 7-63 v New Zealand in
the first Test at Christchurch 2001-02, the best innings return by an England pace
bowler in Tests v New Zealand. Took Test hat-trick (Sarwan, Chanderpaul, Ryan
Hinds) in the third Test v West Indies at Bridgetown 2003-04. His international awards
include Man of the [Test] Series v Bangladesh 2003-04 as well as Man of the Match in
the second Test v Sri Lanka at Edgbaston 2002 (2-55/5-92) and in the fourth Test v
South Africa at Johannesburg 2004-05 (5-144/7-61)

Best batting: 89* Yorkshire v Glamorgan, Headingley 2004
Best bowling: 7-49 Yorkshire v Somerset, Headingley 2003
Stop press: Appointed MBE in 2006 New Year Honours as part of 2005 Ashes-winning England team. Man of the Match in the first Test v India at Nagpur 2005-06

2005 Season

	M	Inns	NO	Runs	HS	Avge	100s	50s	Ct	St	O	M	Runs	Wkts	Avge	Best	5wl	10wM
Test	7	9	2	45	16	6.42	-	-	2	-	172.2	30	654	30	21.80	5-73	1	-
All First	13	16	3	161	64 *	12.38	-	1	4	-	401.1	83	1386	50	27.72	5-73	1	-
1-Day Int																		
C & G	3	2	2	0	0 *	-	-	-	-	-	30	2	106	4	26.50	2-28	-	
tsL	4	0	0	0	0	-	-	-	-	-	34	3	140	5	28.00	2-29	-	
Twenty20	5	1	0	18	18	18.00	-	-	1	-	18	0	198	4	49.50	2-18	-	

Career Performances

	M	Inns	NO	Runs	HS	Avge	100s	50s	Ct	St	Balls	Runs	Wkts	Avge	Best	5wl	10wM
Test	45	59	22	319	38	8.62	-	-	18	-	9223	5126	173	29.63	7-61	5	1
All First	123	154	52	946	89 *	9.27	-	2	36	-	23137	11862	441	26.89	7-49	14	1
1-Day Int	24	5	2	10	5	3.33	-	-	3	-	1204	1034	32	32.31	5-49	1	
C & G	12	3	3	7	7 *	-	-	-	1	-	605	387	18	21.50	5-65	1	
tsL	50	18	10	18	5 *	2.25	-	-	5	-	2247	1578	80	19.72	5-28	2	
Twenty20	6	2	1	19	18	19.00	-	-	1	-	132	221	7	31.57	3-23	-	

HOPKINSON, C. D. Sussex

Name: <u>Carl</u> Daniel Hopkinson
Role: Right-hand bat, right-arm medium-fast bowler; 'batter that bowls'
Born: 14 September 1981, Brighton
Height: 5ft 11in
Nickname: Hoppo
County debut: 2001 (one-day), 2002 (first-class)
Place in batting averages: 176th av. 26.23
Strike rate: (career 93.00)
Parents: Jane and Jerry
Marital status: Single
Family links with cricket: 'Dad played in the local team, which got me interested, and coached me from a young age'
Education: Chailey; Brighton College
Qualifications: 7 GCSEs, 3 A-levels, Level 1 coaching

Overseas tours: Tours to India 1997-98, to South Africa 1999
Overseas teams played for: Rockingham-Mandurah, Western Australia 2000-01
Career highlights to date: 'Playing in my first day/night game on TV; also my debut'
Cricket moments to forget: 'Playing on my debut and taking guard before the incoming batsman was announced; in other words, they didn't know who I was!'
Cricketers particularly admired: Dennis Lillee, Ian Botham, Viv Richards, Graham Thorpe
Other sports played: Rugby ('won Rosslyn Park National Sevens'), squash, football
Other sports followed: Football (West Ham)
Favourite band: 50 Cent
Relaxations: 'Going out in Brighton with my mates, cinema etc.'
Extras: South of England and England squads until U17. Sussex Young Player of the Year 2000. Sussex 2nd XI Fielder of the Year 2001, 2003. Took wicket (John Wood) with his third ball on county debut, in the Norwich Union League v Lancashire at Hove 2001. C&G Man of the Match award v Nottinghamshire at Hove 2005 (51 plus run-out of Stephen Fleming)
Best batting: 64 Sussex v Bangladeshis, Hove 2005
Best bowling: 1-20 Sussex v LUCCE, Hove 2004

2005 Season

	M	Inns	NO	Runs	HS	Avge	100s	50s	Ct	St	O	M	Runs	Wkts	Avge	Best	5wI	10wM
Test																		
All First	8	13	0	341	64	26.23	-	3	3	-	12	1	42	0	-		-	-	-
1-Day Int																		
C & G	3	2	0	66	51	33.00	-	1	-	-								
tsL	16	11	2	181	39	20.11	-	-	8	-	4.3	0	29	2	14.50	2-20	-	
Twenty20	5	3	1	16	8	8.00	-	-	-	-								

Career Performances

	M	Inns	NO	Runs	HS	Avge	100s	50s	Ct	St	Balls	Runs	Wkts	Avge	Best	5wI	10wM
Test																	
All First	11	18	1	403	64	23.70	-	3	5	-	186	119	2	59.50	1-20	-	-
1-Day Int																	
C & G	5	4	0	124	51	31.00	-	1	1	-	90	88	0	-		-	-
tsL	38	28	4	445	67 *	18.54	-	1	22	-	350	337	13	25.92	3-19	-	
Twenty20	7	4	1	20	8	6.66	-	-	-	-							

HORTON, P. J. Lancashire

Name: <u>Paul</u> James Horton
Role: Right-hand bat, right-arm medium/off-spin bowler
Born: 20 September 1982, Sydney, Australia
Height: 5ft 10in **Weight:** 11st 3lbs
Nickname: Horts, Ozzy
County debut: 2003
Place in batting averages: 76th av. 38.88
Parents: Donald William and Norma
Marital status: Single
Education: Colo High School, Sydney/Broadgreen Comprehensive, Liverpool; St Margaret's High School
Qualifications: 11 GCSEs, 3 A-levels, Level 2 ECB coach
Overseas tours: Hawkesbury U15 to New Zealand 1997; Lancashire to Cape Town 2002-03, to Grenada 2003

Overseas teams played for: Hawkesbury, Sydney 1992-93 – 1997-98; Penrith, NSW 2002-03
Career highlights to date: 'First-class debut v Durham UCCE 2003'
Cricket moments to forget: 'First 2nd XI game for Lancashire at Old Trafford – out for 0'
Cricket superstitions: 'None'
Cricketers particularly admired: Dean Jones, Sachin Tendulkar, Mark Waugh
Young players to look out for: Steven Crook, Chris Whelan, Kyle Hogg
Other sports played: Football, golf, squash, tennis, badminton
Other sports followed: Football (Liverpool)
Favourite band: Red Hot Chili Peppers
Relaxations: 'Golf, socialising with friends, watching sport'
Extras: Captained Lancashire U17 and U19. Captained Lancashire Board XI in the C&G 2003. Lancashire Young Player of the Year Award 2001, 2002. Leading run-scorer for Lancashire 2nd XI in the 2nd XI Championship 2003 (861 runs; av. 50.65)
Best batting: 99 Lancashire v Essex, Old Trafford 2005

2005 Season

	M	Inns	NO	Runs	HS	Avge	100s	50s	Ct	St	O	M	Runs	Wkts	Avge	Best	5wI	10wM
Test																		
All First	6	9	0	350	99	38.88	-	2	2	1								
1-Day Int																		
C & G																		
tsL																		
Twenty20	1	1	0	11	11	11.00	-	-	-	-								

Career Performances

	M	Inns	NO	Runs	HS	Avge	100s	50s	Ct	St	Balls	Runs	Wkts	Avge	Best	5wI	10wM
Test																	
All First	8	11	1	374	99	37.40	-	2	3	1							
1-Day Int																	
C & G	3	2	0	49	26	24.50	-	-	-	-							
tsL	3	2	0	46	42	23.00	-	-	-	-							
Twenty20	1	1	0	11	11	11.00	-	-	-	-							

HUGGINS, T. B. Northamptonshire

Name: Thomas (Tom) Benjamin Huggins
Role: Right-hand opening bat, right-arm occasional off-spin bowler
Born: 8 March 1983, Peterborough
Height: 6ft 3in **Weight:** 15st
Nickname: Huggo, Sheep's Head, The Viking
County debut: 2003
Place in batting averages: (2004 148th av. 29.58)
Parents: John and Elizabeth
Marital status: Single
Family links with cricket: 'Dad's a coach; brother plays'
Education: Kimbolton School; De Montfort University, Bedford
Qualifications: 9 GCSEs, 3 A-levels, Level 3 coach
Overseas tours: Huntingdon Cricket 2000 to Zimbabwe 1999
Career highlights to date: 'First-class debut; getting a double hundred against Worcestershire 2nd XI 2003; playing at Lord's'
Cricket moments to forget: 'First TV game against Kent at Canterbury – fielding was distinctly average'

Cricket superstitions: 'Quite a few'
Cricketers particularly admired: Usman Afzaal, Mike Hussey
Other sports played: Football, hockey
Favourite band: Oasis, Libertines, Jay-Z
Relaxations: 'Music; playing snooker; going out with friends'
Extras: Huntingdonshire Young Player of the Year 1997, 1998, 2000. Recorded highest individual score in Huntingdonshire Youth cricket (185* v Norfolk U19 2000). Set three records for Kimbolton School 1st XI in 2001. Released by Northamptonshire at the end of the 2005 season
Best batting: 82* Northamptonshire v Middlesex, Lord's 2004

2005 Season

	M	Inns	NO	Runs	HS	Avge	100s	50s	Ct	St	O	M	Runs	Wkts	Avge	Best	5wI	10wM
Test																		
All First	1	1	0	8	8	8.00	-	-	1	-								
1-Day Int																		
C & G																		
tsL	2	2	0	21	13	10.50	-	-	-	-								
Twenty20	6	3	2	25	19	25.00	-	-	2	-								

Career Performances

	M	Inns	NO	Runs	HS	Avge	100s	50s	Ct	St	Balls	Runs	Wkts	Avge	Best	5wI	10wM
Test																	
All First	11	17	2	403	82 *	26.86	-	2	4	-							
1-Day Int																	
C & G	1	1	0	2	2	2.00	-	-	-	-							
tsL	6	6	1	49	16	9.80	-	-	-	-							
Twenty20	6	3	2	25	19	25.00	-	-	2	-							

HUGHES, J.   Glamorgan

Name: Jonathan Hughes
Role: Right-hand bat, right-arm medium bowler
Born: 30 June 1981, Pontypridd
Height: 5ft 11in
Nickname: Jonny, Tuck Box, Hughesy
County debut: 2001
Place in batting averages: 201st av. 22.21 (2004 190th av. 24.06)
Parents: Steve and Anne
Marital status: Single
Family links with cricket: 'Dad and brothers Matthew and Gareth play for Hopkinstown'
Education: Coed y Lan Comprehensive, Pontypridd

Qualifications: MCC coaching badges
Overseas tours: Hopkinstown to Barbados 1998
Overseas teams played for: Easts-Redlands, Brisbane 2000, 2001
Career highlights to date: 'Debut v Surrey for Glamorgan in County Championship'
Cricketers particularly admired: Matthew Maynard, Ian Botham
Other sports played: Football (Hopkinstown)
Other sports followed: Rugby (Pontypridd), football (Everton)
Relaxations: Going to the pub
Extras: Captained Welsh Schools. Was on Lord's groundstaff 1998-99. Glamorgan 2nd XI Player of the Year 2001. Glamorgan Young Player of the Year 2001. NBC Denis

Compton Award for the most promising young Glamorgan player 2002. Released by Glamorgan at the end of the 2005 season
Best batting: 134* Glamorgan v Middlesex, Southgate 2005

2005 Season

	M	Inns	NO	Runs	HS	Avge	100s	50s	Ct	St	O	M	Runs	Wkts	Avge	Best	5wI	10wM
Test																		
All First	13	25	2	511	134 *	22.21	2	-	10	-								
1-Day Int																		
C & G																		
tsL	4	4	1	29	13	9.66	-	-	2	-								
Twenty20	1	1	0	0	0	0.00	-	-	-	-								

Career Performances

	M	Inns	NO	Runs	HS	Avge	100s	50s	Ct	St	Balls	Runs	Wkts	Avge	Best	5wI	10wM
Test																	
All First	42	69	3	1556	134 *	23.57	3	4	27	-							
1-Day Int																	
C & G	1	1	0	51	51	51.00	-	1	-	-							
tsL	7	7	1	69	30	11.50	-	-	3	-							
Twenty20	4	3	0	8	7	2.66	-	-	-	-							

HUGHES, L. D. Derbyshire

Name: <u>Liam</u> Daniel Hughes
Role: Right-hand bat, right-arm
medium-fast bowler
Born: 21 March 1988, Wordsley,
West Midlands
Height: 6ft 1in **Weight:** 11st
Nickname: Lemming, 2Pac
County debut: No first-team appearance
Other sports played: Football, golf
Favourite band: 50 Cent, Eminem, Dr Dre
Extras: Plays for Wombourne CC. Played for
Staffordshire U15. Selected for ECB
Midlands Regional Academy Squad 2005.
Made 2nd XI Championship debut 2005

HUNTER, I. D. Derbyshire

Name: <u>Ian</u> David Hunter
Role: Right-hand bat, right-arm fast-medium bowler
Born: 11 September 1979, Durham City
Height: 6ft 2in **Weight:** 12st 7lbs
Nickname: Sticks, Hunts
County debut: 1999 (one-day, Durham), 2000 (first-class, Durham),
2004 (Derbyshire)
Place in batting averages: 251st av. 15.14
Place in bowling averages: 120th av. 44.29
Strike rate: 67.50 (career 66.21)
Parents: Ken and Linda
Marital status: Single
Family links with cricket: Brother local village cricketer
Education: Fyndoune Community College, Sacriston; New College, Durham
Qualifications: 9 GCSEs, 1 A-level (PE), BTEC National Diploma in Sports Science,
Level I and II cricket coaching awards
Overseas tours: Durham U21 to Sri Lanka 1996; Durham to Cape Town 2002
Career highlights to date: 'Scoring 63 on first-class debut' (*v Leicestershire at
Riverside 2000 as nightwatchman*)

Cricket superstitions: 'Always put my left pad on first'
Cricketers particularly admired: Allan Donald, Steve Waugh
Other sports played: Football, golf
Other sports followed: Football (Durham City AFC)
Relaxations: Socialising with friends; keeping fit, golf, football
Extras: Set a new Durham best analysis for the 2nd XI Championship with his 11-155 v Lancashire 2nd XI 1999. Represented England U19 1999
Best batting: 65 Durham v Northamptonshire, Northampton 2002
Best bowling: 5-63 Derbyshire v Durham, Riverside 2005

2005 Season

	M	Inns	NO	Runs	HS	Avge	100s	50s	Ct	St	O	M	Runs	Wkts	Avge	Best	5wI	10wM
Test																		
All First	13	20	6	212	40	15.14	-	-	3	-	382.3	56	1506	34	44.29	5-63	1	-
1-Day Int																		
C & G	2	2	0	10	9	5.00	-	-	-	-	19	1	103	2	51.50	2-52	-	
tsL	16	8	3	39	12 *	7.80	-	-	2	-	101	5	555	15	37.00	2-23	-	
Twenty20	8	2	1	12	12	12.00	-	-	3	-	29	0	238	12	19.83	3-26	-	

Career Performances

	M	Inns	NO	Runs	HS	Avge	100s	50s	Ct	St	Balls	Runs	Wkts	Avge	Best	5wI	10wM
Test																	
All First	35	54	10	795	65	18.06	-	2	9	-	5430	3452	82	42.09	5-63	1	-
1-Day Int																	
C & G	5	5	0	26	13	5.20	-	-	1	-	252	195	5	39.00	2-45	-	
tsL	52	29	7	170	21	7.72	-	-	10	-	2124	1767	56	31.55	4-29	-	
Twenty20	11	4	2	39	25 *	19.50	-	-	3	-	234	330	14	23.57	3-26	-	

HUSSEY, D. J. Nottinghamshire

Name: David (Dave) John Hussey
Role: Right-hand middle-order bat, right-arm off-spin bowler
Born: 15 July 1977, Perth, Western Australia
Height: 5ft 11in **Weight:** 13st 5lbs
Nickname: Hussa, Husscat, Huss
County debut: 2004
County cap: 2004
1000 runs in a season: 2
1st-Class 200s: 2
Place in batting averages: 6th av. 68.05 (2004 4th av. 69.21)
Strike rate: (career 84.66)
Parents: Helen and Ted
Marital status: Single
Family links with cricket: Brother Mike plays for Australia, Western Australia and Durham and played for Northamptonshire 2001-03 and Gloucestershire 2004

Education: Prendiville Catholic College; Edith Cowan University
Off-season: Playing for Victoria in Australia
Overseas tours: Commonwealth Bank [Australian] Cricket Academy to Sri Lanka 1997-98
Overseas teams played for: Prahran, Victoria; Victoria 2002-03 –
Career highlights to date: 'Winning Pura Cup final with Victoria 2003-04'
Cricket moments to forget: 'Debut for Victoria – dropped S. Waugh on four; he went on to make 211'
Cricket superstitions: 'Left shoe on first'
Cricketers particularly admired: Damien Martyn, Mark Waugh, Brendon Julian
Young players to look out for: Aaron Finch, Andrew Hodd, Mark Nash
Other sports played: Australian Rules football, squash
Other sports followed: Football (Brighton & Hove Albion)
Favourite band: Counting Crows
Relaxations: Movies, crime novels, shopping
Extras: Played for Western Australia U19 and 2nd XI. Represented Australia U19 1995-96. Has represented Australia A. Scored 212* and won Man of the Match award as Victoria scored 455-7 to beat New South Wales at Newcastle in the Pura Cup 2003-04. His other awards include Man of the Match v New South Wales at Melbourne in the Pura Cup 2003-04 (120/50) and v South Australia at Adelaide in the ING Cup 2003-04 (113). An overseas player with Nottinghamshire since 2004
Opinions on cricket: 'Bowlers should be allowed to bowl as many bouncers per over as they like. No-ball/free hit in first-class cricket.'

Best batting: 232* Nottinghamshire v Warwickshire, Trent Bridge 2005
Best bowling: 4-105 Nottinghamshire v Hampshire, Trent Bridge 2005

2005 Season

	M	Inns	NO	Runs	HS	Avge	100s	50s	Ct	St	O	M	Runs	Wkts	Avge	Best	5wl	10wM
Test																		
All First	16	21	2	1293	232 *	68.05	3	8	30	-	71	11	304	8	38.00	4-105	-	-
1-Day Int																		
C & G	2	2	0	46	26	23.00	-	-	1									
tsL	15	13	0	339	75	26.07	-	2	6	-	3	0	14	0	-		-	-
Twenty20	8	8	0	113	28	14.12	-	-	4	-	3.4	0	22	0	-		-	-

Career Performances

	M	Inns	NO	Runs	HS	Avge	100s	50s	Ct	St	Balls	Runs	Wkts	Avge	Best	5wl	10wM
Test																	
All First	55	79	9	3892	232 *	55.60	15	15	69	-	1016	679	12	56.58	4-105	-	-
1-Day Int																	
C & G	7	7	1	212	118 *	35.33	1	-	5	-	179	182	6	30.33	3-48	-	
tsL	31	29	4	783	87 *	31.32	-	4	8	-	96	91	2	45.50	1-5	-	
Twenty20	13	13	0	172	33	13.23	-	-	9	-	22	22	0	-		-	-

43. Who holds the record for the most successful individual
all-round performance in an ODI? ✎

HUSSEY, M. E. K. Durham

Name: <u>Michael</u> Edward Killeen Hussey
Role: Left-hand bat, right-arm medium
bowler, county captain
Born: 27 May 1975, Perth, Western Australia
Height: 6ft 1in **Weight:** 12st 8lbs
Nickname: Huss, Mr C
County debut: 2001 (Northamptonshire),
2004 (Gloucestershire), 2005 (Durham)
County cap: 2001 (Northamptonshire),
2004 (Gloucestershire), 2005 (Durham)
1000 runs in a season: 4
1st-Class 200s: 6
1st-Class 300s: 3
Place in batting averages: 2nd av. 76.71
(2004 92nd av. 36.83)
Strike rate: (career 74.00)
Parents: Helen and Ted
Wife and date of marriage: Amy,
6 April 2001

Children: Jasmin, 9 February 2004
Family links with cricket: Brother David plays for Victoria and Nottinghamshire
Education: Prendiville College; Curtin University
Qualifications: Teaching degree
Off-season: Playing for Australia
Overseas tours: Australia U19 to India 1993-94; Australian Cricket Academy to
Pakistan 1995; Australia A to Scotland and Ireland 1998, to South Africa 2002-03, to
Pakistan 2005-06; Australia to New Zealand 2004-05, to England 2005 (one-day
series), to New Zealand (one-day series) 2005-06
Overseas teams played for: Western Australia 1994-95 –
Career highlights to date: 'Test century v South Africa, Boxing Day Test MCG
[2005-06]'
Cricket moments to forget: 'Losing ODI to Bangladesh [2005]'
Cricket superstitions: 'None'
Cricketers particularly admired: Mark Taylor, Glenn McGrath
Young players to look out for: Shaun Marsh
Other sports played: AFL, squash
Other sports followed: AFL (West Coast Eagles), football (Man Utd)
Favourite band: U2
Relaxations: 'Relaxing with family'
Extras: Attended Commonwealth Bank [Australian] Cricket Academy 1995. Finished
third in the Sheffield Shield Player of the Year award in his first full season 1995-96.

Sir Donald Bradman Young Cricketer of the Year 1998. Excalibur Award (Western Australia) 1998-2000. Joined Northamptonshire as overseas player for 2001. Leading run-scorer in English first-class cricket 2001 with 2055 runs (all in the Championship) at 79.03. Northamptonshire Player of the Year 2001 and 2002, the first player to win the award twice in succession. Scored third triple century in successive seasons (331*), v Somerset at Taunton 2003, breaking his own record (329*) for the highest individual score by a Northamptonshire player. Captain of Northamptonshire 2002-03. Was an overseas player with Glos July to September 2004 as a replacement for Shoaib Malik/Shabbir Ahmed; an overseas player with Durham (and captain) since 2005. Made Twenty20 international debut v New Zealand at Auckland 2004-05

Opinions on cricket: 'Super sub to be named after the toss. Opposition team choose one of the powerplays.'

Best batting: 331* Northamptonshire v Somerset, Taunton 2003

Best bowling: 3-34 Western Australia v Queensland, Brisbane 2004-05

Stop press: Made Test debut in the first Test v West Indies at Brisbane 2005-06. Man of the Match in the second Test v South Africa at Melbourne 2005-06 (122/31). Named Australia's ODI Player of the Year at the 2006 Allan Border Medal awards

2005 Season

	M	Inns	NO	Runs	HS	Avge	100s	50s	Ct	St	O	M	Runs	Wkts	Avge	Best	5wI	10wM
Test																		
All First	10	18	4	1074	253	76.71	3	5	19	-	12	0	59	1	59.00	1-36	-	-
1-Day Int	10	6	3	273	84	91.00	-	2	3	-	9	0	55	1	55.00	1-31	-	
C & G	1	1	0	29	29	29.00	-	-	1	-								
tsL	9	9	0	280	97	31.11	-	2	4	-								
Twenty20																		

Career Performances

	M	Inns	NO	Runs	HS	Avge	100s	50s	Ct	St	Balls	Runs	Wkts	Avge	Best	5wI	10wM
Test																	
All First	175	315	27	15223	331 *	52.85	39	66	196	-	1332	693	18	38.50	3-34	-	-
1-Day Int	15	10	7	387	84	129.00	-	3	7	-	90	92	1	92.00	1-31	-	
C & G	8	8	0	183	59	22.87	-	1	6	-	66	68	1	68.00	1-20	-	
tsL	59	59	7	2361	123	45.40	5	17	23	-	87	99	1	99.00	1-12	-	
Twenty20	7	7	1	326	88	54.33	-	3	5	-							

44. Which former South Africa batsman and current county cricketer took a wicket with his first ball in ODIs, against Bangladesh at Kimberley in 2002?

HUTCHISON, P. M. Middlesex

Name: <u>Paul</u> Michael Hutchison
Role: Left-hand bat, left-arm seamer
Born: 9 June 1977, Leeds
Height: 6ft 3in **Weight:** 13-14st
Nickname: Hutch, Mantis
County debut: 1995-96 (Yorkshire),
2002 (Sussex), 2004 (Middlesex)
County cap: 1998 (Yorkshire)
50 wickets in a season: 1
Place in bowling averages: (2004 154th
av. 58.63)
Strike rate: (career 49.24)
Parents: Rita Laycock (deceased) and
David Hutchison
Wife and date of marriage: Emma,
18 October 2003
Family links with cricket: Brother Richard
played 17 years at Pudsey St Lawrence
Education: Pudsey Crawshaw
Qualifications: 8 GCSEs, GNVQ Leisure and Tourism, qualified cricket coach,
basic IT ('thanks to PCA')
Career outside cricket: 'Master IT developer'
Overseas tours: England U19 to Zimbabwe 1995-96; England A to Kenya and Sri
Lanka 1997-98, to Zimbabwe and South Africa 1998-99; Yorkshire to Zimbabwe and
Botswana 1996, to South Africa 1998, 1999, 2001; Sussex to Grenada 2002; MCC to
Namibia and Uganda 2004-05
Overseas teams played for: Upper Valley Bears, Wellington, New Zealand 2003-05
Career highlights to date: 'My Championship debut 7-50. My two England A tours.
My two Championship winner's medals'
Cricket moments to forget: 'More and more as the seasons pass by!'
Cricket superstitions: 'Not really'
Cricketers particularly admired: Glenn McGrath
Young players to look out for: Ben Scott, Chris Whelan, Eoin Morgan
Other sports played: Golf, football
Other sports followed: 'Most sports; anything on Sky Sports; any team from my area
(Leeds/Bradford)'
Favourite band: Drifters
Extras: Represented England at U17, U18 and U19 levels. Took 7-38 on first first-
class appearance of 1997, against Pakistan A. Took 7-50 against Hampshire at
Portsmouth 1997, the best Championship debut figures for Yorkshire since Wilfred
Rhodes took 7-24 v Somerset in 1898. Voted Wombwell Cricket Lovers' Young Player
of the Year for 1997. Released by Middlesex at the end of the 2005 season

Best batting: 30 Yorkshire v Essex, Scarborough 1998
Best bowling: 7-31 Yorkshire v Sussex, Hove 1998

2005 Season

	M	Inns	NO	Runs	HS	Avge	100s	50s	Ct	St	O	M	Runs	Wkts	Avge	Best	5wl	10wM
Test																		
All First	2	3	1	28	26 *	14.00	-	-	2	-	53.4	3	255	5	51.00	2-43	-	-
1-Day Int																		
C & G																		
tsL	2	1	0	0	0	0.00	-	-	-	-	18	1	127	2	63.50	1-55	-	
Twenty20	2	0	0	0	0	-	-	-	-	-	3.2	0	38	1	38.00	1-38	-	

Career Performances

	M	Inns	NO	Runs	HS	Avge	100s	50s	Ct	St	Balls	Runs	Wkts	Avge	Best	5wl	10wM
Test																	
All First	62	66	31	305	30	8.71	-	-	14	-	9091	5256	184	28.56	7-31	7	1
1-Day Int																	
C & G	3	1	1	4	4 *	-	-	-	-	-	132	62	5	12.40	3-18	-	
tsL	40	18	7	86	20	7.81	-	-	6	-	1730	1327	51	26.01	4-29	-	
Twenty20	5	1	1	0	0 *	-	-	-	1	-	80	110	4	27.50	2-22	-	

HUTTON, B. L.   Middlesex

Name: Benjamin (Ben) Leonard Hutton
Role: Left-hand bat, right-arm
medium bowler, county captain
Born: 29 January 1977, Johannesburg,
South Africa
Height: 6ft 1½in **Weight:** 12st
Nickname: Gibbo
County debut: 1999
County cap: 2003
1000 runs in a season: 2
Place in batting averages: 104th av. 34.82
(2004 78th av. 40.32)
Strike rate: (career 98.68)
Parents: Charmaine and Richard
Marital status: Single
Family links with cricket: Sir Leonard
Hutton (grandfather) Yorkshire and England;
Richard Hutton (father) Yorkshire and
England; Ben Brocklehurst (grandfather) Somerset; Oliver Hutton (brother) Oxford
University

Education: Radley College; Durham University
Qualifications: 10 GCSEs, 3 A-levels, BA (Hons) Social Sciences, NCA coaching award
Overseas tours: Durham University to Zimbabwe 1997-98; Middlesex to Portugal 1996, 1997, 1998, to South Africa 1999, to Malta 2001, to Bombay 2003; MCC to Italy
Overseas teams played for: Pirates CC, Johannesburg 1996; Wanderers CC, Johannesburg 1997; Gosnells, Perth 2001-02
Cricket moments to forget: 'Breaking my hand v Gloucestershire 2001. Two Championship pairs'
Cricket superstitions: 'None'
Cricketers particularly admired: Sir Leonard Hutton, Justin Langer, Mark Ramprakash, Andy Flower
Young players to look out for: Nick Compton, Eoin Morgan
Other sports played: Golf (12 handicap)
Other sports followed: 'All sport, except motor racing'
Favourite band: 'Too many to mention'
Relaxations: 'Reading and listening to music'
Extras: Played in Durham University's BUSA Championship winning side 1997, 1998 (shared) and 1999. Opened for Middlesex v Essex at Southend 1999 with Andrew Strauss, his former opening partner at Radley. Scored century in each innings (100/107) v Kent at Southgate 2004. Captain of Middlesex since 2005
Best batting: 152 Middlesex v Kent, Lord's 2005
Best bowling: 4-37 Middlesex v Sri Lankans, Shenley 2002

2005 Season

	M	Inns	NO	Runs	HS	Avge	100s	50s	Ct	St	O	M	Runs	Wkts	Avge	Best	5wI	10wM
Test																		
All First	17	31	2	1010	152	34.82	2	4	24	-	93	10	394	1	394.00	1-31	-	-
1-Day Int																		
C & G	2	1	0	0	0	0.00	-	-	1	-	4	0	23	0	-	-	-	-
tsL	16	11	2	146	61	16.22	-	1	12	-	52	0	288	10	28.80	3-42	-	
Twenty20	9	8	2	57	27 *	9.50	-	-	4	-	5	0	57	0	-	-	-	

Career Performances

	M	Inns	NO	Runs	HS	Avge	100s	50s	Ct	St	Balls	Runs	Wkts	Avge	Best	5wI	10wM
Test																	
All First	95	162	14	4933	152	33.33	15	17	117	-	3158	1948	32	60.87	4-37	-	-
1-Day Int																	
C & G	10	8	1	86	27	12.28	-	-	8	-	120	127	4	31.75	2-42	-	
tsL	84	68	14	1131	77	20.94	-	5	38	-	1300	1182	39	30.30	5-45	1	
Twenty20	18	14	3	114	27 *	10.36	-	-	8	-	84	129	4	32.25	2-21	-	

IRANI, R. C. Essex

Name: Ronald (Ronnie) Charles Irani
Role: Right-hand bat, county captain
Born: 26 October 1971, Leigh, Lancashire
Height: 6ft 4in **Weight:** 14st 8lbs
Nickname: Reggie
County debut: 1990 (Lancashire),
1994 (Essex)
County cap: 1994 (Essex)
Benefit: 2003 (Essex)
Test debut: 1996
1000 runs in a season: 6
50 wickets in a season: 1
1st-Class 200s: 1
Place in batting averages: 20th av. 57.23
(2004 18th av. 57.91)
Strike rate: (career 60.15)
Parents: Jimmy and Anne
Wife: Lorraine
Children: Simone, 25 September 2000; Maria, 6 January 2002
Family links with cricket: 'Father played league cricket for over 30 years. Mum did teas for years as well'
Education: Smithills Comprehensive School
Qualifications: 9 GCSEs
Overseas tours: England YC to Australia 1989-90; England A to Pakistan 1995-96, to Bangladesh and New Zealand 1999-2000; England to Zimbabwe and New Zealand 1996-97, to Sri Lanka (ICC Champions Trophy) 2002-03, to Australia 2002-03 (VB Series), to Africa (World Cup) 2002-03; England VI to Hong Kong 2002
Overseas teams played for: Technicol Natal, Durban 1992-93; Eden-Roskill, Auckland 1993-94
Career highlights to date: 'Playing for England. Winning one-day trophies with Essex'
Cricket moments to forget: 'Admiring lady streaker and getting caught on TV cameras doing it!'
Cricketers particularly admired: Graham Gooch, Javed Miandad, Viv Richards, Wasim Akram
Other sports played: Golf, pool
Other sports followed: Football (Manchester United), Muay Thai boxing
Favourite band: Manic Street Preachers, Travis, Joyce Simms, Alexander O'Neal
Relaxations: Fly fishing
Extras: Bull Man of the Series, England YC v Australia YC 1991. Appointed vice-captain of Essex 1999. Achieved double of 1000 first-class runs and 50 first-class

wickets 1999. Took over 1st XI captaincy of Essex at the start of the 2000 season, Nasser Hussain remaining as club captain until his retirement in 2004. Recorded a five-wicket innings return (5-58) and scored a century (119) for Essex v Surrey at Ilford 2001. Man of the Match v India at The Oval in the NatWest Series 2002 (53/5-26); also named 'Fans' Player of the Series'. Captained England XI v Sir Donald Bradman XI at Bowral 2002-03. Granted Freedom of the City of London in April 2003. Forced by knee injury to give up bowling 2003
Best batting: 207* Essex v Northamptonshire, Ilford 2002
Best bowling: 6-71 Essex v Nottinghamshire, Trent Bridge 2002

2005 Season

	M	Inns	NO	Runs	HS	Avge	100s	50s	Ct	St	O	M	Runs	Wkts	Avge	Best	5wI	10wM
Test																		
All First	16	23	2	1202	103	57.23	1	10	5	-								
1-Day Int																		
C & G	2	2	0	48	41	24.00	-	-	-	-								
tsL	14	14	0	363	67	25.92	-	3	8	-								
Twenty20	7	6	0	71	34	11.83	-	-	3	-								

Career Performances

	M	Inns	NO	Runs	HS	Avge	100s	50s	Ct	St	Balls	Runs	Wkts	Avge	Best	5wI	10wM
Test	3	5	0	86	41	17.20	-	-	2	-	192	112	3	37.33	1-22	-	-
All First	212	344	42	11932	207 *	39.50	23	66	174	-	20389	10007	339	29.51	6-71	9	-
1-Day Int	31	30	5	360	53	14.40	-	1	6	-	1283	989	24	41.20	5-26	1	
C & G	30	27	3	945	124	39.37	1	7	10	-	1526	1042	37	28.16	4-41	-	
tsL	180	172	25	4264	158 *	29.00	4	23	46	-	5210	3912	165	23.70	5-33	1	
Twenty20	17	16	1	313	64 *	20.86	-	1	5	-							

JAMES, N. A.   Warwickshire

Name: Nicholas (Nick) Alexander James
Role: Left-hand bat, slow left-arm bowler
Born: 17 September 1986, Sandwell, West Midlands
Height: 5ft 10in **Weight:** 11st
Nickname: Jaymo
County debut: No first-team appearance
Parents: Ann and Mike
Marital status: Single
Family links with cricket: 'Dad coaches youth cricket; Dad and brother Chris play club cricket at Aldridge CC'
Education: King Edward VI, Aston
Qualifications: 10 GCSEs, 3 A-levels
Off-season: 'Training and playing abroad'

Overseas tours: England U19 to Bangladesh 2005-06, to Sri Lanka (U19 World Cup) 2005-06
Career highlights to date: 'Scoring 78 on England U19 "Test" debut v Sri Lanka, summer 2005'
Cricket superstitions: 'None'
Cricketers particularly admired: Brian Lara, Ashley Giles
Young players to look out for: Andrew Miller
Other sports played: Football, golf
Other sports followed: Football (Aston Villa)
Favourite band: 'All types of music'
Relaxations: 'Playing snooker at Rileys; listening to music'
Extras: Captain of Warwickshire U17

County Championship winning side 2004. Member of England U18 Development Squad 2004. Represented England U19 2005. Has won eight Warwickshire Youth awards since the age of 12, including Tiger Smith Memorial Award 2005 for the most promising young player
Opinions on cricket: 'Great game. Can't forget to enjoy yourself!'

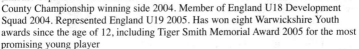

45. Who recently became the 158th Australian to play in ODIs and made the highest debut score for his country?

JAQUES, P. A.   Worcestershire

Name: <u>Philip</u> Anthony Jaques
Role: Left-hand bat, left-arm spin bowler
Born: 3 May 1979, Wollongong, Australia
Height: 6ft 1in
Nickname: Jakesy, Poop
County debut: 2003 (Northamptonshire),
2004 (Yorkshire)
County cap: 2003 (Northamptonshire),
2005 (Yorkshire)
1000 runs in a season: 3
1st-Class 200s: 5
Place in batting averages: 9th av. 64.71
(2004 16th av. 58.84)
Parents: Mary and Stuart
Marital status: Engaged
Family links with cricket: 'Dad played
league cricket in South Lancashire League'
Education: Figtree High School; Australian
College of Physical Education (PE degree)
Qualifications: Fitness trainer, Level II coach
Career outside cricket: Coaching
Overseas tours: New South Wales to New Zealand 2000-01; Australia A to Pakistan
2005-06
Overseas teams played for: Sutherland DCC, Sydney; New South Wales Blues
2000-01 – 2001-02, 2003-04 –
Career highlights to date: '243 v Hampshire [2004] and maiden first-class hundred
for NSW'
Cricket moments to forget: 'Any duck really'
Cricketers particularly admired: Steve Waugh
Favourite band: Coldplay
Extras: Attended Australian Cricket Academy 2000. Scored maiden first-class century
(149*) v Worcestershire at Worcester 2003 and maiden first-class double century (222)
in his next Championship innings v Yorkshire at Northampton 2003. Scored 1409 first-
class runs in his first season of county cricket 2003. Holds a British passport and was
not considered an overseas player with Northamptonshire in 2003. An overseas player
with Yorkshire 2004 (having played for New South Wales 2003-04), deputising for Ian
Harvey and Darren Lehmann, and in 2005. Has joined Worcestershire as an overseas
player for 2006
Best batting: 243 Yorkshire v Hampshire, West End 2004
Stop press: Made Test debut in the second Test v South Africa at Melbourne 2005-06
and ODI debut v South Africa at Melbourne in the VB Series 2005-06, scoring 94.
Named Australia's State Player of the Year at the 2006 Allan Border Medal awards

312

2005 Season

	M	Inns	NO	Runs	HS	Avge	100s	50s	Ct	St	O	M	Runs	Wkts	Avge	Best	5wI	10wM
Test																		
All First	13	23	2	1359	219	64.71	4	6	14	-	3	0	19	0	-	-	-	-
1-Day Int																		
C & G	4	4	1	151	55 *	50.33	-	1	2	-								
tsL	11	11	0	422	98	38.36	-	4	6	-								
Twenty20	8	8	0	275	72	34.37	-	2	1	-	1	0	15	0	-	-	-	

Career Performances

	M	Inns	NO	Runs	HS	Avge	100s	50s	Ct	St	Balls	Runs	Wkts	Avge	Best	5wI	10wM
Test																	
All First	65	114	6	5970	243	55.27	16	28	53	-	66	72	0	-	-	-	-
1-Day Int																	
C & G	7	7	1	216	55 *	36.00	-	2	2	-							
tsL	38	37	2	1591	117	45.45	3	13	15	-							
Twenty20	18	18	1	552	92	32.47	-	3	3	-	6	15	0	-	-	-	

JAYASURIYA, S. T.   Somerset

Name: Sanath Teran Jayasuriya
Role: Left-hand bat, slow left-arm bowler
Born: 30 June 1969, Matara, Sri Lanka
Height: 5ft 6in
County debut: 2005
Test debut: 1990-91
1st-Class 200s: 2
1st-Class 300s: 1
Place in batting averages: 179th av. 25.15
Strike rate: (career 73.13)
Overseas tours: Sri Lankan Young
Cricketers to Australia (U19 World Cup)
1987-88; Sri Lanka B to Pakistan 1988-89;
Sri Lanka U24 to South Africa 1992-93; Sri
Lanka to Australia 1989-90, to England 1990,
to New Zealand 1990-91, to England 1991, to
Pakistan 1991-92, to Australia and New
Zealand (World Cup) 1991-92, to India 1993-

94, to Zimbabwe and South Africa 1994-95, to New Zealand 1994-95, to Pakistan
1995-96, to Australia 1995-96, to India and Pakistan (World Cup) 1995-96, to New
Zealand 1996-97, to West Indies 1996-97, to India 1997-98, to South Africa 1997-98,
to England 1998, to Bangladesh (Wills International Cup) 1998-99, to UK, Ireland and

Holland (World Cup) 1999, to Zimbabwe 1999-2000 (c), to Pakistan 1999-2000 (c), to Kenya (ICC Knockout Trophy) 2000-01 (c), to South Africa 2000-01 (c), to England 2002 (c), to South Africa 2002-03 (c), to Africa (World Cup) 2002-03 (c), to West Indies 2003, to Zimbabwe 2004, to Australia 2004, to England (ICC Champions Trophy) 2004, to Pakistan 2004-05, to New Zealand 2004-05, plus other one-day series and tournaments in Sharjah, India, Singapore, West Indies, Kenya, Pakistan, Australia, Bangladesh, New Zealand and Morocco; FICA World XI to New Zealand 2004-05

Overseas teams played for: Colombo 1988-89 – 1992; Bloomfield C&AC 1994-95 –
Extras: One of *Indian Cricket*'s five Cricketers of the Year 1996. One of *Wisden*'s Five Cricketers of the Year 1997. Is Sri Lanka's leading run-scorer in both Tests and ODIs, becoming the fourth batsman to reach 10,000 runs in the latter format v India at Colombo in the Indian Oil Cup 2005. Holds the records for the highest individual scores for Sri Lanka in Tests (340 v India in the first Test at Colombo 1997) and ODIs (189 v India in the Coca-Cola Champions Trophy in Sharjah 2000-01). Captain of Sri Lanka 1999-2003. Has won many, many international awards, including Man of the Series at the 1995-96 World Cup in India and Pakistan. Was a temporary overseas player with Somerset during the 2005 season. Made his 100th Test appearance in the second Test v Bangladesh at Colombo 2005-06
Best batting: 340 Sri Lanka v India, Colombo 1997-98
Best bowling: 5-34 Sri Lanka v South Africa, Colombo 2004-05

2005 Season

	M	Inns	NO	Runs	HS	Avge	100s	50s	Ct	St	O	M	Runs	Wkts	Avge	Best	5wI	10wM
Test																		
All First	7	13	0	327	73	25.15	-	3	2	-	56.1	7	230	5	46.00	2-2	-	-
1-Day Int																		
C & G	1	1	0	0	0	0.00	-	-	-	-								
tsL	7	7	0	117	61	16.71	-	1	4	-	34	2	189	4	47.25	1-18	-	
Twenty20																		

Career Performances

	M	Inns	NO	Runs	HS	Avge	100s	50s	Ct	St	Balls	Runs	Wkts	Avge	Best	5wI	10wM
Test	100	170	14	6580	340	42.17	14	29	73	-	7397	3016	92	32.78	5-34	2	-
All First	240	379	33	13864	340	40.06	29	65	152	-	13677	6003	187	32.10	5-34	2	-
1-Day Int	339	330	15	10122	189	32.13	18	58	106	-	12203	9701	267	36.33	6-29	4	
C & G	1	1	0	0	0	0.00	-	-	-	-							
tsL	7	7	0	117	61	16.71	-	1	4	-	204	189	4	47.25	1-18	-	
Twenty20																	

JEFFERSON, W. I.   Essex

Name: William (<u>Will</u>) Ingleby Jefferson
Role: Right-hand bat, right-arm
medium bowler
Born: 25 October 1979, Derby ('but native
of Norfolk')
Height: 6ft 10½in   **Weight:** 15st 2lbs
Nickname: Santa, Lemar, Jeffo
County debut: 2000
County cap: 2002
1000 runs in a season: 1
1st-Class 200s: 1
Place in batting averages: 73rd av. 39.08
(2004 20th av. 55.53)
Strike rate: (career 120.00)
Parents: Richard and Pauline
Marital status: Single
Family links with cricket: Grandfather
Jefferson played for the Army and Combined
Services in the 1920s. Father, R. I. Jefferson, played for Cambridge University 1961
and Surrey 1961-66
Education: Oundle School, Northants; Durham University
Qualifications: 9 GCSEs, 3 A-levels, BA (Hons) Sport in the Community, Levels 1
and 2 cricket coaching awards
Overseas tours: Oundle School to South Africa 1995
Overseas teams played for: Young People's Club, Paarl, South Africa 1998-99; South
Perth, Western Australia 2002-03
Career highlights to date: 'Being awarded county cap on final day of the 2002
season. Scoring 165* to help beat Notts and secure 2002 second division
Championship. 222 v Hampshire at Rose Bowl [2004]'
Cricket moments to forget: 'Any dropped catch; any time bowled playing across the
line'
Cricketers particularly admired: Andy Flower, Nasser Hussain
Other sports played: Golf (12 handicap), tennis, swimming
Other sports followed: 'Follow most sports'
Favourite band: Coldplay
Relaxations: 'Listening to music; seeing friends outside cricket'
Extras: Holmwoods School Cricketer of the Year 1998. Represented British
Universities 2000, 2001 and 2002. Played for Durham University CCE 2001 and 2002.
NBC Denis Compton Award for the most promising young Essex player 2002. Scored
century before lunch on the opening day for Essex v Cambridge UCCE at Fenner's
2003. C&G Man of the Match awards for his 97 v Scotland at Edinburgh 2004 and for

his 126 v Nottinghamshire at Trent Bridge in the next round. Essex Player of the Year 2004. Essex Boundary Club Trophy for scoring most runs for Essex 1st XI 2004
Best batting: 222 Essex v Hampshire, West End 2004
Best bowling: 1-16 Essex v Yorkshire, Headingley 2005

2005 Season

	M	Inns	NO	Runs	HS	Avge	100s	50s	Ct	St	O	M	Runs	Wkts	Avge	Best	5wI	10wM
Test																		
All First	15	26	2	938	149	39.08	2	4	11	-	20	6	60	1	60.00	1-16	-	-
1-Day Int																		
C & G	2	2	0	27	27	13.50	-	-	-	-								
tsL	10	10	1	283	88	31.44	-	1	5	-	4	0	9	2	4.50	2-9	-	
Twenty20	1	1	0	1	1	1.00	-	-	-	-								

Career Performances

	M	Inns	NO	Runs	HS	Avge	100s	50s	Ct	St	Balls	Runs	Wkts	Avge	Best	5wI	10wM
Test																	
All First	66	119	11	4295	222	39.76	11	17	58	-	120	60	1	60.00	1-16	-	-
1-Day Int																	
C & G	7	7	0	401	132	57.28	2	1	3	-							
tsL	55	54	4	1710	111 *	34.20	2	10	26	-	24	9	2	4.50	2-9	-	
Twenty20	8	8	1	60	19	8.57	-	-	1	-							

JOHNSON, R. L.   Somerset

Name: <u>Richard</u> Leonard Johnson
Role: Right-hand bat, right-arm fast-medium bowler
Born: 29 December 1974, Chertsey, Surrey
Height: 6ft 2in **Weight:** 14st 3lbs
Nickname: Jono, Lenny, The Greek
County debut: 1992 (Middlesex), 2001 (Somerset)
County cap: 1995 (Middlesex), 2001 (Somerset)
Benefit: 2006 (Somerset)
Test debut: 2003
50 wickets in a season: 4
Place in batting averages: 255th av. 14.53 (2004 180th av. 24.75)
Place in bowling averages: 139th av. 52.40 (2004 75th av. 34.36)
Strike rate: 86.25 (career 52.19)

Parents: Roger and Mary Anne
Wife and date of marriage: Nikki, 4 October 2003
Family links with cricket: Father and grandfather played club cricket
Education: Sunbury Manor School; Spelthorne College
Qualifications: 9 GCSEs, A-level in Physical Education, NCA senior coaching award
Overseas tours: England U18 to South Africa 1992-93; England U19 to Sri Lanka 1993-94; England A to India 1994-95; MCC to Bangladesh 1999-2000, to Canada 2000-01; England to India 2001-02, to Bangladesh and Sri Lanka 2003-04
Career highlights to date: 'Playing in a domestic final for Somerset. Making England debut'
Cricket moments to forget: 'Losing C&G final [2002]'
Cricketers particularly admired: Ian Botham, Richard Hadlee, Angus Fraser
Young players to look out for: James Hildreth
Other sports followed: Football (Tottenham), rugby (London Irish)
Relaxations: 'Eating out with wife and friends; having a few beers with Nashy'
Player website: www.winningwickets.com
Extras: Represented Middlesex at all levels from U11. Took 10 for 45 v Derbyshire at Derby 1994, becoming the first person to take ten wickets in an English first-class innings since 1964. Won Man of the Match awards in his first two Tests: for his 6-33 on debut in the second Test v Zimbabwe at Riverside 2003 and 5-49/4-44 in the second Test v Bangladesh at Chittagong 2003-04. Won Walter Lawrence Trophy 2004 (for the season's fastest hundred) for his 63-ball century v Durham at Riverside
Opinions on cricket: 'Twenty20 cricket has been fantastic for the game, bringing in a new generation of cricket follower. We still need to look at the amount of cricket being played, though!'
Best batting: 118 Somerset v Gloucestershire, Bristol 2003
Best bowling: 10-45 Middlesex v Derbyshire, Derby 1994

2005 Season

	M	Inns	NO	Runs	HS	Avge	100s	50s	Ct	St	O	M	Runs	Wkts	Avge	Best	5wl	10wM
Test																		
All First	11	15	0	218	35	14.53	-	-	5	-	287.3	52	1048	20	52.40	4-118	-	-
1-Day Int																		
C & G	1	1	0	8	8	8.00	-	-	-	-	8	2	22	2	11.00	2-22	-	
tsL	10	5	1	33	19	8.25	-	-	1	-	70	4	395	10	39.50	2-27	-	
Twenty20	2	1	0	0	0	0.00	-	-	1	-	6	0	47	6	7.83	3-21	-	

Career Performances

	M	Inns	NO	Runs	HS	Avge	100s	50s	Ct	St	Balls	Runs	Wkts	Avge	Best	5wl	10wM
Test	3	4	0	59	26	14.75	-	-	-	-	547	275	16	17.18	6-33	2	-
All First	154	211	27	3286	118	17.85	2	7	60	-	26095	13993	500	27.98	10-45	19	3
1-Day Int	10	4	1	16	10	5.33	-	-	-	-	402	239	11	21.72	3-32	-	
C & G	28	17	3	192	45 *	13.71	-	-	4	-	1455	1066	40	26.65	5-50	1	
tsL	113	76	21	700	53	12.72	-	1	11	-	4682	4002	119	33.63	4-45	-	
Twenty20	2	1	0	0	0	0.00	-	-	1	-	36	47	6	7.83	3-21	-	

JONES, C. M. P.   Middlesex

Name: <u>Craig</u> Michael Parry Jones
Role: Right-hand bat, right-arm
fast-medium bowler
Born: 13 April 1978, Tamworth,
New South Wales, Australia
Height: 6ft **Weight:** 13st
Nickname: Bushy, CJ
County debut: 2005
Strike rate: (career 60.66)
Parents: John and Therese
Marital status: Girlfriend Karin
Family links with cricket: 'Grandfather
NSW Colts. Father and brothers played'
Education: St Johns College, Dubbo,
Australia; University of Wollongong,
Australia
Qualifications: BEd (PD/H/PE)
Career outside cricket: 'Manage a teacher
recruitment company – VIBE Teacher Recruitment'
Off-season: '[Intend to spend it] festively plump!'
Overseas tours: Club Cricket Conference to Ireland 2003, to West Indies 2005
Overseas teams played for: St George DCC, Sydney 2000-01; University of
Wollongong 1996-2000
Career highlights to date: 'Playing at Lord's for the first time'
Cricket moments to forget: 'My first ball in senior cricket in a day/night game in
Dubbo at the age of 13. I was hit for six and then turned round to see the umpire
signalling no-ball. 8-0 off 0.0 overs! Not a great start.'
Cricket superstitions: 'Left sock on first'
Cricketers particularly admired: Glenn McGrath, Andrew Flintoff, Simon Jones,
Ricky Ponting
Young players to look out for: Billy Godleman, Nick Compton, 'Chris Goldie'
Other sports played: Rugby, football, hockey
Other sports followed: 'Sport lover – even grown to watch darts and snooker'
Injuries: Out for six weeks with an injured back
Favourite band: Counting Crows
Relaxations: 'Quiet beer with mates; travelling; reading 17th-century French poetry'
Extras: NSW Country Cricketer of the Year 2000. Middlesex County Cricket League
Cricketer of the Year 2004. Played for Middlesex Board XI in the 2003 C&G. Played
one first-class match for Middlesex 2005; not re-engaged for 2006
Opinions on cricket: 'A balance needs to be struck between amount of cricket played
and the quality of competition entered into – e.g. too many one-day competitions

waters down the appeal and diffuses the achievement between too many teams. Counties should look to better develop club junior talent in their own areas to strengthen club competition and ultimately the county and international teams.'

Best bowling: 2-26 Middlesex v CUCCE, Fenner's 2005

2005 Season

	M	Inns	NO	Runs	HS	Avge	100s	50s	Ct	St	O	M	Runs	Wkts	Avge	Best	5wI	10wM
Test																		
All First	1	0	0	0	0	-	-	-	-	-	30.2	6	90	3	30.00	2-26	-	-
1-Day Int																		
C & G																			
tsL																			
Twenty20																			

Career Performances

	M	Inns	NO	Runs	HS	Avge	100s	50s	Ct	St	Balls	Runs	Wkts	Avge	Best	5wI	10wM
Test																	
All First	1	0	0	0	0	-	-	-	-	-	182	90	3	30.00	2-26	-	-
1-Day Int																	
C & G	2	2	1	0	0 *	0.00	-	-	3	-	78	65	1	65.00	1-47	-	
tsL																	
Twenty20																	

46. Two Surrey players have taken a wicket with their first ball in ODIs. Who are they?

JONES, G. O.   Kent

Name: <u>Geraint</u> Owen Jones
Role: Right-hand bat, wicket-keeper
Born: 14 July 1976, Kundiawa,
Papua New Guinea
Height: 5ft 10in **Weight:** 11st
Nickname: Jonesy
County debut: 2001
County cap: 2003
Test debut: 2003-04
50 dismissals in a season: 1
Place in batting averages: 192nd av. 23.57
(2004 101st av. 36.08)
Parents: Emrys, Carol (deceased),
Maureen (stepmother)
Marital status: Single
Family links with cricket: 'Father was star
off-spinner in local school side'
Education: Harristown State High School,
Toowoomba, Queensland; MacGregor SHS, Brisbane
Qualifications: Level 1 coach
Overseas tours: Beenleigh-Logan U19 to New Zealand 1995; Kent to Port Elizabeth
2001-02; England to Bangladesh and Sri Lanka 2003-04, to West Indies 2003-04, to
Zimbabwe (one-day series) 2004-05, to South Africa 2004-05, to Pakistan 2005-06, to
India 2005-06
Overseas teams played for: Beenleigh-Logan, Brisbane 1995-98; Valleys, Brisbane
2001-02
Cricket superstitions: 'Left pad first'
Cricketers particularly admired: Jack Russell, Alec Stewart
Other sports played: Golf
Other sports followed: Rugby (Crickhowell RFC)
Favourite band: Matchbox Twenty
Extras: Set new record for a season's tally of wicket-keeping dismissals in the one-
day league (33; 27/6) 2003; also equalled record for number of wicket-keeping catches
in one match, six v Leicestershire at Canterbury 2003. Made 59 first-class dismissals
plus 985 first-class runs in his first full season of county cricket 2003. Man of the
Match in the second Test v New Zealand at Headingley 2004, in which he scored his
maiden Test century (100). His other international awards include Man of the Match v
Australia in the tied final of the NatWest Series 2005 (71 plus five catches). Made
Twenty20 international debut v Australia at the Rose Bowl 2005
Best batting: 108* Kent v Essex, Chelmsford 2003
Stop press: Appointed MBE in 2006 New Year Honours as part of 2005 Ashes-
winning England team

2005 Season

	M	Inns	NO	Runs	HS	Avge	100s	50s	Ct	St	O	M	Runs	Wkts	Avge	Best	5wI	10wM
Test	7	10	1	229	85	25.44	-	1	28	1								
All First	10	16	2	330	85	23.57	-	1	41	2								
1-Day Int	10	7	2	126	71	25.20	-	1	24	1								
C & G	3	3	1	103	70	51.50	-	1	2	2								
tsL	5	5	1	44	18	11.00	-	-	2	1								
Twenty20																		

Career Performances

	M	Inns	NO	Runs	HS	Avge	100s	50s	Ct	St	Balls	Runs	Wkts	Avge	Best	5wI	10wM
Test	20	29	2	803	100	29.74	1	4	71	3							
All First	53	75	10	2316	108 *	35.63	4	13	161	12	6	4	0	-	-	-	-
1-Day Int	33	26	6	529	80	26.45	-	3	53	2							
C & G	8	6	2	167	70	41.75	-	1	5	3							
tsL	36	33	4	537	74 *	18.51	-	2	35	7							
Twenty20	7	6	1	71	22	14.20	-	-	7	-							

JONES, K. J. F.   Kent

Name: <u>Kevin</u> John Francis Jones
Role: Right-hand bat, right-arm medium bowler; all-rounder
Born: 9 September 1986, Chatham, Kent
Height: 6ft **Weight:** 10st 7lbs
Nickname: Jonesy, The Ghost, Sunbed Kev, Jonah, Buckets
County debut: 2005
Parents: Linda and David
Marital status: Single
Family links with cricket: Brother (Michael) plays local league cricket for Rodmersham
Education: Sittingbourne Community College
Qualifications: 5 GCSEs
Career outside cricket: Floor layer
Off-season: Playing for Melbourne CC in Australia
Overseas teams played for: Melbourne CC 2005-06
Career highlights to date: 'First-class debut v Bangladesh A for Kent CCC 2005'
Cricket moments to forget: 'First innings against Bangladesh A'
Cricketers particularly admired: Martin McCague, Steve Marsh, Michael Atherton

Young players to look out for: Chris Piesley, Sean Piesley
Other sports played: Football
Other sports followed: Football (Arsenal FC)
Favourite band: Oasis
Extras: Kent League Young Cricketer of the Year 2005. Gore Court top bowler, top run-scorer and Player of the Year 2005. Has joined MCC groundstaff for 2006
Opinions on cricket: 'Just love playing the game.'
Best batting: 14 Kent v Bangladesh A, Canterbury 2005

2005 Season

	M	Inns	NO	Runs	HS	Avge	100s	50s	Ct	St	O	M	Runs	Wkts	Avge	Best	5wl	10wM
Test																		
All First	1	2	0	14	14	7.00	-	-	1	-								
1-Day Int																		
C & G																		
tsL																		
Twenty20																		

Career Performances

	M	Inns	NO	Runs	HS	Avge	100s	50s	Ct	St	Balls	Runs	Wkts	Avge	Best	5wl	10wM
Test																	
All First	1	2	0	14	14	7.00	-	-	1	-							
1-Day Int																	
C & G																	
tsL																	
Twenty20																	

JONES, P. S.   Derbyshire

Name: Philip Steffan Jones
Role: Right-hand bat, right-arm fast-medium bowler
Born: 9 February 1974, Llanelli
Height: 6ft 1in **Weight:** 15st
Nickname: Jona
County debut: 1997 (Somerset), 2004 (Northamptonshire)
50 wickets in a season: 1
Place in batting averages: 264th av. 13.00 (2004 236th av. 17.37)
Place in bowling averages: (2004 155th av. 79.20)
Strike rate: (career 66.94)
Parents: Lyndon and Ann
Wife and date of marriage: Alex, 12 October 2002
Family links with cricket: Father played at a high standard and played first-class rugby

Education: Ysgol Gyfun y Strade, Llanelli; Loughborough University; Homerton College, Cambridge University
Qualifications: BSc Sports Science, PGCE in Physical Education
Career outside cricket: Personal fitness trainer
Overseas tours: Wales Minor Counties to Barbados 1996; Somerset CCC to South Africa 1999, 2000
Career highlights to date: 'Winning C&G Trophy with Somerset CCC'
Cricket superstitions: 'Always give 110 per cent effort'
Other sports played: Rugby union (Wales Schools, U18, Youth; Swansea, Bristol, Exeter and Moseley)
Other sports followed: Baseball, rugby union, athletics
Favourite band: Will Young
Relaxations: 'Spending time with my wife and close friends; going back to Wales to see my family'
Extras: Played first-class cricket and first-class rugby for two years. Took nine wickets (6-67/3-81) in the Varsity Match at Lord's 1997. Took 59 first-class wickets in 2001, 'Somerset's most successful season'. Released by Northamptonshire at the end of the 2005 season and has joined Derbyshire for 2006
Best batting: 105 Somerset v New Zealanders, Taunton 1999
Best bowling: 6-67 Cambridge University v Oxford University, Lord's 1997

2005 Season

	M	Inns	NO	Runs	HS	Avge	100s	50s	Ct	St	O	M	Runs	Wkts	Avge	Best	5wI	10wM
Test																		
All First	6	6	0	78	51	13.00	-	1	-	-	144	34	474	9	52.66	4-74	-	-
1-Day Int																		
C & G	3	2	0	25	24	12.50	-	-	-	-	17.3	2	76	2	38.00	2-12	-	
tsL	11	4	1	16	12	5.33	-	-	1	-	70.5	1	339	9	37.66	2-29	-	
Twenty20	7	1	1	1	1*	-	-	-	2	-	25.1	0	197	8	24.62	2-24	-	

Career Performances

	M	Inns	NO	Runs	HS	Avge	100s	50s	Ct	St	Balls	Runs	Wkts	Avge	Best	5wl	10wM
Test																	
All First	83	99	24	1322	105	17.62	1	4	17	-	13857	8179	207	39.51	6-67	5	1
1-Day Int																	
C & G	25	9	5	83	26 *	20.75	-	-	3	-	1217	1071	33	32.45	6-56	1	
tsL	103	57	28	297	27	10.24	-	-	20	-	4510	3989	146	27.32	5-23	1	
Twenty20	12	5	3	27	24 *	13.50	-	-	2	-	247	356	13	27.38	2-24	-	

JONES, R. A. Worcestershire

Name: <u>Richard</u> Alan Jones
Role: Right-hand bat, right-arm medium-fast bowler; all-rounder
Born: 6 November 1986, Wordsley, West Midlands
Height: 6ft 2in **Weight:** 12st 4lbs
Nickname: Jonesy, Jonah
County debut: No first-team appearance
Parents: Robert and Julie
Marital status: Single
Education: Grange High School, Stourbridge; King Edward VI College, Stourbridge
Qualifications: 13 GCSEs, 3 A-levels
Off-season: 'Tour to Bangladesh (Nov), Sri Lanka (Feb)'
Overseas tours: England U19 to Bangladesh 2005-06, to Sri Lanka (U19 World Cup) 2005-06

Career highlights to date: 'Being picked for U19 tour to Bangladesh. Signing contract with Worcestershire last season'
Cricket moments to forget: 'Being run out backing up for 0 without facing a ball'
Cricket superstitions: 'None'
Cricketers particularly admired: Andrew Flintoff, Jacques Kallis
Young players to look out for: Steve Davies, Moeen Ali, Rory Hamilton-Brown, Karl Brown
Other sports played: Football (local schools district U13 and U14)
Other sports followed: Football (West Bromwich Albion)
Injuries: Out for two months with an ankle injury; for one month with a lower back injury
Favourite band: Bloc Party

Relaxations: 'PlayStation, films, listening to music'
Extras: Scored first league hundred aged 17 for local side Old Hill (Birmingham & District Premier League)
Opinions on cricket: 'County sides should contain a minimum number of English-qualified players which would hopefully make the national side stronger and give young English players more of a chance in county cricket.'

JONES, S. P.   Glamorgan

Name: <u>Simon</u> Philip Jones
Role: Left-hand bat, right-arm fast bowler
Born: 25 December 1978, Morriston, Swansea
Height: 6ft 3in   **Weight:** 15st
Nickname: Horse
County debut: 1998
County cap: 2002
Test debut: 2002
Place in bowling averages: 21st av. 24.48 (2004 72nd av. 33.97)
Strike rate: 41.93 (career 50.79)
Parents: Irene and Jeff
Marital status: Single
Family links with cricket: 'Dad played for Glamorgan and England (15 Tests)'
Education: Coedcae Comprehensive School; Millfield School
Qualifications: 12 GCSEs, 1 A-level, basic and senior coaching awards
Overseas tours: Dyfed Schools to Zimbabwe 1994; Glamorgan to South Africa 1998; ECB National Academy to Australia 2001-02; England to Australia 2002-03, to West Indies 2003-04, to Zimbabwe (one-day series) 2004-05, to South Africa 2004-05, to India 2005-06; England A to Malaysia and India 2003-04
Cricket moments to forget: 'Injuring my right knee in Australia'
Cricket superstitions: 'Right boot on first'
Cricketers particularly admired: 'Dad', Allan Donald
Other sports played: Football (trials with Leeds United)
Favourite band: 50 Cent
Extras: NBC Denis Compton Award for the most promising young Glamorgan player 2001. Made Test debut in the first Test v India at Lord's 2002, striking a 43-ball 44 (more runs than his father scored in his Test career); the Joneses are the eleventh father and son to have played in Tests for England. ECB National Academy 2003-04. Recorded maiden Test five-wicket return (5-57) in the second Test v West Indies at Port-of-Spain 2003-04; the Joneses thus became the first father and son to have taken five-wicket hauls for England

Opinions on cricket: 'Game is progressing. Becoming more professional. Just need more sunshine.'
Best batting: 46 Glamorgan v Yorkshire, Scarborough 2001
Best bowling: 6-45 Glamorgan v Derbyshire, Cardiff 2002
Stop press: Appointed MBE in 2006 New Year Honours as part of 2005 Ashes-winning England team. Had best strike rate among Test bowlers taking 20 or more wickets in the calendar year 2005 (38.50 balls/wicket). Forced to return home from England tour to India 2005-06 with a knee injury

2005 Season

	M	Inns	NO	Runs	HS	Avge	100s	50s	Ct	St	O	M	Runs	Wkts	Avge	Best	5wI	10wM
Test	6	6	4	66	20 *	33.00	-	-	1	-	137	27	486	23	21.13	6-53	2	-
All First	9	12	8	85	20 *	21.25	-	-	3	-	230.4	46	808	33	24.48	6-53	2	-
1-Day Int	6	1	0	1	1	1.00	-	-	-	-	42	5	199	4	49.75	2-53	-	
C & G	1	1	1	0	0 *	-	-	-	1	-	10	2	52	2	26.00	2-52	-	
tsL	2	0	0	0	0	-	-	-	-	-	16.2	1	66	3	22.00	3-19	-	
Twenty20																		

Career Performances

	M	Inns	NO	Runs	HS	Avge	100s	50s	Ct	St	Balls	Runs	Wkts	Avge	Best	5wI	10wM
Test	18	18	5	205	44	15.76	-	-	4	-	2821	1666	59	28.23	6-53	3	-
All First	74	88	29	712	46	12.06	-	-	17	-	11031	6804	216	31.50	6-45	11	1
1-Day Int	8	1	0	1	1	1.00	-	-	-	-	348	275	7	39.28	2-43	-	
C & G	3	1	1	0	0 *	-	-	-	1	-	145	146	3	48.66	2-52	-	
tsL	4	1	1	12	12 *	-	-	-	-	-	194	139	5	27.80	3-19	-	
Twenty20																	

47. To date Faisal Iqbal has made one century in 17 ODIs,
but his uncle made eight centuries in his 233-ODI career. Who is he?

JOSEPH, R. H.　　　　　　　　　　Kent

Name: <u>Robert</u> Hartman Joseph Jnr
Role: Right-hand bat, right-arm
fast-medium bowler
Born: 20 January 1982, Antigua
Height: 6ft 1in　**Weight:** 13st 7lbs
Nickname: RJ, Blueie
County debut: 2004
Place in batting averages: (2004 258th
av. 12.83)
Place in bowling averages: (2004 73rd
av. 34.10)
Strike rate: (career 48.00)
Education: Sutton Valence School; St Mary's
University College
Overseas tours: Antigua Young Lions to
England 1997; Antigua and Leeward Islands
U15 to Trinidad and St Lucia
Career highlights to date: 'Playing for the
ECB First-Class XI against New Zealand A'
Cricket moments to forget: 'Losing in a local school final – getting out on 47
needing one to win with four wickets in hand and losing'
Cricketers particularly admired: Sir Vivian Richards, Andy Roberts
Other sports played: Golf
Other sports followed: Football (Arsenal)
Favourite band: Maroon 5
Relaxations: Listening to music
Extras: Made first-class debut for First-Class Counties XI v New Zealand A at Milton
Keynes 2000
Opinions on cricket: 'It's evolving into a faster, more interesting spectator sport,
which is in the best interests of the game.'
Best batting: 26 Kent v Middlesex, Canterbury 2004
Best bowling: 5-19 Kent v Bangladesh A, Canterbury 2005

2005 Season

	M	Inns	NO	Runs	HS	Avge	100s	50s	Ct	St	O	M	Runs	Wkts	Avge	Best	5wI	10wM
Test																		
All First	2	3	1	12	12	6.00	-	-	1	-	41.4	7	179	9	19.88	5-19	1	-
1-Day Int																		
C & G																		
tsL	5	3	1	17	15	8.50	-	-	2	-	31	1	142	5	28.40	2-21	-	
Twenty20																		

Career Performances

	M	Inns	NO	Runs	HS	Avge	100s	50s	Ct	St	Balls	Runs	Wkts	Avge	Best	5wl	10wM
Test																	
All First	10	13	5	89	26	11.12	-	-	4	-	1392	883	29	30.44	5-19	1	-
1-Day Int																	
C & G																	
tsL	11	6	4	23	15	11.50	-	-	2	-	438	339	12	28.25	2-21	-	
Twenty20																	

JOYCE, E. C. Middlesex

Name: Edmund (Ed) Christopher Joyce
Role: Left-hand middle-order bat, occasional right-arm medium bowler
Born: 22 September 1978, Dublin
Height: 5ft 10in **Weight:** 12st 7lbs
Nickname: Joycey, Spud, Piece
County debut: 1999
County cap: 2002
1000 runs in a season: 4
Place in batting averages: 12th av. 61.77 (2004 56th av. 45.86)
Strike rate: (career 111.00)
Parents: Maureen and Jimmy
Marital status: Single
Family links with cricket: 'Two brothers played for Ireland; two sisters currently play for Ireland Ladies'
Education: Presentation College, Bray, County Wicklow; Trinity College, Dublin
Qualifications: Irish Leaving Certificate, BA (Hons) Economics and Geography, Level II coach
Overseas tours: Ireland U19 to Bermuda (International Youth Tournament) 1997, to South Africa (U19 World Cup) 1997-98; Ireland to Zimbabwe (ICC Emerging Nations Tournament) 1999-2000, to Canada (ICC Trophy) 2001; MCC to Namibia and Uganda 2004-05; England A to West Indies 2005-06
Overseas teams played for: Coburg CC, Melbourne 1996-97; University CC, Perth 2001-02
Career highlights to date: 'Making hundred at Lord's in 2001'
Cricket superstitions: 'None'
Cricketers particularly admired: Larry Gomes, Brian Lara
Young players to look out for: Eoin Morgan, Nick Compton

Other sports played: Golf, rugby, soccer, snooker
Other sports followed: Rugby (Leinster), football (Manchester United)
Favourite band: The Mars Volta
Relaxations: Cinema, eating out, listening to music
Extras: NBC Denis Compton Award for the most promising young Middlesex player 2000. Became the first Irish-born-and-bred player to record a century in the County Championship with his 104 v Warwickshire at Lord's 2001. C&G Man of the Match award for his 72 v Northamptonshire at Northampton 2003. Appointed vice-captain of Middlesex in June 2004, captaining the county in the absence of Andrew Strauss on international duty. First batsman to 1000 first-class runs in 2005 (18 June). Represented Ireland in the ICC Trophy 2005. ECB National Academy 2005-06. Is England-qualified
Best batting: 192 Middlesex v Nottinghamshire, Lord's 2005
Best bowling: 2-34 Middlesex v CUCCE, Fenner's 2004

2005 Season

	M	Inns	NO	Runs	HS	Avge	100s	50s	Ct	St	O	M	Runs	Wkts	Avge	Best	5wI	10wM
Test																		
All First	16	29	2	1668	192	61.77	3	13	15	-	32.3	1	204	3	68.00	1-4	-	-
1-Day Int																		
C & G	2	1	0	8	8	8.00	-	-	1	-								
tsL	15	14	4	378	74	37.80	-	2	4	-	3	0	25	0	-		-	-
Twenty20	6	6	0	57	25	9.50	-	-	1	-								

Career Performances

	M	Inns	NO	Runs	HS	Avge	100s	50s	Ct	St	Balls	Runs	Wkts	Avge	Best	5wI	10wM
Test																	
All First	78	130	13	5533	192	47.29	14	31	64	-		999	768	9	85.33	2-34	-	-
1-Day Int																	
C & G	14	13	3	479	100 *	47.90	1	3	2	-							
tsL	73	67	13	1756	77	32.51	-	11	26	-	84	104	2	52.00	2-10	-	
Twenty20	10	10	1	110	31	12.22	-	-	2	-	6	12	0	-	-	-	

48. Which Guyanese spinner with 18 ODI wickets
to his name has uncles named Kanhai and Kallicharran?

KARTIK, M. Lancashire

Name: Murali Kartik
Role: Left-hand bat, slow left-arm bowler
Born: 11 September 1976, Chennai (Madras), India
County debut: 2005
Test debut: 1999-2000
Strike rate: (career 64.22)
Overseas tours: India A to Pakistan 1997-98, to West Indies 1999-2000, to South Africa 2001-02, to Sri Lanka 2002, to England 2003; India to Bangladesh 2000-01, to Australia 2003-04, to Pakistan 2003-04, to Bangladesh 2004-05, to Zimbabwe 2005-06 (Videocon Tri-Series)
Overseas teams played for: Railways 1996-97 –
Extras: Represented India U19. Man of the Match in the fourth Test v Australia at

Mumbai (Bombay) 2004-05 (4-44/3-32). Professional for Ramsbottom in the Lancashire League 2004-05 and was a temporary overseas player with Lancashire during the 2005 season, taking 10-168 (5-93/5-75) on Championship debut v Essex at Chelmsford
Best batting: 79 Railways v Baroda, Baroda 2000-01
Best bowling: 9-70 Rest of India v Mumbai, Mumbai (Bombay) 2000-01

2005 Season

	M	Inns	NO	Runs	HS	Avge	100s	50s	Ct	St	O	M	Runs	Wkts	Avge	Best	5wI	10wM
Test																		
All First	2	3	0	11	7	3.66	-	-	1	-	90	21	260	16	16.25	5-75	2	1
1-Day Int																		
C & G																		
tsL	2	2	1	12	11	12.00	-	-	-	-	16	0	67	5	13.40	3-43	-	
Twenty20																		

Career Performances

	M	Inns	NO	Runs	HS	Avge	100s	50s	Ct	St	Balls	Runs	Wkts	Avge	Best	5wI	10wM
Test	8	10	1	88	43	9.77	-	-	2	-	1932	820	24	34.16	4-44	-	-
All First	87	102	11	1671	79	18.36	-	10	45	-	18881	7538	294	25.63	9-70	17	3
1-Day Int	20	9	4	80	32 *	16.00	-	-	7	-	1032	880	19	46.31	3-36	-	
C & G																		
tsL	2	2	1	12	11	12.00	-	-	-	-	96	67	5	13.40	3-43	-	
Twenty20																		

KASPROWICZ, M. S.   Glamorgan

Name: <u>Michael</u> Scott Kasprowicz
Role: Right-hand bat, right-arm fast bowler
Born: 10 February 1972, Brisbane, Australia
Height: 6ft 4in **Weight:** 15st 5lbs
Nickname: Kasper
County debut: 1994 (Essex), 1999
(Leicestershire), 2002 (Glamorgan)
County cap: 1994 (Essex), 1999
(Leicestershire), 2002 (Glamorgan)
Test debut: 1996-97
50 wickets in a season: 4
Place in batting averages: (2004 252nd
av. 14.00)
Place in bowling averages: 110th av. 41.70
(2004 124th av. 42.52)
Strike rate: 59.40 (career 51.58)
Parents: Wally and Joan
Wife and date of marriage: Lindsay,
5 December 2002

Children: 1
Family links with cricket/rugby: 'Brother Adam represented Queensland U17 and
U19. Brother Simon played for NSW Waratahs in Super 12 rugby competition'
Education: Brisbane State High School
Qualifications: Level 2 cricket coaching
Overseas tours: Australia YC to England 1991; Young Australia (Australia A) to
England and Netherlands 1995; Australia to England 1997, to India 1997-98, to
Malaysia (Commonwealth Games) 1998-99, to Pakistan 1998-99, to Bangladesh
(Wills International Cup) 1998-99, to New Zealand 1999-2000, to India 2000-01, to
Sri Lanka 2003-04, to Zimbabwe (one-day series) 2004, to England (ICC Champions
Trophy) 2004, to India 2004-05, to New Zealand 2004-05, to England 2005, plus other
one-day tournaments in Sharjah, India and Holland
Overseas teams played for: Queensland 1989-90 –
Career highlights to date: 'Representing Australia and receiving baggy green cap'
Cricketers particularly admired: Dennis Lillee, Steve Waugh
Other sports played: Rugby (Australian Schoolboys 1989, including tour of New
Zealand)
Other sports followed: Rugby league (Brisbane Broncos), Australian Rules football
(Brisbane Lions)
Relaxations: 'Fishing, beach, music'
Extras: Made his Queensland debut aged 17. Played for Australia U17. Attended
Australian Cricket Academy 1991. Was Essex's overseas player 1994; was

Leicestershire's overseas player 1999; overseas player at Glamorgan 2002-04 and has returned for 2006. Took 9-36 in Durham's second innings at Cardiff 2003 and 9-45 in Durham's second innings at Riverside 2003. Glamorgan Player of the Year 2003 (jointly with Robert Croft). Cricket Society's Wetherell Award 2003 for the leading all-rounder in English first-class cricket. His international awards include Man of the Match in the fourth ODI v Sri Lanka at Colombo 2003-04 (5-45). Queensland's leading wicket-taker in first-class and Sheffield Shield/Pura Cup cricket. Made Twenty20 international debut v New Zealand at Auckland 2004-05

Best batting: 92 Australians v India A, Nagpur 2000-01
Best bowling: 9-36 Glamorgan v Durham, Cardiff 2003

2005 Season

	M	Inns	NO	Runs	HS	Avge	100s	50s	Ct	St	O	M	Runs	Wkts	Avge	Best	5wI	10wM
Test	2	4	0	44	20	11.00	-	-	3	-	52	6	250	4	62.50	3-80	-	-
All First	4	5	0	52	20	10.40	-	-	5	-	99	15	417	10	41.70	5-67	1	-
1-Day Int	5	1	0	1	1	1.00	-	-	3	-	48	3	240	7	34.28	2-40	-	
C & G																		
tsL																		
Twenty20																		

Career Performances

	M	Inns	NO	Runs	HS	Avge	100s	50s	Ct	St	Balls	Runs	Wkts	Avge	Best	5wI	10wM
Test	35	50	10	423	25	10.57	-	-	15	-	6676	3425	106	32.31	7-36	4	-
All First	225	303	63	4173	92	17.38	-	11	91	-	46011	23652	892	26.51	9-36	49	6
1-Day Int	43	13	9	72	28 *	18.00	-	-	13	-	2225	1674	67	24.98	5-45	2	
C & G	7	5	0	90	25	18.00	-	-	1	-	407	279	14	19.92	5-60	1	
tsL	62	40	10	409	38	13.63	-	-	13	-	2805	2046	76	26.92	4-28	-	
Twenty20	6	6	1	65	31	13.00	-	-	1	-	126	145	5	29.00	2-25	-	

KATICH, S. M.   Hampshire

Name: <u>Simon</u> Mathew Katich
Role: Left-hand bat, left-arm wrist-spin bowler
Born: 21 August 1975, Midland, Western Australia
Height: 6ft   **Weight:** 12st 8lbs
Nickname: Kat
County debut: 2000 (Durham), 2002 (Yorkshire), 2003 (Hampshire)
County cap: 2000 (Durham), 2003 (Hampshire)
Test debut: 2001
1000 runs in a season: 2
1st-Class 200s: 1
Place in batting averages: 84th av. 37.52
Strike rate: (career 63.14)

Parents: Vince and Kerry
Marital status: Engaged to Georgie
Education: Trinity College, Perth; University of Western Australia
Qualifications: Bachelor of Commerce degree
Career outside cricket: Entrepreneur
Overseas tours: Australian Cricket Academy to South Africa 1996; Australia to Sri Lanka and Zimbabwe 1999-2000, to England 2001, to Sri Lanka 2003-04, to India 2004-05, to New Zealand 2004-05, to England 2005, to New Zealand (one-day series) 2005-06; Australia A to South Africa 2002-03 (vice-captain)
Overseas teams played for: Western Australia 1996-97 – 2001-02; New South Wales 2002-03 –; Randwick-Petersham, Sydney

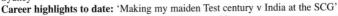

Career highlights to date: 'Making my maiden Test century v India at the SCG'
Cricket moments to forget: 'Any time I drop a catch'
Cricket superstitions: 'Like to wear old gear'
Cricketers particularly admired: Viv Richards
Other sports played: Australian Rules, hockey
Other sports followed: Australian Rules (Richmond), football (Newcastle United)
Favourite band: U2
Relaxations: 'Golf, watching movies and going to the beach in Sydney'
Extras: Attended Commonwealth Bank [Australian] Cricket Academy 1996. *Wisden Australia*'s Sheffield Shield Cricketer of the Year 1998-99. Was Durham's overseas player in 2000. Became the first WA batsman to score a century against each of the other states in a single season 2000-01. Was Yorkshire's overseas player during June 2002. Man of the Match in the Pura Cup final v Queensland at Brisbane 2002-03. Was an overseas player with Hampshire 2003; August to September 2004, deputising for Michael Clarke, and in 2005. Hampshire Cricket Society Player of the Year 2003. Named State Player of the Year at the 2004 Allan Border Medal awards. Made Twenty20 international debut v New Zealand at Auckland 2004-05. Captain of New South Wales since 2004-05
Best batting: 228* Western Australia v South Australia, Perth 2000-01
Best bowling: 7-130 New South Wales v Victoria, Melbourne 2002-03

2005 Season

	M	Inns	NO	Runs	HS	Avge	100s	50s	Ct	St	O	M	Runs	Wkts	Avge	Best	5wI	10wM
Test	5	9	0	248	67	27.55	-	2	4	-	12	1	50	1	50.00	1-36	-	-
All First	14	24	1	863	128	37.52	1	6	12	-	37	5	136	5	27.20	2-25	-	-
1-Day Int	3	2	1	66	36 *	66.00	-	-	2	-								
C & G	2	1	0	0	0	0.00	-	-	-	-								
tsL	5	5	0	144	85	28.80	-	1	4	-	4	0	37	0	-		-	-
Twenty20																		

Career Performances

	M	Inns	NO	Runs	HS	Avge	100s	50s	Ct	St	Balls	Runs	Wkts	Avge	Best	5wI	10wM
Test	21	35	3	1258	125	39.31	2	8	14	-	659	406	12	33.83	6-65	1	-
All First	143	246	33	10514	228 *	49.36	28	55	137	-	4925	2951	78	37.83	7-130	3	-
1-Day Int	18	15	3	344	76	28.66	-	2	8	-							
C & G	6	5	2	166	82 *	55.33	-	1	2	-							
tsL	43	43	5	1569	106	41.28	2	14	29	-	314	315	8	39.37	2-25	-	
Twenty20	5	5	2	179	59 *	59.66	-	2	1	-							

KEEDY, G. Lancashire

Name: Gary Keedy
Role: Left-hand bat, slow left-arm bowler
Born: 27 November 1974, Wakefield
Height: 5ft 11in **Weight:** 12st 6lbs
Nickname: Keeds
County debut: 1994 (Yorkshire),
1995 (Lancashire)
County cap: 2000 (Lancashire)
50 wickets in a season: 2
Place in bowling averages: 12th av. 22.81
(2004 23rd av. 25.68)
Strike rate: 48.27 (career 68.46)
Parents: Roy and Pat
Wife and date of marriage: Andrea,
12 October 2002
Family links with cricket: Twin brother
plays for Castleford in the Yorkshire League
Education: Garforth Comprehensive
Qualifications: 8 GCSEs, Level 2 coaching award
Off-season: 12-month contract
Overseas tours: England U18 to South Africa 1992-93, to Denmark 1993;
England U19 to Sri Lanka 1993-94; Lancashire to Portugal 1995, to Jamaica 1996,
to South Africa 1997

Overseas teams played for: Frankston, Melbourne 1995-96
Career highlights to date: 'Probably bowling Yorkshire out at Headingley. My involvement with Lancashire in general; receiving my county cap was a proud moment'
Cricketers particularly admired: Shane Warne, Graham Gooch
Other sports played: Football, snooker
Other sports followed: Football (Leeds United), rugby league (Leeds Rhinos)
Relaxations: PlayStation
Extras: Player of the Series for England U19 v West Indies U19 1993; also played v India U19 1994. Graduate of the Yorkshire Cricket Academy. Had match figures of 14-227 (7-95/7-132) v Gloucestershire at Old Trafford 2004, the best return by an English spinner since Martyn Ball's 14-169 in 1993. Leading English wicket-taker (second overall) in the Championship 2004 (72 at 25.68)
Best batting: 57 Lancashire v Yorkshire, Headingley 2002
Best bowling: 7-95 Lancashire v Gloucestershire, Old Trafford 2004

2005 Season

	M	Inns	NO	Runs	HS	Avge	100s	50s	Ct	St	O	M	Runs	Wkts	Avge	Best	5wI	10wM
Test																		
All First	9	10	7	47	34	15.66	-	-	1	-	265.3	67	753	33	22.81	6-33	2	1
1-Day Int																		
C & G	2	0	0	0	0	-	-	-	-	-	10	0	44	1	44.00	1-44	-	
tsL	1	0	0	0	0	-	-	-	-	-	5.5	0	34	0	-	-	-	
Twenty20	8	1	0	0	0	0.00	-	-	1	-	25	0	168	7	24.00	3-26	-	

Career Performances

	M	Inns	NO	Runs	HS	Avge	100s	50s	Ct	St	Balls	Runs	Wkts	Avge	Best	5wI	10wM
Test																	
All First	132	151	78	816	57	11.17	-	1	37	-	27112	12640	396	31.91	7-95	20	5
1-Day Int																	
C & G	3	0	0	0	0	-	-	-	-	-	120	84	2	42.00	1-40	-	
tsL	21	7	4	19	10 *	6.33	-	-	1	-	807	698	21	33.23	5-30	1	
Twenty20	15	2	0	0	0	0.00	-	-	2	-	288	306	17	18.00	3-25	-	

KEEGAN, C. B. Middlesex

Name: <u>Chad</u> Blake Keegan
Role: Right-hand bat, right-arm
fast-medium bowler
Born: 30 July 1979, Sandton, Johannesburg,
South Africa
Height: 6ft 1in **Weight:** 12st
Nickname: Wick
County debut: 2001
County cap: 2003
50 wickets in a season: 1
Place in bowling averages: (2004 33rd
av. 27.50)
Strike rate: (career 59.42)
Parents: Sharon and Blake
Marital status: Single
Education: Durban High School
Qualifications: YMCA fitness instructor
Overseas tours: MCC to Argentina and
Chile 2001

Overseas teams played for: Durban High School Old Boys 1994-97; Crusaders,
Durban 1998-99
Career highlights to date: 'Being awarded Player of the Year for Middlesex 2003'
Cricket moments to forget: 'Losing my pants diving for a ball at Lord's'
Cricket superstitions: 'Tapping the bat either side of the crease three times'
Cricketers particularly admired: Malcolm Marshall, Neil Johnson
Other sports played: 'Any extreme sports, golf'
Other sports followed: Football (Liverpool)
Favourite band: Jack Johnson
Relaxations: 'Making and listening to music (guitar); sketching'
Extras: Represented KwaZulu-Natal U13, KwaZulu-Natal Schools, KwaZulu-Natal
U19, KwaZulu-Natal Academy. MCC Young Cricketer. Middlesex Player of the Year
2003. Is not considered an overseas player
Best batting: 44 Middlesex v Surrey, The Oval 2004
Best bowling: 6-114 Middlesex v Leicestershire, Southgate 2003

2005 Season

	M	Inns	NO	Runs	HS	Avge	100s	50s	Ct	St	O	M	Runs	Wkts	Avge	Best	5wI	10wM
Test																		
All First	2	3	0	48	28	16.00	-	-	-	-	70	18	233	1	233.00	1-78	-	-
1-Day Int																		
C & G	1	0	0	0	0	-	-	-	-	-	7	1	44	2	22.00	2-44	-	
tsL	3	2	1	38	26	38.00	-	-	2	-	25	4	109	10	10.90	6-33	1	
Twenty20																		

Career Performances

	M	Inns	NO	Runs	HS	Avge	100s	50s	Ct	St	Balls	Runs	Wkts	Avge	Best	5wI	10wM
Test																	
All First	40	47	5	496	44	11.80	-	-	11	-	7191	4151	121	34.30	6-114	5	-
1-Day Int																	
C & G	7	5	3	97	29 *	48.50	-	-	1	-	364	278	12	23.16	4-35	-	
tsL	55	35	9	395	50	15.19	-	1	15	-	2542	1967	85	23.14	6-33	3	
Twenty20	6	6	1	122	42	24.40	-	-	3	-	138	191	5	38.20	3-34	-	

KEMP, J. M.   Kent

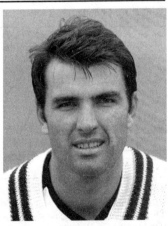

Name: Justin Miles Kemp
Role: Right-hand bat, right-arm
fast-medium bowler
Born: 2 October 1977, Queenstown,
Cape Province, South Africa
Nickname: Kempie
County debut: 2003 (Worcestershire),
2005 (Kent)
County colours: 2003 (Worcestershire)
Test debut: 2000-01
Place in batting averages: 26th av. 52.70
Place in bowling averages: 76th av. 32.63
Strike rate: 59.90 (career 57.70)
Family links with cricket: Grandfather
(J. M. Kemp) played for Border 1947-48;
father (J. W. Kemp) played for Border 1975-
76 – 1976-77; cousin of former South Africa
ODI player Dave Callaghan
Education: Queens College; University of Port Elizabeth
Overseas tours: South Africa U19 to India 1995-96; South African Academy to
Zimbabwe 1998-99; South Africa A to West Indies 2000, to Australia 2002-03, to
Zimbabwe 2004; South Africa to West Indies 2000-01, to Zimbabwe 2001-02, to

Australia 2001-02 (VB Series), to West Indies 2004-05 (one-day series), to India (one-day series) 2005-06, to Australia 2005-06

Overseas teams played for: Eastern Province 1996-97 – 2002-03; Northerns 2003-04 – 2004-05; Titans 2004-05 –

Extras: An overseas player with Worcestershire during the 2003 season as a locum for Andrew Hall; an overseas player with Kent since 2005. Played for African XI v Asian Cricket Council XI in ODI series 2005-06. Has won numerous match awards in domestic and international cricket, including Man of the Match v England in the fifth ODI at East London 2004-05 (50-ball 80) and in the third ODI v Zimbabwe at Port Elizabeth 2004-05 (0-17/78* plus two catches)

Best batting: 188 Eastern Province v North West, Port Elizabeth 2000-01
Best bowling: 6-56 Eastern Province v Border, Port Elizabeth 2000-01
Stop press: Made Twenty20 international debut v New Zealand at Johannesburg 2005-06. Player of the [ODI] Series v New Zealand 2005-06

2005 Season

	M	Inns	NO	Runs	HS	Avge	100s	50s	Ct	St	O	M	Runs	Wkts	Avge	Best	5wl	10wM
Test																		
All First	8	12	2	527	124	52.70	2	2	8	-	109.5	14	359	11	32.63	3-53	-	-
1-Day Int																		
C & G	1	1	1	14	14*	-	-	-	1	-	10	0	43	3	14.33	3-43	-	
tsL	7	7	3	255	84	63.75	-	2	3	-	25.3	1	144	5	28.80	4-52	-	
Twenty20	8	7	1	112	31	18.66	-	-	5	-	14	0	129	7	18.42	2-32	-	

Career Performances

	M	Inns	NO	Runs	HS	Avge	100s	50s	Ct	St	Balls	Runs	Wkts	Avge	Best	5wl	10wM
Test	3	4	0	18	16	4.50	-	-	3	-	395	151	8	18.87	3-33	-	-
All First	76	124	14	4033	188	36.66	8	19	82	-	9099	4218	159	26.52	6-56	4	-
1-Day Int	32	22	4	550	80	30.55	-	5	13	-	863	654	21	31.14	3-20	-	
C & G	2	2	1	27	14*	27.00	-	-	1	-	120	97	3	32.33	3-43	-	
tsL	14	14	5	437	84	48.55	-	3	7	-	329	321	7	45.85	4-52	-	
Twenty20	8	7	1	112	31	18.66	-	-	5	-	84	129	7	18.42	2-32	-	

KENWAY, D. A.   Hampshire

Name: Derek Anthony Kenway
Role: Right-hand bat, right-arm off-spin bowler, part-time wicket-keeper
Born: 12 June 1978, Fareham
Height: 5ft 11in **Weight:** 14st
Nickname: Kenners
County debut: 1997
County cap: 2001
1000 runs in a season: 1

Place in batting averages: (2004 177th av. 25.09)
Strike rate: (career 37.50)
Parents: Keith and Geraldine
Marital status: Single
Family links with cricket: 'Brother Richard plays local cricket and has played some 2nd XI'
Education: St George's, Southampton; Barton Peveril College
Qualifications: 6 GCSEs, Level 2 coaching
Career outside cricket: 'Family own roofing company'
Overseas tours: West of England U15 to West Indies 1993; ECB National Academy to Australia 2001-02
Overseas teams played for: Beaumaris CC, Melbourne 1997-98
Career highlights to date: 'The win against Australia for Hants [2001]'
Cricket moments to forget: 'Leaving a straight one from Welchy on debut'
Cricketers particularly admired: Robin Smith
Other sports played: Golf, football ('locally')
Other sports followed: Football (Southampton FC)
Favourite band: U2
Extras: Southern League Young Player of the Year 1996. NBC Denis Compton Award 1999. Hampshire Cricket Society Player of the Year 2001. Scored half-century (60) in ECB National Academy's innings victory over Commonwealth Bank [Australian] Cricket Academy at Adelaide 2001-02. Released by Hampshire at the end of the 2005 season
Best batting: 166 Hampshire v Nottinghamshire, West End 2001
Best bowling: 1-5 Hampshire v Warwickshire, Southampton 1997

2005 Season

	M	Inns	NO	Runs	HS	Avge	100s	50s	Ct	St	O	M	Runs	Wkts	Avge	Best	5wl	10wM
Test																		
All First	1	2	0	20	20	10.00	-	-	3	-								
1-Day Int																		
C & G	1	1	0	13	13	13.00	-	-	1	-								
tsL	7	6	0	136	65	22.66	-	1	3	-								
Twenty20	5	4	0	19	16	4.75	-	-	2	3								

Career Performances

	M	Inns	NO	Runs	HS	Avge	100s	50s	Ct	St	Balls	Runs	Wkts	Avge	Best	5wI	10wM
Test																	
All First	93	163	15	4382	166	29.60	7	20	85	1	150	159	4	39.75	1-5	-	-
1-Day Int																	
C & G	8	8	0	263	76	32.87	-	2	4	1	17	16	1	16.00	1-16	-	
tsL	86	80	2	1945	115	24.93	1	13	49	5							
Twenty20	10	9	0	134	40	14.88	-	-	4	3							

KEY, R. W. T. Kent

Name: Robert William Trevor Key
Role: Right-hand bat, off-spin bowler,
county captain
Born: 12 May 1979, Dulwich, London
Height: 6ft 1in **Weight:** 12st 7lbs
Nickname: Keysy
County debut: 1998
County cap: 2001
Test debut: 2002
1000 runs in a season: 4
1st-Class 200s: 1
Place in batting averages: 14th av. 59.84
(2004 1st av. 79.00)
Parents: Trevor and Lynn
Marital status: Single
Family links with cricket: Mother played
for Kent Ladies. Father played club cricket in
Derby. Sister Elizabeth played for her junior
school side

Education: Langley Park Boys' School
Qualifications: 10 GCSEs, NCA coaching award, GNVQ Business Studies
Overseas tours: Kent U13 to Holland; England U17 to Bermuda (International Youth
Tournament) 1997 (c); England U19 to South Africa (including U19 World Cup) 1997-
98; England A to Zimbabwe and South Africa 1998-99; ECB National Academy to
Australia 2001-02, to Sri Lanka 2002-03; England to Australia 2002-03, to South
Africa 2004-05
Overseas teams played for: Greenpoint CC, Cape Town 1996-97
Cricketers particularly admired: Min Patel, Neil Taylor, Alan Wells, Mark Ealham
Other sports played: Hockey, football, snooker, tennis (played for county)
Other sports followed: Football (Chelsea), basketball (Chicago Bulls)
Extras: Represented England U19 1997 and was England U19 Man of the Series v

Pakistan U19 1998 (award shared with Graeme Swann). NBC Denis Compton Award for the most promising young Kent player 2001. Scored 221 in the first Test v West Indies 2004, in the process sharing with Andrew Strauss (137) in a record second-wicket stand for Test cricket at Lord's (291). Leading run-scorer in English first-class cricket 2004 with 1896 runs at 79.00, including nine centuries. One of *Wisden*'s Five Cricketers of the Year 2005. Scored twin centuries (112/189) v Surrey at Tunbridge Wells 2005, in the second innings sharing with Martin van Jaarsveld (168) in a new Kent record third-wicket partnership (323). ECB National Academy 2005-06. Appointed captain of Kent for 2006

Best batting: 221 England v West Indies, Lord's 2004

2005 Season

	M	Inns	NO	Runs	HS	Avge	100s	50s	Ct	St	O	M	Runs	Wkts	Avge	Best	5wl	10wM
Test																		
All First	15	27	1	1556	189	59.84	4	8	8	-	1	0	5	0	-	-	-	-
1-Day Int																		
C & G	3	3	0	94	53	31.33	-	1	1	-								
tsL	10	10	1	185	67	20.55	-	1	1	-								
Twenty20	6	6	1	59	15 *	11.80	-	-	2	-								

Career Performances

	M	Inns	NO	Runs	HS	Avge	100s	50s	Ct	St	Balls	Runs	Wkts	Avge	Best	5wl	10wM
Test	15	26	1	775	221	31.00	1	3	11	-							
All First	144	249	12	9694	221	40.90	28	39	91	-	80	49	0	-	-	-	-
1-Day Int	5	5	0	54	19	10.80	-	-	-	-							
C & G	18	18	2	705	77	44.06	-	7	3	-							
tsL	82	78	7	1962	114	27.63	1	12	11	-							
Twenty20	9	9	2	173	66 *	24.71	-	1	2	-							

49. Which India international was dismissed both handled the ball and obstructing the field in ODIs?

KHALID, S. A.   Worcestershire

Name: <u>Shaftab</u> Ahmad Khalid
Role: Right-hand bat, right-arm
off-spin bowler
Born: 6 October 1982, Pakistan
Height: 5ft 11in **Weight:** 10st 6lbs
Nickname: Shafi
County debut: 2003
County colours: 2003
Strike rate: (career 91.42)
Parents: Dr Khalid Mahmood and
Mrs Nuzhat Bano
Marital status: Single
Education: Dormers Wells High School;
West Thames College
Qualifications: 11 GCSEs, 3 A-levels
Overseas tours: England A to Malaysia and
India 2003-04
Extras: ECB National Academy 2003-04.
NBC Denis Compton Award for the most promising young Worcestershire player 2003
Best batting: 20 Worcestershire v LUCCE, Kidderminster 2005
Best bowling: 4-131 Worcestershire v Northamptonshire, Northampton 2003

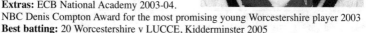

2005 Season

	M	Inns	NO	Runs	HS	Avge	100s	50s	Ct	St	O	M	Runs	Wkts	Avge	Best	5wI	10wM
Test																		
All First	1	2	0	20	20	10.00	-	-	-	-	16	3	39	0	-	-	-	-
1-Day Int																		
C & G																		
tsL																		
Twenty20																		

Career Performances

	M	Inns	NO	Runs	HS	Avge	100s	50s	Ct	St	Balls	Runs	Wkts	Avge	Best	5wI	10wM
Test																	
All First	10	9	2	64	20	9.14	-	-	3	-	1280	712	14	50.85	4-131	-	-
1-Day Int																	
C & G	1	1	1	9	9*	-	-	-	-	-							
tsL	6	2	2	4	3*	-	-	-	1	-	174	138	2	69.00	2-40	-	
Twenty20	1	0	0	0	0	-	-	-	-	-	6	13	0	-	-	-	

KHAN, A.

Name: Amjad Khan
Role: Right-hand bat, right-arm fast bowler
Born: 14 October 1980, Copenhagen,
Denmark
Height: 6ft **Weight:** 11st 6lbs
Nickname: Ammy
County debut: 2001
County cap: 2005
50 wickets in a season: 2
Place in batting averages: 210th av. 21.25
(2004 249th av. 15.28)
Place in bowling averages: 52nd av. 28.27
(2004 105th av. 37.80)
Strike rate: 45.30 (career 47.85)
Parents: Aslam and Raisa
Marital status: Single
Education: Skolen på Duevej, Denmark;
Falkonĕrgårdens Gymnasium

Overseas tours: Denmark U19 to Canada 1996, to Bermuda 1997, to South Africa
(U19 World Cup) 1997-98, to Wales 1998, to Ireland 1999; Denmark to Holland 1998,
to Zimbabwe (ICC Emerging Nations Tournament) 1999-2000, to Canada (ICC
Trophy) 2001
Overseas teams played for: Kjøbenhavns Boldklub, Denmark
Cricket moments to forget: 'I try to forget most of the games where I didn't perform
as well as I would like'
Cricketers particularly admired: Wasim Akram, Dennis Lillee
Other sports followed: Football (Denmark)
Favourite band: Marvin Gaye, George Michael, Nerd (Neptunes)
Relaxations: 'Music, sleeping, reading'
Extras: Made debut for Denmark at the age of 17. Took 50 first-class wickets (63) in
his first full season 2002. NBC Denis Compton Award for the most promising young
Kent player 2002. Is not considered an overseas player
Best batting: 78 Kent v Middlesex, Lord's 2003
Best bowling: 6-52 Kent v Yorkshire, Canterbury 2002

2005 Season

	M	Inns	NO	Runs	HS	Avge	100s	50s	Ct	St	O	M	Runs	Wkts	Avge	Best	5wl	10wM
Test																		
All First	14	17	9	170	58 *	21.25	-	1	2	-	415.2	80	1555	55	28.27	6-73	1	-
1-Day Int																		
C & G	2	1	0	1	1	1.00	-	-	-	-	14	1	51	2	25.50	1-12	-	
tsL	9	3	0	35	33	11.66	-	-	1	-	58.5	3	320	11	29.09	2-16	-	
Twenty20	3	0	0	0	0	-	-	-	-	-	4	0	40	3	13.33	3-24	-	

Career Performances

	M	Inns	NO	Runs	HS	Avge	100s	50s	Ct	St	Balls	Runs	Wkts	Avge	Best	5wl	10wM
Test																	
All First	48	55	16	726	78	18.61	-	3	8	-	7465	5158	156	33.06	6-52	5	-
1-Day Int																	
C & G	8	4	0	16	13	4.00	-	-	3	-	363	283	9	31.44	2-34	-	
tsL	22	13	3	97	33	9.70	-	-	2	-	839	734	26	28.23	4-26	-	
Twenty20	8	3	0	16	15	5.33	-	-	-	-	138	200	11	18.18	3-24	-	

KILLEEN, N.   Durham

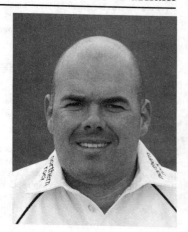

Name: Neil Killeen
Role: Right-hand bat, right-arm medium-fast bowler
Born: 17 October 1975, Shotley Bridge
Height: 6ft 1in **Weight:** 15st
Nickname: Killer, Bully, Quinny, Squeaky, Bull
County debut: 1995
County cap: 1999
Benefit: 2006
50 wickets in a season: 1
Place in batting averages: (2004 246th av. 15.82)
Place in bowling averages: (2004 153rd av. 55.57)
Strike rate: (career 63.80)
Parents: Glen and Thora
Wife and date of marriage: Clare Louise, 5 February 2000
Children: Jonathan David
Family links with cricket: 'Dad best armchair player in the game'
Education: Greencroft Comprehensive School; Derwentside College, University of Teesside

Qualifications: 8 GCSEs, 2 A-levels, first year Sports Science, Level III coaching award, Level I staff coach
Career outside cricket: Cricket coaching
Overseas tours: Durham CCC to Zimbabwe 1992; England U19 to West Indies 1994-95; MCC to Bangladesh 1999-2000
Career highlights to date: 'My county cap and first-class debut'
Cricket moments to forget: 'Injury causing me to miss most of 2001 season'
Cricketers particularly admired: Ian Botham, Curtly Ambrose, Courtney Walsh, David Boon
Other sports played: Athletics (English Schools javelin)
Sports followed: Football (Sunderland AFC), cricket (Anfield Plain CC)
Relaxations: 'Good food, good wine; golf; spending time with wife and family'
Extras: Was first Durham bowler to take five wickets in a Sunday League game (5-26 v Northamptonshire at Northampton 1995). Scored 35 batting at No. 10 as Durham made 453-9 to beat Somerset at Taunton 2004. Had figures of 8.3-7-5-2 v Derbyshire at Riverside in the totesport League 2004
Best batting: 48 Durham v Somerset, Riverside 1995
Best bowling: 7-70 Durham v Hampshire, Riverside 2003

2005 Season

	M	Inns	NO	Runs	HS	Avge	100s	50s	Ct	St	O	M	Runs	Wkts	Avge	Best	5wI	10wM
Test																		
All First	5	5	1	39	23	9.75	-	-	3	-	122.5	37	357	8	44.62	3-40	-	-
1-Day Int																		
C & G	1	1	0	1	1	1.00	-	-	2	-	10	2	65	3	21.66	3-65	-	
tsL	16	4	1	17	8 *	5.66	-	-	4	-	128	14	460	21	21.90	3-15	-	
Twenty20	7	2	2	3	3 *	-	-	-	3	-	25	0	195	6	32.50	1-14	-	

Career Performances

	M	Inns	NO	Runs	HS	Avge	100s	50s	Ct	St	Balls	Runs	Wkts	Avge	Best	5wI	10wM
Test																	
All First	89	131	27	1225	48	11.77	-	-	23	-	14612	7362	229	32.14	7-70	7	-
1-Day Int																	
C & G	12	8	1	53	29	7.57	-	-	3	-	646	411	17	24.17	3-65	-	
tsL	136	73	30	425	32	9.88	-	-	25	-	6171	4380	193	22.69	6-31	4	
Twenty20	17	8	5	43	17 *	14.33	-	-	4	-	366	456	24	19.00	4-7	-	

KING, R. E.   Northamptonshire

Name: <u>Richard</u> Eric King
Role: Right-hand bat, left-arm medium-fast
bowler; all-rounder
Born: 3 January 1984, Hitchin
Height: 6ft **Weight:** 13st
Nickname: Kingy
County debut: 2005
Strike rate: (career 196.50)
Parents: Roger and Rosemary
Marital status: Single
Education: Bedford Modern School;
Loughborough University
Qualifications: 10 GCSEs, 3 A-levels, Level
2 ECB coach
Overseas tours: Bedford Modern to
Barbados 1999; Northamptonshire YC to
South Africa 2002
Cricket superstitions: 'Right pad on before
left'
Cricketers particularly admired: Ian Botham, Shane Warne, Viv Richards,
Chris Park
Other sports played: Rugby (East Midlands), golf
Other sports followed: Football (Arsenal)
Favourite band: Lifehouse
Relaxations: 'Listening to music, socialising, extra training'
Extras: MCC Taverners U15 Young Cricketer of the Year. Played for Northants Board
XI in the C&G 2002 and 2003. Northamptonshire Academy 2002. Captained ECB
Schools XI v India U19 2002. Played for Loughborough UCCE 2003. Released by
Northamptonshire at the end of the 2005 season
Best batting: 17 LUCCE v Somerset, Taunton 2003
Best bowling: 1-32 Northamptonshire v Bangladeshis, Northampton 2005

2005 Season

	M	Inns	NO	Runs	HS	Avge	100s	50s	Ct	St	O	M	Runs	Wkts	Avge	Best	5wl	10wM
Test																		
All First	1	0	0	0	0	-	-	-	-	-	7	2	32	1	32.00	1-32	-	-
1-Day Int																		
C & G																		
tsL	1	0	0	0	0	-	-	-	-	-	2	0	26	0	-	-	-	-
Twenty20																		

Career Performances

	M	Inns	NO	Runs	HS	Avge	100s	50s	Ct	St	Balls	Runs	Wkts	Avge	Best	5wI	10wM
Test																	
All First	4	5	0	19	17	3.80	-	-	-	-	393	345	2	172.50	1-32	-	-
1-Day Int																	
C & G	2	2	0	2	2	1.00	-	-	1	-	90	66	2	33.00	2-39	-	
tsL	1	0	0	0	0	-	-	-	-	-	12	26	0	-	-	-	
Twenty20																	

KIRBY, S. P. Gloucestershire

Name: <u>Steven</u> Paul Kirby
Role: Right-hand bat, right-arm fast bowler
Born: 4 October 1977, Bury, Lancashire
Height: 6ft 3in **Weight:** 13st 5lbs
Nickname: Tango
County debut: 2001 (Yorkshire),
2005 (Gloucestershire)
County cap: 2003 (Yorkshire),
2005 (Gloucestershire)
50 wickets in a season: 1
Place in batting averages: 277th av. 10.50
Place in bowling averages: 30th av. 26.00
(2004 94th av. 36.51)
Strike rate: 46.64 (career 47.63)
Parents: Paul and Alison
Wife and date of marriage: Sasha,
11 October 2003
Education: Elton High School, Walshaw,
Bury, Lancs; Bury College
Qualifications: 10 GCSEs, BTEC/GNVQ Advanced Leisure and Tourism
Career outside cricket: 'Coaching, teaching'
Overseas tours: Yorkshire to Grenada 2001; ECB National Academy to Australia 2001-02; England A to India 2003-04
Overseas teams played for: Egmont Plains, New Zealand 1997-98
Cricket moments to forget: 'Being knocked out by Nixon McLean trying to take a return catch'
Cricketers particularly admired: Steve Waugh, Richard Hadlee, Glenn McGrath, Michael Atherton, Curtly Ambrose, Sachin Tendulkar
Other sports played: Basketball, table tennis, squash, golf – 'anything sporty and competitive'
Other sports followed: Football (Manchester United), rugby (Leicester Tigers)

Relaxations: 'Walking the dog; shooting; spending time with family; socialising with friends'

Extras: Formerly with Leicestershire but did not appear for first team. Took 14 wickets (41-18-47-14) in one day for Egmont Plains v Hawera in a New Zealand club match 1997-98. Took 7-50 in Kent's second innings at Headingley 2001, the best bowling figures by a Yorkshire player on first-class debut; Kirby had replaced Matthew Hoggard (called up by England) halfway through the match. Took 13-154 (5-74/8-80) v Somerset at Taunton 2003, the best match return by a Yorkshire bowler for 36 years

Best batting: 57 Yorkshire v Hampshire, Headingley 2002

Best bowling: 8-80 Yorkshire v Somerset, Taunton 2003

2005 Season

	M	Inns	NO	Runs	HS	Avge	100s	50s	Ct	St	O	M	Runs	Wkts	Avge	Best	5wI	10wM
Test																		
All First	13	21	11	105	15 *	10.50	-	-	-	-	349.5	79	1170	45	26.00	4-20	-	-
1-Day Int																		
C & G																			
tsL	3	1	1	1	1 *	-	-	-	1	-	20.4	2	117	1	117.00	1-45	-	
Twenty20	8	3	1	1	1 *	0.50	-	-	-	-	24	0	170	9	18.88	2-15	-	

Career Performances

	M	Inns	NO	Runs	HS	Avge	100s	50s	Ct	St	Balls	Runs	Wkts	Avge	Best	5wI	10wM
Test																	
All First	61	84	25	447	57	7.57	-	1	13	-	10696	6401	229	27.95	8-80	9	3
1-Day Int																	
C & G	2	1	0	0	0	0.00	-	-	-	-	102	74	2	37.00	1-21	-	
tsL	28	11	4	39	15	5.57	-	-	7	-	1110	1036	23	45.04	3-27	-	
Twenty20	11	3	1	1	1 *	0.50	-	-	1	-	216	289	13	22.23	2-15	-	

KIRTLEY, R. J.   Sussex

Name: Robert James Kirtley
Role: Right-hand bat, right-arm fast-medium bowler
Born: 10 January 1975, Eastbourne
Height: 6ft **Weight:** 12st
Nickname: Ambi
County debut: 1995
County cap: 1998
Benefit: 2006
Test debut: 2003
50 wickets in a season: 7
Place in batting averages: 227th av. 19.40 (2004 242nd av. 16.30)

Place in bowling averages: 20th av. 24.33
(2004 100th av. 37.32)
Strike rate: 50.01 (career 50.01)
Parents: Bob and Pip
Wife and date of marriage: Jenny,
26 October 2002
Family links with cricket: Brother plays
league cricket
Education: St Andrews School, Eastbourne;
Clifton College, Bristol
Qualifications: 9 GCSEs, 2 A-levels, NCA
coaching first level
Overseas tours: Sussex YC to Barbados
1993, to Sri Lanka 1995; Sussex to Grenada
2001; England A to Bangladesh and New
Zealand 1999-2000; England to Zimbabwe
(one-day series) 2001-02, to Sri Lanka (ICC
Champions Trophy) 2002-03, to Australia

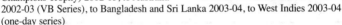

2002-03 (VB Series), to Bangladesh and Sri Lanka 2003-04, to West Indies 2003-04
(one-day series)
Overseas teams played for: Mashonaland, Zimbabwe 1996-97; Namibian Cricket
Board/Wanderers, Windhoek, Namibia 1998-99
Career highlights to date: 'My Test debut at Trent Bridge'
Cricket moments to forget: 'The three times I've bagged a pair'
Cricket superstitions: 'Put my left boot on first!'
Cricketers particularly admired: Curtly Ambrose, Jim Andrew, Darren Gough
Other sports followed: Rugby (England), football (Brighton & Hove Albion)
Relaxations: 'Inviting friends round for a braai (barbeque) and enjoying a cold beer
with them'
Extras: Played in the Mashonaland side which defeated England on their 1996-97 tour
of Zimbabwe, taking seven wickets in the match. Winner of an NBC Denis Compton
Award for promising cricketers 1997. Leading wicket-taker in English first-class
cricket 2001 with 75 wickets (av. 23.32). Sussex Player of the Year 2002. Made Test
debut in the third Test v South Africa at Trent Bridge 2003, taking 6-34 in South
Africa's second innings and winning Man of the Match award. Vice-captain of Sussex
2001-05
Best batting: 59 Sussex v Durham, Eastbourne 1998
Best bowling: 7-21 Sussex v Hampshire, Southampton 1999

2005 Season

	M	Inns	NO	Runs	HS	Avge	100s	50s	Ct	St	O	M	Runs	Wkts	Avge	Best	5wI	10wM
Test																		
All First	17	23	13	194	30	19.40	-	-	7	-	525.1	130	1533	63	24.33	6-80	2	-
1-Day Int																		
C & G	3	0	0	0	0	-	-	-	-	-	29	6	112	6	18.66	3-24	-	
tsL	18	4	2	10	8 *	5.00	-	-	7	-	133	14	593	31	19.12	4-29	-	
Twenty20	8	1	0	2	2	2.00	-	-	-	-	19	0	126	6	21.00	2-19	-	

Career Performances

	M	Inns	NO	Runs	HS	Avge	100s	50s	Ct	St	Balls	Runs	Wkts	Avge	Best	5wI	10wM
Test	4	7	1	32	12	5.33	-	-	3	-	1079	561	19	29.52	6-34	1	-
All First	150	208	68	1761	59	12.57	-	3	50	-	28763	14977	576	26.00	7-21	29	4
1-Day Int	11	2	0	2	1	1.00	-	-	5	-	549	481	9	53.44	2-33	-	
C & G	16	5	3	61	30 *	30.50	-	-	1	-	919	622	33	18.84	5-39	2	
tsL	126	51	26	244	19 *	9.76	-	-	34	-	5256	4121	173	23.82	4-21	-	
Twenty20	14	4	0	2	2	0.50	-	-	1	-	250	287	14	20.50	2-8	-	

KLUSENER, L.   Northamptonshire

Name: Lance Klusener
Role: Left-hand bat, right-arm
medium-fast bowler
Born: 4 September 1971, Durban,
South Africa
Height: 6ft **Weight:** 12st 10lbs
Nickname: Zulu
County debut: 2002 (Nottinghamshire),
2004 (Middlesex)
Test debut: 1996-97
Place in batting averages: (2004 185th
av. 24.28)
Place in bowling averages: (2004 147th
av. 51.76)
Strike rate: (career 57.83)
Parents: Peter and Dawn
Wife and date of marriage: Isabelle,
13 May 2000
Children: Matthew, 17 February 2002
Education: Durban High School; Durban Technikon
Overseas tours: South Africa U24 to Sri Lanka 1995; South Africa A to England
1996; South Africa to India 1996-97, to Pakistan 1997-98, to Australia 1997-98, to

England 1998, to New Zealand 1998-99, to UK, Ireland and Holland (World Cup) 1999, to Zimbabwe 1999-2000, to India 1999-2000, to Sri Lanka 2000, to Kenya (ICC Knockout Trophy) 2000-01, to West Indies 2000-01, to Zimbabwe 2001-02, to Australia 2001-02, to Sri Lanka (ICC Champions Trophy) 2002-03, to New Zealand 2003-04 (one-day series), to Sri Lanka 2004, to England (ICC Champions Trophy) 2004, plus other one-day tournaments in Kenya, Sharjah, Australia, Singapore and Morocco; FICA World XI to New Zealand 2004-05

Overseas teams played for: Natal/KwaZulu-Natal 1993-94 – 2003-04; Dolphins 2004-05 –

Career highlights to date: 'World Cup Man of the Tournament [1999]'

Cricketers particularly admired: Malcolm Marshall

Other sports played: Golf

Other sports followed: Rugby (Sharks)

Extras: Returned the best innings analysis by a South African on Test debut – 8-64 in the second Test v India at Kolkata 1996-97. One of *South African Cricket Annual*'s five Cricketers of the Year 1997, 1999. Scored 174 in the second Test v England at Port Elizabeth 1999-2000, winning Man of the Match award. One of *Wisden*'s Five Cricketers of the Year 2000. His other Test awards include Man of the Series v Sri Lanka 2000. Has won numerous ODI awards, including Player of the Tournament in the World Cup 1999. Man of the Match in the SuperSport Series final v Western Province at Cape Town 2003-04 (7-70/5-90). An overseas player with Nottinghamshire at the start of the 2002 season; an overseas player with Middlesex 2004. Is no longer considered an overseas player

Best batting: 174 South Africa v England, Port Elizabeth 1999-2000

Best bowling: 8-34 Natal v Western Province, Durban 1995-96

2005 Season (did not make any first-class or one-day appearances)

Career Performances

	M	Inns	NO	Runs	HS	Avge	100s	50s	Ct	St	Balls	Runs	Wkts	Avge	Best	5wI	10wM
Test	49	69	11	1906	174	32.86	4	8	34	-	6881	3033	80	37.91	8-64	1	-
All First	134	186	39	5303	174	36.07	8	29	73	-	23078	11033	399	27.65	8-34	15	4
1-Day Int	171	137	50	3576	103 *	41.10	2	19	35	-	7336	5751	192	29.95	6-49	6	
C & G	3	2	0	14	11	7.00	-	-	1	-	144	88	2	44.00	1-20	-	
tsL	9	4	3	85	56 *	85.00	-	1	2	-	396	332	9	36.88	2-31	-	
Twenty20	3	2	1	88	53	88.00	-	1	1	-	66	98	4	24.50	2-32	-	

KNAPPETT, J. P. T.   Worcestershire

Name: Joshua (<u>Josh</u>) Philip
Thomas Knappett
Role: Right-hand bat, wicket-keeper
Born: 15 April 1985, Westminster, London
Height: 6ft **Weight:** 12st 4lbs
Nickname: Badger, Edwin (van der Sar)
County debut: No first-team appearance
Parents: Phil and Janie
Marital status: Girlfriend Kate
Family links with cricket: 'Dad is Cricket
Development Officer of Middlesex and has
played club cricket. Brother, Jon, plays
socially'
Education: East Barnet School; Oxford
Brookes University
Qualifications: 10 GCSEs, 3 A-levels, Level
3 ECB tutor trained and assessor trained

cricket coach, swimming, football and rugby
Level 1 coaching qualifications
Career outside cricket: 'Education, coaching and coach education'
Off-season: 'Perhaps a winter in Oz; otherwise training hard and coaching'
Overseas tours: MCC A to Canada 2005
Career highlights to date: 'Going on MCC A tour to Canada. Scoring 73 against
Bangladesh for BUSA. Winning *Evening Standard* Cup with Finchley CC (Middlesex
Premier League) 2004'
Cricket moments to forget: 'Being hit on the head by Jimmy Ormond on first-class
debut for OUCCE'
Cricketers particularly admired: Jack Russell, Adam Gilchrist
Young players to look out for: Eoin Morgan, Billy Godleman, Richard Jones
Other sports played: Squash, trampolining
Other sports followed: Football (Tottenham Hotspur)
Favourite band: 'Led Zeppelin, Jack Johnson, DJ Shadow, Montana, Hendrix,
Gomez etc.'
Relaxations: 'Listening to music, eating and sleeping (as well as training)'
Extras: Played for Oxford UCCE 2004, 2005. Represented British Universities 2005.
Attended training camp in Mumbai, India 2005 (World Cricket Academy)
Opinions on cricket: 'Fast and furious – will only get better. The more interested the
public are, the more money will be around, which will improve standards.'
Best batting: 73 British Universities v Bangladeshis, Fenner's 2005

2005 Season (did not make any first-class or one-day appearances for his county)

Career Performances

	M	Inns	NO	Runs	HS	Avge	100s	50s	Ct	St	Balls	Runs	Wkts	Avge	Best	5wI	10wM
Test																	
All First	6	8	1	277	73	39.57	-	2	12	1							
1-Day Int																	
C & G																	
tsL																	
Twenty20																	

KNIGHT, N. V. Warwickshire

Name: Nicholas (<u>Nick</u>) Verity Knight
Role: Left-hand bat, right-arm medium-fast bowler, close fielder
Born: 28 November 1969, Watford
Height: 6ft 1in **Weight:** 13st
Nickname: Stitch, Fungus
County debut: 1991 (Essex), 1995 (Warwickshire)
County cap: 1994 (Essex), 1995 (Warwickshire)
Benefit: 2004 (Warwickshire)
Test debut: 1995
1000 runs in a season: 6
1st-Class 200s: 3
1st-Class 300s: 1
Place in batting averages: 51st av. 45.25 (2004 22nd av. 55.16)
Strike rate: (career 195.00)
Parents: John and Rosemary
Wife and date of marriage: Trudie, 3 October 1998
Family links with cricket: Father played for Cambridgeshire. Brother Andy club cricketer in local Cambridge leagues
Education: Felsted School; Loughborough University
Qualifications: 9 O-levels, 3 A-levels, BSc (Hons) Sociology, coaching qualification
Overseas tours: Felsted School to Australia 1986-87; England A to India 1994-95; to Pakistan 1995-96, to Kenya and Sri Lanka 1997-98; England to Zimbabwe and New Zealand 1996-97, to Sharjah (Champions Trophy) 1997-98, to West Indies 1997-98 (one-day series), to Bangladesh (Wills International Cup) 1998-99, to Australia 1998-99 (CUB Series), to Sharjah (Coca-Cola Cup) 1998-99, to South Africa and Zimbabwe

1999-2000 (one-day series), to Sri Lanka 2000-01 (one-day series), to Zimbabwe (one-day series) 2001-02, to India and New Zealand 2001-02 (one-day series), to Sri Lanka (ICC Champions Trophy) 2002-03, to Australia 2002-03 (VB Series), to Africa (World Cup) 2002-03; FICA World XI to New Zealand 2004-05
Overseas teams played for: Northern Districts, Sydney 1991-92; East Torrens, Adelaide 1992-94
Cricketers particularly admired: David Gower, Graham Gooch
Other sports played: Rugby (Eastern Counties), hockey (Essex and Young England)
Relaxations: Eating good food, painting
Extras: Captained England YC v New Zealand YC 1989 and captained Combined Universities 1991. Gray-Nicolls Cricketer of the Year 1988, Cricket Society Most Promising Young Cricketer of the Year 1989, Essex Young Player of the Year 1991 and Essex U19 Player of the Year. Warwickshire vice-captain 1999. Leading English player (second overall) in the 2002 first-class batting averages with 1520 runs at 95.00. Warwickshire Batsman of the Year 2002. His international awards include Man of the Match in the first Test v Zimbabwe at Bulawayo 1996-97, Man of the [ODI] Series v Zimbabwe 2001-02 (302 runs; av. 100.67), and successive ODI Man of the Match awards v West Indies 1997-98. Retired from international cricket in April 2003. Captain of Warwickshire 2004-05
Best batting: 303* Warwickshire v Middlesex, Lord's 2004
Best bowling: 1-61 Essex v Middlesex, Uxbridge 1994

2005 Season

	M	Inns	NO	Runs	HS	Avge	100s	50s	Ct	St	O	M	Runs	Wkts	Avge	Best	5wI	10wM
Test																		
All First	17	30	3	1222	117	45.25	4	5	9	-								
1-Day Int																		
C & G	5	5	1	435	118	108.75	3	1	-	-								
tsL	17	16	2	520	122 *	37.14	2	1	6	-								
Twenty20	9	9	1	135	61	16.87	-	1	3	-								

Career Performances

	M	Inns	NO	Runs	HS	Avge	100s	50s	Ct	St	Balls	Runs	Wkts	Avge	Best	5wI	10wM
Test	17	30	0	719	113	23.96	1	4	26	-							
All First	223	379	42	15102	303 *	44.81	38	71	271	-	195	230	1	230.00	1-61	-	-
1-Day Int	100	100	10	3637	125 *	40.41	5	25	44	-							
C & G	39	39	5	1760	151	51.76	7	7	17	-							
tsL	180	167	20	5163	134	35.12	10	23	74	-	84	85	2	42.50	1-14	-	
Twenty20	19	19	2	496	89	29.17	-	5	7	-	5	4	0	-	-	-	

KREJZA, J. J. Leicestershire

Name: Jason Jan Krejza
Role: Right-hand bat, right-arm
off-spin bowler
Born: 14 January 1983, Sydney, Australia
Height: 6ft 1in
Nickname: Krazy
County debut: 2005
Strike rate: (career 76.66)
Parents: George and Jadwiga
Marital status: Partner
Education: All Saints Catholic Boys College,
Liverpool, NSW; All Saints Catholic Senior
College, Casula, NSW
Qualifications: Level 1 coach
Career outside cricket: 'Currently working
towards property development'
Overseas tours: Australia Cricket Centre of
Excellence to India 2004; New South Wales
to India 2005
Overseas teams played for: Fairfield-Liverpool CC 2000-04; UTS-Balmain CC
2004-06; New South Wales 2004-05 –
Career highlights to date: 'Winning the Pura Cup final last year [2004-05] – first
year of first-class cricket and winning the cup is very rare!'
Cricket moments to forget: 'Injuries. They are terrible'
Cricket superstitions: 'All the conventional ones – certain pad first etc.'
Cricketers particularly admired: Mark Waugh ('long-time hero'), Damien Martyn
Young players to look out for: Travis Birt (Tasmania)
Other sports played: AFL 'the great Australian game' (South West Sydney Magpies),
football ('various teams')
Other sports followed: AFL (Essendon)
Injuries: 'This season I have played only one game. Been out for 16 weeks with a
stress fracture in my shin. Frustrating year'
Favourite band: Foo Fighters
Relaxations: 'Playing guitar, relaxing at the beach, pub lunches with mates'
Player website: 'I wish … I might create my own, though'
Extras: Professional with Greenock CC in Scotland 2005, making club record score
(194*), v SMRH in the Scottish Cup at Glenpark. Played one first-class match for
Leicestershire 2005, v Australians at Leicester
Opinions on cricket: 'Not too many concerns at this time. The game is great and we
shouldn't change it too much.'
Best batting: 63 New South Wales v Victoria, Melbourne 2004-05
Best bowling: 2-11 New South Wales v Victoria, Melbourne 2004-05

2005 Season

	M	Inns	NO	Runs	HS	Avge	100s	50s	Ct	St	O	M	Runs	Wkts	Avge	Best	5wI	10wM
Test																		
All First	1	2	0	57	38	28.50	-	-	-	-	25	0	136	0	-		-	-
1-Day Int																		
C & G																		
tsL																		
Twenty20																		

Career Performances

	M	Inns	NO	Runs	HS	Avge	100s	50s	Ct	St	Balls	Runs	Wkts	Avge	Best	5wI	10wM
Test																		
All First	1	2	0	57	38	28.50	-	-	-	-	150	136	0	-		-	-
1-Day Int																		
C & G																		
tsL																		
Twenty20																		

KRUIS, G. J.   Yorkshire

Name: Gideon (<u>Deon</u>) Jacobus Kruis
Role: Right-hand bat, right-arm
fast-medium bowler
Born: 9 May 1974, Pretoria, South Africa
Height: 6ft 3in **Weight:** 12st 12lbs
Nickname: Kruisie
County debut: 2005
50 wickets in a season: 1
Place in batting averages: 228th av. 19.33
Place in bowling averages: 66th av. 30.64
Strike rate: 54.79 (career 61.48)
Parents: Fanie and Hester
Wife and date of marriage: Marna,
29 June 2002
Family links with cricket: 'Brother-in-law
(P. J. Kootzen) played first-class cricket for
Griquas and Free State'
Education: St Alban's College, Pretoria;
University of Pretoria
Qualifications: BComm Hotel and Tourism Management
Career outside cricket: 'Coaching at St Andrews School in Bloemfontein, cricket
commentary and property investing and development'

Overseas tours: MCC to Bermuda, to Denmark; South African Invitation XI to Malawi
Overseas teams played for: Northern Transvaal 1993-97; Griqualand West 1997-2004; Goodyear Eagles 2004-05
Career highlights to date: 'Playing for Yorkshire and being Player of the Year in 2005'
Cricket moments to forget: 'Any time I bowl badly!'
Cricket superstitions: 'Left boot on first; four knots when batting, five when bowling on left boot'
Cricketers particularly admired: Allan Donald, Clive Rice, Richard Hadlee, Dennis Lillee, Glenn McGrath, Steve Waugh
Young players to look out for: Tim Bresnan, Alastair Cook, Monty Panesar
Other sports played: Golf, squash
Other sports followed: Golf, football (Liverpool)
Favourite band: Green Day
Relaxations: 'Want to get into falconry'
Extras: Yorkshire Player of the Year 2005. Is not considered an overseas player
Opinions on cricket: 'Twenty20 cricket has been good for the game overall. Test cricket healthy although some teams are still weaker. County cricket improved the last few seasons.'
Best batting: 59 Griqualand West v Bangladeshis, Kimberley 2000-01
Best bowling: 7-58 Griqualand West v Northerns, Centurion 1997-98

2005 Season

	M	Inns	NO	Runs	HS	Avge	100s	50s	Ct	St	O	M	Runs	Wkts	Avge	Best	5wI	10wM
Test																		
All First	16	18	9	174	37 *	19.33	-	-	5	-	584.3	135	1961	64	30.64	5-59	4	-
1-Day Int																		
C & G	3	3	2	20	11	20.00	-	-	-	-	27	2	100	2	50.00	1-23	-	
tsL	15	7	4	40	27 *	13.33	-	-	4	-	122	11	504	13	38.76	3-27	-	
Twenty20																		

Career Performances

	M	Inns	NO	Runs	HS	Avge	100s	50s	Ct	St	Balls	Runs	Wkts	Avge	Best	5wI	10wM
Test																	
All First	92	134	36	1406	59	14.34	-	2	39	-	19430	9334	316	29.53	7-58	16	1
1-Day Int																	
C & G	3	3	2	20	11	20.00	-	-	-	-	162	100	2	50.00	1-23	-	
tsL	15	7	4	40	27 *	13.33	-	-	4	-	732	504	13	38.76	3-27	-	
Twenty20																	

KUMBLE, A.   Surrey

Name: Anil Kumble
Role: Right-hand bat, leg-spin bowler
Born: 17 October 1970, Bangalore, India
Height: 6ft 1in **Weight:** 12st 8lbs
County debut: 1995 (Northants),
2000 (Leics)
County cap: 1995 (Northants), 2000 (Leics)
Test debut: 1990
100 wickets in a season: 1
Strike rate: (career 58.42)
Education: National High School,
Bangalore; National College and RV College
of Engineering, Bangalore
Overseas tours: India to England 1990, to
Zimbabwe and South Africa 1992-93, to Sri
Lanka 1993, to New Zealand 1993-94, to
England 1996, to South Africa 1996-97, to
West Indies 1996-97, to Sri Lanka 1997, to

Malaysia (Commonwealth Games) 1998-99, to Zimbabwe 1998-99, to Bangladesh
(Wills International Cup) 1998-99, to New Zealand 1998-99, to UK, Ireland and
Holland (World Cup) 1999, to Australia 1999-2000, to Kenya (ICC Knockout Trophy)
2000-01, to South Africa 2001-02, to West Indies 2001-02, to England 2002, to Sri
Lanka (ICC Champions Trophy) 2002-03, to Africa (World Cup) 2002-03, to Australia
2003-04, to Pakistan 2003-04, to England (ICC Champions Trophy) 2004, to
Bangladesh 2004-05, to Zimbabwe 2005-06, to Pakistan 2005-06, plus other one-day
tournaments and series in Sharjah, Sri Lanka, New Zealand, Singapore, Toronto,
Zimbabwe, Bangladesh and Holland; Asian Cricket Council to Australia (Tsunami
Relief) 2004-05, to South Africa (Afro-Asia Cup) 2005-06
Overseas teams played for: Karnataka, India 1989-90 –
Other sports followed: Tennis, football
Relaxations: Listening to music, watching television
Extras: Represented India U19 1989-90. One of *Indian Cricket*'s five Cricketers of the
Year 1993. One of *Wisden*'s Five Cricketers of the Year 1996. Took 10-74 (14-159 in
the match) in the second Test v Pakistan at Delhi 1998-99, winning Man of the Match
award; it was the first ten-wicket haul by a bowler in Tests since Jim Laker's 10-53 v
Australia at Old Trafford 1956. His numerous other international awards include Man
of the [Test] Series v England 1992-93 and v Zimbabwe 2001-02 and Man of the
Match in the second Test v Australia at Chennai 2004-05 (7-48/6-133). Is India's all-
time leading wicket-taker in Tests and ODIs. Overseas player with Northants 1995;
overseas player with Leics 2000; has joined Surrey as an overseas player for 2006
Best batting: 154* Karnataka v Kerala, Bijapur 1991-92
Best bowling: 10-74 India v Pakistan, Delhi 1998-99

Stop press: Man of the Series v Sri Lanka 2005-06, during which he made his 100th Test appearance

2005 Season (did not make any first-class or one-day appearances)

Career Performances

	M	Inns	NO	Runs	HS	Avge	100s	50s	Ct	St	Balls	Runs	Wkts	Avge	Best	5wI	10wM
Test	97	124	26	1670	88	17.04	-	3	43	-	30660	13204	465	28.39	10-74	29	7
All First	198	256	53	4643	154 *	22.87	6	15	93	-	54213	22961	928	24.72	10-74	63	17
1-Day Int	264	131	46	931	26	10.95	-	-	84	-	14117	10123	329	30.76	6-12	2	
C & G	7	4	2	10	6 *	5.00	-	-	1	-	474	263	17	15.47	5-27	1	
tsL	22	10	2	42	13	5.25	-	-	9	-	1013	693	32	21.65	3-25	-	
Twenty20																	

LAMB, G. A. Hampshire

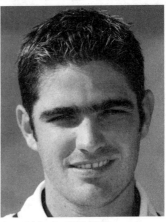

Name: Gregory (<u>Greg</u>) Arthur Lamb
Role: Right-hand bat, right-arm off-spin or medium bowler; all-rounder
Born: 4 March 1981, Harare, Zimbabwe
Height: 6ft **Weight:** 12st
Nickname: Lamby
County debut: 2004
Place in batting averages: 246th av. 16.66
Strike rate: (career 43.31)
Parents: Terry and Jackie
Marital status: Single
Children: Isabella Grace Saskia Lamb
Education: Lomagundi College; Guildford College (both Zimbabwe)
Qualifications: School and coaching qualifications
Overseas tours: Zimbabwe U19 to South Africa (U19 World Cup) 1997-98, to Sri Lanka (U19 World Cup) 1999-2000; Zimbabwe A to Sri Lanka 1999-2000
Overseas teams played for: CFX [Zimbabwe] Academy 1999-2000; Mashonaland A 2000-01
Career highlights to date: 'Playing against Australia. Making my first first-class hundred'
Cricket superstitions: 'Every time I hit a four I have to touch the other side of the pitch'
Cricketers particularly admired: Aravinda de Silva
Other sports played: 'All sports'

Favourite band: Matchbox Twenty
Relaxations: 'Fishing, playing sport'
Extras: Played for Zimbabwe U12, U15 and U19. Represented CFX [Zimbabwe] Academy, ZCU President's XI and Zimbabwe A against various touring sides. Scored 94 on Championship debut for Hampshire v Derbyshire at Derby 2004
Best batting: 100* CFX Academy v Manicaland, Mutare 1999-2000
Best bowling: 7-73 CFX Academy v Midlands, Kwekwe 1999-2000

2005 Season

	M	Inns	NO	Runs	HS	Avge	100s	50s	Ct	St	O	M	Runs	Wkts	Avge	Best	5wI	10wM
Test																		
All First	9	15	0	250	75	16.66	-	2	13	-	36.4	5	145	3	48.33	2-30	-	-
1-Day Int																		
C & G	4	2	0	4	4	2.00	-	-	2	-	10	0	63	0	-		-	-
tsL	12	12	2	292	100 *	29.20	1	-	6	-	25.2	1	105	5	21.00	3-24	-	
Twenty20	7	6	0	151	67	25.16	-	1	3	-	8	0	69	4	17.25	4-28	-	

Career Performances

	M	Inns	NO	Runs	HS	Avge	100s	50s	Ct	St	Balls	Runs	Wkts	Avge	Best	5wI	10wM
Test																	
All First	26	40	4	842	100 *	23.38	1	5	22	-	1256	719	29	24.79	7-73	1	-
1-Day Int																	
C & G	4	2	0	4	4	2.00	-	-	2	-	60	63	0	-		-	-
tsL	18	18	2	421	100 *	26.31	1	1	11	-	164	117	5	23.40	3-24	-	
Twenty20	13	11	0	189	67	17.18	-	1	4	-	48	69	4	17.25	4-28	-	

---

50. To date, who has been run out the highest number
of times in ODI matches?

LANGEVELDT, C. K.

Name: <u>Charl</u> Kenneth Langeveldt
Role: Right-hand bat, right-arm fast-medium bowler
Born: 17 December 1974, Stellenbosch, South Africa
County debut: 2005
County cap: 2005
Test debut: 2004-05
Place in bowling averages: 113th av. 42.46
Strike rate: 86.06 (career 58.41)
Career outside cricket: Formerly a prison officer
Overseas tours: South African Academy to Zimbabwe 1998-99; South Africa A to West Indies 2000, to Australia 2002-03, to Zimbabwe 2004; South Africa to Zimbabwe 2001-02, to Australia 2001-02 (VB Series), to England 2003 (NatWest Series), to Sri Lanka 2004 (one-day series), to England (ICC Champions Trophy) 2004, to West Indies 2004-05, to India (one-day series) 2005-06
Overseas teams played for: Boland 1997-98 – 2002-03; Border 2003-04; Lions 2004-05 –
Extras: Represented South Africa in the 2002-03 World Cup. Took 5-46 on Test debut in the third Test v England at Cape Town 2004-05. Has won several match awards, including Man of the Match v Bangladesh at Edgbaston in the ICC Champions Trophy 2004 (3-17) and v West Indies in the third ODI at Bridgetown 2004-05 (5-62, including hat-trick to secure a one-run victory). Was a temporary overseas player with Somerset during the 2005 season
Best batting: 56 Boland v Eastern Province, Port Elizabeth 1999-2000
Best bowling: 5-19 Boland v Free State, Paarl 2000-01
Stop press: Made Twenty20 international debut v New Zealand at Johannesburg 2005-06

2005 Season

	M	Inns	NO	Runs	HS	Avge	100s	50s	Ct	St	O	M	Runs	Wkts	Avge	Best	5wI	10wM
Test																		
All First	6	6	3	38	18 *	12.66	-	-	-	-	215.1	59	637	15	42.46	3-67	-	-
1-Day Int																		
C & G																		
tsL	7	2	0	9	5	4.50	-	-	-	-	56	1	323	7	46.14	2-33	-	
Twenty20	3	1	1	0	0 *	-	-	-	2	-	10	0	102	0	-	-	-	-

Career Performances

	M	Inns	NO	Runs	HS	Avge	100s	50s	Ct	St	Balls	Runs	Wkts	Avge	Best	5wl	10wM
Test	4	2	1	15	10	15.00	-	-	1	-	483	216	9	24.00	5-46	1	-
All First	56	68	23	666	56	14.80	-	1	14	-	9561	4641	163	28.47	5-19	5	1
1-Day Int	16	2	0	5	3	2.50	-	-	1	-	732	544	26	20.92	5-62	1	
C & G																	
tsL	7	2	0	9	5	4.50	-	-	-	-	336	323	7	46.14	2-33	-	
Twenty20	3	1	1	0	0*	-	-	-	2	-	60	102	0	-	-	-	

LARAMAN, A. W.   Somerset

Name: Aaron William Laraman
Role: Right-hand bat, right-arm
medium-fast bowler
Born: 10 January 1979, London
Height: 6ft 5in   **Weight:** 14st 7lbs
Nickname: Az, Lazza, Shanky, Long
County debut: 1998 (Middlesex),
2003 (Somerset)
Place in batting averages: 222nd av. 19.66
(2004 215th av. 20.66)
Place in bowling averages: 130th av. 46.30
(2004 40th av. 29.00)
Strike rate: 81.69 (career 60.38)
Parents: William and Lynda
Marital status: Single
Education: Enfield Grammar School
Qualifications: 8 GCSEs
Overseas tours: England U17 to Holland
1995; England U19 to South Africa 1997-98
Overseas teams played for: Burnside CC, Christchurch, New Zealand 1999-2000;
Willetton CC, Perth 2000-01
Career highlights to date: 'Making my debut at Lord's in 1998'
Cricketers particularly admired: Steve Waugh, Glenn McGrath, Michael Atherton
Other sports followed: Football (Arsenal)
Relaxations: Working out at the gym, football, golf
Extras: Seaxe 2nd XI Player of the Year 1997. Took 4-39 on NatWest debut v
Nottinghamshire at Lord's 2000. Scored maiden first-class century (148*), having
arrived at 136 for 5, v Gloucestershire at Taunton 2003. Released by Somerset at the
end of the 2005 season
Best batting: 148* Somerset v Gloucestershire, Taunton 2003
Best bowling: 5-58 Somerset v Derbyshire, Taunton 2004

2005 Season

	M	Inns	NO	Runs	HS	Avge	100s	50s	Ct	St	O	M	Runs	Wkts	Avge	Best	5wI	10wM
Test																		
All First	9	13	1	236	53	19.66	-	2	2	-	177	21	602	13	46.30	3-68	-	-
1-Day Int																		
C & G	1	1	0	1	1	1.00	-	-	-	-	3	0	17	0	-		-	-
tsL	6	5	0	90	51	18.00	-	1	2	-	43	3	215	4	53.75	2-17	-	
Twenty20																		

Career Performances

	M	Inns	NO	Runs	HS	Avge	100s	50s	Ct	St	Balls	Runs	Wkts	Avge	Best	5wI	10wM
Test																	
All First	47	56	11	1378	148 *	30.62	1	7	17	-	5555	3214	92	34.93	5-58	1	-
1-Day Int																	
C & G	7	4	2	69	50 *	34.50	-	1	3	-	267	178	9	19.77	4-39	-	
tsL	38	33	7	343	51	13.19	-	1	8	-	1462	1272	39	32.61	6-42	2	
Twenty20	7	5	1	35	28 *	8.75	-	-	-	-	123	151	9	16.77	4-15	-	

LATOUF, K. J.   Hampshire

Name: <u>Kevin</u> John Latouf
Role: Right-hand bat, right-arm medium bowler
Born: 7 September 1985, Pretoria, South Africa
Height: 5ft 10in **Weight:** 12st
Nickname: Poindexter, Mushy, Latsy, Kev
County debut: 2005 (one-day)
Parents: Colin and Josephine
Marital status: Single
Family links with cricket: 'Uncle Brian Venables was a batsman who played in Dublin and now plays cricket in Kent'
Education: Millfield School; Barton Peveril Sixth Form College
Qualifications: 11 GCSEs, 4 AS-Levels
Overseas tours: West of England U15 to West Indies 2000, 2001
Overseas teams played for: Melville CC, Perth ('briefly')
Cricket moments to forget: 'Golden duck in England U15 trial match'
Cricket superstitions: 'Don't believe in superstition'
Cricketers particularly admired: Ricky Ponting, Jonty Rhodes, Allan Donald

Young players to look out for: Anthony Latouf, James Hildreth, Tom Burrows, Chris Benham, Tom Cledwyn

Other sports played: Tennis (county trials), rugby (Bristol and Somerset trials), golf ('fun'), surfing, snowboarding

Other sports followed: Rugby (Natal Sharks), football (Arsenal), AFL (Collingwood)

Favourite band: Coldplay

Relaxations: 'Prefer listening to R&B and hip hop; going out with mates from cricket, Millfield and BP'

Extras: Played for West of England U13, U14 and U15. Played for ECB U17 and ECB U19. Played in Hampshire's 2nd XI Trophy winning side 2003. Represented England U19 2005

2005 Season

	M	Inns	NO	Runs	HS	Avge	100s	50s	Ct	St	O	M	Runs	Wkts	Avge	Best	5wl	10wM
Test																		
All First																		
1-Day Int																		
C & G	3	2	1	25	25	25.00	-	-	2	-								
tsL	6	6	1	41	14	8.20	-	-	4	-								
Twenty20																			

Career Performances

	M	Inns	NO	Runs	HS	Avge	100s	50s	Ct	St	Balls	Runs	Wkts	Avge	Best	5wl	10wM
Test																	
All First																		
1-Day Int																		
C & G	3	2	1	25	25	25.00	-	-	2	-							
tsL	6	6	1	41	14	8.20	-	-	4	-							
Twenty20																		

LAW, S. G.   Lancashire

Name: <u>Stuart</u> Grant Law
Role: Right-hand bat, county vice-captain
Born: 18 October 1968, Brisbane, Australia
Height: 6ft **Weight:** 13st 7lbs
Nickname: Lawman, Judge
County debut: 1996 (Essex), 2002 (Lancashire)
County cap: 1996 (Essex), 2002 (Lancashire)
Test debut: 1995-96
1000 runs in a season: 8
1st-Class 200s: 5
Place in batting averages: 75th av. 39.00 (2004 37th av. 51.00)

Strike rate: (career 101.67)
Parents: Grant and Pam
Wife and date of marriage: Debbie-Lee,
31 December 1998
Children: Max, 9 January 2002
Family links with cricket: 'Dad, grandad
and uncles played'
Education: Craigslea State High School,
Brisbane
Qualifications: Level 2 cricket coach
Career outside cricket: 'Desperately need to
find one!'
Off-season: 'Training, family and keeping
warm'
Overseas tours: Australia B to Zimbabwe
1991-92; Young Australia (Australia A) to
England and Netherlands 1995 (c); Australia
to India and Pakistan (World Cup) 1995-96,

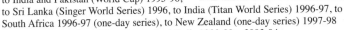

to Sri Lanka (Singer World Series) 1996, to India (Titan World Series) 1996-97, to
South Africa 1996-97 (one-day series), to New Zealand (one-day series) 1997-98
Overseas teams played for: Queensland Bulls 1988-89 – 2003-04
Career highlights to date: 'Playing for Australia. Winning first Sheffield Shield for
Queensland [1994-95]'
Cricket moments to forget: 'None. There is always a funny side to things that
happen. Some take longer to become funny!'
Cricket superstitions: 'None'
Cricketers particularly admired: Greg Chappell, Viv Richards
Young players to look out for: Mitchell Johnson (Queensland)
Other sports played: Golf ('very socially')
Other sports followed: Rugby league (Brisbane Broncos)
Injuries: Out for two weeks with a frozen shoulder
Relaxations: 'Spending time with friends/family; lying on a beach'
Extras: Sheffield Shield Player of the Year 1990-91. Captain of Queensland 1994-95 –
1996-97 and 1999-2000 – 2001-02; is the most successful captain in modern-day
Australian domestic cricket, having captained his state to five Sheffield Shield/Pura
Cup titles and to three one-day titles. One of *Wisden*'s Five Cricketers of the Year
1998. PCA Player of the Year 1999. Scored century (168) v Warwickshire at
Edgbaston 2003, sharing with Carl Hooper (177) in a Lancashire record fifth-wicket
partnership of 360 as the county scored 781. Lancashire Player of the Year 2003. Is
Queensland's all-time leading run-scorer in first-class cricket. Retired from Australian
cricket at the end of 2003-04. Vice-captain of Lancashire since 2005. Is a UK citizen
and no longer considered an overseas player
Opinions on cricket: 'There are too many players with too many wrong opinions on
the game. We all love it – that's why we play it. If you don't love it, then find an office
job that will give you more satisfaction.'

Best batting: 263 Essex v Somerset, Chelmsford 1999
Best bowling: 5-39 Queensland v Tasmania, Brisbane 1995-96

2005 Season

	M	Inns	NO	Runs	HS	Avge	100s	50s	Ct	St	O	M	Runs	Wkts	Avge	Best	5wl	10wM
Test																		
All First	15	24	2	858	143	39.00	3	2	18	-								
1-Day Int																		
C & G	4	4	0	126	47	31.50	-	-	-	-								
tsL	15	15	0	464	82	30.93	-	5	12	-								
Twenty20	9	9	1	387	101	48.37	1	3	4	-								

Career Performances

	M	Inns	NO	Runs	HS	Avge	100s	50s	Ct	St	Balls	Runs	Wkts	Avge	Best	5wl	10wM
Test	1	1	1	54	54 *	-	-	1	1	-	18	9	0	-	-	-	-
All First	322	531	58	23957	263	50.64	71	109	361	-	8337	4165	82	50.79	5-39	1	-
1-Day Int	54	51	5	1237	110	26.89	1	7	12	-	807	635	12	52.91	2-22	-	
C & G	29	26	1	1015	107	40.60	3	4	19	-	439	366	8	45.75	2-36	-	
tsL	136	133	7	4557	133	36.16	8	25	54	-	954	832	25	33.28	4-37	-	
Twenty20	17	17	1	509	101	31.81	1	3	6	-	6	10	0	-	-	-	-

LAWSON, M. A. K.   Yorkshire

Name: <u>Mark</u> Anthony Kenneth Lawson
Role: Right-hand bat, right-arm
leg-spin bowler
Born: 24 November 1985, Leeds
Height: 5ft 8in **Weight:** 12st ('approx')
Nickname: Sauce
County debut: 2004
Strike rate: (career 59.06)
Parents: Anthony and Dawn
Marital status: Single
Family links with cricket: 'Father played
local league cricket and encouraged me to
take up the game'
Education: Castle Hall Language College,
Mirfield, West Yorkshire
Qualifications: 11 GCSEs
Overseas tours: England U19 to Australia
2002-03, to Bangladesh (U19 World Cup)
2003-04, to India 2004-05
Cricketers particularly admired: Shane Warne, Gareth Batty

Other sports played: Football (school), rugby union (school, Cleckheaton 'in early teens'), rugby league (Dewsbury Moor ARLFC 'in early teens')

Other sports followed: Rugby league (Bradford Bulls)

Relaxations: Music, dining out, cinema

Extras: Played for Yorkshire Schools U11-U16 (captain U13-U15); ESCA North of England U14 and U15; North of England Development of Excellence U17 and U19. Represented England U15, U17 and U19. Awarded Brian Johnston Scholarship. Part of Terry Jenner Elite Wrist Spin Program. Voted Yorkshire Supporters' Young Player of the Year 2003

Best batting: 20* Yorkshire v Leicestershire, Scarborough 2005

Best bowling: 5-62 Yorkshire v Durham, Scarborough 2004

2005 Season

	M	Inns	NO	Runs	HS	Avge	100s	50s	Ct	St	O	M	Runs	Wkts	Avge	Best	5wI	10wM
Test																		
All First	3	4	1	31	20*	10.33	-	-	-	-	82	9	372	7	53.14	5-155	1	-
1-Day Int																		
C & G																		
tsL	2	2	0	23	20	11.50	-	-	1	-	5.4	0	53	1	53.00	1-27	-	
Twenty20	2	1	1	4	4*	-	-	-	1	-	8	0	87	3	29.00	2-34	-	

Career Performances

	M	Inns	NO	Runs	HS	Avge	100s	50s	Ct	St	Balls	Runs	Wkts	Avge	Best	5wI	10wM
Test																	
All First	6	9	2	64	20*	9.14	-	-	1	-	945	680	16	42.50	5-62	2	-
1-Day Int																	
C & G																	
tsL	2	2	0	23	20	11.50	-	-	1	-	34	53	1	53.00	1-27	-	
Twenty20	2	1	1	4	4*	-	-	-	1	-	48	87	3	29.00	2-34	-	

---

51. Who was called up from league cricket with Pudsey St Lawrence to make his ODI debut in 1990 and holds the record for the most ODI wickets in a calendar year for New Zealand?

LEATHERDALE, D. A.   Worcestershire

Name: <u>David</u> Anthony Leatherdale
Role: Right-hand bat, right-arm medium bowler, cover fielder
Born: 26 November 1967, Bradford
Height: 5ft 10in **Weight:** 11st
Nickname: Lugsy, Spock
County debut: 1988
County cap: 1994; colours 2002
Benefit: 2003
1000 runs in a season: 1
Strike rate: (career 53.88)
Parents: Paul and Rosalyn
Wife: Vanessa
Children: Callum Edward, 6 July 1990; Christian Ellis, 21 March 1995
Family links with cricket: Father played local cricket; brother-in-law played for England YC in 1979
Education: Pudsey Grangefield Secondary School
Qualifications: 8 O-levels, 3 A-levels, NCA coaching award (stage 1)
Career outside cricket: Commercial director at Worcestershire CCC
Overseas tours: England Indoor to Australia and New Zealand 1994-95
Overseas teams played for: Pretoria Police, South Africa 1987-88
Career highlights to date: '5-10 v Australia 1997' (*In one-day match against the Australian tourists at Worcester*)
Cricketers particularly admired: Mark Scott, George Batty, Peter Kippax
Other sports followed: Football, American football
Relaxations: Golf
Extras: Scored century (120) v Nottinghamshire at Trent Bridge 2002, in the process sharing with Steve Rhodes (124) in a new record seventh-wicket partnership for Worcestershire (256). Recorded career best C&G/NatWest score (80) v Yorkshire at Worcester 2003, winning Man of the Match award. Worcestershire One-Day Player of the Year 2003. Retired from county cricket in the 2005-06 off-season to become full-time commercial director at Worcestershire
Best batting: 157 Worcestershire v Somerset, Worcester 1991
Best bowling: 5-20 Worcestershire v Gloucestershire, Worcester 1998

2005 Season

	M	Inns	NO	Runs	HS	Avge	100s	50s	Ct	St	O	M	Runs	Wkts	Avge	Best	5wI	10wM
Test																		
All First	1	1	0	14	14	14.00	-	-	-	-	17	4	47	1	47.00	1-18	-	-
1-Day Int																		
C & G	1	0	0	0	0	-	-	-	-	-	5	0	18	2	9.00	2-18	-	
tsL	13	10	2	156	72 *	19.50	-	1	2	-	65.1	1	343	11	31.18	2-19	-	
Twenty20	7	6	1	89	32	17.80	-	-	2	-	25.4	0	199	6	33.16	2-21	-	

Career Performances

	M	Inns	NO	Runs	HS	Avge	100s	50s	Ct	St	Balls	Runs	Wkts	Avge	Best	5wI	10wM
Test																		
All First	215	347	41	10017	157	32.73	14	54	151	-	7113	4158	132	31.50	5-20	2	-
1-Day Int																		
C & G	41	34	4	776	80	25.86	-	4	18	-	666	548	21	26.09	3-9	-	
tsL	233	197	29	3451	72 *	20.54	-	14	93	-	3642	3022	132	22.89	5-9	2	
Twenty20	18	17	5	212	52 *	17.66	-	1	8	-	304	386	15	25.73	2-14	-	

LEHMANN, D. S. — Yorkshire

Name: <u>Darren</u> Scott Lehmann
Role: Left-hand bat, slow left-arm bowler
Born: 5 February 1970, Gawler,
South Australia
Nickname: Boof
Height: 5ft 11in **Weight:** 14st 2lbs
County debut: 1997
County cap: 1997
Test debut: 1997-98
1000 runs in a season: 4
1st-Class 200s: 9
Place in batting averages: (2004 15th
av. 59.20)
Place in bowling averages: (2004 1st
av. 17.40)
Strike rate: (career 74.63)
Wife: Andrea
Overseas tours: Australia to Sri Lanka
(Singer World Series) 1996-97, to New Zealand (one-day series) 1997-98, to Sharjah
(Coca-Cola Cup) 1997-98, to India 1997-98, to Pakistan 1998-99, to Bangladesh
(Wills International Cup) 1998-99, to West Indies 1998-99 (one-day series), to UK,
Ireland and Holland (World Cup) 1999, to Sri Lanka 1999-2000 (one-day series), to

Zimbabwe 1999-2000 (one-day series), to India 2000-01 (one-day series), to South Africa 2001-02, to Sri Lanka (ICC Champions Trophy) 2002-03, to Africa (World Cup) 2002-03, to West Indies 2002-03, to Sri Lanka 2003-04, to Zimbabwe (one-day series) 2004, to Holland (Videocon Cup) 2004, to England (ICC Champions Trophy) 2004, to India 2004-05

Overseas teams played for: Salisbury District CC (now Northern Districts), Adelaide; South Australia 1987-88 – 1989-90; Victoria 1990-91 – 1992-93; South Australia 1993-94 –

Other sports followed: Australian Football League (Adelaide Crows)

Relaxations: Golf, watching sport

Extras: Scored 1142 runs (av. 57.10) in his first full Australian season 1989-90. Pura Milk Cup Player of the Year 1999-2000. Was voted Interstate Cricketer of the Year 1999-2000 at the inaugural Allan Border Medal awards, also winning the award in 2000-01 and 2001-02. An overseas player with Yorkshire 1997-98, 2000-02, 2004 and has returned for 2006. Won the EDS Walter Lawrence Trophy for the fastest first-class century of the 2000 season – 89 balls for Yorkshire v Kent at Canterbury. One of *Wisden*'s Five Cricketers of the Year 2001. Yorkshire Player of the Year 2001. Is highest-scoring batsman in Sheffield Shield/Pura Cup history. His international awards include Man of the Match v Sri Lanka in the VB Series at Perth 2002-03 and in the third Test v Sri Lanka at Colombo 2003-04 (153 plus match figures of 6-92). Vice-captain of Yorkshire 2001; captain of Yorkshire 2002, the first overseas player to be appointed to the office. Captain of South Australia since 1998-99. *Wisden Australia*'s Cricketer of the Year 2003-04. Book *Darren Lehmann: Worth the Wait* published 2004

Best batting: 255 South Australia v Queensland, Adelaide 1996-97

Best bowling: 4-35 Yorkshire v Essex, Chelmsford 2004

Stop press: Scored maiden first-class triple century (301*) v Western Australia at Adelaide in the Pura Cup 2005-06

2005 Season (did not make any first-class or one-day appearances)

Career Performances

	M	Inns	NO	Runs	HS	Avge	100s	50s	Ct	St	Balls	Runs	Wkts	Avge	Best	5wl	10wM
Test	27	42	2	1798	177	44.95	5	10	11	-	974	412	15	27.46	3-42	-	-
All First	248	420	28	21991	255	56.09	70	100	129	-	7165	3359	96	34.98	4-35	-	-
1-Day Int	117	101	22	3078	119	38.96	4	17	26	-	1793	1446	52	27.80	4-7	-	
C & G	16	13	3	492	105	49.20	1	4	3	-	416	268	16	16.75	4-26	-	
tsL	73	73	10	2963	191	47.03	3	23	24	-	1537	1143	46	24.84	3-31	-	
Twenty20																	

LEWIS, J.   Gloucestershire

Name: Jonathan (Jon) Lewis
Role: Right-hand bat, right-arm
fast-medium bowler, county captain
Born: 26 August 1975, Aylesbury
Height: 6ft 3in **Weight:** 14st
Nickname: Lewy, JJ, King Black
County debut: 1995
County cap: 1998
50 wickets in a season: 5
Place in batting averages: 181st av. 24.92
(2004 235th av. 17.54)
Place in bowling averages: 64th av. 30.44
(2004 19th av. 25.26)
Strike rate: 59.51 (career 53.32)
Parents: John and Jane
Marital status: Married
Education: Churchfields School, Swindon;

Swindon College
Qualifications: 9 GCSEs, BTEC in Leisure and Hospitality, Level III coach
Overseas tours: Bath Schools to New South Wales 1993; England A to West Indies
2000-01, to Sri Lanka 2004-05; England to South Africa 2004-05
Overseas teams played for: Marist, Christchurch, New Zealand 1994-95; Richmond
City, Melbourne 1995-96; Wanderers, Johannesburg 1996-98; Techs CC, Cape Town
1998-99; Randwick-Petersham, Sydney 2003-04
Cricket moments to forget: 'Any injury'
Cricket superstitions: 'I always get a haircut if I go for a gallon'
Cricketers particularly admired: Courtney Walsh, Jack Russell, Jonty Rhodes
Young players to look out for: Alex Gidman
Other sports played: Golf (7 handicap), football (Bristol North West FC)
Other sports followed: Football (Swindon Town FC)
Favourite band: Brand New Heavies
Relaxations: Movies
Extras: Was on Northamptonshire staff in 1994 but made no first-team appearance.
Took Championship hat-trick (Gallian, Afzaal and Morris) v Nottinghamshire at Trent
Bridge 2000. Leading first-class wicket-taker among English bowlers in 2000 with 72
wickets (av. 20.91). Gloucestershire Player of the Year 2000. C&G Man of the Match
award for his 4-39 v Hampshire at Bristol 2004. ECB National Academy 2004-05.
Took 4-24 v Australia at the Rose Bowl in Twenty20 international 2005. Made ODI
debut v Bangladesh at The Oval in the NatWest Series 2005. Appointed captain of
Gloucestershire for 2006
Best batting: 62 Gloucestershire v Worcestershire, Cheltenham 1999
Best bowling: 8-95 Gloucestershire v Zimbabweans, Gloucester 2000

2005 Season

	M	Inns	NO	Runs	HS	Avge	100s	50s	Ct	St	O	M	Runs	Wkts	Avge	Best	5wI	10wM
Test																		
All First	12	19	6	324	55	24.92	-	1	5	-	426.3	106	1309	43	30.44	5-57	2	-
1-Day Int	3	1	1	7	7*	-	-	-	-	-	25	1	124	4	31.00	3-32	-	
C & G	2	2	0	4	4	2.00	-	-	1	-	17	1	79	4	19.75	3-47	-	
tsL	11	8	4	73	40	18.25	-	-	2	-	82.2	9	382	19	20.10	5-19	1	
Twenty20	2	1	0	34	34	34.00	-	-	-	-	6.1	0	34	0	-	-	-	

Career Performances

	M	Inns	NO	Runs	HS	Avge	100s	50s	Ct	St	Balls	Runs	Wkts	Avge	Best	5wI	10wM
Test																	
All First	145	205	45	2244	62	14.02	-	4	34	-	27407	13898	514	27.03	8-95	26	3
1-Day Int	3	1	1	7	7*	-	-	-	-	-	150	124	4	31.00	3-32	-	
C & G	17	10	5	30	9*	6.00	-	-	7	-	886	553	26	21.26	4-39	-	
tsL	94	56	20	368	40	10.22	-	-	15	-	4035	3217	117	27.49	5-19	2	
Twenty20	10	2	1	35	34	35.00	-	-	-	-	211	246	15	16.40	3-21	-	

LEWIS, J. J. B.   Durham

Name: Jonathan (<u>Jon</u>) James Benjamin Lewis
Role: Right-hand bat
Born: 21 May 1970, Isleworth, Middlesex
Height: 5ft 10in   **Weight:** 12st 7lbs
Nickname: JJ, Judge
County debut: 1990 (Essex), 1997 (Durham)
County cap: 1994 (Essex), 1998 (Durham)
Benefit: 2004 (Durham)
1000 runs in a season: 4
1st-Class 200s: 1
Place in batting averages: 136th av. 30.93
(2004 175th av. 25.23)
Strike rate: (career 120.00)
Parents: Ted and Nina
Wife and date of marriage: Fiona,
6 July 1999
Children: Candice, Michael and Heather
Family links with cricket: Father played

County Schools. Uncle is a lifelong Somerset supporter. Sister is right-arm medium-fast bowler for Cisco
Education: King Edward VI School, Chelmsford; Roehampton Institute of Higher Education

Qualifications: 5 O-levels, 3 A-levels, BSc (Hons) Sports Science, NCA Senior Coach
Career outside cricket: 'Really should be thinking seriously'
Off-season: 'Working at Surridge Sport'
Overseas tours: Durham to Cape Town 2002, to Sharjah and Dubai 2005
Overseas teams played for: Old Hararians, Zimbabwe 1991-92; Taita District, New Zealand 1992-93; Eshowe and Zululand, South Africa 1994-95; Richards Bay, South Africa 1996-97; Empangeni, Natal 1997-98; Eshowe 1998-2002
Career highlights to date: 'Captaining Durham CCC'
Cricket moments to forget: 'Even the bad days are worth remembering: you always learn something'
Cricketers particularly admired: John Childs, Greg Matthews, Alan Walker, Shane Warne
Other sports followed: Soccer (West Ham United), rugby (Newcastle Falcons), 'most sports really'
Injuries: Out for two and a half months with a multiple fracture of the collarbone
Relaxations: Sleep
Extras: Hit century (116*) on first-class debut in Essex's final Championship match of the 1990 season, v Surrey at The Oval. Scored a double century on his debut for Durham (210* v Oxford University at The Parks 1997), placing him in a small club of players who have scored centuries on debut for two different counties. Scored 112 v Nottinghamshire at Riverside 2001, in the process sharing in Durham's highest Championship partnership for any wicket (258) with Martin Love. Became Durham's leading first-class run-scorer when he passed John Morris's record of 5670 runs during his 124 v Yorkshire at Headingley 2003. Durham Player of the Year and Batsman of the Year 2003. Captain of Durham 2000-04
Best batting: 210* Durham v Oxford University, The Parks 1997
Best bowling: 1-73 Durham v Surrey, Riverside 1998

2005 Season

	M	Inns	NO	Runs	HS	Avge	100s	50s	Ct	St	O	M	Runs	Wkts	Avge	Best	5wI	10wM
Test																		
All First	10	17	1	495	68	30.93	-	3	8	-								
1-Day Int																		
C & G	1	1	0	45	45	45.00	-	-	-	-								
tsL	8	8	0	111	34	13.87	-	-	3	-								
Twenty20																		

Career Performances

	M	Inns	NO	Runs	HS	Avge	100s	50s	Ct	St	Balls	Runs	Wkts	Avge	Best	5wI	10wM
Test																	
All First	196	349	26	10466	210 *	32.40	16	64	112	-	120	121	1	121.00	1-73	-	-
1-Day Int																	
C & G	21	20	4	352	65 *	22.00	-	1	1	-							
tsL	171	152	32	3258	102	27.15	1	15	30	-	8	35	0	-	-	-	-
Twenty20	10	9	4	132	49 *	26.40	-	-	6	-							

LEWIS, M. L.   Durham

Name: Michael (Mick) Llewellyn Lewis
Role: Right-hand bat, right-arm fast bowler
Born: 29 June 1974, Greensborough,
Victoria, Australia
Height: 6ft **Weight:** 13st 3lbs
Nickname: Brown Snake
County debut: 2004 (Glamorgan),
2005 (Durham)
Place in bowling averages: 18th av. 23.61
Strike rate: 39.00 (career 51.69)
Parents: Melva and Graeme
Marital status: Single
Family links with cricket: 'Older brother
played'
Education: Parade College, Victoria
Qualifications: Horticultural Certificate III
(Turf Management)
Career outside cricket: Greenkeeper
Off-season: 'No such thing these days'
Overseas tours: Australia A to Pakistan 2005-06; Australia to New Zealand (one-day
series) 2005-06
Overseas teams played for: Northcote CC, Victoria; Victorian Bushrangers
1999-2000 –
Career highlights to date: '2003-04 Pura Cup final (winning)'
Cricket moments to forget: '2000-01 Pura Cup final (losing)'
Cricket superstitions: 'None'
Cricketers particularly admired: Michael Holding, Rodney Hogg
Young players to look out for: Cameron White
Other sports played: Aussie Rules (Greensborough Football Club)
Other sports followed: AFL (Carlton)
Favourite band: Live
Relaxations: Golf, horse racing
Extras: Victoria's leading wicket-taker in the Pura Cup 2002-03 (32; av. 28.53), 2003-
04 (34; av. 27.85) and 2004-05 (38: av. 22.05). Was an overseas player with
Glamorgan August to September 2004, deputising for Michael Kasprowicz. Was an
overseas player with Durham for parts of 2005 as a replacement for the injured Ashley
Noffke; has returned for 2006
Opinions on cricket: 'We don't need to change the game that much. There is still too
much tradition, but some should be kept forever.'
Best batting: 54* Victoria v New South Wales, Sydney 2001-02
Best bowling: 6-59 Victoria v Queensland, Melbourne 2003-04

Stop press: Made ODI debut v New Zealand at Wellington 2005-06. Made Twenty20 international debut v South Africa at Brisbane 2005-06

2005 Season

	M	Inns	NO	Runs	HS	Avge	100s	50s	Ct	St	O	M	Runs	Wkts	Avge	Best	5wI	10wM
Test																		
All First	5	6	1	44	20	8.80	-	-	2	-	169	27	614	26	23.61	5-80	1	-
1-Day Int																		
C & G	1	1	0	0	0	0.00	-	-	-	-	10	0	59	0	-	-	-	-
tsL	5	0	0	0	0	-	-	-	3	-	36.2	3	156	13	12.00	5-48	1	
Twenty20																		

Career Performances

	M	Inns	NO	Runs	HS	Avge	100s	50s	Ct	St	Balls	Runs	Wkts	Avge	Best	5wI	10wM
Test																	
All First	56	74	18	507	54 *	9.05	-	1	27	-	10257	5633	198	28.44	6-59	7	-
1-Day Int																	
C & G	1	1	0	0	0	0.00	-	-	-	-	60	59	0	-	-	-	-
tsL	9	1	0	0	0	0.00	-	-	4	-	398	313	19	16.47	5-48	1	
Twenty20																	

LEWRY, J. D.   Sussex

Name: <u>Jason</u> David Lewry
Role: Left-hand bat, left-arm
fast-medium bowler
Born: 2 April 1971, Worthing
Height: 6ft 3in **Weight:** 14st 7lbs
('depending on time of year!')
Nickname: Lewie, Urco
County debut: 1994
County cap: 1996
Benefit: 2002
50 wickets in a season: 4
Place in batting averages: (2004 245th
av. 15.90)
Place in bowling averages: 8th av. 21.75
(2004 58th av. 31.44)
Strike rate: 43.75 (career 49.07)
Parents: David and Veronica
Wife and date of marriage: Naomi
Madeleine, 18 August 1997
Children: William, 14 February 1998; Louis, 20 November 2000

Family links with cricket: Father coaches
Education: Durrington High School, Worthing; Worthing Sixth Form College
Qualifications: 6 O-levels, 3 GCSEs, City and Guilds, NCA Award
Career outside cricket: 'Still looking, but with more urgency with each passing year!'
Overseas tours: Goring CC to Isle of Wight 1992, 1993; England A to Zimbabwe and South Africa 1998-99
Career highlights to date: 'Winning County Championship 2003 and the month of debauchery that followed'
Cricket moments to forget: 'King pair, Eastbourne 1995'
Cricketers particularly admired: David Gower, Martin Andrews
Other sports played: Golf, squash; darts, pool ('anything you can do in a pub')
Other sports followed: Football (West Ham United)
Favourite band: REM
Relaxations: Golf, pub games, films
Extras: Took seven wickets in 14 balls v Hampshire at Hove 2001, the second most (most by a seamer) outstanding spell of wicket-taking in first-class cricket (after Pat Pocock's seven in 11 for Surrey v Sussex at Eastbourne in 1972)
Best batting: 72 Sussex v Surrey, The Oval 2004
Best bowling: 8-106 Sussex v Leicestershire, Hove 2003

2005 Season

	M	Inns	NO	Runs	HS	Avge	100s	50s	Ct	St	O	M	Runs	Wkts	Avge	Best	5wl	10wM
Test																		
All First	12	16	3	90	23	6.92	-	-	3	-	350	80	1044	48	21.75	6-65	4	-
1-Day Int																		
C & G	1	0	0	0	0	-	-	-	-	-	10	1	31	3	10.33	3-31	-	
tsL	1	1	1	14	14*	-	-	-	-	-	9	0	42	2	21.00	2-42	-	
Twenty20	3	1	0	1	1	1.00	-	-	2	-	5	0	38	1	38.00	1-18	-	

Career Performances

	M	Inns	NO	Runs	HS	Avge	100s	50s	Ct	St	Balls	Runs	Wkts	Avge	Best	5wl	10wM
Test																	
All First	136	186	42	1520	72	10.55	-	2	31	-	23558	12727	480	26.51	8-106	29	4
1-Day Int																	
C & G	10	6	3	37	16	12.33	-	-	1	-	612	385	19	20.26	4-42	-	
tsL	44	26	9	97	16*	5.70	-	-	9	-	1853	1497	59	25.37	4-29	-	
Twenty20	11	4	1	10	8*	3.33	-	-	4	-	197	239	14	17.07	3-34	-	

LIDDLE, C. J. Leicestershire

Name: Christopher (<u>Chris</u>) John Liddle
Role: Right-hand lower-order bat,
left-arm fast bowler
Born: 1 February 1984, Middlesbrough
Height: 6ft 4in **Weight:** 12st 7lbs
Nickname: Lids
County debut: 2005
Parents: Pat and John
Marital status: Engaged
Family links with cricket: 'Brother plays for
Marton CC and Cleveland Schools county
team'
Education: Nunthorpe Comprehensive
School, Middlesbrough; Teesside Tertiary
College; TTE Advanced Modern
Apprenticeship
Qualifications: 9 GCSEs, qualified
instrument technician, Level 1 coaching
Career highlights to date: 'Signing [as] professional for Leicestershire'
Cricket superstitions: 'Right bowling boot on first for bowling; left pad on first
for batting'
Cricketers particularly admired: Brett Lee, Brad Hodge
Young players to look out for: John Sadler, Tom New, John Maunders,
Andrew Liddle
Other sports played: Football, squash
Other sports followed: Football (Middlesbrough)
Favourite band: 'Have not really got a favourite band – just like lots of different
songs, mostly R&B'
Relaxations: 'Going to the gym; playing Championship Manager on the PC or Tiger
Woods Golf on the PlayStation'
Extras: Yorkshire area Bowler of the Year 2001-02
Opinions on cricket: 'There should be a limit on Kolpak players [*see page 9*] at
each club.'

2005 Season

	M	Inns	NO	Runs	HS	Avge	100s	50s	Ct	St	O	M	Runs	Wkts	Avge	Best	5wI	10wM
Test																		
All First	1	0	0	0	0	-	-	-	-	-	14	2	45	0	-	-	-	-
1-Day Int																		
C & G																		
tsL																		
Twenty20																		

Career Performances

	M	Inns	NO	Runs	HS	Avge	100s	50s	Ct	St	Balls	Runs	Wkts	Avge	Best	5wI	10wM
Test																	
All First	1	0	0	0	0	-	-	-	-	-	84	45	0	-	-	-	-
1-Day Int																	
C & G																	
tsL																	
Twenty20																	

LINLEY, T. E. Sussex

Name: Timothy (Tim) Edward Linley
Role: Right-hand lower-order bat,
right-arm medium-fast bowler
Born: 23 March 1982, Leeds
Height: 6ft 2in **Weight:** 12st
Nickname: Joe Club, Sheephead, Sloth,
Bambi
County debut: No first-team appearance
Strike rate: (career 54.46)
Parents: Francis and Jane
Marital status: Single
Education: St Mary's RC Comprehensive;
Notre Dame Sixth Form College; Oxford
Brookes University
Qualifications: 10 GCSEs, 4 A-levels, BSc
(Hons) Geography/Theology
Off-season: 'Two months' training in Cape
Town with London County Cricket Club'
Career highlights to date: 'Playing for British Universities v New Zealand in 2004.
Signing my first professional contract in 2005 for Sussex'
Cricket moments to forget: 'Being hit for six by my mate Pete "The Lumberjack"
Lawrence in a friendly held at Horsforth CC in 2005. I've never lived it down'
Cricketers particularly admired: Glenn McGrath, Shaun Pollock, Andrew Flintoff,
Jonty Rhodes
Young players to look out for: Steve Moreton
Other sports played: Pool, hockey (Leeds VIth team), badminton
Other sports followed: Football (Halifax Town FC)
Injuries: Out for most of OUCCE's season with spondylolisthesis
Relaxations: 'Playing most other sports; historical fiction books, especially Conn
Iggulden, Bernard Cornwell, Christian Jacq; also Paulo Coelho books; watching films
or *Lost* or *Orange County* on TV'

Extras: Played for Oxford UCCE 2003-05. Represented British Universities 2004. Won London County CC 'Search 4 A Star' bowling competition 2005
Opinions on cricket: 'Lunch and tea breaks are not long enough. By the time I've taken my size 13s off, it's time to go out again.'
Best batting: 42 OUCCE v Derbyshire, The Parks 2005
Best bowling: 3-44 OUCCE v Surrey, The Parks 2004

2005 Season (did not make any first-class or one-day appearances for his county)

Career Performances

	M	Inns	NO	Runs	HS	Avge	100s	50s	Ct	St	Balls	Runs	Wkts	Avge	Best	5wI	10wM
Test																	
All First	7	7	0	75	42	10.71	-	-	1	-	708	480	13	36.92	3-44	-	-
1-Day Int																	
C & G																	
tsL																	
Twenty20																	

LOGAN, R. J. Hampshire

Name: <u>Richard</u> James Logan
Role: Right-hand bat, right-arm fast bowler
Born: 28 January 1980, Cannock, Staffordshire
Height: 6ft 1in **Weight:** 14st
Nickname: Bungle
County debut: 1999 (Northants), 2001 (Notts), 2005 (Hants)
Place in bowling averages: (2004 84th av. 35.30)
Strike rate: (career 56.40)
Parents: Margaret and Robert
Marital status: Single
Family links with cricket: 'Dad played local cricket for Cannock'
Education: Wolverhampton Grammar School
Qualifications: 11 GCSEs, 1 A-level
Overseas tours: England U17 to Bermuda

(International Youth Tournament) 1997; England U19 to South Africa (including U19 World Cup) 1997-98, to New Zealand 1998-99
Overseas teams played for: St George, Sydney 1999-2000; Lancaster Park, New Zealand; Rovers, Durban; Northerns Goodwood, Cape Town
Career highlights to date: 'Winning junior World Cup'

Cricketers particularly admired: Malcolm Marshall, Dennis Lillee
Other sports played: Hockey
Other sports followed: Football (Wolverhampton Wanderers)
Relaxations: 'Spending time with my mates. Training'
Extras: Played for Staffordshire U11-U19 (captain U13-U17); Midlands U14 and U15 (both as captain); HMC Schools U15. 1995 *Daily Telegraph*/Lombard U15 Midlands Bowler and Batsman of the Year. Played for Northamptonshire U17 and U19 national champions 1997. Played for England U15, U17 and U19. C&G Man of the Match award for his 5-24 v Suffolk at Mildenhall 2001
Best batting: 37* Nottinghamshire v Hampshire, Trent Bridge 2001
Best bowling: 6-93 Nottinghamshire v Derbyshire, Trent Bridge 2001

2005 Season

	M	Inns	NO	Runs	HS	Avge	100s	50s	Ct	St	O	M	Runs	Wkts	Avge	Best	5wI	10wM
Test																		
All First	6	9	2	61	28	8.71	-	-	-	-	128.4	15	572	7	81.71	3-59	-	-
1-Day Int																		
C & G	2	0	0	0	0	-	-	-	1	-	11.5	0	62	3	20.66	3-37	-	
tsL	4	3	2	31	28 *	31.00	-	-	4	-	19	0	111	1	111.00	1-23	-	
Twenty20	7	1	0	0	0	0.00	-	-	-	-	14	0	115	5	23.00	4-37	-	

Career Performances

	M	Inns	NO	Runs	HS	Avge	100s	50s	Ct	St	Balls	Runs	Wkts	Avge	Best	5wI	10wM
Test																	
All First	43	61	13	486	37 *	10.12	-	-	14	-	6430	4295	114	37.67	6-93	4	-
1-Day Int																	
C & G	6	2	0	9	9	4.50	-	-	2	-	311	196	10	19.60	5-24	1	
tsL	45	25	10	192	28 *	12.80	-	-	17	-	1727	1748	44	39.72	4-32	-	
Twenty20	17	8	4	39	11 *	9.75	-	-	-	-	244	315	17	18.52	5-26	1	

LOUDON, A. G. R.   Warwickshire

Name: Alexander (Alex) Guy Rushworth Loudon
Role: Right-hand bat, right-arm off-spin bowler
Born: 6 September 1980, London
Height: 6ft 3in **Weight:** 14st 8lbs
Nickname: Noisy, Minor, A-Lo, Minotaur
County debut: 2002 (one-day, Kent), 2003 (first-class, Kent), 2005 (Warwickshire)
Place in batting averages: 126th av. 32.07 (2004 109th av. 35.11)
Place in bowling averages: 92nd av. 36.64 (2004 55th av. 31.09)
Strike rate: 67.51 (career 65.28)
Parents: Jane and James
Marital status: Single

Family links with cricket: Brother and father played for Hampshire 2nd XI
Education: Eton College; Durham University
Qualifications: 9 GCSEs, 1 AO-level, 3 A-levels, 2.1 degree, ECB Level 1 coaching
Overseas tours: Kent U12 to Holland 1991; Eton College to South Africa 1995; England U19 to Malaysia and (U19 World Cup) Sri Lanka 1999-2000 (c); Kent to South Africa 2002; England to Pakistan 2005-06; England A to West Indies 2005-06
Cricket moments to forget: 'Being bowled by Gimli in the nets'
Cricket superstitions: 'Avoiding them'
Cricketers particularly admired: Steve Waugh, Michael Atherton, Michael Bevan, Brian Lara
Other sports played: Golf, squash, rackets, tennis
Other sports followed: Rugby (England), football (Man Utd)
Favourite band: Red Hot Chili Peppers
Relaxations: 'Eating, sleeping, reading, Sky Sports and MTV'
Extras: Captained England U15 in U15 World Cup 1996. Len Newbery Award for Best Schools Cricketer 1999. NBC Denis Compton Award for the most promising young Kent player 1999. Silk Trophy batting award 1999. Played for Durham UCCE 2001, 2002 and 2003, and was captain of Durham's BUSA winning side 2003. Represented British Universities 2003
Opinions on cricket: 'Twenty20 has heightened interest in the game. The competition's expansion should be considered, perhaps with more games being played throughout the season. The Kolpak situation [*see page 9*] needs attention.'
Best batting: 172 DUCCE v Durham, Durham 2003
Best bowling: 6-47 Kent v Middlesex, Canterbury 2004

2005 Season

	M	Inns	NO	Runs	HS	Avge	100s	50s	Ct	St	O	M	Runs	Wkts	Avge	Best	5wI	10wM
Test																		
All First	17	30	4	834	95 *	32.07	-	5	12	-	416.2	48	1356	37	36.64	6-66	2	-
1-Day Int																		
C & G	5	5	0	72	29	14.40	-	-	4	-	31.3	1	143	7	20.42	3-32	-	
tsL	17	15	2	422	73 *	32.46	-	4	6	-	101.2	7	479	12	39.91	3-26	-	
Twenty20	9	7	0	32	13	4.57	-	-	3	-	20	0	148	8	18.50	5-33	1	

Career Performances

	M	Inns	NO	Runs	HS	Avge	100s	50s	Ct	St	Balls	Runs	Wkts	Avge	Best	5wI	10wM
Test																	
All First	39	65	5	1954	172	32.56	1	12	28	-	4374	2561	67	38.22	6-47	4	-
1-Day Int																	
C & G	6	6	0	125	53	20.83	-	1	4	-	195	147	7	21.00	3-32	-	
tsL	32	30	4	688	73 *	26.46	-	6	11	-	833	680	21	32.38	4-48	-	
Twenty20	14	12	0	110	25	9.16	-	-	5	-	120	148	8	18.50	5-33	1	

LOUW, J. Middlesex

Name: Johann Louw
Role: Right-hand bat, right-arm
medium-fast bowler
Born: 12 April 1979, Cape Town,
South Africa
County debut: 2004 (Northants)
50 wickets in a season: 1
Place in batting averages: 247th av. 16.29
(2004 232nd av. 18.00)
Place in bowling averages: 74th av. 32.36
(2004 28th av. 26.51)
Strike rate: 56.70 (career 57.29)
Overseas teams played for: Griqualand West
2000-01 – 2002-03; Eastern Province 2003-
04; Dolphins 2004-05; Eagles 2005-06 –
Extras: His awards include Man of the
Match v Boland at Port Elizabeth in the
SuperSport Series 2003-04 (124 and match

figures of 5-131). Played for Northamptonshire 2004-05 (2004 as an overseas player),
in 2004 taking 60 first-class wickets at 26.51 and finishing as leading wicket-taker in
Division One of the totesport League (34; av. 15.67). Has joined Middlesex as an
overseas player for 2006
Best batting: 124 Eastern Province v Boland, Port Elizabeth, 2003-04
Best bowling: 6-51 Northamptonshire v Essex, Northampton 2005

2005 Season

	M	Inns	NO	Runs	HS	Avge	100s	50s	Ct	St	O	M	Runs	Wkts	Avge	Best	5wl	10wM
Test																		
All First	15	20	3	277	64	16.29	-	2	2	-	415.5	94	1424	44	32.36	6-51	2	-
1-Day Int																		
C & G	2	2	0	7	4	3.50	-	-	-	-	20	1	116	5	23.20	3-65	-	
tsL	16	7	3	92	25	23.00	-	-	2	-	122	9	576	22	26.18	4-39	-	
Twenty20	7	1	0	0	0	0.00	-	-	3	-	23.5	0	183	6	30.50	3-25	-	

Career Performances

	M	Inns	NO	Runs	HS	Avge	100s	50s	Ct	St	Balls	Runs	Wkts	Avge	Best	5wl	10wM
Test																	
All First	56	82	11	1450	124	20.42	1	7	23	-	9912	5274	173	30.48	6-51	6	-
1-Day Int																	
C & G	5	4	0	37	20	9.25	-	-	2	-	276	266	9	29.55	3-65	-	
tsL	32	19	5	236	36	16.85	-	-	5	-	1544	1109	56	19.80	5-27	1	
Twenty20	12	5	1	32	17	8.00	-	-	3	-	235	298	11	27.09	3-25	-	

LOVE, M. L. Northamptonshire

Name: <u>Martin</u> Lloyd Love
Role: Right-hand bat
Born: 30 March 1974, Mundubbera, Queensland, Australia
Height: 6ft **Weight:** 13st
Nickname: Handles
County debut: 2001 (Durham), 2004 (Northamptonshire)
County cap: 2001 (Durham)
Test debut: 2002-03
1000 runs in a season: 2
1st-Class 200s: 7
1st-Class 300s: 1
Place in batting averages: 22nd av. 56.04
Strike rate: (career 30.00)
Parents: Ormond and Evelyn
Wife: Deborah
Education: Toowoomba Grammar School; University of Queensland
Qualifications: Bachelor of Physiotherapy, Level 2 coach
Career outside cricket: Physiotherapist
Overseas tours: Australia U19 to New Zealand 1992-93; Young Australia (Australia A) to England and Netherlands 1995; Australia to West Indies 2002-03

Overseas teams played for: Queensland Bulls 1992-93 –
Career highlights to date: 'Member of Queensland's first ever Sheffield Shield winning team 1994-95'
Cricket moments to forget: 'Any duck'
Cricket superstitions: 'Left pad on first'
Cricketers particularly admired: Allan Border
Other sports played: Golf
Other sports followed: AFL (Brisbane Lions), rugby union (Queensland Reds)
Extras: Made debut for Queensland in 1992-93 Sheffield Shield final v New South Wales. Won the Ian Healy Trophy for Queensland Player of the Year 2000-01. An overseas player with Durham 2001-03. Scored 149* v Nottinghamshire at Riverside 2001, in the process sharing in Durham's highest Championship partnership for any wicket (258) with Jon Lewis. Named State Player of the Year at the 2003 Allan Border Medal awards. Scored 273 v Hampshire at Riverside 2003, setting a new record for the highest individual score made by a Durham batsman. Scored 300* v Victoria at Melbourne 2003-04, becoming the first player to score a first-class triple century for Queensland. An overseas player with Northamptonshire July to August 2004, deputising for Martin van Jaarsveld, and in 2005
Best batting: 300* Queensland v Victoria, Melbourne 2003-04
Best bowling: 1-5 Queensland v Western Australia, Brisbane 1997-98

2005 Season

	M	Inns	NO	Runs	HS	Avge	100s	50s	Ct	St	O	M	Runs	Wkts	Avge	Best	5wI	10wM
Test																		
All First	15	25	1	1345	177	56.04	4	6	36	-								
1-Day Int																		
C & G	3	3	0	46	42	15.33	-	-	1	-								
tsL	15	15	2	579	111*	44.53	1	4	8	-								
Twenty20	3	3	0	104	53	34.66	-	1	-	-								

Career Performances

	M	Inns	NO	Runs	HS	Avge	100s	50s	Ct	St	Balls	Runs	Wkts	Avge	Best	5wI	10wM
Test	5	8	3	233	100*	46.60	1	1	7	-							
All First	184	320	30	14620	300*	50.41	36	68	233	-	30	11	1	11.00	1-5	-	-
1-Day Int																	
C & G	8	7	0	178	51	25.42	-	1	2	-							
tsL	46	46	3	1427	111*	33.18	1	8	21	-	12	7	0	-		-	-
Twenty20	6	6	0	166	53	27.66	-	2	2	-							

LOWE, J. A.   Durham

Name: <u>James</u> Adam Lowe
Role: Right-hand bat, right-arm
off-spin bowler
Born: 4 November 1982, Bury St Edmunds
Height: 6ft 2in **Weight:** 14st 10lbs
Nickname: Lowey, J-Lo
County debut: 2003
Parents: Jim and Pat
Marital status: Single
Family links with cricket: 'Dad played for
Northallerton CC and is a qualified coach'
Education: Northallerton College
Qualifications: Coaching Level 2
Overseas tours: Durham to India 2004
Overseas teams played for: Gosnells CC,
Perth 2003-04
Career highlights to date: '80 on my first-
class debut v Hampshire'

Cricketers particularly admired: Ritchie Storr, Paul Collingwood, Danny Law
Young players to look out for: Graham Onions
Other sports played: Football ('played for school and town as a youngster')
Other sports followed: Football (Middlesbrough)
Favourite band: Stone Roses
Relaxations: Eating out; watching Middlesbrough
Extras: Scored 80 on first-class debut v Hampshire at West End 2003
Best batting: 80 Durham v Hampshire, West End 2003

2005 Season

	M	Inns	NO	Runs	HS	Avge	100s	50s	Ct	St	O	M	Runs	Wkts	Avge	Best	5wI	10wM
Test																		
All First	1	2	0	40	26	20.00	-	-	-	-								
1-Day Int																		
C & G																		
tsL																		
Twenty20																		

Career Performances

	M	Inns	NO	Runs	HS	Avge	100s	50s	Ct	St	Balls	Runs	Wkts	Avge	Best	5wI	10wM
Test																	
All First	4	8	0	211	80	26.37	-	1	2	-							
1-Day Int																	
C & G																	
tsL																	
Twenty20																	

LOYE, M. B. Lancashire

Name: <u>Malachy</u> Bernard Loye
Role: Right-hand bat, off-spin bowler, occasional wicket-keeper
Born: 27 September 1972, Northampton
Height: 6ft 3in **Weight:** 14st
Nickname: Mal, Chairman, Jacko, Shermenator
County debut: 1991 (Northamptonshire), 2003 (Lancashire)
County cap: 1994 (Northamptonshire), 2003 (Lancashire)
1000 runs in a season: 4
1st-Class 200s: 2
1st-Class 300s: 1
Place in batting averages: 36th av. 49.91 (2004 43rd av. 49.15)
Strike rate: (career 55.00)
Parents: Patrick and Anne
Marital status: Single
Family links with cricket: Father and brother played for Cogenhoe CC in Northampton
Education: Moulton Comprehensive School
Qualifications: GCSEs, 'numerous coaching certificates'
Overseas tours: England U18 to Canada (International Youth Tournament) 1991; England U19 to Pakistan 1991-92; England A to South Africa 1993-94, to Zimbabwe and South Africa 1998-99; Northamptonshire to Cape Town 1993, to Zimbabwe 1995, 1998, to Johannesburg 1996, to Grenada 2001, 2002
Overseas teams played for: Riccarton, Christchurch, New Zealand 1992-95; Onslow, Wellington, New Zealand 1995-96; North Perth, Australia 1997-98; Claremont, Perth 2001
Career highlights to date: 'PCA Player of the Year 1998'

Cricket moments to forget: 'Not being picked for 1995 and 1996 cup finals'
Cricket superstitions: 'None'
Cricketers particularly admired: Wayne Larkins, Gordon Greenidge, Curtly Ambrose, Devon Malcolm, Peter Carlstein, David Capel
Other sports followed: Football (Liverpool, Northampton Town), rugby union (Ireland), boxing
Relaxations: 'Playing the guitar, swimming, singing, reading. Having the odd large night out!'
Extras: Played for England YC and for England U19. PCA Young Player of the Year and Whittingdale Young Player of the Year 1993. Scored 322* v Glamorgan at Northampton 1998 (the then highest individual first-class score for the county), in the process sharing with David Ripley in a new record partnership for any wicket for Northamptonshire (401). PCA Player of the Year 1998. Scored century (126) on Championship debut for Lancashire v Surrey at The Oval 2003 and another (113) in the next match v Nottinghamshire at Old Trafford to become the first batsman to score centuries in his first two matches for the county
Best batting: 322* Northamptonshire v Glamorgan, Northampton 1998
Best bowling: 1-8 Lancashire v Kent, Blackpool 2003

2005 Season

	M	Inns	NO	Runs	HS	Avge	100s	50s	Ct	St	O	M	Runs	Wkts	Avge	Best	5wl	10wM
Test																		
All First	16	25	1	1198	200	49.91	4	3	11	-								
1-Day Int																		
C & G	4	4	0	148	66	37.00	-	1	1	-								
tsL	15	15	2	313	94 *	24.07	-	2	3	-								
Twenty20	10	10	0	373	100	37.30	1	2	5	-								

Career Performances

	M	Inns	NO	Runs	HS	Avge	100s	50s	Ct	St	Balls	Runs	Wkts	Avge	Best	5wl	10wM
Test																	
All First	196	312	28	11543	322 *	40.64	32	46	98	-	55	61	1	61.00	1-8	-	-
1-Day Int																	
C & G	32	31	6	1013	124 *	40.52	2	5	7	-							
tsL	164	160	16	4608	122	32.00	4	31	40	-							
Twenty20	21	21	1	600	100	30.00	1	3	8	-							

LUCAS, D. S.   Yorkshire

Name: <u>David</u> Scott Lucas
Role: Right-hand bat, left-arm
medium-fast bowler
Born: 19 August 1978, Nottingham
Height: 6ft 3in **Weight:** 13st 3lbs
Nickname: Muke, Lukey
County debut: 1999 (Nottinghamshire),
2005 (Yorkshire)
Strike rate: (career 55.23)
Parents: Mary and Terry
Marital status: Married
Education: Djanogly City Technology
College, Nottingham

Qualifications: 6 GCSEs, pass in Computer-
Aided Design
Overseas tours: England (Indoor) to
Australia (Indoor Cricket World Cup) 1998
Overseas teams played for: Bankstown-
Canterbury Bulldogs, Sydney 1996-97; Wanneroo, Perth 2001-02
Career highlights to date: 'Getting Man of the Match against Derbyshire in a
close fixture' (*4-27 v Derbyshire at Derby in the NUL 2000*)
Cricket superstitions: 'Always walk back to the left of my mark when bowling.
Always put left pad on first'
Cricketers particularly admired: Wasim Akram, Glenn McGrath, Steve Waugh,
Damien Martyn
Young players to look out for: Bilal Shafayat
Other sports played: Indoor cricket, football
Other sports followed: Football (Arsenal FC)
Relaxations: 'Food, cars, PS2, movies'
Extras: Won Yorkshire League with Rotherham in 1996. NBC Denis Compton Award
for the most promising young Nottinghamshire player 2000. Released by Yorkshire at
the end of the 2005 season
Best batting: 49 Nottinghamshire v DUCCE, Trent Bridge 2002
Best bowling: 5-49 Yorkshire v Bangladesh A, Headingley 2005

2005 Season

	M	Inns	NO	Runs	HS	Avge	100s	50s	Ct	St	O	M	Runs	Wkts	Avge	Best	5wI	10wM
Test																		
All First	1	0	0	0	0	-	-	-	-	-	29.4	4	84	8	10.50	5-49	1	-
1-Day Int																		
C & G																			
tsL	5	2	0	40	32	20.00	-	-	1	-	30	1	187	3	62.33	2-39	-	
Twenty20																			

Career Performances

	M	Inns	NO	Runs	HS	Avge	100s	50s	Ct	St	Balls	Runs	Wkts	Avge	Best	5wI	10wM
Test																	
All First	23	28	8	436	49	21.80	-	-	3	-	3314	1993	60	33.21	5-49	2	-
1-Day Int																	
C & G	1	1	1	14	14 *	-	-	-	-	-	36	40	0	-	-	-	-
tsL	31	11	2	92	32	10.22	-	-	4	-	1293	1223	42	29.11	4-27	-	
Twenty20																		

LUMB, M. J. *Yorkshire*

Name: Michael John Lumb
Role: Left-hand bat, right-arm
medium bowler
Born: 12 February 1980, Johannesburg,
South Africa
Height: 6ft **Weight:** 13st
Nickname: China, Joe
County debut: 2000
County cap: 2003
1000 runs in a season: 1
Place in batting averages: 109th av. 34.35
(2004 179th av. 24.81)
Strike rate: (career 48.00)
Parents: Richard and Sue
Marital status: Single
Family links with cricket: Father played for
Yorkshire. Uncle played for Natal
Education: St Stithians College
Qualifications: Matriculation
Overseas tours: Transvaal U19 to Barbados; Yorkshire to Cape Town 2001, to
Grenada 2002; England A to Malaysia and India 2003-04
Overseas teams played for: Pirates CC, Johannesburg; Wanderers CC, Johannesburg

Career highlights to date: 'Getting my Yorkshire cap'
Cricket moments to forget: 'Relegation in 2002'
Cricket superstitions: 'None'
Cricketers particularly admired: Graham Thorpe, Darren Lehmann, Craig White, Stephen Fleming
Other sports played: Golf
Other sports followed: Rugby union (Sharks in Super 14, Leeds Tykes)
Favourite band: Oasis
Relaxations: 'Golf, socialising with friends'
Extras: Scored maiden first-class century (122) v Leicestershire at Headingley 2001; the Lumbs thus became only the fourth father and son to have scored centuries for Yorkshire. Yorkshire Young Player of the Year 2002, 2003. ECB National Academy 2003-04. C&G Man of the Match award in the quarter-final v Northamptonshire at Headingley 2005 (89)
Best batting: 130 Yorkshire v Somerset, Taunton 2005
Best bowling: 2-10 Yorkshire v Kent, Canterbury 2001

2005 Season

	M	Inns	NO	Runs	HS	Avge	100s	50s	Ct	St	O	M	Runs	Wkts	Avge	Best	5wI	10wM
Test																		
All First	11	21	4	584	130	34.35	2	1	10	-	23	2	92	2	46.00	1-7	-	-
1-Day Int																		
C & G	3	3	0	147	89	49.00	-	1	-	-								
tsL	18	18	1	598	69	35.17	-	6	2	-	2	0	28	0	-		-	-
Twenty20	7	7	1	60	23 *	10.00	-	-	1	-								

Career Performances

	M	Inns	NO	Runs	HS	Avge	100s	50s	Ct	St	Balls	Runs	Wkts	Avge	Best	5wI	10wM
Test																	
All First	65	112	10	3323	130	32.57	6	18	38	-	288	206	6	34.33	2-10	-	-
1-Day Int																	
C & G	12	11	1	408	89	40.80	-	3	3	-							
tsL	64	62	4	1705	92	29.39	-	13	18	-	12	28	0	-		-	-
Twenty20	17	17	2	224	55	14.93	-	2	2	-	36	65	3	21.66	3-32	-	

LUNGLEY, T.   Derbyshire

Name: Tom Lungley
Role: Left-hand bat, right-arm
medium bowler
Born: 25 July 1979, Derby
Height: 6ft 2in **Weight:** 13st
Nickname: Lungfish, Monkfish, Sweaty, Full
Moon, Half Moon, Lungo
County debut: 2000
Strike rate: (career 51.31)
Parents: Richard and Christina
Marital status: 'Taken'
Family links with cricket: 'Dad was captain
of Derby Road CC. Grandad was bat maker
in younger days'
Education: Saint John Houghton School;
South East Derbyshire College
Qualifications: 9 GCSEs, Sport and
Recreation Levels 1 and 2, pool lifeguard
qualification, coaching qualifications in cricket, tennis, basketball, football and
volleyball
Career outside cricket: Painter and decorator
Overseas teams played for: Delacombe Park, Melbourne 1999-2000
Cricket moments to forget: 'Unable to speak when interviewed by Sybil Ruscoe on
Channel 4 Cricket Roadshow (live)'
Cricket superstitions: 'Always eat Jaffa Cake before play'
Cricketers particularly admired: Ian Botham, Dennis Lillee, Courtney Walsh, Curtly
Ambrose, Brian Lara, Richard Hadlee, Glenn McGrath
Other sports played: 'Enjoy playing most sports, mainly football and basketball'
Other sports followed: Football (Derby County), basketball
Extras: First home-grown cricketer to become professional from Ockbrook and
Borrowash CC. Took 4-13 v Nottinghamshire at Derby in the Twenty20 2003. NBC
Denis Compton Award for the most promising young Derbyshire player 2003
Best batting: 47 Derbyshire v Warwickshire, Derby 2001
Best bowling: 4-101 Derbyshire v Glamorgan, Swansea 2003

2005 Season

	M	Inns	NO	Runs	HS	Avge	100s	50s	Ct	St	O	M	Runs	Wkts	Avge	Best	5wI	10wM
Test																		
All First	3	3	0	41	36	13.66	-	-	1	-	79	12	320	5	64.00	2-54	-	-
1-Day Int																		
C & G	2	2	0	27	14	13.50	-	-	-	-	14	0	82	2	41.00	2-40	-	
tsL	14	7	2	76	22 *	15.20	-	-	3	-	54	6	273	4	68.25	1-13	-	
Twenty20	8	5	2	46	25	15.33	-	-	2	-	19	0	145	8	18.12	3-21	-	

Career Performances

	M	Inns	NO	Runs	HS	Avge	100s	50s	Ct	St	Balls	Runs	Wkts	Avge	Best	5wI	10wM
Test																	
All First	22	35	5	397	47	13.23	-	-	7	-	2412	1654	47	35.19	4-101	-	-
1-Day Int																	
C & G	7	6	1	34	14	6.80	-	-	2	-	263	227	6	37.83	2-18	-	
tsL	39	23	7	274	45	17.12	-	-	7	-	1401	1157	41	28.21	4-28	-	
Twenty20	13	8	3	83	25	16.60	-	-	3	-	216	271	14	19.35	4-13	-	

MADDY, D. L. Leicestershire

Name: Darren Lee Maddy
Role: Right-hand bat, right-arm medium bowler
Born: 23 May 1974, Leicester
Height: 5ft 9in **Weight:** 12st 7lbs
Nickname: Roaster, Dazza, Fire Starter
County debut: 1993 (one-day), 1994 (first-class)
County cap: 1996
Benefit: 2006
Test debut: 1999
1000 runs in a season: 4
1st-Class 200s: 2
Place in batting averages: 174th av. 26.40 (2004 133rd av. 32.14)
Place in bowling averages: 118th av. 43.69 (2004 137th av. 45.73)
Strike rate: 83.53 (career 58.05)
Parents: William Arthur and Hilary Jean
Wife and date of marriage: Justine Marie, 7 October 2000
Family links with cricket: Father and younger brother, Greg, play club cricket
Education: Roundhill, Thurmaston; Wreake Valley, Syston

Qualifications: 8 GCSEs, Level 1 coach

Career outside cricket: Fitness advisor

Overseas tours: Leicestershire to Bloemfontein 1995, to Western Transvaal 1996, to Durban 1997, to Barbados 1998, to Anguilla 2000, to Potchefstroom 2001; England A to Kenya and Sri Lanka 1997-98, to Zimbabwe and South Africa 1998-99; England to South Africa and Zimbabwe 1999-2000; England VI to Hong Kong 2003, 2004, 2005

Overseas teams played for: Wanderers, Johannesburg 1992-93; Northern Free State, South Africa 1993-95; Rhodes University, South Africa 1995-97; Sunshine CC, Grenada 2002; Perth CC, 2002-04

Career highlights to date: 'Winning two Championship medals. Playing for England. Winning Twenty20 final [2004]'

Cricket moments to forget: 'Too many to mention. I hate losing a cricket match and I hate getting out – losing two Lord's finals, finishing second in the Norwich Union League, and being relegated'

Cricket superstitions: 'Always put my left pad on first'

Cricketers particularly admired: Graham Gooch, Michael Atherton, Ian Botham, Viv Richards, Richard Hadlee

Young players to look out for: Stuart Broad

Other sports played: Touch rugby, golf, squash, 5-a-side football

Other sports followed: Rugby (Leicester Tigers), football (Leicester City), baseball, golf, boxing – 'most sports really except for horse racing and motor racing'

Favourite band: 'Too many to mention – Two Tone Deaf, Bon Jovi, Def Leppard, Stereophonics, Aerosmith'

Relaxations: 'Going to the gym, playing sport, spending time with my wife, Justine; listening to music, watching TV, going on holiday, scuba diving, bungee jumping, playing the drums'

Extras: Rapid Cricketline 2nd XI Championship Player of the Year 1994. Was leading run-scorer on England A's 1997-98 tour (687; av. 68.7). In 1998, broke the season record for runs scored in the B&H (629; av. 125.80), winning five Gold Awards. Scored 229* v Loughborough UCCE at Leicester 2003, in the process sharing with Brad Hodge (202*) in a record partnership for any wicket for Leicestershire (436*). Struck 60-ball 111 v Yorkshire at Headingley in the Twenty20 2004, in the process sharing with Brad Hodge (78) in a competition record partnership for any wicket (167). President of the Leicestershire School Sports Federation. Vice-captain of Leicestershire July 2004-2005

Opinions on cricket: 'There are too many non-English players playing county cricket. If we don't put some kind of restriction on the influx of such players it will have a detrimental effect on the England team in the very near future! We've already started to see counties releasing home-grown players and substituting them with non-English-qualified players who are not necessarily any better cricketers.'

Best batting: 229* Leicestershire v LUCCE, Leicester 2003

Best bowling: 5-37 Leicestershire v Hampshire, West End 2002

2005 Season

	M	Inns	NO	Runs	HS	Avge	100s	50s	Ct	St	O	M	Runs	Wkts	Avge	Best	5wI	10wM
Test																		
All First	15	25	0	660	124	26.40	1	1	17	-	181	36	568	13	43.69	4-65	-	-
1-Day Int																		
C & G	2	2	0	10	10	5.00	-	-	1	-	11	1	58	2	29.00	2-37	-	
tsL	17	17	2	621	107 *	41.40	1	5	7	-	74.3	8	315	10	31.50	2-14	-	
Twenty20	9	9	1	224	72 *	28.00	-	2	7	-	17	0	146	6	24.33	2-18	-	

Career Performances

	M	Inns	NO	Runs	HS	Avge	100s	50s	Ct	St	Balls	Runs	Wkts	Avge	Best	5wI	10wM
Test	3	4	0	46	24	11.50	-	-	4	-	84	40	0	-	-	-	-
All First	203	331	20	10135	229 *	32.58	19	49	212	-	9405	5170	162	31.91	5-37	4	-
1-Day Int	8	6	0	113	53	18.83	-	1	1	-							
C & G	26	24	2	465	89	21.13	-	2	11	-	587	483	17	28.41	3-44	-	
tsL	185	169	21	4296	107 *	29.02	2	30	63	-	3616	3130	104	30.09	4-16	-	
Twenty20	22	22	1	756	111	36.00	1	6	9	-	266	358	11	32.54	2-18	-	

MAHER, J. P. Durham

Name: James (<u>Jimmy</u>) Patrick Maher
Role: Left-hand bat, right-arm medium bowler, occasional wicket-keeper
Born: 27 February 1974, Innisfail, Queensland, Australia
Height: 6ft **Weight:** 13st 5lbs
Nickname: Rock, Mahbo
County debut: 2001 (Glamorgan), 2005 (Durham)
County cap: 2001 (Glamorgan)
1000 runs in a season: 1
1st-Class 200s: 3
Strike rate: (career 85.20)
Parents: Marie Ann and Warren George
Wife and date of marriage: Debbie, 6 April 2001
Children: Lily Matilda, 2002
Family links with cricket: Father and uncle played for Queensland Country
Education: St Augustine's College, Cairns; Nudgee College, Brisbane
Overseas tours: Australia U19 to New Zealand 1992-93; Queensland Academy to South Africa 1993; Australia to South Africa 2001-02 (one-day series), to Kenya (PSO

Tri-Nation Tournament) 2002, to Sri Lanka (ICC Champions Trophy) 2002-03, to Africa (World Cup) 2002-03, to West Indies 2002-03 (one-day series), to India (TVS Cup) 2003-04

Overseas teams played for: Queensland 1993-94 –

Career highlights to date: 'Playing for Australia. Being part of Queensland's first ever Sheffield Shield title win at The Gabba [1994-95]'

Cricket moments to forget: 'Running out Allan Border on my debut'

Cricketers particularly admired: Allan Border, Matt Hayden, Shane Warne, Glenn McGrath

Young players to look out for: Mark Wallace, Mitchell Johnson

Other sports played: Squash ('played State titles U12-U16'), tennis ('ranked in top ten in Queensland at U14')

Other sports followed: Rugby union (Queensland Reds), rugby league (Canterbury Bulldogs)

Relaxations: 'Golf, dinner with friends, couple of lagers with mates'

Extras: Represented Australia U17 and U19. Attended Australian Cricket Academy 1993. Was Glamorgan's overseas player in 2001, returning in 2003. Pura Cup Player of the Year 2001-02 (jointly with Brad Hodge of Victoria) and *Wisden Australia*'s Pura Cup Cricketer of the Year 2001-02. Recalled to Australia's one-day squad for tour of South Africa 2001-02 and was Man of the Match in his first two ODIs since 1997-98 (95 and 43*). His other match awards include Man of the Match in the ING Cup final 2004-05 v Tasmania at The Gabba (104). Captain of Queensland since 2002-03 and has captained Australia A. Was an overseas player with Durham during the 2005 season as a locum for Mike Hussey

Best batting: 217 Glamorgan v Essex, Cardiff 2001

Best bowling: 3-11 Queensland v Western Australia, Perth 1995-96

2005 Season

	M	Inns	NO	Runs	HS	Avge	100s	50s	Ct	St	O	M	Runs	Wkts	Avge	Best	5wI	10wM
Test																		
All First	2	4	0	18	9	4.50	-	-	3	-								
1-Day Int																		
C & G																		
tsL	4	4	0	194	70	48.50	-	2	1	-								
Twenty20																		

Career Performances

	M	Inns	NO	Runs	HS	Avge	100s	50s	Ct	St	Balls	Runs	Wkts	Avge	Best	5wI	10wM
Test																	
All First	151	268	27	10024	217	41.59	21	49	157	2	852	504	10	50.40	3-11	-	-
1-Day Int	26	20	3	438	95	25.76	-	1	18	-							
C & G	1	1	0	30	30	30.00	-	-	1	-							
tsL	29	29	1	942	142	33.64	1	6	13	-	18	29	3	9.66	3-29	-	
Twenty20																	

MAHMOOD, S. I. Lancashire

Name: Sajid Iqbal Mahmood
Role: Right-hand bat, right-arm
fast-medium bowler
Born: 21 December 1981, Bolton
Height: 6ft 4in **Weight:** 12st 7lbs
Nickname: Saj, King
County debut: 2002
Place in batting averages: 236th av. 17.70
(2004 213th av. 21.18)
Place in bowling averages: 94th av. 37.21
(2004 131st av. 43.91)
Strike rate: 60.57 (career 54.14)
Parents: Shahid and Femida
Marital status: Single
Family links with cricket: Father played in
Bolton League; younger brother plays in
Bolton League
Education: Smithills School; North College,
Bolton (sixth form)

Qualifications: 9 GCSEs, 3 A-levels
Overseas tours: Lancashire to South Africa 2003; England A to Malaysia and India
2003-04, to Sri Lanka 2004-05, to West Indies 2005-06
Overseas teams played for: Napier, New Zealand 2002-03
Career highlights to date: 'Making first-team debut and selection for academy'
Cricket moments to forget: 'None'
Cricket superstitions: 'None'
Cricketers particularly admired: Brett Lee, Shoaib Akhtar
Favourite band: Nelly, Eminem
Relaxations: 'Music and chillin' with mates'
Extras: Took 5-62 for England A v East Zone at Amritsar 2003-04. NBC Denis
Compton Award for the most promising young Lancashire player 2003. Struck 66-ball
94 in Championship v Sussex at Old Trafford 2004. ECB National Academy 2003-04,
2004-05, 2005-06. Is cousin of Olympic silver medal winning boxer Amir Khan
Best batting: 94 Lancashire v Sussex, Old Trafford 2004
Best bowling: 5-37 Lancashire v DUCCE, Durham 2003

	M	Inns	NO	Runs	HS	Avge	100s	50s	Ct	St	O	M	Runs	Wkts	Avge	Best	5wI	10wM
Test																		
All First	8	10	0	177	57	17.70	-	1	-	-	141.2	22	521	14	37.21	3-21	-	-
1-Day Int																		
C & G	2	1	1	8	8 *	-	-	-	1	-	7	0	28	2	14.00	2-28	-	
tsL	13	10	1	79	17 *	8.77	-	-	2	-	86	3	441	10	44.10	2-23	-	
Twenty20																		

Career Performances

	M	Inns	NO	Runs	HS	Avge	100s	50s	Ct	St	Balls	Runs	Wkts	Avge	Best	5wI	10wM
Test																	
All First	29	37	6	540	94	17.41	-	2	4	-	3628	2376	67	35.46	5-37	2	-
1-Day Int	1	1	0	1	1	1.00	-	-	-	-	42	56	0	-	-	-	
C & G	7	4	2	53	29	26.50	-	-	1	-	231	207	10	20.70	3-56	-	
tsL	34	17	5	109	17 *	9.08	-	-	3	-	1448	1216	43	28.27	4-39	-	
Twenty20	8	4	0	22	21	5.50	-	-	-	-	168	216	3	72.00	1-20	-	

MALIK, M. N. Worcestershire

Name: Muhammad Nadeem Malik
Role: Right-hand bat, right-arm
fast-medium bowler
Born: 6 October 1982, Nottingham
Height: 6ft 5in **Weight:** 14st 7lbs
Nickname: Nad, Busta, Nigel, Gerz
County debut: 2001 (Nottinghamshire),
2004 (Worcestershire)
County colours: 2004 (Worcestershire)
Place in bowling averages: 49th av. 27.83
(2004 67th av. 32.54)
Strike rate: 45.08 (career 49.40)
Parents: Abdul and Arshad
Marital status: Single
Family links with cricket: Brother plays
club cricket for Carrington
Education: Wilford Meadows Secondary
School; Bilborough College
Qualifications: 9 GCSEs
Career outside cricket: Personal trainer
Overseas tours: ZRK to Pakistan 2000; Nottinghamshire to South Africa 2001;
England U19 to India 2000-01, to Australia and (U19 World Cup) New Zealand
2001-02

Career highlights to date: '5-57 against Derbyshire 2001'
Cricket moments to forget: 'Norwich Union match v Yorkshire at Scarborough 2001 – Lehmann 191'
Cricketers particularly admired: Glenn McGrath, Wasim Akram, Curtly Ambrose
Young players to look out for: Steve Davies, Will Gifford
Other sports played: Football
Other sports followed: Football, boxing
Relaxations: Music, games consoles
Extras: Made Nottinghamshire 2nd XI debut in 1999, aged 16, and took 15 wickets at an average of 19.40 for the 2nd XI 2000. Represented England U19 2001 and 2002
Best batting: 39* Worcestershire v New Zealanders, Worcester 2004
Best bowling: 5-57 Nottinghamshire v Derbyshire, Trent Bridge 2001

2005 Season

	M	Inns	NO	Runs	HS	Avge	100s	50s	Ct	St	O	M	Runs	Wkts	Avge	Best	5wl	10wM
Test																		
All First	9	14	5	61	21*	6.77	-	-	-	-	270.3	58	1002	36	27.83	5-71	1	-
1-Day Int																		
C & G																		
tsL	9	5	3	31	9	15.50	-	-	1	-	58	1	317	10	31.70	2-34	-	
Twenty20	6	2	0	0	0	0.00	-	-	-	-	24	0	235	6	39.16	2-40	-	

Career Performances

	M	Inns	NO	Runs	HS	Avge	100s	50s	Ct	St	Balls	Runs	Wkts	Avge	Best	5wl	10wM
Test																	
All First	31	39	14	209	39*	8.36	-	-	3	-	4693	2986	95	31.43	5-57	4	-
1-Day Int																	
C & G	3	1	1	1	1*	-	-	-	-	-	90	83	0	-	-	-	-
tsL	31	16	10	66	11	11.00	-	-	5	-	1277	1114	34	32.76	4-42	-	
Twenty20	12	4	2	4	3*	2.00	-	-	1	-	264	391	16	24.43	3-23	-	

52. Which former ODI captain had a father
who kept goal for Stenhousemuir?

MARSHALL, H. J. H. — Gloucestershire

Name: <u>Hamish</u> John Hamilton Marshall
Role: Right-hand bat, right-arm medium bowler
Born: 15 February 1979, Warkworth, Auckland, New Zealand
County debut: No first-team appearance
Test debut: 2000-01
Strike rate: (career 90.00)
Family links with cricket: Twin brother James Marshall also plays for Northern Districts and New Zealand
Overseas tours: New Zealand U19 to South Africa (U19 World Cup) 1997-98; New Zealand to South Africa 2000-01, to Pakistan (one-day series) 2003-04, to England 2004 (NatWest Series), to England (ICC Champions Trophy) 2004, to Bangladesh 2004-05, to Australia 2004-05, to Zimbabwe 2005-06, to South Africa (one-day series) 2005-06

Overseas teams played for: Northern Districts 1998-99 –
Extras: MCC Young Cricketer 1998. Attended New Zealand Cricket Academy 1999. Played for Buckinghamshire in the 2004 C&G competition. Represented New Zealand v FICA World XI 2004-05. One of *New Zealand Cricket Almanack*'s two Players of the Year 2005. His match awards include Man of the Match v West Indies at Cardiff in the NatWest Series 2004 (75*) and v Australia in the first ODI at Melbourne 2004-05 (50*). Made Twenty20 international debut v Australia at Auckland 2004-05. Has joined Gloucestershire as an overseas player for 2006
Best batting: 160 New Zealand v Sri Lanka, Napier 2004-05
Best bowling: 1-12 New Zealand A v Sri Lanka A, Christchurch 2003-04

2005 Season (did not make any first-class or one-day appearances)

Career Performances

	M	Inns	NO	Runs	HS	Avge	100s	50s	Ct	St	Balls	Runs	Wkts	Avge	Best	5wI	10wM
Test	9	13	1	583	160	48.58	2	2	-	-	6	4	0	-	-	-	-
All First	58	94	5	2620	160	29.43	3	12	29	-	180	113	2	56.50	1-12	-	-
1-Day Int	40	37	6	1058	101 *	34.12	1	10	11	-							
C & G	1	1	1	66	66 *	-	-	-	1	-							
tsL																	
Twenty20																	

MARSHALL, S. J.   Lancashire

Name: <u>Simon</u> James Marshall
Role: Right-hand bat, right-arm leg-spin
bowler; all-rounder
Born: 20 September 1982, Wirral
Height: 6ft 3in **Weight:** 12st 12lbs
Nickname: Marsh
County debut: 2005
Place in batting averages: (2004 96th
av. 36.33)
Strike rate: (career 133.95)
Parents: Jim and Dinah
Marital status: Single
Family links with cricket: Father captained
Radley School and Liverpool University
Education: Birkenhead School; Cambridge
University
Qualifications: 9 GCSEs, 4 A-levels, BA
(Cantab) Land Economy
Overseas tours: ESCA and ECB age-group tours 1996-2001; British Universities to
South Africa 2004
Overseas teams played for: Adelaide Buffalos CC, South Australia 2004-05
Career highlights to date: 'Taking 6-128 and scoring 99 against Essex in my debut
first-class season for Cambridge. Maiden first-class century. The 2005 A-Grade one-
day final for Adelaide under lights at the Adelaide Oval'
Cricket moments to forget: 'Making a 27-ball duck against Kent 2003, which only
included two balls hitting the bat, both of which were dropped at first slip by Greg
Blewett'
Cricketers particularly admired: Carl Hooper, Jack Smith, Ben Johnson,
Luke Williams
Young players to look out for: Dan Cullen
Other sports played: Hockey (Cambridge Blue)
Other sports followed: Football (Everton FC), hockey (Cambridge University HC)
Favourite band: Dire Straits
Relaxations: 'Spending time with a fantastic group of friends; painting'
Extras: Played for Cheshire in the C&G 2002, 2003. Played for Cambridge UCCE
2002, (as captain) 2003, and 2004; took 6-128 then followed up with 99 in CUCCE's
second innings v Essex at Fenner's 2002. Cambridge Blue 2002-04. Represented
British Universities 2004. Cambridge University Sportsman of the Year 2004
Opinions on cricket: 'Having recently experienced a season of Australian grade
cricket, it seems that the league set-up in the UK is hugely inadequate for developing
cricketers into first-class players. The best players need to be playing against each

other week in week out, allowing county selectors to have a realistic chance of selecting proven run-scorers and wicket-takers to take the next step. The grade system also allows young players to see a clear path into the first-class game through consistent performances rather than the talent-spotting of junior representative coaches.'

Best batting: 126* Cambridge University v Oxford University, Fenner's 2003
Best bowling: 6-128 CUCCE v Essex, Fenner's 2002

2005 Season

	M	Inns	NO	Runs	HS	Avge	100s	50s	Ct	St	O	M	Runs	Wkts	Avge	Best	5wI	10wM
Test																		
All First	4	6	3	104	35 *	34.66	-	-	1	-	94.3	15	266	7	38.00	2-23	-	-
1-Day Int																		
C & G																		
tsL	1	1	0	0	0	0.00	-	-	-	-	5.1	0	31	0	-		-	-
Twenty20																		

Career Performances

	M	Inns	NO	Runs	HS	Avge	100s	50s	Ct	St	Balls	Runs	Wkts	Avge	Best	5wI	10wM
Test																	
All First	16	26	6	733	126 *	36.65	1	3	4	-	3215	1729	24	72.04	6-128	1	-
1-Day Int																	
C & G	2	2	0	7	4	3.50	-	-	-	-	96	85	0	-		-	-
tsL	1	1	0	0	0	0.00	-	-	-	-	31	31	0	-		-	-
Twenty20																	

53. Which ground has hosted the most ODI matches?

MARTIN-JENKINS, R. S. C.   Sussex

Name: <u>Robin</u> Simon Christopher
Martin-Jenkins
Role: Right-hand bat, right-arm
fast-medium bowler
Born: 28 October 1975, Guildford
Height: 6ft 5in **Weight:** 14st
Nickname: Tucker
County debut: 1995
County cap: 2000
1000 runs in a season: 1
1st-Class 200s: 1
Place in batting averages: 96th av. 36.62
(2004 223rd av. 19.27)
Place in bowling averages: 109th av. 41.20
(2004 112th av. 38.86)
Strike rate: 85.10 (career 66.14)
Parents: Christopher and Judy
Wife and date of marriage: Flora,
19 February 2000
Family links with cricket: Father is *The Times* chief cricket correspondent and BBC
TMS commentator. Brother plays for the Radley Rangers
Education: Radley College, Oxon; Durham University
Qualifications: 10 GCSEs, 3 A-levels, 1 AS-level, Grade 3 bassoon (with merit),
BA (Hons) Social Sciences, Don Mackenzie School of Professional Photography
Certificate, SWPP (Society of Wedding and Portrait Photographers), BPPA (British
Professional Photographers Associates)
Overseas tours: Radley College to Barbados 1992; Sussex U19 to Sri Lanka 1995;
Durham University to Vienna 1995; MCC to Kenya 1999; Sussex to Grenada 2001,
2002
Overseas teams played for: Lima CC, Peru 1994; Bellville CC, Cape Town 2000-01
Career highlights to date: 'Winning National League Division Two in 1999. Scoring
maiden first-class century in same match that Sussex won to take second division
Championship 2001. Scoring maiden first-class 200 v Somerset at Taunton 2002.
Winning first division Championship 2003'
Cricket superstitions: 'Never bowl first at Colwyn Bay'
Other sports played: Golf, tennis, Rugby fives
Other sports followed: Rugby, football (Liverpool)
Relaxations: Photography, guitar, reading, TV, films
Extras: Played for ESCA U15-U19. European Player of the Year, Vienna 1995. Best
Performance Award for Sussex 1998. NBC Denis Compton Award for the most
promising young Sussex player 1998, 1999, 2000. Scored 205* v Somerset at Taunton

2002, in the process sharing with Mark Davis (111) in a record eighth-wicket stand for Sussex (291); the stand fell one run short of the record eighth-wicket partnership in English first-class cricket, set in 1896. BBC South Cricketer of the Year 2002

Best batting: 205* Sussex v Somerset, Taunton 2002
Best bowling: 7-51 Sussex v Leicestershire, Horsham 2002

2005 Season

	M	Inns	NO	Runs	HS	Avge	100s	50s	Ct	St	O	M	Runs	Wkts	Avge	Best	5wl	10wM
Test																		
All First	15	20	4	586	88	36.62	-	2	4	-	283.4	71	824	20	41.20	4-31	-	-
1-Day Int																		
C & G	2	2	2	14	8 *	-	-	-	1	-	15	2	72	1	72.00	1-48	-	
tsL	16	10	1	163	37	18.11	-	-	6	-	116	4	491	14	35.07	3-32	-	
Twenty20																		

Career Performances

	M	Inns	NO	Runs	HS	Avge	100s	50s	Ct	St	Balls	Runs	Wkts	Avge	Best	5wl	10wM
Test																	
All First	116	180	22	4765	205 *	30.15	3	24	33	-	16470	8555	249	34.35	7-51	5	-
1-Day Int																	
C & G	11	10	5	170	61 *	34.00	-	1	4	-	556	357	11	32.45	2-24	-	
tsL	121	86	10	1027	68 *	13.51	-	2	32	-	5153	3546	126	28.14	4-39	-	
Twenty20	8	8	2	135	56 *	22.50	-	1	2	-	169	225	10	22.50	4-20	-	

54. Which former Yorkshire overseas player became the first son to follow his father into India's ODI side?

MASCARENHAS, D. A.   Hampshire

Name: <u>Dimitri</u> Adrian Mascarenhas
Role: Right-hand bat, right-arm
medium bowler
Born: 30 October 1977, Chiswick, London
Height: 6ft 1in **Weight:** 12st 2lbs
Nickname: Dimi, D-Train
County debut: 1996
County cap: 1998
50 wickets in a season: 1
Place in batting averages: 39th av. 49.09
(2004 205th av. 21.68)
Place in bowling averages: 17th av. 23.55
(2004 2nd av. 18.67)
Strike rate: 48.29 (career 60.95)
Parents: Malik and Pauline
Marital status: Single
Family links with cricket: Uncle played in
Sri Lanka and brothers both play for Melville
CC in Perth, Western Australia
Education: Trinity College, Perth
Qualifications: Level 2 coaching
Career outside cricket: Personal trainer
Overseas tours: England VI to Hong Kong 2004, 2005
Overseas teams played for: Melville CC, Perth 1991 –
Career highlights to date: 'Debut for Hampshire 1996 – 6-88 v Glamorgan'
Cricketers particularly admired: Sir Viv Richards, Malcolm Marshall,
Shane Warne
Young players to look out for: Beau Casson (Western Australia)
Other sports followed: Australian Rules (Collingwood)
Favourite band: Red Hot Chili Peppers
Relaxations: Tennis, golf, Australian Rules
Extras: Played for Western Australia at U17 and U19 level as captain. Took 6-88 on
first-class debut, for Hampshire v Glamorgan at Southampton 1996. Won NatWest
Man of the Match awards in semi-final v Lancashire at Southampton 1998 (3-28/73)
and in quarter-final v Middlesex at Lord's 2000 (4-25). Scorer of the first
Championship century at the Rose Bowl (104) v Worcestershire 2001. Took 5-14 v
Sussex at Hove in the Twenty20 2004, including the competition's first hat-trick
(Davis, Mushtaq Ahmed, Lewry)
Opinions on cricket: 'I think that two overseas players [per county] is great for the
game. It definitely raises the standard, and you also get a chance to play against the
best players worldwide.'

Best batting: 104 Hampshire v Worcestershire, West End 2001
104 Hampshire v Durham, Riverside 2004
Best bowling: 6-25 Hampshire v Derbyshire, West End 2004

2005 Season

	M	Inns	NO	Runs	HS	Avge	100s	50s	Ct	St	O	M	Runs	Wkts	Avge	Best	5wI	10wM
Test																		
All First	11	18	7	540	103 *	49.09	2	1	5	-	273.4	65	801	34	23.55	5-55	2	-
1-Day Int																		
C & G	5	3	0	26	12	8.66	-	-	1	-	39	3	152	4	38.00	2-7	-	
tsL	9	9	3	231	50 *	38.50	-	2	2	-	66.1	2	332	10	33.20	2-32	-	
Twenty20	1	1	1	9	9 *	-	-	-	-	-	3	0	31	0	-	-	-	

Career Performances

	M	Inns	NO	Runs	HS	Avge	100s	50s	Ct	St	Balls	Runs	Wkts	Avge	Best	5wI	10wM
Test																	
All First	130	196	24	4295	104	24.97	6	16	54	-	18653	8668	306	28.32	6-25	12	-
1-Day Int																	
C & G	21	17	4	439	73	33.76	-	4	3	-	1020	607	28	21.67	4-25	-	
tsL	122	109	20	1868	79	20.98	-	10	36	-	5111	3673	157	23.39	5-27	1	
Twenty20	12	12	4	223	52	27.87	-	1	6	-	215	283	15	18.86	5-14	1	

MASON, M. S.   Worcestershire

Name: Matthew (<u>Matt</u>) Sean Mason
Role: Right-hand bat, right-arm
fast-medium bowler
Born: 20 March 1974, Perth, Western
Australia
Height: 6ft 5in **Weight:** 16st
Nickname: Mase, Moose
County debut: 2002
County colours: 2002
50 wickets in a season: 3
Place in batting averages: 252nd av. 14.83
(2004 250th av. 14.64)
Place in bowling averages: 50th av. 28.03
(2004 50th av. 30.42)
Strike rate: 56.22 (career 60.22)
Parents: Bill and Sue
Wife and date of marriage: Kellie,
8 October 2005
Family links with cricket: Brother Simon plays first-grade cricket in Perth

Education: Mazenod College, Perth; Curtin University of Technology
Qualifications: Level 1 ACB coach
Career outside cricket: 'Would like to get into sports management'
Off-season: 'Heading to Perth for six weeks with Kellie'
Overseas tours: Worcestershire to South Africa 2003
Overseas teams played for: Western Australia 1996-1998; Wanneroo District CC 1999-2001
Career highlights to date: 'Two Lord's finals'
Cricket moments to forget: 'Losing both Lord's finals, and 2005 season'
Cricket superstitions: 'Don't go out with Gareth Batty during a game (joking)'
Cricketers particularly admired: Justin Langer, Dennis Lillee, Darren Gough
Young players to look out for: Steve Davies
Other sports played: 'Very bad golf and love Aussie Rules football'
Other sports followed: 'Follow all sports'
Injuries: 'Struggled with shoulder a bit but nothing serious'
Favourite band: 'Loving Coldplay at the moment'
Relaxations: 'Spending time with my wife, friends and family'
Extras: Scored maiden first-class fifty (50) from 27 balls v Derbyshire at Worcester 2002. Dick Lygon Award for the [Worcestershire] Clubman of the Year 2003. Is England-qualified by residency
Opinions on cricket: 'The game just keeps going from strength to strength as can be seen with the quality of the England side now.'
Best batting: 63 Worcestershire v Warwickshire, Worcester 2004
Best bowling: 6-68 Worcestershire v Durham, Worcester 2003

2005 Season

	M	Inns	NO	Runs	HS	Avge	100s	50s	Ct	St	O	M	Runs	Wkts	Avge	Best	5wI	10wM
Test																		
All First	16	23	5	267	38	14.83	-	-	2	-	496.4	137	1486	53	28.03	5-34	1	-
1-Day Int																		
C & G	1	0	0	0	0	-	-	-	-	-	5	0	33	0	-	-	-	-
tsL	3	2	1	9	9 *	9.00	-	-	-	-	24	1	116	4	29.00	3-20	-	
Twenty20	1	1	1	8	8 *	-	-	-	1	-	4	1	21	1	21.00	1-21	-	

Career Performances

	M	Inns	NO	Runs	HS	Avge	100s	50s	Ct	St	Balls	Runs	Wkts	Avge	Best	5wI	10wM
Test																	
All First	58	76	18	839	63	14.46	-	3	11	-	11082	5074	184	27.57	6-68	5	-
1-Day Int																	
C & G	13	7	3	7	3 *	1.75	-	-	2	-	663	434	16	27.12	3-28	-	
tsL	38	19	6	129	25	9.92	-	-	7	-	1703	1244	45	27.64	4-34	-	
Twenty20	5	3	1	11	8 *	5.50	-	-	2	-	115	124	4	31.00	1-21	-	

MASTERS, D. D. Leicestershire

Name: David Daniel Masters
Role: Right-hand bat, right-arm medium-fast bowler
Born: 22 April 1978, Chatham, Kent
Height: 6ft 4ins **Weight:** 12st 5lbs
Nickname: Hod, Race Horse, Hoddy
County debut: 2000 (Kent), 2003 (Leicestershire)
Place in batting averages: 225th av. 19.50
Place in bowling averages: 35th av. 26.55 (2004 109th av. 38.07)
Strike rate: 53.88 (career 60.60)
Parents: Kevin and Tracey
Marital status: Single
Family links with cricket: 'Dad was on staff at Kent 1983-86'
Education: Fort Luton High School; Mid-Kent College
Qualifications: 8 GCSEs, GNVQ in Leisure and Tourism, qualified coach in cricket, football and athletics, bricklayer and plasterer
Career outside cricket: Builder
Overseas teams played for: Double View, Perth 1998-99
Cricketers particularly admired: Ian Botham
Other sports played: Football, boxing 'and most other sports'
Other sports followed: Football (Manchester United)
Relaxations: 'Going out with mates'
Extras: Joint Kent Player of the Year 2000 (with Martin Saggers). NBC Denis Compton Award for the most promising young Kent player 2000
Best batting: 119 Leicestershire v Sussex, Hove 2003
Best bowling: 6-27 Kent v Durham, Tunbridge Wells 2000

2005 Season

	M	Inns	NO	Runs	HS	Avge	100s	50s	Ct	St	O	M	Runs	Wkts	Avge	Best	5wI	10wM
Test																		
All First	13	16	6	195	36	19.50	-	-	4	-	305.2	85	903	34	26.55	6-74	1	-
1-Day Int																		
C & G	1	1	0	2	2	2.00	-	-	-	-	4	0	27	0	-	-	-	-
tsL	13	5	5	39	17*	-	-	-	2	-	81	11	293	9	32.55	3-32	-	
Twenty20	8	3	2	14	7	14.00	-	-	3	-	24	0	208	4	52.00	2-15	-	

Career Performances

	M	Inns	NO	Runs	HS	Avge	100s	50s	Ct	St	Balls	Runs	Wkts	Avge	Best	5wl	10wM
Test																	
All First	64	78	19	734	119	12.44	1	1	20	-	9878	5321	163	32.64	6-27	5	-
1-Day Int																	
C & G	5	4	1	27	24 *	9.00	-	-	-	-	209	159	5	31.80	4-15	-	
tsL	50	31	15	193	27	12.06	-	-	5	-	1891	1544	35	44.11	5-20	1	
Twenty20	14	6	3	15	7	5.00	-	-	4	-	252	343	11	31.18	2-15	-	

MAUNDERS, J. K.   Leicestershire

Name: <u>John</u> Kenneth Maunders
Role: Left-hand opening bat, right-arm medium bowler
Born: 4 April 1981, Ashford, Middlesex
Height: 5ft 10in **Weight:** 13st
Nickname: Rod, Weaz
County debut: 1999 (Middlesex), 2003 (Leicestershire)
Place in batting averages: 163rd av. 28.11 (2004 214th av. 20.95)
Place in bowling averages: 39th av. 27.42
Strike rate: 45.00 (career 51.00)
Parents: Lynn and Kenneth
Marital status: Single
Family links with cricket: Grandfather and two uncles club cricketers for Thames Valley Ramblers
Education: Ashford High School; Spelthorne College
Qualifications: 10 GCSEs, coaching certificates
Career outside cricket: Cricket coach
Overseas tours: England U19 to New Zealand 1998-99, to Malaysia and (U19 World Cup) Sri Lanka 1999-2000
Overseas teams played for: University CC, Perth 2001-02
Career highlights to date: 'Scoring maiden first-class hundred v Surrey at Grace Road'
Cricket moments to forget: 'Not any one in particular; getting 0 and dropping catches are not great moments!'
Cricket superstitions: 'Just a few small ones'
Cricketers particularly admired: Brad Hodge, Justin Langer
Other sports played: Football, hockey, squash
Other sports followed: Horse racing

Extras: Has been Seaxe Player of Year. Represented England U17 and U19. NBC Denis Compton Award 1999
Best batting: 171 Leicestershire v Surrey, Leicester 2003
Best bowling: 4-28 Leicestershire v Lancashire, Old Trafford 2005

2005 Season

	M	Inns	NO	Runs	HS	Avge	100s	50s	Ct	St	O	M	Runs	Wkts	Avge	Best	5wI	10wM
Test																		
All First	16	27	0	759	148	28.11	1	3	7	-	105	16	384	14	27.42	4-28	-	-
1-Day Int																		
C & G	1	1	0	25	25	25.00	-	-	1	-	4	0	16	2	8.00	2-16	-	
tsL	2	2	0	11	10	5.50	-	-	1	-								
Twenty20	9	6	2	18	10	4.50	-	-	1	-								

Career Performances

	M	Inns	NO	Runs	HS	Avge	100s	50s	Ct	St	Balls	Runs	Wkts	Avge	Best	5wI	10wM
Test																	
All First	40	73	2	2010	171	28.30	4	8	17	-	816	506	16	31.62	4-28	-	-
1-Day Int																	
C & G	4	4	0	61	25	15.25	-	-	1	-	37	34	2	17.00	2-16	-
tsL	9	9	0	95	49	10.55	-	-	2	-							
Twenty20	9	6	2	18	10	4.50	-	-	1	-							

MAYNARD, M. P.   Glamorgan

Name: <u>Matthew</u> Peter Maynard
Role: Right-hand middle-order bat, right-arm medium bowler, occasional wicket-keeper
Born: 21 March 1966, Oldham, Lancashire
Height: 5ft 11in **Weight:** 13st
Nickname: Ollie, Wilf
County debut: 1985
County cap: 1987
Benefit: 1996; testimonial 2005
Test debut: 1988
1000 runs in a season: 12
1st-Class 200s: 3
Place in batting averages: (2004 66th av. 43.14)
Strike rate: (career 195.16)
Parents: Ken (deceased) and Pat
Wife and date of marriage: Susan, 27 September 1986

Children: Tom, 25 March 1989; Ceri Lloyd, 5 August 1993
Family links with cricket: Father played for many years for Duckinfield. Brother Charles plays for St Fagans. Son Tom has played for Glamorgan 2nd XI
Education: Ysgol David Hughes, Menai Bridge, Anglesey
Qualifications: Level 3 coach
Overseas tours: North Wales XI to Barbados 1982; Glamorgan to Barbados 1982, to South Africa 1993; unofficial England XI to South Africa 1989-90; HKCC (Australia) to Bangkok and Hong Kong 1990; England VI to Hong Kong 1992, 1994, 2001 (c), 2002 (c), 2003 (c), 2004 (c); England to West Indies 1993-94; England XI to New Zealand (Cricket Max) 1997 (c); England Classics to Grenada (Grenada Classics) 2003-04
Overseas teams played for: St Joseph's, Whakatane, New Zealand 1986-88; Gosnells, Perth, Western Australia 1988-89; Papakura and Northern Districts, New Zealand 1990-91; Morrinsville College and Northern Districts, New Zealand 1991-92; Otago, New Zealand 1996-97
Career highlights to date: 'Leading Glamorgan to the County Championship in 1997. Playing for England'
Cricket moments to forget: 'Losing B&H final in 2000' (*Was nevertheless Gold Award winner for his 118-ball 104*)
Cricketers particularly admired: Ian Botham, Viv Richards, David Gower
Young players to look out for: Tom Maynard
Other sports played: Golf, football
Other sports followed: Rugby, football
Relaxations: 'Spending time with my wife and family and relaxing'
Extras: Scored century (102) on first-class debut v Yorkshire at Swansea 1985, reaching his 100 with three successive straight sixes; scored 1000 first-class runs in his first full season 1986. Cricket Writers' Club Young Cricketer of the Year 1988. Captained Glamorgan for most of 1992 in Alan Butcher's absence; Glamorgan captain 1996-2000. Voted Wombwell Cricket Lovers' Society captain of the year for 1997. One of *Wisden*'s Five Cricketers of the Year 1998. Appointed honorary fellow of University of Wales, Bangor. Published *On the Attack: the Batsman's Story* (with Paul Rees) 2001. Glamorgan Player of the Year 2002. Is Glamorgan's leading century-maker and third highest run-scorer in first-class cricket and the county's leading century-maker and highest run-scorer in one-day cricket. Appointed assistant coach to England one-day squad for tours to Zimbabwe and South Africa 2004-05. Retired during the 2005 season to take up post as Assistant Coach to England teams
Best batting: 243 Glamorgan v Hampshire, Southampton 1991
Best bowling: 3-21 Glamorgan v Oxford University, The Parks 1987

2005 Season

	M	Inns	NO	Runs	HS	Avge	100s	50s	Ct	St	O	M	Runs	Wkts	Avge	Best	5wl	10wM
Test																		
All First	1	2	0	20	20	10.00	-	-	1	-								
1-Day Int																		
C & G																		
tsL	1	0	0	0	0	-	-	-	-	-								
Twenty20																		

Career Performances

	M	Inns	NO	Runs	HS	Avge	100s	50s	Ct	St	Balls	Runs	Wkts	Avge	Best	5wl	10wM
Test	4	8	0	87	35	10.87	-	-	3	-							
All First	395	643	60	24799	243	42.53	59	131	372	7	1171	895	6	149.16	3-21	-	-
1-Day Int	14	12	1	156	41	14.18	-	-	3	-							
C & G	49	47	4	1893	151 *	44.02	3	13	23	1	18	8	0	-	-	-	-
tsL	272	260	32	8027	132	35.20	6	53	120	4	64	64	1	64.00	1-13	-	
Twenty20	12	12	0	424	72	35.33	-	4	9	-							

McGRATH, A.   Yorkshire

Name: Anthony McGrath
Role: Right-hand bat, right-arm
medium bowler
Born: 6 October 1975, Bradford
Height: 6ft 2in   **Weight:** 14st 7lbs
Nickname: Gripper, Mags, Terry
County debut: 1995
County cap: 1999
Test debut: 2003
1000 runs in a season: 1
Place in batting averages: 15th av. 59.37
(2004 57th av. 45.50)
Place in bowling averages: 126th av. 45.43
Strike rate: 86.62 (career 64.74)
Parents: Terry and Kath
Marital status: Single
Education: Yorkshire Martyrs Collegiate
School

Qualifications: 9 GCSEs, BTEC National Diploma in Leisure Studies, senior
coaching award
Overseas tours: England U19 to West Indies 1994-95; England A to Pakistan 1995-
96, to Australia 1996-97; MCC to Bangladesh 1999-2000; England to Bangladesh and
Sri Lanka 2003-04 (one-day series), to West Indies 2003-04 (one-day series)

Overseas teams played for: Deep Dene, Melbourne 1998-99; Wanneroo, Perth 1999-2001
Cricket moments to forget: 'Losing semi-final to Lancashire 1996. Relegation to Division Two 2002'
Cricketers particularly admired: Darren Lehmann, Robin Smith
Other sports followed: 'Most sports', football (Manchester United)
Relaxations: 'Music; spending time with friends; eating out'
Extras: Captained Yorkshire Schools U13, U14, U15, U16; captained English Schools U17. Bradford League Young Cricketer of the Year 1992 and 1993. Played for England U17 and U19. Captain of Yorkshire 2003. Recorded maiden first-class five-wicket return (5-39) v Derbyshire at Derby 2004, scoring career best 174 in the same match
Best batting: 174 Yorkshire v Derbyshire, Derby 2004
Best bowling: 5-39 Yorkshire v Derbyshire, Derby 2004

2005 Season

	M	Inns	NO	Runs	HS	Avge	100s	50s	Ct	St	O	M	Runs	Wkts	Avge	Best	5wI	10wM
Test																		
All First	16	28	4	1425	173 *	59.37	5	5	20	-	231	36	727	16	45.43	3-35	-	-
1-Day Int																		
C & G	4	4	0	130	74	32.50	-	1	-	-	10	0	55	1	55.00	1-11	-	
tsL	18	18	1	517	68	30.41	-	3	6	-	81.5	4	395	10	39.50	2-29	-	
Twenty20	8	8	1	107	33 *	15.28	-	-	3	-	16	0	139	7	19.85	3-27	-	

Career Performances

	M	Inns	NO	Runs	HS	Avge	100s	50s	Ct	St	Balls	Runs	Wkts	Avge	Best	5wI	10wM
Test	4	5	0	201	81	40.20	-	2	3	-	102	56	4	14.00	3-16	-	-
All First	155	266	20	8523	174	34.64	18	37	104	-	4985	2489	77	32.32	5-39	1	-
1-Day Int	14	12	2	166	52	16.60	-	1	4	-	228	175	4	43.75	1-13	-	
C & G	28	25	4	909	84	43.28	-	9	9	-	331	301	8	37.62	4-56	-	
tsL	132	123	20	3240	102	31.45	1	20	41	-	1705	1384	42	32.95	4-41	-	
Twenty20	12	11	1	154	37	15.40	-	-	4	-	143	237	8	29.62	3-27	-	

McLEAN, J. J.   Hampshire

Name: Jonathan (Jono) James McLean
Role: Right-hand bat, right-arm seam bowler
Born: 11 July 1980, Johannesburg, South Africa
Height: 6ft 1in **Weight:** 12st 8lbs
County debut: 2005
Place in batting averages: 150th av. 30.25
Parents: Brian and Rosey
Marital status: Single
Education: St Stithians College, Gauteng

Overseas teams played for: University of Cape Town 2000-04; Western Province 2001-02 – 2003-04
Career highlights to date: 'Making my first-class debut'
Cricketers particularly admired: Sachin Tendulkar, Jacques Kallis
Other sports played: Hockey (Provincial U15), golf (social)
Other sports followed: Rugby
Relaxations: Golf, listening to music, reading
Extras: Made first-class debut for Western Province v Northerns at Centurion 2001-02. Played for Hampshire 2nd XI 2004
Opinions on cricket: 'The game is getting more exciting and challenging all the time, which means players and teams are having to

adjust their tactics quicker to stay ahead of the pack. With Twenty20, specialised skills are being tested to the limit.'
Best batting: 68 Hampshire v Gloucestershire, Cheltenham 2005

2005 Season

	M	Inns	NO	Runs	HS	Avge	100s	50s	Ct	St	O	M	Runs	Wkts	Avge	Best	5wI	10wM
Test																		
All First	6	9	1	242	68	30.25	-	3	4	-								
1-Day Int																		
C & G	1	0	0	0	0	-	-	-	-	-								
tsL	7	4	1	56	36	18.66	-	-	5	-								
Twenty20																		

Career Performances

	M	Inns	NO	Runs	HS	Avge	100s	50s	Ct	St	Balls	Runs	Wkts	Avge	Best	5wI	10wM
Test																		
All First	12	17	1	404	68	25.25	-	4	11	-								
1-Day Int																		
C & G	1	0	0	0	0	-	-	-	-	-								
tsL	7	4	1	56	36	18.66	-	-	5	-								
Twenty20																		

McLEAN, N. A. M. Somerset

Name: <u>Nixon</u> Alexei McNamara McLean
Role: Left-hand bat, right-arm fast bowler
Born: 20 July 1973, Stubbs, St Vincent
Height: 6ft 5in
Nickname: Nicko
County debut: 1998 (Hampshire), 2003 (Somerset)
County cap: 1998 (Hampshire), 2003 (Somerset)
Test debut: 1997-98
50 wickets in a season: 2
Place in bowling averages: 112th av. 42.25 (2004 26th av. 26.20)
Strike rate: 61.50 (career 51.89)
Marital status: Single
Education: Carapan SS, St Vincent
Overseas tours: West Indies to Australia 1996-97, to Bangladesh (Wills International

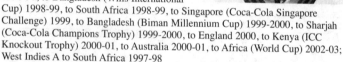

Cup) 1998-99, to South Africa 1998-99, to Singapore (Coca-Cola Singapore Challenge) 1999, to Bangladesh (Biman Millennium Cup) 1999-2000, to Sharjah (Coca-Cola Champions Trophy) 1999-2000, to England 2000, to Kenya (ICC Knockout Trophy) 2000-01, to Australia 2000-01, to Africa (World Cup) 2002-03; West Indies A to South Africa 1997-98
Overseas teams played for: Windward Islands 1992-93 – 2000-01; St Vincent and the Grenadines 2002-03; KwaZulu-Natal 2001-02 – 2003-04; Canterbury 2005-06 –
Extras: Took 44 wickets (av. 16.27) in KwaZulu-Natal's Supersport Series title win 2001-02, including 6-84 in the Northerns first innings in the final at Durban; also took 15 wickets at 15.33 in KwaZulu-Natal's successful Standard Bank Cup campaign 2001-02. Overseas player with Hampshire 1998-99; an overseas player with Somerset 2003-05, taking 5-87 on debut v Gloucestershire at Bristol
Best batting: 76 Somerset v Gloucestershire, Taunton 2003
Best bowling: 7-28 West Indians v Free State, Bloemfontein 1998-99

2005 Season

	M	Inns	NO	Runs	HS	Avge	100s	50s	Ct	St	O	M	Runs	Wkts	Avge	Best	5wI	10wM
Test																		
All First	6	7	1	59	40	9.83	-	-	1	-	123	27	507	12	42.25	3-107	-	-
1-Day Int																		
C & G																		
tsL	3	2	1	6	6*	6.00	-	-	-	-	7.1	0	39	0	-		-	-
Twenty20																		

Career Performances

	M	Inns	NO	Runs	HS		Avge	100s	50s	Ct	St	Balls	Runs	Wkts	Avge	Best	5wI	10wM
Test	19	32	2	368	46		12.26	-	-	5	-	3299	1873	44	42.56	3-53	-	-
All First	145	216	32	2458	76		13.35	-	3	42	-	25739	13649	496	27.51	7-28	19	3
1-Day Int	45	34	8	314	50	*	12.07	-	1	8	-	2120	1729	46	37.58	3-21	-	
C & G	10	8	4	118	36		29.50	-	-	1	-	511	295	12	24.58	3-27	-	
tsL	56	40	10	436	32		14.53	-	-	7	-	2260	1941	77	25.20	4-35	-	
Twenty20																		

McMAHON, P. J. Nottinghamshire

Name: <u>Paul</u> Joseph McMahon
Role: Right-hand bat, off-spin bowler
Born: 12 March 1983, Wigan
Height: 6ft 1in **Weight:** 12st
Nickname: Vince, Macca, Boffin
County debut: 2002
Place in bowling averages: 42nd av. 27.66
(2004 138th av. 45.91)
Strike rate: 68.91 (career 73.13)
Parents: Gerry and Teresa
Marital status: Single
Family links with cricket: 'Dad was club
professional in Lancashire and Cheshire
leagues; now plays for Notts Over 50s and
for Wollaton in Notts Premier League. Mum
now an expert at finding out scores on
Teletext'
Education: Trinity RC Comprehensive,
Nottingham; Wadham College, Oxford University
Qualifications: 11 GCSEs, 4 A-levels, BA (Hons) Law
Career outside cricket: 'Potentially something related to the legal profession'
Off-season: 'Playing grade cricket in Sydney'
Overseas tours: England U19 to Australia and (U19 World Cup) New Zealand 2001-
02; Nottinghamshire to South Africa 2002, 2003; WCA spin bowling camp, Mumbai
2004
Overseas teams played for: Sydney University 2005-06
Career highlights to date: 'Captaining England U19 against India U19 [2002], and
taking eight wickets [4-47 and 4-58] in the victory at Northampton in the deciding
final "Test"'
Cricketers particularly admired: Mike Atherton, Steve Waugh, Nasser Hussain
Young players to look out for: Michael Munday, Will Smith, Ed Cowan (NSW),
Amit Suman (Delhi)

Other sports played: Football (OUAFC reserve goalkeeper in 2005 Varsity Match), darts (Wadham College 2nd VIII), tennis ('badly'), golf ('even worse')
Other sports followed: Football (AFC Wimbledon)
Injuries: 'Lower back problem – no cricket missed'
Favourite band: End of Fashion
Relaxations: 'Reading, current affairs, music'
Extras: Has played for Notts from U11 to 1st XI. Captained England U19 v India U19 2002; leading wicket-taker in 'Test' series with ten wickets (av. 22.20). Nottinghamshire Young Player of the Year 2003. Oxford UCCE 2003-05 (captain 2004, during which season OUCCE won the UCCE Championship and One-Day Challenge). Oxford University 2003-05 (captain 2004-05). Represented British Universities 2004. Oxford University Sportsman of the Year 2004
Best batting: 99 Oxford University v Cambridge University, The Parks 2004
Best bowling: 5-30 Oxford University v Cambridge University, Fenner's 2005

2005 Season

	M	Inns	NO	Runs	HS	Avge	100s	50s	Ct	St	O	M	Runs	Wkts	Avge	Best	5wl	10wM
Test																		
All First	3	3	1	79	62 *	39.50	-	1	5	-	137.5	46	332	12	27.66	5-30	1	-
1-Day Int																		
C & G																		
tsL																		
Twenty20	1	0	0	0	0	-	-	-	1	-	4	0	22	1	22.00	1-22	-	

Career Performances

	M	Inns	NO	Runs	HS	Avge	100s	50s	Ct	St	Balls	Runs	Wkts	Avge	Best	5wl	10wM
Test																	
All First	17	21	3	340	99	18.88	-	2	11	-	3218	1581	44	35.93	5-30	1	-
1-Day Int																	
C & G																	
tsL	1	1	0	0	0	0.00	-	-	-	-	30	33	0	-	-	-	-
Twenty20	1	0	0	0	0	-	-	-	1	-	24	22	1	22.00	1-22	-	

McMILLAN, C. D.   Hampshire

Name: Craig Douglas McMillan
Role: Right-hand bat, right-arm medium bowler
Born: 13 September 1976, Christchurch, New Zealand
County debut: 2005 (Hampshire; *see Extras*)
Test debut: 1997-98
Place in batting averages: 189th av. 21.14
Strike rate: (career 74.55)
Family links with cricket: Cousin James McMillan plays for Otago

Overseas tours: New Zealand U19 to Pakistan 1993-94, to Australia 1995-96, to England 1996; New Zealand Academy to South Africa 1997; New Zealand to India (Pepsi Independence Cup) 1996-97, to Zimbabwe 1997-98, to Australia 1997-98, to Sri Lanka 1998, to Malaysia (Commonwealth Games) 1998-99, to Bangladesh (Wills International Cup) 1998-99, to UK, Ireland and Holland (World Cup) 1999, to England 1999, to India 1999-2000, to Zimbabwe 2000-01, to Kenya (ICC Knockout Trophy) 2000-01, to South Africa 2000-01, to Australia 2001-02, to Pakistan 2002, to West Indies 2002, to Africa (World Cup) 2002-03, to India 2003-04, to England 2004, to England (ICC Champions Trophy) 2004, to Australia 2004-05, plus other one-day series

and tournaments in Sharjah, Singapore, Sri Lanka, Bangladesh, Zimbabwe and South Africa

Overseas teams played for: Canterbury 1994-95 –

Extras: One of *New Zealand Cricket Almanack*'s two Players of the Year 2001. Struck 26 off an over from Younis Khan in the third Test v Pakistan at Hamilton 2000-01, a Test record until superseded by Brian Lara (28 from an over) in 2003-04. Played for Gloucestershire in a 50-over match v India A at Cheltenham 2003. Has won numerous domestic and international match awards, including Man of the Match in the third Test v England at Old Trafford 1999 (107*) and v Bangladesh at Kimberley in the World Cup 2002-03 (75). Made Twenty20 international debut v Australia at Auckland 2004-05. Was an overseas player with Hampshire during the 2005 season as a locum for Simon Katich

Best batting: 168* New Zealanders v President's XI, Jodhpur 1999-2000

Best bowling: 6-71 Central Conference v Pakistan A, Blenheim 1998-99

2005 Season

	M	Inns	NO	Runs	HS	Avge	100s	50s	Ct	St	O	M	Runs	Wkts	Avge	Best	5wI	10wM
Test																		
All First	4	8	1	169	52	24.14	-	1	-	-	41	7	150	3	50.00	2-49	-	-
1-Day Int																		
C & G	1	1	0	42	42	42.00	-	-	-	-	2	0	20	0	-		-	-
tsL	4	4	1	90	49 *	30.00	-	-	-	-	4	0	23	0	-		-	-
Twenty20	7	6	1	183	65 *	36.60	-	1	2	-	10	0	102	6	17.00	2-21	-	

Career Performances

	M	Inns	NO	Runs	HS	Avge	100s	50s	Ct	St	Balls	Runs	Wkts	Avge	Best	5wl	10wM
Test	55	91	10	3116	142	38.46	6	19	22	-	2502	1257	28	44.89	3-48	-	-
All First	125	205	23	7131	168 *	39.18	13	42	51	-	6039	2894	81	35.72	6-71	1	-
1-Day Int	167	157	13	4031	105	27.99	2	24	43	-	1541	1394	39	35.74	3-20	-	
C & G	1	1	0	42	42	42.00	-	-	-	-	12	20	0	-	-	-	-
tsL	4	4	1	90	49 *	30.00	-	-	-	-	24	23	0	-	-	-	-
Twenty20	7	6	1	183	65 *	36.60	-	1	2	-	60	102	6	17.00	2-21	-	

McNALLY, J. D. Worcestershire

Name: Jason David McNally
Role: Right-hand bat, right-arm
medium-fast bowler
Born: 18 December 1986, Romford, Essex
Height: 6ft 1in **Weight:** 14st 3lbs
Nickname: 'None yet!'
County debut: No first-team appearance
Parents: Mark and Sue
Marital status: Single
Education: Gaynes School, Upminster;
South East Essex College; Worcester
University
Qualifications: 10 GCSEs, BTEC National
Diploma Sport and Exercise Science, Sports
Leader Certificate, currently studying BSc
Sports Coaching
Career outside cricket: Student
Off-season: Fitness training; playing hockey
and golf
Career highlights to date: 'Being hit for three sixes by Graham Gooch'
Cricket moments to forget: 'Breaking two bats in one game – cost my dad a
fortune!'
Cricket superstitions: 'None (watch the ball)'
Cricketers particularly admired: Graham Thorpe, Ian Botham
Other sports played: Hockey (Upminster, Worcester University), golf
Other sports followed: Football (Chelsea, Dagenham & Redbridge), rugby league
(Bradford Bulls)
Favourite band: The Police, The Jam, Faithless
Relaxations: 'All things sport'
Extras: Jack Petchey Award June 2004 (Outstanding Achievement). Upminster 1st XI
Bowler of the Year 2005

Opinions on cricket: 'The Ashes success has boosted the profile of the game to new heights; far more youngsters are taking up the game directly due to this. Cricket even got an A2-size poster in *Zoo* magazine! I am a big fan of Twenty20 because it is all action and a big crowd-puller. Some ardent cricket fans have not warmed to this new game but I feel we have to move forward and give the public what they want, as well as holding on to the main fan base. There has been much discussion about changing the amount of overseas players in the County Championship; personally I feel the current level is fine because it gives our English players the opportunity to mix with overseas legends and implement new styles learned from them.'

MEES, T.   Warwickshire

Name: Thomas (<u>Tom</u>) Mees
Role: Right-hand bat, right-arm fast-medium bowler
Born: 8 June 1981, Wolverhampton
Height: 6ft 3in   **Weight:** 13st
Nickname: Meesy, Meesdog
County debut: 2005
Strike rate: (career 74.55)
Parents: Mark and Christina
Marital status: Single
Family links with cricket: 'Cousin Simon played for Worcestershire Youth. Dad played for Cosely and umpires'
Education: Worcester Royal Grammar School; King Edward VI College, Stourbridge; Oxford Brookes University
Qualifications: 9 GCSEs, 3 A-levels, ECB Level 1 coaching award
Overseas tours: British Universities to South Africa 2002
Overseas teams played for: Railways, Albany, Western Australia 1999-2000
Career highlights to date: 'Taking 6-64 v Middlesex on first-class debut for Oxford UCCE 2001'
Cricket moments to forget: 'Playing in a Birmingham League match for Old Hill v Walsall, mistaking the umpire for the wicket-keeper and throwing the ball over the umpire's head for four overthrows off the last ball of the game with the opposition needing two to win!'
Cricketers particularly admired: Ian Botham, Andrew Flintoff
Other sports played: Golf, football, tennis
Other sports followed: Football (Liverpool FC)
Relaxations: Playing golf, spending time with friends, shopping, going out
Extras: Played for Worcestershire Board XI in the NatWest 1999. Played for Oxford

UCCE 2001, 2002 and 2003. Recorded maiden first-class five-wicket return (6-64) for OUCCE on first-class debut v Middlesex at The Parks 2001. Played for Warwickshire Board XI in the C&G 2001 and 2002, taking 3-19 v Cambridgeshire at March in the 2002 competition and winning the Man of the Match award. Represented British Universities 2002 and 2003. Released by Warwickshire at the end of the 2005 season
Best batting: 36* OUCCE v Hampshire, The Parks 2003
Best bowling: 6-64 OUCCE v Middlesex, The Parks 2001

2005 Season

	M	Inns	NO	Runs	HS	Avge	100s	50s	Ct	St	O	M	Runs	Wkts	Avge	Best	5wI	10wM
Test																		
All First	1	0	0	0	0	-	-	-	-	-	10	2	49	0	-	-	-	-
1-Day Int																		
C & G																		
tsL																		
Twenty20																		

Career Performances

	M	Inns	NO	Runs	HS	Avge	100s	50s	Ct	St	Balls	Runs	Wkts	Avge	Best	5wI	10wM
Test																		
All First	9	12	2	110	36 *	11.00	-	-	1	-	1491	966	20	48.30	6-64	1	-
1-Day Int																		
C & G	4	2	1	4	4 *	4.00	-	-	-	-	198	144	3	48.00	3-19	-	
tsL																		
Twenty20																		

MIDDLEBROOK, J. D.   Essex

Name: <u>James</u> Daniel Middlebrook
Role: Right-hand bat, off-spin bowler
Born: 13 May 1977, Leeds
Height: 6ft 1in **Weight:** 13st
Nickname: Brooky, Midi, Midders, Midhouse, Dog
County debut: 1998 (Yorkshire), 2002 (Essex)
County cap: 2003 (Essex)
50 wickets in a season: 1
Place in batting averages: 116th av. 33.83 (2004 126th av. 32.86)
Place in bowling averages: 119th av. 44.28 (2004 126th av. 42.91)
Strike rate: 87.65 (career 72.85)
Parents: Ralph and Mavis
Marital status: Single
Family links with cricket: 'Dad is a senior staff coach'
Education: Crawshaw, Pudsey ('at this school with Paul Hutchison')

Qualifications: NVQ Level 2 in Coaching Sport and Recreation, ECB senior coach
Overseas tours: Yorkshire CCC to Guernsey
Overseas teams played for: Stokes Valley CC, New Zealand; Gold Coast Dolphins, Brisbane; Surfers Paradise CC, Brisbane
Cricket superstitions: 'Always put my batting gear on the same way'
Cricketers particularly admired: John Emburey, Ian Botham
Young players to look out for: Alastair Cook, Ravinder Bopara
Other sports played: Golf, tennis, squash, badminton
Other sports followed: Football (Leeds United), athletics
Relaxations: 'Any music – MTV – sleeping, socialising, catching up with old friends'
Extras: Played for Yorkshire from U11 to 1st XI. His 6-82 v Hampshire at Southampton 2000 included a spell of four wickets in five balls. Took Championship hat-trick (Saggers, Muralitharan, Sheriyar) v Kent at Canterbury 2003
Best batting: 115 Essex v Somerset, Taunton 2004
Best bowling: 6-82 Yorkshire v Hampshire, Southampton 2000

2005 Season

	M	Inns	NO	Runs	HS	Avge	100s	50s	Ct	St	O	M	Runs	Wkts	Avge	Best	5wI	10wM
Test																		
All First	16	23	5	609	71	33.83	-	3	9	-	467.3	97	1417	32	44.28	5-54	1	-
1-Day Int																		
C & G	2	2	1	11	7 *	11.00	-	-	-	-	15	2	45	2	22.50	2-19	-	
tsL	14	11	1	196	46	19.60	-	-	2	-	102.3	2	421	18	23.38	3-30	-	
Twenty20	7	6	0	91	29	15.16	-	-	2	-	22	0	137	6	22.83	3-25	-	

Career Performances

	M	Inns	NO	Runs	HS	Avge	100s	50s	Ct	St	Balls	Runs	Wkts	Avge	Best	5wI	10wM
Test																	
All First	89	131	15	2718	115	23.43	2	10	41	-	15226	8049	209	38.51	6-82	6	1
1-Day Int																	
C & G	9	5	3	70	47	35.00	-	-	4	-	344	239	7	34.14	2-19	-	
tsL	72	50	12	596	46 *	15.68	-	-	15	-	2691	2032	68	29.88	4-33	-	
Twenty20	12	10	0	131	29	13.10	-	-	4	-	186	200	8	25.00	3-25	-	

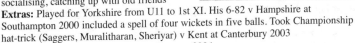

MILLER, D. J.   Surrey

Name: <u>Daniel</u> James Miller
Role: Left-hand bat, right-arm fast bowler
Born: 12 June 1983, Hammersmith, London
Height: 6ft 4in   **Weight:** 14st 4lbs
Nickname: Windy, Funky
County debut: 2002 (one-day)
Parents: Gillian and Keith
Marital status: Single
Family links with cricket: 'My dad's got the name but no ability'
Education: Ewell Castle Senior School; Kingston College
Qualifications: 9 GCSEs, 4 A-levels
Overseas tours: Surrey Cricket Board to Barbados 1999
Career highlights to date: 'Making first-team debut at Surrey in NUL'
Cricket superstitions: 'Copying the preparation of a good day'
Cricketers particularly admired: David Morgan, Ian Botham, Alec Stewart, Graham Thorpe, Glenn McGrath
Young players to look out for: Neil Saker, Chris Murtagh, Simon Day
Other sports played: Football (Kingstonian Youth)
Other sports followed: Football (Tottenham Hotspur), 'all rugby union'
Extras: Attended Surrey Academy

2005 Season (did not make any first-class or one-day appearances)

Career Performances

	M	Inns	NO	Runs	HS	Avge	100s	50s	Ct	St	Balls	Runs	Wkts	Avge	Best	5wI	10wM
Test																	
All First																	
1-Day Int																	
C & G																	
tsL	1	1	0	1	1	1.00	-	-	-	-	42	32	0	-		-	-
Twenty20																	

MITCHELL, D. K. H.   Worcestershire

Name: <u>Daryl</u> Keith Henry Mitchell
Role: Right-hand bat, part-time right-arm medium bowler
Born: 25 November 1983, Evesham
Height: 5ft 10in **Weight:** 11st 4lbs
Nickname: Mitch, Peggy
County debut: 2005
County colours: 2005
Place in batting averages: 185th av. 24.50
Strike rate: (career 90.00)
Parents: Keith and Jane
Marital status: Single
Family links with cricket: 'Dad played club cricket and coaches WYC U13'
Education: Prince Henry's, Evesham; University College Worcester
Qualifications: 10 GCSEs, 3 A-levels, 1 AS-level, BSc (Hons) Sports Studies and Geography
Off-season: 'Australia'
Overseas teams played for: Midland-Guildford, Perth 2005-06
Career highlights to date: 'Beating Warwickshire by one run in Twenty20 Cup in front of 19,000 fans. Maiden Championship 50 against Leicestershire'
Cricket moments to forget: '2nd XI Championship v Warwickshire 2004 – lbw first ball of game, dropped two catches, bowled two overs 0-22'
Cricket superstitions: 'Put gloves on before helmet'
Cricketers particularly admired: Michael Atherton, Ian Botham, Graeme Hick
Young players to look out for: Steve Davies
Other sports played: Golf
Other sports followed: Football (Aston Villa)
Favourite band: Oasis
Relaxations: 'Watching any sport; playing golf'
Extras: Made 2nd XI Championship debut for Worcestershire 2002
Opinions on cricket: 'Best game in the world! The more cricket the better!'
Best batting: 63* Worcestershire v Leicestershire, Leicester 2005
Best bowling: 1-59 Worcestershire v Essex, Worcester 2005

2005 Season

	M	Inns	NO	Runs	HS	Avge	100s	50s	Ct	St	O	M	Runs	Wkts	Avge	Best	5wI	10wM
Test																		
All First	6	10	2	196	63 *	24.50	-	2	6	-	15	1	99	1	99.00	1-59	-	-
1-Day Int																		
C & G																		
tsL																		
Twenty20	6	4	2	9	4	4.50	-	-	-	-	13	0	108	5	21.60	2-26	-	

Career Performances

	M	Inns	NO	Runs	HS	Avge	100s	50s	Ct	St	Balls	Runs	Wkts	Avge	Best	5wI	10wM
Test																	
All First	6	10	2	196	63 *	24.50	-	2	6	-	90	99	1	99.00	1-59	-	-
1-Day Int																	
C & G																	
tsL																	
Twenty20	6	4	2	9	4	4.50	-	-	-	-	78	108	5	21.60	2-26	-	

MOHAMMAD AKRAM Surrey

Name: Mohammad Akram Awan
Role: Right-hand bat, right-arm fast bowler
Born: 10 September 1974, Islamabad, Pakistan
Height: 6ft 2in **Weight:** 13st 7lbs
Nickname: Haji, Akee
County debut: 1997 (Northamptonshire), 2003 (Essex), 2004 (Sussex), 2005 (Surrey)
Test debut: 1995-96
Place in batting averages: (2004 220th av. 19.90)
Place in bowling averages: 89th av. 35.86 (2004 76th av. 34.36)
Strike rate: 51.16 (career 47.66)
Parents: Mohammad Akbar
Wife and date of marriage: Hamera Akram, May 1999
Children: Imaan Akram; Amaar Akram
Education: Modern Secondary School; Gordon College, Rawalpindi
Career outside cricket: Business
Overseas tours: Pakistan to Australia 1995-96, to England 1996, to South Africa and Zimbabwe 1997-98, to Australia 1999-2000, to West Indies 1999-2000, to New

Zealand 2000-01, plus one-day tournaments in Sharjah, Singapore, Toronto, Bangladesh and Sri Lanka
Overseas teams played for: Rawalpindi Cricket Association 1992-93 – 2002-03; Allied Bank 1996-97 – 2000-01
Career highlights to date: 'When I played Test cricket'
Cricket moments to forget: 'All good'
Cricket superstitions: 'None'
Cricketers particularly admired: Wasim, Waqar, Michael Holding
Young players to look out for: Matthew Prior, Alastair Cook
Other sports played: Football, gulee danda (traditional Pakistani game)
Other sports followed: Football, boxing
Favourite band: 'Not into music'
Relaxations: 'Meeting friends, swimming, eating out'
Extras: Was Northamptonshire's overseas player in 1997. Took 5-98 on Championship debut for Essex v Sussex at Colchester 2003. Took career best 8-49 v Surrey at The Oval 2003, including the first four wickets without conceding a run. No longer classed as an overseas player, having qualified by residency
Opinions on cricket: 'I don't like too much technology involved in decision-making. Leave it natural. That is the beauty of this game.'
Best batting: 35* Sussex v Warwickshire, Edgbaston 2004
Best bowling: 8-49 Essex v Surrey, The Oval 2003

2005 Season

	M	Inns	NO	Runs	HS	Avge	100s	50s	Ct	St	O	M	Runs	Wkts	Avge	Best	5wI	10wM
Test																		
All First	14	15	5	79	27 *	7.90	-	-	1	-	366.4	54	1542	43	35.86	5-41	2	-
1-Day Int																		
C & G	1	0	0	0	0	-	-	-	1	-	10	0	71	2	35.50	2-71	-	
tsL	5	3	1	11	8	5.50	-	-	-	-	44	3	277	7	39.57	2-19	-	
Twenty20	2	0	0	0	0	-	-	-	1	-	8	1	61	2	30.50	2-22	-	

Career Performances

	M	Inns	NO	Runs	HS	Avge	100s	50s	Ct	St	Balls	Runs	Wkts	Avge	Best	5wI	10wM
Test	9	15	6	24	10 *	2.66	-	-	4	-	1477	859	17	50.52	5-138	1	-
All First	108	138	39	863	35 *	8.71	-	-	28	-	17541	10433	368	28.35	8-49	16	1
1-Day Int	23	9	7	14	7 *	7.00	-	-	8	-	989	790	19	41.57	2-28	-	
C & G	4	3	1	2	1	1.00	-	-	1	-	252	221	9	24.55	4-61	-	
tsL	25	13	6	46	14	6.57	-	-	5	-	1140	931	26	35.80	4-19	-	
Twenty20	3	1	1	7	7 *	-	-	-	2	-	66	96	3	32.00	2-22	-	

MOHAMMAD ALI   Middlesex

Name: Syed Mohammad Ali Bukhari
Role: Right-hand bat, left-arm
fast-medium bowler
Born: 8 November 1973, Bahawalpur,
Punjab
County debut: 2002 (Derbyshire),
2005 (one-day, Middlesex)
Place in bowling averages: (2004 143rd
av. 48.60)
Strike rate: (career 51.84)
Family links with cricket: Uncle Taslim Arif
played for Pakistan 1979-80
Overseas teams played for: Numerous,
including Bahawalpur, Islamabad Cricket
Association, Lahore Cricket Association,
Railways and United Bank

Extras: Played for Glamorgan 2nd XI 2000
and 2001. Struck a 38-ball 53 on debut for
Derbyshire v Durham at Derby 2002, batting at No. 9. Is England-qualified
Best batting: 92 Bahawalpur v Lahore City, Rahimyarkhan 1998-99
Best bowling: 6-37 Railways v National Bank, Faisalabad 1993-94

2005 Season

	M	Inns	NO	Runs	HS	Avge	100s	50s	Ct	St	O	M	Runs	Wkts	Avge	Best	5wI	10wM
Test																		
All First																		
1-Day Int																		
C & G																		
tsL	1	0	0	0	0	-	-	-	-	-	9	1	50	2	25.00	2-50	-	
Twenty20																		

Career Performances

	M	Inns	NO	Runs	HS	Avge	100s	50s	Ct	St	Balls	Runs	Wkts	Avge	Best	5wI	10wM
Test																	
All First	84	112	26	1247	92	14.50	-	5	25	-	13688	8607	264	32.60	6-37	11	2
1-Day Int																	
C & G	3	2	1	36	19	36.00	-	-	-	-	138	113	1	113.00	1-28	-	
tsL	20	10	5	37	10*	7.40	-	-	1	-	832	710	27	26.29	3-22	-	
Twenty20	4	0	0	0	0	-	-	-	-	-	90	95	10	9.50	3-24	-	

MOHAMMAD ASIF   Leicestershire

Name: Mohammad Asif
Role: Left-hand bat, right-arm
fast-medium bowler
Born: 20 December 1982, Sheikhupura,
Pakistan
County debut: No first-team appearance
Test debut: 2004-05
Strike rate: (career 47.21)
Overseas tours: Pakistan A to Sri Lanka
2004-05, to Namibia and Zimbabwe 2004-05;
Pakistan to Australia 2004-05
Overseas teams played for: Lahore Division
1999-2000; Sheikhupura 2000-01 – 2001-02;
Khan Research Laboratories 2001-02 – 2003-
04; Quetta 2003-04; National Bank of
Pakistan 2004-05; Sialkot 2004-05 –
Extras: Has represented Pakistan A against
various touring teams. Played one game for

Leicestershire 2nd XI 2004. Has joined Leicestershire as an overseas player for 2006
Best batting: 42 KRL v Allied Bank, Karachi 2002-03
Best bowling: 7-35 Sialkot v Multan, Multan 2004-05
Stop press: Returned match figures of 10-106 (7-62/3-44) for Pakistan A v England
XI at Lahore 2005-06. Made ODI debut in the fifth ODI v England at Rawalpindi
2005-06

2005 Season (did not make any first-class or one-day appearances)

Career Performances

	M	Inns	NO	Runs	HS	Avge	100s	50s	Ct	St	Balls	Runs	Wkts	Avge	Best	5wI	10wM
Test	1	2	2	12	12*	-	-	-	1	-	108	88	0	-	-	-	-
All First	45	64	27	350	42	9.45	-	-	21	-	7648	4306	162	26.58	7-35	6	1
1-Day Int																	
C & G																	
tsL																	
Twenty20																	

MOHAMMAD YOUSUF Derbyshire

Name: Mohammad Yousuf (formerly known as Yousuf Youhana)
Role: Right-hand bat
Born: 27 August 1974, Lahore, Pakistan
County debut: No first-team appearance
Test debut: 1997-98
1st-Class 200s: 2
Overseas teams played for: Bahawalpur 1996-97; Lahore City 1997-98; WAPDA 1997-98 – ; Pakistan International Airlines 1999-2000 – 2001-02; Lahore Blues 2000-01; Zarai Taraqiati Bank 2002-03; Lahore 2003-04
Overseas tours: Pakistan to South Africa 1997-98, to Zimbabwe 1997-98, to India 1998-99, to UK, Ireland and Holland (World Cup) 1999, to Australia 1999-2000, to West Indies 1999-2000, to Sri Lanka 2000, to

Kenya (ICC Knockout Trophy) 2000-01, to New Zealand 2000-01, to England 2001, to Bangladesh 2001-02, to Sharjah (v West Indies) 2001-02, to Sri Lanka (ICC Champions Trophy) 2002-03, to Zimbabwe 2002-03, to South Africa 2002-03, to Africa (World Cup) 2002-03, to New Zealand 2003-04, to England (ICC Champions Trophy) 2004, to Australia 2004-05, to India 2004-05, to West Indies 2005, plus other one-day tournaments and series in India, Sharjah, Toronto, Bangladesh, Singapore, Australia, Morocco, Sri Lanka, England and Holland; Asian Cricket Council to Australia (Tsunami Relief) 2004-05, to South Africa (Afro-Asia Cup) 2005-06
Extras: Known as Yousuf Youhana until his conversion from Christianity to Islam in September 2005. His numerous international awards include Man of the [Test] Series v England 2000-01, Man of the Match v India at Edgbaston in the ICC Champions Trophy 2004 (81*) and Man of the Match v West Indies at Perth in the VB Series 2004-05 (105). Has joined Derbyshire as an overseas player for early 2006
Best batting: 204* Pakistan v Bangladesh, Chittagong 2001-02
Stop press: Man of the Match for his 223 in the third Test v England at Lahore 2005-06

Career Performances

	M	Inns	NO	Runs	HS	Avge	100s	50s	Ct	St	Balls	Runs	Wkts	Avge	Best	5wI	10wM
Test	59	98	8	4272	204 *	47.46	13	22	53	-	6	3	0	-	-	-	-
All First	96	157	14	6497	204 *	45.43	17	37	69	-	18	24	0	-	-	-	-
1-Day Int	202	191	27	6761	141 *	41.22	11	43	45	-	1	1	0	-		-	-
C & G																	
tsL																	
Twenty20																	

MONGIA, D. Leicestershire

Name: Dinesh Mongia
Role: Left-hand bat, slow left-arm bowler
Born: 17 April 1977, Chandigarh, India
County debut: 2004 (Lancashire), 2005 (Leicestershire)
County cap: 2005 (Leicestershire)
1st-Class 200s: 3
1st-Class 300s: 1
Place in batting averages: 69th av. 40.23 (2004 6th av. 67.14)
Strike rate: (career 84.38)
Overseas tours: India to Zimbabwe 2001 (Coca-Cola Cup), to Sri Lanka 2001, to West Indies 2001-02, to England 2002, to Sri Lanka (ICC Champions Trophy) 2002-03, to New Zealand 2002-03 (one-day series), to Africa (World Cup) 2002-03, to Bangladesh (TVS Cup) 2003, to Bangladesh 2004-05 (one-day series)
Overseas teams played for: Punjab (India) 1995-96 –
Extras: Represented India U19 1995-96. Awards include Man of the Match in ODI v Zimbabwe at Guwahati 2001-02 (159*; also Man of the Series) and in ODI v West Indies in Barbados 2001-02 (74). An overseas player with Lancashire June to August 2004, deputising first for Carl Hooper, then for Stuart Law; an overseas player with Leicestershire since 2005
Best batting: 308* Punjab v Jammu & Kashmir, Jullundur 2000-01
Best bowling: 4-34 Punjab v Kerala, Palakkad 2003-04

2005 Season

	M	Inns	NO	Runs	HS	Avge	100s	50s	Ct	St	O	M	Runs	Wkts	Avge	Best	5wI	10wM
Test																		
All First	11	17	0	684	164	40.23	1	5	5	-	76.2	14	209	5	41.80	2-8	-	-
1-Day Int																		
C & G	2	2	0	5	5	2.50	-	-	-	-	10	0	30	1	30.00	1-30	-	
tsL	15	15	2	481	92 *	37.00	-	5	5	-	73.3	4	318	15	21.20	4-12	-	
Twenty20	8	8	0	117	39	14.62	-	-	2	-	23	0	156	8	19.50	3-30	-	

Career Performances

	M	Inns	NO	Runs	HS	Avge	100s	50s	Ct	St	Balls	Runs	Wkts	Avge	Best	5wI	10wM
Test																	
All First	100	148	13	6668	308 *	49.39	21	26	109	-	2194	995	26	38.26	4-34	-	-
1-Day Int	51	45	6	1073	159 *	27.51	1	3	21	-	400	370	8	46.25	3-31	-	
C & G	3	3	0	36	31	12.00	-	-	3	-	120	72	3	24.00	2-42	-	
tsL	23	22	4	722	104 *	40.11	1	6	6	-	676	518	18	28.77	4-12	-	
Twenty20	12	11	0	229	50	20.81	-	1	4	-	216	208	16	13.00	3-19	-	

MONTGOMERIE, R. R.   Sussex

Name: <u>Richard</u> Robert Montgomerie
Role: Right-hand opening bat, occasional right-arm slow bowler
Born: 3 July 1971, Rugby
Height: 5ft 10in **Weight:** 13st
Nickname: Monty
County debut: 1991 (Northamptonshire), 1999 (Sussex)
County cap: 1995 (Northamptonshire), 1999 (Sussex)
1000 runs in a season: 5
Place in batting averages: 146th av. 30.39 (2004 102nd av. 36.07)
Strike rate: (career 141.00)
Parents: Robert and Gillian
Wife and date of marriage: Frances Elizabeth, 23 October 2004
Family links with cricket: Father captained Oxfordshire
Education: Rugby School; Worcester College, Oxford University
Qualifications: 12 O-levels, 4 A-levels, BA (Hons) Chemistry, Level II coaching
Career outside cricket: Teacher

Off-season: 'Training and Open University PGCE (teacher training)'
Overseas tours: Oxford University to Namibia 1991; Northamptonshire to Zimbabwe and Johannesburg; Christians in Sport to South Africa 2000; Sussex to Grenada 2001, 2002
Overseas teams played for: Sydney University CC 1995-96
Career highlights to date: 'Winning Championship [2003]'
Cricket moments to forget: 'Running [Northants] captain Allan Lamb out on my Championship debut … as his runner'
Other sports followed: Golf, rackets, real tennis 'and many others'
Favourite band: The Police
Relaxations: Any sport, good television, reading and 'occasionally testing my brain'
Extras: Oxford rackets Blue 1990. Faced first ball delivered by Durham in first-class cricket, for Oxford University at The Parks 1992. Captained Oxford University and Combined Universities 1994. Scored 108 v Essex at Hove in the Norwich Union League 2001, in the process sharing with Murray Goodwin in a Sussex record opening partnership in the one-day league (176). Man of the Match award for his 157 in the Vodafone Challenge match against the Australians at Hove 2001. Joint Sussex Player of the Year (with Murray Goodwin) 2001. Sussex 1st XI Fielder of the Year 2003. 'Two first-class wickets!'
Opinions on cricket: 'It's going well!'
Best batting: 196 Sussex v Hampshire, Hove 2002
Best bowling: 1-0 Sussex v Middlesex, Lord's 2001

2005 Season

	M	Inns	NO	Runs	HS	Avge	100s	50s	Ct	St	O	M	Runs	Wkts	Avge	Best	5wI	10wM
Test																		
All First	18	30	2	851	184 *	30.39	2	3	11	-	6	1	13	0	-	-	-	-
1-Day Int																		
C & G																		
tsL	9	9	2	375	132 *	53.57	1	2	3	-								
Twenty20																		

Career Performances

	M	Inns	NO	Runs	HS	Avge	100s	50s	Ct	St	Balls	Runs	Wkts	Avge	Best	5wI	10wM
Test																	
All First	217	376	32	12303	196	35.76	26	66	200	-	282	147	2	73.50	1-0	-	-
1-Day Int																	
C & G	18	18	4	799	126 *	57.07	2	6	5	-							
tsL	116	114	11	3298	132 *	32.01	2	23	33	-							
Twenty20																	

MOORE, S. C.   Worcestershire

Name: <u>Stephen</u> Colin Moore
Role: Right-hand opening bat, right-arm
medium bowler
Born: 4 November 1980, Johannesburg,
South Africa
Height: 6ft 1in **Weight:** 13st
Nickname: Mandy, Circles, Mork
County debut: 2003
County colours: 2003
1000 runs in a season: 2
1st-Class 200s: 1
Place in batting averages: 42nd av. 48.24
(2004 83rd av. 38.61)
Strike rate: (career 57.00)
Parents: Shane and Carrol
Marital status: Single
Education: St Stithians College, South
Africa; Exeter University

Qualifications: MEng (Hons) Electronic Engineering
Off-season: 'Academy in India and playing club cricket in South Africa'
Overseas teams played for: Midland-Guildford, Perth 2002-04
Career highlights to date: 'First-class debut and Lord's final 2004'
Cricket moments to forget: 'Losing Lord's final 2004 and getting a duck!'
Cricket superstitions: 'Left pad first!'
Other sports played: Hockey, tennis (both Exeter University 1st team), golf, squash
Other sports followed: Tennis
Favourite band: Soul Jazz Collective
Relaxations: 'My music (guitar and saxophone); watersports and wildlife'
Extras: Scored 1000 first-class runs in his first full season 2004. Is not considered an
overseas player
Opinions on cricket: 'I think county cricket has grown in strength, reflected in the
success of the national team. Twenty20 is exciting for players and crowds. Hopefully
we the players can use the buzz generated by the summer of 2005 and produce even
better players and cricket over the coming years.'
Best batting: 246 Worcestershire v Derbyshire, Worcester 2005
Best bowling: 1-13 Worcestershire v Lancashire, Worcester 2004

2005 Season

	M	Inns	NO	Runs	HS	Avge	100s	50s	Ct	St	O	M	Runs	Wkts	Avge	Best	5wI	10wM
Test																		
All First	18	33	4	1399	246	48.24	2	6	11	-	11	1	44	1	44.00	1-36	-	-
1-Day Int																		
C & G	2	2	1	69	57 *	69.00	-	1	-	-								
tsL	15	15	1	420	104	30.00	1	-	5	-	2.2	0	13	0	-		-	-
Twenty20	7	7	0	124	53	17.71	-	1	3	-								

Career Performances

	M	Inns	NO	Runs	HS	Avge	100s	50s	Ct	St	Balls	Runs	Wkts	Avge	Best	5wI	10wM
Test																	
All First	37	66	8	2500	246	43.10	5	10	20	-	228	171	4	42.75	1-13	-	-
1-Day Int																	
C & G	6	5	1	173	57 *	43.25	-	2	-	-							
tsL	29	29	3	799	104	30.73	1	3	9	-	29	33	1	33.00	1-1	-	
Twenty20	18	16	3	255	53	19.61	-	1	9	-							

MORGAN, E. J. G.   Middlesex

Name: Eoin Joseph Gerard Morgan
Role: Left-hand bat, right-arm
medium bowler
Born: 10 September 1986, Dublin
Height: 5ft 10in **Weight:** 11st 11lbs
Nickname: Moggie
County debut: 2005 (one-day)
Parents: Joseph and Olivia
Marital status: Single
Family links with cricket: 'My father, three
brothers, two sisters, grandfather and great-
grandfather all played'
Education: Catholic University School,
Dublin
Overseas tours: Ireland U15 to Holland
(European U15 Championships) 2000, to
Denmark (European U15 Championships)
2002; Ireland U17 to Scotland (European
U17 Championships) 2002; Ireland U19 to Holland (European U19 Championships)
2003, to Bangladesh (U19 World Cup) 2003-04, to Sri Lanka (U19 World Cup) 2005-
06; Ireland to Namibia (ICC Inter-Continental Cup) 2005
Overseas teams played for: St Henry's Marist School U19, Durban 2003

Career highlights to date: 'Winning the Inter-Continental Cup with Ireland in Namibia'
Cricketers particularly admired: Ricky Ponting, Brian Lara
Young players to look out for: Billy Godleman
Other sports played: Rugby (Schools), Gaelic football
Other sports followed: Gaelic football (Dublin GAA – 'The Dubs'), rugby, snooker, darts
Favourite band: Aslan
Relaxations: 'Watching sports and listening to music'
Extras: Player of the Tournament at European U15 Championships 2000, 2002 and at European U17 Championships 2002. Became youngest player to represent Ireland 2003. NBC Denis Compton Award for the most promising young Middlesex player 2003. Made first-class debut for Ireland v Scotland at Dublin in the ICC Inter-Continental Cup 2004. Represented Ireland in the ICC Trophy 2005 and in the C&G 2004 and 2005, winning C&G Man of the Match award v Yorks in Belfast 2005 (59)
Best batting: 151 Ireland v United Arab Emirates, Windhoek 2005

2005 Season

	M	Inns	NO	Runs	HS	Avge	100s	50s	Ct	St	O	M	Runs	Wkts	Avge	Best	5wI	10wM
Test																		
All First																		
1-Day Int																		
C & G	1	1	0	59	59	59.00	-	1	-	-								
tsL	1	1	1	5	5*	-	-	-	-	-	-							
Twenty20																		

Career Performances

	M	Inns	NO	Runs	HS	Avge	100s	50s	Ct	St	Balls	Runs	Wkts	Avge	Best	5wI	10wM
Test																	
All First	1	2	0	7	7	3.50	-	-	-	-							
1-Day Int																	
C & G	4	2	1	72	59	72.00	-	1	2	-	30	44	0	-	-	-	-
tsL	1	1	1	5	5*	-	-	-	-	-							
Twenty20																	

55. Which Pakistan player took a wicket with his first ball in ODIs when he had Brian Lara caught behind at Faisalabad in 1991?

MORRIS, R. K.   Hampshire

Name: <u>Richard</u> Kyle Morris
Role: Right-hand bat, right-arm
medium-fast bowler
Born: 26 September 1987, Newbury
Height: 6ft 1in **Weight:** 12st
Nickname: Mozza, Moz, Bruno, Woody
County debut: No first-team appearance
Parents: David and Debbie
Marital status: Single
Family links with cricket: 'Brother Jimmy
plays, and captains Durham UCCE'
Education: Bradfield College;
Loughborough University
Qualifications: Level 1 coaching
Career outside cricket: Student
Off-season: 'Studying! Training at
Loughborough; working hard at the gym'
Overseas tours: Bradfield College to Cape
Town 2001, to Sri Lanka 2004
Career highlights to date: 'Signing for Hampshire. Representing England U17. 81
and 61 v Essex 2nd XI 2005'
Cricket moments to forget: 'Any dropped catch!'
Cricket superstitions: 'Always turn to my left at my bowling mark'
Cricketers particularly admired: Shane Warne, Dimi Mascarenhas, Shane Watson,
Nic Pothas, John Crawley
Young players to look out for: Richard King, Ruel Braithwaite, Liam Dawson, James
Morris, Will Chaloner, Hamza Riazuddin
Other sports played: Football (Reading Academy)
Other sports followed: Football (Reading FC)
Injuries: Out for six months with a lumbar stress fracture
Favourite band: Oasis, The Killers, 3 Doors Down, The Coral
Relaxations: 'Live music; Pro Evo Soccer; cooking'
Extras: Represented England U17. Made Hampshire 2nd XI debut aged 16 v
Bangladesh U19, taking 3-25 from ten overs. *Cricketer* Cup winner with Bradfield
Waifs 2005. Is a sport scholar at Loughborough University
Opinions on cricket: 'The emergence of Twenty20 has brought a whole new
dimension to the game. The number of new fans watching the sport is raising the
profile of the game rapidly. The game is moving forward quickly and it's an exciting
time to be involved.'

MOSS, J.   Derbyshire

Name: Jonathan Moss
Role: Right-hand bat, right-arm medium
bowler; all-rounder
Born: 4 May 1975, Manly, Sydney, Australia
Height: 6ft 1in **Weight:** 13st 7lbs
Nickname: Mossy
County debut: 2004
County cap: 2004
1000 runs in a season: 1
Place in batting averages: 113th av. 34.03
(2004 123rd av. 33.77)
Place in bowling averages: 97th av. 37.76
(2004 139th av. 46.14)
Strike rate: 78.28 (career 71.53)
Parents: David and Shirley
Wife and date of marriage: Lori,
16 April 2004
Family links with cricket: 'Father grew up
in Manchester and played league cricket with Didsbury; also went to strong cricket
school, Manchester Grammar'
Education: Sydney C of E Grammar School (Shore), Sydney; Australian College of
Physical Education
Qualifications: Bachelor of Physical Education, Level 2 cricket coach
Career outside cricket: Business development in sport (possible player-manager);
public relations in sport
Overseas tours: Antipodeans to UK 1991
Overseas teams played for: Gordon DCC, Sydney 1992-97; Manly-Warringah DCC,
Sydney 1998-2000; Prahran CC, Melbourne; Victorian Bushrangers 2000-01 –
Career highlights to date: 'Debut for Victorian Bushrangers 2001; winning Pura Cup
with Victoria 2003-04; captaining Victoria v Western Australia, December 2003;
maiden first-class hundred v NSW at SCG; contributing with 98 and three wickets in
Pura Cup final at MCG v Queensland 2003-04'
Cricket moments to forget: 'Without forgetting the man himself, the death of David
Hookes – a coach who helped me achieve new and greater heights with my cricket'
Cricket superstitions: 'A couple of pieces of toast with honey morning of game day'
Cricketers particularly admired: Mark Waugh, Shane Warne, Darren Berry
Players to look out for: David Hussey, Cameron White
Other sports played: Soccer, golf
Other sports followed: Football (Manchester United)
Favourite band: U2, INXS
Relaxations: 'Travelling the world; reading a newspaper sipping on a latte at a nice
cafe'

Extras: Played for Berkshire in the C&G Trophy 2001. Awarded inaugural Bill Lawry Medal for Victorian Pura Cup Cricketer of the Year 2002-03. Left Derbyshire at the end of the 2005 season

Opinions on cricket: 'The Twenty20 competition has invigorated the game and has shown what success can be achieved by a progressive and innovative attitude – great concept. I think county cricket is primarily quite strong in terms of talent. However, due to the amount of cricket played, the intensity is poor and the levels of desire to achieve lack. Essentially I think first-class and one-day league games should be modelled on international cricket to fully prepare players for the next level (i.e. 50 overs per side and less than 104 overs per day – compromise in between).'

Best batting: 172* Victoria v Western Australia, Perth 2003-04

Best bowling: 4-40 Derbyshire v Lancashire, Derby 2005

2005 Season

	M	Inns	NO	Runs	HS	Avge	100s	50s	Ct	St	O	M	Runs	Wkts	Avge	Best	5wI	10wM
Test																		
All First	17	31	1	1021	109 *	34.03	2	7	11	-	326.1	98	944	25	37.76	4-40	-	-
1-Day Int																		
C & G	2	2	0	33	26	16.50	-	-	-	-	12	0	60	1	60.00	1-46	-	
tsL	17	17	3	418	79	29.85	-	2	5	-	117	8	516	27	19.11	4-28	-	
Twenty20	8	8	1	225	83	32.14	-	1	2	-	4	0	41	1	41.00	1-41	-	

Career Performances

	M	Inns	NO	Runs	HS	Avge	100s	50s	Ct	St	Balls	Runs	Wkts	Avge	Best	5wI	10wM
Test																	
All First	66	112	8	3905	172 *	37.54	7	26	33	-	6867	3218	96	33.52	4-40	-	-
1-Day Int																	
C & G	5	5	0	67	28	13.40	-	-	1	-	252	204	6	34.00	3-52	-	
tsL	32	31	5	857	104	32.96	1	5	12	-	1178	947	38	24.92	4-28	-	
Twenty20	12	12	1	373	83	33.90	-	2	2	-	90	114	3	38.00	1-16	-	

56. Twelve players made their debuts when India played their first ODI in 1974 and all were born in India. Who was the Simla-born player representing England?

MUCHALL, G. J.   Durham

Name: <u>Gordon</u> James Muchall
Role: Right-hand bat, right-arm medium
'part-time' bowler
Born: 2 November 1982,
Newcastle upon Tyne
Height: 6ft **Weight:** 13st 5lbs
Nickname: Much
County debut: 2002
County cap: 2005
Place in batting averages: 143rd av. 30.56
(2004 124th av. 33.62)
Strike rate: (career 58.13)
Parents: Mary and Arthur
Marital status: Single
Family links with cricket: Grandfather
played for Northumberland. Younger brother
(Paul) was in England U15 squad
Education: Durham School
Qualifications: 8 GCSEs, 2 A-levels
Career outside cricket: 'Cricket coaching for SCK'
Off-season: 'Perth, Oz – Claremont-Nedlands'
Overseas tours: England U19 to India 2000-01, to Australia and (U19 World Cup)
New Zealand 2001-02; ECB National Academy to Australia and Sri Lanka 2002-03
Overseas teams played for: Fremantle 2001-02; Claremont-Nedlands, Perth 2005-06
Career highlights to date: '100 at Lord's. One-day 100 against Yorkshire. 254 for
England U19 v India U19. Getting first-team cap'
Cricket moments to forget: 'With the opposition needing four off the last ball to win,
going into the long barrier position and the ball bouncing over my head for four'
Cricketers particularly admired: Jacques Kallis, Ian Botham, Steve Waugh,
Darren Gough
Young players to look out for: Paul Muchall, Kyle Coetzer
Other sports played: Rugby (Durham School – played in *Daily Mail* cup final at
Twickenham)
Other sports followed: Football (Newcastle United), rugby (Newcastle Falcons)
Relaxations: Listening to music, socialising with friends
Extras: Represented England U19, scoring 254 in the first 'Test' v India U19 at
Cardiff 2002. Cricket Society's Most Promising Young Cricketer of the Year Award
2002. NBC Denis Compton Award for the most promising young Durham player 2002.
Durham Batsman of the Year 2004
Best batting: 142* Durham v Yorkshire, Scarborough 2004
Best bowling: 3-26 Durham v Yorkshire, Headingley 2003

2005 Season

	M	Inns	NO	Runs	HS	Avge	100s	50s	Ct	St	O	M	Runs	Wkts	Avge	Best	5wl	10wM
Test																		
All First	17	29	4	764	123	30.56	1	3	6	-	7	0	18	0	-	-	-	-
1-Day Int																		
C & G	1	1	1	21	21 *	-	-	-	-	-								
tsL	17	14	4	462	101 *	46.20	1	3	1	-								
Twenty20	7	7	2	227	64 *	45.40	-	1	3	-								

Career Performances

	M	Inns	NO	Runs	HS	Avge	100s	50s	Ct	St	Balls	Runs	Wkts	Avge	Best	5wl	10wM
Test																	
All First	64	115	6	3231	142 *	29.64	5	16	40	-	860	581	15	38.73	3-26	-	-
1-Day Int																	
C & G	6	5	1	69	22	17.25	-	-	2	-	84	76	0	-	-	-	-
tsL	46	40	8	1165	101 *	36.40	1	6	10	-	78	61	1	61.00	1-15	-	
Twenty20	15	13	3	315	64 *	31.50	-	1	7	-	12	8	1	8.00	1-8	-	

MULLALLY, A. D.   Hampshire

Name: <u>Alan</u> David Mullally
Role: Right-hand bat, left-arm fast bowler
Born: 12 July 1969, Southend
Height: 6ft 4in **Weight:** 14st
Nickname: Spider
County debut: 1988 (Hampshire),
1990 (Leicestershire)
County cap: 1993 (Leicestershire),
2000 (Hampshire; *see* **Extras**)
Benefit: 2005 (Hampshire)
Test debut: 1996
50 wickets in a season: 5
Place in bowling averages: (2004 117th
av. 39.50)
Strike rate: (career 61.64)
Parents: Mick and Ann
Wife and date of marriage: Chelsey, 1997
Education: Cannington High School, Perth,
Australia; Wembley and Carlisle Technical College
Overseas tours: Western Australia to India 1989-90; Leicestershire to Jamaica 1992-93; England to Zimbabwe and New Zealand 1996-97, to Australia 1998-99, to Sharjah (Coca-Cola Cup) 1998-99, to South Africa and Zimbabwe 1999-2000, to Sri Lanka 2000-01 (one-day series)

Overseas teams played for: Western Australia 1987-90; Victoria 1990-91
Career highlights to date: 'Career best 9-93 v Derbyshire. Man of the Match in World Cup [v Zimbabwe 1999] and CUB Series v Australia [1998-99]'
Cricket moments to forget: 'Sunday League v Middlesex' (*At the Rose Bowl in 2001, Middlesex took 35 runs off the last 13 deliveries of the game to win*)
Cricketers particularly admired: Robin Smith
Other sports followed: Australian Rules football, basketball, most sports
Relaxations: Fishing, music
Extras: Made first-class debut for Western Australia in the 1987-88 Sheffield Shield final v Queensland at Perth. Represented Australia YC v West Indies YC and in the U19 World Cup 1987-88. Played one match for Hampshire in 1988 before joining Leicestershire. Represented England in the 1999 World Cup. Left Leicestershire at end of 1999 season and rejoined Hampshire for 2000. Took 5-18 as Hampshire bowled out the Australians for 97 at West End 2001. Retired at the end of the 2005 season
Best batting: 75 Leicestershire v Middlesex, Leicester 1996
Best bowling: 9-93 Hampshire v Derbyshire, Derby 2000

2005 Season

	M	Inns	NO	Runs	HS	Avge	100s	50s	Ct	St	O	M	Runs	Wkts	Avge	Best	5wI	10wM
Test																		
All First																		
1-Day Int																		
C & G																		
tsL	3	3	1	18	9	9.00	-	-	-	-	14	1	75	3	25.00	2-30	-	
Twenty20																		

Career Performances

	M	Inns	NO	Runs	HS	Avge	100s	50s	Ct	St	Balls	Runs	Wkts	Avge	Best	5wI	10wM
Test	19	27	4	127	24	5.52	-	-	6	-	4525	1812	58	31.24	5-105	1	-
All First	230	258	70	1615	75	8.59	-	2	44	-	43645	19953	708	28.18	9-93	31	4
1-Day Int	50	25	10	86	20	5.73	-	-	8	-	2698	1728	63	27.42	4-18	-	
C & G	30	11	6	58	19 *	11.60	-	-	3	-	1806	1027	50	20.54	5-18	1	
tsL	155	71	30	315	38	7.68	-	-	27	-	6929	4828	167	28.91	5-15	1	
Twenty20	6	3	0	0	0	0.00	-	-	1	-	102	123	2	61.50	1-16	-	

57. Which American-born national swimming champion has recently featured in Sri Lanka's ODI team?

MUNDAY, M. K.

Name: <u>Michael</u> Kenneth Munday
Role: Right-hand bat, leg-spin bowler
Born: 22 October 1984, Nottingham
Height: 5ft 8in **Weight:** 12st
County debut: 2005
Place in bowling averages: (2004 24th av. 25.70)
Strike rate: (career 43.12)
Parents: John and Maureen
Marital status: Single
Family links with cricket: 'Dad, brother and sister have played league cricket in Cornwall'
Education: Truro School; Corpus Christi College, Oxford University
Qualifications: 10 GCSEs, 3 A-levels
Career outside cricket: Student
Overseas tours: Cornwall Schools U13 to South Africa 1998; ESCA West U15 to West Indies 2000
Career highlights to date: 'Playing in the Oxford University side that beat Cambridge by an innings at Fenner's 2003 and representing England U19 in summer 2004'
Cricket moments to forget: 'Being part of a Cornwall Minor Counties team that dropped 17 catches against Dorset'
Cricket superstitions: 'None'
Cricketers particularly admired: Shane Warne, Graham Gooch
Young players to look out for: Joe Sayers, Paul McMahon, Luke Parker, Rob Woodman
Other sports played: Chess ('Yes, it is a sport')
Other sports followed: Football (Liverpool)
Favourite band: 'None in particular'
Relaxations: Swimming, reading
Extras: Played for Cornwall in the C&G 2001. Played for Oxford UCCE 2003-05. Oxford Blue 2003-05, taking 5-83 v Cambridge University in the Varsity Match at Fenner's 2003. Represented England U19 2004
Opinions on cricket: 'Less cricket during the summer to enable more time for practice.'
Best batting: 14 OUCCE v Surrey, The Parks 2004
Best bowling: 5-83 Oxford University v Cambridge University, Fenner's 2003

2005 Season

	M	Inns	NO	Runs	HS	Avge	100s	50s	Ct	St	O	M	Runs	Wkts	Avge	Best	5wI	10wM
Test																		
All First	4	2	2	1	1*	-	-	-	3	-	89.3	13	360	8	45.00	2-45	-	-
1-Day Int																		
C & G																		
tsL																		
Twenty20																		

Career Performances

	M	Inns	NO	Runs	HS	Avge	100s	50s	Ct	St	Balls	Runs	Wkts	Avge	Best	5wI	10wM
Test																	
All First	12	8	5	16	14	5.33	-	-	5	-	1380	922	32	28.81	5-83	1	-
1-Day Int																	
C & G	1	0	0	0	0	-	-	-	-	-	30	39	1	39.00	1-39	-	
tsL																	
Twenty20																	

MURALITHARAN, M.   Lancashire

Name: Muttiah Muralitharan
Role: Right-hand bat, off-spin bowler
Born: 17 April 1972, Kandy, Sri Lanka
Height: 5ft 5in
Nickname: Murali
County debut: 1999 (Lancashire),
2003 (Kent)
County cap: 1999 (Lancashire), 2003 (Kent)
Test debut: 1992-93
50 wickets in a season: 2
Place in batting averages: 263rd av. 13.00
Place in bowling averages: 1st av. 15.00
Strike rate: 38.88 (career 48.55)
Wife and date of marriage: Madhimalar,
21 March 2005
Education: St Anthony's College, Kandy
Overseas tours: Sri Lanka U24 to South
Africa 1992-93; Sri Lanka to England 1991,
to India 1993-94, to Zimbabwe 1994-95, to South Africa 1994-95, to New Zealand
1994-95, to Pakistan 1995-96, to Australia 1995-96, to India and Pakistan (World Cup)
1995-96, to New Zealand 1996-97, to West Indies 1996-97, to India 1997-98, to South
Africa 1997-98, to England 1998, to Bangladesh (Wills International Cup) 1998-99, to

UK, Ireland and Holland (World Cup) 1999, to Zimbabwe 1999-2000, to Pakistan 1999-2000, to Kenya (ICC Knockout Trophy) 2000-01, to South Africa 2000-01, to England 2002, to South Africa 2002-03, to Africa (World Cup) 2002-03, to West Indies 2003, to Zimbabwe 2004, to India 2005-06, plus numerous other one-day series and tournaments in Sharjah, India, Singapore, West Indies, Kenya, Pakistan, Australia, Bangladesh, New Zealand and Morocco; Asian Cricket Council XI to Australia (Tsunami Relief) 2004-05, to South Africa (Afro-Asia Cup) 2005-06; FICA World XI to New Zealand 2004-05; ICC World XI to Australia (Super Series) 2005-06

Overseas teams played for: Tamil Union Cricket and Athletic Club 1991-92 –

Extras: One of *Wisden's* Five Cricketers of the Year 1999. Was an overseas player with Lancashire 1999 (taking 66 wickets in the 12 Championship innings in which he bowled), 2001 and 2005; Lancashire Player of the Year 1999. Took 7-30 v India in the Champions Trophy in Sharjah 2000, at the time the best return in ODI history. Highest wicket-taker in Test cricket for the calendar year 2000 with 75 wickets in ten matches. Has won numerous international series and match awards, including Man of the Match v England at The Oval 1998 (7-155/9-65 from 113.5 overs), in the first Test at Galle 2000 in Sri Lanka's first Test win over South Africa (6-87/7-84) and in the second Test v Zimbabwe at Kandy 2001-02 (9-51/4-64). Was an overseas player with Kent July to September 2003. Took 500th Test wicket (Michael Kasprowicz) in the second Test v Australia on his home ground, Kandy, 2003-04, becoming the third bowler to reach the milestone

Best batting: 67 Sri Lanka v India, Kandy 2001-02
Best bowling: 9-51 Sri Lanka v Zimbabwe, Kandy 2001-02

2005 Season

	M	Inns	NO	Runs	HS	Avge	100s	50s	Ct	St	O	M	Runs	Wkts	Avge	Best	5wI	10wM
Test																		
All First	6	8	2	78	24 *	13.00	-	-	3	-	233.2	69	540	36	15.00	6-50	4	-
1-Day Int																		
C & G	1	0	0	0	0	-	-	-	-	-	10	0	49	1	49.00	1-49	-	
tsL	6	2	0	1	1	0.50	-	-	2	-	39.2	1	149	8	18.62	2-5	-	
Twenty20	5	2	1	16	9	16.00	-	-	2	-	17	1	90	10	9.00	4-19	-	

Career Performances

	M	Inns	NO	Runs	HS	Avge	100s	50s	Ct	St	Balls	Runs	Wkts	Avge	Best	5wI	10wM
Test	95	121	43	1023	67	13.11	-	1	51	-	31897	12475	563	22.15	9-51	47	14
All First	185	226	65	1896	67	11.77	-	1	101	-	52178	20238	1082	18.70	9-51	94	26
1-Day Int	247	113	44	386	19	5.59	-	-	101	-	13429	8456	381	22.19	7-30	8	
C & G	6	2	0	15	15	7.50	-	-	-	-	348	235	6	39.16	3-21	-	
tsL	26	8	3	41	13 *	8.20	-	-	7	-	1222	698	36	19.38	5-34	1	
Twenty20	5	2	1	16	9	16.00	-	-	2	-	102	90	10	9.00	4-19	-	

MURTAGH, C. P.   Surrey

Name: Christopher (<u>Chris</u>) Paul Murtagh
Role: Right-hand bat, 'very occasional'
leg-spin bowler
Born: 14 October 1984, Lambeth, London
Height: 5ft 11in **Weight:** 11st
Nickname: Murts, Baby, Brow
County debut: 2005 (one-day)
Parents: Dominic and Elizabeth
Marital status: Single
Family links with cricket: Elder brother Tim
plays for Surrey; Uncle Andy (A. J. Murtagh)
played for Hampshire
Education: John Fisher, Purley, Surrey;
Loughborough University
Qualifications: 10 GCSEs, 2 A-levels
Overseas tours: Surrey U19 to Sri Lanka
2002, to Perth 2004
Overseas teams played for: Parramatta,
Sydney 2004
Cricket moments to forget: 'Dislocating finger in first training session in Australia –
unable to play for two weeks'
Cricket superstitions: 'Left pad on first'
Cricketers particularly admired: Sachin Tendulkar, Andrew Flintoff,
Curtly Ambrose
Young players to look out for: Tim Murtagh, Danny Miller, Neil Saker,
Jade Dernbach
Other sports played: Rugby, football, golf
Other sports followed: Football (Liverpool FC)
Relaxations: 'Playing golf; watching sport'
Extras: Played for Surrey age groups and attended Surrey Academy. Made 2nd XI
Championship debut 2002. Played for Loughborough UCCE 2005
Opinions on cricket: 'Too many EU-type players in county cricket. Twenty20 a
good idea.'
Best batting: 37* LUCCE v Nottinghamshire, Trent Bridge 2005

2005 Season

	M	Inns	NO	Runs	HS	Avge	100s	50s	Ct	St	O	M	Runs	Wkts	Avge	Best	5wl	10wM
Test																		
All First	3	5	2	52	37 *	17.33	-	-	2	-								
1-Day Int																		
C & G																		
tsL	2	2	2	34	30 *	-	-	-	2	-								
Twenty20																		

Career Performances

	M	Inns	NO	Runs	HS	Avge	100s	50s	Ct	St	Balls	Runs	Wkts	Avge	Best	5wl	10wM
Test																		
All First	3	5	2	52	37 *	17.33	-	-	2	-								
1-Day Int																		
C & G																		
tsL	2	2	2	34	30 *	-	-	-	2	-								
Twenty20																		

MURTAGH, T. J.   Surrey

Name: Timothy (Tim) James Murtagh
Role: Left-hand bat, right-arm
fast-medium bowler
Born: 2 August 1981, Lambeth, London
Height: 6ft 2in **Weight:** 12st
Nickname: Hairy Faced Dingo
County debut: 2000 (one-day),
2001 (first-class)
Place in batting averages: 89th av. 37.00
(2004 74th av. 41.55)
Place in bowling averages: 132nd av. 46.91
(2004 129th av. 43.65)
Strike rate: 81.66 (career 61.88)
Parents: Dominic and Elizabeth
Marital status: Single
Family links with cricket: Younger brother
Chris plays for Surrey; Uncle Andy
(A. J. Murtagh) played for Hampshire
Education: John Fisher, Purley, Surrey; St Mary's University, Twickenham
Qualifications: 10 GCSEs, 2 A-levels
Overseas tours: Surrey U17 to South Africa 1997; England U19 to Malaysia and
(U19 World Cup) Sri Lanka 1999-2000; British Universities to South Africa 2002

Cricketers particularly admired: Darren Gough, Glenn McGrath
Young players to look out for: Neil Saker, Chris Murtagh, Danny Miller
Other sports played: Rugby (was captain of John Fisher 2nd XV), skiing ('in the past')
Other sports followed: Football (Liverpool FC), rugby
Relaxations: Playing golf, watching sport, films, reading
Extras: Represented British Universities 2000, 2001, 2002 and 2003. Represented England U19 2000. NBC Denis Compton Award for the most promising young Surrey player 2001. Took 6-24 v Middlesex at Lord's in the Twenty20 2005
Best batting: 74* Surrey v Middlesex, The Oval 2004
                 74* Surrey v Warwickshire, Croydon 2005
Best bowling: 6-86 British Universities v Pakistanis, Trent Bridge 2001

2005 Season

	M	Inns	NO	Runs	HS	Avge	100s	50s	Ct	St	O	M	Runs	Wkts	Avge	Best	5wI	10wM
Test																		
All First	9	11	3	296	74 *	37.00	-	2	4	-	163.2	30	563	12	46.91	3-71	-	-
1-Day Int																		
C & G	2	2	1	3	3	3.00	-	-	-	-	18.5	2	99	5	19.80	3-36	-	
tsL	16	9	2	89	31 *	12.71	-	-	3	-	130	17	605	30	20.16	4-14	-	
Twenty20	10	6	2	54	24 *	13.50	-	-	2	-	30.3	0	272	14	19.42	6-24	1	

Career Performances

	M	Inns	NO	Runs	HS	Avge	100s	50s	Ct	St	Balls	Runs	Wkts	Avge	Best	5wI	10wM
Test																	
All First	35	50	20	851	74 *	28.36	-	6	15	-	4270	2595	69	37.60	6-86	3	-
1-Day Int																	
C & G	4	4	1	16	11	5.33	-	-	1	-	221	185	7	26.42	3-36	-	
tsL	46	31	13	256	31 *	14.22	-	-	8	-	2177	1841	65	28.32	4-14	-	
Twenty20	19	10	2	66	24 *	8.25	-	-	4	-	357	525	24	21.87	6-24	1	

---

58. Who holds the record for the most ODI wickets in a calendar year for England with 43 in 1987?

MUSHTAQ AHMED   Sussex

Name: Mushtaq Ahmed
Role: Right-hand bat, leg-spin bowler
Born: 28 June 1970, Sahiwal, Pakistan
Height: 5ft 4in
Nickname: Mushie
County debut: 1993 (Somerset),
2002 (Surrey), 2003 (Sussex)
County cap: 1993 (Somerset), 2003 (Sussex)
Test debut: 1991-92
50 wickets in a season: 5
100 wickets in a season: 1
Place in batting averages: 231st av. 18.94
(2004 199th av. 22.31)
Place in bowling averages: 36th av. 26.73
(2004 34th av. 27.59)
Strike rate: 45.06 (career 52.00)
Wife and date of marriage: Uzma,
18 December 1994
Children: Bazal, Nawal, Habiba
Overseas tours: Pakistan YC to Australia (U19 World Cup) 1987-88; Pakistan to Sharjah (Sharjah Cup) 1988-89, to Australia 1989-90, to New Zealand and Australia (World Cup) 1991-92, to England 1992, to New Zealand 1992-93, to West Indies 1992-93, to New Zealand 1993-94, to Sri Lanka 1994-95, to Australia 1995-96, to New Zealand 1995-96, to England 1996, to Sri Lanka 1996-97, to South Africa 1997-98, to Zimbabwe 1997-98, to India 1998-99, to UK, Ireland and Holland (World Cup) 1999, to Australia 1999-2000, to West Indies 1999-2000, to Sri Lanka 2000, to New Zealand 2000-01, to England 2001, plus numerous other one-day tournaments in India, Sharjah, Australia, South Africa, Zimbabwe, Singapore, Toronto and Bangladesh
Overseas teams played for: Numerous, including Multan, United Bank, and National Bank 2001-02 –
Career highlights to date: 'Winning the 1992 cricket World Cup final'
Cricket moments to forget: 'Losing the 1996 World Cup quarter-final to India at Bangalore'
Cricket superstitions: 'None'
Cricketers particularly admired: Imran Khan
Other sports followed: Hockey, football (Brazil)
Relaxations: 'Spending time with family, prayer'
Extras: Somerset's overseas player 1993-95 and 1997-98; Player of the Year 1993. Had match figures of 9-198 and 9-186 in successive Tests (Man of the Match in the latter) v Australia 1995-96, following up with 10-171 in next Test v New Zealand eight days later, winning Man of the Match award. His other international awards include

Man of the [Test] Series v England 1996 and v South Africa 1997-98. One of *Wisden*'s Five Cricketers of the Year 1997. Was Surrey's overseas player during August 2002; an overseas player with Sussex since 2003. Took 103 Championship wickets (av. 24.65) 2003. Sussex Player of the Year 2003. PCA Player of the Year 2003. Took 1000th first-class wicket (Martin Bicknell) v Surrey at The Oval 2004. Took 80 wickets (av. 26.73) in the Championship 2005 to become the competition's leading wicket-taker for the third consecutive season

Best batting: 90* Sussex v Kent, Hove 2005
Best bowling: 9-93 Multan v Peshawar, Sahiwal 1990-91

2005 Season

	M	Inns	NO	Runs	HS	Avge	100s	50s	Ct	St	O	M	Runs	Wkts	Avge	Best	5wI	10wM
Test																		
All First	16	22	3	360	90 *	18.94	-	2	4	-	600.5	82	2139	80	26.73	6-44	4	1
1-Day Int																		
C & G	3	1	1	9	9*	-	-	-	-	-	30	4	103	4	25.75	3-48	-	
tsL	17	8	2	50	15	8.33	-	-	1	-	127	3	635	20	31.75	4-36	-	
Twenty20	8	1	0	1	1	1.00	-	-	1	-	21.3	1	115	14	8.21	5-11	1	

Career Performances

	M	Inns	NO	Runs	HS	Avge	100s	50s	Ct	St	Balls	Runs	Wkts	Avge	Best	5wI	10wM
Test	52	72	16	656	59	11.71	-	2	23	-	12531	6100	185	32.97	7-56	10	3
All First	269	337	45	4649	90 *	15.92	-	19	110	-	61308	30780	1179	26.10	9-93	82	24
1-Day Int	144	76	34	399	34 *	9.50	-	-	30	-	7543	5361	161	33.29	5-36	1	
C & G	18	11	4	128	35	18.28	-	-	4	-	1174	621	30	20.70	5-26	1	
tsL	98	63	19	504	41	11.45	-	-	8	-	4243	3089	97	31.84	4-36	-	
Twenty20	16	6	0	29	16	4.83	-	-	1	-	303	289	23	12.56	5-11	1	

59. Which of *Wisden*'s Five Cricketers of the Year in 2004 has played 73 ODIs to date but has never been capped at Test level?

MUSTARD, P.   Durham

Name: Philip Mustard
Role: Left-hand bat, wicket-keeper
Born: 8 October 1982, Sunderland
Height: 5ft 11in   **Weight:** 13st 3lbs
Nickname: Colonel
County debut: 2002
Place in batting averages: 175th av. 26.27
Parents: Maureen and Alan
Marital status: Single
Family links with cricket: 'Dad played local
cricket; two brothers play local cricket'
Education: Usworth Comprehensive
Off-season: 'Adelaide'
Overseas teams played for: Bulleen,
Melbourne 2002; Glenorchy, Tasmania 2003;
Bankstown, Sydney 2004
Cricket moments to forget: 'First ball
against Jimmy Anderson on debut in C&G'
(Caught Flintoff, bowled Anderson)

Cricketers particularly admired: Alec Stewart
Young players to look out for: Ben Harmison
Other sports played: Golf, football
Other sports followed: Football (Middlesbrough)
Favourite band: U2
Relaxations: 'Socialising, reading, football'
Extras: Scored 77-ball 75 on first-class debut v Sri Lankans at Riverside 2002.
Represented England U19 2002
Best batting: 80 Durham v Northamptonshire, Northampton 2005

2005 Season

	M	Inns	NO	Runs	HS	Avge	100s	50s	Ct	St	O	M	Runs	Wkts	Avge	Best	5wl	10wM
Test																		
All First	17	23	1	578	80	26.27	-	3	45	3								
1-Day Int																		
C & G	1	1	0	5	5	5.00	-	-	1	-								
tsL	17	8	1	135	53*	19.28	-	1	22	3								
Twenty20	7	7	0	90	31	12.85	-	-	2	5								

	M	Inns	NO	Runs	HS	Avge	100s	50s	Ct	St	Balls	Runs	Wkts	Avge	Best	5wI	10wM
Test																	
All First	34	52	2	1287	80	25.74	-	6	98	6							
1-Day Int																	
C & G	8	7	1	52	33	8.66	-	-	10	3							
tsL	33	21	1	301	53 *	15.05	-	1	37	4							
Twenty20	17	17	0	325	64	19.11	-	2	2	8							

NAPIER, G. R. Essex

Name: <u>Graham</u> Richard Napier
Role: Right-hand bat, right-arm medium bowler
Born: 6 January 1980, Colchester
Height: 5ft 10in **Weight:** 12st 7lbs
Nickname: Plank, Napes
County debut: 1997
Place in batting averages: 203rd av. 21.85 (2004 125th av. 33.52)
Place in bowling averages: 125th av. 45.28 (2004 108th av. 37.97)
Strike rate: 71.28 (career 60.82)
Parents: Roger and Carol
Marital status: Single
Family links with cricket: Father played for Palmers Boys School 1st XI (1965-68), Essex Police divisional teams, and Harwich Immigration CC
Education: Gilberd School, Colchester
Qualifications: NCA coaching award
Overseas tours: England U17 to Bermuda (International Youth Tournament) 1997; England U19 to South Africa (including U19 World Cup) 1997-98; England A to Malaysia and India 2003-04; England VI to Hong Kong 2004; MCC to Namibia and Uganda 2004-05
Overseas teams played for: Campbelltown CC, Sydney 2000-01; North Perth, Western Australia 2001-02
Career highlights to date: 'Testing myself against the world's best and scoring some runs'
Cricket moments to forget: 'Being 12th man at Lord's and after a drinks break dropping the empties on a tray, towels, jumpers and anything else thrown at me in front of the MCC members'

Young players to look out for: Will Jefferson, Mark Pettini
Other sports followed: Football ('The Tractor Boys' – Ipswich Town FC)
Extras: Represented England U19 1999. Man of the Match award for Essex Board XI v Lancashire Board XI in the NatWest 2000. ECB National Academy 2003-04. Included in preliminary England one-day squad of 30 for ICC Champions Trophy 2004
Best batting: 106* Essex v Nottinghamshire, Trent Bridge 2004
Best bowling: 5-56 Essex v Derbyshire, Derby 2004

2005 Season

	M	Inns	NO	Runs	HS	Avge	100s	50s	Ct	St	O	M	Runs	Wkts	Avge	Best	5wI	10wM
Test																		
All First	8	7	0	153	55	21.85	-	2	2	-	166.2	32	634	14	45.28	3-25	-	-
1-Day Int																		
C & G	1	1	0	15	15	15.00	-	-	-	-								
tsL	5	2	1	17	17	17.00	-	-	-	-	21	1	117	2	58.50	2-34	-	
Twenty20																		

Career Performances

	M	Inns	NO	Runs	HS	Avge	100s	50s	Ct	St	Balls	Runs	Wkts	Avge	Best	5wI	10wM
Test																	
All First	65	95	17	2298	106 *	29.46	2	14	29	-	7962	5196	131	39.66	5-56	2	-
1-Day Int																	
C & G	11	9	1	156	79	19.50	-	1	2	-	339	295	13	22.69	3-11	-	
tsL	88	68	10	984	78	16.96	-	5	19	-	2285	1827	92	19.85	6-29	1	
Twenty20	10	8	0	105	38	13.12	-	-	1	-	230	280	13	21.53	3-13	-	

60. Two West Indies cricketers have scored a century in their one hundredth ODI. Who are they?

NASH, C. D. Sussex

Name: Christopher (Chris) David Nash
Role: Right-hand bat, right-arm
off-spin bowler
Born: 19 May 1983, Cuckfield
Height: 5ft 11in **Weight:** 12st 8lbs
Nickname: Nashy, Nashdog, Spidey
County debut: 2002
Strike rate: (career 112.40)
Parents: Nick and Jane
Marital status: Single
Family links with cricket: Brother played
Sussex 2nd XI and Sussex age groups
Education: Collyers Sixth Form College;
Loughborough University
Qualifications: 11 GCSEs, 3 A-levels
Overseas tours: Sussex Academy to Cape
Town 1999
Career highlights to date: 'First-class debut
v Warwickshire at Edgbaston July 2002, taking first wicket in third over'
Cricket moments to forget: 'Getting out first ball on debut (lbw Carter), then having
to stand at the non-striker's end for four balls to see if I had to face on a pair in the
second innings'
Other sports played: Squash (county level; Loughborough University team), football
(Horsham FC)
Other sports followed: Rugby, football (Horsham), cricket (Horsham)
Relaxations: 'Fishing, listening to music, going out with friends, training, squash'
Extras: Represented England U15, U17, U18, U19, captaining at U17 and U18 levels.
Sussex League Young Player of the Year 2001. Played for Loughborough UCCE 2002,
2003, 2004. Represented British Universities 2004
Best batting: 63 LUCCE v Somerset, Taunton 2004
Best bowling: 1-5 LUCCE v Sussex, Hove 2004

2005 Season

	M	Inns	NO	Runs	HS	Avge	100s	50s	Ct	St	O	M	Runs	Wkts	Avge	Best	5wI	10wM
Test																		
All First	1	0	0	0	0	-	-	-	1	-								
1-Day Int																		
C & G																		
tsL																		
Twenty20																		

Career Performances

	M	Inns	NO	Runs	HS	Avge	100s	50s	Ct	St	Balls	Runs	Wkts	Avge	Best	5wl	10wM
Test																	
All First	9	13	2	363	63	33.00	-	4	5	-	562	457	5	91.40	1-5	-	-
1-Day Int																	
C & G																	
tsL																	
Twenty20																	

NASH, D. C. Middlesex

Name: <u>David</u> Charles Nash
Role: Right-hand bat, wicket-keeper
Born: 19 January 1978, Chertsey, Surrey
Height: 5ft 7in **Weight:** 11st 5lbs
Nickname: Nashy, Knocker
County debut: 1995 (one-day), 1997 (first-class)
County cap: 1999
50 dismissals in a season: 1
Place in batting averages: (2004 76th
av. 40.69)
Strike rate: (career 61.00)
Parents: David and Christine
Marital status: Single
Family links with cricket: 'Father played
club cricket; brother plays now and again for
Ashford CC; mother is avid watcher and tea
lady'

Education: Sunbury Manor; Malvern
College
Qualifications: 9 O-levels, 1 A-level, Levels 1 and 2 cricket coaching, qualified
football referee
Career outside cricket: Qualified cricket coach
Overseas tours: England U15 to South Africa 1993; British Airways Youth Team to
West Indies 1993-94; England U19 to Zimbabwe 1995-96, to Pakistan 1996-97;
England A to Kenya and Sri Lanka 1997-98
Overseas teams played for: Fremantle, Perth 2000-01, 2002-03
Career highlights to date: 'Touring with England A and scoring first hundred for
Middlesex at Lord's v Somerset'
Cricket moments to forget: 'All golden ducks'
Cricket superstitions: 'Too many to mention'
Cricketers particularly admired: Angus Fraser

Young players to look out for: Ed Joyce

Other sports played: Rugby, football ('played for Millwall U15 and my district side'), 'and most other sports'

Other sports followed: Rugby (London Irish), football (Chelsea)

Relaxations: 'Listening to music, watching sport and socialising with friends'

Extras: Represented Middlesex at all ages. Played for England U14, U15, U17 and U19. Once took six wickets in six balls, aged 11 – 'when I could bowl!' Seaxe Young Player of the Year 1993

Best batting: 114 Middlesex v Somerset, Lord's 1998

Best bowling: 1-8 Middlesex v Essex, Chelmsford 1997

2005 Season

	M	Inns	NO	Runs	HS	Avge	100s	50s	Ct	St	O	M	Runs	Wkts	Avge	Best	5wI	10wM
Test																		
All First	1	2	0	12	12	6.00	-	-	-	-								
1-Day Int																		
C & G																		
tsL																		
Twenty20																		

Career Performances

	M	Inns	NO	Runs	HS	Avge	100s	50s	Ct	St	Balls	Runs	Wkts	Avge	Best	5wI	10wM
Test																	
All First	116	164	33	4295	114	32.78	7	20	239	19	61	52	1	52.00	1-8	-	-
1-Day Int																	
C & G	8	5	1	95	58	23.75	-	1	5	-							
tsL	84	64	13	1034	62	20.27	-	3	59	11							
Twenty20																	

61. Greg Campbell made 12 ODI appearances for Australia in 1989-90 as a seam bowler, but who is his more illustrious nephew?

NAVED-UL-HASAN Sussex

Name: Rana Naved-ul-Hasan
Role: Right-hand bat, right-arm
medium-fast bowler
Born: 28 February 1978, Sheikhupura,
Pakistan
County debut: 2005
Test debut: 2004-05
50 wickets in a season: 1
Place in batting averages: 160th av. 28.83
Place in bowling averages: 4th av. 19.92
Strike rate: 34.79 (career 42.97)
Overseas tours: Pakistan U19 to New
Zealand 1994-95; Pakistan to Sharjah (Cherry
Blossom Sharjah Cup) 2002-03, to England
(ICC Champions Trophy) 2004, to Australia
2004-05, to India 2004-05, to West Indies
2004-05, plus other one-day matches in
England and India

Overseas teams played for: Lahore Division 1999-2000; Pakistan Customs 2000-01;
Sheikhupura 2000-01 – 2001-02; Allied Bank 2001-02; WAPDA 2002-03 – 2003-04;
Sialkot 2003-04 –
Extras: Played for Herefordshire in the 2003 C&G competition. Played one game for
Essex 2nd XI 2003. Has won several awards, including Player of the [ODI] Series v
India 2004-05. An overseas player with Sussex since 2005
Best batting: 139 Sussex v Middlesex, Lord's 2005
Best bowling: 7-49 Sheikhupura v Sialkot, Muridke 2001-02

2005 Season

	M	Inns	NO	Runs	HS	Avge	100s	50s	Ct	St	O	M	Runs	Wkts	Avge	Best	5wI	10wM
Test																		
All First	9	14	2	346	139	28.83	1	-	5	-	313.1	53	1076	54	19.92	5-41	2	-
1-Day Int																		
C & G	1	1	0	8	8	8.00	-	-	-	-	10	0	39	3	13.00	3-39	-	
tsL	11	7	1	91	45	15.16	-	-	1	-	83.5	8	349	18	19.38	5-30	1	
Twenty20	3	1	1	7	7 *	-	-	-	-	-	9	0	53	2	26.50	2-17	-	

Career Performances

	M	Inns	NO	Runs	HS	Avge	100s	50s	Ct	St	Balls	Runs	Wkts	Avge	Best	5wI	10wM
Test	5	9	2	99	38 *	14.14	-	-	3	-	917	613	8	76.62	3-83	-	-
All First	72	104	13	2202	139	24.19	2	7	43	-	14355	7876	334	23.58	7-49	18	2
1-Day Int	31	21	8	178	29	13.69	-	-	8	-	1549	1353	55	24.60	6-27	1	
C & G	2	2	0	33	25	16.50	-	-	1	-	113	88	7	12.57	4-49	-	
tsL	11	7	1	91	45	15.16	-	-	1	-	503	349	18	19.38	5-30	1	
Twenty20	3	1	1	7	7 *	-	-	-	-	-	54	53	2	26.50	2-17	-	

NEEDHAM, J. — Derbyshire

Name: Jake Needham
Role: Right-hand bat, right-arm off-spin bowler; all-rounder
Born: 30 September 1986, Portsmouth, Hampshire
Height: 6ft 1in **Weight:** 11st 7lbs
County debut: 2005
Strike rate: (career 45.00)
Extras: Man of the Match playing for Ockbrook & Borrowash v Kibworth in the Cockspur Cup final at Lord's 2004 (51/4-27). Derbyshire Academy Player of the Year 2005
Best batting: 6 Derbyshire v Essex, Derby 2005
Best bowling: 2-42 Derbyshire v Essex, Derby 2005

2005 Season

	M	Inns	NO	Runs	HS	Avge	100s	50s	Ct	St	O	M	Runs	Wkts	Avge	Best	5wI	10wM
Test																		
All First	1	2	1	7	6	7.00	-	-	-	-	15	4	68	2	34.00	2-42	-	-
1-Day Int																		
C & G																		
tsL	4	2	1	9	9 *	9.00	-	-	-	-	16	0	102	2	51.00	1-35	-	
Twenty20																		

Career Performances

	M	Inns	NO	Runs	HS	Avge	100s	50s	Ct	St	Balls	Runs	Wkts	Avge	Best	5wI	10wM
Test																	
All First	1	2	1	7	6	7.00	-	-	-	-	90	68	2	34.00	2-42	-	-
1-Day Int																	
C & G																	
tsL	4	2	1	9	9*	9.00	-	-	-	-	96	102	2	51.00	1-35	-	
Twenty20																	

NEL, A. Essex

Name: Andre Nel
Role: Right-hand bat, right-arm fast-medium bowler
Born: 15 July 1977, Germiston, Gauteng, South Africa
County debut: 2003 (Northants), 2005 (Essex)
County cap: 2003 (Northants)
Test debut: 2001-02
Strike rate: (career 54.25)
Education: Hoërskool Dr E.G. Jansen, Boksburg
Overseas tours: South African Academy to Ireland and Scotland 1999; South Africa A to Zimbabwe 2002-03, to Australia 2002-03; South Africa to West Indies 2000-01, to Zimbabwe 2001-02, to England 2003 (NatWest Series), to Pakistan 2003-04, to New Zealand 2003-04, to West Indies 2004-05, to India (one-day series) 2005-06, to Australia 2005-06
Overseas teams played for: Easterns 1996-97 – ; Titans 2004-05 –
Extras: Was an overseas player with Northamptonshire 2003. One of *South African Cricket Annual*'s five Cricketers of the Year 2004, 2005. His match awards include Man of the Match in the fourth ODI v Pakistan at Rawalpindi 2003-04 (4-39) and in the third Test v West Indies in Barbados 2004-05 (4-56/6-32). Was an overseas player with Essex during the 2005 season as a locum for André Adams, taking a wicket (Matthew Wood) with his first ball for the county, v Somerset at Colchester
Best batting: 44 Easterns v Free State, Benoni 2000-01
Best bowling: 6-25 Easterns v Gauteng, Johannesburg 2001-02
Stop press: Made Twenty20 international debut v New Zealand at Johannesburg 2005-06

2005 Season

	M	Inns	NO	Runs	HS	Avge	100s	50s	Ct	St	O	M	Runs	Wkts	Avge	Best	5wI	10wM
Test																		
All First	1	0	0	0	0	-	-	-	1	-	23	3	88	4	22.00	2-12	-	-
1-Day Int																		
C & G																		
tsL	2	1	1	5	5 *	-	-	-	2	-	16.2	3	65	2	32.50	1-32	-	
Twenty20																		

Career Performances

	M	Inns	NO	Runs	HS	Avge	100s	50s	Ct	St	Balls	Runs	Wkts	Avge	Best	5wI	10wM
Test	15	12	4	32	7	4.00	-	-	3	-	3273	1578	62	25.45	6-32	3	1
All First	73	77	29	718	44	14.95	-	-	24	-	14540	6503	268	24.26	6-25	12	1
1-Day Int	34	6	4	8	3 *	4.00	-	-	11	-	1644	1311	43	30.48	4-39	-	
C & G	1	1	0	14	14	14.00	-	-	-	-	60	36	0				
tsL	17	8	4	38	15 *	9.50	-	-	6	-	791	475	24	19.79	3-20	-	
Twenty20	5	2	0	22	12	11.00	-	-	-	-	114	126	6	21.00	2-29	-	

NEW, T. J.   Leicestershire

Name: Thomas (Tom) James New
Role: Left-hand bat, wicket-keeper
Born: 18 January 1985, Sutton-in-Ashfield
Height: 5ft 10in **Weight:** 9st 8lbs
Nickname: Newy
County debut: 2004
Place in batting averages: 120th av. 32.90
Parents: Martin and Louise
Marital status: Single
Education: Quarrydale Comprehensive
Qualifications: GCSEs
Overseas tours: England U19 to Bangladesh
(U19 World Cup) 2003-04
Overseas teams played for: Geelong
Cement, Victoria 2001-02
Cricket moments to forget: 'Losing semi-
final of Costcutter World Challenge 2000
to Pakistan'
Cricket superstitions: 'None'
Cricketers particularly admired: Ian Healy, Jack Russell
Other sports played: Rugby (County U14/U15), football
Other sports followed: Football (Mansfield Town FC)

Relaxations: 'Golf, music'
Extras: Played for Nottinghamshire U12, U13, U15, U16 and Midlands U13, U14, U15. Captained England U15 in Costcutter World Challenge [U15 World Cup] 2000. Sir John Hobbs Silver Jubilee Memorial Prize 2000. Represented England U19 2003 and 2004. NBC Denis Compton Award for the most promising young Leicestershire player 2003
Best batting: 89 Leicestershire v Derbyshire, Leicester 2005

2005 Season

	M	Inns	NO	Runs	HS	Avge	100s	50s	Ct	St	O	M	Runs	Wkts	Avge	Best	5wl	10wM
Test																		
All First	7	11	1	329	89	32.90	-	2	7	1								
1-Day Int																		
C & G																		
tsL	8	8	0	217	47	27.12	-	-	-	-								
Twenty20																		

Career Performances

	M	Inns	NO	Runs	HS	Avge	100s	50s	Ct	St	Balls	Runs	Wkts	Avge	Best	5wl	10wM
Test																	
All First	12	18	4	423	89	30.21	-	3	18	2							
1-Day Int																	
C & G	2	2	0	9	6	4.50	-	-	-	-							
tsL	8	8	0	217	47	27.12	-	-	-	-							
Twenty20																	

62. Who was the Lambeth-born wicket-keeper who added 71 for the ninth wicket with Ian Bradshaw to defeat England in the 2004 ICC Champions Trophy final?

NEWBY, O. J. — Lancashire

Name: Oliver James Newby
Role: Right-hand bat, right-arm
fast-medium bowler
Born: 26 August 1984, Blackburn
Height: 6ft 5in **Weight:** 13st
Nickname: Newbz, Uncle, Flipper
County debut: 2003 (*see Extras*)
Strike rate: (career 83.25)
Parents: Frank and Carol
Marital status: Single
Family links with cricket: 'Dad played
league cricket for Read CC'
Education: Ribblesdale High School;
Myerscough College
Qualifications: 10 GCSEs, ND Sports
Science, Level 1 coaching
Career highlights to date: 'First-class debut'
Other sports played: Golf
Favourite band: Eminem, Counting Crows
Relaxations: Music
Extras: Played for Lancashire v India A in a 50-over match at Blackpool 2003, taking
a wicket in each of his first two overs. Played two Championship matches for
Nottinghamshire on loan 2005
Best batting: 38* Nottinghamshire v Kent, Trent Bridge 2005
Best bowling: 2-32 Lancashire v Northamptonshire, Liverpool 2004

2005 Season

	M	Inns	NO	Runs	HS	Avge	100s	50s	Ct	St	O	M	Runs	Wkts	Avge	Best	5wI	10wM
Test																		
All First	2	3	1	49	38 *	24.50	-	-	-	-	47	10	223	5	44.60	2-78	-	-
1-Day Int																		
C & G																		
tsL	1	1	1	7	7 *	-	-	-	-	-	5	0	36	0	-		-	-
Twenty20																		

Career Performances

	M	Inns	NO	Runs	HS	Avge	100s	50s	Ct	St	Balls	Runs	Wkts	Avge	Best	5wI	10wM
Test																	
All First	4	4	2	49	38 *	24.50	-	-	-	-	666	412	8	51.50	2-32	-	-
1-Day Int																	
C & G	2	1	1	3	3 *	-	-	-	1	-	110	104	1	104.00	1-45	-	
tsL	2	2	2	9	7 *	-	-	-	-	-	54	73	2	36.50	2-37	-	
Twenty20	2	0	0	0	0	-	-	-	-	-	24	32	1	32.00	1-20	-	

NEWMAN, S. A.   Surrey

Name: Scott Alexander Newman
Role: Left-hand bat
Born: 3 November 1979, Epsom
Height: 6ft 1in **Weight:** 13st 7lbs
Nickname: Ronaldo
County debut: 2001 (one-day),
2002 (first-class)
County cap: 2005
1000 runs in a season: 2
1st-Class 200s: 1
Place in batting averages: 44th av. 47.62
(2004 60th av. 44.03)
Parents: Ken and Sandy
Marital status: Married
Children: Lemoy, 1985; Brandon,
8 September 2002
Family links with cricket: 'Dad and brother

both played'
Education: Trinity School, Croydon; Brighton University
Qualifications: 10 GCSEs, GNVQ (Advanced) Business Studies
Career outside cricket: 'Father'
Overseas tours: SCB to Barbados; England A to Malaysia and India 2003-04
Overseas teams played for: Mount Lawley CC, Perth
Cricket moments to forget: 'Any time I fail'
Cricket superstitions: 'None'
Cricketers particularly admired: 'All of Surrey CCC'
Young players to look out for: Alastair Cook, Neil Saker, Brandon Newman,
Ben Scott
Other sports played: 'Most sports'
Other sports followed: Football (Man Utd)
Favourite band: Nas

Relaxations: 'Music, relaxing with family'
Extras: Scored 99 on first-class debut v Hampshire at The Oval 2002. Scored 284 v Derbyshire 2nd XI at The Oval 2003, in the process sharing with Nadeem Shahid (266) in an opening partnership of 552, just three runs short of the English all-cricket record first-wicket stand of 555 set in 1932. Scored 117 and 219 v Glamorgan at The Oval 2005, becoming the first Surrey batsman to score a double hundred and a hundred in the same Championship match. ECB National Academy 2003-04
Best batting: 219 Surrey v Glamorgan, The Oval 2005

2005 Season

	M	Inns	NO	Runs	HS	Avge	100s	50s	Ct	St	O	M	Runs	Wkts	Avge	Best	5wl	10wM
Test																		
All First	16	27	0	1286	219	47.62	4	4	14	-	3	0	17	0	-	-	-	-
1-Day Int																		
C & G	2	2	0	20	20	10.00	-	-	-	-								
tsL	9	9	1	238	80 *	29.75	-	1	5	-								
Twenty20	9	8	1	124	52 *	17.71	-	1	2	-								

Career Performances

	M	Inns	NO	Runs	HS	Avge	100s	50s	Ct	St	Balls	Runs	Wkts	Avge	Best	5wl	10wM
Test																	
All First	41	72	2	3045	219	43.50	8	15	32	-	24	22	0	-	-	-	-
1-Day Int																	
C & G	5	5	0	120	49	24.00	-	-	1	-							
tsL	29	28	1	562	106	20.81	1	1	7	-							
Twenty20	17	16	1	298	59	19.86	-	2	6	-							

63. Which former Middlesex opener holds the
record for the highest score by a debutant in an ODI?

NICHOLSON, M. J.   Northamptonshire

Name: <u>Matthew</u> James Nicholson
Role: Right-hand bat, right-arm
fast-medium bowler
Born: 2 October 1974, Sydney, Australia
Height: 6ft 6in
Nickname: Nicho
County debut: No first-team appearance
Test debut: 1998-99
Strike rate: (career 53.63)
Overseas tours: Australia U19 to New
Zealand 1992-93, to India 1993-94; Australia
to Zimbabwe 1999-2000
Overseas teams played for: Western
Australia 1996-97 – 2002-03; New South
Wales 2003-04 –
Extras: Australia U19 Player of the Year
1992-93. Attended Commonwealth Bank
[Australian] Cricket Academy 1994-95. Had
first innings figures of 7-77 (and scored 58*) for Western Australia v England XI at
Perth 1998-99; it was his first first-class match after 18 months out with glandular
fever and chronic fatigue syndrome (CFS). Man of the Match v South Australia at
Adelaide in the Pura Cup 2001-02 (4-58/4-60). Had second innings figures of 5-60 v
Queensland at Brisbane in the final of the Pura Cup 2004-05. Has played for Australia
A against touring sides. Has joined Northamptonshire as an overseas player for 2006
Best batting: 101* Western Australia v South Africans, Perth 2001-02
Best bowling: 7-77 Western Australia v England XI, Perth 1998-99

2005 Season (did not make any first-class or one-day appearances)

Career Performances

	M	Inns	NO	Runs	HS	Avge	100s	50s	Ct	St	Balls	Runs	Wkts	Avge	Best	5wI	10wM
Test	1	2	0	14	9	7.00	-	-	-	-	150	115	4	28.75	3-56	-	-
All First	63	94	17	1518	101 *	19.71	1	3	34	-	12659	6481	236	27.46	7-77	8	-
1-Day Int																	
C & G																	
tsL																	
Twenty20																	

NIXON, P. A. Leicestershire

Name: <u>Paul</u> Andrew Nixon
Role: Left-hand bat, wicket-keeper
Born: 21 October 1970, Carlisle
Height: 6ft **Weight:** 12st 10lbs
Nickname: Badger, Nico, Nobby
County debut: 1989 (Leicestershire),
2000 (Kent)
County cap: 1994 (Leicestershire),
2000 (Kent)
1000 runs in a season: 1
50 dismissals in a season: 7
Place in batting averages: 100th av. 35.40
(2004 217th av. 20.05)
Parents: Brian and Sylvia
Wife and date of marriage: Jen,
9 October 1999
Family links with cricket: 'Grandad and
father played local league cricket. Mum made
the teas for Edenhall CC, Penrith'
Education: Ullswater High
Qualifications: 2 O-levels, 6 GCSEs, coaching certificates
Overseas tours: Cumbria Schools U15 to Denmark 1985; Leicestershire to Barbados,
to Jamaica, to Holland, to Johannesburg, to Bloemfontein; MCC to Bangladesh 1999-
2000; England A to India and Bangladesh 1994-95; England to Pakistan and Sri Lanka
2000-01
Overseas teams played for: Melville, Western Australia; North Fremantle, Western
Australia; Mitchells Plain, Cape Town 1993; Primrose CC, Cape Town 1995-96
Career highlights to date: 'Winning the Championship in 1996 with Leicestershire.
Receiving phone call from David Graveney advising me of England [tour] selection'
Cricket moments to forget: 'Losing Lord's one-day finals'
Cricketers particularly admired: David Gower, Ian Botham, Ian Healy, Viv Richards
Other sports played: Golf, football (played for Carlisle United)
Other sports followed: Football (Leicester City, Carlisle United, Liverpool),
rugby (Leicester Tigers)
Relaxations: Watching England rugby
Extras: Played for England U15. Played in Minor Counties Championship for
Cumberland at 16. MCC Young Pro 1988. Took eight catches in debut match v
Warwickshire at Hinckley 1989. Leicestershire Young Player of the Year two years
running. In 1994 became only second Leicestershire wicket-keeper to score 1000 runs
in a season (1046). Voted Cumbria Sports Personality of the Year 1994-95. Captained
First-Class Counties Select XI v New Zealand A at Milton Keynes 2000. Released by
Kent at the end of the 2002 season and rejoined Leicestershire for 2003

Best batting: 134* Kent v Hampshire, Canterbury 2000

2005 Season

	M	Inns	NO	Runs	HS	Avge	100s	50s	Ct	St	O	M	Runs	Wkts	Avge	Best	5wl	10wM
Test																		
All First	16	27	7	708	85	35.40	-	6	40	4								
1-Day Int																		
C & G	2	2	1	46	38 *	46.00	-	-	-	2								
tsL	17	12	4	248	47 *	31.00	-	-	18	6								
Twenty20	9	8	4	131	32 *	32.75	-	-	6	1								

Career Performances

	M	Inns	NO	Runs	HS	Avge	100s	50s	Ct	St	Balls	Runs	Wkts	Avge	Best	5wl	10wM
Test																	
All First	281	414	91	10227	134 *	31.66	14	46	743	62	33	22	0	-	-	-	-
1-Day Int																	
C & G	37	31	12	644	57	33.89	-	2	46	12							
tsL	235	203	37	3687	96 *	22.21	-	14	234	58							
Twenty20	22	20	5	292	43	19.46	-	-	11	5							

NOFFKE, A. A.   Durham

Name: Ashley Allan Noffke
Role: Right-hand bat, right-arm fast bowler; all-rounder
Born: 30 April 1977, Sunshine Coast, Queensland, Australia
Height: 6ft 3in **Weight:** 14st
Nickname: Noffers, Wombat
County debut: 2002 (Middlesex), 2005 (Durham)
County cap: 2003 (Middlesex)
Place in batting averages: 197th av. 23.00
Place in bowling averages: 65th av. 30.56
Strike rate: 63.00 (career 58.90)
Parents: Rob and Lesley Simpson, and Allan Noffke
Wife and date of marriage: Michelle, 8 April 2000
Family links with cricket: Father played club cricket
Education: Immanuel Lutheran College; Sunshine Coast University
Qualifications: Bachelor of Business, ACB Level 2 coaching certificate

Overseas tours: Commonwealth Bank [Australian] Cricket Academy to Zimbabwe 1998-99; Australia to England 2001, to West Indies 2002-03
Overseas teams played for: Queensland 1999-2000 –
Career highlights to date: 'Man of the Match in a winning Pura Cup final for Queensland. Being selected for Australia for 2001 Ashes tour'
Cricket moments to forget: 'Rolling my ankle playing for Australia v Sussex, forcing me home from the Ashes tour'
Cricket superstitions: 'None'
Cricketers particularly admired: Steve Waugh
Young players to look out for: Ed Joyce
Other sports played: Golf
Other sports followed: Rugby league, rugby union, 'enjoy all sports'
Favourite band: Powderfinger
Relaxations: Fishing
Extras: Queensland Academy of Sport Player of the Year 1998-99. Awarded an ACB contract 2001-02 after just six first-class matches. Has represented Australia A. Sunshine Coast Sportstar of the Year 2001. His awards include Man of the Match in the Pura Cup final v Victoria 2000-01 for his 7-120 match return and 43 runs batting as nightwatchman. Was Middlesex overseas player for two periods during the 2002 season; returned as an overseas player for 2003. Was an overseas player with Durham in 2005 but was ruled out with a back injury from late July
Best batting: 114* Queensland v South Australia, Brisbane 2003-04
Best bowling: 8-24 Middlesex v Derbyshire, Derby 2002

2005 Season

	M	Inns	NO	Runs	HS	Avge	100s	50s	Ct	St	O	M	Runs	Wkts	Avge	Best	5wI	10wM
Test																		
All First	6	8	2	138	65	23.00	-	1	1	-	168	45	489	16	30.56	4-19	-	-
1-Day Int																		
C & G																		
tsL	5	3	0	21	13	7.00	-	-	-	-	40	9	136	9	15.11	3-16	-	
Twenty20																		

Career Performances

	M	Inns	NO	Runs	HS	Avge	100s	50s	Ct	St	Balls	Runs	Wkts	Avge	Best	5wI	10wM
Test																	
All First	70	86	18	1704	114 *	25.05	1	6	24	-	13542	7131	230	31.00	8-24	9	1
1-Day Int																	
C & G	2	1	0	19	19	19.00	-	-	3	-	120	84	1	84.00	1-47	-	
tsL	12	7	2	34	13	6.80	-	-	-	-	532	325	15	21.66	3-16	-	
Twenty20	3	1	0	7	7	7.00	-	-	2	-	72	97	8	12.12	3-22	-	

NORTH, M. J. Lancashire

Name: Marcus James North
Role: Left-hand bat, right-arm
off-spin bowler
Born: 28 July 1979, Pakenham,
Melbourne, Australia
Height: 6ft 1in **Weight:** 12st 10lbs
County debut: 2004 (Durham),
2005 (Lancashire)
1st-Class 200s: 2
Place in batting averages: (2004 131st
av. 32.30)
Strike rate: (career 81.47)
Wife: Joanne
Overseas tours: Australia U19 to Pakistan
1996-97, to South Africa (U19 World Cup)
1997-98; Commonwealth Bank [Australian]
Cricket Academy to Zimbabwe 1998-99;
Australia A to Pakistan 2005-06

Overseas teams played for: Western Australia 1999-2000 –
Extras: Commonwealth Bank [Australian] Cricket Academy 1998. Won President's
Silver Trophy (season's best individual performance for Western Australia) for his
200* v Victoria at Melbourne in the Pura Cup 2001-02. Scored 200* and 132 in the
second 'Test' v Pakistan U19 at Sheikhupura 1996-97, winning Man of the Match
award (also Australia's Man of the 'Test' Series). Other awards include Man of the
Match for Australia A v Zimbabweans at Adelaide 2003-04 (115). An overseas player
with Durham 2004, originally as a temporary stand-in for Herschelle Gibbs; an
overseas player with Lancashire during the 2005 season as a locum for Brad Hodge
Best batting: 219 Durham v Glamorgan, Cardiff 2004
Best bowling: 4-16 Durham v DUCCE, Riverside 2004

2005 Season

	M	Inns	NO	Runs	HS	Avge	100s	50s	Ct	St	O	M	Runs	Wkts	Avge	Best	5wI	10wM
Test																		
All First	3	4	0	101	60	25.25	-	1	2	-	56	10	176	2	88.00	1-16	-	-
1-Day Int																		
C & G	2	2	0	45	38	22.50	-	-	-	-	8	0	31	3	10.33	3-31	-	
tsL	5	5	0	108	56	21.60	-	1	1	-	5	0	26	0	-		-	-
Twenty20	1	1	0	1	1	1.00	-	-	1	-								

Career Performances

	M	Inns	NO	Runs	HS	Avge	100s	50s	Ct	St	Balls	Runs	Wkts	Avge	Best	5wl	10wM
Test																	
All First	72	125	11	4553	219	39.93	9	28	43	-	2930	1643	38	43.23	4-16	-	-
1-Day Int																	
C & G	9	9	1	246	69 *	30.75	-	1	4	-	366	254	10	25.40	4-26	-	
tsL	21	21	1	619	121 *	30.95	2	3	3	-	162	144	4	36.00	2-10	-	
Twenty20	3	3	0	26	21	8.66	-	-	2	-	12	10	0	-	-	-	-

NTINI, M.   Warwickshire

Name: Makhaya Ntini
Role: Right-hand bat, right-arm fast bowler
Born: 6 July 1977, Mdingi, near King William's Town, South Africa
Height: 6ft
Nickname: George
County debut: 2005
Test debut: 1997-98
Place in batting averages: 275th av. 10.57
Place in bowling averages: 78th av. 32.77
Strike rate: 52.40 (career 54.99)
Education: Dale College; East London Technical College

Overseas tours: South Africa U19 to England 1995, to India 1995-96; South Africa to Australia 1997-98, to England 1998, to Malaysia (Commonwealth Games) 1998-99, to Sri Lanka 2000, to West Indies 2000-01, to Zimbabwe 2001-02, to Australia 2001-02, to Sri Lanka (ICC Champions Trophy) 2002-03, to Bangladesh 2003, to England 2003, to Pakistan 2003-04, to New Zealand 2003-04, to Sri Lanka 2004, to England (ICC Champions Trophy) 2004, to India 2004-05, to West Indies 2004-05, plus other one-day series and tournaments in Sharjah, Australia, Singapore, Morocco and India; ICC World XI to Australia (Super Series) 2005-06
Overseas teams played for: Border 1995-96 – 2003-04; Warriors 2004-05 –
Extras: Represented South African Schools 1995. One of *South African Cricket Annual*'s five Cricketers of the Year 2001, 2003, 2004, 2005. Became first South Africa bowler to take ten wickets in a Lord's Test (5-75/5-145) in the second Test v England 2003, sharing the Man of the Match award with Graeme Smith. Returned 13-132 (6-95/7-37), the best match analysis by a South Africa bowler in Tests, in the second

Test v West Indies at Trinidad 2004-05, winning the Man of the Match award. His other awards include Man of the [Test] Series v Pakistan 2002-03 and Man of the [ODI] Series v West Indies 2003-04. Was an overseas player with Warwickshire during the 2005 season as a locum for Heath Streak, taking wickets with his first balls for the county on both home and away Championship debuts

Best batting: 34* Border v India, Centurion 2001-02
Best bowling: 7-37 South Africa v West Indies, Port of Spain 2004-05
Stop press: Made Twenty20 international debut v New Zealand at Johannesburg 2005-06

2005 Season

	M	Inns	NO	Runs	HS	Avge	100s	50s	Ct	St	O	M	Runs	Wkts	Avge	Best	5wI	10wM
Test																		
All First	6	8	1	74	27 *	10.57	-	-	1	-	192.1	29	721	22	32.77	5-69	1	-
1-Day Int																		
C & G	2	1	0	0	0	0.00	-	-	1	-	17	3	55	2	27.50	2-12	-	
tsL	2	1	0	5	5	5.00	-	-	1	-	17	2	97	2	48.50	2-42	-	
Twenty20																		

Career Performances

	M	Inns	NO	Runs	HS	Avge	100s	50s	Ct	St	Balls	Runs	Wkts	Avge	Best	5wI	10wM
Test	59	61	17	455	32 *	10.34	-	-	16	-	12349	6457	221	29.21	7-37	9	2
All First	122	137	41	943	34 *	9.82	-	-	30	-	22439	12206	409	29.84	7-37	14	2
1-Day Int	115	26	14	144	42 *	12.00	-	-	24	-	5778	4183	183	22.85	5-31	2	
C & G	2	1	0	0	0	0.00	-	-	1	-	102	55	2	27.50	2-12	-	
tsL	2	1	0	5	5	5.00	-	-	1	-	102	97	2	48.50	2-42	-	
Twenty20																	

64. Who holds the record for having the longest gap between a Test debut and an ODI debut?

O'BRIEN, N. J.   Kent

Name: <u>Niall</u> John O'Brien
Role: Left-hand bat, leg-spin bowler,
wicket-keeper
Born: 8 November 1981, Dublin
Height: 5ft 7in **Weight:** 10st 7lbs
Nickname: Nobby, Spud, Paddy, Irish
County debut: 2004
50 dismissals in a season: 1
Place in batting averages: 184th av. 24.55
(2004 152nd av. 29.26)
Parents: Brendan and Camilla
Marital status: Single
Family links with cricket: Father a past
captain of Ireland; brother Kevin an U19
international and an MCC Young Cricketer
Education: Marian College, Ballsbridge,
Dublin
Qualifications: Cricket coach

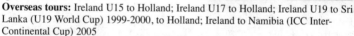

Overseas tours: Ireland U15 to Holland; Ireland U17 to Holland; Ireland U19 to Sri
Lanka (U19 World Cup) 1999-2000, to Holland; Ireland to Namibia (ICC Inter-
Continental Cup) 2005
Overseas teams played for: Railway Union CC, Dublin; Mosman DCC, Sydney
2000-02; University of Port Elizabeth Academy, South Africa 2002; North Sydney
DCC 2003-04
Career highlights to date: 'Gaining first international cap for Ireland; first hundred
for Ireland (111 v MCC); making first-class debut for Kent'
Cricket moments to forget: 'Getting a duck on Sky, bowled Warne'
Cricket superstitions: 'None'
Cricketers particularly admired: Steve Waugh, Brett Lee
Young players to look out for: Kevin O'Brien ('brother')
Other sports played: Hockey (Railway Union, Dublin), 'love soccer (especially
beating the old guys at warm-ups)'
Other sports followed: Football (Everton), rugby (Ireland)
Favourite band: Oasis
Relaxations: 'Music; walking dog; going to my local in the winter with mates'
Extras: Made Ireland senior debut v Denmark 2002 and played for Ireland in the
C&G 2003. Ireland Cricketer of the Year 2002. Scored 58* as Ireland defeated West
Indians in 50-over game in Belfast 2004, winning Man of the Match award
Best batting: 69 Kent v Warwickshire, Edgbaston 2004

2005 Season

	M	Inns	NO	Runs	HS	Avge	100s	50s	Ct	St	O	M	Runs	Wkts	Avge	Best	5wI	10wM
Test																		
All First	14	22	4	442	64	24.55	-	3	46	5								
1-Day Int																		
C & G																		
tsL	12	8	0	108	43	13.50	-	-	8	3								
Twenty20	8	4	3	9	5 *	9.00	-	-	1	3								

Career Performances

	M	Inns	NO	Runs	HS	Avge	100s	50s	Ct	St	Balls	Runs	Wkts	Avge	Best	5wI	10wM
Test																	
All First	28	41	8	881	69	26.69	-	6	79	10							
1-Day Int																	
C & G	1	1	0	13	13	13.00	-	-	-	-							
tsL	24	14	1	164	43	12.61	-	-	17	6							
Twenty20	11	6	3	32	12	10.66	-	-	1	3							

O'SHEA, M. P.   Glamorgan

Name: Michael Peter O'Shea
Role: Right-hand middle/top-order bat, right-arm off-spin bowler; all-rounder
Born: 4 September 1987, Cardiff
Height: 5ft 11in **Weight:** 12st 6lbs
Nickname: Rik, O'Sh, Mosh
County debut: 2005
Parents: Paul and June
Marital status: Single
Education: Barry Comprehensive School; Millfield School
Qualifications: 13 GCSEs
Off-season: England U19 tour
Overseas tours: England U19 to India 2004-05, to Bangladesh 2005-06
Career highlights to date: 'Championship debut v Kent'
Cricket moments to forget: 'Getting 0 on Championship debut'
Cricket superstitions: 'Put left pad on first'
Cricketers particularly admired: Damien Martyn, Andrew Flintoff
Young players to look out for: Chris Thompson, Rory Hamilton-Brown, Karl Brown, Andy Miller, Ben Wright, Greg Wood

Other sports played: Rugby (Millfield 1st XV – won national XVs competition)
Other sports followed: Rugby (Cardiff Blues, Wales)
Favourite band: Oasis, Westlife
Relaxations: 'Girlfriend, music, PS2, rugby'
Extras: Has represented England U15, U16, U17, U19
Opinions on cricket: 'Improving every year, with great forward thinking, drawing bigger crowds – e.g. Twenty20.'
Best batting: 24 Glamorgan v Kent, Canterbury 2005

2005 Season

	M	Inns	NO	Runs	HS	Avge	100s	50s	Ct	St	O	M	Runs	Wkts	Avge	Best	5wI	10wM
Test																		
All First	3	5	0	52	24	10.40	-	-	1	-								
1-Day Int																		
C & G	1	1	0	0	0	0.00	-	-	1	-								
tsL																		
Twenty20																		

Career Performances

	M	Inns	NO	Runs	HS	Avge	100s	50s	Ct	St	Balls	Runs	Wkts	Avge	Best	5wI	10wM
Test																	
All First	3	5	0	52	24	10.40	-	-	1	-							
1-Day Int																	
C & G	1	1	0	0	0	0.00	-	-	1	-							
tsL																	
Twenty20																	

ONIONS, G.   Durham

Name: Graham Onions
Role: Right-hand bat, right-arm medium bowler
Born: 9 September 1982, Gateshead
Height: 6ft 2in **Weight:** 11st 3lbs
Nickname: Thierry Williamson
County debut: 2004
Place in batting averages: (2004 265th av. 10.85)
Strike rate: (career 98.61)
Parents: Maureen and Richard
Marital status: Single
Education: St Thomas More RC School, Blaydon
Qualifications: 10 GCSEs, GNVQ Advanced Science (Distinction), Level 2 coach
Career outside cricket: Coaching

Off-season: 'Getting fit/strong; tour India 28 January'
Overseas tours: Durham to Dubai 2005
Overseas teams played for: South Perth CC 2004
Career highlights to date: 'Signing my pro contract 2003'
Cricket moments to forget: 'Getting out to my dad in a charity game!'
Cricket superstitions: 'Licking my fingers before I run in to bowl in case the ball slips'
Cricketers particularly admired: Darren Gough, Glenn McGrath
Young players to look out for: Liam Plunkett, Ben Harmison
Other sports played: Badminton (England U17; plays for Durham County first team)
Other sports followed: Football (Newcastle)
Injuries: Out for five weeks with a broken bone in a hand
Favourite band: Take That
Relaxations: 'Sleep, TV'
Extras: Attended UPE International Cricket Academy, Port Elizabeth 2005
Opinions on cricket: 'The game is going forward due to help of England-contracted players playing more for their counties. Counties should only have two overseas players a year. If they get called up for their country or injured, then tough luck.'
Best batting: 20* Durham v Leicestershire, Riverside 2004
Best bowling: 3-110 Durham v Leicestershire, Leicester 2004

2005 Season

	M	Inns	NO	Runs	HS	Avge	100s	50s	Ct	St	O	M	Runs	Wkts	Avge	Best	5wI	10wM
Test																		
All First	4	4	2	13	9 *	6.50	-	-	1	-	67	8	309	4	77.25	2-83	-	-
1-Day Int																		
C & G																		
tsL	1	0	0	0	0	-	-	-	-	-	9	0	39	3	13.00	3-39	-	
Twenty20	3	0	0	0	0	-	-	-	1	-	12	0	71	3	23.66	1-20	-	

Career Performances

	M	Inns	NO	Runs	HS	Avge	100s	50s	Ct	St	Balls	Runs	Wkts	Avge	Best	5wI	10wM
Test																	
All First	12	16	7	89	20 *	9.88	-	-	3	-	1282	902	13	69.38	3-110	-	-
1-Day Int																	
C & G	1	1	0	5	5	5.00	-	-	-	-	60	59	2	29.50	2-59	-	
tsL	13	2	2	5	4 *	-	-	-	1	-	440	339	13	26.07	3-39	-	
Twenty20	7	1	0	0	0	0.00	-	-	2	-	168	155	7	22.14	2-25	-	

ORMOND, J.   Surrey

Name: James Ormond
Role: Right-hand bat, right-arm fast'ish'
bowler, can also bowl off spin
Born: 20 August 1977, Walsgrave, Coventry
Height: 6ft 3in **Weight:** 15st
Nickname: Jimmy, Horse
County debut: 1995 (Leicestershire),
2002 (Surrey)
County cap: 1999 (Leicestershire),
2003 (Surrey)
Test debut: 2001
50 wickets in a season: 4
Place in batting averages: 256th av. 14.33
(2004 237th av. 17.36)
Place in bowling averages: 47th av. 27.80
(2004 96th av. 36.71)
Strike rate: 50.16 (career 53.69)
Parents: Richard and Margaret
Marital status: Single
Family links with cricket: 'Dad played years of cricket in Warwickshire'
Education: St Thomas More, Nuneaton; North Warwickshire College of Further
Education
Qualifications: 6 GCSEs
Overseas tours: England U19 to Zimbabwe 1995-96; England A to Kenya and Sri
Lanka 1997-98; England to India and New Zealand 2001-02
Overseas teams played for: Sydney University CC 1996, 1998, 1999
Cricketers particularly admired: Curtly Ambrose, Courtney Walsh, Allan Donald,
Sachin Tendulkar, Brian Lara, Steve Griffin
Other sports played: Football, mountain biking, 'anything'
Other sports followed: Football (Coventry City)
Relaxations: Spending time with friends and family
Extras: Played for the Development of Excellence side and England U19. NBC Denis
Compton Award for the most promising young Leicestershire player 1998, 1999, 2000.
Took 5-26 v Middlesex at The Oval in the Twenty20 2003 and was Man of the Match
(4-11) at Trent Bridge in the inaugural final. Took four wickets in an over, all left-
handers and including hat-trick (Hutton, Joyce, Weekes), in the Championship v
Middlesex at Guildford 2003
Best batting: 57 Surrey v Gloucestershire, Bristol 2004
Best bowling: 7-63 Surrey v Glamorgan, Cardiff 2005

474

2005 Season

	M	Inns	NO	Runs	HS	Avge	100s	50s	Ct	St	O	M	Runs	Wkts	Avge	Best	5wI	10wM
Test																		
All First	9	11	2	129	35	14.33	-	-	2	-	301	65	1001	36	27.80	7-63	1	-
1-Day Int																		
C & G	2	1	1	0	0 *	-	-	-	-	-	19.5	1	100	3	33.33	3-29	-	
tsL	4	4	0	39	32	9.75	-	-	-	-	31	2	180	1	180.00	1-63	-	
Twenty20	3	2	1	9	6	9.00	-	-	-	-	9	0	66	2	33.00	1-18	-	

Career Performances

	M	Inns	NO	Runs	HS	Avge	100s	50s	Ct	St	Balls	Runs	Wkts	Avge	Best	5wI	10wM
Test	2	4	1	38	18	12.66	-	-	-	-	372	185	2	92.50	1-70	-	-
All First	119	144	34	1682	57	15.29	-	2	26	-	22392	12045	417	28.88	7-63	20	1
1-Day Int																	
C & G	18	10	6	39	18 *	9.75	-	-	3	-	948	743	18	41.27	3-29	-	
tsL	76	46	22	248	32	10.33	-	-	16	-	3324	2428	93	26.10	4-12	-	
Twenty20	12	5	3	17	6	8.50	-	-	2	-	264	259	16	16.18	5-26	1	

PAGET, C. D.   Derbyshire

Name: Christopher (<u>Chris</u>) David Paget
Role: Right-hand bat, right-arm off-spin bowler
Born: 2 November 1987, Stafford
Height: 6ft **Weight:** 11st 11lbs
Nickname: Padge, Inna
County debut: 2004
Strike rate: (career 112.00)
Parents: Anne and Andrew
Marital status: Single
Family links with cricket: 'Grandad was a keen follower of county cricket. Brother (Alex) plays junior league cricket in Staffordshire'
Education: Repton School, Derby
Qualifications: 9 GCSEs
Overseas tours: Repton School to Goa 2002, to Sri Lanka 2004-05; Staffordshire to Barbados 2003
Career highlights to date: 'Making my first-class debut v West Indies; making my County Championship debut v Yorkshire at Headingley'
Cricket moments to forget: 'Losing to Notts in a massive collapse that I was involved in in the 2004 season at Derby'

Cricket superstitions: 'Always mark my guard twice'
Cricketers particularly admired: Matthew Hayden, Jacques Kallis
Other sports played: Tennis ('used to play junior county level for Staffordshire'), hockey, golf
Other sports followed: Football (Everton), rugby, Formula One
Favourite band: REM, Snow Patrol, Oasis, Keane
Extras: Played Staffordshire age group cricket for six years. Took 3-63 (Joseph, Bravo, Dwayne Smith) on first-class debut v West Indians at Derby 2004. Became youngest player to represent Derbyshire in the Championship, v Yorkshire at Headingley 2004, aged 16 years 283 days. Selected for England U17 winter squad 2004-05
Opinions on cricket: 'There are too many games, too frequently, so there isn't enough time for practice and preparation. But Twenty20 is brilliant; it's bringing big crowds and making cricket more popular.'
Best batting: 7 Derbyshire v Yorkshire, Headingley 2004
Best bowling: 3-63 Derbyshire v West Indians, Derby 2004

2005 Season (did not make any first-class or one-day appearances)

Career Performances

	M	Inns	NO	Runs	HS	Avge	100s	50s	Ct	St	Balls	Runs	Wkts	Avge	Best	5wl	10wM
Test																	
All First	4	4	2	7	7	3.50	-	-	-	-	336	206	3	68.66	3-63	-	-
1-Day Int																	
C & G																		
tsL																		
Twenty20																		

PALLADINO, A. P.   Essex

Name: Antonio (Tony) Paul Palladino
Role: Right-hand bat, right-arm fast-medium bowler
Born: 29 June 1983, Whitechapel, London
Height: 6ft **Weight:** 11st 6lbs
Nickname: Dino, TP, Italian Stallion
County debut: 2003
Place in batting averages: 237th av. 17.66
Place in bowling averages: 124th av. 44.92
Strike rate: 74.76 (career 85.77)
Parents: Antonio and Kathleen
Marital status: Single
Family links with cricket: 'Dad played cricket in the Kent League'
Education: Cardinal Pole Secondary School; Anglia Polytechnic University

Qualifications: 9 GCSEs, Advanced GNVQ Leisure and Tourism
Career highlights to date: 'Taking 6-41 against Kent in my second Championship match for Essex'
Cricket moments to forget: 'Getting hit for 78 off 10 overs against Durham in AON Trophy semi-final'
Cricket superstitions: 'Paint three dots as my run-up mark'
Cricketers particularly admired: Ian Botham
Other sports played: Football, golf, snooker
Other sports followed: Football (Chelsea), baseball (Boston Red Sox)
Favourite band: 'Various artists'
Relaxations: Playing computer games; watching films

Extras: Hackney Young Sportsman of the Year. London Schools Bowler of the Year five years running. Represented England U17. Represented ECB U19 2000 and 2001. Played for Cambridge UCCE 2003, 2004, 2005. Recorded maiden first-class five-wicket return (6-41) v Kent at Canterbury 2003 in only his second Championship match. Represented British Universities 2005
Opinions on cricket: 'Tea should be longer.'
Best batting: 41 Essex v Nottinghamshire, Trent Bridge 2004
Best bowling: 6-41 Essex v Kent, Canterbury 2003

2005 Season

	M	Inns	NO	Runs	HS	Avge	100s	50s	Ct	St	O	M	Runs	Wkts	Avge	Best	5wI	10wM
Test																		
All First	8	11	5	106	30	17.66	-	-	3	-	162	36	584	13	44.92	4-74	-	-
1-Day Int																		
C & G																		
tsL	3	0	0	0	0	-	-	-	-	-	13	2	55	2	27.50	2-27	-	
Twenty20	6	0	0	0	0	-	-	-	-	-	17	0	123	6	20.50	2-3	-	

Career Performances

	M	Inns	NO	Runs	HS	Avge	100s	50s	Ct	St	Balls	Runs	Wkts	Avge	Best	5wI	10wM
Test																	
All First	17	18	8	171	41	17.10	-	-	5	-	2316	1445	27	53.51	6-41	1	-
1-Day Int																	
C & G	2	1	0	16	16	16.00	-	-	1	-	113	90	3	30.00	3-56	-	
tsL	8	2	1	1	1 *	1.00	-	-	-	-	283	211	9	23.44	3-32	-	
Twenty20	6	0	0	0	0	-	-	-	-	-	102	123	6	20.50	2-3	-	

PANESAR, M. S.   Northamptonshire

Name: <u>Mudhsuden</u> Singh Panesar
Role: Left-hand bat, slow left-arm bowler
Born: 25 April 1982, Luton
Height: 6ft 1in **Weight:** 12st 7lbs
Nickname: Monty
County debut: 2001
50 wickets in a season: 1
Place in bowling averages: 9th av. 22.47
Strike rate: 50.50 (career 58.51)
Parents: Paramjit and Gursharan
Marital status: Single
Family links with cricket: 'Dad played local cricket'
Education: Stopsley High School; Bedford Modern School; Loughborough University
Qualifications: 10 GCSEs, 3 A-levels
Overseas tours: Bedford Modern School to Barbados 1999; England U19 to India 2000-01; Northamptonshire to Grenada 2001-02; British Universities to South Africa 2002; ECB National Academy to Australia and Sri Lanka 2002-03; England to India 2005-06
Cricketers particularly admired: Sachin Tendulkar, Steve Waugh, Matthew Hayden, Rahul Dravid
Other sports played: Badminton, tennis, snooker
Other sports followed: Football (Arsenal)
Relaxations: Music, cars, wildlife
Extras: Represented England U19. Had match figures of 8-131 on first-class debut v Leicestershire at Northampton 2001, including 4-11 in the second innings. NBC Denis Compton Award for the most promising young Northamptonshire player 2001. Played for Loughborough University CCE 2002, 2004. Represented British Universities 2002, 2004, 2005
Best batting: 39* Northamptonshire v Worcestershire, Northampton 2005
Best bowling: 7-181 Northamptonshire v Essex, Chelmsford 2005
Stop press: Made Test debut in the first Test v India at Nagpur 2005-06

2005 Season

	M	Inns	NO	Runs	HS	Avge	100s	50s	Ct	St	O	M	Runs	Wkts	Avge	Best	5wI	10wM
Test																		
All First	9	12	4	75	39 *	9.37	-	-	2	-	429.2	106	1146	51	22.47	7-181	4	1
1-Day Int																		
C & G																		
tsL	1	1	0	1	1	1.00	-	-	-	-	9	1	30	0	-		-	-
Twenty20																		

Career Performances

	M	Inns	NO	Runs	HS	Avge	100s	50s	Ct	St	Balls	Runs	Wkts	Avge	Best	5wI	10wM
Test																	
All First	28	34	14	156	39 *	7.80	-	-	10	-	6261	3021	107	28.23	7-181	5	1
1-Day Int																	
C & G																	
tsL	3	3	2	23	16 *	23.00	-	-	-	-	144	92	1	92.00	1-36	-	
Twenty20																	

PARK, G. T.   Durham

Name: <u>Garry</u> Terence Park
Role: Right-hand bat, wicket-keeper
Born: 19 April 1983, Empangeni, South Africa
Height: 5ft 7in **Weight:** 10st 8lbs
Nickname: Porky
County debut: No first-team appearance (*see **Extras***)
Parents: Michael Park and Christine Reeves
Marital status: Single
Education: Eshowe High School, South Africa; Anglia Ruskin University
Qualifications: Matric, Levels 1 and 2 cricket coaching
Off-season: 'Cricket season in Durban, South Africa'
Career highlights to date: 'Getting a two-year contract for Durham CCC'
Cricket superstitions: 'None'
Cricketers particularly admired: Jonty Rhodes
Other sports played: Hockey, rugby (both KwaZulu-Natal), golf
Other sports followed: Rugby (Natal Sharks)

Favourite band: Blink-182

Relaxations: Golf, music, fishing

Extras: Played for Cambridge UCCE 2003-05. Played for Durham v Bangladesh A in a 50-over match at Riverside 2005 but has yet to appear for the county in first-class or competitive one-day cricket

Opinions on cricket: 'I believe cricket is heading in the right direction in terms of the popularity of the game.'

Best batting: 68 CUCCE v Northamptonshire, Fenner's 2003

2005 Season (did not make any first-class or one-day appearances for his county)

Career Performances

	M	Inns	NO	Runs	HS	Avge	100s	50s	Ct	St	Balls	Runs	Wkts	Avge	Best	5wl	10wM
Test																	
All First	9	13	2	331	68	30.09	-	1	15	-	300	261	0	-	-	-	-
1-Day Int																	
C & G																	
tsL																	
Twenty20																	

PARKER, L. C.   Warwickshire

Name: <u>Luke</u> Charles Parker

Role: Right-hand bat, right-arm medium bowler

Born: 27 September 1983, Coventry

Height: 6ft **Weight:** 13st

Nickname: Parks

Place in batting averages: 94th av. 36.66

Strike rate: (career 55.50)

Parents: Linda and Neil

Marital status: Single

Family links with cricket: 'Dad played for Lincolnshire'

Education: Finham Park; Oxford Brookes University

Qualifications: 8 GCSEs, 3 A-levels, ECB Level 1 coach, 'third year of business degree'

Off-season: 'At uni; trip to Mumbai to World Cricket Academy'

Overseas teams played for: United, Cape Town 2002-03

Career highlights to date: 'Making first-class debut for Warwickshire CCC in 2005. Captaining Oxford UCCE 2005'

Cricket moments to forget: 'Dropping Matt Windows three times in an innings of 200-plus'
Cricket superstitions: 'Not really'
Cricketers particularly admired: Nick Knight, Damien Martyn
Young players to look out for: Thomas Beaney, Josh Knappett, Mike Munday, Navdeep Poonia
Other sports played: Football (Coventry City Academy U10-15)
Other sports followed: Football (Coventry City)
Injuries: Out for two weeks with a broken thumb
Favourite band: Mylo
Relaxations: 'Playing golf; uni life'
Extras: Played for Warwickshire Board XI in the 2002 C&G. Played for Oxford UCCE 2004-05 (captain 2005). Represented British Universities 2005
Opinions on cricket: 'Tea break is not long enough.'
Best batting: 89 OUCCE v Derbyshire, The Parks 2005
Best bowling: 2-37 OUCCE v Gloucestershire, The Parks 2005

2005 Season

	M	Inns	NO	Runs	HS	Avge	100s	50s	Ct	St	O	M	Runs	Wkts	Avge	Best	5wI	10wM
Test																		
All First	9	15	3	440	89	36.66	-	2	5	-	36	4	131	4	32.75	2-37	-	-
1-Day Int																		
C & G																		
tsL																		
Twenty20																		

Career Performances

	M	Inns	NO	Runs	HS	Avge	100s	50s	Ct	St	Balls	Runs	Wkts	Avge	Best	5wI	10wM
Test																	
All First	12	18	3	472	89	31.46	-	2	6	-	222	144	4	36.00	2-37	-	-
1-Day Int																	
C & G	2	2	1	23	17	23.00	-	-	1	-	12	11	0	-		-	-
tsL																	
Twenty20																	

65. Who was the first super sub to win a Man of the Match award in an ODI?

PARSONS, K. A.   Somerset

Name: <u>Keith</u> Alan Parsons
Role: Right-hand bat, right-arm medium bowler
Born: 2 May 1973, Taunton
Height: 6ft 1in **Weight:** 14st 7lbs
Nickname: Pilot, Pars, Orv
County debut: 1992
County cap: 1999
Benefit: 2004
Place in batting averages: 54th av. 44.55
Strike rate: (career 78.09)
Parents: Alan and Lynne
Wife and date of marriage: Sharon, 12 January 2002
Children: Joseph Luke, 17 October 2002; Alex Mathew, 23 March 2005
Family links with cricket: Identical twin brother, Kevin, was on the Somerset staff 1992-94 and then captained the Somerset Board XI. Father played six seasons for Somerset 2nd XI and captained National Civil Service XI
Education: The Castle School, Taunton; Richard Huish Sixth Form College, Taunton
Qualifications: 8 GCSEs, 3 A-levels, NCA senior coach
Career outside cricket: 'Working for Sporting Spectrum Ltd, a corporate hospitality company specialising in sporting events throughout England'
Off-season: 'Setting up and establishing Sporting Spectrum Ltd'
Overseas tours: Castle School to Barbados 1989; Somerset CCC to Cape Town 1999, 2000, 2001
Overseas teams played for: Kapiti Old Boys, Horowhenua, New Zealand 1992-93; Taita District, Wellington, New Zealand 1993-96; Wembley Downs CC, Perth 1998
Career highlights to date: 'C&G final 2001 v Leicestershire – great to win a trophy, and Man of the Match capped a dream day'
Cricket moments to forget: 'Any bad days at Taunton'
Cricket superstitions: 'None'
Cricketers particularly admired: Andy Caddick, Marcus Trescothick, Glenn McGrath, Saqlain Mushtaq
Other sports followed: Rugby union (Bath RFC), football (Nottingham Forest FC), golf, horse racing
Relaxations: Playing golf, watching movies, listening to music 'and the odd social pint of beer'
Extras: Captained two National Cup winning sides – Taunton St Andrews in National U15 Club Championship and Richard Huish College in National U17 School Championship. Represented English Schools at U15 and U19 level. Somerset Young

Player of the Year 1993. C&G Man of the Match award for his 52-ball 60* (including sixes from the last two balls of the innings) and 2-40 in the final v Leicestershire at Lord's 2001

Best batting: 193* Somerset v West Indians, Taunton 2000
Best bowling: 5-13 Somerset v Lancashire, Taunton 2000

2005 Season

	M	Inns	NO	Runs	HS	Avge	100s	50s	Ct	St	O	M	Runs	Wkts	Avge	Best	5wI	10wM
Test																		
All First	8	12	3	401	94	44.55	-	2	5	-	112.1	19	428	7	61.14	3-81	-	-
1-Day Int																		
C & G	1	1	0	0	0	0.00	-	-	-	-								
tsL	18	17	4	558	91 *	42.92	-	4	9	-	75.5	0	407	10	40.70	4-34	-	
Twenty20	11	10	3	215	57 *	30.71	-	1	1	-	26	0	172	10	17.20	3-12	-	

Career Performances

	M	Inns	NO	Runs	HS	Avge	100s	50s	Ct	St	Balls	Runs	Wkts	Avge	Best	5wI	10wM
Test																	
All First	120	194	21	4813	193 *	27.82	5	26	106	-	7419	4286	95	45.11	5-13	2	-
1-Day Int																	
C & G	32	29	8	818	121	38.95	1	3	9	-	1292	969	37	26.18	4-43	-	
tsL	168	146	22	3665	115 *	29.55	1	22	69	-	3844	3268	89	36.71	5-39	1	
Twenty20	21	20	6	340	57 *	24.28	-	1	4	-	204	255	12	21.25	3-12	-	

66. Which Bangladesh player carried his bat for 33* v Zimbabwe at Harare in 2001?

PARSONS, M.   Somerset

Name: Michael Parsons
Role: Right-hand bat, right-arm
fast-medium bowler
Born: 26 November 1984, Taunton
Height: 6ft **Weight:** 11st 11lbs
Nickname: Pars
County debut: 2002 (one-day),
2005 (first-class)
Parents: Dave and Hilary
Marital status: Single
Education: Ladymead; Richard Huish
College, Taunton
Qualifications: 10 GCSEs, 1 A-level, Level
1 ECB coach
Overseas tours: ESCA West Region U15 to
West Indies 2000; Somerset Academy U19 to
Australia 2002
Career highlights to date: 'Somerset v New
Zealand 2004 – 10-1-30-6'
Cricket moments to forget: 'Dropped catch live on Sky TV'
Cricket superstitions: 'None'
Cricketers particularly admired: Allan Donald, Glenn McGrath
Young players to look out for: James Hildreth
Other sports followed: Football (Man United)
Relaxations: 'Music, PlayStation'
Extras: England U15 and U17. Bowler of ESCA West Region U15 tour to West Indies
2000. Played for Somerset Board XI in the C&G 2003. Represented England U19
2003. Took 6-30 in 10 overs v New Zealanders in 50-over match at Taunton 2004
Opinions on cricket: 'More day/night cricket.'
Best batting: 6* Somerset v Lancashire, Taunton 2005

2005 Season

	M	Inns	NO	Runs	HS	Avge	100s	50s	Ct	St	O	M	Runs	Wkts	Avge	Best	5wI	10wM
Test																		
All First	2	3	1	11	6 *	5.50	-	-	-	-	27	3	135	0	-		-	-
1-Day Int																		
C & G																		
tsL	1	0	0	0	0	-	-	-	1	-	5	0	43	0	-		-	-
Twenty20	1	1	0	0	0	0.00	-	-	-	-	4	0	39	0	-		-	-

Career Performances

	M	Inns	NO	Runs	HS	Avge	100s	50s	Ct	St	Balls	Runs	Wkts	Avge	Best	5wI	10wM
Test																	
All First	2	3	1	11	6 *	5.50	-	-	-	-	162	135	0	-		-	-
1-Day Int																	
C & G	1	1	0	0	0	0.00	-	-	-	-	60	70	3	23.33	3-70	-	
tsL	8	4	1	1	1 *	0.33	-	-	3	-	315	305	5	61.00	2-60	-	
Twenty20	1	1	0	0	0	0.00	-	-	-	-	24	39	0	-		-	

PATEL, M. M.   Kent

Name: Minal (<u>Min</u>) Mahesh Patel
Role: Right-hand bat, slow left-arm
orthodox bowler, county vice-captain
Born: 7 July 1970, Mumbai, India
Height: 5ft 7in **Weight:** 10st
Nickname: Ho Chi, Diamond, Geez
County debut: 1989
County cap: 1994
Benefit: 2004
Test debut: 1996
50 wickets in a season: 4
Place in batting averages: 161st av. 28.64
(2004 256th av. 13.22)
Place in bowling averages: 41st av. 27.55
(2004 39th av. 28.89)
Strike rate: 60.88 (career 71.04)
Parents: Mahesh and Aruna
Wife and date of marriage: Karuna,
8 October 1995
Family links with cricket: Father played good club cricket in India,
Africa and England
Education: Dartford Grammar School; Manchester Polytechnic
Qualifications: 6 O-levels, 3 A-levels, BA (Hons) Economics
Overseas tours: Dartford GS to Barbados 1988; England A to India and Bangladesh
1994-95; MCC to Malta 1997, 1999, to Fiji, Sydney and Hong Kong 1998, to East and
Central Africa 1999, to Bangladesh 1999-2000 (c), to Argentina and Chile 2001, to
Namibia and Uganda 2004-05 (c); Kent to Port Elizabeth 2001; Club Cricket
Conference to Australia 2002
Overseas teams played for: St Augustine's, Cape Town 1993-94; Alberton,
Johannesburg 1997-98
Career highlights to date: 'Winning 2001 Norwich Union League at Edgbaston. First
Test cap. Any match-winning performance for Kent'

Cricket moments to forget: 'Being left out of the final XI for the Lord's Test v India 1996'
Cricketers particularly admired: Derek Underwood, Aravinda de Silva
Other sports played: Golf, snooker
Other sports followed: Football (Tottenham Hotspur), 'most sports that you can name'
Favourite band: 'A lot of 1970s/80s soul – Phyllis Hyman, Loose Ends, Keni Burke etc.'
Extras: Played for English Schools 1988, 1989 and NCA England South 1989. Was voted Kent League Young Player of the Year 1987 while playing for Blackheath. Whittingdale Young Player of the Year 1994. Appointed vice-captain of Kent for 2006
Best batting: 87 Kent v Glamorgan, Cardiff 2005
Best bowling: 8-96 Kent v Lancashire, Canterbury 1994

2005 Season

	M	Inns	NO	Runs	HS	Avge	100s	50s	Ct	St	O	M	Runs	Wkts	Avge	Best	5wl	10wM
Test																		
All First	16	21	4	487	87	28.64	-	4	3	-	598.4	132	1626	59	27.55	6-53	3	-
1-Day Int																		
C & G																			
tsL																			
Twenty20																			

Career Performances

	M	Inns	NO	Runs	HS	Avge	100s	50s	Ct	St	Balls	Runs	Wkts	Avge	Best	5wl	10wM
Test	2	2	0	45	27	22.50	-	-	2	-	276	180	1	180.00	1-101	-	-
All First	189	254	49	3650	87	17.80	-	15	92	-	41063	17526	578	30.32	8-96	28	9
1-Day Int																	
C & G	14	5	2	45	27 *	15.00	-	-	5	-	662	399	11	36.27	2-29	-	
tsL	42	25	7	148	26	8.22	-	-	13	-	1762	1335	50	26.70	3-22	-	
Twenty20																	

67. Who hit nine sixes while making the highest score by a New Zealand player in an ODI, v Zimbabwe at Bulawayo in 2005?

PATEL, S. R.　　　　　　　　　Nottinghamshire

Name: <u>Samit</u> Rohit Patel
Role: Right-hand bat, left-arm orthodox spin bowler; all-rounder
Born: 30 November 1984, Leicester
Height: 5ft 8in **Weight:** 12st
Nickname: Pilchy Patel
County debut: 2002
Strike rate: (career 85.16)
Parents: Rohit and Sejal
Marital status: Single
Family links with cricket: Father local league cricketer and brother has played for Nottinghamshire U15
Education: Worksop College
Qualifications: 7 GCSEs, 2 A-levels
Career outside cricket: 'Want to be a coach'
Overseas tours: England U17 to Australia 2001; England U19 to Australia and (U19 World Cup) New Zealand 2001-02, to Australia 2002-03, to Bangladesh (U19 World Cup) 2003-04
Career highlights to date: 'Scoring 122 against South Africa U19 at Arundel [2003], because we were 90-6 at the time'
Cricket moments to forget: 'Playing at Headingley in the Twenty20 Cup against Yorkshire, where I got hit for 28 in an over by Michael Lumb'
Cricket superstitions: 'Put my right pad on first'
Cricketers particularly admired: Sachin Tendulkar, Brian Lara
Young players to look out for: Akhil Patel, Bilal Shafayat, Ravinder Bopara
Other sports played: Rugby, hockey (both for Worksop College 1st XI)
Other sports followed: Football (Nottingham Forest)
Favourite band: G-Unit
Relaxations: 'Listening to music; playing snooker; just generally relaxing'
Extras: Made Nottinghamshire 2nd XI debut in 1999, aged 14. Winner of inaugural BBC *Test Match Special* U15 Young Cricketer of the Year Award 2000. Represented England U19 2002, 2003 (captain in one-day series 2003) and 2004
Best batting: 55 Nottinghamshire v Lancashire, Trent Bridge 2003
Best bowling: 3-73 Nottinghamshire v Kent, Trent Bridge 2005

2005 Season

	M	Inns	NO	Runs	HS	Avge	100s	50s	Ct	St	O	M	Runs	Wkts	Avge	Best	5wl	10wM
Test																		
All First	3	4	0	27	12	6.75	-	-	-	-	77.1	17	218	6	36.33	3-73	-	-
1-Day Int																		
C & G	2	2	2	74	61 *	-	-	-	1	-	8	0	50	1	50.00	1-50	-	
tsL	14	10	2	239	82	29.87	-	1	3	-	42	3	169	4	42.25	2-33	-	
Twenty20	7	7	1	110	32	18.33	-	-	1	-	24.5	0	176	10	17.60	2-22	-	

Career Performances

	M	Inns	NO	Runs	HS	Avge	100s	50s	Ct	St	Balls	Runs	Wkts	Avge	Best	5wl	10wM
Test																	
All First	5	7	0	126	55	18.00	-	1	1	-	511	228	6	38.00	3-73	-	-
1-Day Int																	
C & G	2	2	2	74	61 *	-	-	1	-	-	48	50	1	50.00	1-50	-	
tsL	26	19	4	373	82	24.86	-	1	4	-	456	343	11	31.18	2-14	-	
Twenty20	14	14	4	192	32	19.20	-	-	4	-	197	259	12	21.58	2-22	-	

PATHAN, I. K.   Middlesex

Name: <u>Irfan</u> Khan Pathan
Role: Left-hand bat, left-arm medium-fast bowler
Born: 27 October 1984, Baroda, India
County debut: 2005
Test debut: 2003-04
Strike rate: (career 63.12)
Family links with cricket: Brother Yusuf Pathan plays first-class cricket for Baroda in India
Overseas tours: India U19 to New Zealand (U19 World Cup) 2001-02, to England 2002, to Pakistan (Asia U19 Tournament) 2003-04; India A to Sri Lanka 2002, to England 2003; India to Australia 2003-04, to Pakistan 2003-04, to England (ICC Champions Trophy) 2004, to Bangladesh 2004-05, to Zimbabwe 2005-06, plus other one-day tournaments in Sri Lanka, Holland and England
Overseas teams played for: Baroda 2000-01 –
Extras: ICC Emerging Player of the Year award 2004. Has won numerous international awards, including Man of the [Test] Series v Bangladesh 2004-05 and v Zimbabwe 2005-06, in which he equalled the record for wickets in a two-match series

(21). Was an overseas player with Middlesex during the 2005 season as a locum for Nantie Hayward

Best batting: 68 Middlesex v Surrey, Lord's 2005
Best bowling: 7-59 India v Zimbabwe, Harare 2005-06
Stop press: Took hat-trick (Salman Butt, Younis Khan, Mohammad Yousuf) in the first over of the third Test v Pakistan at Karachi 2005-06

2005 Season

	M	Inns	NO	Runs	HS	Avge	100s	50s	Ct	St	O	M	Runs	Wkts	Avge	Best	5wI	10wM
Test																		
All First	3	4	2	126	68	63.00	-	1	1	-	89	13	324	5	64.80	4-81	-	-
1-Day Int																		
C & G																		
tsL	4	2	0	18	15	9.00	-	-	1	-	27.2	0	148	6	24.66	3-42	-	
Twenty20	7	4	1	37	21 *	12.33	-	-	-	-	24	0	153	12	12.75	4-27	-	

Career Performances

	M	Inns	NO	Runs	HS	Avge	100s	50s	Ct	St	Balls	Runs	Wkts	Avge	Best	5wI	10wM
Test	15	18	2	359	55	22.43	-	2	6	-	3253	1726	66	26.15	7-59	6	2
All First	50	61	15	1019	68	22.15	-	5	17	-	9670	5080	168	30.23	7-59	9	3
1-Day Int	38	27	10	412	64	24.23	-	2	6	-	2009	1671	63	26.52	5-27	1	
C & G																	
tsL	4	2	0	18	15	9.00	-	-	1	-	164	148	6	24.66	3-42	-	
Twenty20	7	4	1	37	21 *	12.33	-	-	-	-	144	153	12	12.75	4-27	-	

68. Who played in just one ODI for New Zealand v Zimbabwe at Dhaka in 1998, didn't bat, didn't bowl but fielded for 50 overs?

PATTERSON, S. A. Yorkshire

Name: <u>Steven</u> Andrew Patterson
Role: Right-hand bat, right-arm
medium-fast bowler
Born: 3 October 1983, Hull
Height: 6ft 4in **Weight:** 14st
Nickname: Patto
County debut: 2005
Parents: Sue and Alan
Marital status: Single
Education: Malet Lambert School; St Mary's
Sixth Form College; Leeds University
Qualifications: 11 GCSEs, 3 A-levels, BSc
Maths, Level 2 cricket coach
Off-season: 'Playing abroad in New Zealand
and possibly travelling'
Overseas tours: MCC A to UAE and Oman
2004
Overseas teams played for: Suburbs New
Lynn CC, Auckland 2005-06
Career highlights to date: 'Making my first-class debut for Yorkshire'
Cricket moments to forget: 'Going in as nightwatchman and getting a first-ball
duck!'
Cricket superstitions: 'Not really'
Cricketers particularly admired: Glenn McGrath
Other sports played: Football, golf, skiing, mountain biking
Injuries: Shin splints
Favourite band: Foo Fighters
Relaxations: 'Playing guitar, travelling, reading'
Extras: Played for Yorkshire Board XI in the 2003 C&G

2005 Season

	M	Inns	NO	Runs	HS	Avge	100s	50s	Ct	St	O	M	Runs	Wkts	Avge	Best	5wI	10wM
Test																		
All First	1	0	0	0	0	-	-	-	1	-	18	0	53	0	-	-	-	-
1-Day Int																		
C & G																			
tsL	4	3	2	18	11 *	18.00	-	-	1	-	29	4	125	1	125.00	1 22	-	
Twenty20																		

Career Performances

	M	Inns	NO	Runs	HS	Avge	100s	50s	Ct	St	Balls	Runs	Wkts	Avge	Best	5wI	10wM
Test																	
All First	1	0	0	0	0	-	-	-	1	-	108	53	0	-	-	-	-
1-Day Int																	
C & G	2	1	1	1	1*	-	-	-	-	-	104	88	4	22.00	3-11	-	
tsL	4	3	2	18	11*	18.00	-	-	1	-	174	125	1	125.00	1-22	-	
Twenty20																	

PEARSON, J. A.   Gloucestershire

Name: <u>James</u> Alexander Pearson
Role: Left-hand bat
Born: 11 September 1983, Bristol
Height: 5ft 10in **Weight:** 12st 7lbs
Nickname: JP
County debut: 2002
County cap: 2005
Place in batting averages: 199th av. 22.88
Parents: Milverton and Faith
Marital status: Single
Family links with cricket: 'Dad played club cricket'
Education: Clifton College
Qualifications: 5 GCSEs, 3 A-levels, GNVQ
Overseas tours: England U19 to Australia 2002-03
Career highlights to date: 'Making 51 opening the batting on debut v Northamptonshire'
Cricketers particularly admired: Brian Lara, Courtney Walsh, Ricky Ponting
Young players to look out for: Alex Gidman
Other sports played: 'A bit of footy now and then'
Other sports followed: Football (Arsenal)
Relaxations: 'Listening to music and going clubbing'
Extras: Played for Gloucestershire Board XI in the C&G 2001 and 2002. Represented England U19 2002. Released by Gloucestershire at the end of the 2005 season
Best batting: 68 Gloucestershire v Nottinghamshire, Bristol 2005

2005 Season

	M	Inns	NO	Runs	HS	Avge	100s	50s	Ct	St	O	M	Runs	Wkts	Avge	Best	5wl	10wM
Test																		
All First	5	10	1	206	68	22.88	-	2	2	-								
1-Day Int																		
C & G																		
tsL																		
Twenty20																		

Career Performances

	M	Inns	NO	Runs	HS	Avge	100s	50s	Ct	St	Balls	Runs	Wkts	Avge	Best	5wl	10wM
Test																	
All First	8	16	2	320	68	22.85	-	3	4	-							
1-Day Int																	
C & G	2	2	0	7	7	3.50	-	-	-	-	18	29	1	29.00	1-29	-	
tsL																	
Twenty20																	

PENG, N.   Glamorgan

Name: Nicky Peng
Role: Right-hand bat
Born: 18 September 1982,
Newcastle upon Tyne
Height: 6ft 3in **Weight:** 14st 5lbs
Nickname: Pengy
County debut: 2000 (Durham)
County cap: 2001 (Durham)
Place in batting averages: 234th av. 18.80
(2004 193rd av. 23.16)
Parents: Linda and Wilf
Marital status: Single
Education: Royal Grammar School,
Newcastle upon Tyne
Qualifications: 10 GCSEs
Off-season: 'Club cricket, Perth, Australia'
Overseas tours: England U19 to India 2000-
01, to Australia and (U19 World Cup) New
Zealand 2001-02 (captain); ECB National Academy to Australia 2001-02; Durham to
South Africa 2002
Overseas teams played for: Subiaco Floreat, Perth
Career highlights to date: 'Double promotion at Durham. Signing for Glamorgan.
PCA Young Player of the Year 2001'

Cricketers particularly admired: Steve Waugh, Jacques Kallis, Paul Collingwood
Young players to look out for: Gordon Muchall, Ben Harmison, Mark Turner
Other sports followed: Football (Newcastle United), rugby (Newcastle Falcons)
Extras: Full name Nicky Peng Gillender. Has represented England at U14, U15, U17 and U19 levels. Represented Minor Counties at age 15. Sir John Hobbs Silver Jubilee Memorial Prize 1998. Scored 98 on Championship debut, v Surrey at Riverside 2000. NBC Denis Compton Award for the most promising young Durham player 2000, 2001. Durham CCC Young Player of the Year 2001. PCA Young Player of the Year 2001. Left Durham at the end of the 2005 season and has joined Glamorgan for 2006
Best batting: 158 Durham v DUCCE, Durham 2003

2005 Season

	M	Inns	NO	Runs	HS	Avge	100s	50s	Ct	St	O	M	Runs	Wkts	Avge	Best	5wI	10wM
Test																		
All First	10	15	0	282	87	18.80	-	1	-	-								
1-Day Int																		
C & G	1	1	0	3	3	3.00	-	-	-	-								
tsL	10	10	1	269	63	29.88	-	3	1	-								
Twenty20	7	7	0	97	37	13.85	-	-	2	-								

Career Performances

	M	Inns	NO	Runs	HS	Avge	100s	50s	Ct	St	Balls	Runs	Wkts	Avge	Best	5wI	10wM
Test																		
All First	68	116	2	2732	158	23.96	4	12	35	-	6	2	0	-	-	-	-
1-Day Int																		
C & G	9	9	0	246	119	27.33	1	-	1	-							
tsL	70	70	5	1734	121	26.67	2	10	17	-							
Twenty20	12	12	0	207	49	17.25	-	-	8	-							

69. Clive Lloyd took a wicket with his first ball in ODIs, but which opener – later Middlesex's scorer – did he dismiss?

PENNEY, T. L.   Warwickshire

Name: <u>Trevor</u> Lionel Penney
Role: Right-hand bat, leg-break bowler, occasional wicket-keeper
Born: 12 June 1968, Harare, Zimbabwe
Height: 6ft **Weight:** 11st 2lbs
Nickname: TP, Blondie
County debut: 1992
County cap: 1994
Benefit: 2003
1000 runs in a season: 2
Strike rate: (career 43.16)
Parents: George and Bets
Wife and date of marriage: Deborah-Anne, 19 December 1992
Children: Samantha Anne, 20 August 1995; Kevin, 7 June 1998
Family links with cricket: Father played club cricket. Brother Stephen captained Zimbabwe Schools
Education: Prince Edward Boys High School, Zimbabwe
Qualifications: 3 O-levels
Overseas tours: Zimbabwe U24 to England 1984; Zimbabwe to Sri Lanka 1987; ICC Associates to Australia (U19 World Cup) 1987-88 (c)
Overseas teams played for: Old Hararians, Zimbabwe 1983-89, 1992-98; Scarborough, Perth 1989-90; Avendale, South Africa 1990-91; Boland, South Africa 1991-92; Mashonaland, Zimbabwe 1993-94, 1997-98 – 2000-01
Cricketers particularly admired: Colin Bland, Ian Botham, Allan Donald, Steve Waugh
Other sports played: Hockey (Zimbabwe and Africa), squash, tennis, golf and white water rafting
Other sports followed: Basketball (Chicago Bulls), American football (San Francisco 49ers), Formula One motor racing
Relaxations: 'Spending time with my family'
Extras: Played for Zimbabwe v Sri Lanka B 1987-88. Scored century (102*) on first-class debut for Warwickshire, v Cambridge University at Fenner's 1992. Qualified to play for England in 1992. Warwickshire 2nd XI captain 2002 and 2003. Retired at the end of the 2005 season to become Assistant Coach to Sri Lanka
Best batting: 151 Warwickshire v Middlesex, Lord's 1992
Best bowling: 3-18 Mashonaland v Mashonaland U24, Harare 1993-94

2005 Season

	M	Inns	NO	Runs	HS	Avge	100s	50s	Ct	St	O	M	Runs	Wkts	Avge	Best	5wI	10wM
Test																		
All First																		
1-Day Int																		
C & G	5	5	2	136	51 *	45.33	-	2	2	-								
tsL	16	13	3	217	45	21.70	-	-	10	-								
Twenty20	3	3	2	82	35 *	82.00	-	-	2	-								

Career Performances

	M	Inns	NO	Runs	HS	Avge	100s	50s	Ct	St	Balls	Runs	Wkts	Avge	Best	5wI	10wM
Test																	
All First	158	248	45	7975	151	39.28	15	36	94	2	259	184	6	30.66	3-18	-	-
1-Day Int																	
C & G	47	42	12	1014	90	33.80	-	5	24	-	13	16	1	16.00	1-8	-	
tsL	187	159	52	3102	88 *	28.99	-	12	71	1	6	2	0	-	-	-	-
Twenty20	15	14	5	322	52	35.77	-	1	6	-							

PEPLOE, C. T.   Middlesex

Name: Christopher (<u>Chris</u>) Thomas Peploe
Role: Left-hand lower-order bat,
slow-left arm bowler
Born: 26 April 1981, Hammersmith, London
Height: 6ft 4in **Weight:** 13st 7lbs
Nickname: Peps, Pepsy
County debut: 2003
Place in batting averages: 235th av. 18.37
(2004 253rd av. 14.00)
Place in bowling averages: 122nd av. 44.50
(2004 130th av. 43.82)
Strike rate: 83.00 (career 90.21)
Parents: Trevor and Margaret
Marital status: Single
Education: Twyford C of E High School;
University of Surrey, Roehampton
Qualifications: 9 GCSEs, 3 A-levels, Sports
Science degree, ECB Level 2 coach, YMCA
gym instructor

Career outside cricket: Cricket coach
Overseas tours: MCC Young Cricketers to South Africa 2002, to Sri Lanka 2003;
Middlesex to India 2004

Career highlights to date: 'Making my debut at Lord's for Middlesex. Taking career best figures against Sussex (4-65) at Hove'
Cricket moments to forget: 'Bowling at Nick Knight and Craig Spearman when they both scored 300-plus in 2004'
Cricket superstitions: 'None'
Cricketers particularly admired: Daniel Vettori, Andrew Strauss, Phil Tufnell
Young players to look out for: Ed Joyce
Other sports played: Golf
Other sports followed: English rugby
Favourite band: Linkin Park
Relaxations: 'Music, movies, golf'
Extras: MCC Young Cricketer 2002-03
Opinions on cricket: 'Twenty20 great for game.'
Best batting: 42 Middlesex v Sussex, Lord's 2005
Best bowling: 4-65 Middlesex v Sussex, Hove 2004

2005 Season

	M	Inns	NO	Runs	HS	Avge	100s	50s	Ct	St	O	M	Runs	Wkts	Avge	Best	5wl	10wM
Test																		
All First	7	10	2	147	42	18.37	-	-	2	-	249	57	801	18	44.50	3-77	-	-
1-Day Int																		
C & G																		
tsL	6	4	1	17	14 *	5.66	-	-	2	-	51	2	209	10	20.90	4-38	-	
Twenty20	9	3	3	4	3 *	-	-	-	4	-	26	0	229	8	28.62	3-35	-	

Career Performances

	M	Inns	NO	Runs	HS	Avge	100s	50s	Ct	St	Balls	Runs	Wkts	Avge	Best	5wl	10wM
Test																	
All First	17	24	5	300	42	15.78	-	-	7	-	3338	1785	37	48.24	4-65	-	-
1-Day Int																	
C & G																	
tsL	7	4	1	17	14 *	5.66	-	-	2	-	324	228	10	22.80	4-38	-	
Twenty20	9	3	3	4	3 *	-	-	-	4	-	156	229	8	28.62	3-35	-	

70. Who is the only Australia player to have scored over 1000 runs and taken more than 200 wickets in ODIs?

PETERS, S. D. Northamptonshire

Name: <u>Stephen</u> David Peters
Role: Right-hand bat, leg-break bowler
Born: 10 December 1978, Harold Wood, Essex
Height: 5ft 11in **Weight:** 11st 9lbs
Nickname: Pedro, Geezer
County debut: 1996 (Essex), 2002 (Worcestershire)
County colours: 2002 (Worcestershire)
1000 runs in a season: 1
Place in batting averages: 233rd av. 18.80 (2004 135th av. 31.27)
Strike rate: (career 35.00)
Parents: Lesley and Brian
Marital status: Single
Family links with cricket: 'All family is linked with Upminster CC'
Education: Coopers Company and Coborn School

Qualifications: 9 GCSEs, Level 2 coaching
Off-season: 'Training'
Overseas tours: Essex U14 to Barbados; Essex U15 to Hong Kong; England U19 to Pakistan 1996-97, to South Africa (including U19 World Cup) 1997-98
Overseas teams played for: Cornwall CC, Auckland 2001-02; Willetton CC, Perth 2002-03
Career highlights to date: 'Winning B&H Cup in 1998 with Essex'
Cricket moments to forget: 'Running myself out for a pair against Durham in 2003'
Cricketers particularly admired: 'Anyone who has played at the top level'
Other sports played: Football, golf
Other sports followed: Football (West Ham United)
Injuries: Out for two Twenty20 games with a hamstring injury
Favourite band: Rooster
Relaxations: 'My sofa'
Extras: Sir John Hobbs Silver Jubilee Memorial Prize 1994. Represented England at U14, U15, U17 and U19. Scored century (110) on Essex first-class debut v Cambridge University at Fenner's 1996, aged 17 years 194 days. Essex Young Player of the Year 1996. Man of the Match (107) in the U19 World Cup final in South Africa 1997-98. Released by Worcs at the end of the 2005 season and has joined Northants for 2006
Opinions on cricket: 'Twenty20 great for crowds. EU/Kolpak [*see page 9*] – is it good for the future of English cricket?'
Best batting: 165 Worcestershire v Somerset, Bath 2003
Best bowling: 1-19 Essex v Oxford University, Chelmsford 1999

2005 Season

	M	Inns	NO	Runs	HS	Avge	100s	50s	Ct	St	O	M	Runs	Wkts	Avge	Best	5wI	10wM
Test																		
All First	9	16	1	282	88	18.80	-	2	6	-								
1-Day Int																		
C & G																		
tsL	1	1	1	41	41 *	-	-	-	-	-								
Twenty20	6	6	1	54	26 *	10.80	-	-	-	-								

Career Performances

	M	Inns	NO	Runs	HS	Avge	100s	50s	Ct	St	Balls	Runs	Wkts	Avge	Best	5wI	10wM
Test																	
All First	116	193	17	5278	165	29.98	9	27	86	-	35	31	1	31.00	1-19	-	-
1-Day Int																	
C & G	11	11	0	127	58	11.54	-	1	5	-							
tsL	82	73	4	1326	82	19.21	-	6	20	-							
Twenty20	10	9	1	82	26 *	10.25	-	-	3	-							

PETTINI, M. L.   Essex

Name: <u>Mark</u> Lewis Pettini
Role: Right-hand bat, occasional wicket-keeper
Born: 7 August 1983, Brighton
Height: 5ft 11in **Weight:** 11st 7lbs
Nickname: Swampy, Michelle
County debut: 2001
Parents: Pauline and Max
Marital status: Single
Family links with cricket: 'Brother Tom plays. Mum and Dad watch'
Education: Comberton Village College and Hills Road Sixth Form College, Cambridge; Cardiff University
Qualifications: 10 GCSEs, 3 A-levels, Level 1 cricket coaching award
Overseas tours: England U19 to Australia and (U19 World Cup) New Zealand 2001-02; MCC to Sierra Leone and Nigeria; Essex to Cape Town
Career highlights to date: 'Any first-team cricket played'
Cricket moments to forget: 'Losing three U19 ODIs to India [2002]'
Cricketers particularly admired: 'All the Essex first team', Graham Gooch, Damien West

Extras: Captained Cambridgeshire U11-U16. Played for Development of Excellence XI (South) 2001. Represented England U19 2002. Essex 2nd XI Player of the Year 2002. Represented British Universities 2003 and 2004
Best batting: 78 Essex v Warwickshire, Chelmsford 2003

2005 Season

	M	Inns	NO	Runs	HS	Avge	100s	50s	Ct	St	O	M	Runs	Wkts	Avge	Best	5wI	10wM
Test																		
All First	1	1	1	41	41 *	-	-	-	2	-								
1-Day Int																		
C & G																		
tsL	5	3	0	17	13	5.66	-	-	1	-								
Twenty20	6	4	0	98	60	24.50	-	1	-	-								

Career Performances

	M	Inns	NO	Runs	HS	Avge	100s	50s	Ct	St	Balls	Runs	Wkts	Avge	Best	5wI	10wM
Test																	
All First	11	19	2	516	78	30.35	-	5	9	-							
1-Day Int																	
C & G	3	3	2	113	92 *	113.00	-	1	2	-							
tsL	34	29	1	504	75	18.00	-	3	5	-							
Twenty20	12	10	3	196	60	28.00	-	1	4	-							

PHILLIPS, B. J.   Northamptonshire

Name: <u>Ben</u> James Phillips
Role: Right-hand bat, right-arm
fast-medium bowler
Born: 30 September 1975, Lewisham,
London
Height: 6ft 6in   **Weight:** 15st
Nickname: Bennyphil, Bus
County debut: 1996 (Kent),
2002 (Northamptonshire)
County cap: 2005 (Northamptonshire)
Place in batting averages: 128th av. 31.92
(2004 230th av. 18.16)
Place in bowling averages: 86th av. 34.66
(2004 106th av. 37.90)
Strike rate: 72.57 (career 61.04)
Parents: Glynis and Trevor
Wife and date of marriage: Sarah Jane,
20 January 2003

Family links with cricket: Father and brother both keen club cricketers for Hayes CC (Kent)
Education: Langley Park School for Boys, Beckenham
Qualifications: 9 GCSEs, 3 A-levels
Overseas tours: Northamptonshire to Grenada 2002
Overseas teams played for: University of Queensland, Australia 1993-94; Cape Technikon Greenpoint, Cape Town 1994-95, 1996-98; University of Western Australia, Perth 1998-99; Valley, Brisbane 2001-02
Career highlights to date: '100* v Lancashire, Old Trafford 1997'
Cricket moments to forget: 'Having to leave the field in a televised game against Worcestershire with a shoulder injury that kept me out for most of [2002] season – that would be up there'
Cricket superstitions: 'Arrive at the ground early – hate rushing!'
Cricketers particularly admired: Glenn McGrath, Jason Gillespie
Other sports followed: Football (West Ham United), rugby (Northampton Saints)
Relaxations: 'Enjoy swimming, watching a good movie, and just generally like spending time with family and friends'
Extras: Set Langley Park School record for the fastest half-century, off 11 balls. Represented England U19 Schools 1993-94
Best batting: 100* Kent v Lancashire, Old Trafford 1997
Best bowling: 5-47 Kent v Sussex, Horsham 1997

2005 Season

	M	Inns	NO	Runs	HS	Avge	100s	50s	Ct	St	O	M	Runs	Wkts	Avge	Best	5wl	10wM
Test																		
All First	13	20	6	447	58	31.92	-	2	2	-	254	73	728	21	34.66	3-42	-	-
1-Day Int																		
C & G	3	2	0	3	2	1.50	-	-	1	-	22	3	90	5	18.00	2-32	-	
tsL	14	11	4	135	26 *	19.28	-	-	3	-	102.2	6	579	14	41.35	4-48	-	
Twenty20	7	6	2	126	41 *	31.50	-	-	3	-	25	0	209	12	17.41	4-18	-	

Career Performances

	M	Inns	NO	Runs	HS	Avge	100s	50s	Ct	St	Balls	Runs	Wkts	Avge	Best	5wl	10wM
Test																	
All First	63	89	15	1494	100 *	20.18	1	7	13	-	8668	4258	142	29.98	5-47	3	-
1-Day Int																	
C & G	9	6	1	66	33	13.20	-	-	3	-	408	321	9	35.66	3-14	-	
tsL	60	38	9	485	44 *	16.72	-	-	17	-	2418	1968	62	31.74	4-25	-	
Twenty20	16	14	6	216	41 *	27.00	-	-	6	-	336	474	20	23.70	4-18	-	

PHILLIPS, T. J.   Essex

Name: Timothy (Tim) James Phillips
Role: Left-hand bat, slow left-arm bowler
Born: 13 March 1981, Cambridge
Height: 6ft 1in **Weight:** 13st
Nickname: Pips
County debut: 1999
Strike rate: (career 80.65)
Parents: Carolyn and Martin (deceased)
Marital status: Single
Family links with cricket: 'Father played in
Lancashire League then village cricket in
Essex. Brother Nick plays for local village,
Lindsell'
Education: Felsted School; Durham
University
Qualifications: 10 GCSEs, 3 A-levels,
BA (Hons) Sport in the Community

Overseas tours: Felsted School to Australia
1995-96; England U19 to Malaysia and (U19 World Cup) Sri Lanka 1999-2000
Career highlights to date: '4-42 on first-class debut v Sri Lanka A'
Cricket moments to forget: '2003 season' (*Out for the whole of the season with
cartilage and ligament damage to a knee*)
Cricketers particularly admired: Phil Tufnell
Other sports played: Golf, hockey (Essex Schools U14, U15; East of England
U21 trials)
Other sports followed: Rugby union
Favourite band: The Libertines, Coldplay, The White Stripes
Relaxations: 'Music, gigs, socialising, fishing'
Extras: Holmwoods School Cricketer of the Year runner-up 1997 and 1998. Broke
Nick Knight's and Elliott Wilson's record for runs in a season for Felsted School,
scoring 1213 in 1999. NBC Denis Compton Award 1999. Played for Durham UCCE
2001 and 2002
Best batting: 89 Essex v Worcestershire, Worcester 2005
Best bowling: 4-42 Essex v Sri Lanka A, Chelmsford 1999

2005 Season

	M	Inns	NO	Runs	HS	Avge	100s	50s	Ct	St	O	M	Runs	Wkts	Avge	Best	5wl	10wM
Test																		
All First	3	4	2	116	89	58.00	-	1	-	-	81	13	322	6	53.66	3-24	-	-
1-Day Int																		
C & G	2	1	1	24	24 *	-	-	-	-	-	14	0	67	3	22.33	2-43	-	
tsL	3	1	1	9	9 *	-	-	-	1	-	20	0	108	6	18.00	3-31	-	
Twenty20																		

Career Performances

	M	Inns	NO	Runs	HS	Avge	100s	50s	Ct	St	Balls	Runs	Wkts	Avge	Best	5wl	10wM
Test																	
All First	20	29	5	504	89	21.00	-	2	7	-	3065	2026	38	53.31	4-42	-	-
1-Day Int																	
C & G	3	2	2	28	24 *	-	-	-	-	-	114	94	3	31.33	2-43	-	
tsL	9	7	3	25	9 *	6.25	-	-	3	-	330	290	12	24.16	3-31	-	
Twenty20																	

PHYTHIAN, M. J.   Northamptonshire

Name: <u>Mark</u> John Phythian
Role: Right-hand bat, wicket-keeper; also off-spin bowler
Born: 26 April 1985, Peterborough
Height: 5ft 9in **Weight:** 12st
Nickname: Phythers, Phyth, Monty
County debut: No first-team appearance
Parents: John and Julie
Marital status: Single
Family links with cricket: 'Parents are both very keen supporters'
Education: Oundle School; Durham University
Qualifications: 10 GCSEs, 3 A-levels, ECB Level 1 coaching award
Career outside cricket: 'Student at Durham'
Off-season: 'Studying at Durham and trip to World Academy, Mumbai'
Overseas tours: Oundle School to Sri Lanka 2003; Northamptonshire U17 to South Africa 2000; Northamptonshire U19 to South Africa 2002; MCC to Namibia and Uganda 2004-05
Overseas teams played for: Young Peoples CC, Paarl, South Africa 2003-04

Career highlights to date: 'First-class debut v Somerset at Taunton 2005'
Cricket moments to forget: 'Scoring 0 in my first first-class innings'
Cricket superstitions: 'None'
Cricketers particularly admired: Mark Boucher, Adam Gilchrist, Steve Waugh
Young players to look out for: Nick Lamb, David Balcombe, Will Smith, Patrick Foster
Other sports played: Rugby (school and county), football (school), golf, squash
Other sports followed: Rugby (Leicester Tigers)
Favourite band: Coldplay
Relaxations: 'Cooking, golf, socialising'
Extras: Made 2nd XI Championship debut 2003. Played for Durham UCCE 2005. Northamptonshire Academy Player of the Year 2005
Opinions on cricket: 'I feel that it's important for promising young players to be given the opportunities to prove themselves and that when given these opportunities they take them so that counties are not forced to look overseas to bring in established foreign players on EU passports and Kolpak [*see page 9*].'

2005 Season (did not make any first-class or one-day appearances for his county)

Career Performances

	M	Inns	NO	Runs	HS	Avge	100s	50s	Ct	St	Balls	Runs	Wkts	Avge	Best	5wl	10wM
Test																	
All First	2	1	0	0	0	0.00	-	-	6	-							
1-Day Int																	
C & G																	
tsL																	
Twenty20																	

71. Which Bedfordshire-born batsman had a gap of almost ten years between his sixth and seventh ODI appearances?

PIETERSEN, C.

Northamptonshire

Name: Charl Pietersen
Role: Left-hand bat, left-arm medium-fast opening bowler
Born: 6 January 1983, Kimberley, South Africa
Height: 6ft **Weight:** 13st
County debut: 2005
Strike rate: (career 68.37)
Parents: Thinus and Dalena
Marital status: Single
Family links with cricket: 'Younger brother selected for SA Schools in 2005 and Griqualand West amateur squad (first-class cricket in South Africa)'
Education: Northern Cape High School, Kimberley
Qualifications: Grade 12 (Matriculation)
Off-season: 'Going back to South Africa and preparing for the next cricket season'
Overseas teams played for: Griqualand West 2001-02 – 2003-04
Cricket moments to forget: 'When in 2004 there was no longer a place for me in SA cricket'
Cricket superstitions: 'None'
Cricketers particularly admired: Allan Donald, Steve Harmison, Gary Kirsten, Steve Waugh, Shane Warne
Other sports played: Indoor cricket (Griqualand West)
Other sports followed: Rugby (Blue Bulls)
Injuries: Out for two weeks with a side strain
Favourite band: Rolling Stones, Blink-182
Relaxations: 'Play a little bit of golf'
Extras: South African indoor cricketer of 1999. Represented South African Schools 2001. Man of the Match v KwaZulu-Natal at Pietermaritzburg in the Standard Bank Cup 2002-03 (4-32). C&G Man of the Match award on county debut for his 7-10 (8-3-10-7) v Denmark at Brøndby 2005; it was the best one-day return by a Northamptonshire bowler. Is not considered an overseas player
Opnions on cricket: 'International cricket is very competitive between countries – e.g. Australia have to work hard for a win; they are not unbeatable any more – and that is good for cricket. I don't think any politics should interfere with cricket. Just look at the cricket in Zimbabwe!'
Best batting: 45 Griqualand West v North West, Kimberley 2003-04
Best bowling: 6-43 Griqualand West v Boland, Kimberley 2002-03

2005 Season

	M	Inns	NO	Runs	HS	Avge	100s	50s	Ct	St	O	M	Runs	Wkts	Avge	Best	5wI	10wM
Test																		
All First	4	3	0	1	1	0.33	-	-	2	-	48	1	204	4	51.00	3-74	-	-
1-Day Int																		
C & G	1	0	0	0	0	-	-	-	-	-	8	3	10	7	1.42	7-10	1	
tsL	2	0	0	0	0	-	-	-	-	-	18	0	96	2	48.00	1-45	-	
Twenty20																		

Career Performances

	M	Inns	NO	Runs	HS	Avge	100s	50s	Ct	St	Balls	Runs	Wkts	Avge	Best	5wI	10wM
Test																	
All First	18	28	7	327	45	15.57	-	-	4	-	2735	1604	40	40.10	6-43	1	-
1-Day Int																	
C & G	1	0	0	0	0	-	-	-	-	-	48	10	7	1.42	7-10	1	
tsL	2	0	0	0	0	-	-	-	-	-	108	96	2	48.00	1-45	-	
Twenty20																	

PIETERSEN, K. P.   Hampshire

Name: <u>Kevin</u> Peter Pietersen
Role: Right-hand bat, right-arm off-spin bowler
Born: 27 June 1980, Pietermaritzburg, South Africa
Height: 6ft 4in **Weight:** 14st 9lbs
Nickname: KP, Kelv, Kapes
County debut: 2001 (Nottinghamshire), 2005 (Hampshire)
County cap: 2002 (Nottinghamshire), 2005 (Hampshire)
Test debut: 2005
1000 runs in a season: 3
1st-Class 200s: 3
Place in batting averages: 53rd av. 44.85 (2004 32nd av. 52.20)
Strike rate: (career 84.94)
Parents: Jannie and Penny
Marital status: Single
Education: Maritzburg College; University of South Africa
Qualifications: 3 A-levels
Overseas tours: Natal to Zimbabwe 1999-2000, to Australia 2000-01; Nottinghamshire to South Africa 2001, 2002; England A to Malaysia and India 2003-

04; England to Zimbabwe (one-day series) 2004-05, to South Africa 2004-05 (one-day series), to Pakistan 2005-06, to India 2005-06; ICC World XI to Australia (Super Series) 2005-06

Overseas teams played for: Berea Rovers, Durban 1997 – 2001-02; KwaZulu-Natal 1997-98 – 2000-01; Sydney University 2002-03

Cricket moments to forget: 'Breaking my leg against Glamorgan in August 2002 in an NUL game'

Cricket superstitions: 'Left pad first'

Cricketers particularly admired: Shaun Pollock, Errol Stewart

Other sports played: Golf, swimming ('represented my state in 1992-93'), running

Other sports followed: Formula One (Ferrari), rugby (Natal Sharks)

Extras: Played for South African Schools B 1997. Merit award for cricket from Natal 1997. Scored 61* and had figures of 4-141 from 56 overs for KwaZulu-Natal v England XI 1999-2000. Scored 1275 first-class runs in first season of county cricket 2001. Became first batsman to hit a ball over the pavilion at Riverside, v Durham in the NCL 2003. Player of the [ODI] Series v South Africa 2004-05 (454 runs at 151.33, including the fastest hundred for England in ODIs, from 69 balls). Man of the Match v Australia in Twenty20 international at the Rose Bowl 2005 and v Australia at Bristol in the NatWest Series 2005 (65-ball 91*). Made Test debut in the first Test v Australia at Lord's 2005, scoring 57 and 64*. Scored maiden Test century (158, including an Ashes record seven sixes) in the fifth Test v Australia at The Oval 2005, winning Man of the Match award. ECB National Academy 2003-04, 2004-05. ICC Emerging Player of the Year and ICC ODI Player of the Year awards 2005

Best batting: 254* Nottinghamshire v Middlesex, Trent Bridge 2002

Best bowling: 4-31 Nottinghamshire v DUCCE, Trent Bridge 2003

Stop press: Appointed MBE in 2006 New Year Honours as part of 2005 Ashes-winning England team

2005 Season

	M	Inns	NO	Runs	HS	Avge	100s	50s	Ct	St	O	M	Runs	Wkts	Avge	Best	5wl	10wM
Test	5	10	1	473	158	52.55	1	3	-	-								
All First	11	21	1	897	158	44.85	3	4	4	-	2	1	7	0	-		-	-
1-Day Int	10	6	1	228	91 *	45.60	-	2	8	-								
C & G	3	3	1	150	76	75.00	-	2	-	-								
tsL	6	6	0	140	80	23.33	-	1	-	-	1	0	1	1	1.00	1-1	-	
Twenty20																		

Career Performances

	M	Inns	NO	Runs	HS	Avge	100s	50s	Ct	St	Balls	Runs	Wkts	Avge	Best	5wl	10wM
Test	5	10	1	473	158	52.55	1	3	-	-							
All First	83	134	12	6409	254 *	52.53	22	28	80	-	4672	2605	55	47.36	4-31	-	-
1-Day Int	21	15	6	786	116	87.33	3	4	14	-	12	22	0	-	-	-	-
C & G	10	8	1	202	76	28.85	-	2	4	-	108	81	1	81.00	1-19	-	
tsL	67	65	10	2348	147	42.69	4	14	26	-	1018	954	22	43.36	3-14	-	
Twenty20	10	10	0	256	67	25.60	-	2	-	-	108	136	6	22.66	2-9	-	

PIPE, D. J.   Derbyshire

Name: David James Pipe
Role: Right-hand bat, wicket-keeper
Born: 16 December 1977, Bradford
Height: 5ft 11in **Weight:** 12st
Nickname: Pipey
County debut: 1998 (Worcestershire)
County colours: 2002 (Worcestershire)
Place in batting averages: 229th av. 19.17
Parents: David and Dorothy
Marital status: Single
Family links with cricket: 'My dad and
uncle played in the local league'
Education: Queensbury Upper School; BICC
Qualifications: 8 GCSEs, BTEC National in
Business and Finance, HND Leisure
Management, senior coaching award,
Diploma in Personal Training, Diploma in
Sports Therapy
Overseas teams played for: Leeming Spartans CC/South Metropolitan Cricket
Association, Perth 1998-99; Manly CC, Australia 1999-2004
Career highlights to date: 'Getting first hundred'
Cricket moments to forget: 'Any game we lose'
Cricketers particularly admired: Adam Gilchrist, Ian Healy
Other sports followed: Rugby league (Bradford Bulls, Manly Sea Eagles), boxing
('all British fighters'), AFL (West Coast Eagles)
Relaxations: Training
Extras: MCC School of Merit Wilf Slack Memorial Trophy winner 1995. Took eight
catches v Hertfordshire at Hertford in the C&G 2001 to set a new NatWest/C&G
record for most dismissals in a match by a wicket-keeper. Dick Lygon Award 2002
(Worcestershire Club Man of the Year). Released by Worcestershire at the end of the
2005 season and has joined Derbyshire for 2006
Best batting: 104* Worcestershire v Hampshire, West End 2003

2005 Season

	M	Inns	NO	Runs	HS	Avge	100s	50s	Ct	St	O	M	Runs	Wkts	Avge	Best	5wl	10wM
Test																		
All First	12	19	2	326	80 *	19.17	-	1	43	2								
1-Day Int																		
C & G	2	1	1	1	1 *	-	-	-	3	1								
tsL	8	5	2	64	33 *	21.33	-	-	3	6								
Twenty20	7	7	2	32	9	6.40	-	-	3	2								

Career Performances

	M	Inns	NO	Runs	HS	Avge	100s	50s	Ct	St	Balls	Runs	Wkts	Avge	Best	5wI	10wM
Test																	
All First	31	47	5	781	104 *	18.59	1	2	81	7							
1-Day Int																	
C & G	5	3	1	61	56	30.50	-	1	14	1							
tsL	22	18	5	251	45	19.30	-	-	9	11							
Twenty20	13	10	3	51	14	7.28	-	-	6	2							

PIPER, K. J. Warwickshire

Name: <u>Keith</u> John Piper
Role: Right-hand bat, wicket-keeper
Born: 18 December 1969, Leicester
Height: 5ft 7in **Weight:** 10st 8lbs
Nickname: Tubbsy, Garden Boy
County debut: 1989
County cap: 1992
Benefit: 2001
50 dismissals in a season: 2
Strike rate: (career 34.00)
Parents: John and Charlotte
Marital status: Single
Family links with cricket: Father club
cricketer in Leicester
Education: Somerset Senior
Qualifications: Senior coaching award,
basketball coaching award, volleyball
coaching award
Overseas tours: Haringey Cricket College to Barbados 1986, to Trinidad 1987, to
Jamaica 1988; Warwickshire to La Manga 1989, to St Lucia 1990; England A to India
1994-95, to Pakistan 1995-96
Overseas teams played for: Desmond Haynes's XI, Barbados v Haringey Cricket College
Cricketers particularly admired: Jack Russell, Alec Stewart, Dermot Reeve,
Colin Metson
Other sports followed: Snooker, football, tennis
Relaxations: Music, eating
Extras: London Young Cricketer of the Year 1989 and in the last five 1992. Played for
England YC 1989. Was batting partner (116*) to Brian Lara when he reached his 501*,
v Durham at Edgbaston 1994. Took six catches v Leics at Edgbaston in the NCL 2003,
equalling the record for the one-day league. Retired at the end of the 2005 season
Best batting: 116* Warwickshire v Durham, Edgbaston 1994
Best bowling: 1-57 Warwickshire v Nottinghamshire, Edgbaston 1992

2005 Season

	M	Inns	NO	Runs	HS	Avge	100s	50s	Ct	St	O	M	Runs	Wkts	Avge	Best	5wI	10wM
Test																		
All First	1	0	0	0	0	-	-	-	2	2								
1-Day Int																		
C & G																		
tsL	1	0	0	0	0	-	-	-	-	-								
Twenty20																		

Career Performances

	M	Inns	NO	Runs	HS	Avge	100s	50s	Ct	St	Balls	Runs	Wkts	Avge	Best	5wI	10wM
Test																	
All First	200	275	44	4618	116 *	19.99	2	14	504	36	34	60	1	60.00	1-57	-	-
1-Day Int																	
C & G	41	21	10	181	19	16.45	-	-	47	7							
tsL	146	71	35	548	38 *	15.22	-	-	148	38							
Twenty20	6	2	2	1	1 *	-	-	-	3	1							

PLUNKETT, L. E.   Durham

Name: <u>Liam</u> Edward Plunkett
Role: Right-hand bat, right-arm fast bowler
Born: 6 April 1985, Middlesbrough
Height: 6ft 3in **Weight:** 13st
Nickname: Pudsey
County debut: 2003
50 wickets in a season: 1
Place in batting averages: 243rd av. 17.06
(2004 176th av. 25.16)
Place in bowling averages: 68th av. 30.84
(2004 56th av. 31.09)
Strike rate: 49.76 (career 49.59)
Parents: Alan and Marie
Marital status: Engaged to Lisa
Education: Nunthorpe Comprehensive;
Teesside Tertiary
Qualifications: 9 GCSEs, volleyball
coaching badge
Overseas tours: England U19 to Australia 2002-03, to Bangladesh (U19 World Cup)
2003-04; England to Pakistan 2005-06, to India 2005-06
Career highlights to date: 'Taking five wickets on Championship debut against
Yorkshire'

Cricket moments to forget: 'Bowling too many wides in first game on TV'
Cricket superstitions: 'None'
Cricketers particularly admired: Glenn McGrath, Stephen Harmison, Allan Donald, Jacques Kallis
Young players to look out for: Ravinder Bopara
Other sports played: Football, swimming
Other sports followed: Football (Arsenal, Middlesbrough)
Favourite band: 'Any R&B'
Relaxations: Swimming, gym, cinema
Extras: Became only the second bowler to record a five-wicket innings return on Championship debut for Durham, 5-53 v Yorkshire at Headingley 2003. Represented England U19 2003. NBC Denis Compton Award for the most promising young Durham player 2003. ECB National Academy 2004-05 (part-time), 2005-06
Opinions on cricket: 'Twenty20 good game, which brings the crowds in, and is fun to watch.'
Best batting: 74* Durham v Somerset, Stockton 2005
Best bowling: 6-74 Durham v Hampshire, Riverside 2004
Stop press: Made Test debut in the third Test v Pakistan at Lahore 2005-06 and ODI debut in the first ODI v Pakistan at Lahore 2005-06

2005 Season

	M	Inns	NO	Runs	HS	Avge	100s	50s	Ct	St	O	M	Runs	Wkts	Avge	Best	5wI	10wM
Test																		
All First	14	19	4	256	74 *	17.06	-	1	6	-	423	80	1573	51	30.84	5-43	2	-
1-Day Int																		
C & G																			
tsL	15	7	4	62	14	20.66	-	-	2	-	117	9	553	19	29.10	4-28	-	
Twenty20	7	5	4	27	8	27.00	-	-	2	-	18.4	0	155	1	155.00	1-38	-	

Career Performances

	M	Inns	NO	Runs	HS	Avge	100s	50s	Ct	St	Balls	Runs	Wkts	Avge	Best	5wI	10wM
Test																	
All First	31	47	13	722	74 *	21.23	-	2	10	-	5009	3209	101	31.77	6-74	4	-
1-Day Int																	
C & G	2	1	0	3	3	3.00	-	-	1	-	84	87	4	21.75	3-63	-	
tsL	25	15	7	151	21	18.87	-	-	4	-	1146	888	29	30.62	4-28	-	
Twenty20	9	6	4	29	8	14.50	-	-	4	-	160	205	5	41.00	2-18	-	

POONIA, N. S.
Warwickshire

Name: Navdeep (<u>Navi</u>) Singh Poonia
Role: Right-hand bat, right-arm medium bowler
Born: 11 May 1986, Glasgow
Height: 6ft 3in **Weight:** 14st
Nickname: Nav, Sat Nav
County debut: No first-team appearance
Parents: Jaipal and Bindy Poonia
Marital status: Single
Family links with cricket: 'Dad played club cricket at Walsall CC'
Education: Moseley Park School; Wolverhampton University
Qualifications: 10 GCSEs, 2 A-levels, Levels 1 and 2 coaching
Off-season: 'Completing my second year at university'
Overseas tours: Warwickshire Academy to South Africa 2005

Career highlights to date: 'Scoring 199 against Worcestershire 2nd XI. Getting signed on to Warwickshire CCC staff'
Cricket superstitions: 'None'
Cricketers particularly admired: Sachin Tendulkar, Brian Lara, Allan Donald
Young players to look out for: Jasbir Poonia
Other sports played: Football, badminton
Other sports followed: Football (Man Utd and Glasgow Rangers)
Favourite band: 112, Jagged Edge
Relaxations: 'Playing snooker with mates and cousins'
Extras: Played for Warwickshire Board XI in the 2003 C&G. Cyril Goodway (Warwickshire Old County Cricketers' Association) Trophy U17
Opinions on cricket: 'Better cricketing wickets for both batters and bowlers'

2005 Season (did not make any first-class or one-day appearances)

Career Performances

	M	Inns	NO	Runs	HS	Avge	100s	50s	Ct	St	Balls	Runs	Wkts	Avge	Best	5wI	10wM
Test																	
All First																	
1-Day Int																	
C & G	1	1	0	17	17	17.00	-	-	-	-							
tsL																	
Twenty20																	

POTHAS, N.

Hampshire

Name: Nicolas (<u>Nic</u>) Pothas
Role: Right-hand bat, wicket-keeper
Born: 18 November 1973, Johannesburg,
South Africa
Height: 6ft 1in **Weight:** 13st 7lbs
Nickname: Skeg
County debut: 2002
County cap: 2003
50 dismissals in a season: 2
Place in batting averages: 31st av. 51.21
(2004 81st av. 39.71)
Parents: Emmanuel and Penelope
Marital status: 'Very single'
Family links with cricket: 'Greek by
nationality, therefore clearly none'
Education: King Edward VII High School;
Rand Afrikaans University

Overseas tours: South Africa A to England
1996, to Sri Lanka 1998-99, to West Indies 2000-01; Gauteng to Australia 1997; South
Africa to Singapore (Singapore Challenge) 2000-01
Overseas teams played for: Transvaal/Gauteng 1993-94 – 2001-02
Career highlights to date: 'First tour for South Africa A. Playing for South Africa'
Cricket superstitions: 'Too many to mention'
Cricketers particularly admired: Ray Jennings, Jimmy Cook, Robin Smith
Other sports played: Hockey (South Africa U21, Transvaal)
Other sports followed: Football (Manchester United)
Favourite band: Counting Crows, Gin Blossoms, Just Jinger
Relaxations: 'Shopping; designing clothes; sleeping; gym'
Extras: Scored maiden first-class century (147) for South African Students v England
tourists at Pietermaritzburg 1995-96. Benson and Hedges Young Player of the Year
1996. Transvaal Player of the Year 1996, 1998. C&G Man of the Match award v
Glamorgan at Cardiff 2005 (114*). Scored 139 v Gloucestershire at Cheltenham 2005,
in the process sharing with Andy Bichel (138) in a new Hampshire record partnership
for the eighth wicket (257). Made 51 first-class dismissals in 2005, also scoring 973
runs. Holds a Greek passport and is not considered an overseas player
Best batting: 165 Gauteng v KwaZulu-Natal, Johannesburg 1998-99

2005 Season

	M	Inns	NO	Runs	HS	Avge	100s	50s	Ct	St	O	M	Runs	Wkts	Avge	Best	5wI	10wM
Test																		
All First	15	24	5	973	139	51.21	3	5	48	3								
1-Day Int																		
C & G	5	5	3	289	114 *	144.50	1	2	8	3								
tsL	14	14	0	300	76	21.42	-	1	12	4								
Twenty20	7	6	1	137	59	27.40	-	2	4	-								

Career Performances

	M	Inns	NO	Runs	HS	Avge	100s	50s	Ct	St	Balls	Runs	Wkts	Avge	Best	5wI	10wM
Test																	
All First	146	227	36	7103	165	37.18	15	35	399	36	6	5	0	-	-	-	-
1-Day Int	3	1	0	24	24	24.00	-	-	4	1							
C & G	10	9	4	380	114 *	76.00	1	2	14	3							
tsL	51	47	15	1259	83 *	39.34	-	8	52	13							
Twenty20	18	14	5	218	59	24.22	-	2	12	1							

POWELL, M. J.   Warwickshire

Name: <u>Michael</u> James Powell
Role: Right-hand opening/middle-order bat, right-arm medium bowler
Born: 5 April 1975, Bolton
Height: 5ft 10in **Weight:** 12st 2lbs
Nickname: Arthur, Powelly
County debut: 1996
County cap: 1999
1000 runs in a season: 1
1st-Class 200s: 1
Place in batting averages: 145th av. 30.40 (2004 61st av. 43.80)
Strike rate: (career 108.54)
Parents: Terry and Pat
Marital status: Single
Family links with cricket: 'Father loves the game. Brother John played for Warwickshire youth teams'
Education: Lawrence Sheriff Grammar School, Rugby
Qualifications: 6 GCSEs, 2 A-levels, Levels I-III ECB coaching awards
Career outside cricket: Coaching

Overseas tours: England U18 to South Africa 1992-93 (c), to Denmark 1993 (c); England U19 to Sri Lanka 1993-94; England A to West Indies 2000-01
Overseas teams played for: Avendale CC, Cape Town 1994-95, 1996-97, 2000-01; Griqualand West, South Africa 2001-02
Career highlights to date: 'B&H Cup winners 2002. Frizzell County Champions 2004'
Cricket moments to forget: 'My first pair against my old friend Gary Keedy v Lancs 2004'
Cricket superstitions: 'None'
Cricketers particularly admired: Dermot Reeve, Shaun Pollock, Allan Donald
Young players to look out for: Moeen Ali
Other sports played: Golf, rugby (Warwickshire U16-U18)
Other sports followed: Football
Favourite band: 'No band, just Robbie!! (Williams, that is)'
Extras: Captained Warwickshire U14-U19 and England U17 and U18. Became first uncapped Warwickshire player for 49 years to carry his bat, for 70* out of 130 v Nottinghamshire at Edgbaston 1998. Captain of Warwickshire 2001-03
Opinions on cricket: 'The England set-up is superb. If this is to be maintained, then two quality overseas players is a must, with nine English-born players learning from them. "Kolpak" [see page 9] will do to English cricket what "quota system" is doing to South African first-class and Zimbabwean cricket.'
Best batting: 236 Warwickshire v OUCCE, The Parks 2001
Best bowling: 2-16 Warwickshire v Oxford University, The Parks 1998

2005 Season

	M	Inns	NO	Runs	HS	Avge	100s	50s	Ct	St	O	M	Runs	Wkts	Avge	Best	5wl	10wM
Test																		
All First	13	22	2	608	146	30.40	1	2	8	-	11	4	30	1	30.00	1-16	-	-
1-Day Int																		
C & G	1	1	1	44	44*	-	-	-	1	-								
tsL	7	5	2	92	39	30.66	-	-	2	-								
Twenty20	3	3	1	61	40*	30.50	-	-	3	-								

Career Performances

	M	Inns	NO	Runs	HS	Avge	100s	50s	Ct	St	Balls	Runs	Wkts	Avge	Best	5wl	10wM
Test																	
All First	125	208	9	6511	236	32.71	12	35	89	-	1194	657	11	59.72	2-16	-	-
1-Day Int																	
C & G	12	12	2	215	44*	21.50	-	-	9	-	42	40	5	8.00	5-40	1	
tsL	66	52	9	1079	78	25.09	-	2	27	-	467	415	14	29.64	3-44	-	
Twenty20	3	3	1	61	40*	30.50	-	-	3	-							

POWELL, M. J. Glamorgan

Name: <u>Michael</u> John Powell
Role: Right-hand bat
Born: 3 February 1977, Abergavenny
Height: 6ft 1in **Weight:** 14st 8lbs
Nickname: Powelly
County debut: 1997
County cap: 2000
1000 runs in a season: 4
1st-Class 200s: 1
Place in batting averages: 105th av. 34.80
(2004 103rd av. 36.00)
Strike rate: (career 82.00)
Parents: Linda and John
Marital status: Single
Family links with cricket: 'Dad John and
Uncle Mike both played for Abergavenny'
Education: Crickhowell Secondary School;
Pontypool College
Qualifications: 5 GCSEs, BTEC National Diploma in Sports Science, Level 1
coaching award
Overseas tours: Glamorgan to Cape Town 1999, 2002; England A to Sri Lanka
2004-05
Overseas teams played for: Wests, Brisbane 1996-97; Cornwall CC, Auckland
1998-99, 2000-01
Cricket moments to forget: 'You wouldn't want to forget any of it'
Cricket superstitions: 'None'
Other sports played: Rugby (Crickhowell RFC)
Other sports followed: Rugby (Cardiff)
Relaxations: Eating and sleeping
Extras: Scored 200* on first-class debut v Oxford University at The Parks 1997.
Second XI Championship Player of the Year 1997 (1210 runs at 75.63). NBC Denis
Compton Award for the most promising young Glamorgan player 2000. Acted as 12th
man in the third Test v Sri Lanka at Old Trafford 2002, taking the catch that ended Sri
Lanka's second innings. Included in England one-day squad for NatWest Series 2004.
ECB National Academy 2004-05
Best batting: 200* Glamorgan v Oxford University, The Parks 1997
Best bowling: 2-39 Glamorgan v Oxford University, The Parks 1999

2005 Season

	M	Inns	NO	Runs	HS	Avge	100s	50s	Ct	St	O	M	Runs	Wkts	Avge	Best	5wl	10wM
Test																		
All First	17	32	2	1044	111	34.80	1	6	10	-								
1-Day Int																		
C & G	2	2	0	56	56	28.00	-	1	-	-								
tsL	14	12	2	432	83 *	43.20	-	4	14	-								
Twenty20	7	6	1	178	68 *	35.60	-	2	2	-								

Career Performances

	M	Inns	NO	Runs	HS	Avge	100s	50s	Ct	St	Balls	Runs	Wkts	Avge	Best	5wl	10wM
Test																	
All First	138	233	20	8118	200 *	38.11	17	42	87	-	164	132	2	66.00	2-39	-	-
1-Day Int																	
C & G	15	15	2	223	56	17.15	-	2	5	-	24	26	1	26.00	1-26	-	
tsL	124	115	17	3035	91 *	30.96	-	16	49	-							
Twenty20	17	16	2	327	68 *	23.35	-	3	7	-							

POYNTER, A. D.   Middlesex

Name: <u>Andrew</u> David Poynter
Role: Right-hand bat, right-arm
off-spin bowler
Born: 25 April 1987, Hammersmith, London
Height: 5ft 8in **Weight:** 12st
Nickname: AP, Poyntz
County debut: 2005
Parents: Wendy and David
Marital status: Single
Family links with cricket: 'Mum scored for
the 1st XI at Sunbury and later made teas.
Dad played in the 4th XI on Saturdays and
my uncle (Deryck Vincent) played for
Ireland'
Education: Teddington School; Esher
College; St Mary's College, Twickenham
Qualifications: 9 GCSEs, 3 A-levels, Level 1
cricket coaching
Career outside cricket: 'Full-time student; part-time cricket coach'
Off-season: 'Training for and going to the U19 World Cup with Ireland. Playing
hockey for Sunbury and studying for degree'
Overseas tours: Sunbury CC to Tobago 2004; Ireland U19 to Sri Lanka (U19 World
Cup) 2005-06

Career highlights to date: 'Making my first-class debut for Middlesex and being selected for the Ireland U19 World Cup squad'

Cricket moments to forget: 'All the ducks in my career'

Cricket superstitions: 'Always put my helmet and gloves on whilst on the way to the wicket'

Cricketers particularly admired: Sachin Tendulkar, Andrew Flintoff, Adam Stanier, Michael Vaughan

Young players to look out for: Billy Godleman, Eoin Morgan, Stuart Poynter

Other sports played: Hockey (South East of England U13, U15 and U17)

Other sports followed: Football (Tottenham Hotspur FC)

Favourite band: Kaiser Chiefs

Relaxations: 'Spending time with my girlfriend, Victoria; socialising with my friends outside of cricket'

Extras: Middlesex Youth Player of the Year 2004. Seaxe Best Batsman Award 2001, 2003

Opinions on cricket: 'Cricketers should be paid more according to their increased workload.'

Best batting: 1 Middlesex v CUCCE, Fenner's 2005

2005 Season

	M	Inns	NO	Runs	HS	Avge	100s	50s	Ct	St	O	M	Runs	Wkts	Avge	Best	5wI	10wM
Test																		
All First	1	1	0	1	1	1.00	-	-	2	-								
1-Day Int																		
C & G																		
tsL																		
Twenty20																		

Career Performances

	M	Inns	NO	Runs	HS	Avge	100s	50s	Ct	St	Balls	Runs	Wkts	Avge	Best	5wI	10wM
Test																	
All First	1	1	0	1	1	1.00	-	-	2	-							
1-Day Int																	
C & G																	
tsL																	
Twenty20																	

PRATT, G. J. Durham

Name: <u>Gary</u> Joseph Pratt
Role: Left-hand bat, right-arm spin bowler, wicket-keeper ('if I need to')
Born: 22 December 1981, Bishop Auckland
Height: 5ft 10in **Weight:** 10st 7lbs
Nickname: Gonzo, Gazza, Gates
County debut: 2000
1000 runs in a season: 1
Place in batting averages: (2004 224th av. 19.05)
Parents: Gordon and Brenda
Marital status: Single
Family links with cricket: Father played for many years in Durham and one brother was on Lord's groundstaff (MCC Young Cricketers). Brother Andrew also played for Durham

Education: Parkside Comprehensive
Qualifications: 9 GCSEs
Overseas tours: England U19 to Malaysia and (U19 World Cup) Sri Lanka 1999-2000, to India 2000-01
Overseas teams played for: Melville, Perth 2001-02
Cricket moments to forget: 'Getting my first pair in my cricket career v Gloucestershire'
Cricket superstitions: 'Right pad first'
Cricketers particularly admired: Steve Waugh, Graham Thorpe, David Gower
Young players to look out for: Mark Turner
Other sports played: Golf (14 handicap)
Other sports followed: Football ('all northern teams')
Favourite band: Stereophonics
Relaxations: 'Golf, TV, singing, socialising'
Extras: Represented England U17 and U19. NBC Denis Compton Award 1999. On his first-class debut, against Lancashire at Old Trafford 2000, he and brother Andrew became the first brothers to play in a Championship match for Durham. Durham Player of the Year 2002. Durham Fielder of the Year 2002, 2003. Durham Young Player of the Year 2003. Ran out Australia captain Ricky Ponting with a direct hit while fielding as a substitute for England in the fourth Test at Trent Bridge 2005
Best batting: 150 Durham v Northamptonshire, Riverside 2003

2005 Season

	M	Inns	NO	Runs	HS	Avge	100s	50s	Ct	St	O	M	Runs	Wkts	Avge	Best	5wI	10wM
Test																		
All First																		
1-Day Int																		
C & G																		
tsL	6	5	3	102	38 *	51.00	-	-	2	-								
Twenty20	7	7	0	69	23	9.85	-	-	3	-								

Career Performances

	M	Inns	NO	Runs	HS	Avge	100s	50s	Ct	St	Balls	Runs	Wkts	Avge	Best	5wI	10wM
Test																	
All First	47	84	1	2217	150	26.71	1	14	32	-	33	19	0	-	-	-	-
1-Day Int																	
C & G	6	6	1	154	89	30.80	-	1	-	-							
tsL	57	52	15	1314	101 *	35.51	1	9	29	-							
Twenty20	17	17	2	248	62 *	16.53	-	1	6	-							

PRETORIUS, D. Warwickshire

Name: Dewald Pretorius
Role: Right-hand bat, right-arm fast bowler
Born: 6 December 1977, Pretoria, South Africa
County debut: 2003 (Durham), 2004 (Warwickshire)
Test debut: 2001-02
Place in bowling averages: 102nd av. 38.66 (2004 115th av. 39.00)
Strike rate: 63.25 (career 49.40)
Overseas tours: South African Academy to Ireland and Scotland 1999; South Africa A to Australia 2002-03; South Africa to England 2003
Overseas teams played for: Free State 1998-99 – 2003-04
Extras: Was leading wicket-taker in South African first-class cricket 2001-02 with 42 wickets (av. 23.35) in nine matches. Represented South Africa A v Australians at Port Elizabeth 2001-02, taking 5-148 in the tourists' only innings. An overseas player with Durham for part of 2003; an overseas player with Warwickshire 2004; not considered an overseas player for 2005. Retired at the end of the 2005 season

Best batting: 43 Free State v Western Province, Bloemfontein 1998-99
Best bowling: 6-49 South Africa A v India A, Bloemfontein 2001-02

2005 Season

	M	Inns	NO	Runs	HS	Avge	100s	50s	Ct	St	O	M	Runs	Wkts	Avge	Best	5wI	10wM
Test																		
All First	6	6	2	56	22	14.00	-	-	3	-	126.3	13	464	12	38.66	3-88	-	-
1-Day Int																		
C & G																		
tsL	5	0	0	0	0	-	-	-	-	-	41.3	3	188	10	18.80	5-32	1	
Twenty20	9	7	3	59	22	14.75	-	-	8	-	18.2	0	156	6	26.00	2-22	-	

Career Performances

	M	Inns	NO	Runs	HS	Avge	100s	50s	Ct	St	Balls	Runs	Wkts	Avge	Best	5wI	10wM
Test	4	4	1	22	9	7.33	-	-	-	-	570	430	6	71.66	4-115	-	-
All First	67	71	19	508	43	9.76	-	-	16	-	11413	6330	231	27.40	6-49	7	-
1-Day Int																	
C & G	3	1	0	2	2	2.00	-	-	1	-	180	103	8	12.87	3-32	-	
tsL	15	6	1	9	7*	1.80	-	-	4	-	665	502	29	17.31	5-32	1	
Twenty20	11	7	3	59	22	14.75	-	-	9	-	140	196	8	24.50	2-22	-	

PRICE, R. W. — Worcestershire

Name: Raymond (Ray) William Price
Role: Right-hand bat, slow left-arm spin bowler
Born: 12 June 1976, Harare, Zimbabwe
Height: 6ft 1in **Weight:** 13st
Nickname: Razor, Razorback
County debut: 2004
County colours: 2004
Test debut: 1999-2000
Place in bowling averages: 73rd av. 32.13 (2004 121st av. 42.00)
Strike rate: 74.50 (career 70.04)
Parents: Tim and Pam
Wife and date of marriage: Julie, 13 July 2003
Family links with cricket: Father captained Zimbabwe Schools XI
Education: Watershed College, Zimbabwe
Qualifications: 7 GCEs, 2 A-levels, refrigeration and air conditioning mechanic
Career outside cricket: 'Fishing'

Overseas tours: Zimbabwe A to Sri Lanka 1999-2000, to Kenya 2001-02; Zimbabwe to India 2001-02, to Sri Lanka (ICC Champions Trophy) 2002-03, to Sharjah (Cherry Blossom Sharjah Cup) 2002-03, to England 2003, to Australia 2003-04
Overseas teams played for: Midlands, Zimbabwe 1999-2000 – 2003-04; Old Hararians
Career highlights to date: 'Six wickets v Australia at Sydney 2003-04. Tendulkar twice in same Test' (*In the second Test v India at Delhi 2001-02*)
Cricket moments to forget: 'Missed stumping off first ball in Test cricket'
Cricket superstitions: 'None'
Cricketers particularly admired: Steve Waugh, Heath Streak, Andy Flower, Sachin Tendulkar, Shane Warne
Other sports played: Tennis, squash, golf
Other sports followed: BASS League USA (Jerry Joost)
Favourite band: Dire Straits
Relaxations: Fishing, walking
Extras: Took 33 wickets in six Tests 2003-04, including 6-121 in Australia's first innings of the second Test at Sydney and 19 wickets (av. 20.84) in two-Test home series v West Indies. Zimbabwe Cricketer of the Year. Is nephew of golfer Nick Price. Is not considered an overseas player
Opinions on cricket: 'Twenty20 should be played at schools to get more young people interested.'
Best batting: 117* Midlands v Manicaland, Mutare 2003-04
Best bowling: 8-35 Midlands v CFX Academy, Kwekwe 2001-02

2005 Season

	M	Inns	NO	Runs	HS	Avge	100s	50s	Ct	St	O	M	Runs	Wkts	Avge	Best	5wI	10wM
Test																		
All First	10	13	1	101	20	8.41	-	-	6	-	372.3	90	964	30	32.13	4-64	-	-
1-Day Int																		
C & G	2	0	0	0	0	-	-	-	-	-	20	1	74	4	18.50	2-37	-	
tsL	15	8	1	18	7	2.57	-	-	4	-	122	9	447	19	23.52	4-21	-	
Twenty20	3	0	0	0	0	-	-	-	1	-	8	0	89	1	89.00	1-26	-	

Career Performances

	M	Inns	NO	Runs	HS	Avge	100s	50s	Ct	St	Balls	Runs	Wkts	Avge	Best	5wI	10wM
Test	18	30	7	224	36	9.73	-	-	3	-	5135	2475	69	35.86	6-73	5	1
All First	71	114	20	1502	117 *	15.97	1	6	24	-	17861	8170	255	32.03	8-35	15	3
1-Day Int	26	12	5	90	20 *	12.85	-	-	1	-	1322	917	15	61.13	2-16	-	
C & G	3	1	1	2	2 *	-	-	-	-	-	174	125	5	25.00	2-37	-	
tsL	18	8	1	18	7	2.57	-	-	4	-	798	511	21	24.33	4-21	-	
Twenty20	3	0	0	0	0	-	-	-	1	-	48	89	1	89.00	1-26	-	

PRIOR, M. J.

Sussex

Name: Matthew (<u>Matt</u>) James Prior
Role: Right-hand bat, wicket-keeper
Born: 26 February 1982, Johannesburg,
South Africa
Height: 5ft 11in **Weight:** 13st
Nickname: MP, Cheese
County debut: 2001
County cap: 2003
1000 runs in a season: 2
1st-Class 200s: 1
Place in batting averages: 117th av. 33.61
(2004 52nd av. 46.32)
Parents: Michael and Teresa
Marital status: Engaged
Education: Brighton College, East Sussex
Qualifications: 9 GCSEs, 3 A-levels, Level 1
coaching certificate

Overseas tours: Brighton College to India
1997-98; Sussex Academy to Cape Town 1999; Sussex to Grenada 2001, 2002;
England A to Malaysia and India 2003-04, to Sri Lanka 2004-05; England to
Zimbabwe (one-day series) 2004-05, to Pakistan 2005-06, to India 2005-06
Cricket moments to forget: 'Falling on to stumps at the Rose Bowl on Sky TV!'
Cricket superstitions: 'Too many to name all of them'
Cricketers particularly admired: Steve Waugh, Alec Stewart, Mushtaq Ahmed,
Murray Goodwin
Young players to look out for: Bilal Shafayat, Michael Lumb
Other sports played: Golf
Other sports followed: Football (Arsenal), golf, rugby
Favourite band: Red Hot Chili Peppers
Relaxations: 'Gym, listening to music'
Extras: Has played for Sussex since U12. Represented England U14-U19, captaining
England U17. NBC Denis Compton Award for the most promising young Sussex
player 2001, 2002, 2003. Umer Rashid Award for Most Improved [Sussex] Player
2003. ECB National Academy 2003-04, 2004-05
Best batting: 201* Sussex v LUCCE, Hove 2004

2005 Season

	M	Inns	NO	Runs	HS	Avge	100s	50s	Ct	St	O	M	Runs	Wkts	Avge	Best	5wI	10wM
Test																		
All First	17	27	1	874	109	33.61	2	6	45	1								
1-Day Int																		
C & G	3	3	0	117	59	39.00	-	1	3	2								
tsL	17	17	1	660	144	41.25	1	5	16	4								
Twenty20	6	4	1	159	66 *	53.00	-	2	5	-								

Career Performances

	M	Inns	NO	Runs	HS	Avge	100s	50s	Ct	St	Balls	Runs	Wkts	Avge	Best	5wI	10wM
Test																	
All First	88	138	13	4742	201 *	37.93	11	25	190	7							
1-Day Int	1	1	0	35	35	35.00	-	-	1	-							
C & G	12	11	0	205	59	18.63	-	1	15	2							
tsL	72	64	6	1660	144	28.62	2	11	44	9							
Twenty20	15	13	2	363	68 *	33.00		3	11	1							

PRITTIPAUL, L. R.　　　　Hampshire

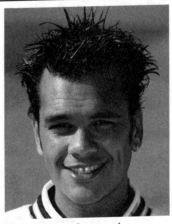

Name: <u>Lawrence</u> Roland Prittipaul
Role: Right-hand bat, right-arm
medium-fast bowler; all-rounder
Born: 19 October 1979, Portsmouth
Height: 6ft **Weight:** 12st 7lbs
Nickname: Lozza, Lawrie, Throat
County debut: 1999 (one-day),
2000 (first-class)
Place in batting averages: (2004 172nd
av. 25.66)
Strike rate: (career 84.33)
Parents: Roland and Christine
Marital status: Single
Family links with cricket: Cousin
Shivnarine Chanderpaul plays for West Indies
Education: St John's College, Southsea
Qualifications: GCSEs, GNVQ, Level 2
coaching, first aid
Overseas tours: Hampshire to Cape Town 2001; MCC to Sierra Leone and
Nigeria 2003
Overseas teams played for: Milnerton, Cape Town 2000-02; Old Edwardian
(Old Eds), Johannesburg 2003; Rockingham, Perth 2003-04

Career highlights to date: '152 v Derbyshire on home debut'
Cricketers particularly admired: Carl Hooper, Shane Warne
Young players to look out for: David Griffiths, Archie Ayling, Deano Wilson
Other sports played: Football
Other sports followed: Football ('Pompey!!')
Favourite band: Counting Crows
Relaxations: 'Films, spending time with friends, holidays'
Extras: Played for Hants Colts from age 11 to 18. Represented England U17. Won Player of the Year award in Southern League 1998. Scored over 1000 runs for Hampshire 2nd XI in 1999. Scored 152 on home debut, v Derbyshire at Southampton 2000. Hampshire Young Player of the Year 2000. Released by Hampshire at the end of the 2005 season
Opinions on cricket: 'More games need to end in results – need to play to win more.'
Best batting: 152 Hampshire v Derbyshire, Southampton 2000
Best bowling: 3-17 Hampshire v Worcestershire, West End 2003

2005 Season

	M	Inns	NO	Runs	HS	Avge	100s	50s	Ct	St	O	M	Runs	Wkts	Avge	Best	5wI	10wM
Test																		
All First																		
1-Day Int																		
C & G																		
tsL	3	2	0	26	23	13.00	-	-	-	-								
Twenty20	7	5	1	54	35	13.50	-	-	3	-	4	0	42	0	-		-	-

Career Performances

	M	Inns	NO	Runs	HS	Avge	100s	50s	Ct	St	Balls	Runs	Wkts	Avge	Best	5wI	10wM
Test																	
All First	23	36	2	975	152	28.67	1	4	17	-	759	443	9	49.22	3-17	-	-
1-Day Int																	
C & G	5	5	0	76	30	15.20	-	-	4	-	180	136	7	19.42	3-11	-	
tsL	55	42	5	488	61	13.18	-	1	13	-	748	697	15	46.46	3-33	-	
Twenty20	13	9	1	84	35	10.50	-	-	5	-	83	109	2	54.50	2-17	-	

72. Who captained his country in 86 ODIs between 1996 and 2002 and was awarded honorary life membership of MCC in 2005?

PYRAH, R. M. *Yorkshire*

Name: Richard (<u>Rich</u>) Michael Pyrah
Role: Right-hand bat, right-arm
medium bowler
Born: 1 November 1982, Dewsbury
Height: 6ft **Weight:** 12st
Nickname: RP, Pyro
County debut: 2004
Place in batting averages: (2004 168th
av. 26.33)
Strike rate: (career 32.00)
Parents: Mick and Lesley
Marital status: Single
Family links with cricket: 'Dad and
Grandad both played for Ossett CC'
Education: Ossett High School;
Wakefield College
Qualifications: 10 GCSEs, Level 1 coaching
Overseas teams played for: Kaponga, New
Zealand 2000-02; Taranaki, New Zealand 2003-04
Career highlights to date: 'Making my debut for Yorkshire on Sky. Man of the
Match in my second NCL game at Scarborough'
Cricket moments to forget: 'First ever pair!'
Cricket superstitions: 'Left pad on first. Bat in some whites'
Cricketers particularly admired: Michael Vaughan, Matthew Wood
Young players to look out for: Mark Lawson, John Sadler
Other sports played: Golf
Other sports followed: Football (Leeds United)
Favourite band: Oasis, Evanescence
Relaxations: Xbox
Extras: C&G Man of the Match award for his 5-50 (plus 26 runs) for Yorkshire Board
XI v Somerset at Scarborough in the third round 2002
Best batting: 78 Yorkshire v Worcestershire, Worcester 2005
Best bowling: 1-4 Yorkshire v Bangladesh A, Headingley 2005

2005 Season

	M	Inns	NO	Runs	HS	Avge	100s	50s	Ct	St	O	M	Runs	Wkts	Avge	Best	5wl	10wM
Test																		
All First	2	3	0	78	78	26.00	-	1	1	-	10	2	34	3	11.33	1-4	-	-
1-Day Int																		
C & G	2	2	0	12	11	6.00	-	-	1	-	2	0	20	0	-		-	-
tsL	8	8	2	78	28*	13.00	-	-	2	-	10	0	87	1	87.00	1-41	-	
Twenty20	8	7	3	100	33*	25.00	-	-	3	-	3	0	26	0	-		-	-

Career Performances

	M	Inns	NO	Runs	HS	Avge	100s	50s	Ct	St	Balls	Runs	Wkts	Avge	Best	5wl	10wM
Test																	
All First	6	10	1	236	78	26.22	-	1	1	-	96	36	3	12.00	1-4	-	-
1-Day Int																	
C & G	6	6	0	118	27	19.66	-	-	3	-	114	118	7	16.85	5-50	1	
tsL	10	10	2	122	42	15.25	-	-	2	-	90	104	3	34.66	2-17	-	
Twenty20	8	7	3	100	33 *	25.00	-	-	3	-	18	26	0	-	-	-	

RAMPRAKASH, M. R.   Surrey

Name: <u>Mark</u> Ravindra Ramprakash
Role: Right-hand bat, right arm off-spin bowler
Born: 5 September 1969, Bushey, Herts
Height: 5ft 10in **Weight:** 12st 4lbs
Nickname: Ramps, Bloodaxe
County debut: 1987 (Middlesex), 2001 (Surrey)
County cap: 1990 (Middlesex), 2002 (Surrey)
Benefit: 2000 (Middlesex)
Test debut: 1991
1000 runs in a season: 15
1st-Class 200s: 10
Place in batting averages: 3rd av. 74.66 (2004 7th av. 65.16)
Strike rate: (career 122.50)
Parents: Deonarine and Jennifer
Date of marriage: 24 September 1993
Children: Two
Family links with cricket: Father played club cricket in Guyana
Education: Gayton High School; Harrow Weald Sixth Form College
Qualifications: 6 O-levels, 2 A-levels, Level 3 cricket coach, Level 2 FA football coach
Overseas tours: England YC to Sri Lanka 1986-87, to Australia (U19 World Cup) 1987-88; England A to Pakistan 1990-91, to West Indies 1991-92, to India 1994-95 (vc); Lion Cubs to Barbados 1993; England to New Zealand 1991-92, to West Indies 1993-94, to Australia 1994-95, to South Africa 1995-96, to West Indies 1997-98, to Australia 1998-99, to South Africa 1999-2000, to Zimbabwe (one-day series) 2001-02, to India and New Zealand 2001-02
Overseas teams played for: Nairobi Jafferys, Kenya 1988; North Melbourne 1989; University of Perth 1996-97; Clico-Preysal, Trinidad 2004

Career highlights to date: 'My two Test hundreds, v West Indies and Australia'
Cricket moments to forget: 'There are so many bad days!'
Cricket superstitions: 'Same piece of chewing gum in innings'
Cricketers particularly admired: 'All the great all-rounders'; Alec Stewart
Young players to look out for: Arun Harinath
Other sports played: Football (Corinthian Casuals FC, Arsenal Pro-Celeb XI)
Other sports followed: Football (Arsenal FC)
Favourite band: 'Have lost touch!'
Extras: Voted Best U15 Schoolboy of 1985 by Cricket Society (Sir John Hobbs Silver Jubilee Memorial Prize) and Cricket Society's Most Promising Young Cricketer of the Year 1988. Man of the Match for his 56 in Middlesex's NatWest Trophy final win in 1988, on his debut in the competition. Represented England YC. Cricket Writers' Young Cricketer of the Year 1991. Middlesex captain May 1997 to the end of the 1999 season. Man of the Match in the fifth Test v West Indies at Bridgetown 1997-98 (154). Leading run-scorer in the single-division four-day era of the County Championship with 8392 runs (av. 56.32) 1993-99. Became first player to score a Championship century against all 18 first-class counties with his 110 v Middlesex at Lord's 2003. Scored century in each innings of a Championship match (130/100*) for the fifth time, v Worcestershire at The Oval 2004. Surrey Players' Player of the Year 2003, 2004; Surrey Supporters' Player of the Year 2003, 2004. Vice-captain of Surrey 2004-05
Best batting: 279* Surrey v Nottinghamshire, Croydon 2003
Best bowling: 3-32 Middlesex v Glamorgan, Lord's 1998

2005 Season

	M	Inns	NO	Runs	HS	Avge	100s	50s	Ct	St	O	M	Runs	Wkts	Avge	Best	5wI	10wM
Test																		
All First	14	23	2	1568	252	74.66	6	5	8	-	2	0	6	0	-	-	-	-
1-Day Int																		
C & G	3	3	1	138	84	69.00	-	1	-									
tsL	15	15	1	445	89 *	31.78	-	3	6	-	16	0	99	1	99.00	1-26	-	
Twenty20	2	2	1	79	45	79.00	-	-	-									

Career Performances

	M	Inns	NO	Runs	HS	Avge	100s	50s	Ct	St	Balls	Runs	Wkts	Avge	Best	5wI	10wM
Test	52	92	6	2350	154	27.32	2	12	39	-	895	477	4	119.25	1-2	-	-
All First	371	612	77	26355	279 *	49.26	79	121	209	-	4165	2178	34	64.05	3-32	-	-
1-Day Int	18	18	4	376	51	26.85	-	1	8	-	132	108	4	27.00	3-28	-	
C & G	43	42	4	1453	107 *	38.23	3	6	20	-	396	255	10	25.50	2-15	-	
tsL	223	214	35	7287	147 *	40.70	6	54	68	-	654	602	18	33.44	5-38	1	
Twenty20	16	16	5	400	76 *	36.36	-	2	7	-							

RANKIN, W. B. Middlesex

Name: William Boyd Rankin
Role: Left-hand bat, right-arm
medium-fast bowler
Born: 5 July 1984, Londonderry
Height: 6ft 7in **Weight:** 16st 5lbs
Nickname: Boydo
County debut: No first-team appearance
Parents: Robert and Dawn
Marital status: Single
Family links with cricket: 'Both brothers –
Robert and David – play cricket for Ireland
youth teams'
Education: Strabane Grammar School;
Harper Adams University College
Qualifications: 11 GCSEs, 3 A-levels, Level
1 cricket coaching
Career outside cricket: 'University, farmer'
Off-season: 'Work placement; university;
cricket training with Ireland'
Overseas tours: Ireland U17 to Denmark 2000; Ireland A to Holland 2002, 2005;
Ireland U19 to Bangladesh (U19 World Cup) 2003-04
Career highlights to date: 'Making full debut for Ireland 2003. U19 World Cup,
Bangladesh 2004'
Cricket superstitions: 'None'
Cricketers particularly admired: Glenn McGrath
Young players to look out for: Eoin Morgan, Billy Godleman
Other sports played: Rugby, badminton, football
Other sports followed: Football (Liverpool FC)
Favourite band: Coldplay
Relaxations: 'Shooting; listening to music; reading autobiographies'
Extras: Attended European Cricket Academy in Spain

73. Which member of the 1997-98 Akai-Singer Champions Trophy
winning team had a great-grandfather, Charles Leslie, who played four
Tests for England in Australia in 1892-93?

RAYNER, O. P. Sussex

Name: Oliver (<u>Ollie</u>) Philip Rayner
Role: Right-hand bat, right-arm
off-spin bowler
Born: 1 November 1985, Walsrode, Germany
Height: 6ft 5¼in **Weight:** 16st
Nickname: Mervin, Rocket, Rain-cakes, KP
('Kelvin Pietersen, not Kevin!')
County debut: No first-team appearance
Parents: Mark and Penny
Marital status: Single (girlfriend)
Education: St Bede's, The Dicker,
East Sussex
Qualifications: 7 GCSEs, 2 A-levels, Level 1
coaching
Off-season: 'Overseas player (South Africa)'
Overseas tours: Sussex Academy to Sri
Lanka 2001, to South Africa 2003
Overseas teams played for: University of
Cape Town; Western Province

Career highlights to date: 'Getting contracted to Sussex. Getting into Sussex Academy. South of England U15. England Development Squad U19'
Cricket moments to forget: 'Chirping at Somerset, then getting a pair!'
Cricketers particularly admired: Andrew Flintoff, Shane Warne, Chris Gayle
Young players to look out for: Tom Smith, Krishna Singh
Other sports played: Football (Eastbourne Town Reserves; Eastbourne United 1st XI)
Other sports followed: Football (Brighton & Hove Albion)
Favourite band: Kanye West, Common, Talib Kwali
Relaxations: 'Body-boarding, skiing, chilling with mates'
Extras: Sussex 2nd XI Player of the Year 2005
Opinions on cricket: 'Progressing. Twenty20 good idea – exciting, appealing to audience. Ashes win will do no end of good to England cricket.'

READ, C. M. W.   Nottinghamshire

Name: Christopher (<u>Chris</u>) Mark Wells Read
Role: Right-hand bat, wicket-keeper
Born: 10 August 1978, Paignton
Height: 5ft 8in **Weight:** 11st
Nickname: Readie, Reados
County debut: 1997 (one-day, Glos),
1998 (Notts)
County cap: 1999 (Notts)
Test debut: 1999
50 dismissals in a season: 3
Place in batting averages: 55th av. 44.47
(2004 38th av. 50.43)
Parents: Geoffrey and Carolyn
Wife and date of marriage: Louise,
2 October 2004
Education: Torquay Boys' Grammar School;
University of Bath; Loughborough University
Qualifications: 9 GCSEs, 4 A-levels, senior
coaching award

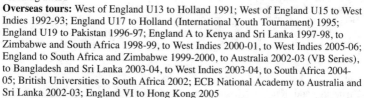

Overseas tours: West of England U13 to Holland 1991; West of England U15 to West
Indies 1992-93; England U17 to Holland (International Youth Tournament) 1995;
England U19 to Pakistan 1996-97; England A to Kenya and Sri Lanka 1997-98, to
Zimbabwe and South Africa 1998-99, to West Indies 2000-01, to West Indies 2005-06;
England to South Africa and Zimbabwe 1999-2000, to Australia 2002-03 (VB Series),
to Bangladesh and Sri Lanka 2003-04, to West Indies 2003-04, to South Africa 2004-
05; British Universities to South Africa 2002; ECB National Academy to Australia and
Sri Lanka 2002-03; England VI to Hong Kong 2005
Career highlights to date: 'Winning Test series v West Indies 2004'
Cricket moments to forget: 'Ducking a slower ball from Chris Cairns in second Test
v New Zealand at Lord's 1999'
Cricketers particularly admired: Adam Gilchrist, Bruce French, Alan Knott,
Bob Taylor, Jack Russell, Ian Healy
Young players to look out for: James Hildreth
Other sports played: Hockey (Devon U18, U21; West of England U17; South
Nottingham)
Other sports followed: Football (Torquay United)
Favourite band: Stereophonics
Relaxations: 'Reading, listening to music, keeping fit and going out with friends'
Extras: Played for Devon 1995-97. Represented England U18 1996 and England U19
1997. Was selected for the England A tour to Kenya and Sri Lanka 1997-98 aged 18
and without having played a first-class game. Recorded eight dismissals on Test debut

in the first Test v New Zealand at Edgbaston 1999. Man of the Match in the first ODI v West Indies at Georgetown 2003-04 after striking a match-winning 15-ball 27 including three sixes and a four. ECB National Academy 2005-06

Opinions on cricket: 'Temporary floodlights at domestic day/night games (totesport League) often inadequate. Too many non-English-qualified players!'

Best batting: 160 Nottinghamshire v Warwickshire, Trent Bridge 1999

2005 Season

	M	Inns	NO	Runs	HS	Avge	100s	50s	Ct	St	O	M	Runs	Wkts	Avge	Best	5wl	10wM
Test																		
All First	16	21	4	756	103 *	44.47	1	7	62	2								
1-Day Int																		
C & G	2	1	0	16	16	16.00	-	-	2	-								
tsL	14	12	2	342	68 *	34.20	-	1	13	2								
Twenty20	8	8	2	235	44 *	39.16	-	-	6	1								

Career Performances

	M	Inns	NO	Runs	HS	Avge	100s	50s	Ct	St	Balls	Runs	Wkts	Avge	Best	5wl	10wM
Test	11	16	3	199	38 *	15.30	-	-	31	4							
All First	155	233	36	5838	160	29.63	5	33	440	22	18	25	0	-	-	-	-
1-Day Int	28	17	6	239	30 *	21.72	-	-	36	2							
C & G	18	14	4	334	77 *	33.40	-	2	16	7							
tsL	114	96	21	2045	119 *	27.26	1	4	120	28							
Twenty20	13	13	3	339	44 *	33.90	-	-	11	2							

---

74. Which two South Africans who appeared in their country's international comeback series of ODIs against India in 1991-92 subsequently played for Somerset?

REES, G. P. Glamorgan

Name: <u>Gareth</u> Peter Rees
Role: Left-hand opening bat
Born: 8 April 1985, Swansea
Height: 6ft 1in **Weight:** 14st 8lbs
Nickname: Gums
County debut: No first-team appearance
Parents: Peter and Diane
Marital status: Single
Education: Coedcae Comprehensive, Llanelli; Coleg Sir Gar; Bath University
Qualifications: 10 GCSEs, 3 A-levels, 'doing Maths and Physics degree'
Career outside cricket: Student
Off-season: 'Final year at university'
Career highlights to date: 'Getting first hundred for 2nd team'
Cricket moments to forget: 'Getting out first ball next game'
Cricket superstitions: 'Left pad on first'
Cricketers particularly admired: Brian Lara
Young players to look out for: Ben Wright, Mike O'Shea
Other sports played: Rugby (Wales U17, Llanelli Scarlets U21)
Favourite band: Oasis
Extras: Made 2nd XI Championship debut 2003. Played for Wales Minor Counties in the C&G 2004, 2005. Is on a development contract at Glamorgan
Opinions on cricket: 'The game today is becoming much more entertaining.'

2005 Season (did not make any first-class or one-day appearances for his county)

Career Performances

	M	Inns	NO	Runs	HS	Avge	100s	50s	Ct	St	Balls	Runs	Wkts	Avge	Best	5wI	10wM
Test																	
All First																	
1-Day Int																	
C & G	3	3	0	38	15	12.66	-	-	1	-							
tsL																	
Twenty20																	

RICHARDSON, A.   Middlesex

Name: Alan Richardson
Role: Right-hand bat, right-arm
medium bowler
Born: 6 May 1975, Newcastle-under-Lyme,
Staffs
Height: 6ft 2in **Weight:** 13st
Nickname: Richo
County debut: 1995 (Derbyshire),
1999 (Warwickshire), 2005 (Middlesex)
County cap: 2002 (Warwickshire),
2005 (Middlesex)
50 wickets in a season: 1
Place in batting averages: 266th av. 12.45
Place in bowling averages: 23rd av. 25.22
Strike rate: 49.64 (career 63.03)
Parents: Roy and Sandra
Marital status: Single
Family links with cricket: 'Dad captained
Little Stoke 3rd XI and now patrols the boundary with pint in hand at the Sid Jenkins
Cricket Ground'
Education: Alleyne's High School, Stone; Stafford College of Further Education
Qualifications: 8 GCSEs, 2 A-levels, 2 AS-levels, Level 2 cricket coach
Career outside cricket: Landscape gardener
Overseas tours: Derbyshire to Malaga 1995; Warwickshire to Bloemfontein 2000,
to Cape Town 2001, 2002, to Portugal 2003
Overseas teams played for: Northern Natal, South Africa 1994-96; Hawkesbury CC,
Sydney 1997-99; Northern Districts, Sydney 1999-2000, 2001-03; Avendale, Cape
Town 2000-01; Kyriang Mountains, Australia 2003-04
Cricket superstitions: 'None'
Cricketers particularly admired: Angus Fraser, Neil Smith, Ian Carr
Players to look out for: Moeen Ali
Other sports followed: Football (Stoke City – 'bordering on fanatical')
Favourite band: The Zutons, Kasabian
Extras: *Cricket World* award for best bowling performance in Oxford U19 Festival
(8-60 v Devon). Topped Minor Counties bowling averages with Staffordshire 1998 and
won Minor Counties bowling award. Most Improved 2nd XI Player 1999. Outstanding
Performance of the Year 1999 for his 8-51 v Gloucestershire on home debut. Scored
91 v Hampshire at Edgbaston 2002, in the process sharing with Nick Knight (255*) in
a Warwickshire record tenth-wicket stand of 214. Had first innings figures of 7-113 on
first-class debut for Middlesex v Nottinghamshire at Lord's 2005. Took 50 first-class
wickets (57) in a season for the first time 2005
Opinions on cricket: 'Longer teas. Less bouncers at tail-enders!'

Best batting: 91 Warwickshire v Hampshire, Edgbaston 2002
Best bowling: 8-46 Warwickshire v Sussex, Edgbaston 2002

2005 Season

	M	Inns	NO	Runs	HS	Avge	100s	50s	Ct	St	O	M	Runs	Wkts	Avge	Best	5wl	10wM
Test																		
All First	13	16	5	137	25	12.45	-	-	2	-	471.4	109	1438	57	25.22	7-113	3	-
1-Day Int																		
C & G	2	1	1	1	1 *	-	-	-	-	-	17	3	68	3	22.66	3-46	-	
tsL	11	4	3	35	21 *	35.00	-	-	1	-	90.3	3	426	8	53.25	2-45	-	
Twenty20	2	0	0	0	0	-	-	-	-	-	8	0	68	1	68.00	1-29	-	

Career Performances

	M	Inns	NO	Runs	HS	Avge	100s	50s	Ct	St	Balls	Runs	Wkts	Avge	Best	5wl	10wM
Test																	
All First	77	78	30	529	91	11.02	-	1	20	-	14056	6857	223	30.74	8-46	7	1
1-Day Int																	
C & G	8	6	3	5	3	1.66	-	-	2	-	408	298	10	29.80	5-35	1	
tsL	40	16	11	89	21 *	17.80	-	-	7	-	1732	1394	36	38.72	3-17	-	
Twenty20	5	1	1	6	6 *	-	-	-	1	-	102	120	4	30.00	3-13	-	

ROBERTS, T. W. Northamptonshire

Name: Timothy (<u>Tim</u>) William Roberts
Role: Right-hand bat, right-arm off-spin bowler
Born: 4 March 1978, Kettering
Height: 5ft 8in **Weight:** 11st
Nickname: Robbo
County debut: 2001 (Lancashire), 2003 (Northamptonshire)
Place in batting averages: (2004 162nd av. 27.70)
Strike rate: (career 114.00)
Parents: Dave and Shirley
Marital status: Single
Family links with cricket: 'Brother Andy was a leg-spinner at Northants; Dad had trials for Northants'
Education: Bishop Stopford School, Kettering; Durham University
Qualifications: 2.1 degree in Geology, Level 3 cricket coach
Career outside cricket: Teaching/coaching

Overseas tours: England U17 to Holland (International Youth Tournament) 1995; Lancashire to South Africa 2000, 2001
Overseas teams played for: Eastern Suburbs, Wellington, New Zealand 1999-2000
Cricketers particularly admired: Andy Roberts, Mike Hussey
Other sports played: Golf, football, squash, badminton
Other sports followed: Football (Rushden & Diamonds FC)
Favourite band: Oasis
Relaxations: 'Having a few Coronas with the lads at Finedon Dolben CC'
Extras: Represented British Universities 1999. Scored 83 on Championship debut for Northamptonshire v Somerset at Northampton 2003, his first two scoring strokes being a four and a six. Released by Northamptonshire at the end of the 2005 season
Best batting: 89 Northamptonshire v Lancashire, Northampton 2004
Best bowling: 1-10 Northamptonshire v DUCCE, Northampton 2004

2005 Season

	M	Inns	NO	Runs	HS	Avge	100s	50s	Ct	St	O	M	Runs	Wkts	Avge	Best	5wI	10wM
Test																		
All First	3	5	0	114	53	22.80	-	1	-	-								
1-Day Int																		
C & G	2	2	1	51	31	51.00	-	-	-	-								
tsL	5	4	0	122	90	30.50	-	1	1	-								
Twenty20	7	7	1	77	43	12.83	-	-	-	-								

Career Performances

	M	Inns	NO	Runs	HS	Avge	100s	50s	Ct	St	Balls	Runs	Wkts	Avge	Best	5wI	10wM
Test																	
All First	32	51	2	1235	89	25.20	-	9	21	-	114	20	1	20.00	1-10	-	-
1-Day Int																	
C & G	6	6	1	153	48	30.60	-	-	1	-							
tsL	35	34	0	926	131	27.23	2	5	8	-	36	35	0	-	-	-	
Twenty20	12	11	2	167	43	18.55	-	-	1	-							

75. Who holds the record for the most ODI wickets in a calendar year and has recorded two ODI hat-tricks against Zimbabwe?

ROBINSON, D. D. J.   Leicestershire

Name: <u>Darren</u> David John Robinson
Role: Right-hand bat, leg-spin bowler
Born: 2 March 1973, Braintree, Essex
Height: 5ft 11in **Weight:** 14st
Nickname: Pies, Pie Shop, Robbo
County debut: 1993 (Essex),
2004 (Leicestershire)
County cap: 1997 (Essex)
1000 runs in a season: 3
1st-Class 200s: 1
Place in batting averages: 63rd av. 42.61
(2004 82nd av. 38.82)
Strike rate: (career 272.00)
Parents: Dorothy (deceased) and David
Wife and date of marriage: Alyssa,
2 December 2001
Children: Kalli, 20 July 1998; Cameron, 20
May 2000; Evie, 30 October 2002
Family links with cricket: Father club cricketer for Halstead
Education: Tabor High School, Braintree; Chelmsford College of Further Education
Qualifications: 5 GCSEs, BTEC National Diploma in Building and Construction
Career outside cricket: Site investigation and surveying
Overseas tours: England U18 to Canada (International Youth Tournament) 1991;
England U19 to Pakistan 1991-92
Overseas teams played for: Waverley, Sydney 1992-94; Eden Roskill CC,
Auckland 1995-96
Career highlights to date: 'Every trophy won'
Cricket moments to forget: 'Being bowled out for 57 against Lancashire in the
NatWest final [1996]'
Cricket superstitions: 'None'
Cricketers particularly admired: Steve Hale, David Denny
Young players to look out for: Alastair Cook, Ravinder Bopara
Other sports played: Football, golf, squash
Other sports followed: Golf, football, rugby, swimming
Relaxations: Reading, music
Extras: International Youth Tournament in Canada batting award 1991. Scored two
centuries (102/118*) in match v Leicestershire at Chelmsford 2001. Essex Player of
the Year 2002. Scored 81 v Australians at Leicester 2005, in the process sharing with
Chris Rogers (209) in a record opening partnership for a county against an Australian
touring side (247)
Best batting: 200 Essex v New Zealanders, Chelmsford 1999
Best bowling: 1-7 Essex v Middlesex, Chelmsford 2003

2005 Season

	M	Inns	NO	Runs	HS	Avge	100s	50s	Ct	St	O	M	Runs	Wkts	Avge	Best	5wl	10wM
Test																		
All First	16	27	1	1108	139	42.61	4	4	13	-	2	0	3	0	-	-	-	-
1-Day Int																		
C & G																			
tsL	6	6	0	138	61	23.00	-	1	2	-								
Twenty20																			

Career Performances

	M	Inns	NO	Runs	HS	Avge	100s	50s	Ct	St	Balls	Runs	Wkts	Avge	Best	5wl	10wM
Test																	
All First	168	295	14	9344	200	33.25	20	46	142	-	272	282	1	282.00	1-7	-	-
1-Day Int																	
C & G	21	19	1	475	70	26.38	-	5	6	-							
tsL	128	123	10	2915	129 *	25.79	2	14	37	-	17	26	1	26.00	1-7	-	
Twenty20	2	2	0	12	7	6.00	-	-	1	-							

ROGERS, C. J. L.   Northamptonshire

Name: Christopher (Chris) John Llewellyn Rogers
Role: Left-hand bat, leg-spin/right-arm medium bowler
Born: 31 August 1977, Sydney, Australia
Height: 5ft 11in **Weight:** 12st 8lbs
County debut: 2004 (Derbyshire), 2005 (Leicestershire)
1st-Class 200s: 1
Place in batting averages: 4th av. 73.50 (2004 21st av. 55.33)
Family links with cricket: Father played for New South Wales and became cricket administrator
Overseas teams played for: Western Australia 1998-99 –
Extras: Represented Australia U19 1995-96. Has represented Australia A. Scored two centuries (101*/102*) in Pura Cup match v South Australia at Perth 2001-02, winning Man of the Match award. Won three Western Australia awards 2002-03 – Lawrie Sawle Medal (leading first-class and one-day player), President's Silver Trophy (season's best individual performance – for his 194 v NSW in the Pura Cup), and

Excalibur Award (spirit of WA cricket). An overseas player with Derbyshire 2004 but forced to return home early injured; an overseas player with Leicestershire during the 2005 season as a locum for Dinesh Mongia. Scored 209 v Australians at Leicester 2005, in the process sharing with Darren Robinson (81) in a record opening partnership for a county against an Australian touring side (247). Has joined Northamptonshire as an overseas player for 2006
Best batting: 209 Leicestershire v Australians, Leicester 2005

2005 Season

	M	Inns	NO	Runs	HS	Avge	100s	50s	Ct	St	O	M	Runs	Wkts	Avge	Best	5wI	10wM
Test																		
All First	3	6	0	441	209	73.50	1	2	4	-	5	0	14	0	-	-	-	-
1-Day Int																		
C & G																		
tsL	1	1	1	5	5*	-	-	-	-	2	-							
Twenty20	1	1	0	35	35	35.00	-	-	-	-								

Career Performances

	M	Inns	NO	Runs	HS	Avge	100s	50s	Ct	St	Balls	Runs	Wkts	Avge	Best	5wI	10wM
Test																	
All First	52	94	6	4040	209	45.90	11	19	52	-	48	26	0	-	-	-	-
1-Day Int																	
C & G	2	2	0	142	93	71.00	-	1	-	-							
tsL	4	4	1	46	27	15.33	-	-	4	-							
Twenty20	1	1	0	35	35	35.00	-	-	-	-							

76. What did New Zealand international batsman John F Reid's cousin achieve in 1986 at Sydney?

RUDGE, W. D.

Gloucestershire

Name: <u>William</u> Douglas Rudge
Role: Right-hand bat, right-arm
medium-fast bowler
Born: 15 July 1983, Bristol
County debut: 2005
County cap: 2005
Place in bowling averages: 91st av. 36.07
Strike rate: 47.21 (career 47.21)
Extras: Played for Gloucestershire Board XI
in the C&G 2002, 2003. NBC Denis
Compton Award for the most promising
young Gloucestershire player 2004
Best batting: 15 Gloucestershire v Surrey,
The Oval 2005
Best bowling: 3-46 Gloucestershire v
Bangladesh A, Bristol 2005

2005 Season

	M	Inns	NO	Runs	HS	Avge	100s	50s	Ct	St	O	M	Runs	Wkts	Avge	Best	5wI	10wM
Test																		
All First	5	8	1	35	15	5.00	-	-	2	-	110.1	21	505	14	36.07	3-46	-	-
1-Day Int																		
C & G																		
tsL																		
Twenty20																		

Career Performances

	M	Inns	NO	Runs	HS	Avge	100s	50s	Ct	St	Balls	Runs	Wkts	Avge	Best	5wI	10wM
Test																	
All First	5	8	1	35	15	5.00	-	-	2	-	661	505	14	36.07	3-46	-	-
1-Day Int																	
C & G	2	2	1	4	3	4.00	-	-	-	-	72	75	0	-	-	-	-
tsL																	
Twenty20																	

RUDOLPH, J. A. Derbyshire

Name: Jacobus (Jacques) Andries Rudolph
Role: Left-hand bat, right-arm
leg-spin bowler
Born: 4 May 1981, Springs, South Africa
County debut: No first-team appearance
Test debut: 2003
1st-Class 200s: 1
Strike rate: (career 66.44)
Overseas tours: South Africa U19 to
Pakistan 1998-99, to Sri Lanka (U19 World
Cup) 1999-2000; South Africa A to
Zimbabwe 2002-03, to Sri Lanka 2005-06;
South Africa to Australia 2001-02, to
Bangladesh 2003, to England 2003, to
Pakistan 2003-04, to New Zealand 2003-04,
to Sri Lanka 2004, to England (ICC
Champions Trophy) 2004, to India 2004-05,
to West Indies 2004-05, to Australia 2005-06

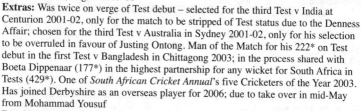

Overseas teams played for: Northerns B/Northerns 1997-98 – 2003-04;
Titans 2004-05; Eagles 2005-06
Extras: Was twice on verge of Test debut – selected for the third Test v India at
Centurion 2001-02, only for the match to be stripped of Test status due to the Denness
Affair; chosen for the third Test v Australia in Sydney 2001-02, only for his selection
to be overruled in favour of Justing Ontong. Man of the Match for his 222* on Test
debut in the first Test v Bangladesh in Chittagong 2003; in the process shared with
Boeta Dippenaar (177*) in the highest partnership for any wicket for South Africa in
Tests (429*). One of *South African Cricket Annual*'s five Cricketers of the Year 2003.
Has joined Derbyshire as an overseas player for 2006; due to take over in mid-May
from Mohammad Yousuf
Best batting: 222* South Africa v Bangladesh, Chittagong 2003
Best bowling: 5-87 Northerns B v Griqualand West B, Centurion 1998-99
Stop press: Scored second innings 102* to help save the first Test v Australia at Perth
2005-06. Made Twenty20 international debut v Australia at Brisbane 2005-06

Career Performances

	M	Inns	NO	Runs	HS	Avge	100s	50s	Ct	St	Balls	Runs	Wkts	Avge	Best	5wI	10wM
Test	27	47	6	1587	222 *	38.70	4	7	16	-	516	309	4	77.25	1-1	-	-
All First	76	135	9	5121	222 *	40.64	13	24	54	-	2857	1594	43	37.06	5-87	2	-
1-Day Int	39	33	5	1018	81	36.35	-	6	9	-	24	26	0	-	-	-	-
C & G																	
tsL																	
Twenty20																	

SADLER, J. L.   Leicestershire

Name: John Leonard Sadler
Role: Left-hand top-order bat,
leg-spin bowler
Born: 19 November 1981, Dewsbury
Height: 5ft 11in **Weight:** 12st 7lbs
Nickname: Sads
County debut: 2003 (*see Extras*)
Place in batting averages: 35th av. 50.33
(2004 182nd av. 24.60)
Strike rate: (career 87.00)
Parents: Michael and Sue
Marital status: Single
Family links with cricket: Father played for
25 years and now coaches. Brothers Dave and
Jamie play local league cricket; both played
for Yorkshire youth teams
Education: St Thomas à Becket RC School,
Wakefield
Qualifications: 9 GCSEs, Levels I and II coaching awards
Overseas tours: England U19 to Malaysia and (U19 World Cup) Sri Lanka
1999-2000, to India 2000-01; Yorkshire to Grenada 2002
Overseas teams played for: Tuart Hill, Perth 2001-04
Career highlights to date: 'First first-class 50 v Warwickshire; first first-class century
v Surrey; winning Twenty20 competition'
Cricket moments to forget: 'Injury to knee in Sri Lanka January 2000, leading to
early return to England from U19 World Cup squad'
Cricket superstitions: 'None'
Cricketers particularly admired: Robin Smith, Sachin Tendulkar, Graham Thorpe,
Darren Lehmann, Brian Lara

Young players to look out for: Stuart Broad, Tom New, Richard Pyrah
Other sports played: 'Five-a-side football, squash and occasional golf'
Other sports followed: Football (Leeds United), rugby league (Leeds Rhinos)
Favourite band: Oasis
Relaxations: 'Music, relaxing, socialising with friends, keeping fit, PlayStation 2'
Extras: Played for Yorkshire Schools at all levels; attended Yorkshire Academy; awarded Yorkshire 2nd XI cap. Yorkshire Supporters' Club Young Player of the Year 1998. Represented England U14, U15, U17, U18 and U19. Played for Yorkshire v West Indies A in a one-day fixture at Headingley 2002 but did not appear for the county in first-class cricket or one-day competition; joined Leicestershire for 2003
Best batting: 145 Leicestershire v Surrey, Leicester 2003
　　　　　　　145 Leicestershire v Sussex, Hove 2003
Best bowling: 1-22 Leicestershire v New Zealanders, Leicester 2004

2005 Season

	M	Inns	NO	Runs	HS	Avge	100s	50s	Ct	St	O	M	Runs	Wkts	Avge	Best	5wI	10wM
Test																		
All First	6	10	4	302	82 *	50.33	-	3	4	-								
1-Day Int																		
C & G	2	2	0	31	27	15.50	-	-	-	-								
tsL	10	10	3	263	50	37.57	-	1	3	-								
Twenty20	7	7	1	210	73	35.00	-	1	1	-								

Career Performances

	M	Inns	NO	Runs	HS	Avge	100s	50s	Ct	St	Balls	Runs	Wkts	Avge	Best	5wI	10wM
Test																	
All First	27	46	7	1302	145	33.38	2	7	16	-	87	98	1	98.00	1-22	-	-
1-Day Int																	
C & G	5	5	0	58	27	11.60	-	-	-	-							
tsL	37	33	4	668	88	23.03	-	2	7	-							
Twenty20	19	18	5	264	73	20.30	-	1	8	-							

77. Which South African Barbarians rugby star played 40 ODIs
and also appeared for both Derbyshire and Sussex?

SAGGERS, M. J. Kent

Name: <u>Martin</u> John Saggers
Role: Right-hand bat, right-arm
fast-medium bowler
Born: 23 May 1972, King's Lynn
Height: 6ft 2in **Weight:** 14st 2lbs
Nickname: Saggs, Saggy Bits, Bits of Aloo,
Jurgen Burgen
County debut: 1996 (Durham), 1999 (Kent)
County cap: 2001 (Kent)
Test debut: 2003-04
50 wickets in a season: 4
Place in batting averages: 168th av. 27.00
Place in bowling averages: 114th av. 42.70
(2004 57th av. 31.17)
Strike rate: 77.55 (career 48.06)
Parents: Brian and Edna
Wife and date of marriage: Samantha,
27 February 2004

Children: Ethan, 9 October 2005
Family links with cricket: Grandfather played in the Essex League
Education: Springwood High School; University of Huddersfield
Qualifications: BA (Hons) Architectural Studies International
Career outside cricket: Runs a website (www.africanwildlife.co.uk) devoted to African wildlife photography
Overseas tours: Kent to South Africa 2001; England VI to Hong Kong 2002; England to Bangladesh 2003-04
Overseas teams played for: Randburg CC, Johannesburg 1996-98, 2000-04; Southern Suburbs CC, Johannesburg 1998-99
Career highlights to date: 'Winning the Norwich Union League 2001. Making my Test debut in Bangladesh. Taking a wicket with my first delivery in Test cricket on English soil'
Cricket moments to forget: 'Any form of injury'
Cricket superstitions: 'Getting a corner spot in the changing room'
Cricketers particularly admired: Neil Foster, Graham Dilley, Allan Donald, Richard Ellison
Other sports played: Golf (10 handicap), 'base jumping, snail racing'
Other sports followed: Football (Spurs), 'any form of motor sport'
Favourite band: Metallica
Relaxations: 'Going on safari in the Kruger National Park in South Africa. Wildlife photography'
Extras: Won Most Promising Uncapped Player Award 2000. Joint Kent Player of the Year 2000 (with David Masters). Underwood Award (Kent leading wicket-taker) 2001,

2002, 2003. *Kent Messenger* Group Readers Player of the Season 2002. Shepherd Neame Award for Best Bowler 2002. Cowdrey Award (Kent Player of the Year) 2002. Scored career best 64 as nightwatchman as Kent scored a county record fourth-innings 429-5 to beat Worcestershire at Canterbury 2004. Took wicket (Mark Richardson) with his first delivery in Test cricket on English soil, in the second Test v New Zealand at Headingley 2004

Best batting: 64 Kent v Worcestershire, Canterbury 2004
Best bowling: 7-79 Kent v Durham, Riverside 2000

2005 Season

	M	Inns	NO	Runs	HS	Avge	100s	50s	Ct	St	O	M	Runs	Wkts	Avge	Best	5wI	10wM
Test																		
All First	9	13	5	216	45	27.00	-	-	5	-	258.3	55	854	20	42.70	5-48	1	-
1-Day Int																		
C & G	3	1	1	5	5 *	-	-	-	-	-	22.1	3	76	3	25.33	3-21	-	
tsL	15	7	3	41	21	10.25	-	-	-	-	111.3	9	499	13	38.38	3-29	-	
Twenty20	3	0	0	0	0	-	-	-	1	-	7	0	48	1	48.00	1-33	-	

Career Performances

	M	Inns	NO	Runs	HS	Avge	100s	50s	Ct	St	Balls	Runs	Wkts	Avge	Best	5wI	10wM
Test	3	3	0	1	1	0.33	-	-	1	-	493	247	7	35.28	2-29	-	-
All First	93	117	31	1008	64	11.72	-	2	26	-	16677	8520	347	24.55	7-79	16	-
1-Day Int																	
C & G	16	7	4	12	5 *	4.00	-	-	1	-	829	555	22	25.22	4-6	-	
tsL	81	41	19	193	21 *	8.77	-	-	14	-	3510	2616	109	24.00	5-22	1	
Twenty20	5	1	0	5	5	5.00	-	-	2	-	84	93	3	31.00	2-14	-	

SAKER, N. C. Surrey

Name: Neil Clifford Saker
Role: Right-hand bat, right-arm fast bowler
Born: 20 September 1984, Tooting, London
Height: 6ft 4in **Weight:** 12st
Nickname: Sakes, For Goodness, Bulbus
County debut: 2003
Strike rate: (career 171.50)
Parents: Pauline and Steve
Marital status: Single
Family links with cricket: 'Dad plays for Guildford CC'
Education: Raynes Park High; Nescot College
Qualifications: 2 GCSEs, City & Guilds Carpentry and Joinery
Overseas tours: Guildford CC to Trinidad and Tobago 2001; Surrey U19 to Sri Lanka 2002

Overseas teams played for: Randwick-Petersham, Sydney 2003-04
Career highlights to date: 'Championship debut v Essex at The Oval 2003'
Cricket moments to forget: 'Once bowled a 13-ball over in a club game'
Cricket superstitions: 'Bowling marker has to be lying on surface, <u>not</u> pushed into ground!'
Cricketers particularly admired: Ian Botham, Brett Lee, Allan Donald
Young players to look out for: Jade Dernbach, Chris Murtagh, Danny Miller
Other sports played: Snooker, 'occasionally like to hack my way around a golf course'
Other sports followed: Football (Tottenham)
Favourite band: Powderfinger
Extras: Attended University of Port Elizabeth International Cricket Academy 2002-03
Opinions on cricket: 'Would like to see one overseas [player] as opposed to two – would give youngsters more opportunities to fill their spot in the team.'
Best batting: 5 Surrey v India A, The Oval 2003
Best bowling: 1-62 Surrey v Bangladesh A, The Oval 2005

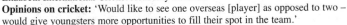

2005 Season

	M	Inns	NO	Runs	HS	Avge	100s	50s	Ct	St	O	M	Runs	Wkts	Avge	Best	5wI	10wM
Test																		
All First	1	1	0	0	0	0.00	-	-	-	-	22	3	93	1	93.00	1-62	-	-
1-Day Int																		
C & G	2	0	0	0	0	-	-	-	-	-	17	0	70	1	70.00	1-32	-	
tsL	10	4	3	6	2 *	6.00	-	-	2	-	61	0	396	11	36.00	4-43	-	
Twenty20																		

Career Performances

	M	Inns	NO	Runs	HS	Avge	100s	50s	Ct	St	Balls	Runs	Wkts	Avge	Best	5wI	10wM
Test																	
All First	3	4	0	6	5	1.50	-	-	-	-	343	272	2	136.00	1-62	-	-
1-Day Int																	
C & G	2	0	0	0	0	-	-	-	-	-	102	70	1	70.00	1-32	-	
tsL	10	4	3	6	2 *	6.00	-	-	2	-	366	396	11	36.00	4-43	-	
Twenty20																	

SALES, D. J. G. Northamptonshire

Name: <u>David</u> John Grimwood Sales
Role: Right-hand bat, right-arm medium
bowler, county captain
Born: 3 December 1977, Carshalton, Surrey
Height: 6ft **Weight:** 14st 7lbs
Nickname: Jumble
County debut: 1994 (one-day),
1996 (first-class)
County cap: 1999
1000 runs in a season: 3
1st-Class 200s: 4
1st-Class 300s: 1
Place in batting averages: 47th av. 46.84
(2004 12th av. 61.50)
Strike rate: (career 35.66)
Parents: Daphne and John
Wife and date of marriage: Abigail,
22 September 2001

Children: James, 11 February 2003
Family links with cricket: Father played club cricket
Education: Caterham Boys' School
Qualifications: 7 GCSEs, cricket coach
Overseas tours: England U15 to South Africa 1993; England U19 to West Indies
1994-95, to Zimbabwe 1995-96, to Pakistan 1996-97; England A to Kenya and Sri Lanka
1997-98, to Bangladesh and New Zealand 1999-2000, to West Indies 2000-01;
Northamptonshire to Grenada 2000
Overseas teams played for: Wellington Firebirds, New Zealand 2001-02
Career highlights to date: '303 not out v Essex; 104 v Pakistan 2003'
Cricket moments to forget: 'Watching White and Powell for five hours, then getting
0' (*Rob White and Mark Powell shared in a new record Northamptonshire opening
partnership of 375 v Gloucestershire at Northampton 2002*)
Cricket superstitions: 'None'
Cricketers particularly admired: Graham Gooch, Steve Waugh
Other sports followed: Rugby (Northampton Saints), football (Crystal Palace), golf
Favourite band: Coldplay
Relaxations: Fishing and golf
Extras: Sir John Hobbs Silver Jubilee Memorial Prize 1993. Scored 56-ball 70* v
Essex at Chelmsford in the Sunday League 1994, aged 16 years 289 days. Scored 210*
on Championship debut v Worcs at Kidderminster 1996, aged 18 years 237 days.
Became the youngest Englishman to score a first-class 300 (303*) v Essex at
Northampton 1999, aged 21 years 240 days. PCA/CGU Young Player of the Year

1999. Man of the Match for Wellington v Canterbury in the final of New Zealand's State Shield at Wellington 2001-02 (62). Captain of Northamptonshire since 2004
Best batting: 303* Northamptonshire v Essex, Northampton 1999
Best bowling: 4-25 Northamptonshire v Sri Lanka A, Northampton 1999

2005 Season

	M	Inns	NO	Runs	HS	Avge	100s	50s	Ct	St	O	M	Runs	Wkts	Avge	Best	5wI	10wM
Test																		
All First	16	27	2	1171	190	46.84	3	6	20	-								
1-Day Int																		
C & G	3	2	0	50	40	25.00	-	-	3	-	5	0	26	0	-	-	-	-
tsL	16	14	1	417	77	32.07	-	2	7	-	3	0	11	0	-	-	-	-
Twenty20	7	7	1	246	78 *	41.00	-	2	7	-	2	0	23	1	23.00	1-10	-	

Career Performances

	M	Inns	NO	Runs	HS	Avge	100s	50s	Ct	St	Balls	Runs	Wkts	Avge	Best	5wI	10wM
Test																	
All First	138	216	19	7717	303 *	39.17	15	41	117	-	321	169	9	18.77	4-25	-	-
1-Day Int																	
C & G	18	17	1	563	67	35.18	-	5	11	-	42	39	0	-	-	-	-
tsL	131	122	17	3237	133 *	30.82	1	21	53	-	42	28	0	-	-	-	-
Twenty20	17	17	2	403	78 *	26.86	-	3	10	-	12	23	1	23.00	1-10	-	

SALISBURY, I. D. K. Surrey

Name: <u>Ian</u> David Kenneth Salisbury
Role: Right-hand bat, leg-break bowler
Born: 21 January 1970, Moulton, Northampton
Height: 5ft 11in **Weight:** 12st 7lbs
Nickname: Solly, Dingle, Sals
County debut: 1989 (Sussex), 1997 (Surrey)
County cap: 1991 (Sussex), 1998 (Surrey)
Test debut: 1992
50 wickets in a season: 6
Place in batting averages: (2004 191st av. 23.75)
Place in bowling averages: (2004 144th av. 50.76)
Strike rate: (career 64.27)
Parents: Dave and Margaret
Wife and date of marriage: Emma Louise, 25 September 1993

Children: Anya-Rose, 10 August 2002
Family links with cricket: 'Dad is vice-president of my first club, Brixworth. He also re-lays cricket squares (e.g. Lord's, Northampton, Leicester)'
Education: Moulton Comprehensive, Northampton
Qualifications: 7 O-levels, NCA coaching certificate
Overseas tours: England A to Pakistan 1990-91, to Bermuda and West Indies 1991-92, to India 1994-95, to Pakistan 1995-96; England to India and Sri Lanka 1992-93, to West Indies 1993-94, to Pakistan 2000-01; World Masters XI v Indian Masters XI November 1996 ('Masters aged 26?')
Overseas teams played for: University of New South Wales, Sydney 1997-2000
Cricketers particularly admired: 'Any that keep performing day in, day out, for both country and county'
Other sports played: 'Most sports'
Other sports followed: Football (Southampton FC, Northampton Town FC), rugby union (Northampton Saints), 'any England team'
Relaxations: 'Spending time with wife Emma; meeting friends and relaxing with them and eating out with good wine'
Extras: In 1992 was named Young Player of the Year by both the Wombwell Cricket Lovers and the Cricket Writers. One of *Wisden*'s Five Cricketers of the Year 1993. Won Bill O'Reilly Medal for Sydney first-grade player of the year 1999-2000
Best batting: 101* Surrey v Leicestershire, The Oval 2003
Best bowling: 8-60 Surrey v Somerset, The Oval 2000

2005 Season

	M	Inns	NO	Runs	HS	Avge	100s	50s	Ct	St	O	M	Runs	Wkts	Avge	Best	5wI	10wM
Test																		
All First	5	5	2	141	59 *	47.00	-	1	4	-	82.3	4	359	7	51.28	3-73	-	-
1-Day Int																		
C & G																			
tsL	8	7	3	51	14	12.75	-	-	6	-	55.2	1	371	6	61.83	3-47	-	
Twenty20	10	7	2	57	20	11.40	-	-	3	-	9	0	85	0	-		-	-

Career Performances

	M	Inns	NO	Runs	HS	Avge	100s	50s	Ct	St	Balls	Runs	Wkts	Avge	Best	5wI	10wM
Test	15	25	3	368	50	16.72	-	1	5	-	2492	1539	20	76.95	4-163	-	-
All First	289	372	75	6082	101 *	20.47	2	21	184	-	50134	25519	780	32.71	8-60	34	6
1-Day Int	4	2	1	7	5	7.00	-	-	1	-	186	177	5	35.40	3-41	-	
C & G	30	18	5	168	34 *	12.92	-	-	5	-	1745	1024	34	30.11	3-28	-	
tsL	158	108	28	1077	59 *	13.46	-	1	61	-	5817	4904	137	35.79	5-30	1	
Twenty20	15	11	3	77	20	9.62	-	-	5	-	138	178	3	59.33	2-20	-	

SAMPSON, P. J. Surrey

Name: <u>Philip</u> James Sampson
Role: Right-hand bat, right-arm
fast-medium bowler
Born: 6 September 1980, Manchester
Height: 6ft 1in **Weight:** 14st 7lbs
Nickname: Sammo, Rhino
County debut: 2000 (one-day),
2002 (first-class)
Strike rate: (career 34.70)
Parents: Les and Kay
Marital status: Single
Family links with cricket: Father played
league cricket and was chairman of the
Harlequins club in Pretoria. Brother was
captain of Northern Transvaal (Northerns) at
Youth level
Education: Pretoria Boys High School
Qualifications: Matriculation (A-level
equivalent)
Overseas teams played for: Harlequins CC, Pretoria 1990-98, 2002
Career highlights to date: 'Playing in front of 26,000 at Lord's in Twenty20 v
Middlesex [2004]'
Cricket moments to forget: 'Not getting a hand on a catch in Twenty20 semi-final
v Lancs'
Cricket superstitions: 'Tying my left shoelace first'
Cricketers particularly admired: Allan Donald, Adam Hollioake
Young players to look out for: Jade Dernbach, Neil Saker
Other sports played: Football, golf
Other sports followed: Football (Manchester United), 'all sports'
Favourite band: Counting Crows, Powderfinger
Extras: Represented Northerns at U15, U18, U19. Played for Buckinghamshire in the
Minor Counties 1999. Is not considered an overseas player. Left Surrey at the end of
the 2005 season
Opinions on cricket: 'Reduce the number of National League games and increase
Twenty20 games.'
Best batting: 42 Surrey v CUCCE, Fenner's 2002
Best bowling: 5-121 Surrey v Warwickshire, Guildford 2004

2005 Season

	M	Inns	NO	Runs	HS	Avge	100s	50s	Ct	St	O	M	Runs	Wkts	Avge	Best	5wI	10wM
Test																		
All First																		
1-Day Int																		
C & G	1	0	0	0	0	-	-	-	-	-	7	0	32	1	32.00	1-32	-	
tsL	2	2	1	16	12 *	16.00	-	-	1	-	14	0	115	1	115.00	1-85	-	
Twenty20	4	0	0	0	0	-	-	-	2	-	6	0	77	0	-	-	-	

Career Performances

	M	Inns	NO	Runs	HS	Avge	100s	50s	Ct	St	Balls	Runs	Wkts	Avge	Best	5wI	10wM
Test																	
All First	5	9	4	91	42	18.20	-	-	-	-	590	415	17	24.41	5-121	1	-
1-Day Int																	
C & G	3	2	2	9	5 *	-	-	-	2	-	138	91	1	91.00	1-32	-	
tsL	19	9	2	39	16	5.57	-	-	3	-	744	722	18	40.11	3-48	-	
Twenty20	15	3	2	7	4 *	7.00	-	-	7	-	264	364	13	28.00	2-26	-	

SAQLAIN MUSHTAQ   Surrey

Name: Saqlain Mushtaq
Role: Right-hand bat, off-spin bowler
Born: 29 December 1976, Lahore, Pakistan
Height: 5ft 9in **Weight:** 11st 4lbs
Nickname: Saqi, Baba
County debut: 1997
County cap: 1998
Test debut: 1995-96
50 wickets in a season: 5
Place in bowling averages: 93rd av. 37.06
Strike rate: 71.18 (career 53.60)
Parents: Nasim Akhtar and Mushtaq Ahmed
Wife and date of marriage: Sana ('Sunny')
Saqlain, 11 April 2000
Education: Lahore MAO College
Overseas tours: Pakistan U19 to New
Zealand 1994-95; Pakistan to Australia 1995-
96, to England 1996, to Australia 1996-97, to
Sri Lanka 1996 97, to India 1996-97, to South Africa and Zimbabwe 1997-98, to India
1998-99, to Bangladesh (Wills International Cup) 1998-99, to UK, Ireland and Holland
(World Cup) 1999, to Australia 1999-2000, to West Indies 1999-2000, to Kenya (ICC
Knockout Trophy) 2000-01, to New Zealand 2000-01, to England 2001, to Bangladesh

2001-02, to Sharjah (v West Indies) 2001-02, to Sri Lanka and Sharjah (v Australia) 2002-03, to South Africa and Zimbabwe 2002-03, to Africa (World Cup) 2002-03, plus other one-day tournaments in Sri Lanka, Toronto, Sharjah, Kenya, Bangladesh, Singapore and Morocco

Overseas teams played for: PIA 1994-95 – 2003-04; Islamabad 1994-95, 1998; Lahore 2003-04

Cricketers particularly admired: Imran Khan, Wasim Akram, Waqar Younis

Other sports played: Squash

Other sports followed: Hockey (Pakistan), football (Manchester United and Arsenal)

Relaxations: 'I like listening to music when free or travelling'

Extras: Scored 79 in the first Test v Zimbabwe at Sheikhupura 1996-97, sharing with Wasim Akram (257*) in a world record eighth-wicket partnership in Tests (313). Took only the second hat-trick in World Cup cricket (Olonga, Huckle and Mbangwa), v Zimbabwe at The Oval 1999; it was his second hat-trick in ODIs v Zimbabwe. Topped the English first-class bowling averages in 1999, taking 58 wickets at 11.37 in seven games. One of *Wisden*'s Five Cricketers of the Year 2000. His international awards include Man of the [Test] Series v India 1998-99 and v Zimbabwe 2002-03. Holds record for taking fewest matches to reach 100 (53 matches), 150 (78), 200 (104) and 250 (138) ODI wickets, and also for the most ODI wickets in a calendar year (69 in 1997). An overseas player with Surrey 1997-2004 and in August-September 2005

Best batting: 101* Pakistan v New Zealand, Christchurch 2000-01

Best bowling: 8-65 Surrey v Derbyshire, The Oval 1998

2005 Season

	M	Inns	NO	Runs	HS	Avge	100s	50s	Ct	St	O	M	Runs	Wkts	Avge	Best	5wI	10wM
Test																		
All First	5	5	1	55	31	13.75	-	-	3	-	189.5	28	593	16	37.06	4-80	-	-
1-Day Int																		
C & G																		
tsL																		
Twenty20																		

Career Performances

	M	Inns	NO	Runs	HS	Avge	100s	50s	Ct	St	Balls	Runs	Wkts	Avge	Best	5wI	10wM
Test	49	78	14	927	101 *	14.48	1	2	14	-	14070	6206	208	29.83	8-164	13	3
All First	176	242	54	3111	101 *	16.54	1	12	63	-	41544	18026	775	23.25	8-65	56	15
1-Day Int	169	98	39	709	37 *	12.01	-	-	40	-	8770	6276	288	21.79	5-20	6	
C & G	21	8	2	52	24	8.66	-	-	1	-	1141	764	32	23.87	4-17	-	
tsL	58	36	12	308	38 *	12.83	-	-	13	-	2542	1810	63	28.73	3-12	-	
Twenty20	3	2	0	5	5	2.50	-	-	1	-	66	87	4	21.75	2-35	-	

SARWAN, R. R.   Gloucestershire

Name: <u>Ramnaresh</u> Ronnie Sarwan
Role: Right-hand bat, leg-break bowler
Born: 23 June 1980, Wakenaam Island,
Essequibo, Guyana
County debut: 2005
County cap: 2005
Test debut: 1999-2000
1st-Class 200s: 1
Place in batting averages: 131st av. 31.57
Strike rate: (career 74.73)
Overseas tours: West Indies U19 to South
Africa (U19 World Cup) 1997-98; West
Indies A to South Africa 1997-98, to
Bangladesh and India 1998-99; West Indies to
England 2000, to Australia 2000-01, to
Zimbabwe and Kenya 2001, to Sri Lanka
2001-02, to Sri Lanka (ICC Champions
Trophy) 2002-03, to India and Bangladesh

2002-03, to Africa (World Cup) 2002-03, to Zimbabwe and South Africa 2003-04, to
England 2004, to England (ICC Champions Trophy) 2004, to Australia (VB Series)
2004-05, to Australia 2005-06
Overseas teams played for: Guyana 1995-96 –
Extras: Scored 84* in his maiden Test innings, in the second Test v Pakistan in
Barbados 1999-2000. One of *Indian Cricket*'s five Cricketers of the Year 2004. Has
won numerous domestic and international awards, including Man of the [Test] Series v
Bangladesh 2004 and Player of the Tournament at the ICC Champions Trophy in
England 2004. Was an overseas player with Gloucestershire 2005
Best batting: 261* West Indies v Bangladesh, Kingston 2003-04
Best bowling: 6-62 Guyana v Leeward Islands, St John's 2000-01

2005 Season

	M	Inns	NO	Runs	HS	Avge	100s	50s	Ct	St	O	M	Runs	Wkts	Avge	Best	5wI	10wM
Test																		
All First	7	14	0	442	117	31.57	1	2	9	-	32	5	99	2	49.50	2-38	-	-
1-Day Int																		
C & G																		
tsL	8	8	1	210	118*	30.00	1	-	2	-	5	0	31	0	-	-	-	-
Twenty20																		

Career Performances

	M	Inns	NO	Runs	HS	Avge	100s	50s	Ct	St	Balls	Runs	Wkts	Avge	Best	5wI	10wM
Test	55	98	7	3720	261 *	40.87	8	22	37	-	1536	833	20	41.65	4-37	-	-
All First	140	237	18	8258	261 *	37.70	18	47	104	-	3363	1657	45	36.82	6-62	1	-
1-Day Int	87	82	20	2761	104 *	44.53	2	16	25	-	340	336	7	48.00	3-31	-	
C & G																	
tsL	8	8	1	210	118 *	30.00	1	-	2	-	30	31	0	-	-	-	-
Twenty20																	

SAYERS, J. J. — Yorkshire

Name: Joseph (<u>Joe</u>) John Sayers
Role: Left-hand bat, right-arm off-spin bowler
Born: 5 November 1983, Leeds
Height: 6ft **Weight:** 13st
Nickname: Leo, JJ, Ralph
County debut: 2003 (one-day), 2004 (first-class)
Place in batting averages: 90th av. 37.00 (2004 80th av. 39.84)
Parents: Geraldine and Roger
Marital status: Single
Family links with cricket: 'Father played at school, but otherwise none'
Education: St Mary's RC Comprehensive School, Menston; Worcester College, Oxford University
Qualifications: 12 GCSEs, 4 A-levels, BA Physics (Oxon)
Overseas tours: Leeds Schools to South Africa 1998; Yorkshire U17 to South Africa 2001; England U17 to Australia 2001
Overseas teams played for: Manly-Warringah, Sydney 2004-05
Career highlights to date: 'Making my Championship debut for Yorkshire. Scoring 144* at Lord's in 2004 [one-day] Varsity Match victory for Oxford. Maiden first-class century v Hampshire 2003'
Cricketers particularly admired: Rahul Dravid, Andrew Strauss, Michael Vaughan
Young players to look out for: Tim Bresnan
Other sports played: Football ('played as goalkeeper for Bradford City AFC for three years'), rowing (Worcester College)
Favourite band: Coldplay
Relaxations: 'Playing guitar; drawing/painting; reading autobiographies; listening to music'

Extras: Captained England U17 v Australia U17 at Adelaide 2001. Played for Oxford UCCE 2002, 2003, 2004 (captain 2003). Oxford Blue 2002, 2003, 2004. Represented England U19 2002, 2003 (captain in the third 'Test' 2003)

Opinions on cricket: 'The presence of two overseas players per county team has led to an improved standard of first-class cricket and has fuelled the development of many emerging young players. However, the introduction and employment of players who are not qualified to play for England must not be allowed to further hinder the progress of future prospects.'

Best batting: 147 Oxford University v Cambridge University, The Parks 2004

2005 Season

	M	Inns	NO	Runs	HS	Avge	100s	50s	Ct	St	O	M	Runs	Wkts	Avge	Best	5wI	10wM
Test																		
All First	10	17	1	592	115	37.00	2	2	11	-	7	0	35	0	-		-	-	-
1-Day Int																		
C & G																		
tsL	7	7	2	130	54 *	26.00	-	1	-	-	9	0	71	1	71.00	1-31	-	
Twenty20	3	1	0	12	12	12.00	-	-	2	-								

Career Performances

	M	Inns	NO	Runs	HS	Avge	100s	50s	Ct	St	Balls	Runs	Wkts	Avge	Best	5wI	10wM
Test																	
All First	26	44	2	1505	147	35.83	4	8	14	-	60	47	0	-	-	-	-
1-Day Int																	
C & G																	
tsL	9	9	2	199	62	28.42	-	2	-	-	54	71	1	71.00	1-31	-	
Twenty20	3	1	0	12	12	12.00	-	-	2	-							

SCOTT, B. J. M.   Middlesex

Name: Benjamin (<u>Ben</u>) James Matthew Scott
Role: Right-hand bat, wicket-keeper, leg-spin bowler
Born: 4 August 1981, Isleworth
Height: 'Small' (5ft 9in) **Weight:** 11st 7lbs
Nickname: Scotty
County debut: 2002 (one-day, Surrey), 2003 (first-class, Surrey), 2004 (Middlesex)
50 dismissals in a season: 1
Place in batting averages: 183rd av. 24.55 (2004 169th av. 26.22)
Parents: Terry and Edna
Marital status: Single
Family links with cricket: Father played for the Primitives; brother played local cricket
Education: Whitton School, Richmond; Richmond College

Qualifications: 9 GCSEs, 3 A-levels studied, ECB Level 1 coach, YMCA Fitness Instructor's Award
Overseas tours: MCC YC to Cape Town 1999-2000; Mumbai, India 2005
Overseas teams played for: Portland CC, Victoria 1999-2000; Mt Gambia, South Australia 2001-02
Career highlights to date: 'Scoring 101* at Lord's v Northants; just getting there with Nantie Hayward down the other end'
Cricket moments to forget: 'Getting a first-baller against Alex Loudon's "other one" at Kent'
Cricket superstitions: 'None'
Cricketers particularly admired: Alec Stewart, Jack Russell, Nad Shahid
Young players to look out for: Eoin Morgan
Other sports played: Golf
Favourite band: Michael Jackson, The Jacksons, Usher
Relaxations: Music, golf, TV
Extras: Middlesex YC cap. Represented ESCA U14 and U15. Played for Development of Excellence XI 1999. Finchley CC Player of the Season 2000
Opinions on cricket: 'One-day and Twenty20 cricket has dramatically enhanced the profile of cricket in England. England winning Test matches now is awesome.'
Best batting: 101* Middlesex v Northamptonshire, Lord's 2004

2005 Season

	M	Inns	NO	Runs	HS	Avge	100s	50s	Ct	St	O	M	Runs	Wkts	Avge	Best	5wI	10wM
Test																		
All First	16	23	5	442	64 *	24.55	-	3	44	6								
1-Day Int																		
C & G	2	1	0	2	2	2.00	-	-	-	1								
tsL	16	8	3	119	50 *	23.80	-	1	12	2								
Twenty20	9	5	2	21	17 *	7.00	-	-	4	4								

Career Performances

	M	Inns	NO	Runs	HS	Avge	100s	50s	Ct	St	Balls	Runs	Wkts	Avge	Best	5wI	10wM
Test																	
All First	25	39	10	757	101 *	26.10	1	4	58	9							
1-Day Int																	
C & G	5	3	1	21	11	10.50	-	-	-	2							
tsL	35	16	4	193	50 *	16.08	-	1	36	10							
Twenty20	13	8	4	22	17 *	5.50	-	-	5	4							

SCOTT, G. M.   Durham

Name: <u>Gary</u> Michael Scott
Role: Right-hand bat, right-arm
off-spin bowler; all-rounder
Born: 21 July 1984, Sunderland
Height: 6ft **Weight:** 13st
Nickname: Dirk, Scotty
County debut: 2001
Place in batting averages: 164th av. 27.90
Parents: Mary and Michael
Marital status: Engaged
Family links with cricket: 'Brother (Martin)
played with me at Hetton Lyons CC'
Education: Hetton Comprehensive
Qualifications: 7 GCSEs
Career outside cricket: 'Love to stay
in sport'
Off-season: 'I've played abroad, worked at
home, but resting and training this winter'
Overseas tours: England U17 to Australia 2000-01; Durham to Sharjah and Dubai
2005; Durham Development Team to India 2005
Overseas teams played for: Northern Districts, Adelaide 2002-03
Career highlights to date: 'First-class debut'
Cricket moments to forget: 'Getting my first pair – against Warwickshire in the same
day for the 2nd XI (first year with Durham)'
Cricket superstitions: 'None'
Cricketers particularly admired: Shane Warne, Jacques Kallis, Steve Waugh
Young players to look out for: Liam Plunkett, Alastair Cook
Other sports played: Football (represented Sunderland Schools as goalkeeper)
Other sports followed: 'Love golf. Like to see all northeast teams do well (soft spot
for Newcastle)'
Injuries: Hamstring strain
Favourite band: Usher, 50 Cent
Relaxations: 'Golf, eating out; spending time with family and friends'
Extras: Sir John Hobbs Silver Jubilee Memorial Prize 1999. C&G Man of the Match
award (for Durham Board XI) for his 100 v Herefordshire at Darlington in the 2003
competition. Became youngest to play first-class cricket for Durham, v Derbyshire at
Riverside 2001 aged 17 years and 19 days
Opinions on cricket: 'Not enough practice and rest time during season.'
Best batting: 61* Durham v Somerset, Taunton 2005

2005 Season

	M	Inns	NO	Runs	HS	Avge	100s	50s	Ct	St	O	M	Runs	Wkts	Avge	Best	5wl	10wM
Test																		
All First	7	13	2	307	61 *	27.90	-	1	2	-	10	1	48	0	-	-	-	-
1-Day Int																		
C & G																		
tsL	1	0	0	0	0	-	-	-	1	-								
Twenty20	7	5	2	52	31	17.33	-	-	6	-	8	0	80	7	11.42	3-27	-	

Career Performances

	M	Inns	NO	Runs	HS	Avge	100s	50s	Ct	St	Balls	Runs	Wkts	Avge	Best	5wl	10wM
Test																	
All First	8	15	2	340	61 *	26.15	-	1	3	-	78	59	0	-	-	-	-
1-Day Int																	
C & G	3	3	0	130	100	43.33	1	-	2	-	174	107	4	26.75	2-32	-	
tsL	1	0	0	0	0	-	-	-	1	-							
Twenty20	7	5	2	52	31	17.33	-	-	6	-	48	80	7	11.42	3-27	-	

SHAFAYAT, B. M.　　Northamptonshire

Name: Bilal Mustafa Shafayat
Role: Right-hand bat, right-arm medium-fast bowler, occasional wicket-keeper
Born: 10 July 1984, Nottingham
Height: 5ft 7in **Weight:** 10st 7lbs
Nickname: Billy, Muzzy, Our Kid
County debut: 2001 (Nottinghamshire), 2005 (Northamptonshire)
1000 runs in a season: 1
Place in batting averages: 82nd av. 37.78
Strike rate: (career 367.00)
Parents: Mohammad Shafayat and Mahfooza Begum
Marital status: Single
Family links with cricket: 'Brother Rashid played for Notts up to 2nd XI and is now playing in Staffordshire Premier (took ten wickets in a game 2003). Uncle Nadeem played for PCC. Father just loves it!'
Education: Greenwood Dale; Nottingham Bluecoat School and Sixth Form College
Qualifications: 9 GCSEs, 2 A-levels, Level 1 coaching
Overseas tours: ZRK to Pakistan 2000; Sparkhill ('Kadeer Ali's dad's academy') to

Pakistan; England U17 to Australia 2000-01; England U19 to Australia and (U19 World Cup) New Zealand 2001-02, to Australia 2002-03 (c); Nottinghamshire to South Africa 2002, 2003; England A to Malaysia and India 2003-04

Career highlights to date: 'Making my first-class debut for Notts v Middlesex (scoring 72). Scoring a hundred and double hundred v India in final U19 "Test" 2002. Scoring crucial hundred v Worcestershire for promotion in Championship. Beating Australia U19 in first "Test" 2002-03, scoring 66, 108 and taking six wickets'

Cricket moments to forget: 'Losing U19 "Test" series to Australia'

Cricketers particularly admired: Sachin Tendulkar, Carl Hooper, Andrew Jackman

Young players to look out for: Ravinder Bopara, Samit Patel, Moeen and Kadeer Ali, Nadeem Malik, Aaqib Afzaal, Kamani, Sajid and Rakib Mahmood, Shaftab Khalid

Other sports played: Football, badminton, squash, pool

Other sports followed: Football (Liverpool), boxing, snooker

Favourite band: Sean Paul, 50 Cent, Tupac, Nusrat Fateh Ali Khan

Relaxations: 'Praying Namaz; chilling with loved ones'

Extras: Scored 72 on Championship debut v Middlesex at Trent Bridge 2001, aged 16 years 360 days. NBC Denis Compton Award for the most promising young Nottinghamshire player 2001, 2002. Scored record-equalling four 'Test' centuries for England U19. BBC East Midlands Junior Sportsman of the Year 2003. ECB National Academy 2003-04

Best batting: 161 Northamptonshire v Derbyshire, Derby 2005

Best bowling: 1-22 Nottinghamshire v DUCCE, Trent Bridge 2003

2005 Season

	M	Inns	NO	Runs	HS	Avge	100s	50s	Ct	St	O	M	Runs	Wkts	Avge	Best	5wI	10wM
Test																		
All First	17	28	0	1058	161	37.78	2	6	21	-	20.5	2	61	0	-	-	-	-
1-Day Int																		
C & G	3	3	0	96	46	32.00	-	-	1	-	7	0	34	0	-	-	-	
tsL	15	15	3	425	97 *	35.41	-	3	5	-	35	0	156	8	19.50	4-33	-	
Twenty20	7	7	0	140	40	20.00	-	-	2	-	9	0	96	3	32.00	2-13	-	

Career Performances

	M	Inns	NO	Runs	HS	Avge	100s	50s	Ct	St	Balls	Runs	Wkts	Avge	Best	5wI	10wM
Test																	
All First	44	76	1	2390	161	31.86	4	13	31	1	367	253	1	253.00	1-22	-	-
1-Day Int																	
C & G	9	9	1	172	46	21.50	-	-	1	-	54	55	0	-	-	-	
tsL	46	44	3	960	97 *	23.41	-	4	20	1	502	417	17	24.52	4-33	-	
Twenty20	14	14	1	218	40	16.76	-	-	4	1	90	150	3	50.00	2-13	-	

SHAH, O. A.   Middlesex

Name: <u>Owais</u> Alam Shah
Role: Right-hand bat, off-spin bowler
Born: 22 October 1978, Karachi, Pakistan
Height: 6ft 1in **Weight:** 13st 7lbs
Nickname: Ace, The Mauler
County debut: 1995 (one-day),
1996 (first-class)
County cap: 1999
1000 runs in a season: 5
1st-Class 200s: 1
Place in batting averages: 8th av. 66.46
(2004 27th av. 53.44)
Strike rate: (career 71.85)
Parents: Jamshed and Mehjabeen
Wife and date of marriage: Gemma,
25 September 2004
Family links with cricket: Father played for
his college side
Education: Isleworth and Syon School; Lampton School; Westminster
University, Harrow
Qualifications: 7 GCSEs, 2 A-levels
Overseas tours: England U19 to Zimbabwe 1995-96, to South Africa (including U19
World Cup) 1997-98 (c); England A to Australia 1996-97, to Kenya and Sri Lanka
1997-98, to Sri Lanka 2004-05, to West Indies 2005-06; ECB National Academy to
Australia 2001-02; England to Zimbabwe (one-day series) 2001-02, to India and New
Zealand 2001-02 (one-day series), to Sri Lanka (ICC Champions Trophy) 2002-03, to
Australia 2002-03 (VB Series), to India 2005-06
Overseas teams played for: University of Western Australia, Perth
Career highlights to date: 'England debut v Australia [2001]. Fifty [62] against
Pakistan at Lord's [2001]'
Cricket moments to forget: 'Getting a pair in first-class cricket'
Cricketers particularly admired: Viv Richards, Sachin Tendulkar, Mark Waugh
Young players to look out for: Ben Scott, Chris Whelan
Other sports played: Snooker
Other sports followed: Football ('like to watch Man Utd play')
Favourite band: 'Too many to mention'
Relaxations: 'Movies, eating out'
Extras: Man of the U17 'Test' series v India 1994. Captained England U19 to success
in the 1997-98 U19 World Cup in South Africa, scoring 54* in the final; captain of
England U19 v Pakistan U19 1998. Cricket Writers' Young Player of the Year 2001.
Middlesex Player of the Year 2002. *Evening Standard* Player of the Month August

2004. Vice-captain of Middlesex 2002 to June 2004. Leading run-scorer in English first-class cricket 2005 (1728; av. 66.46). ECB National Academy 2004-05, 2005-06
Best batting: 203 Middlesex v Derbyshire, Southgate 2001
Best bowling: 3-33 Middlesex v Gloucestershire, Bristol 1999
Stop press: Called up as a replacement to the England tour to India 2005-06

2005 Season

	M	Inns	NO	Runs	HS	Avge	100s	50s	Ct	St	O	M	Runs	Wkts	Avge	Best	5wI	10wM
Test																		
All First	17	31	5	1728	173*	66.46	7	8	22	-	48.3	3	220	3	73.33	2-95	-	-
1-Day Int																		
C & G	2	1	0	2	2	2.00	-	-	-	-	7	0	34	0	-	-	-	-
tsL	16	15	1	527	96	37.64	-	6	6	-								
Twenty20	9	9	2	410	79	58.57	-	5	1	-								

Career Performances

	M	Inns	NO	Runs	HS	Avge	100s	50s	Ct	St	Balls	Runs	Wkts	Avge	Best	5wI	10wM
Test																	
All First	149	251	23	9528	203	41.78	26	50	114	-	1509	992	21	47.23	3-33	-	-
1-Day Int	15	15	2	283	62	21.76	-	2	6	-							
C & G	19	18	1	313	49	18.41	-	-	4	-	72	70	1	70.00	1-36	-	
tsL	138	129	15	3841	134	33.69	6	23	48	-	151	176	3	58.66	1-4	-	
Twenty20	18	18	5	566	79	43.53	-	5	6	-	1	1	0	-	-	-	

---

78. Which two sons of Test-playing fathers have scored over 4000 ODI runs and taken over 200 ODI wickets for the same country?

SHAHZAD, A.   Yorkshire

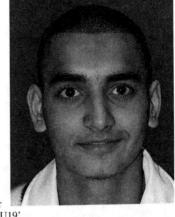

Name: Ajmal Shahzad
Role: Right-hand bat, right-arm fast bowler
Born: 27 July 1985, Huddersfield
Height: 6ft **Weight:** 12st
Nickname: Ajy
County debut: 2004 (one-day)
Parents: Parveen and Mohammed
Marital status: Single
Family links with cricket: 'Dad played
some Bradford League cricket'
Education: Woodhouse Grove School;
Bradford University
Qualifications: GCSEs and A-levels
Career outside cricket: Studying
pharmacology at Bradford University
Overseas tours: England U18 to Holland
2003; Woodhouse Grove to Grenada 2004
Career highlights to date: 'Being chosen for
Yorkshire first team and playing for England U19'
Cricket moments to forget: 'England U19 v Ireland'
Cricketers particularly admired: Wasim Akram
Young players to look out for: Tim Bresnan
Other sports played: Badminton (Yorkshire U15)
Favourite band: Niche
Relaxations: 'Gym, clubbing'
Extras: First British-born Asian to play for Yorkshire first team

2005 Season (did not make any first-class or one-day appearances)

Career Performances

	M	Inns	NO	Runs	HS	Avge	100s	50s	Ct	St	Balls	Runs	Wkts	Avge	Best	5wI	10wM
Test																	
All First																	
1-Day Int																	
C & G																	
tsL	1	1	0	5	5	5.00	-	-	-	-	36	35	0	-		-	-
Twenty20																	

SHANTRY, A. J.   Warwickshire

Name: <u>Adam</u> John Shantry
Role: Left-hand bat, left-arm
fast-medium bowler; all-rounder
Born: 13 November 1982, Bristol
Height: 6ft 3in   **Weight:** 14st 6lbs
Nickname: Shants
County debut: 2003 (Northamptonshire),
2005 (one-day, Warwickshire)
Strike rate: (career 49.00)
Parents: Brian and Josephine
Marital status: Single
Family links with cricket: Father played for
Gloucestershire; younger brother played for
Shropshire U17
Education: The Priory School, Shrewsbury;
Shrewsbury Sixth Form College
Qualifications: 11 GCSEs, 4 A-levels,
Level 2 coaching
Overseas teams played for: Balwyn, Melbourne 2001-02
Career highlights to date: '5-37 v New Zealand 2004; 3-8 on Championship debut v
Somerset 2003; four wickets in four balls v Warwickshire 2nd XI 2004'
Cricket superstitions: 'None'
Cricketers particularly admired: Brian Shantry, Andre Nel
Young players to look out for: Jack Shantry
Other sports played: Football (Shrewsbury Area)
Other sports followed: Football (Bristol City – 'only team in Bristol')
Favourite band: Feeder
Relaxations: 'Listening to proper music – My Chemical Romance, Lostprophets, Bloc
Party, Funeral for a Friend'
Extras: England U17 squad. Represented ESCA U18 2001. Radio Shropshire Young
Player of the Year 2001. Took 5-37 v New Zealanders in 50-over match at
Northampton 2004, winning Carlsberg Man of the Match award. His 5-15 v
Warwickshire 2nd XI at Kenilworth 2004 included four wickets in four balls (bowled,
bowled, lbw, bowled)
Opinions on cricket: 'More cricket on TV and other exposure in the media can only
be good for the game.'
Best batting: 38* Northamptonshire v Somerset, Northampton 2003
Best bowling: 3-8 Northamptonshire v Somerset, Northampton 2003

2005 Season

	M	Inns	NO	Runs	HS	Avge	100s	50s	Ct	St	O	M	Runs	Wkts	Avge	Best	5wI	10wM
Test																		
All First																		
1-Day Int																		
C & G																		
tsL	1	0	0	0	0	-	-	-	3	-	7	0	44	0	-	-	-	-
Twenty20																		

Career Performances

	M	Inns	NO	Runs	HS	Avge	100s	50s	Ct	St	Balls	Runs	Wkts	Avge	Best	5wI	10wM
Test																	
All First	5	6	4	62	38 *	31.00	-	-	2	-	490	263	10	26.30	3-8	-	-
1-Day Int																	
C & G	1	1	0	15	15	15.00	-	-	-	-	42	21	2	10.50	2-21	-	
tsL	2	1	0	4	4	4.00	-	-	4	-	54	61	0	-	-	-	-
Twenty20	1	0	0	0	0	-	-	-	-	-	12	31	0	-	-	-	-

SHAW, A. D.   Glamorgan

Name: Adrian David Shaw
Role: Right-hand bat, wicket-keeper;
2nd XI coach
Born: 17 February 1972, Neath
Height: 6ft **Weight:** 13st
Nickname: Shawsy
County debut: 1992 (one-day),
1994 (first-class)
County cap: 1999
50 dismissals in a season: 1
Parents: David Colin and Christina
Wife and date of marriage: Wendy,
December 2002
Children: Seren Georgia, 8 January 2002
Education: Llangatwg Comprehensive;
Neath Tertiary College
Qualifications: 9 O-levels, 3 A-levels
Overseas tours: Welsh Schools U17 to
Barbados 1987; England YC to New Zealand 1990-91; Glamorgan pre-season tours,
including to Cape Town 1999
Overseas teams played for: Welkom Police, Free State 1995-96
Cricket superstitions: 'Never whistle with a mouth full of custard'

Cricketers particularly admired: 'Anyone who stays modest with success'
Other sports played: Rugby (formerly centre with Neath RFC – Back of the Year 1993-94; Welsh U19 and U21 squad member)
Other sports followed: Rugby (Neath)
Favourite band: Massive Attack
Extras: Voted Glamorgan 2nd XI Player of the Year and Glamorgan Young Player of the Year 1995. Claimed eight catches in the second innings and 12 for the match v Gloucestershire 2nd XI at Usk 1998. Scored eleventh century for Glamorgan 2nd XI (103) v Somerset 2nd XI at Cardiff 2003, surpassing Tony Cottey's record of ten centuries in 2nd XI cricket for Glamorgan. Glamorgan 2nd XI player/coach 2002-05; retired at the end of the 2005 season to become 2nd XI coach full-time
Best batting: 140 Glamorgan v Oxford University, The Parks 1999

2005 Season (did not make any first-class or one-day appearances)

Career Performances

	M	Inns	NO	Runs	HS	Avge	100s	50s	Ct	St	Balls	Runs	Wkts	Avge	Best	5wI	10wM
Test																	
All First	77	103	16	1906	140	21.90	1	9	180	14	6	7	0	-		-	-	-
1-Day Int																	
C & G	9	8	2	151	47	25.16	-	-	13	-							
tsL	56	38	9	436	48	15.03	-	-	29	10							
Twenty20																		

79. To date, who holds the record for the
highest individual score in an ODI by a batsman
finishing on the losing side?

SHEIKH, M. A.   Derbyshire

Name: <u>Mohammed</u> Avez Sheikh
Role: Left-hand bat, right-arm
medium bowler
Born: 2 July 1973, Birmingham
Height: 6ft
Nickname: Sheikhy
County debut: 1997 (Warwickshire),
2004 (Derbyshire)
Place in batting averages: 242nd av. 17.12
(2004 207th av. 21.58)
Place in bowling averages: 100th av. 38.30
(2004 91st av. 36.34)
Strike rate: 81.15 (career 77.65)
Education: Broadway School
Overseas teams played for: Western
Province CC 1997-98
Extras: Played for Warwickshire U19.
Played for the Warwickshire Board side that

won the last ECB 38-County competition 2002, taking 4-37 in the final. Returned first
innings figures of 11-7-9-4 v Durham at Riverside 2004
Best batting: 58* Warwickshire v Northamptonshire, Northampton 2000
Best bowling: 4-9 Derbyshire v Durham, Riverside 2004

2005 Season

	M	Inns	NO	Runs	HS	Avge	100s	50s	Ct	St	O	M	Runs	Wkts	Avge	Best	5wI	10wM
Test																		
All First	5	8	0	137	55	17.12	-	1	-	-	175.5	44	498	13	38.30	4-67	-	-
1-Day Int																		
C & G																		
tsL	11	6	1	46	18	9.20	-	-	2	-	79	11	292	6	48.66	1-16	-	
Twenty20	6	4	1	29	20	9.66	-	-	1	-	16	0	165	5	33.00	2-25	-	

Career Performances

	M	Inns	NO	Runs	HS	Avge	100s	50s	Ct	St	Balls	Runs	Wkts	Avge	Best	5wI	10wM
Test																	
All First	38	53	13	968	58 *	24.20	-	3	4	-	5824	2834	75	37.78	4-9	-	-
1-Day Int																	
C & G	11	7	3	50	14	12.50	-	-	2	-	606	420	10	42.00	2-18	-	
tsL	77	43	16	334	50 *	12.37	-	1	11	-	3219	2257	74	30.50	4-17	-	
Twenty20	10	5	2	29	20	9.66	-	-	3	-	157	217	8	27.12	2-20	-	

SHERIYAR, A.   Kent

Name: Alamgir Sheriyar
Role: Right-hand bat, left-arm fast bowler
Born: 15 November 1973, Birmingham
Height: 6ft 1in **Weight:** 13st
Nickname: Sheri
County debut: 1993 (one-day, Leics),
1994 (first-class, Leics), 1996 (Worcs),
2003 (Kent)
County cap: 1997; colours, 2002 (both
Worcs)
50 wickets in a season: 4
Place in bowling averages: (2004 125th
av. 42.88)
Strike rate: (career 51.46)
Parents: Mohammed Zaman (deceased) and
Safia Sultana
Marital status: Single
Family links with cricket: Brothers play
a bit
Education: George Dixon Secondary School, Birmingham; Joseph Chamberlain Sixth
Form College, Birmingham; Oxford Brookes University
Qualifications: 6 O-levels
Overseas tours: Leicestershire to South Africa 1995; Worcestershire to Barbados
1996; England A to Bangladesh and New Zealand 1999-2000
Cricketers particularly admired: Wasim Akram
Other sports followed: Football, basketball
Relaxations: Time at home, music
Extras: Played for English Schools U17. Became only the second player to take a hat-
trick on his Championship debut, for Leicestershire v Durham at Durham University
1994. First bowler to reach 50 first-class wickets in 1999 and ended season as leading
wicket-taker with 92 wickets (av. 24.70). Took second first-class hat-trick of his career
v Kent at Worcester 1999. Played for Worcestershire on loan from Kent 2005.
Released by Kent at the end of the 2005 season
Best batting: 21 Worcestershire v Nottinghamshire, Trent Bridge 1997
                21 Worcestershire v Pakistan A, Worcester 1997
Best bowling: 7-130 Worcestershire v Hampshire, Southampton 1999

2005 Season

	M	Inns	NO	Runs	HS	Avge	100s	50s	Ct	St	O	M	Runs	Wkts	Avge	Best	5wI	10wM
Test																		
All First	2	3	1	13	5	6.50	-	-	-	-	58.5	13	181	5	36.20	3-48	-	-
1-Day Int																		
C & G																		
tsL	2	0	0	0	0	-	-	-	-	-	11	2	61	0	-		-	-
Twenty20																		

Career Performances

	M	Inns	NO	Runs	HS	Avge	100s	50s	Ct	St	Balls	Runs	Wkts	Avge	Best	5wI	10wM
Test																	
All First	152	165	65	829	21	8.29	-	-	22	-	25888	15085	503	29.99	7-130	23	3
1-Day Int																	
C & G	11	5	2	16	10	5.33	-	-	1	-	468	371	10	37.10	2-47	-	
tsL	82	24	13	88	19	8.00	-	-	5	-	2884	2488	88	28.27	4-18	-	
Twenty20	3	2	2	13	9 *	-	-	-	-	-	60	64	2	32.00	1-18	-	

SHOAIB AKHTAR   Worcestershire

Name: Shoaib Akhtar
Role: Right-hand bat, right-arm fast bowler
Born: 13 August 1975, Rawalpindi, Pakistan
Height: 6ft
County debut: 2001 (Somerset; *see Extras*),
2003 (Durham), 2005 (Worcestershire)
County colours: 2005 (Worcestershire)
Test debut: 1997-98
Place in batting averages: 258th av. 14.00
Place in bowling averages: 55th av. 28.92
Strike rate: 37.07 (career 43.22)
Education: Elliott High School, Rawalpindi;
Asghar Mal Government College, Rawalpindi
Overseas tours: Pakistan A to England 1997;
Pakistan to South Africa 1997-98,
to Zimbabwe 1997-98, to Malaysia
(Commonwealth Games) 1998-99, to India
1998-99, to UK, Ireland and Holland (World

Cup) 1999, to Australia 1999-2000, to West Indies 1999-2000, to England 2001, to
Bangladesh 2001-02, to Sharjah (v West Indies) 2001-02, to Sri Lanka (ICC
Champions Trophy) 2002-03, to Sri Lanka and Sharjah (v Australia) 2002-03, to
Zimbabwe 2002-03, to South Africa 2002-03, to Africa (World Cup) 2002-03, to

England (NatWest Challenge) 2003, to New Zealand 2003-04, to England (ICC Champions Trophy) 2004, to Australia 2004-05, plus other one-day series and tournaments in Bangladesh, India, Sharjah, New Zealand, Kenya, Australia, Holland and Sri Lanka; Asian Cricket Council XI to South Africa (Afro-Asia Cup) 2005-06; ICC World XI to Australia (Super Series) 2005-06

Overseas teams played for: Rawalpindi 1993-94 – 1998-99, 2003-04; Pakistan International Airlines 1994-95 – 1995-96; Agriculture Development Bank of Pakistan 1996-97 – 1997-98; Khan Research Labs 2001-02 – 2004-05

Extras: Nicknamed the Rawalpindi Express. Represented Pakistan U19. Played one first-class match for Somerset 2001, v Australians at Taunton. Took 6-11 from 8.2 overs as New Zealand were bowled out for 73 in their first innings of the first Test at Lahore 2001-02. Bowled the first official 100mph delivery (timed at 100.23mph) to Nick Knight v England at Cape Town in the World Cup 2002-03. An overseas player with Durham June to September 2003 and in 2004. Durham Bowler of the Year 2003. His Test awards include Man of the Match in the second Test v Bangladesh at Peshawar 2003-04 (6-50/4-30) and in the second Test v New Zealand at Wellington 2003-04 (5-48/6-30). His ODI awards include Man of the Series in the Coca-Cola Sharjah Cup 1998-99 and in the Super Challenge II v Australia 2002. An overseas player with Worcestershire 2005. Took 6-16 v Gloucestershire at Worcester in the totesport League 2005, the best ever one-day league figures by a Worcestershire bowler

Best batting: 59* KRL v PIA, Lahore 2001-02
Best bowling: 6-11 Pakistan v New Zealand, Lahore 2001-02

2005 Season

	M	Inns	NO	Runs	HS	Avge	100s	50s	Ct	St	O	M	Runs	Wkts	Avge	Best	5wI	10wM
Test																		
All First	4	7	1	84	35	14.00	-	-	1	-	86.3	15	405	14	28.92	6-47	2	-
1-Day Int																		
C & G																		
tsL	5	3	2	39	36 *	39.00	-	-	-	-	39	4	198	7	28.28	6-16	1	
Twenty20	3	2	1	8	8	8.00	-	-	-	-	10	1	57	1	57.00	1-33	-	

Career Performances

	M	Inns	NO	Runs	HS	Avge	100s	50s	Ct	St	Balls	Runs	Wkts	Avge	Best	5wI	10wM
Test	36	54	10	360	37	8.18	-	-	9	-	6386	3568	144	24.77	6-11	11	2
All First	114	160	45	1326	59 *	11.53	-	1	35	-	17591	10622	407	26.09	6-11	27	2
1-Day Int	123	59	29	317	43	10.56	-	-	15	-	5761	4392	192	22.87	6-16	3	
C & G																	
tsL	18	14	2	201	36 *	16.75	-	-	1	-	855	637	37	17.21	6-16	2	
Twenty20	4	3	1	8	8	4.00	-	-	-	-	84	88	2	44.00	1-31	-	

SHRECK, C. E.   Nottinghamshire

Name: Charles (<u>Charlie</u>) Edward Shreck
Role: Right-hand bat, right-arm
fast-medium bowler
Born: 6 January 1978, Truro
Height: 6ft 7in **Weight:** 15st 7lbs
Nickname: Shrecker, Ogre, Stoat, Chough
County debut: 2002 (one-day),
2003 (first-class)
Place in bowling averages: (2004 29th
av. 26.54)
Strike rate: (career 51.35)
Parents: Peter and Sheila
Marital status: Single
Family links with cricket: 'Grandfather
watched Southampton'
Education: Truro School
Qualifications: Level 1 coaching

Career outside cricket: 'Sleeping'
Off-season: Playing cricket in New Zealand
Overseas tours: Cornwall U17 to South Africa 1997
Overseas teams played for: Merewether District CC, NSW 1997-98;
Hutt District CC, New Zealand 2000-03
Cricket moments to forget: 'Being run out off the last ball of the game against
Shropshire, walking off – we lost!'
Cricket superstitions: 'None'
Cricketers particularly admired: Viv Richards, Michael Holding, Ian Botham
Young players to look out for: Michael Munday, Carl Gazzard
Injuries: Out for the entire 2005 season after back surgery
Relaxations: 'Swimming, music'
Extras: C&G Man of the Match award for his 5-19 for Cornwall v Worcestershire at
Truro 2002. Took wicket (Vikram Solanki) with his third ball in county cricket v
Worcestershire at Trent Bridge in the NUL 2002, going on to record maiden one-day
league five-wicket return (5-35)
Best batting: 19 Nottinghamshire v Essex, Chelmsford 2003
Best bowling: 6-46 Nottinghamshire v Durham, Riverside 2004

2005 Season (did not make any first-class or one-day appearances)

Career Performances

	M	Inns	NO	Runs	HS	Avge	100s	50s	Ct	St	Balls	Runs	Wkts	Avge	Best	5wI	10wM
Test																	
All First	19	21	10	67	19	6.09	-	-	3	-	2773	1701	54	31.50	6-46	3	-
1-Day Int																	
C & G	7	3	1	11	9	5.50	-	-	2	-	360	298	12	24.83	5-19	1	
tsL	2	2	2	3	2*	-	-	-	1	-	96	97	6	16.16	5-35	1	
Twenty20	1	1	1	1	1*	-	-	-	-	-	24	25	1	25.00	1-25	-	

SIDEBOTTOM, R. J. Nottinghamshire

Name: Ryan Jay Sidebottom
Role: Left-hand bat, left-arm fast bowler
Born: 15 January 1978, Huddersfield
Height: 6ft 4in **Weight:** 14st 7lbs
Nickname: Siddy, Sexual, Jazz
County debut: 1997 (Yorkshire),
2004 (Nottinghamshire)
County cap: 2000 (Yorkshire),
2004 (Nottinghamshire)
Test debut: 2001
50 wickets in a season: 1
Place in batting averages: 271st av. 11.72
Place in bowling averages: 11th av. 22.64
(2004 37th av. 28.63)
Strike rate: 52.04 (career 51.62)
Parents: Arnie and Gillian
Marital status: Single
Family links with cricket: Father played
cricket for Yorkshire and England and football for Manchester United and
Huddersfield Town
Education: King James Grammar School, Almondbury
Qualifications: 5 GCSEs
Overseas tours: England U17 to Holland 1995; MCC to Bangladesh 1999-2000;
England A to West Indies 2000-01; England to Zimbabwe (one-day series) 2001-02;
ECB National Academy to Australia 2001-02
Overseas teams played for: Ringwood, Melbourne 1998
Cricketers particularly admired: Darren Gough, Chris Silverwood, Glenn McGrath
Young players to look out for: Joe Sayers
Other sports played: Football (once with Sheffield United), 'all sports'

Other sports followed: 'Love rugby league (any team)', football (Man Utd)
Relaxations: 'Music (R&B), films, clubbing, going out with my team-mates'
Extras: NBC Denis Compton Award for the most promising young Yorkshire player 1999, 2000. Took 5-31 (8-65 in match) for England A v Jamaica at Kingston in the Busta Cup 2000-01, winning the Man of the Match award; topped tour first-class bowling averages (16 wickets; av. 16.81). Made Test debut in the first Test v Pakistan at Lord's 2001 (England's 100th Test at the ground), becoming the tenth player to follow his father into the England Test team
Best batting: 54 Yorkshire v Glamorgan, Cardiff 1998
Best bowling: 7-97 Yorkshire v Derbyshire, Headingley 2003

2005 Season

	M	Inns	NO	Runs	HS	Avge	100s	50s	Ct	St	O	M	Runs	Wkts	Avge	Best	5wI	10wM
Test																		
All First	15	15	4	129	31	11.72	-	-	6	-	433.4	130	1132	50	22.64	5-61	1	-
1-Day Int																		
C & G	1	1	1	1	1 *	-	-	-	-	-	10	1	26	2	13.00	2-26	-	
tsL	12	6	2	57	32	14.25	-	-	4	-	76.5	10	302	17	17.76	3-13	-	
Twenty20																		

Career Performances

	M	Inns	NO	Runs	HS	Avge	100s	50s	Ct	St	Balls	Runs	Wkts	Avge	Best	5wI	10wM
Test	1	1	0	4	4	4.00	-	-	-	-	120	64	0	-	-	-	-
All First	85	104	30	802	54	10.83	-	1	32	-	13371	6420	259	24.78	7-97	10	1
1-Day Int	2	1	1	2	2 *	-	-	-	-	-	84	84	2	42.00	1-42	-	
C & G	16	4	2	23	9	11.50	-	-	4	-	762	492	22	22.36	4-39	-	
tsL	88	41	20	275	32	13.09	-	-	15	-	3586	2667	94	28.37	6-40	2	
Twenty20	10	3	2	11	10	11.00	-	-	3	-	205	270	12	22.50	3-20	-	

80. Which country has had the most ODI captains
since the first fixture in 1971?

SILLENCE, R. J. — Worcestershire

Name: <u>Roger</u> John Sillence
Role: Right-hand bat, right-arm
fast-medium bowler
Born: 29 June 1977, Salisbury, Wiltshire
Height: 6ft 3in **Weight:** 13st 7lbs
Nickname: Sillo
County debut: 2001 (Gloucestershire)
County cap: 2004 (Gloucestershire)
Strike rate: (career 55.17)
Parents: Angela
Marital status: Single
Family links with cricket: Father played
cricket
Education: Highbury, Salisbury; Salisbury
Art College
Qualifications: 7 GCSEs, ND and HND
Graphic Design, ECB Level 2 coach
Career outside cricket: 'Setting up my own
design agency and working for Willowwizard, my bat sponsor'
Off-season: Player/coach for South Melbourne CC
Overseas teams played for: Napier Old Boys, New Zealand 1997-98; St Augustine's,
Cape Town 1998-99; East Keilor, Melbourne 2000-01; Hamersley Carine, Perth
2001-02; South Melbourne 2002-03, 2005-06
Career highlights to date: 'Getting five wickets on debut v Sussex at Hove and then
getting 100 on home debut v Derby'
Cricket moments to forget: 'Whenever I drop a catch'
Cricket superstitions: 'Always bowl in a short-sleeved shirt'
Cricketers particularly admired: Mike Smith, Jack Russell
Young players to look out for: Steve Davies
Other sports followed: 'Follow football but not really one team, and look out for my
mate who plays AFL for St Kilda'
Injuries: Out for about five weeks with a side strain
Favourite band: Jamiroquai, Razorlight, Coldplay
Relaxations: 'Enjoy a good coffee with a slice of carrot cake. Other interests such as
design, photography, fashion design, music – the normal same old same old'
Extras: Wiltshire Player of the Year 2000. Recorded maiden first-class five-wicket
return (5-97) on debut v Sussex at Hove 2001. Scored maiden first-class century (101)
v Derbyshire at Bristol 2002 on home debut, batting at No. 9. Released by
Gloucestershire at the end of the 2005 season and has joined Worcestershire for 2006
Opinions on cricket: 'Two quality overseas players, and the rest of us all qualify to
play for England.'

Best batting: 101 Gloucestershire v Derbyshire, Bristol 2002
Best bowling: 5-63 Gloucestershire v Durham, Bristol 2002

2005 Season

	M	Inns	NO	Runs	HS	Avge	100s	50s	Ct	St	O	M	Runs	Wkts	Avge	Best	5wI	10wM
Test																		
All First	1	2	0	12	12	6.00	-	-	-	-	30	3	144	2	72.00	2-90	-	-
1-Day Int																		
C & G																		
tsL																		
Twenty20																		

Career Performances

	M	Inns	NO	Runs	HS	Avge	100s	50s	Ct	St	Balls	Runs	Wkts	Avge	Best	5wI	10wM
Test																	
All First	13	18	0	379	101	21.05	1	1	3	-	1876	1236	34	36.35	5-63	2	-
1-Day Int																	
C & G	4	3	0	89	82	29.66	-	1	-	-	96	75	4	18.75	3-47	-	
tsL	1	1	0	11	11	11.00	-	-	-	-							
Twenty20																	

SILVERWOOD, C. E. W. Yorkshire

Name: Christopher (Chris) Eric Wilfred Silverwood
Role: Right-hand bat, right-arm fast bowler
Born: 5 March 1975, Pontefract
Height: 6ft 1in **Weight:** 12st 9lbs
Nickname: Spoons, Silvers, Chubby
County debut: 1993
County cap: 1996
Benefit: 2004
Test debut: 1996-97
50 wickets in a season: 1
Place in batting averages: 171st av. 26.57 (2004 226th av. 18.75)
Place in bowling averages: (2004 25th av. 25.90)
Strike rate: (career 51.33)
Parents: Brenda
Marital status: Single
Family links with cricket: 'Dad played a bit'

Education: Garforth Comprehensive
Qualifications: 8 GCSEs, City and Guilds in Leisure and Recreation
Overseas tours: England A to Kenya and Sri Lanka 1997-98, to Bangladesh and New Zealand 1999-2000, to West Indies 2000-01; England to Zimbabwe and New Zealand 1996-97, to West Indies 1997-98, to Bangladesh (Wills International Cup) 1998-99, to South Africa 1999-2000, to Zimbabwe (one-day series) 2001-02, to Australia 2002-03; England VI to Hong Kong 2002, 2003
Overseas teams played for: Wellington, Cape Town 1993-94, 1995-96
Career highlights to date: 'Making Test debut. Winning the Championship [2001]'
Cricketers particularly admired: Ian Botham, Allan Donald
Other sports played: Karate (black belt), rugby league (Kippax Welfare), athletics (represented Yorkshire)
Other sports followed: Rugby league (Castleford)
Extras: Attended Yorkshire Academy. Represented England U19. C&G Man of the Match awards v Northamptonshire at Northampton 2002 (61/2-35) and v Dorset at Dean Park 2004 (4-18)
Best batting: 80 Yorkshire v Durham, Riverside 2005
Best bowling: 7-93 Yorkshire v Kent, Headingley 1997

2005 Season

	M	Inns	NO	Runs	HS	Avge	100s	50s	Ct	St	O	M	Runs	Wkts	Avge	Best	5wI	10wM
Test																		
All First	6	7	0	186	80	26.57	-	2	3	-	142.2	28	479	9	53.22	3-73	-	-
1-Day Int																		
C & G																		
tsL																		
Twenty20																		

Career Performances

	M	Inns	NO	Runs	HS	Avge	100s	50s	Ct	St	Balls	Runs	Wkts	Avge	Best	5wI	10wM
Test	6	7	3	29	10	7.25	-	-	5	-	828	444	11	40.36	5-91	1	-
All First	148	197	38	2511	80	15.79	-	8	37	-	24129	12748	470	27.12	7-93	20	1
1-Day Int	7	4	0	17	12	4.25	-	-	-	-	306	244	6	40.66	3-43	-	
C & G	26	12	3	161	61	17.88	-	1	7	-	1325	841	27	31.14	4-18	-	
tsL	106	64	27	555	58	15.00	-	2	11	-	4420	3168	146	21.69	4-11	-	
Twenty20	9	5	2	32	13 *	10.66	-	-	4	-	204	264	7	37.71	2-22	-	

SINGH, A.   Nottinghamshire

Name: Anurag Singh
Role: Right-hand bat, right-arm 'all sorts'
Born: 9 September 1975, Kanpur, India
Height: 5ft 11½in   **Weight:** 11st
Nickname: Ragi
County debut: 1995 (Warwickshire), 2001 (Worcestershire), 2004 (Nottinghamshire)
County colours: 2002 (Worcestershire)
1000 runs in a season: 2
Place in batting averages: 152nd av. 30.10 (2004 48th av. 47.42)
Parents: Vijay and Rajul
Marital status: Single
Family links with cricket: 'Brother (Rudi) has played first-class cricket for Cambridge Uni and has a Cambridge Blue'
Education: King Edward's School, Birmingham; Gonville and Caius College, Cambridge; College of Law, London
Qualifications: 12 GCSEs, 1 AO-level, 4 A-levels, passed Law School exams
Career outside cricket: Solicitor
Overseas tours: England U19 to West Indies 1994-95; Warwickshire U21 to South Africa; Warwickshire CCC to South Africa; Quidnuncs to South Africa 2002; Worcestershire to South Africa 2003
Overseas teams played for: Gordon CC, Sydney; Avendale CC, Cape Town
Cricket moments to forget: 'Losing two cup finals to Gloucestershire'
Cricket superstitions: 'None'
Cricketers particularly admired: Steve Waugh, Sachin Tendulkar, Michael Atherton, Brian Lara
Young players to look out for: Samit Patel, Mark Footitt
Other sports played: Hockey ('college and school'), football ('college and firm')
Other sports followed: Football (Aston Villa FC)
Favourite band: 'Too many to mention'
Relaxations: Reading, socialising with friends
Extras: Cambridge Blue 1996-98; captain of Cambridge University 1997-98. Scored 1000 first-class runs in each of his first two full seasons of county cricket (2001 and 2002). C&G Man of the Match award for his 74 v Leicestershire in the quarter-final at Leicester 2003
Opinions on cricket: 'The effect of Kolpak [*see page 9*], EU and overseas players needs to be carefully regulated, otherwise the game in this country will suffer greatly. I think the number of EU and Kolpak players on a county's staff should affect the

number of overseas players they can register – e.g. if you have two Kolpak/EU players, then you can only have one overseas; if you have three or more, then no overseas; if none or one, then two overseas players.'

Best batting: 187 Worcestershire v Gloucestershire, Bristol 2002

2005 Season

	M	Inns	NO	Runs	HS	Avge	100s	50s	Ct	St	O	M	Runs	Wkts	Avge	Best	5wI	10wM
Test																		
All First	7	10	0	301	131	30.10	1	1	2	-	1	0	13	0	-	-	-	-
1-Day Int																		
C & G																		
tsL	9	8	1	198	47	28.28	-	-	2	-								
Twenty20																		

Career Performances

	M	Inns	NO	Runs	HS	Avge	100s	50s	Ct	St	Balls	Runs	Wkts	Avge	Best	5wI	10wM
Test																	
All First	107	175	7	5437	187	32.36	11	24	42	-	101	124	0	-	-	-	-
1-Day Int																	
C & G	13	13	0	471	85	36.23	-	4	3	-							
tsL	76	74	4	1897	97	27.10	-	11	18	-							
Twenty20																	

SMITH, B. F. Worcestershire

Name: Benjamin (<u>Ben</u>) Francis Smith
Role: Right-hand bat, right-arm medium bowler
Born: 3 April 1972, Corby
Height: 5ft 9in **Weight:** 11st
Nickname: Turnip, Sven
County debut: 1990 (Leicestershire), 2002 (Worcestershire)
County cap: 1995 (Leicestershire), 2002 (Worcestershire colours)
1000 runs in a season: 7
1st-Class 200s: 2
Place in batting averages: 19th av. 57.25 (2004 49th av. 47.09)
Strike rate: (career 193.66)
Parents: Keith and Janet
Wife and date of marriage: Lisa, 10 October 1998

Children: Ruby Frances, 6 November 2005
Family links with cricket: Father, grandfather and uncles all played club and representative cricket
Education: Kibworth High School; Robert Smyth, Market Harborough
Qualifications: 5 O-levels, 8 GCSEs, NCA coaching certificate
Off-season: 'Being a dad; keeping fit'
Overseas tours: England YC to New Zealand 1990-91; MCC to Bangladesh 1999-2000; 'numerous pre-season tours to South Africa, Caribbean and Sri Lanka'
Overseas teams played for: Alexandria, Zimbabwe 1990; Bankstown-Canterbury, Sydney 1993-96; Central Hawke's Bay CC, New Zealand 1997-98; Central Districts, New Zealand 2000-02
Career highlights to date: 'Winning 1996 County Championship'
Cricket moments to forget: 'Lord's finals'
Cricketers particularly admired: Viv Richards, David Gower, Steve Waugh
Other sports played: Tennis (Leicestershire aged 12), golf, touch rugby
Other sports followed: Rugby union (Leicester Tigers)
Favourite band: Coldplay
Relaxations: 'Music, DIY, good wine'
Extras: Cricket Society Young Player of the Year 1991. Vice-captain of Leicestershire 2001. Scored century (137) on first-class debut for Worcestershire v OUCCE at The Parks and another (129) on Championship debut for the county v Gloucestershire at Worcester 2002 to become the first player to achieve this 'double' for Worcestershire. Worcestershire Supporters' Player of the Year 2002. Worcestershire Player of the Year 2003. Scored 187 v Gloucestershire at Worcester 2004, in the process sharing with Graeme Hick (262) in the highest first-class partnership ever made at New Road (417). Captain of Worcestershire 2003 until standing down in August 2004
Best batting: 204 Leicestershire v Surrey, The Oval 1998
Best bowling: 1-5 Leicestershire v Essex, Ilford 1991

2005 Season

	M	Inns	NO	Runs	HS	Avge	100s	50s	Ct	St	O	M	Runs	Wkts	Avge	Best	5wI	10wM
Test																		
All First	18	30	3	1546	172	57.25	6	5	20	-	7	1	41	0	-	-	-	-
1-Day Int																		
C & G	2	1	0	19	19	19.00	-	-	2	-								
tsL	15	13	2	253	58	23.00	-	1	5	-								
Twenty20	7	7	0	227	105	32.42	1	-	2	-								

Career Performances

	M	Inns	NO	Runs	HS	Avge	100s	50s	Ct	St	Balls	Runs	Wkts	Avge	Best	5wl	10wM
Test																	
All First	266	414	48	15319	204	41.85	38	74	150	-	581	391	3	130.33	1-5	-	-
1-Day Int																	
C & G	37	34	5	889	91	30.65	-	6	18	-	24	17	1	17.00	1-2	-	
tsL	218	211	32	5561	115	31.06	1	34	60	-	31	36	0	-	-	-	
Twenty20	17	17	1	330	105	20.62	1	-	8	-							

SMITH, E. T.   Middlesex

Name: Edward (<u>Ed</u>) Thomas Smith
Role: Right-hand bat, right-arm
medium bowler .
Born: 19 July 1977, Pembury, Kent
Height: 6ft 2in **Weight:** 13st
Nickname: Smudge
County debut: 1996 (Kent),
2005 (Middlesex)
County cap: 2001 (Kent), 2005 (Middlesex)
Test debut: 2003
1000 runs in a season: 6
1st-Class 200s: 2
Place in batting averages: 71st av. 39.81
(2004 44th av. 49.11)
Parents: Jonathan and Gillie
Marital status: Single
Family links with cricket: 'Dad wrote *Good
Enough?* with Chris Cowdrey'
Education: Tonbridge School; Peterhouse, Cambridge University
Qualifications: 11 GCSEs, 3 A-levels, degree in History
Career outside cricket: Journalism; broadcasting
Overseas tours: England A to Malaysia and India 2003-04
Overseas teams played for: University CC, Perth, Western Australia
Career highlights to date: 'My Test debut'
Cricket moments to forget: 'Getting a pair at Chelmsford 2003'
Cricket superstitions: 'Left pad on first'
Cricketers particularly admired: Steve Waugh, Rahul Dravid
Young players to look out for: Simon Cusden
Other sports played: Squash, golf
Other sports followed: Football (Arsenal FC), baseball (New York Mets)
Favourite band: Bob Dylan

Relaxations: 'Listening to music, reading, going to concerts'

Extras: Scored century (101) on first-class debut v Glamorgan 1996; was also the first person to score 50 or more in each of his first six first-class games. Cambridge Blue 1996. Represented England U19. Scored century in each innings (149/113) v Nottinghamshire at Maidstone 2003. Equalled Kent record of four consecutive first-class centuries with his 108 v Essex at Canterbury 2003. *Kent Messenger* Readers Player of the Year 2003. Denness Award (Kent leading run-scorer) 2003. Cowdrey Award (Kent Player of the Season) 2003. Slazenger 'Sheer Instinct' award for 2003. Books *Playing Hard Ball* (about baseball) published 2001 and *On and Off the Field* published 2004; series *Peak Performance* (comparing sporting and musical performance) broadcast on Radio 3 2005

Opinions on cricket: 'We need good wickets, good practice facilities and enough time between games to prepare properly.'

Best batting: 213 Kent v Warwickshire, Canterbury 2003

2005 Season

	M	Inns	NO	Runs	HS	Avge	100s	50s	Ct	St	O	M	Runs	Wkts	Avge	Best	5wI	10wM
Test																		
All First	17	32	0	1274	145	39.81	2	7	12	-								
1-Day Int																		
C & G	2	2	1	138	96 *	138.00	-	1	1	-								
tsL	16	16	1	476	93	31.73	-	3	6	-								
Twenty20	9	9	0	265	85	29.44	-	1	1	-								

Career Performances

	M	Inns	NO	Runs	HS	Avge	100s	50s	Ct	St	Balls	Runs	Wkts	Avge	Best	5wI	10wM
Test	3	5	0	87	64	17.40	-	1	5	-							
All First	151	259	14	9964	213	40.66	24	44	61	-	72	59	0	-	-	-	-
1-Day Int																	
C & G	9	9	2	248	96 *	35.42	-	1	1	-							
tsL	71	68	4	2021	122	31.57	2	14	13	-							
Twenty20	11	11	0	330	85	30.00	-	2	2	-							

SMITH, G. C.   Somerset

Name: <u>Graeme</u> Craig Smith
Role: Left-hand bat, right-arm
off-spin bowler
Born: 1 February 1981, Johannesburg,
South Africa
County debut: 2005
County cap: 2005
Test debut: 2001-02
1st-Class 200s: 4
1st-Class 300s: 1
Place in batting averages: 7th av. 67.42
Strike rate: (career 145.30)
Overseas tours: South Africa U19 to
Pakistan 1998-99, to Sri Lanka (U19 World
Cup) 1999-2000; South Africa A to West
Indies 2000, to Zimbabwe 2002-03; South
Africa to Morocco (Morocco Cup) 2002, to
Sri Lanka (ICC Champions Trophy) 2002-03,

to Bangladesh 2002-03 (c), to England 2003 (c), to Pakistan 2003-04 (c), to New
Zealand 2003-04 (c), to Sri Lanka 2004 (c), to England (ICC Champions Trophy) 2004
(c), to India 2004-05 (c), to West Indies 2004-05 (c), to India (one-day series) 2005-06
(c), to Australia 2005-06 (c); ICC World XI to Australia (Super Series) 2005-06
Overseas teams played for: Gauteng 1999-2000; Western Province 2000-01 –
2003-04; Western Province Boland 2004-05
Extras: Made first-class debut for UCBSA Invitation XI v Griqualand West at
Kimberley 1999-2000, scoring 187 in first innings. One of *South African Cricket
Annual*'s Five Cricketers of the Year 2002, 2003. Scored 151 in the second Test v
Pakistan at Cape Town 2002-03, sharing with Herschelle Gibbs (228) in a South
African record opening partnership for Test cricket (368). His 277 in the first Test v
England at Edgbaston 2003 is the highest individual score for South Africa in Tests.
One of *Wisden*'s Five Cricketers of the Year 2004. His international awards include
South Africa's Man of the [Test] Series v England 2003 (714 runs at 79.33) and Man
of the Match in the third Test v New Zealand at Wellington 2003-04 (47/125*).
Captain of South Africa (youngest ever) since March 2003. An overseas player with
Somerset and captain 2005. Man of the Match in the Twenty20 Cup final v Lancashire
at The Oval 2005 (64*)
Best batting: 311 Somerset v Leicestershire, Taunton 2005
Best bowling: 2-145 South Africa v West Indies, St John's 2004-05
Stop press: Made Twenty20 international debut v New Zealand at Johannesburg
2005-06

	M	Inns	NO	Runs	HS	Avge	100s	50s	Ct	St	O	M	Runs	Wkts	Avge	Best	5wl	10wM
Test																		
All First	4	8	1	472	311	67.42	1	1	7	-	20	4	71	1	71.00	1-34	-	-
1-Day Int																		
C & G																		
tsL	4	4	1	218	74	72.66	-	3	3	-	17	0	95	1	95.00	1-51	-	
Twenty20	11	11	1	380	105	38.00	1	2	7	-	2	0	21	0	-	-	-	

Career Performances

	M	Inns	NO	Runs	HS	Avge	100s	50s	Ct	St	Balls	Runs	Wkts	Avge	Best	5wl	10wM
Test	39	67	5	3441	277	55.50	11	12	48	-	1085	611	7	87.28	2-145	-	-
All First	74	127	10	6270	311	53.58	19	21	102	-	1453	858	10	85.80	2-145	-	-
1-Day Int	69	68	3	2609	117	40.13	4	16	28	-	314	334	4	83.50	1-24	-	
C & G	1	1	0	4	4	4.00	-	-	-	-							
tsL	4	4	1	218	74	72.66	-	3	3	-	102	95	1	95.00	1-51	-	
Twenty20	11	11	1	380	105	38.00	1	2	7	-	12	21	0	-	-	-	

SMITH, G. J.   Nottinghamshire

Name: Gregory (<u>Greg</u>) James Smith
Role: Right-hand bat, left-arm fast bowler
Born: 30 October 1971, Pretoria,
South Africa
Height: 6ft 4in **Weight:** 15st
Nickname: Claw, Smudge, G
County debut: 2001
County cap: 2001
50 wickets in a season: 3
Place in batting averages: 276th av. 10.53
(2004 198th av. 22.33)
Place in bowling averages: 26th av. 25.76
(2004 43rd av. 29.76)
Strike rate: 46.33 (career 53.77)
Parents: Fred and Nellie
Wife and date of marriage: Thea,
5 September 1999
Children: Rob, 1989; Keeghan, 1999
Education: Pretoria BHS
Overseas tours: South Africa A to England 1996
Overseas teams played for: Northern Transvaal/Northerns Titans 1993-94 –
2001-02

Career highlights to date: 'Playing for South Africa A. Being capped by Notts'
Cricket moments to forget: 'Losing to Surrey in semi-final of B&H Cup [2001].
Losing to Natal in final of Standard Bank Cup [2000-01]'
Cricketers particularly admired: Wasim Akram, Fanie de Villiers, Kepler Wessels
Other sports played: Golf
Other sports followed: Football (Arsenal), South African rugby
Relaxations: 'Spending time with my family and friends'
Extras: Attended National Academy in South Africa. Took hat-trick (Mitchell, Drakes, Henderson) v Border at East London in semi-final (second leg) of Standard Bank Cup 2000-01; took 3-15 in deciding leg at East London, winning Man of the Match award. Nottinghamshire Player of the Year 2001. Holds a British passport and is not considered an overseas player
Best batting: 68 Northerns v Western Province, Centurion 1995-96
Best bowling: 8-53 Nottinghamshire v Essex, Trent Bridge 2002

2005 Season

	M	Inns	NO	Runs	HS	Avge	100s	50s	Ct	St	O	M	Runs	Wkts	Avge	Best	5wl	10wM
Test																		
All First	15	16	3	137	26	10.53	-	-	4	-	393.5	97	1314	51	25.76	5-19	1	-
1-Day Int																		
C & G	1	0	0	0	0	-	-	-	-	-	3	1	12	2	6.00	2-12	-	
tsL	12	6	3	45	16 *	15.00	-	-	1	-	83.2	4	418	11	38.00	3-49	-	
Twenty20	7	3	3	16	11 *	-	-	-	2	-	26.4	0	226	4	56.50	1-17	-	

Career Performances

	M	Inns	NO	Runs	HS	Avge	100s	50s	Ct	St	Balls	Runs	Wkts	Avge	Best	5wl	10wM
Test																	
All First	140	173	56	1597	68	13.64	-	2	29	-	23930	12233	445	27.48	8-53	17	2
1-Day Int																	
C & G	9	3	1	5	4 *	2.50	-	-	1	-	462	305	17	17.94	4-25	-	
tsL	59	26	11	134	17 *	8.93	-	-	8	-	2581	1934	75	25.78	4-28	-	
Twenty20	9	4	3	18	11 *	18.00	-	-	2	-	202	269	5	53.80	1-17	-	

81. Which West Indies bowler holds the record for
the most economical ten-over bowling stint in an ODI?

SMITH, G. M.   Derbyshire

Name: Gregory (<u>Greg</u>) Marc Smith
Role: Right-hand bat, right-arm medium bowler; all-rounder
Born: 20 April 1983, Johannesburg, South Africa
Nickname: Smithy
County debut: No first-team appearance
Strike rate: (career 74.00)
Parents: Ian and Nadine
Marital status: Single
Family links with cricket: Father used to work for United Cricket Board of South Africa
Education: St Stithians College; UNISA (University of South Africa)
Overseas tours: South Africa U19 to New Zealand (U19 World Cup) 2001-02
Overseas teams played for: Griqualand West 2003-04
Career highlights to date: 'Playing in the U19 World Cup final'
Cricketers particularly admired: Jacques Kallis
Other sports played: Tennis, golf
Favourite band: Coldplay
Relaxations: 'Movies'
Extras: Represented Gauteng Schools U13, U15, U19. South Africa Academy 2003-04
Opinions on cricket: 'Getting much stronger which is great to see.'
Best batting: 56* South Africa Academy v Sri Lanka A, Potchefstroom 2003-04
Best bowling: 2-60 Griqualand West v Border, East London 2003-04

2005 Season (did not make any first-class or one-day appearances)

Career Performances

	M	Inns	NO	Runs	HS	Avge	100s	50s	Ct	St	Balls	Runs	Wkts	Avge	Best	5wI	10wM
Test																	
All First	9	18	1	311	56*	18.29	-	2	1	-	444	251	6	41.83	2-60	-	-
1-Day Int																	
C & G																	
tsL																	
Twenty20																	

SMITH, T. C.   Lancashire

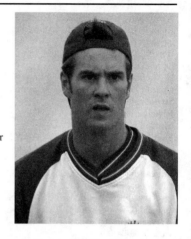

Name: Thomas (Tom) Christopher Smith
Role: Left-hand bat, right-arm medium-fast bowler; all-rounder
Born: 26 December 1985, Liverpool
Height: 6ft 3in **Weight:** 14st
Nickname: Smudger, Yeti
County debut: 2005
Strike rate: (career 120.00)
Parents: Mark and Jacqui
Marital status: Single
Family links with cricket: Brother plays for Lancashire U19. Father and stepfather play for local village teams
Education: Parklands High School; Runshaw College
Qualifications: 10 GCSEs, 4 A-levels
Off-season: National Academy
Overseas tours: England U19 to India 2004-05
Career highlights to date: 'Contract with Lancs and being picked for National Academy 2005-06'
Cricket moments to forget: 'First-ball duck on my first-class debut'
Cricket superstitions: 'Right pad on first'
Cricketers particularly admired: Andrew Flintoff, Ricky Ponting
Young players to look out for: Karl Brown
Other sports played: Football, golf, swimming
Other sports followed: Football (Liverpool FC)
Favourite band: Oasis, Goo Goo Dolls, Kelly Clarkson
Relaxations: 'Watching films and socialising with friends'
Extras: Represented England U19 2005. ECB National Academy 2005-06
Opinions on cricket: 'The game today has improved in all areas – technically, tactically and physically – making it a more exciting game to be involved in.'
Best bowling: 1-24 Lancashire v OUCCE, The Parks 2005

2005 Season

	M	Inns	NO	Runs	HS	Avge	100s	50s	Ct	St	O	M	Runs	Wkts	Avge	Best	5wI	10wM
Test																		
All First	1	1	0	0	0	0.00	-	-	1	-	20	8	46	1	46.00	1-24	-	-
1-Day Int																		
C & G																		
tsL	1	1	0	8	8	8.00	-	-	-	-	5	0	42	0	-	-	-	-
Twenty20																		

Career Performances

	M	Inns	NO	Runs	HS	Avge	100s	50s	Ct	St	Balls	Runs	Wkts	Avge	Best	5wI	10wM
Test																	
All First	1	1	0	0	0	0.00	-	-	1	-	120	46	1	46.00	1-24	-	-
1-Day Int																	
C & G																	
tsL	1	1	0	8	8	8.00	-	-	-	-	30	42	0	-		-	-
Twenty20																	

SMITH, W. R.   Nottinghamshire

Name: William (<u>Will</u>) Rew Smith
Role: Right-hand opening bat, occasional right-arm off-spin bowler, occasional wicket-keeper
Born: 28 September 1982, Luton
Height: 5ft 10in **Weight:** 12st
Nickname: Smudge, Jiggy, Posh Kid
County debut: 2002
Place in batting averages: 92nd av. 36.88
Strike rate: (career 95.50)
Parents: Jim and Barbara
Marital status: Single
Family links with cricket: 'Brother played a lot of county age group; Dad an avid follower and statistician!'
Education: Bedford School; Durham University
Qualifications: 11 GCSEs, 3 A-levels, BSc Molecular Biology and Biochemistry
Career outside cricket: 'Wannabe professional gambler! And repairing the body'
Off-season: 'Rest and rehab from two operations (hernia and shoulder)'
Overseas tours: Bedford School to Barbados (Sir Garfield Sobers International Tournament) 1998; British Universities to South Africa 2004
Overseas teams played for: Gordon DCC, Sydney 2001-02
Career highlights to date: 'Being part of Notts CCC Championship winning side 2005'
Cricket moments to forget: 'Still bagging pair at Rose Bowl for Notts 2nd XI 2001'
Cricket superstitions: 'None'
Cricketers particularly admired: Ian Botham, Steve Waugh, Graeme Fowler
Young players to look out for: Billy Godleman, Josh Mierkalns
Other sports played: 'Used to play everything; now concentrate on cricket as keep getting injured'

Other sports followed: Horse racing, football (Rushden & Diamonds, Luton Town), rugby union
Injuries: Double hernia; shoulder cartilage tear
Favourite band: Athlete
Relaxations: 'Watching horse racing, music, film etc'
Extras: Represented England U16-U18. Played for Durham UCCE 2003-05 (captain 2004-05). Represented British Universities 2004, 2005 (captain 2005). Nottinghamshire 2nd XI Player of the Year 2005
Opinions on cricket: 'Success of England team and Twenty20 cricket has been brilliant for the stature of the game, and long may it continue.'
Best batting: 156 DUCCE v Somerset, Taunton 2005
Best bowling: 3-34 DUCCE v Leicestershire, Leicester 2005

2005 Season

	M	Inns	NO	Runs	HS	Avge	100s	50s	Ct	St	O	M	Runs	Wkts	Avge	Best	5wl	10wM
Test																		
All First	7	10	1	332	156	36.88	1	1	4	-	60.3	4	321	4	80.25	3-34	-	-
1-Day Int																		
C & G																			
tsL	8	6	0	87	36	14.50	-	-	1	-								
Twenty20	8	7	0	158	55	22.57	-	2	3	-								

Career Performances

	M	Inns	NO	Runs	HS	Avge	100s	50s	Ct	St	Balls	Runs	Wkts	Avge	Best	5wl	10wM
Test																	
All First	15	23	3	548	156	27.40	1	1	10	-	573	448	6	74.66	3-34	-	-
1-Day Int																	
C & G																		
tsL	14	11	0	128	36	11.63	-	-	2	-							
Twenty20	10	8	0	159	55	19.87	-	2	4	-							

82. Who were Sri Lanka's opponents when Chaminda Vaas recorded the best bowling figures in ODIs, 8-19?

SNAPE, J. N.   Leicestershire

Name: <u>Jeremy</u> Nicholas Snape
Role: Right-hand bat, off-spin bowler,
county captain
Born: 27 April 1973, Stoke-on-Trent
Height: 5ft 8in **Weight:** 12st
Nickname: Snapey, Coot, Jez, Snapper
County debut: 1992 (Northamptonshire),
1999 (Gloucestershire), 2003 (Leicestershire)
County cap: 1999 (Glos), 2003 (Leics)
Place in batting averages: (2004 218th
av. 20.00)
Strike rate: (career 94.62)
Parents: Keith and Barbara
Wife and date of marriage: Joanne,
4 October 2003
Family links with cricket: 'Brother Jonathan
plays league cricket for Rode Park CC in
Cheshire. Dad loves cricket now, and Mum
hates the sweep shot!'
Education: Denstone College, Staffordshire; Durham University; Loughborough
University (studying for masters degree in Sports Psychology)
Qualifications: 8 GCSEs, 3 A-levels, BSc Natural Science
Overseas tours: England U18 to Canada (International Youth Tournament) 1991 (c);
England U19 to Pakistan 1991-92; Durham University to South Africa 1993, to Vienna
(European Indoor Championships) 1994; Northamptonshire to Cape Town 1993;
Christians in Sport to Zimbabwe 1994-95; Troubadours to South Africa 1997;
Gloucestershire to South Africa 1999; England to Zimbabwe (one-day series) 2001-02,
to India and New Zealand 2001-02 (one-day series), to Sri Lanka (ICC Champions
Trophy) 2002-03, to Australia 2002-03 (VB Series)
Overseas teams played for: Petone, Wellington, New Zealand 1994-95; Wainuiamata,
Wellington, New Zealand 1995-96; Techs CC, Cape Town 1996-99
Career highlights to date: 'Playing for England'
Cricket moments to forget: 'Breaking my thumb in Australia 2003 and being ruled
out of World Cup'
Cricketers particularly admired: Allan Lamb, Jack Russell
Relaxations: Travelling, music, cooking, good food and wine
Extras: Sir John Hobbs Silver Jubilee Memorial Prize 1988. B&H Gold Award for his
3-34 for Combined Universities v Worcestershire at The Parks 1992. Player of the
Tournament at European Indoor 6-a-side Championships 1994. Made ODI debut in
first ODI v Zimbabwe at Harare 2001-02, winning Man of the Match award for his
2-39 and brilliant catch. BBC West Country Sports Cricketer of the Year for 2001.

Struck 16-ball 34*, including winning runs, in the Twenty20 Cup final at Edgbaston 2004. Appointed captain of Leicestershire for 2006
Best batting: 131 Gloucestershire v Sussex, Cheltenham 2001
Best bowling: 5-65 Northamptonshire v Durham, Northampton 1995

2005 Season

	M	Inns	NO	Runs	HS	Avge	100s	50s	Ct	St	O	M	Runs	Wkts	Avge	Best	5wl	10wM
Test																		
All First	2	4	0	101	31	25.25	-	-	-	-	11	1	39	1	39.00	1-23	-	-
1-Day Int																		
C & G	1	1	0	8	8	8.00	-	-	-	-								
tsL	15	12	5	167	41 *	23.85	-	-	1	-	67.3	1	344	13	26.46	3-41	-	
Twenty20	9	9	1	127	39 *	15.87	-	-	2	-	23	1	156	11	14.18	3-18	-	

Career Performances

	M	Inns	NO	Runs	HS	Avge	100s	50s	Ct	St	Balls	Runs	Wkts	Avge	Best	5wl	10wM
Test																	
All First	113	169	30	3975	131	28.59	3	22	71	-	10409	5400	110	49.09	5-65	1	-
1-Day Int	10	7	3	118	38	29.50	-	-	5	-	529	403	13	31.00	3-43	-	
C & G	26	22	4	351	54	19.50	-	1	12	-	625	438	10	43.80	2-19	-	
tsL	156	126	36	2185	104 *	24.27	1	6	44	-	4427	3480	131	26.56	4-27	-	
Twenty20	22	21	8	278	39 *	21.38	-	-	9	-	390	446	18	24.77	3-14	-	

SNELL, S. D.   Gloucestershire

Name: <u>Steven</u> David Snell
Role: Right-hand bat, wicket-keeper, 'right-arm fast/rapid bowler'
Born: 27 February 1983, Winchester
Height: 6ft **Weight:** 11st 7lbs
Nickname: Snelly, Glove Monkey, Gonzo, Jaws
County debut: 2005
County cap: 2005
Parents: Jonathan and Sandra
Marital status: Single
Family links with cricket: 'Grandad and Dad both keen amateur cricketers. Brothers Rob and Peter both play at Ventnor Cricket Club (the real home of cricket!) on the Isle of Wight'
Education: Sandown High School
Qualifications: 10 GCSEs, 2 A-levels, ECB

Level 2 cricket coach, FA Level 1 football coach, EBA basketball coach, YMCA fitness instructor
Career outside cricket: 'Underwater fireman or journalist'
Off-season: 'Working in the marketing department for Gloucestershire CCC or playing club cricket in Melbourne'
Overseas tours: MCC Young Cricketers to Cape Town 2002, to Lanzarote 2003, to Sri Lanka 2004; MCC B to USA 2004
Overseas teams played for: Hermanus, Cape Town 2001-02; Brighton, Melbourne 2003-05
Career highlights to date: '83* on first-class debut against Bangladesh A'
Cricket moments to forget: 'Breaking my jaw in three places during nets at Lord's'
Cricket superstitions: 'Always have to ask somebody if I have the right shirt on. Bordering on obsessive-compulsive...'
Cricketers particularly admired: Jack Russell, Ian Healy, Jonty Rhodes
Young players to look out for: Will Rudge, Tom Stayt, Ben Woodhouse, Peter Snell
Other sports played: Football, squash ('thought I was half-decent till I played Matt Windows')
Other sports followed: Football (Portsmouth FC), 'aerobics Oz-style'
Favourite band: John Mayer, The Killers
Relaxations: 'Enjoy writing about the game; meals out; lying on Sandown beach on the Isle of Wight'
Extras: Played for Hampshire Board XI in the 2002 C&G. Attended World Cricket Academy, Mumbai 2003; International Cricket Academy, Port Elizabeth 2005
Opinions on cricket: 'Controversial decisions are an interesting part of the game! Leave the decisions to the guys in the middle and only use the third umpire for run-outs/stumpings. Creates some great talking points. It should be compulsory for wicket-keepers to bowl an over in every match in every competition.'
Best batting: 83* Gloucestershire v Bangladesh A, Bristol 2005

2005 Season

	M	Inns	NO	Runs	HS	Avge	100s	50s	Ct	St	O	M	Runs	Wkts	Avge	Best	5wI	10wM
Test																		
All First	2	4	1	141	83 *	47.00	-	1	4	-								
1-Day Int																		
C & G																		
tsL	7	5	0	26	17	5.20	-	-	8	-								
Twenty20																		

Career Performances

	M	Inns	NO	Runs	HS	Avge	100s	50s	Ct	St	Balls	Runs	Wkts	Avge	Best	5wl	10wM
Test																	
All First	2	4	1	141	83 *	47.00	-	1	4	-							
1-Day Int																	
C & G	1	1	0	3	3	3.00	-	-	1	-							
tsL	7	5	0	26	17	5.20	-	-	8	-							
Twenty20																	

SOLANKI, V. S.   Worcestershire

Name: <u>Vikram</u> Singh Solanki
Role: Right-hand bat, right-arm
off-spin bowler, county captain
Born: 1 April 1976, Udaipur, India
Height: 6ft **Weight:** 12st
Nickname: Vik
County debut: 1993 (one-day),
1995 (first-class)
County cap: 1998; colours, 2002
1000 runs in a season: 2
Place in batting averages: 138th av. 30.78
(2004 73rd av. 42.05)
Strike rate: (career 78.89)
Parents: Mr Vijay Singh and Mrs Florabel
Solanki
Marital status: Single
Family links with cricket: 'Father played in
India. Brother Vishal is a keen cricketer'
Education: Regis School, Wolverhampton; Open University
Qualifications: 9 GCSEs, 3 A-levels
Overseas tours: England U18 to South Africa 1992-93, to Denmark (ICC Youth
Tournament) 1994; England U19 to West Indies 1994-95; Worcestershire CCC
to Barbados 1996, to Zimbabwe 1997; England A to Zimbabwe and South Africa
1998-99, to Bangladesh and New Zealand 1999-2000, to West Indies 2000-01, to Sri
Lanka 2004-05, to West Indies 2005-06 (c); England to South Africa and Zimbabwe
1999-2000 (one-day series), to Kenya (ICC Knockout Trophy) 2000-01, to Pakistan
2000-01 (one-day series), to Bangladesh and Sri Lanka 2003-04 (one-day series), to
Zimbabwe (one-day series) 2004-05, to South Africa 2004-05 (one-day series), to
Pakistan 2005-06 (one-day series)
Overseas teams played for: Midland-Guildford, Perth, Western Australia
Career highlights to date: 'Playing for England'

Cricket moments to forget: 'Losing to Scotland (NatWest 1998)'
Cricketers particularly admired: Sachin Tendulkar, Graeme Hick
Other sports played: 'Enjoy most sports'
Relaxations: 'Reading; spending time with family and friends'
Extras: Scored more first-class runs (1339) in 1999 season than any other English player. Scored 106 v South Africa at The Oval in the NatWest Series 2003, winning the Man of the Match award and sharing with Marcus Trescothick (114*) in a record England opening partnership in ODIs (200). Man of the Match in the third ODI v Zimbabwe at Bulawayo 2004-05 (100*). C&G Man of the Match awards for his 127 (plus three catches and a run-out) in the semi-final v Warwickshire at Edgbaston 2004 and for his 115 in the final v Gloucestershire at Lord's 2004. Made Twenty20 international debut v Australia at the Rose Bowl 2005. Captain of Worcs since 2005
Best batting: 185 England A v Bangladesh, Chittagong 1999-2000
Best bowling: 5-40 Worcestershire v Middlesex, Lord's 2004

2005 Season

	M	Inns	NO	Runs	HS	Avge	100s	50s	Ct	St	O	M	Runs	Wkts	Avge	Best	5wI	10wM
Test																		
All First	13	21	2	585	80	30.78	-	4	9	-	11	0	49	0	-	-	-	-
1-Day Int	6	4	1	108	53*	36.00	-	1	-	-	2	0	14	0	-	-	-	
C & G	2	2	1	79	74*	79.00	-	1	-	-								
tsL	14	14	1	468	119	36.00	1	2	10	-	2	0	6	0	-	-	-	
Twenty20																		

Career Performances

	M	Inns	NO	Runs	HS	Avge	100s	50s	Ct	St	Balls	Runs	Wkts	Avge	Best	5wI	10wM
Test																	
All First	184	299	21	9767	185	35.13	15	56	218	-	6160	3606	78	46.23	5-40	4	1
1-Day Int	41	37	3	920	106	27.05	2	5	9	-	12	14	0	-	-	-	
C & G	26	25	2	1002	164*	43.56	4	4	10	-	225	174	3	58.00	1-25	-	
tsL	158	141	14	3897	122	30.68	5	22	62	-	258	258	7	36.85	2-5	-	
Twenty20	6	6	0	138	50	23.00	-	1	4	-							

SPEARMAN, C. M.　　　　Gloucestershire

Name: <u>Craig</u> Murray Spearman
Role: Right-hand opening bat
Born: 4 July 1972, Auckland, New Zealand
Height: 6ft **Weight:** 13st 7lbs
Nickname: Spears
County debut: 2002
County cap: 2002
Test debut: 1995-96
1000 runs in a season: 2
1st-Class 200s: 2
1st-Class 300s: 1
Place in batting averages: 108th av. 34.44
(2004 19th av. 56.23)
Strike rate: (career 78.00)
Parents: Murray and Sandra
Wife and date of marriage: Maree,
4 March 2004
Education: Kelston Boys High School,
Auckland; Massey University, Palmerston North, New Zealand
Qualifications: Bachelor of Business Studies (BBS; Finance major)
Overseas tours: New Zealand to India and Pakistan (World Cup) 1995-96, to West Indies 1995-96, to Sharjah (Singer Champions Trophy) 1996-97, to Pakistan 1996-97, to Zimbabwe 1997-98, to Australia 1997-98 (CUB Series), to Sri Lanka 1998, to India 1999-2000, to Zimbabwe 2000-01, to Kenya (ICC Knockout Trophy) 2000-01, to South Africa 2000-01; FICA World XI to New Zealand 2004-05
Overseas teams played for: Auckland 1993-96; Central Districts 1996-97 – 2000-01, 2002-03 – 2004-05
Career highlights to date: 'Playing international cricket; Test century; winning ICC Knockout Trophy [2000-01] with New Zealand; winning two C&G finals with Gloucestershire; scoring 341 for Gloucestershire v Middlesex (highest score for Gloucestershire)'
Cricket moments to forget: 'Misfielding on the boundary at the SCG in the fifth over and hearing about it for the next 45 overs'
Cricket superstitions: 'None'
Cricketers particularly admired: Gordon Greenidge
Other sports played: Golf, tennis
Other sports followed: Rugby, golf, football
Favourite band: U2
Relaxations: 'Sleeping'
Extras: Gloucestershire Players' Player of the Year 2002. Scored 123-ball 153 v Warwickshire at Gloucester in the NCL 2003 to set a new individual record score for Gloucestershire in the one-day league. Vice-captain of Gloucestershire 2003. Scored

341, the highest individual score for Gloucestershire in first-class cricket, v Middlesex at Gloucester 2004. C&G Man of the Match award for his 122-ball 143* in the semi-final v Yorkshire at Bristol 2004. 'Qualify to play for Gloucestershire because of my mother's Welsh background'

Best batting: 341 Gloucestershire v Middlesex, Gloucester 2004
Best bowling: 1-37 Central Districts v Wellington, New Plymouth 1999-2000

2005 Season

	M	Inns	NO	Runs	HS	Avge	100s	50s	Ct	St	O	M	Runs	Wkts	Avge	Best	5wI	10wM
Test																		
All First	14	27	0	930	216	34.44	1	3	13	-								
1-Day Int																		
C & G	2	2	0	20	11	10.00	-	-	1	-								
tsL	15	15	0	326	109	21.73	1	1	9	-								
Twenty20	8	6	0	125	39	20.83	-	-	2	-								

Career Performances

	M	Inns	NO	Runs	HS	Avge	100s	50s	Ct	St	Balls	Runs	Wkts	Avge	Best	5wI	10wM
Test	19	36	2	920	112	27.05	1	3	21	-							
All First	162	293	16	10543	341	38.06	22	49	154	-	78	55	1	55.00	1-37	-	-
1-Day Int	51	50	0	936	86	18.72	-	5	15	-	3	6	0	-	-	-	
C & G	15	15	2	687	143 *	52.84	2	5	5	-							
tsL	61	60	1	2103	153	35.64	4	11	25	-							
Twenty20	19	16	2	316	88	22.57	-	1	4	-							

83. Who helped Hampshire to victory in the 2005 C&G final and also boasts the best bowling figures recorded against England in an ODI?

SPENDLOVE, B. L. Derbyshire

Name: Benjamin (Ben) Lee Spendlove
Role: Right-hand bat, right-arm
off-spin bowler
Born: 4 November 1978, Derby
Height: 6ft 2in **Weight:** 13st
Nickname: Silky
County debut: 1997
Parents: Lee and Christine
Marital status: Single
Children: Zack, 8 September 1999
Family links with cricket: Father played
local leagues
Education: Trent College, Long Eaton
Qualifications: 9 GCSEs, ECB Level 1
coaching
Overseas tours: England U17 to Holland
(International Youth Tournament) 1995
Overseas teams played for: Gold Coast
Dolphins, Queensland 1996-97

Career highlights to date: 'Taking two catches as 12th man for England against
South Africa at Edgbaston [1998]'
Cricket moments to forget: 'Scoring no runs and ending up on the losing side in the
NatWest final [1998]'
Cricketers particularly admired: Robin Smith, Allan Lamb, Alec Stewart
Other sports played: Hockey (Derbyshire U15), rugby (Midlands U16)
Other sports followed: Football (Arsenal, Chesterfield)
Favourite band: Keane, Snow Patrol
Extras: Represented England U15, U17 and U19. Fielded as 12th man for England in
the first Test v South Africa at Edgbaston 1998, taking two catches. Played for
Derbyshire 1997-2000; rejoined the county 2004; released at the end of the 2005
season
Opinions on cricket: 'Enjoying seeing the national side playing positive and
aggressive Test cricket. Also good to see players I grew up playing with doing really
well at the top level.'
Best batting: 63 Derbyshire v Warwickshire, Edgbaston 1999

2005 Season

	M	Inns	NO	Runs	HS	Avge	100s	50s	Ct	St	O	M	Runs	Wkts	Avge	Best	5wI	10wM
Test																		
All First																		
1-Day Int																		
C & G	2	2	0	12	8	6.00	-	-	1	-								
tsL	2	2	0	15	11	7.50	-	-	1	-								
Twenty20																		

Career Performances

	M	Inns	NO	Runs	HS	Avge	100s	50s	Ct	St	Balls	Runs	Wkts	Avge	Best	5wI	10wM
Test																	
All First	20	36	2	656	63	19.29	-	2	10	-							
1-Day Int																	
C & G	10	9	0	223	58	24.77	-	2	3	-							
tsL	19	18	0	166	26	9.22	-	-	5	-							
Twenty20																	

SPURWAY, S. H. P.   Somerset

Name: Samuel (<u>Sam</u>) Harold Patrick Spurway
Role: Left-hand bat, wicket-keeper
Born: 13 March 1987, Taunton
Height: 6ft 1in **Weight:** 12st 7lbs
Nickname: Spurs, Speedy
County debut: No first-team appearance (*see* **Extras**)
Parents: Susan and Colin
Marital status: Single
Family links with cricket: 'Dad and older brother Tom play local cricket'
Education: Wadham Community School; Richard Huish College
Qualifications: 11 GCSEs, 3 A-levels
Off-season: 'Three weeks at the World Cricket Academy, Mumbai, India'
Overseas tours: West Region to West Indies 2001; Somerset to Cape Town 2006
Career highlights to date: 'Making my debut for Somerset in the International 20:20 v Leicestershire'
Cricket moments to forget: 'Getting my three front teeth knocked out whilst playing for my local club side Ilminster'

Cricket superstitions: 'None'
Cricketers particularly admired: Adam Gilchrist, Tim Crawley
Young players to look out for: Jack Cooper, William Spurway
Other sports played: Football, skittles
Other sports followed: Football (Yeovil and Man Utd)
Injuries: Twice broke nose – out for one week on each occasion
Favourite band: 'Tick in the Box'
Extras: Played for Somerset v Leicestershire in the International 20:20 Club Championship 2005 but has yet to appear for the county in first-class cricket or domestic one-day competition
Opinions on cricket: 'The future of English cricket looks in good shape with England winning the Ashes and many young talented players coming through.'

STEVENS, D. I.　　　　　　　　　Kent

Name: <u>Darren</u> Ian Stevens
Role: Right-hand bat, right-arm medium bowler
Born: 30 April 1976, Leicester
Height: 5ft 11in **Weight:** 12st
Nickname: Stevo
County debut: 1997 (Leicestershire), 2005 (Kent)
County cap: 2002 (Leicestershire), 2005 (Kent)
1000 runs in a season: 1
1st-Class 200s: 1
Place in batting averages: 38th av. 49.11 (2004 98th av. 36.26)
Place in bowling averages: 101st av. 38.52
Strike rate: 70.47 (career 81.17)
Parents: Maddy and Bob
Marital status: Single

Family links with cricket: Father and grandfather played league cricket in Leicestershire
Education: Mount Grace High School; John Cleveland College, Hinckley; Hinckley Tech; Charles Klein College
Qualifications: 5 GCSEs, BTEC National in Sports Studies
Overseas tours: Leicestershire U19 to South Africa 1994-95; Leicestershire to Barbados 1998, to Sri Lanka 1999, to Potchefstroom 2001; ECB National Academy to Australia and Sri Lanka 2002-03
Overseas teams played for: Wanderers CC, Johannesburg, South Africa 1996-97;

Rhodes University, Grahamstown, South Africa 1997-98; Fairfield CC, Sydney 1998-99; Hawthorn-Waverley, Melbourne 1999-2000; Taita CC, Wellington, New Zealand 2000-01; Ringwood CC, Melbourne 2001-02

Career highlights to date: 'The build-up to my first final at Lord's'

Cricket moments to forget: 'Losing in my first final in the C&G against Somerset 2001'

Cricketers particularly admired: Steve Waugh, Viv Richards, Ian Botham

Other sports played: Golf, squash

Other sports followed: Football (Leicester City), rugby union (Leicester Tigers)

Favourite band: U2

Relaxations: 'Music, spending time with close friends'

Extras: Received painting from Sir Colin Cowdrey on day of maiden first-class 100 (130 in fourth Championship match), v Sussex at Arundel 1999. Won Sir Ron Brierley/Crusaders Scholarship 1999. Included in provisional England squad of 30 for the 2002-03 World Cup. Scored 101 v Hampshire at West End 2005, in the process passing 1000 first-class runs in a season for the first time

Best batting: 208 Kent v Glamorgan, Canterbury 2005

Best bowling: 3-19 Kent v Gloucestershire, Maidstone 2005

2005 Season

	M	Inns	NO	Runs	HS	Avge	100s	50s	Ct	St	O	M	Runs	Wkts	Avge	Best	5wI	10wM
Test																		
All First	16	27	1	1277	208	49.11	4	6	13	-	199.4	28	655	17	38.52	3-19	-	-
1-Day Int																		
C & G	3	3	1	84	47 *	42.00	-	-	1	-	24	2	81	2	40.50	2-35	-	
tsL	17	16	2	385	76	27.50	-	3	6	-	69	4	344	11	31.27	5-32	1	
Twenty20	8	7	0	80	19	11.42	-	-	1	-	7	0	75	2	37.50	1-13	-	

Career Performances

	M	Inns	NO	Runs	HS	Avge	100s	50s	Ct	St	Balls	Runs	Wkts	Avge	Best	5wI	10wM
Test																	
All First	96	161	9	4819	208	31.70	8	29	77	-	1867	1068	23	46.43	3-19	-	-
1-Day Int																	
C & G	17	16	1	522	133	34.80	1	2	6	-	228	163	4	40.75	2-26	-	
tsL	105	98	8	2350	125	26.11	1	16	46	-	615	501	15	33.40	5-32	1	
Twenty20	21	20	1	324	39	17.05	-	-	7	-	54	91	3	30.33	1-13	-	

STEYN, D. W. Essex

Name: <u>Dale</u> Willem Steyn
Role: Right-hand bat, right-arm fast bowler
Born: 27 June 1983, Phalaborwa,
South Africa
County debut: 2005
Test debut: 2004-05
Place in bowling averages: 144th av. 59.85
Strike rate: 85.42 (career 65.86)
Overseas tours: South Africa A to Sri Lanka
2005-06
Overseas teams played for: Northerns
2003-04; Titans 2004-05 –
Extras: Played for African XI v Asian
Cricket Council XI in the Afro-Asia Cup
2005-06 in South Africa. His match awards
include Man of the Match v Warriors at East
London in the SuperSport Series 2004-05 (5-
30/4-66). Was an overseas player with Essex

during the 2005 season as a locum for Danish Kaneria
Best batting: 82 Essex v Durham, Riverside 2005
Best bowling: 5-30 Titans v Warriors, East London 2004-05
Stop press: Made ODI debut for African XI v Asian Cricket Council XI at Centurion
and played for South Africa v Australia at Melbourne in the VB Series 2005-06

2005 Season

	M	Inns	NO	Runs	HS	Avge	100s	50s	Ct	St	O	M	Runs	Wkts	Avge	Best	5wI	10wM
Test																		
All First	6	7	2	94	82	18.80	-	1	2	-	199.2	38	838	14	59.85	3-69	-	-
1-Day Int																		
C & G	1	1	1	2	2*	-	-	-	-	-	10	0	32	0	-		-	-
tsL	2	0	0	0	0	-	-	-	1	-	14	1	65	4	16.25	3-34	-	
Twenty20																		

Career Performances

	M	Inns	NO	Runs	HS	Avge	100s	50s	Ct	St	Balls	Runs	Wkts	Avge	Best	5wI	10wM
Test	3	5	3	25	8	12.50	-	-	1	-	602	416	8	52.00	2-26	-	-
All First	19	24	8	193	82	12.06	-	1	6	-	3491	2141	53	40.39	5-30	1	-
1-Day Int	2	2	0	4	3	2.00	-	-	-	-	61	42	2	21.00	1-2	-	
C & G	1	1	1	2	2*	-	-	-	-	-	60	32	0	-		-	-
tsL	2	0	0	0	0	-	-	-	1	-	84	65	4	16.25	3-34	-	
Twenty20																		

STIFF, D. A.   Kent

Name: <u>David</u> Alexander Stiff
Role: Right-hand bat, right-arm fast bowler
Born: 20 October 1984, Dewsbury
Height: 6ft 6in **Weight:** 15st
Nickname: Stiffy, Stiffler
County debut: 2004
Strike rate: (career 70.00)
Parents: Christine and Ian
Marital status: Single
Family links with cricket: Eldest brother,
Peter, played club cricket in Yorkshire.
Youngest brother, William, has played for
Yorkshire Schools and North of England
Schools age group teams
Education: Batley Grammar School
Qualifications: 6 GCSEs
Overseas tours: England U17 to Australia
2001; Yorkshire to Grenada 2002; England
U19 to Australia 2002-03, to Bangladesh (U19 World Cup) 2003-04
Career highlights to date: 'Taking five wickets in the first innings of the third U19
"Test" match v Australia at Bankstown, Sydney [2002-03]'
Cricket moments to forget: 'Losing that same match [*see above*] and the series by
14 runs'
Cricketers particularly admired: Allan Donald, Brett Lee, Jason Gillespie,
Courtney Walsh
Young players to look out for: Mark Lawson
Favourite band: Radiohead
Relaxations: Music
Extras: Yorkshire Cricket Academy 1999-2003. Took 5-35 for England U19 in the
third 'Test' v Australia U19 at Bankstown Oval, Sydney 2002-03. Represented
England U19 2004. ECB National Academy 2004-05 (part-time)
Best batting: 18 Kent v Lancashire, Tunbridge Wells 2004
Best bowling: 3-88 Kent v New Zealanders, Canterbury 2004

2005 Season

	M	Inns	NO	Runs	HS	Avge	100s	50s	Ct	St	O	M	Runs	Wkts	Avge	Best	5wI	10wM
Test																		
All First	1	2	2	27	15 *	-	-	-	-	-	17	1	85	2	42.50	1-41	-	-
1-Day Int																		
C & G																		
tsL																		
Twenty20																		

Career Performances

	M	Inns	NO	Runs	HS	Avge	100s	50s	Ct	St	Balls	Runs	Wkts	Avge	Best	5wI	10wM
Test																	
All First	7	6	3	57	18	19.00	-	-	1	-	630	504	9	56.00	3-88	-	-
1-Day Int																	
C & G	1	0	0	0	0	-	-	-	-	-	30	27	1	27.00	1-27	-	
tsL																	
Twenty20																	

STOKES, M. S. T.   Hampshire

Name: <u>Mitchell</u> Sam Thomas Stokes
Role: Right-hand bat, right-arm off-spin bowler; all-rounder
Born: 27 March 1987, Basingstoke
Height: 5ft 8in **Weight:** 10st
Nickname: Stokesy
County debut: 2005 (one-day)
Parents: Paul and Janice
Marital status: Single
Education: Cranbourne School; Basingstoke College of Technology
Qualifications: Level 1 cricket coaching
Off-season: 'Working, training, passing driving test'
Overseas tours: West of England U15 to West Indies 2002; England U19 to India 2004-05
Career highlights to date: 'Twenty20 debut at The Oval. England U19 tour to India'
Young players to look out for: Liam Dawson
Other sports played: Football (Aldershot Youth – national champions 2003-04)
Other sports followed: Football (Spurs)

Favourite band: 'Don't have one – I like R&B, hip hop, old school'
Relaxations: 'Music, shopping for me'
Extras: Bunbury U15 Festival Bowler of the Tournament. Basingstoke Sports Awards Sportsman of the Year
Opinions on cricket: 'I think there should be an international Twenty20 competition after the success it's had in the county game.'

2005 Season

	M	Inns	NO	Runs	HS	Avge	100s	50s	Ct	St	O	M	Runs	Wkts	Avge	Best	5wI	10wM
Test																		
All First																		
1-Day Int																		
C & G																		
tsL																		
Twenty20	6	4	0	54	22	13.50	-	-	1	-	1	0	14	0	-		-	-

Career Performances

	M	Inns	NO	Runs	HS	Avge	100s	50s	Ct	St	Balls	Runs	Wkts	Avge	Best	5wI	10wM
Test																	
All First																	
1-Day Int																	
C & G																	
tsL																	
Twenty20	6	4	0	54	22	13.50	-	-	1	-	6	14	0	-		-	-

84. Name the two Zimbabwe bowlers who have taken six wickets in an ODI?

STONEMAN, M. D.   Durham

Name: <u>Mark</u> Daniel Stoneman
Role: Left-hand top-order bat,
'right-arm variations'
Born: 26 June 1987, Newcastle upon Tyne
Height: 5ft 11in **Weight:** 12st 5lbs
Nickname: Rocky, Doug
County debut: No first-team appearance
Parents: Ian and Pauline
Marital status: Single
Family links with cricket: 'Father played.
Grandfather played and was also an umpire'
Education: Whickham Comprehensive
School
Qualifications: 11 GCSEs, 3 A-levels
Career outside cricket: 'Casual work'
Off-season: 'Temporary work pre-Christmas.
Beating on local game shoot. Darren
Lehmann Talent Squad, Adelaide'
Overseas tours: Durham Development Squad to Mumbai 2004-05; England U19 to
Sri Lanka (U19 World Cup) 2005-06
Career highlights to date: '155 for North Region in U19 trials. 46 on 2nd XI debut'
Cricket moments to forget: 'None. All experiences can provide positives and
lessons learned'
Cricket superstitions: 'Right pad on first'
Cricketers particularly admired: Brian Lara
Young players to look out for: Mark Turner, Ben Harmison, Karl Turner
Other sports followed: Football (Newcastle United FC)
Favourite band: 'None in particular. Like dance, R&B music'
Relaxations: 'Watching films, socialising with friends'
Extras: Attended Darren Lehmann Talent Squad, Adelaide, January-March 2006
Opinions on cricket: 'Starting to gain recognition it deserves due to successful Ashes
series in summer 2005. More varieties in forms of the game providing additional
challenges to help advance players in terms of roles they can play – Championship,
one-day, Twenty20 etc. – which takes the game forward.'

STRAUSS, A. J.   Middlesex

Name: <u>Andrew</u> John Strauss
Role: Left-hand bat, left-arm medium bowler
Born: 2 March 1977, Johannesburg, South Africa
Height: 5ft 11in **Weight:** 13st
Nickname: Straussy, Johann, Levi, Mareman, Muppet, Lord Brocket
County debut: 1997 (one-day), 1998 (first-class)
County cap: 2001
Test debut: 2004
1000 runs in a season: 3
Place in batting averages: 156th av. 29.40 (2004 41st av. 50.28)
Strike rate: (career 48.00)
Parents: David and Dawn
Wife and date of marriage: Ruth, 18 October 2003
Children: Samuel David, December 2005
Education: Radley College; Durham University
Qualifications: 4 A-levels, BA (Hons) Economics
Overseas tours: Durham University to Zimbabwe 1997-98; Middlesex to South Africa 2000; ECB National Academy to Australia 2001-02; England to Bangladesh and Sri Lanka 2003-04 (one-day series), to West Indies 2003-04, to Zimbabwe (one-day series) 2004-05, to South Africa 2004-05, to Pakistan 2005-06, to India 2005-06
Overseas teams played for: Sydney University 1998-99; Mosman, Sydney 1999-2001
Cricket moments to forget: 'Getting out second ball of the season 2001'
Cricketers particularly admired: Allan Donald, Brian Lara, Saqlain Mushtaq
Other sports played: Golf (Durham University 1998), rugby (Durham University 1996-97)
Other sports followed: 'Anything with a ball'
Extras: Middlesex Player of the Year 2001. Scored century (112) plus 83 in second innings on Test debut in the first Test v New Zealand at Lord's (his home ground) 2004, winning Man of the Match award. Scored century (100) v West Indies, also at Lord's, in the NatWest Series 2004, in the process sharing with Andrew Flintoff (123) in a new record partnership for England in ODIs (226). Wombwell Cricket Lovers' Society George Spofforth Cricketer of the Year 2004. Captain of Middlesex 2002-04. Scored 126 in the first Test v South Africa at Port Elizabeth 2004-05, achieving feat of scoring a Test century on home and away debuts and becoming first player to score a Test century in his first innings against each of first three opponents. His other international awards include Man of the [Test] Series v South Africa 2004-05 (656 runs at 72.88). Vodafone England Cricketer of the Year 2004-05. One of *Wisden*'s Five

Cricketers of the Year 2005. Made Twenty20 international debut v Australia at the Rose Bowl 2005
Best batting: 176 Middlesex v Durham, Lord's 2001
Best bowling: 1-27 Middlesex v Nottinghamshire, Lord's 2003
Stop press: Appointed MBE in 2006 New Year Honours as part of 2005 Ashes-winning England team. Man of the Match in the first ODI v Pakistan at Lahore 2005-06 (94)

2005 Season

	M	Inns	NO	Runs	HS	Avge	100s	50s	Ct	St	O	M	Runs	Wkts	Avge	Best	5wI	10wM
Test	7	12	0	470	129	39.16	2	1	9	-								
All First	11	20	0	588	129	29.40	2	1	12	-								
1-Day Int	10	10	1	466	152	51.77	1	2	3	-								
C & G	2	1	0	24	24	24.00	-	-	1	-								
tsL	4	3	0	26	12	8.66	-	-	4	-								
Twenty20																		

Career Performances

	M	Inns	NO	Runs	HS	Avge	100s	50s	Ct	St	Balls	Runs	Wkts	Avge	Best	5wI	10wM
Test	19	36	2	1716	147	50.47	7	5	25	-							
All First	106	187	12	7435	176	42.48	18	34	71	-	48	58	1	58.00	1-27	-	-
1-Day Int	39	38	6	1228	152	38.37	2	6	10	-	6	3	0	-	-	-	
C & G	12	11	0	339	75	30.81	-	3	1	-							
tsL	74	70	4	1832	127	27.75	2	13	14	-							
Twenty20	7	7	0	194	60	27.71	-	2	4	-							

STREAK, H. H.   Warwickshire

Name: Heath Hilton Streak
Role: Right-hand bat, right-arm fast bowler, county captain
Born: 16 March 1974, Bulawayo, Zimbabwe
Height: 6ft 1in **Weight:** 15st
Nickname: Streaky, Stack
County debut: 1995 (Hampshire), 2004 (Warwickshire)
County cap: 2005 (Warwickshire)
Test debut: 1993-94
50 wickets in a season: 1
Place in batting averages: 206th av. 21.55 (2004 171st av. 25.71)
Place in bowling averages: 38th av. 27.23 (2004 7th av. 21.75)
Strike rate: 58.69 (career 60.48)
Parents: Denis and Sheona
Wife and date of marriage: Nadine, 18 August 2000
Children: Holly, 23 December 1992; Charlotte, 14 August 2002

Family links with cricket: 'Denis, my father, played for Rhodesia and Zimbabwe'
Education: Falcon College, Zimbabwe
Qualifications: Pro safari guide
Career outside cricket: Farming/safari guide
Overseas tours: Zimbabwe to England 1993, to India (Hero Cup) 1993-94, to Pakistan 1993-94, to New Zealand 1995-96, to India and Pakistan (World Cup) 1995-96, to Sri Lanka 1996, 1997-98, to New Zealand 1997-98, to Malaysia (Commonwealth Games) 1998-99, to Bangladesh (Wills International Cup) 1998-99, to Pakistan 1998-99, to UK, Ireland and Holland (World Cup) 1999, to West Indies 1999-2000, to England 2000, to Kenya (ICC Knockout Trophy) 2000-01 (c), to India 2000-01 (c), to New Zealand 2000-01 (c), to Bangladesh 2001-02, to Sri Lanka 2001-02, to India 2001-02, to Sri Lanka (ICC Champions Trophy) 2002-03 (c), to England 2003 (c), to Australia 2003-04 (c), to South Africa 2004-05, plus other one-day tournaments in Australia, South Africa, Sharjah, India and Bangladesh; FICA World XI to New Zealand 2004-05

Overseas teams played for: Matabeleland 1993-94 – 2003-04
Career highlights to date: 'Inaugural Test win, v Pakistan [1994-95]'
Cricket moments to forget: 'None – some are embarrassing but funny on reflection!'
Cricket superstitions: 'Nelson!'
Cricketers particularly admired: Dennis Lillee, Ian Botham
Other sports played: Rugby (Zimbabwe U19), fishing
Other sports followed: Football (Liverpool)
Favourite band: U2
Relaxations: 'Time with family and watersports'
Extras: First Zimbabwe player to 100 and 200 wickets in both Tests and ODIs. Has won several ODI awards, including Man of the Match v West Indies at Sydney in the CUB Series 2000-01 (45/4-8) and Man of the Series v Bangladesh 2003-04. His Test awards include Zimbabwe's Man of the Series v England in 2000 and 2003. Captain of Zimbabwe 2000-01 and 2002-04, including the 2002-03 World Cup. An overseas player with Hampshire 1995; an overseas player with Warwickshire since 2004. Had match figures of 13-158 (7-80/6-78) in his first game for Warwickshire, v Northamptonshire at Edgbaston 2004. Announced retirement from international cricket in October 2005. Appointed captain of Warwickshire for 2006
Opinions on cricket: 'Introduction of Twenty20 great for the game. It will generate well needed support for the game and draw youngsters to watch.'
Best batting: 131 Matabeleland v Midlands, Bulawayo 2003-04
Best bowling: 7-55 Matabeleland v Mashonaland, Bulawayo 2003-04

2005 Season

	M	Inns	NO	Runs	HS	Avge	100s	50s	Ct	St	O	M	Runs	Wkts	Avge	Best	5wI	10wM
Test																		
All First	9	11	2	194	51	21.55	-	1	8	-	254.2	67	708	26	27.23	6-31	2	-
1-Day Int																		
C & G	3	1	1	28	28 *	-	-	-	1	-	28	7	83	6	13.83	4-27	-	
tsL	8	5	2	28	13	9.33	-	-	1	-	64.1	8	261	19	13.73	4-22	-	
Twenty20	6	4	1	89	59	29.66	-	1	1	-	14	0	115	4	28.75	3-21	-	

Career Performances

	M	Inns	NO	Runs	HS	Avge	100s	50s	Ct	St	Balls	Runs	Wkts	Avge	Best	5wI	10wM
Test	65	107	18	1990	127 *	22.35	1	11	17	-	13559	6079	216	28.14	6-73	7	-
All First	149	225	39	4893	131	26.30	6	23	54	-	26905	12189	445	27.39	7-55	14	1
1-Day Int	189	159	55	2943	79 *	28.29	-	13	46	-	9468	7129	239	29.82	5-32	1	
C & G	3	1	1	28	28 *	-	-	-	1	-	168	83	6	13.83	4-27	-	
tsL	28	18	8	199	32 *	19.90	-	-	3	-	1274	1077	48	22.43	4-22	-	
Twenty20	7	5	1	107	59	26.75	-	1	2	-	102	147	4	36.75	3-21	-	

STUBBINGS, S. D.   Derbyshire

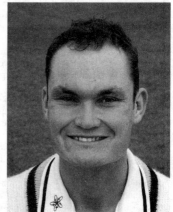

Name: <u>Stephen</u> David Stubbings
Role: Left-hand bat, occasional right-arm medium/spin bowler, 'very occasional wicket-keeper'
Born: 31 March 1978, Huddersfield
Height: 6ft 3in **Weight:** 15st
Nickname: Stubbo
County debut: 1997
County cap: 2001
1000 runs in a season: 3
Place in batting averages: 70th av. 40.21 (2004 163rd av. 27.51)
Parents: Marie and David
Marital status: Single
Family links with cricket: 'My father used to play in Cambridge, while my brother Jonathan plays his cricket at my old club Delacombe Park in Melbourne, Australia'
Education: Frankston High School; Swinburne University – both Melbourne, Australia
Qualifications: Victorian Certificate of Education (VCE), ACB Level 1 coaching
Overseas tours: Derbyshire to Portugal 2000

Overseas teams played for: Delacombe Park CC, Melbourne 1990-94; Frankston Peninsula CC, Victoria 1994-2000, 2002-03; Kingborough CC, Tasmania 2000-02
Career highlights to date: 'Being presented with my Derbyshire county cap at the end of the 2001 season and receiving Player of the Year award'
Cricket moments to forget: 'Making a pair of noughts against Glamorgan at Derby during the 2002 season'
Cricketers particularly admired: Mark Taylor, Michael Atherton, Steve Waugh, Ricky Ponting 'and a couple of Derbyshire players who shall remain anonymous!'
Young players to look out for: Sam Patel
Other sports followed: Australian Rules football (Essendon Bombers)
Relaxations: 'Chris Bassano fishing adventures; eating, drinking, sleeping'
Extras: Represented Victoria at all junior levels. Spent two years on the cricket programme at the Victorian Institute of Sport. Scored 135* v Kent at Canterbury 2000, taking part in an unbroken opening partnership of 293 with Steve Titchard (141*); it was the first occasion on which Derbyshire had batted all day without losing a wicket. Derbyshire Player of the Year 2001
Best batting: 151 Derbyshire v Somerset, Taunton 2005

2005 Season

	M	Inns	NO	Runs	HS	Avge	100s	50s	Ct	St	O	M	Runs	Wkts	Avge	Best	5wl	10wM
Test																		
All First	16	29	1	1126	151	40.21	2	8	9	-								
1-Day Int																		
C & G																		
tsL	14	14	1	524	98	40.30	-	4	1	-								
Twenty20	1	1	0	8	8	8.00	-	-	1	-								

Career Performances

	M	Inns	NO	Runs	HS	Avge	100s	50s	Ct	St	Balls	Runs	Wkts	Avge	Best	5wl	10wM
Test																	
All First	88	159	7	4823	151	31.73	8	27	36	-	54	77	0	-	-	-	-
1-Day Int																	
C & G	3	2	0	63	47	31.50	-	-	-	-							
tsL	67	65	4	1558	98 *	25.54	-	8	8	-							
Twenty20	1	1	0	8	8	8.00	-	-	1	-							

STYRIS, S. B.   Middlesex

Name: <u>Scott</u> Bernard Styris
Role: Right-hand bat, right-arm
medium-fast bowler; all-rounder
Born: 10 July 1975, Brisbane, Australia
Height: 5ft 10in **Weight:** 14st
Nickname: The Rus
County debut: 2005
Test debut: 2002
1st-Class 200s: 1
Place in batting averages: 149th av. 30.25
(2004 155th av. 28.58)
Place in bowling averages: 16th av. 23.54
Strike rate: 44.67 (career 60.13)
Parents: Bernie and Heather
Marital status: Partner Nicky
Education: Hamilton Boys High School
Off-season: 'First-class cricket in
New Zealand'
Overseas tours: New Zealand A to England 2002; New Zealand to India 1999-2000
(one-day series), to Zimbabwe and South Africa 2000-01, to Kenya (ICC Knockout
Trophy) 2000-01, to Australia 2001-02 (VB Series), to Pakistan 2002, to West Indies
2002, to Sri Lanka (ICC Champions Trophy) 2002-03, to Africa (World Cup) 2002-03,
to Sri Lanka 2003, to India 2003-04, to England 2004, to England (ICC Champions
Trophy) 2004, to Bangladesh 2004-05, to Australia 2004-05, to Zimbabwe 2005-06, to
South Africa 2005-06 plus one-day tournaments in Singapore and Sharjah
Overseas teams played for: Northern Districts 1994-95 – 2004-05; Auckland
2005-06 –
Career highlights to date: 'Test century on debut'
Cricket superstitions: 'None'
Cricketers particularly admired: Jacques Kallis
Other sports played: Golf
Other sports followed: Baseball (Oakland), football (Man U), rugby (All Blacks)
Injuries: Out for three months with knee surgery; for one month with a hamstring
injury
Favourite band: Green Day
Extras: Made Test debut in the second Test v West Indies in Grenada 2002, scoring
107 and 69*. His ODI awards include Man of the Series v Bangladesh 2004-05 and
Man of the Match in the fourth ODI v West Indies at Port of Spain 2002 (63*/6-25)
and in the first ODI v Pakistan at Auckland 2003-04 (3-34/101*). Made Twenty20
international debut v Australia at Auckland 2004-05. An overseas player with
Middlesex since 2005

Best batting: 212* Northern Districts v Otago, Hamilton 2001-02
Best bowling: 6-32 Northern Districts v Otago, Gisborne 1999-2000
Stop press: ODI Man of the Match award v Australia at Christchurch 2005-06 (101)

2005 Season

	M	Inns	NO	Runs	HS	Avge	100s	50s	Ct	St	O	M	Runs	Wkts	Avge	Best	5wI	10wM
Test																		
All First	9	17	1	484	100*	30.25	1	3	4	-	230.5	44	730	31	23.54	6-73	2	1
1-Day Int																		
C & G	2	1	0	26	26	26.00	-	-	1	-	20	1	107	3	35.66	2-55	-	
tsL	12	12	0	363	82	30.25	-	3	5	-	90.4	2	420	20	21.00	4-56	-	
Twenty20	9	8	1	199	73*	28.42	-	1	1	-	32	0	223	9	24.77	2-20	-	

Career Performances

	M	Inns	NO	Runs	HS	Avge	100s	50s	Ct	St	Balls	Runs	Wkts	Avge	Best	5wI	10wM
Test	19	33	2	1233	170	39.77	4	5	16	-	1587	841	16	52.56	3-28	-	-
All First	88	148	15	4131	212*	31.06	7	19	63	-	10367	5070	174	29.13	6-32	8	1
1-Day Int	96	82	12	1900	141	27.14	2	10	38	-	3597	2819	95	29.67	6-25	1	
C & G	2	1	0	26	26	26.00	-	-	1	-	120	107	3	35.66	2-55	-	
tsL	12	12	0	363	82	30.25	-	3	5	-	544	420	20	21.00	4-56	-	
Twenty20	9	8	1	199	73*	28.42	-	1	1	-	192	223	9	24.77	2-20	-	

SUPPIAH, A. V. Somerset

Name: Arul Vivasvan Suppiah
Role: Right-hand bat, left-arm orthodox spin bowler
Born: 30 August 1983, Kuala Lumpur, Malaysia
Height: 6ft **Weight:** 12st 7lbs
Nickname: Ruley, Ja Rule
County debut: 2002
Place in batting averages: 124th av. 32.23
Strike rate: (career 56.50)
Parents: Suppiah and Baanumathi
Marital status: Single
Family links with cricket: Brother Rohan Vishnu Suppiah has played cricket for Malaysia
Education: Millfield School; Exeter University
Qualifications: 9 GCSEs, 4 A-levels, BA in Accounting and Finance, Level 1 coaching qualification

Overseas tours: Millfield School to South Africa 1997, to Sri Lanka 1999; West of England U15 to West Indies 1998; Malaysia to Sharjah (Asian Cricket Council Trophy) 2000-01

Career highlights to date: 'Making my first-class debut v West Indies A for Somerset 2002; making my debut in the NUL for Somerset v Durham 2002; being the youngest ever cricketer to play for Malaysia; playing for England through the age groups'

Cricket moments to forget: 'Being bowled out for a golden duck off the seventh ball of the over'

Cricket superstitions: 'Right pad first'

Cricketers particularly admired: Sachin Tendulkar, Wasim Akram, Marcus Trescothick

Young players to look out for: Richard Timms, Bilal Shafayat, Kadeer Ali, Matthew Wood

Other sports played: Hockey (Somerset U16), badminton (Millfield School 1st team)

Other sports followed: Football (Manchester United)

Favourite band: Red Hot Chili Peppers

Relaxations: 'Web surfing, listening to music'

Extras: Made debut for Malaysia aged 15. Has represented England U14, U15, U17 and U18. Somerset U15 Player of the Year 1998. West of England U15 Player of the Year 1998. Most Promising Sportsman for Malaysia 2000. NBC Denis Compton Award for the most promising young Somerset player 2002

Best batting: 123 Somerset v Derbyshire, Derby 2005

Best bowling: 3-46 Somerset v West Indies A, Taunton 2002

2005 Season

	M	Inns	NO	Runs	HS	Avge	100s	50s	Ct	St	O	M	Runs	Wkts	Avge	Best	5wI	10wM
Test																		
All First	7	13	0	419	123	32.23	1	2	1	-	43.1	8	191	2	95.50	1-28	-	-
1-Day Int																		
C & G	1	1	0	8	8	8.00	-	-	-	-	6	0	42	0	-		-	-
tsL	8	8	1	215	79	30.71	-	1	3	-	28.1	0	144	6	24.00	3-41	-	
Twenty20	6	3	1	31	18 *	15.50	-	-	1	-								

Career Performances

	M	Inns	NO	Runs	HS	Avge	100s	50s	Ct	St	Balls	Runs	Wkts	Avge	Best	5wI	10wM
Test																	
All First	12	21	0	506	123	24.09	1	2	3	-	565	395	10	39.50	3-46	-	-
1-Day Int																	
C & G	5	5	0	142	70	28.40	-	1	2	-	162	144	2	72.00	1-24	-	
tsL	14	14	1	296	79	22.76	-	1	4	-	265	235	9	26.11	3-41	-	
Twenty20	6	3	1	31	18 *	15.50	-	-	1	-							

SUTCLIFFE, I. J. Lancashire

Name: Iain John Sutcliffe
Role: Left-hand bat, leg-spin bowler
Born: 20 December 1974, Leeds
Height: 6ft 2in **Weight:** 13st
Nickname: Sutty
County debut: 1995 (Leicestershire),
2003 (Lancashire)
County cap: 1997 (Leicestershire),
2003 (Lancashire)
1000 runs in a season: 3
1st-Class 200s: 1
Place in batting averages: 45th av. 47.54
(2004 119th av. 34.26)
Strike rate: (career 49.00)
Parents: John and Valerie
Marital status: Single
Education: Leeds Grammar School;
Oxford University
Qualifications: 10 GCSEs, 4 A-levels, 2.1 PPE degree
Overseas tours: Leeds GS to Kenya; Leicestershire to South Africa, to West Indies,
to Sri Lanka
Career highlights to date: 'Championship winner's medal 1998'
Cricketers particularly admired: Brian Lara, David Gower
Other sports played: Boxing (Oxford Blue 1994, 1995; British Universities
Light-middleweight Champion 1993)
Other sports followed: Football (Liverpool)
Relaxations: Socialising, cinema
Extras: Played NCA England U14 and NCA Development Team U18/U19. Scored 55
of Leicestershire's first innings total of 96 v Pakistanis at Leicester 2001.
Leicestershire vice-captain 2002. Leicestershire Player of the Year 2002. Scored
century (102*) v Surrey at Whitgift School in the totesport League 2004, in the
process sharing with Mark Chilton (115) in a new Lancashire record opening stand in
one-day cricket (223)
Best batting: 203 Leicestershire v Glamorgan, Cardiff 2001
Best bowling: 2-21 Oxford University v Cambridge University, Lord's 1996

2005 Season

	M	Inns	NO	Runs	HS	Avge	100s	50s	Ct	St	O	M	Runs	Wkts	Avge	Best	5wI	10wM
Test																		
All First	15	25	3	1046	153	47.54	2	7	15	-								
1-Day Int																		
C & G	1	1	0	0	0	0.00	-	-	1	-								
tsL	9	9	0	156	54	17.33	-	1	1	-								
Twenty20																		

Career Performances

	M	Inns	NO	Runs	HS	Avge	100s	50s	Ct	St	Balls	Runs	Wkts	Avge	Best	5wI	10wM
Test																	
All First	162	258	22	8250	203	34.95	13	46	91	-	441	329	9	36.55	2-21	-	-
1-Day Int																	
C & G	15	15	3	579	103 *	48.25	1	3	7	-							
tsL	77	75	6	1847	104 *	26.76	2	10	17	-							
Twenty20	4	3	0	4	4	1.33	-	-	-	-							

SUTTON, L. D.   Lancashire

Name: <u>Luke</u> David Sutton
Role: Right-hand bat, wicket-keeper,
'right-arm rubbish'
Born: 4 October 1976, Keynsham
Height: 5ft 11in **Weight:** 12st 13lbs
Nickname: Sutts
County debut: 1997 (Somerset),
2000 (Derbyshire)
County cap: 2002 (Derbyshire)
50 dismissals in a season: 1
Place in batting averages: 119th av. 33.32
(2004 138th av. 31.12)
Parents: David and Molly
Marital status: Single
Education: Millfield School; Durham
University
Qualifications: 9 GCSEs, 4 A-levels, 2.1
degree in Economics, CeMAP 1, 2 and 3,
Level 1 coaching
Career outside cricket: 'Running sports camps business Activate Sport. Giving
mortgage and insurance advice with Mortgage Pulse'
Off-season: 'Relaxing, training and the above work'

Overseas tours: Various Somerset Schools tours to Holland; West of England U15 to West Indies 1991; Millfield School to Zimbabwe 1993, to Sri Lanka 1994; Durham University to Zimbabwe 1997

Overseas teams played for: UNSW, Sydney 1998-99; Northville, Port Elizabeth, South Africa 1999-2000; Subiaco Marist, Perth 2000-01

Career highlights to date: 'Scoring my maiden first-class 100 v Warwickshire in 2001. Carrying my bat v Sussex in 2001, scoring 140 not out. Captaining Derbyshire in final two games of 2002 season. Being appointed vice-captain of Derbyshire for 2004 season; captaining Derbyshire in 2004 and 2005' (*see Extras*)

Cricket moments to forget: 'Scoring 0 on my Championship debut for Somerset v Leicestershire in 1997. Losing C&G semi in 2003 by one wicket'

Cricket superstitions: 'Plenty, but it's a superstition to keep them a secret'

Cricketers particularly admired: Ian Healy, Jack Russell, Alec Stewart, Steve Waugh

Young players to look out for: 'Some at Derbyshire and no doubt there will be some at Lancashire'

Other sports followed: Football (Derby County), rugby (Bath)

Injuries: 'Little bit of a dodgy back and groin but lost no days of cricket'

Relaxations: 'Quality time with family and friends'

Extras: Captained England U15 and also represented England U18 and U19. Won Sir John Hobbs Silver Jubilee Memorial Prize for the U16 Cricketer of the Year in 1992 and the Gray-Nicolls Award for the English Schools Cricketer of the Year in 1995. Voted Derbyshire 2nd XI Player of the Year 2000. NBC Denis Compton Award for the most promising young Derbyshire player 2000, 2001, 2002. Captain of Derbyshire 2004-05 (originally appointed vice-captain 2004 but assumed the captaincy when back surgery prevented Michael DiVenuto from taking up the post). 'Set up a charity with my brother Noel called Freddie Fright, which raises money for CAH research; CAH is a condition suffered by my nephew Freddie.' Left Derbyshire at the end of the 2005 season and has joined Lancashire for 2006

Opinions on cricket: 'I like two-division cricket; not sure I support going back to one division. Fixture list is always crazily busy, but I'm not arguing – it's a great game.'

Best batting: 140* Derbyshire v Sussex, Derby 2001

2005 Season

	M	Inns	NO	Runs	HS	Avge	100s	50s	Ct	St	O	M	Runs	Wkts	Avge	Best	5wI	10wM
Test																		
All First	17	29	4	833	95	33.32	-	4	52	-								
1-Day Int																		
C & G	2	2	0	48	41	24.00	-	-	-	-								
tsL	18	18	3	321	63*	21.40	-	1	19	3								
Twenty20	8	7	2	211	61*	42.20	-	1	3	3								

Career Performances

	M	Inns	NO	Runs	HS	Avge	100s	50s	Ct	St	Balls	Runs	Wkts	Avge	Best	5wl	10wM
Test																	
All First	87	154	20	4098	140 *	30.58	5	14	181	7							
1-Day Int																	
C & G	11	9	1	144	45	18.00	-	-	11	-							
tsL	85	76	16	1132	83	18.86	-	4	89	10							
Twenty20	16	14	4	306	61 *	30.60	-	1	9	7							

SWANN, G. P.   Nottinghamshire

Name: <u>Graeme</u> Peter Swann
Role: Right-hand bat, right-arm off-spin
bowler, 'benefit wicket-keeper'
Born: 24 March 1979, Northampton
Height: 6ft **Weight:** 13st
Nickname: Swanny, G-spot, Chin
County debut: 1997 (one-day, Northants),
1998 (first-class, Northants), 2005 (Notts)
County cap: 1999 (Northamptonshire)
50 wickets in a season: 1
Place in batting averages: 209th av. 21.46
(2004 202nd av. 22.04)
Place in bowling averages: 105th av. 39.60
(2004 114th av. 38.93)
Strike rate: 75.15 (career 63.37)
Parents: Ray and Mavis
Marital status: Single
Family links with cricket: Father played
Minor Counties cricket for Bedfordshire and Northumberland and also for England
Amateurs. Brother was contracted to Northamptonshire and Lancashire. 'Cat is named
after Gus Logie'
Education: Sponne School, Towcester
Qualifications: 10 GCSEs, 4 A-levels, Levels 1 and 2 coaching awards
Overseas tours: England U19 to South Africa (including U19 World Cup) 1997-98;
England A to Zimbabwe and South Africa 1998-99, to West Indies 2000-01, to Sri
Lanka 2004-05; England to South Africa 1999-2000; ECB National Academy to
Australia 2001-02
Overseas teams played for: Old Colts, Christchurch 2002-03
Career highlights to date: 'Dismissing my brother in a totesport pyjama game'
Cricket moments to forget: 'Being hit for an enormous six by Peter Such'
Cricketers particularly admired: Neil Foster, Devon Malcolm

Other sports played: Golf, rugby (Northants U14, U15, U16), football (Old Northamptonians Chenecks FC)
Other sports followed: Football (Newcastle United)
Favourite band: Oasis, The Libertines, Charlatans, Stone Roses
Relaxations: 'Playing guitar and golf'
Extras: Played for England U14, U15, U17 and U19. Gray-Nicolls Len Newbery Schools Cricketer of the Year 1996. Took 8-118 for England U19 in second 'Test' v Pakistan U19 1998, the best ever figures for England in an U19 'Test'. Completed Championship double of 500 runs and 50 wickets 1999. Man of the Match for England A v Windward Islands in St Lucia in the Busta Cup 2000-01. ECB National Academy 2004-05
Opinions on cricket: 'Still the greatest game in the world, apart from football and golf.'
Best batting: 183 Northamptonshire v Gloucestershire, Bristol 2002
Best bowling: 7-33 Northamptonshire v Derbyshire, Northampton 2003

2005 Season

	M	Inns	NO	Runs	HS	Avge	100s	50s	Ct	St	O	M	Runs	Wkts	Avge	Best	5wI	10wM
Test																		
All First	16	17	2	322	63	21.46	-	2	7	-	413.2	89	1307	33	39.60	6-57	1	-
1-Day Int																		
C & G	2	2	0	12	11	6.00	-	-	1	-	16	3	59	2	29.50	1-24	-	
tsL	14	9	0	118	37	13.11	-	-	2	-	81.3	1	349	12	29.08	3-46	-	
Twenty20	8	8	0	157	62	19.62	-	1	2	-	30	0	201	11	18.27	3-32	-	

Career Performances

	M	Inns	NO	Runs	HS	Avge	100s	50s	Ct	St	Balls	Runs	Wkts	Avge	Best	5wI	10wM
Test																	
All First	126	181	10	4386	183	25.64	4	20	85	-	20721	10504	327	32.12	7-33	14	2
1-Day Int	1	0	0	0	0	-	-	-	-	-	30	24	0	-	-	-	-
C & G	15	13	1	297	50	24.75	-	1	9	-	724	542	14	38.71	4-40	-	
tsL	101	80	6	1495	83	20.20	-	9	24	-	3526	2664	104	25.61	5-35	1	
Twenty20	18	17	3	278	62	19.85	-	1	4	-	384	441	17	25.94	3-32	-	

85. How many overs did the shortest completed ODI last?

SYMONDS, A.   Lancashire

Name: Andrew Symonds
Role: Right-hand bat, right-arm
medium or off-spin bowler
Born: 9 June 1975, Birmingham, England
Height: 6ft 1in **Weight:** 13st 5lbs
Nickname: Roy
County debut: 1995 (Gloucestershire),
1999 (Kent), 2005 (Lancashire)
County cap: 1999 (Kent), 2005 (Lancashire)
Test debut: 2003-04
1000 runs in a season: 2
1st-Class 200s: 1
Place in batting averages: 11th av. 62.30
(2004 2nd av. 72.28)
Place in bowling averages: 61st av. 30.25
(2004 45th av. 29.92)
Strike rate: 66.37 (career 72.20)
Parents: Ken and Barbara

Wife and date of marriage: Brooke, April 2004
Family links with cricket: Father played Minor Counties cricket
Education: All Saints Anglican School, Gold Coast, Australia; Ballarat and Clarendon
College, Australia
Qualifications: Level 2 coaching, professional fisherman
Overseas tours: Australia U19 to India 1993-94; Australia A to Los Angeles
(Moov America Challenge) 1999, to South Africa 2002-03; Australia to Pakistan 1998-
99 (one-day series), to Sri Lanka and Zimbabwe 1999-2000 (one-day series), to New
Zealand 1999-2000 (one-day series), to India 2000-01 (one-day series), to England
2001 (one-day series), to Kenya (Nairobi Triangular) 2002, to Africa (World Cup)
2002-03, to West Indies 2002-03 (one-day series), to India (TVS Cup) 2003-04, to Sri
Lanka 2003-04, to Zimbabwe (one-day series) 2004, to Holland (Videocon Cup) 2004,
to England (ICC Champions Trophy) 2004, to New Zealand 2004-05 (one-day series),
to England (NatWest Series/Challenge) 2005, to New Zealand (one-day series)
2005-06
Overseas teams played for: Queensland Academy of Sport 1992-93 – 1997-98;
Queensland 1994-95 –
Cricketers particularly admired: Viv Richards, Shane Warne, Michael Holding
Other sports followed: Hockey, rugby, football
Relaxations: Fishing, camping and hunting
Extras: Nickname 'Roy' reportedly coined by his father after comic-book character
'Roy of the Rovers'. Attended Commonwealth Bank [Australian] Cricket Academy
1994. Set world record for number of sixes in a first-class innings (16) and match (20)

v Glamorgan at Abergavenny 1995. PCA Young Player of the Year and Cricket Writers' Club Young Cricketer of the Year 1995. Turned down the invitation to tour with England A in 1995 so that he could remain eligible to play for Australia. His ODI awards include Man of the NatWest Series 2005 in England and Man of the Match v Pakistan at Johannesburg in the World Cup 2002-03 (143*; the highest World Cup score for Australia). Made Twenty20 international debut v New Zealand at Auckland 2004-05. Named ODI Player of the Year at the 2005 Allan Border Medal awards. An overseas player with Kent 1999, 2001-04; an overseas player with Lancashire during the 2005 season as a locum for Muttiah Muralitharan. C&G Man of the Match award in the quarter-final v Sussex at Old Trafford 2005 (101/2-46 plus three catches and a run-out)

Best batting: 254* Gloucestershire v Glamorgan, Abergavenny 1995
Best bowling: 6-105 Kent v Sussex, Tunbridge Wells 2002
Stop press: ODI Man of the Match award for his 156 (127 balls; eight sixes) v New Zealand at Wellington 2005-06

2005 Season

	M	Inns	NO	Runs	HS	Avge	100s	50s	Ct	St	O	M	Runs	Wkts	Avge	Best	5wI	10wM
Test																		
All First	7	10	0	623	146	62.30	3	1	4	-	177	37	484	16	30.25	3-80	-	-
1-Day Int	8	6	2	229	74	57.25	-	2	3	-	57.2	4	203	6	33.83	5-18	1	
C & G	2	2	0	109	101	54.50	1	-	4	-	20	0	89	3	29.66	2-46	-	
tsL	9	9	1	406	129	50.75	1	2	-	-	68	3	303	7	43.28	2-25	-	
Twenty20	3	3	2	121	57 *	121.00	-	2	1	-	8	0	63	2	31.50	1-21	-	

Career Performances

	M	Inns	NO	Runs	HS	Avge	100s	50s	Ct	St	Balls	Runs	Wkts	Avge	Best	5wI	10wM
Test	2	4	0	53	24	13.25	-	-	4	-	144	85	1	85.00	1-68	-	-
All First	187	313	28	12269	254 *	43.04	37	49	133	-	14224	7208	197	36.58	6-105	2	-
1-Day Int	124	96	19	2833	143 *	36.79	2	15	48	-	4245	3413	93	36.69	5-18	1	
C & G	18	16	1	595	101	39.66	1	3	8	-	617	421	22	19.13	5-21	1	
tsL	83	82	6	2426	146	31.92	2	12	36	-	2115	1575	61	25.81	5-18	1	
Twenty20	13	13	3	443	112	44.30	1	3	8	-	242	296	9	32.88	2-35	-	

TAHIR, N. Warwickshire

Name: Naqaash Tahir
Role: Right-hand bat, right-arm fast bowler
Born: 14 November 1983, Birmingham
Height: 5ft 10in **Weight:** 11st
Nickname: Naq, Naqy
County debut: 2004
Place in batting averages: (2004 209th av. 21.42)
Place in bowling averages: 53rd av. 28.45 (2004 36th av. 28.25)
Strike rate: 45.27 (career 44.71)
Parents: Mohammed Amin and Ishrat Nasreen
Marital status: Single
Family links with cricket: 'Dad played club cricket and brother played for Worcestershire and Warwickshire'
Education: Moseley School; Spring Hill College

Qualifications: 3 GCSEs, Level 1 coaching
Overseas tours: Warwickshire U15 to South Africa 1999
Overseas teams played for: Mirpur, Pakistan; Subiaco-Floreat, Perth
Cricket superstitions: 'Putting my pads on in a certain way'
Cricketers particularly admired: Waqar Younis, Wasim Akram, Darren Gough, Brett Lee
Young players to look out for: Moeen Ali
Other sports played: Football
Other sports followed: Football (Man Utd)
Relaxations: 'Watching TV; PlayStation 2'
Extras: Has been Moseley Ashfield U15 Player of the Year, Warwickshire U15 Youth Player of the Year, Warwickshire U19 Players' Player of the Year and Warwickshire U19 Player of the Year (Coney Edmonds Trophy). Had match figures of 8-90 (4-47/4-43) on Championship debut v Worcestershire at Edgbaston 2004
Opinions on cricket: 'The game is more competitive now.'
Best batting: 49 Warwickshire v Worcestershire, Worcester 2004
Best bowling: 4-43 Warwickshire v Worcestershire, Edgbaston 2004

2005 Season

	M	Inns	NO	Runs	HS	Avge	100s	50s	Ct	St	O	M	Runs	Wkts	Avge	Best	5wI	10wM
Test																		
All First	5	7	3	95	32	23.75	-	-	-	-	83	11	313	11	28.45	3-28	-	-
1-Day Int																		
C & G	1	0	0	0	0	-	-	-	1	-	5	0	29	0	-		-	-
tsL	5	3	2	2	1*	2.00	-	-	-	-	24	1	110	1	110.00	1-23	-
Twenty20																		

Career Performances

	M	Inns	NO	Runs	HS	Avge	100s	50s	Ct	St	Balls	Runs	Wkts	Avge	Best	5wI	10wM
Test																	
All First	17	19	8	245	49	22.27	-	-	1	-	1744	1104	39	28.30	4-43	-	-
1-Day Int																	
C & G	1	0	0	0	0	-	-	-	1	-	30	29	0	-		-	-
tsL	5	3	2	2	1*	2.00	-	-	-	-	144	110	1	110.00	1-23	-
Twenty20																	

TAYLOR, B. V.   Hampshire

Name: <u>Billy</u> Victor Taylor
Role: Left-hand bat, right-arm medium-fast bowler
Born: 11 January 1977, Southampton
Height: 6ft 3in **Weight:** 14st
Nickname: Tav
County debut: 1999 (Sussex), 2004 (Hampshire)
Place in batting averages: (2004 233rd av. 17.70)
Place in bowling averages: 69th av. 30.89 (2004 59th av. 31.48)
Strike rate: 59.26 (career 61.48)
Parents: Jackie and Victor
Marital status: Single
Family links with cricket: 'Learnt from and played cricket with both my brothers, Martin and James'
Education: Bitterne Park; Southampton Tech College; Sparsholt Agricultural College, Hampshire
Qualifications: 5 GCSEs, NVQ Level 2 Carpentry and Joinery, NTPC Tree Surgery, Level 2 coaching

Career outside cricket: 'Tree surgery'
Overseas tours: Sussex/Hampshire to Cyprus 1999; Sussex to Grenada 2002
Overseas teams played for: Central Hawke's Bay, New Zealand 1996-97; Manawatu Foxton CC and Horowhenua rep team, New Zealand 1998-99, 2000-01; Te Puke 2002
Career highlights to date: 'Winning the County Championship in 2003 [with Sussex]. Playing for Hampshire'
Cricket moments to forget: 'Don't want to forget any moments as it's such a great career and too short a one'
Cricket superstitions: 'Have a towel hanging out of back of trousers'
Cricketers particularly admired: Malcolm Marshall, Robin Smith, Mushtaq Ahmed
Other sports played: Golf
Other sports followed: Football (Havant & Waterlooville)
Favourite band: Dido, Black Eyed Peas
Extras: Took 98 wickets in New Zealand club cricket in 1998-99. Sussex 2nd XI Player of the Year 1999, 2000. Took hat-trick (Ormond, Sampson, Giddins) v Surrey at Hove in the B&H and another (G. Flower, Maddy, Malcolm) v Leicestershire at Leicester in the C&G, both in 2002
Opinions on cricket: 'We should play exactly the same format as international cricket, as that should be the aim – to play for England and improve English cricket at international level.'
Best batting: 40 Hampshire v Essex, West End 2004
Best bowling: 6-45 Hampshire v Gloucestershire, West End 2005

2005 Season

	M	Inns	NO	Runs	HS	Avge	100s	50s	Ct	St	O	M	Runs	Wkts	Avge	Best	5wI	10wM
Test																		
All First	8	14	6	66	24	8.25	-	-	-	-	187.4	34	587	19	30.89	6-45	1	-
1-Day Int																		
C & G	2	0	0	0	0	-	-	-	-	-	12	1	75	1	75.00	1-7	-	
tsL	5	3	0	6	3	2.00	-	-	1	-	38	3	172	3	57.33	2-24	-	
Twenty20																		

Career Performances

	M	Inns	NO	Runs	HS	Avge	100s	50s	Ct	St	Balls	Runs	Wkts	Avge	Best	5wl	10wM
Test																	
All First	47	62	23	426	40	10.92	-	-	5	-	7587	4119	123	33.48	6-45	3	-
1-Day Int																	
C & G	11	1	0	1	1	1.00	-	-	1	-	570	419	18	23.27	4-26	-	
tsL	77	41	17	150	21 *	6.25	-	-	16	-	3266	2448	94	26.04	4-22	-	
Twenty20	6	3	3	15	12 *	-	-	-	2	-	126	143	4	35.75	1-14	-	

TAYLOR, C. G.   Gloucestershire

Name: Christopher (<u>Chris</u>) Glyn Taylor
Role: Right-hand bat, right-arm
off-spin bowler
Born: 27 September 1976, Bristol
Height: 5ft 8in **Weight:** 10st
Nickname: Tales, Tootsie
County debut: 2000
County cap: 2001
1000 runs in a season: 1
Place in batting averages: 102nd av. 35.18
(2004 58th av. 44.87)
Strike rate: (career 93.75)
Parents: Chris and Maggie
Wife and date of marriage: Sarah,
8 December 2001
Family links with cricket: Father and
grandfather both played local club cricket
Education: Colston's Collegiate School
Qualifications: GCSEs and A-levels
Overseas teams played for: Harbord CC, Manly, Australia 2000
Cricket moments to forget: 'B&H loss to Surrey at Lord's [2001]'
Cricketers particularly admired: Jonty Rhodes, Mark Waugh
Other sports played: Rugby, hockey (both county level); squash, tennis
Other sports followed: Rugby
Relaxations: Fishing
Extras: Represented England Schools U18. In 1995 won the Cricket Society's
A. A. Thomson Fielding Prize and Wetherell Award for Leading All-rounder in English
Schools Cricket. Scored maiden first-class century (104) v Middlesex 2000, becoming
the first player to score a century at Lord's on Championship debut; also the first
player to score a century for Gloucestershire in match that was both first-class and
Championship debut. NBC Denis Compton Award for the most promising young
Gloucestershire player 2000. Four-day captain of Gloucestershire 2004-05
Best batting: 196 Gloucestershire v Nottinghamshire, Trent Bridge 2001
Best bowling: 3-126 Gloucestershire v Northamptonshire, Cheltenham 2000

2005 Season

	M	Inns	NO	Runs	HS	Avge	100s	50s	Ct	St	O	M	Runs	Wkts	Avge	Best	5wl	10wM
Test																		
All First	9	17	1	563	176	35.18	1	2	5	-	13	1	43	1	43.00	1-26	-	-
1-Day Int																		
C & G	2	2	0	131	74	65.50	-	2	-	-								
tsL	6	6	1	54	24	10.80	-	-	2	-	7.2	0	45	1	45.00	1-22	-	
Twenty20	8	6	2	98	33 *	24.50	-	-	4	-								

Career Performances

	M	Inns	NO	Runs	HS	Avge	100s	50s	Ct	St	Balls	Runs	Wkts	Avge	Best	5wl	10wM
Test																	
All First	68	121	7	3897	196	34.18	10	12	43	-	375	265	4	66.25	3-126	-	-
1-Day Int																	
C & G	18	17	4	337	74	25.92	-	2	10	-							
tsL	58	51	7	796	63 *	18.09	-	3	16	1	98	74	4	18.50	2-5	-	
Twenty20	18	14	4	246	36	24.60	-	-	7	-	6	11	0	-	-	-	

TAYLOR, C. R.   Derbyshire

Name: Christopher (Chris) Robert Taylor
Role: Right-hand opening bat, right-arm fast-medium bowler
Born: 21 February 1981, Leeds
Height: 6ft 4in **Weight:** 14st 6lbs
Nickname: CT
County debut: 2001 (Yorkshire)
Parents: Phil and Elaine
Marital status: Single
Family links with cricket: 'Brother Matthew plays in Bradford League, Dad slogged a few in Dales Council League and Mum gives good throw-downs'
Education: Benton Park High School, Leeds
Qualifications: 9 GCSEs, 4 A-levels
Overseas tours: Yorkshire to Grenada 2002
Overseas teams played for: Western Suburbs Magpies, Sydney 1999-2003; Fairfield-Liverpool Lions, Sydney 2003-05
Career highlights to date: 'To have played in County Championship winning team 2001. On a personal note, my maiden first-class half-century v Surrey at Headingley, April 2002' (*A 3¼-hour rearguard action of 52**)

Cricket moments to forget: 'To have bagged 'em in my first Roses match v Lancashire, which also just happened to be my first game live on Sky TV (I turned my phone off for a week after it!)'

Cricket superstitions: 'Keeping them to myself!'

Cricketers particularly admired: Geoffrey Boycott, Michael Vaughan, John Wilkinson ('aka "Mad John"')

Young players to look out for: Mark Lawson

Other sports played: Rugby, football, tennis, basketball (all for Benton Park HS first teams)

Other sports followed: Football (Everton – 'since I was four years old'), 'enjoy watching all sports'

Favourite band: Matchbox Twenty

Extras: Represented Yorkshire U10-U17. Represented North of England at Bunbury Festival 1996 and was awarded Neil Lloyd Trophy for top run-scorer in festival. Selected for England U15 team for Lombard World Cup 1996. Has also represented England U17 and U19. Yorkshire CCC Supporters' Club Young Player of the Year 1999. Left Yorkshire at the end of the 2005 season and has joined Derbyshire for 2006

Best batting: 52* Yorkshire v Surrey, Headingley 2002

2005 Season

	M	Inns	NO	Runs	HS	Avge	100s	50s	Ct	St	O	M	Runs	Wkts	Avge	Best	5wI	10wM
Test																		
All First	1	2	1	14	14 *	14.00	-	-	1	-								
1-Day Int																		
C & G																		
tsL																		
Twenty20																		

Career Performances

	M	Inns	NO	Runs	HS	Avge	100s	50s	Ct	St	Balls	Runs	Wkts	Avge	Best	5wI	10wM
Test																		
All First	16	27	3	416	52 *	17.33	-	2	8	-							
1-Day Int																		
C & G	1	0	0	0	0	-	-	-	-	-							
tsL	3	3	0	57	28	19.00	-	-	-	-							
Twenty20																		

TEN DOESCHATE, R. N.   Essex

Name: <u>Ryan</u> Neil ten Doeschate
Role: Right-hand bat, right-arm
medium-fast bowler
Born: 30 June 1980, Port Elizabeth,
South Africa
Height: 5ft 11in **Weight:** 12st 8lbs
Nickname: Tendo
County debut: 2003
Strike rate: (career 63.50)
Parents: Boudewyn and Ingrid
Marital status: Single
Education: Fairbairn College; University of
Cape Town
Qualifications: Business science degree
Overseas tours: Holland to Ireland (ICC
Trophy) 2005
Overseas teams played for: Western
Province; Western Province B; Bloemendaal,
Holland
Cricket moments to forget: 'My county debut at Chelmsford'
Cricketers particularly admired: Jacques Kallis, Kepler Wessels
Young players to look out for: Jono McLean
Other sports played: Rugby
Other sports followed: Football (Arsenal), rugby (Stormers)
Favourite band: Phil Collins
Relaxations: Golf, tennis, reading
Extras: Played for Holland in the ICC Inter-Continental Cup 2005. Is not considered
an overseas player
Best batting: 98 Essex v Worcestershire, Worcester 2005
Best bowling: 3-29 Essex v CUCCE, Fenner's 2004

2005 Season

	M	Inns	NO	Runs	HS	Avge	100s	50s	Ct	St	O	M	Runs	Wkts	Avge	Best	5wl	10wM
Test																		
All First	2	1	0	98	98	98.00	-	1	1	-	19	2	118	0	-		-	-	-
1-Day Int																		
C & G																		
tsL	13	9	5	266	89 *	66.50	-	2	7	-	14	1	81	2	40.50	1-23	-	
Twenty20	6	5	2	84	42 *	28.00	-	-	1	-	2	0	20	0	-		-	-

Career Performances

	M	Inns	NO	Runs	HS	Avge	100s	50s	Ct	St	Balls	Runs	Wkts	Avge	Best	5wI	10wM
Test																	
All First	6	6	0	153	98	25.50	-	1	3	-	479	357	7	51.00	3-29	-	-
1-Day Int																	
C & G																	
tsL	14	9	5	266	89 *	66.50	-	2	7	-	132	120	3	40.00	1-23	-	
Twenty20	11	7	2	93	42 *	18.60	-	-	2	-	121	167	5	33.40	2-27	-	

THOMAS, I. J.   Glamorgan

Name: Ian James Thomas
Role: Left-hand bat, right-arm off-spin
bowler, wicket-keeper 'when needed'
Born: 9 May 1979, Newport, Gwent
Height: 6ft **Weight:** 14st 7lbs
Nickname: Bolts
County debut: 1998
Place in batting averages: 248th av. 16.12
Strike rate: (career 61.00)
Parents: Amanda and Alun
Marital status: Single
Family links with cricket: 'Brother Rhys is
captain of local village team, Machen CC;
father still slogging for them. Mother brings
up the whites lovely'
Education: Bedwas and Bassaleg
Comprehensive Schools; University of Wales
Institute Cardiff (UWIC)

Qualifications: 9 GCSEs, 2 A-levels, BSc (Hons) Sports Development
Overseas tours: Wales U16 to Jersey and Isle of Wight; British Universities to Port
Elizabeth 1999; Glamorgan to Cape Town 2002; Forest Nomads CC to Trinidad and
Tobago 2003
Overseas teams played for: Mt Lawley Hawks, Perth 2001-02; Subiaco Marist CC,
Perth 2003-04
Career highlights to date: 'Winning two National League titles 2002, 2004;
playing for Glamorgan; holding the joint record (116*) with Graeme Hick in the
Twenty20 Cup'
Cricket moments to forget: 'First-class pair, v Derbys 2002'
Cricket superstitions: 'Too many to mention'
Cricketers particularly admired: Matthew Maynard, Brian Lara
Young players to look out for: Michael O'Shea, James Hildreth

Other sports played: Golf (Peterstone Lakes GC), rugby (Machen RFC)
Other sports followed: Rugby (Newport-Gwent Dragons), golf (European Tour)
Favourite band: 'A big fan of Phil Collins'
Relaxations: 'Fishing, golf, swimming'
Extras: Captained Welsh Schools at all age groups. Underwent major back surgery in 1997. Glamorgan Young Player of the Month June, July, August and September 2000. Equalled record for the highest individual score in the Twenty20 Cup (116*, set only hours earlier by Graeme Hick) v Somerset at Taunton 2004. Released by Glamorgan at the end of the 2005 season
Best batting: 82 Glamorgan v Essex, Southend 2000
Best bowling: 1-26 Glamorgan v Nottinghamshire, Colwyn Bay 2002

2005 Season

	M	Inns	NO	Runs	HS	Avge	100s	50s	Ct	St	O	M	Runs	Wkts	Avge	Best	5wI	10wM
Test																		
All First	4	8	0	129	40	16.12	-	-	2	-								
1-Day Int																		
C & G	2	2	0	63	36	31.50	-	-	1	-	6	1	24	1	24.00	1-24	-	
tsL	3	3	0	63	45	21.00	-	-	-	-								
Twenty20	4	4	0	53	32	13.25	-	-	3	-								

Career Performances

	M	Inns	NO	Runs	HS	Avge	100s	50s	Ct	St	Balls	Runs	Wkts	Avge	Best	5wI	10wM
Test																	
All First	32	54	4	1070	82	21.40	-	6	21	-	61	38	1	38.00	1-26	-	-
1-Day Int																	
C & G	6	6	0	224	93	37.33	-	1	3	-	36	24	1	24.00	1-24	-	
tsL	38	37	4	859	72	26.03	-	5	10	-	66	60	1	60.00	1-27	-	
Twenty20	14	14	1	250	116 *	19.23	1	-	7	-	42	63	2	31.50	1-5	-	

THOMAS, S. D.   Glamorgan

Name: Stuart Darren Thomas
Role: Left-hand bat, right-arm fast-medium bowler; all-rounder
Born: 25 January 1975, Morriston, Swansea
Height: 6ft **Weight:** 13st
Nickname: Ted, Stu
County debut: 1992
County cap: 1997
Benefit: 2006
50 wickets in a season: 5
Place in batting averages: 224th av. 19.57 (2004 104th av. 35.64)
Place in bowling averages: (2004 97th av. 36.82)

Strike rate: (career 52.71)
Parents: Stu and Ann
Wife and date of marriage: Claire,
30 September 2000
Children: Ellie Sofia, 20 August 2002
Family links with cricket: 'Father was a
good striker of the ball for Llanelli CC'
Education: Graig Comprehensive, Llanelli;
Neath Tertiary College
Qualifications: 5 GCSEs, BTEC National
Diploma in Sports Studies, Level 2 coaching
award
Overseas tours: Glamorgan to Cape Town
1993, 1999, 2002, to Zimbabwe 1994,
to Pretoria 1995, to Portugal 1996, to Jersey
1998; England U18 to South Africa
1992-93; England U19 to Sri Lanka 1993-94;
England A to Zimbabwe and South Africa
1998-99, to Bangladesh and New Zealand 1999-2000
Overseas teams played for: Rovers CC, Welkom, Free State 1994; Burnside West
University CC, Christchurch, New Zealand 2003
Career highlights to date: 'Winning County Championship 1997 by far, followed by
my two England A tours'
Cricket moments to forget: 'There are too many to mention'
Cricket superstitions: 'None'
Cricketers particularly admired: Allan Donald, Malcolm Marshall, Ian Botham,
'and now Freddie'
Young players to look out for: Gareth Rees, Alastair Cook
Other sports followed: 'All kinds on Sky Sports'
Favourite band: 'Don't have band but Robbie Williams is quality'
Relaxations: 'Spending time with family; training; enjoy seeing the globe; eating out'
Extras: Took 5-80 on debut v Derbyshire 1992, aged 17 years 217 days, and finished
eighth in national bowling averages. BBC Welsh Young Sports Personality 1992.
Represented England U19. Returned Glamorgan best B&H bowling figures (6-20) on
competition debut v Combined Universities at Cardiff 1995. Took 7-16 v Surrey at
Swansea in the Sunday League 1998, a competition best by a Glamorgan bowler.
Glamorgan Player of the Year 1998. Took 8-50 for England A v Zimbabwe A at Harare
1998-99 – the first eight-wicket haul by an England A tourist. Became the second 12th
man to score a century (105*) in a first-class match, v Hampshire at West End 2004
Opinions on cricket: 'The EU and Kolpak system [*see page 9*] is a disgrace. The
younger players will suffer by the introduction of these players, and you even might
find overseas [players] being barred in the future, which is sad. We have to do
something about it!!'
Best batting: 138 Glamorgan v Essex, Chelmsford 2001
Best bowling: 8-50 England A v Zimbabwe A, Harare 1998-99

	M	Inns	NO	Runs	HS	Avge	100s	50s	Ct	St	O	M	Runs	Wkts	Avge	Best	5wI	10wM
Test																		
All First	7	14	0	274	63	19.57	-	1	-	-	122.3	9	611	9	67.88	3-63	-	-
1-Day Int																		
C & G	2	2	1	45	40 *	45.00	-	-	-	-	8	1	36	1	36.00	1-14	-	
tsL	3	1	0	14	14	14.00	-	-	-	-	13	1	91	2	45.50	1-35	-	
Twenty20	4	4	0	18	9	4.50	-	-	1	-	10	0	119	1	119.00	1-49	-	

Career Performances

	M	Inns	NO	Runs	HS	Avge	100s	50s	Ct	St	Balls	Runs	Wkts	Avge	Best	5wI	10wM
Test																	
All First	169	234	43	3976	138	20.81	2	18	56	-	26518	16023	504	31.79	8-50	18	1
1-Day Int																	
C & G	18	15	4	283	71 *	25.72	-	1	3	-	957	806	30	26.86	5-74	1	
tsL	92	68	14	752	38 *	13.92	-	-	15	-	3210	2753	107	25.72	7-16	1	
Twenty20	14	13	3	169	43 *	16.90	-	-	2	-	234	394	11	35.81	3-32	-	

THOMPSON, C. E. J.   Surrey

Name: Christopher (<u>Chris</u>) Everton
Junior Thompson
Role: Right-hand bat, right-arm
medium bowler
Born: 26 June 1987, Lambeth, London
Height: 5ft 7in **Weight:** 12st 8lbs
Nickname: Thommo
County debut: No first-team appearance
Parents: Bery Roberts and Everton
Thompson
Family links with cricket: 'Dad plays club
cricket. Brother played Surrey U19'
Education: Archbishop Tenison School;
South Thames College
Qualifications: 3 GCSEs
Career outside cricket: 'Musician'
Off-season: 'Training; playing drums;
England U19'
Overseas tours: Surrey Academy to Perth 2004, to Cape Town 2005; England U19 to
Bangladesh 2005-06
Career highlights to date: '118 [for South] v West at Loughborough [in ECB U19
tournament]. 186 v Glamorgan at The Oval for Surrey 2nds'

Cricket superstitions: 'Don't have any'
Cricketers particularly admired: Brian Lara, Courtney Walsh, Curtly Ambrose, Sachin Tendulkar
Young players to look out for: Moeen Ali, Rory Hamilton-Brown, David Burton
Other sports played: Football, basketball, table tennis
Other sports followed: Football (Man Utd)
Injuries: Out for six weeks with a broken left index finger
Favourite band: 'Too many to list'
Relaxations: 'Listening to music; playing drums; sleeping; chilling with friends; walking dog; going to church'
Extras: Represented England U19 2005. Girdlers Award (Young Player of the Year)
Opinions on cricket: 'Too technical – e.g. third umpire for lbws, Hawk-Eye.'

THORNELY, D. J.   Hampshire

Name: <u>Dominic</u> John Thornely
Role: Right-hand bat, right-arm medium bowler; all-rounder
Born: 1 October 1978, Albury, New South Wales, Australia
County debut: 2005 (Surrey)
1st-Class 200s: 1
Strike rate: (career 100.66)
Overseas tours: Australia U19 to Pakistan 1996-97, to South Africa (U19 World Cup) 1997-98; Australia A to Pakistan 2005-06
Overseas teams played for: New South Wales 2001-02 –
Extras: Has represented Australia A in home one-day matches against the Zimbabweans, West Indians and Pakistanis. Scored 261* v Western Australia in the Pura Cup at Sydney 2004-05, in the process sharing with Stuart

MacGill (27) in a last-wicket stand of 219 and winning the Man of the Match award. His other match awards include Man of the Match v Queensland at Brisbane in the ING Cup final 2001-02 (20*/3-36) and v South Australia at Adelaide in the Pura Cup 2004-05 (74/102). Was an overseas player with Surrey during the 2005 season as a locum for Azhar Mahmood; has joined Hampshire as an overseas player for 2006
Best batting: 261* New South Wales v Western Australia, Sydney 2004-05
Best bowling: 3-52 New South Wales v Victoria, Melbourne 2003-04

2005 Season

	M	Inns	NO	Runs	HS	Avge	100s	50s	Ct	St	O	M	Runs	Wkts	Avge	Best	5wI	10wM
Test																		
All First	2	2	0	154	81	77.00	-	2	1	-	28	4	108	2	54.00	2-40	-	-
1-Day Int																		
C & G																			
tsL	1	1	0	12	12	12.00	-	-	-	-	9	0	60	2	30.00	2-60	-	
Twenty20	3	3	1	72	67 *	36.00	-	1	2	-	2.3	0	22	3	7.33	3-22	-	

Career Performances

	M	Inns	NO	Runs	HS	Avge	100s	50s	Ct	St	Balls	Runs	Wkts	Avge	Best	5wI	10wM
Test																	
All First	22	37	3	1591	261 *	46.79	5	9	12	-	930	479	9	53.22	3-52	-	-
1-Day Int																	
C & G																		
tsL	1	1	0	12	12	12.00	-	-	-	-	54	60	2	30.00	2-60	-	
Twenty20	3	3	1	72	67 *	36.00	-	1	2	-	15	22	3	7.33	3-22	-	

THORNICROFT, N. D.   Yorkshire

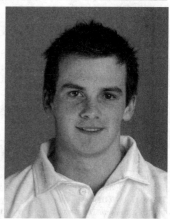

Name: Nicholas (<u>Nick</u>) David Thornicroft
Role: Left-hand bat, right-arm fast bowler
Born: 23 January 1985, York
Height: 5ft 11in **Weight:** 12st 8lbs
Nickname: Thorny, Mad Dog, Harry Potter
County debut: 2002 (*see Extras*)
Strike rate: (career 77.18)
Parents: Lyn and David
Marital status: Single
Education: Easingwold
Overseas tours: Yorkshire U16 to Cape Town, to Jersey; England U19 to Australia 2002-03
Career highlights to date: 'Getting Neil Fairbrother as my first first-class wicket'
Cricketers particularly admired: Darren Gough, Brett Lee, Ian Botham, Craig White, Andrew Flintoff
Young players to look out for: Charlie Thornicroft, Haroon Rashid, Andrew Gale
Other sports played: Athletics, football, basketball
Other sports followed: Football (York City FC), horse racing
Relaxations: 'Spending time with family; music; shooting'

Extras: Made first-class debut in Roses match v Lancashire at Old Trafford 2002, aged 17. Represented England U19 2002 and 2003. Played for Essex on loan 2005
Best batting: 30 Yorkshire v Nottinghamshire, Headingley 2004
Best bowling: 2-27 Yorkshire v Durham, Riverside 2004

2005 Season

	M	Inns	NO	Runs	HS	Avge	100s	50s	Ct	St	O	M	Runs	Wkts	Avge	Best	5wl	10wM
Test																		
All First	1	2	1	4	4 *	4.00	-	-	-	-	22	6	70	1	70.00	1-70	-	-
1-Day Int																		
C & G																		
tsL																		
Twenty20	1	1	1	0	0 *	-	-	-	-	-	1	0	20	0	-		-	-

Career Performances

	M	Inns	NO	Runs	HS	Avge	100s	50s	Ct	St	Balls	Runs	Wkts	Avge	Best	5wl	10wM
Test																	
All First	7	12	5	54	30	7.71	-	-	1	-	849	543	11	49.36	2-27	-	-
1-Day Int																	
C & G	1	0	0	0	0	-	-	-	-	-	30	19	0	-		-	-
tsL	7	3	3	8	8 *	-	-	-	1	-	258	252	11	22.90	5-42	1	
Twenty20	1	1	1	0	0 *	-	-	-	-	-	6	20	0	-		-	-

THORP, C. D.   Durham

Name: <u>Callum</u> David Thorp
Role: Right-hand bat, right-arm
fast-medium bowler
Born: 11 January 1975, Perth,
Western Australia
Height: 6ft 3in
County debut: 2005
Strike rate: (career 97.28)
Parents: Annette and David
Marital status: Single
Education: Servite College
Overseas teams played for: Western
Warriors 2002-03 – 2003-04; Wanneroo DCC
Career highlights to date: 'First-class debut.
Winning first final with Wanneroo DCC'
Cricket superstitions: 'Left shoe on first'
Cricketers particularly admired:
Steve Waugh

Young players to look out for: Liam Plunkett
Other sports followed: AFL (West Coast Eagles), football (West Ham United)
Relaxations: 'Golf, beach'
Extras: Took 4-58 for Western Australia v England XI in two-day match at Perth 2002-03. Attended Commonwealth Bank [Australian] Cricket Academy 2003. Has British parents and is not considered an overseas player
Best batting: 26 Western Australia v New South Wales, Newcastle 2002-03
Best bowling: 3-10 Durham v Northamptonshire, Riverside 2005

2005 Season

	M	Inns	NO	Runs	HS	Avge	100s	50s	Ct	St	O	M	Runs	Wkts	Avge	Best	5wI	10wM
Test																		
All First	5	6	0	49	23	8.16	-	-	3	-	71	13	227	4	56.75	3-10	-	-
1-Day Int																		
C & G																		
tsL	4	2	0	5	4	2.50	-	-	-	-	28	4	84	3	28.00	1-11	-	
Twenty20	3	1	0	12	12	12.00	-	-	-	-	8	0	88	0	-	-	-	

Career Performances

	M	Inns	NO	Runs	HS	Avge	100s	50s	Ct	St	Balls	Runs	Wkts	Avge	Best	5wI	10wM
Test																	
All First	11	14	0	115	26	8.21	-	-	5	-	1362	758	14	54.14	3-10	-	-
1-Day Int																	
C & G																	
tsL	4	2	0	5	4	2.50	-	-	-	-	168	84	3	28.00	1-11	-	
Twenty20	3	1	0	12	12	12.00	-	-	-	-	48	88	0	-	-	-	

THORPE, G. P.   Surrey

Name: Graham Paul Thorpe
Role: Left-hand bat, occasional right-arm medium bowler
Born: 1 August 1969, Farnham
Height: 5ft 10in **Weight:** 12st 9lbs
Nickname: Chalky
County debut: 1988
County cap: 1991
Benefit: 2000
Test debut: 1993
1000 runs in a season: 9
1st-Class 200s: 4
Place in batting averages: 67th av. 41.27 (2004 24th av. 55.00)
Strike rate: (career 91.80)
Parents: 'Mr and Mrs Thorpe'

Children: Henry and Amelia
Education: Weydon Comprehensive;
Farnham College
Qualifications: 7 O-levels, PE Diploma
Overseas tours: England A to Zimbabwe and
Kenya 1989-90, to Pakistan 1990-91,
to Bermuda and West Indies 1991-92, to
Australia 1992-93; England to West Indies
1993-94, to Australia 1994-95, to South
Africa 1995-96, to India and Pakistan
(World Cup) 1995-96, to Zimbabwe and New
Zealand 1996-97, to Sharjah (Champions
Trophy) 1997-98, to West Indies 1997-98, to
Australia 1998-99, to Sharjah (Coca-Cola
Cup) 1998-99, to Kenya (ICC Knockout
Trophy) 2000-01, to Pakistan and Sri Lanka
2000-01, to India and New Zealand 2001-02,
to Bangladesh and Sri Lanka 2003-04, to
West Indies 2003-04, to South Africa 2004-05

Cricketers particularly admired: Grahame Clinton, Waqar Younis, Ian Botham,
Viv Richards
Other sports followed: Football (Chelsea FC), golf
Relaxations: Sleeping
Extras: Played for English Schools cricket U15 and U19 and England Schools
football U18. Scored a century (114*) v Australia on his Test debut at Trent Bridge
1993. Cornhill England Player of the Year 1997-98. One of *Wisden*'s Five Cricketers
of the Year 1998. Captained England in one-day series v Sri Lanka 2000-01. Scored
200* v New Zealand in the first Test at Christchurch 2001-02, sharing with Andrew
Flintoff in a new record sixth-wicket partnership for England in Tests (281). Retired
from ODI cricket after the NatWest Series 2002. Recalled to the England Test side for
the fifth Test v South Africa 2003 at his home ground of The Oval, scoring century
(124). His international awards include England's Player of the Series in the 1997
Ashes campaign; Man of the Match in the third Test v Sri Lanka at Colombo 2000-01
(113*/32*); in the third Test v West Indies at Bridgetown 2003-04 (119*); in the third
Test v New Zealand at Trent Bridge 2004 (45/104*) and in the third Test v West Indies
at Old Trafford 2004 (114). Made 100th Test appearance in the second Test v
Bangladesh at Riverside 2005. Autobiography *Graham Thorpe: Rising from the Ashes*
published 2005. Retired from county cricket at the end of the 2005 season, taking up a
player/coach post in Sydney. Received Special Merit Award at the PCA awards dinner
at the Royal Albert Hall 2005
Best batting: 223* England XI v South Australia, Adelaide 1998-99
Best bowling: 4-40 Surrey v Australians, The Oval 1993

2005 Season

	M	Inns	NO	Runs	HS	Avge	100s	50s	Ct	St	O	M	Runs	Wkts	Avge	Best	5wI	10wM
Test	2	2	2	108	66 *	-		-	1	4	-							
All First	10	14	3	454	95	41.27	-	4	5	-								
1-Day Int																		
C & G	2	2	0	73	60	36.50	-	1	2	-								
tsL	4	4	0	148	69	37.00	-	1	3	-								
Twenty20																		

Career Performances

	M	Inns	NO	Runs	HS	Avge	100s	50s	Ct	St	Balls	Runs	Wkts	Avge	Best	5wI	10wM
Test	100	179	28	6744	200 *	44.66	16	39	105	-	138	37	0	-	-	-	-
All First	341	567	80	21937	223 *	45.04	49	122	290	-	2387	1378	26	53.00	4-40	-	-
1-Day Int	82	77	13	2380	89	37.18	-	21	43	-	120	97	2	48.50	2-15	-	
C & G	35	34	9	1376	145 *	55.04	2	10	21	-	13	12	0	-	-	-	
tsL	149	138	21	4510	126 *	38.54	6	30	65	-	318	307	8	38.37	3-21	-	
Twenty20	5	4	0	95	50	23.75	-	1	1	-							

TOMLINSON, J. A.   Hampshire

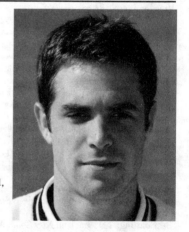

Name: <u>James</u> Andrew Tomlinson
Role: Left-hand lower-order bat, left-arm fast-medium bowler
Born: 12 June 1982, Appleshaw, Hants
Height: 6ft 2in **Weight:** 13st
Nickname: Tommo, Mr T
County debut: 2002
Strike rate: (career 72.06)
Parents: Ian and Janet
Marital status: Single
Family links with cricket: 'Grandfathers played cricket in Yorkshire and Lancashire leagues. Brothers Hugh and Ralph play for South Wilts and Dulwich cricket clubs'
Education: Harrow Way Community School, Andover; Cricklade College, Andover; Cardiff University
Qualifications: 9 GCSEs, 3 A-levels, 2.1 degree in Education and Psychology
Off-season: 'Having operation on rib and spending time rehabbing in Sydney and Perth'
Overseas teams played for: South Perth 2004-05

Career highlights to date: 'Playing for Hampshire. Any Hampshire win I'm involved in. 6-63 v Derbyshire 2003. Scoring 51 for South Perth v Scarborough 2005'
Cricket moments to forget: 'Being injured for the whole of the 2005 season; feeling miserable and frustrated for most of the 2005 season'
Cricket superstitions: 'None'
Cricketers particularly admired: Robin Smith, Dimi Mascarenhas, Shane Warne, Nic Pothas, Shaun Udal, Chris Tremlett, Shane Watson, John Crawley, Jimmy Adams 'and any quick bowler with a "never-say-die" attitude'
Young players to look out for: Richard Morris, Liam Dawson
Other sports played: Darts (played for Walnut Tree, Appleshaw – Andover League and Cup winners), chess, occasional hockey and football
Other sports followed: Football (West Ham)
Injuries: 'Damaged eleventh rib on right-hand side whilst bowling in April 2005. Had part of that rib removed October 2005. Missed all but one game of 2005 season'
Favourite band: Razorlight, The Killers, Aha, ABC, Nik Kershaw, Human League, U2
Relaxations: 'British wildlife, ornithology, travelling, criticising my brothers'
Extras: Played for Development of Excellence XI (South) 2001. Played for Cardiff UCCE 2002-03. Represented British Universities 2002-03. NBC Denis Compton Award for the most promising young Hampshire player 2003. Cardiff University Sportsperson of the Year award 2003
Opinions on cricket: 'There should be a Twenty20 World Cup.'
Best batting: 23 Hampshire v Indians, West End 2002
Best bowling: 6-63 Hampshire v Derbyshire, Derby 2003

2005 Season (did not make any first-class or one-day appearances)

Career Performances

	M	Inns	NO	Runs	HS	Avge	100s	50s	Ct	St	Balls	Runs	Wkts	Avge	Best	5wI	10wM
Test																	
All First	15	24	11	73	23	5.61	-	-	5	-	2162	1585	30	52.83	6-63	1	-
1-Day Int																	
C & G	2	2	0	4	4	2.00	-	-	-	-	102	46	1	46.00	1-29	-	
tsL	12	6	3	10	6	3.33	-	-	1	-	500	413	11	37.54	2-15	-	
Twenty20																	

TREDWELL, J. C. Kent

Name: <u>James</u> Cullum Tredwell
Role: Left-hand bat, right-arm
off-spin bowler
Born: 27 February 1982, Ashford, Kent
Height: 5ft 11in **Weight:** 14st 2lbs
Nickname: Tredders, Pingu, Chad
County debut: 2001
Place in batting averages: (2004 122nd
av. 33.85)
Strike rate: (career 73.84)
Parents: John and Rosemary
Marital status: Single
Family links with cricket: Father played for
Ashford and Folkestone in Kent League
Education: Southlands Community
Comprehensive
Qualifications: 10 GCSEs, 2 A-levels,
ECB Level 1 coach
Overseas tours: Kent U17 to Sri Lanka 1998-99; Kent to Port Elizabeth 2002;
England A to Malaysia and India 2003-04
Overseas teams played for: Redlands Tigers, Brisbane 2000-02
Cricket moments to forget: 'Being hit for six in a crucial B&H Cup match v Essex,
which probably cost Kent's qualification to next stage'
Cricketers particularly admired: 'All the great spinners'
Young players to look out for: Rob Ferley, Joe Denly
Extras: Represented England U19 2001 (captain in second 'Test'). Kent Most
Improved Player Award 2003. ECB National Academy 2003-04. Took over captaincy
of England A in India after Alex Gidman was forced to return home with a hand
injury. NBC Denis Compton Award for the most promising young Kent player 2003
Best batting: 61 Kent v Yorkshire, Headingley 2002
Best bowling: 5-101 England A v East Zone, Amritsar 2003-04

2005 Season

	M	Inns	NO	Runs	HS	Avge	100s	50s	Ct	St	O	M	Runs	Wkts	Avge	Best	5wI	10wM
Test																		
All First	3	5	0	55	27	11.00	-	-	1	-	36.5	8	146	3	48.66	2-37	-	-
1-Day Int																		
C & G																		
tsL	9	7	3	95	29 *	23.75	-	-	9	-	65.2	3	294	13	22.61	4-16	-	
Twenty20	7	4	2	56	33 *	28.00	-	-	1	-	22	0	152	7	21.71	2-16	-	

Career Performances

	M	Inns	NO	Runs	HS	Avge	100s	50s	Ct	St	Balls	Runs	Wkts	Avge	Best	5wI	10wM
Test																	
All First	32	45	6	827	61	21.20	-	3	34	-	4800	2825	65	43.46	5-101	1	-
1-Day Int																	
C & G	13	9	1	203	71	25.37	-	2	5	-	540	333	8	41.62	3-7	-	
tsL	49	39	12	382	30 *	14.14	-	-	26	-	1810	1354	49	27.63	4-16	-	
Twenty20	17	13	2	186	34	16.90	-	-	3	-	264	352	12	29.33	2-16	-	

TREGO, P. D. Somerset

Name: <u>Peter</u> David Trego
Role: Right-hand bat, right-arm
medium-fast bowler
Born: 12 June 1981, Weston-super-Mare
Height: 6ft **Weight:** 12st 7lbs
Nickname: Tregs
County debut: 2000 (Somerset),
2003 (Kent), 2005 (Middlesex)
Place in batting averages: 177th av. 26.00
Place in bowling averages: 90th av. 36.00
Strike rate: 49.12 (career 57.35)
Parents: Carol and Paul
Marital status: Single
Family links with cricket: Brother Sam
played for Somerset 2nd XI
Education: Wyvern Comprehensive
Cricketers particularly admired:
Ian Botham, Graham Rose
Other sports played: Football
Other sports followed: Football (Man Utd), darts, golf
Relaxations: Golf, snooker, music, socialising with friends
Extras: Represented England U19. NBC Denis Compton Award for the most
promising young Somerset player 2000. Scored 140 at Taunton 2002 as Somerset,
chasing 454 to win, tied with West Indies A. Left Somerset at the end of the 2002
season; played for Kent in 2003; played for Middlesex in 2005, leaving the club at
the end of the season to rejoin Somerset for 2006
Best batting: 140 Somerset v West Indies A, Taunton 2002
Best bowling: 6-59 Middlesex v Nottinghamshire, Trent Bridge 2005

2005 Season

	M	Inns	NO	Runs	HS	Avge	100s	50s	Ct	St	O	M	Runs	Wkts	Avge	Best	5wI	10wM
Test																		
All First	7	10	1	234	72	26.00	-	2	2	-	131	21	576	16	36.00	6-59	1	-
1-Day Int																		
C & G																		
tsL	6	4	1	35	15	11.66	-	-	3	-	34	3	199	4	49.75	2-31	-	
Twenty20																		

Career Performances

	M	Inns	NO	Runs	HS	Avge	100s	50s	Ct	St	Balls	Runs	Wkts	Avge	Best	5wI	10wM
Test																	
All First	22	32	4	768	140	27.42	1	3	8	-	2581	1848	45	41.06	6-59	1	-
1-Day Int																	
C & G	4	3	0	13	11	4.33	-	-	-	-	163	115	8	14.37	2-21	-	
tsL	27	22	5	238	31 *	14.00	-	-	6	-	806	759	23	33.00	4-39	-	
Twenty20	4	4	0	15	11	3.75	-	-	-	-	18	34	4	8.50	2-17	-	

TREMLETT, C. T.   Hampshire

Name: Christopher (<u>Chris</u>) Timothy Tremlett
Role: Right-hand bat, right-arm
fast-medium bowler
Born: 2 September 1981, Southampton
Height: 6ft 7in **Weight:** 16st 1lb
Nickname: Twiggy, Goober
County debut: 2000
County cap: 2004
Place in batting averages: 187th av. 24.33
(2004 222nd av. 19.36)
Place in bowling averages: 37th av. 26.78
(2004 8th av. 22.23)
Strike rate: 43.56 (career 46.03)
Parents: Timothy and Carolyn
Marital status: Single
Family links with cricket: Grandfather
[Maurice] played for Somerset and in three
Tests for England. Father played for
Hampshire and is now director of cricket at the county
Education: Thornden School, Chandlers Ford; Taunton's College, Southampton
Qualifications: 5 GCSEs, BTEC National Diploma in Sports Science, Level 2 coach
Overseas tours: West of England U15 to West Indies 1997; Hampshire U16 to Jersey;

England U17 to Northern Ireland (ECC Colts Festival) 1999; England U19 to India 2000-01; ECB National Academy to Australia 2001-02, to Australia and Sri Lanka 2002-03; England VI to Hong Kong 2004
Cricketers particularly admired: Glenn McGrath, Mark Waugh, Shane Warne
Young players to look out for: John Francis
Other sports played: Basketball, volleyball
Other sports followed: Football (Arsenal)
Relaxations: 'Socialising with friends; cinema'
Extras: Took wicket (Mark Richardson) with first ball in first-class cricket v New Zealand A at Portsmouth 2000; finished with debut match figures of 6-91. Represented England U19. NBC Denis Compton Award for the most promising young Hampshire player 2000, 2001. Hampshire Young Player of the Year 2001. Took Championship hat-trick (Ealham, Swann, G. Smith) v Nottinghamshire at Trent Bridge 2005. Made ODI debut v Bangladesh at Trent Bridge in the NatWest Series 2005
Best batting: 64 Hampshire v Gloucestershire, West End 2005
Best bowling: 6-44 Hampshire v Sussex, Hove 2005

2005 Season

	M	Inns	NO	Runs	HS	Avge	100s	50s	Ct	St	O	M	Runs	Wkts	Avge	Best	5wI	10wM
Test																		
All First	11	14	5	219	64	24.33	-	1	3	-	334	57	1232	46	26.78	6-44	2	-
1-Day Int	3	1	0	8	8	8.00	-	-	-	-	24.2	1	111	5	22.20	4-32	-	
C & G	4	3	1	11	7	5.50	-	-	1	-	37	0	184	7	26.28	3-32	-	
tsL	12	8	2	48	20 *	8.00	-	-	4	-	86.2	5	481	23	20.91	3-30	-	
Twenty20																		

Career Performances

	M	Inns	NO	Runs	HS	Avge	100s	50s	Ct	St	Balls	Runs	Wkts	Avge	Best	5wI	10wM
Test																	
All First	52	70	21	939	64	19.16	-	2	16	-	8442	4766	180	26.47	6-44	5	-
1-Day Int	3	1	0	8	8	8.00	-	-	-	-	146	111	5	22.20	4-32	-	
C & G	11	6	2	83	38 *	20.75	-	-	1	-	542	413	14	29.50	3-20	-	
tsL	57	35	11	227	30 *	9.45	-	-	14	-	2520	1882	93	20.23	4-25	-	
Twenty20	5	3	1	31	13	15.50	-	-	3	-	102	110	8	13.75	3-20	-	

86. Which of England's captains has the only unbeaten record in ODIs?

TRESCOTHICK, M. E.   Somerset

Name: <u>Marcus</u> Edward Trescothick
Role: Left-hand bat, right-arm swing bowler, reserve wicket-keeper
Born: 25 December 1975, Keynsham, Bristol
Height: 6ft 3in **Weight:** 14st 7lbs
Nickname: Banger, Tres
County debut: 1993
County cap: 1999
Test debut: 2000
1st-Class 200s: 1
Place in batting averages: 41st av. 48.44
(2004 28th av. 53.41)
Strike rate: (career 74.27)
Parents: Martyn and Lin
Wife and date of marriage: Hayley, 24 January 2004
Children: Ellie, April 2005
Family links with cricket: Father played for Somerset 2nd XI; uncle played club cricket
Education: Sir Bernard Lovell School
Qualifications: 7 GCSEs

Overseas tours: England U18 to South Africa 1992-93; England U19 to Sri Lanka 1993-94, to West Indies 1994-95 (c); England A to Bangladesh and New Zealand 1999-2000; England to Kenya (ICC Knockout Trophy) 2000-01, to Pakistan and Sri Lanka 2000-01, to Zimbabwe (one-day series) 2001-02, to India and New Zealand 2001-02, to Sri Lanka (ICC Champions Trophy) 2002-03, to Australia 2002-03, to Africa (World Cup) 2002-03, to Bangladesh and Sri Lanka 2003-04, to West Indies 2003-04, to South Africa 2004-05, to Pakistan 2005-06, to India 2005-06
Overseas teams played for: Melville CC, Perth 1997-99
Cricketers particularly admired: Adam Gilchrist, Andy Caddick
Other sports followed: Golf, football (Bristol City FC)
Relaxations: 'Spending time at home (it's such a rare thing), playing golf'
Extras: Scored more than 1000 runs for England U19. Took hat-trick (Gilchrist, Angel, McIntyre) for Somerset v Young Australia at Taunton 1995. PCA Player of the Year 2000. Sports.com Cricketer of the Year 2001. BBC West Country Sports Sportsman of the Year 2001. One of *Indian Cricket*'s five Cricketers of the Year 2002. Scored 114* v South Africa at The Oval in the NatWest Series 2003, sharing with Vikram Solanki (106) in a record England opening partnership in ODIs (200). Scored century in each innings (105/107) in the second Test v West Indies at Edgbaston 2004. Man of the Match in his 100th ODI v Bangladesh at The Oval in the NatWest Series 2005 (100*). His Test awards include England's Man of the Series v Bangladesh 2005

and Man of the Match in the fifth Test v South Africa at The Oval 2003 (219/69*). His other ODI awards include Man of the Series v West Indies 2003-04 and Man of the Match v Australia at Headingley in the NatWest Challenge 2005 (104*). One of *Wisden*'s Five Cricketers of the Year 2005. Made Twenty20 international debut v Australia at the Rose Bowl 2005

Best batting: 219 England v South Africa, The Oval 2003
Best bowling: 4-36 Somerset v Young Australia, Taunton 1995
Stop press: Appointed MBE in 2006 New Year Honours as part of 2005 Ashes-winning England team. Returned home from England tour to India 2005-06 for personal reasons

2005 Season

	M	Inns	NO	Runs	HS	Avge	100s	50s	Ct	St	O	M	Runs	Wkts	Avge	Best	5wl	10wM
Test	7	12	0	776	194	64.66	2	3	7	-								
All First	11	18	0	872	194	48.44	2	3	13	-								
1-Day Int	10	10	3	379	104 *	54.14	2	1	3	-								
C & G	1	1	0	11	11	11.00	-	-	-	-								
tsL	1	1	0	52	52	52.00	-	1	-	-								
Twenty20	2	2	0	35	25	17.50	-	-	3	-								

Career Performances

	M	Inns	NO	Runs	HS	Avge	100s	50s	Ct	St	Balls	Runs	Wkts	Avge	Best	5wl	10wM
Test	66	125	10	5206	219	45.26	12	27	76	-	300	155	1	155.00	1-34	-	-
All First	192	332	18	11362	219	36.18	21	61	214	-	2674	1541	36	42.80	4-36	-	-
1-Day Int	109	108	6	3848	137	37.72	10	20	44	-	232	219	4	54.75	2-7	-	
C & G	22	20	1	870	133	45.78	4	1	6	-	174	141	4	35.25	2-23	-	
tsL	90	81	11	2063	110	29.47	1	12	30	-	978	823	31	26.54	4-50	-	
Twenty20	3	3	0	91	56	30.33	-	1	3	-							

87. Which current county player has made the most
ODI catches as an outfielder for England?

TROTT, I. J. L.   Warwickshire

Name: Ian <u>Jonathan</u> Leonard Trott
Role: Right-hand bat, right-arm medium bowler; all-rounder
Born: 22 April 1981, Cape Town, South Africa
Height: 6ft **Weight:** 13st 5lbs
Nickname: Booger
County debut: 2003
County cap: 2005
1000 runs in a season: 2
1st-Class 200s: 1
Place in batting averages: 65th av. 41.46 (2004 30th av. 53.18)
Strike rate: (career 69.43)
Parents: Ian and Donna
Marital status: Single
Family links with cricket: Father a professional cricket coach. Brother (Kenny

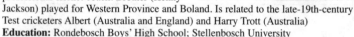

Jackson) played for Western Province and Boland. Is related to the late-19th-century Test cricketers Albert (Australia and England) and Harry Trott (Australia)
Education: Rondebosch Boys' High School; Stellenbosch University
Qualifications: Level 2 coaching
Overseas tours: South Africa U15 to England (U15 World Cup) 1996; South Africa U19 to Pakistan 1998-99, to Sri Lanka (U19 World Cup) 1999-2000
Overseas teams played for: Boland 1999-2000 – 2000-01; Western Province 2001-02; Otago 2005-06
Cricket moments to forget: 'Losing in the final of the Standard Bank Cup 2002'
Cricket superstitions: 'Personal'
Cricketers particularly admired: Sachin Tendulkar, Adam Hollioake, Steve Waugh
Other sports played: Hockey (Western Province U16, U18, U21), golf
Other sports followed: Football (Tottenham Hotspur)
Favourite band: Roxette, Robbie Williams
Relaxations: 'Music, watching sport'
Extras: Represented South Africa A. Struck 245 on debut for Warwickshire 2nd XI v Somerset 2nd XI at Knowle & Dorridge 2002. Scored century (134) on Championship debut for Warwickshire v Sussex at Edgbaston 2003. Became the first player to bat for the full 20 overs in the Twenty20, for a 54-ball 65* v Gloucestershire at Edgbaston 2003. Is a British passport-holder and is not considered an overseas player
Best batting: 210 Warwickshire v Sussex, Edgbaston 2005
Best bowling: 7-39 Warwickshire v Kent, Canterbury 2003

2005 Season

	M	Inns	NO	Runs	HS	Avge	100s	50s	Ct	St	O	M	Runs	Wkts	Avge	Best	5wI	10wM
Test																		
All First	18	30	2	1161	210	41.46	4	2	32	-	129.5	15	449	9	49.88	2-19	-	-
1-Day Int																		
C & G	5	5	0	57	49	11.40	-	-	-	-	10	0	70	3	23.33	3-35	-	
tsL	16	15	5	608	112 *	60.80	2	4	5	-	64.5	3	351	12	29.25	3-46	-	
Twenty20	9	7	0	180	41	25.71	-	-	5	-	14	0	129	5	25.80	2-19	-	

Career Performances

	M	Inns	NO	Runs	HS	Avge	100s	50s	Ct	St	Balls	Runs	Wkts	Avge	Best	5wI	10wM
Test																	
All First	62	108	11	3894	210	40.14	7	24	61	-	1597	980	23	42.60	7-39	1	-
1-Day Int																	
C & G	9	7	1	122	65 *	20.33	-	1	-	-	78	86	3	28.66	3-35	-	
tsL	40	39	10	1290	112 *	44.48	2	9	16	-	407	370	12	30.83	3-46	-	
Twenty20	19	16	4	359	65 *	29.91	-	1	6	-	102	159	7	22.71	2-19	-	

TROUGHTON, J. O.   Warwickshire

Name: Jamie (<u>Jim</u>) Oliver Troughton
Role: Left-hand bat, slow left-arm bowler
Born: 2 March 1979, London
Height: 5ft 11in **Weight:** 12st 12lbs
Nickname: Troughts
County debut: 2001
County cap: 2002
1000 runs in a season: 1
Place in batting averages: 123rd av. 32.38
(2004 117th av. 34.52)
Strike rate: (career 111.63)
Parents: Ali and David
Wife and date of marriage: Naomi,
28 September 2002
Family links with cricket: Father was a
Middlesex Colt. Great-grandfather Henry
Crichton played for Warwickshire. 'Young
brother Wigsy plays for Stratford CC'
Education: Trinity School, Leamington Spa; Birmingham University
Qualifications: 8 GCSEs, 3 A-levels, BSc Sport & Exercise Psychology
Career outside cricket: Coaching/acting
Overseas tours: Warwickshire Development of Excellence squad to Cape Town 1998;

MCC to Australia and Singapore 2001; ECB National Academy to Australia and Sri Lanka 2002-03

Overseas teams played for: Harvinia CC, Free State, South Africa 2000; Avendale CC, Cape Town 2001-02; Belville CC, Cape Town 2003-04; Claremont-Nedlands CC, Perth 2004-05

Career highlights to date: 'Winning the Championship 2004'

Cricket moments to forget: 'Being relegated in one-day league [2004]'

Cricket superstitions: 'None'

Cricketers particularly admired: Graham Thorpe, Steve Waugh, Allan Donald, Ashley Giles

Young players to look out for: Jonathan Trott, Ian Westwood, Naqaash Tahir, Moeen Ali

Other sports played: Football (Stoke City youth player)

Other sports followed: 'Hooked on Manchester United since going to their soccer school aged five'

Favourite band: Red Hot Chili Peppers, Coldplay, Stone Roses

Relaxations: 'Music, films, playing my guitar, spending time with Naomi, going abroad'

Extras: Is grandson of *Dr Who* actor Patrick Troughton; father also an actor. County colours U12-U19. Has represented England U15, U16 and U17. Represented ECB Midlands U19 1998. Has won the Alec Hastilow Trophy and the Coney Edmonds Trophy (Warwickshire awards). Warwickshire 2nd XI Player of the Year 2001. Scored 1067 first-class runs in his first full season 2002. NBC Denis Compton Award for the most promising young Warwickshire player 2002. Warwickshire Young Player and Most Improved Player of the Year 2002

Opinions on cricket: 'There has got to be a gentleman's agreement by all county chairmen not to sign them [Kolpak players; *see page 9*]. With two overseas [players], EU players and Kolpaks we will stifle the English youth and prevent the "cream" rising to the top.'

Best batting: 131* Warwickshire v Hampshire, West End 2002

Best bowling: 3-1 Warwickshire v CUCCE, Fenner's 2004

2005 Season

	M	Inns	NO	Runs	HS	Avge	100s	50s	Ct	St	O	M	Runs	Wkts	Avge	Best	5wI	10wM
Test																		
All First	12	18	0	583	119	32.38	1	5	6	-	44.2	6	220	5	44.00	2-63	-	-
1-Day Int																		
C & G	5	4	0	76	34	19.00	-	-	4	-	4	0	20	0	-		-	-
tsL	15	15	1	465	82	33.21	-	3	7	-	20	0	122	1	122.00	1-17	-	
Twenty20	9	7	0	147	51	21.00	-	1	2	-	6	0	44	4	11.00	2-10	-	

Career Performances

	M	Inns	NO	Runs	HS	Avge	100s	50s	Ct	St	Balls	Runs	Wkts	Avge	Best	5wI	10wM
Test																	
All First	55	86	7	3177	131 *	40.21	9	18	26	-	1228	764	11	69.45	3-1	-	-
1-Day Int	6	5	1	36	20	9.00	-	-	1	-							
C & G	14	12	1	437	115 *	39.72	1	2	7	-	154	103	7	14.71	4-23	-	
tsL	48	43	5	993	82	26.13	-	6	16	-	354	318	8	39.75	2-36	-	
Twenty20	15	12	1	220	51	20.00	-	1	4	-	60	69	6	11.50	2-10	-	

TUDOR, A. J. Essex

Name: Alexander (<u>Alex</u>) Jeremy Tudor
Role: Right-hand bat, right-arm fast bowler
Born: 23 October 1977, West Brompton, London
Height: 6ft 4in **Weight:** 13st 7lbs
Nickname: Big Al, Bambi, Tudes
County debut: 1995 (Surrey), 2005 (Essex)
County cap: 1999 (Surrey)
Test debut: 1998-99
Strike rate: (career 47.14)
Parents: Daryll and Jennifer
Marital status: Engaged to Francesca
Children: Sienna
Family links with cricket: Brother was on the staff at The Oval
Education: St Mark's C of E, Fulham; City of Westminster College
Overseas tours: England U15 to South Africa 1992-93; England U19 to Zimbabwe 1995-96, to Pakistan 1996-97; England to Australia 1998-99, to South Africa 1999-2000, to Pakistan 2000-01, to Australia 2002-03; England A to West Indies 2000-01; ECB National Academy to Australia 2001-02, 2002-03
Cricketers particularly admired: Curtly Ambrose, Brian Lara
Other sports followed: Basketball, football (QPR)
Relaxations: Listening to music
Extras: Played for London Schools at all ages from U8. Represented England U17. MCC Young Cricketer. Took 4-89 in Australia's first innings on Test debut at Perth 1998-99; his victims included both Waugh twins. Scored 99* in second innings of the first Test v New Zealand at Edgbaston 1999, bettering the highest score by a nightwatchman for England (Harold Larwood's 98 v Australia at Sydney 1932-33) and winning Man of the Match award. Cricket Writers' Club Young Cricketer of the Year 1999. Recorded match figures of 7-109 in the third Test v Sri Lanka at Old Trafford 2002, winning Man of the Match award

Best batting: 116 Surrey v Essex, The Oval 2001
Best bowling: 7-48 Surrey v Lancashire, The Oval 2000

2005 Season

	M	Inns	NO	Runs	HS	Avge	100s	50s	Ct	St	O	M	Runs	Wkts	Avge	Best	5wl	10wM
Test																		
All First	3	2	0	86	57	43.00	-	1	2	-	56	13	165	8	20.62	2-30	-	-
1-Day Int																		
C & G	1	1	0	7	7	7.00	-	-	-	-	7	1	34	2	17.00	2-34	-	
tsL	4	1	0	7	7	7.00	-	-	3	-	26	0	154	4	38.50	2-29	-	
Twenty20																		

Career Performances

	M	Inns	NO	Runs	HS	Avge	100s	50s	Ct	St	Balls	Runs	Wkts	Avge	Best	5wl	10wM
Test	10	16	4	229	99 *	19.08	-	1	3	-	1512	963	28	34.39	5-44	1	-
All First	95	122	27	2127	116	22.38	1	7	29	-	13577	8073	288	28.03	7-48	13	-
1-Day Int	3	2	1	9	6	9.00	-	-	1	-	127	136	4	34.00	2-30	-	
C & G	8	4	2	35	17 *	17.50	-	-	2	-	441	303	12	25.25	4-39	-	
tsL	43	30	9	267	56	12.71	-	1	14	-	1661	1363	56	24.33	4-26	-	
Twenty20																		

TURK, N. R. K.   Sussex

Name: Neil Richard Keith Turk
Role: Left-hand bat, right-arm medium bowler
Born: 28 April 1983, Cuckfield
Height: 6ft **Weight:** 11st 8lbs
Nickname: Turkish, Neilo
County debut: 2002 (one-day)
Parents: Keith and Lorraine
Marital status: Single
Family links with cricket: 'Father PE teacher and grade coach. Brother county junior. Mother junior cricket coach/manager'
Education: Sackville Community College, East Grinstead; Exeter University
Qualifications: 9 GCSEs, 1 AS-level, 3 A-levels, FIFA-approved referee
Career highlights to date: 'County debut 2002 v Essex Eagles. Maiden 2nd XI Championship century (123) v Hampshire'

Cricket moments to forget: 'Being dismissed by Hampshire's wicket-keeper in a match for Sussex 2nd XI, having scored a century in the first innings; his only wicket to date'

Cricket superstitions: 'I don't believe you need superstitions to help you'

Cricketers particularly admired: Brian Lara, Jacques Kallis

Young players to look out for: Arul Suppiah

Other sports played: Hockey (West of England U21, Exeter University, ISCA HC), golf, football

Other sports followed: Football (Liverpool FC), rugby league (Wigan Warriors), hockey (East Grinstead HC)

Favourite band: Usher

Relaxations: 'I enjoy most sports; I also like to spend time on the golf course when I'm not playing cricket'

Extras: Sussex U17 Player of the Year. Played for Sussex Board XI in the C&G 2003. Attended Sussex Academy

---

2005 Season (did not make any first-class or one-day appearances)

Career Performances

	M	Inns	NO	Runs	HS	Avge	100s	50s	Ct	St	Balls	Runs	Wkts	Avge	Best	5wI	10wM
Test																	
All First																	
1-Day Int																	
C & G	1	1	0	20	20	20.00	-	-	-	-	12	21	0	-		-	-
tsL	2	2	0	44	36	22.00	-	-	-	-							
Twenty20																	

88. Which New Zealand cricketer, awarded an MBE for services to cricket, dismissed Allan Border more times than any other bowler in ODIs?

TURNER, M. L. Durham

Name: <u>Mark</u> Leif Turner
Role: Right-hand lower-middle-order bat, right-arm fast-medium bowler
Born: 23 October 1984, Sunderland
Height: 5ft 11in **Weight:** '12 stoneish'
Nickname: Tina, Stella
County debut: 2005
Strike rate: (career 147.00)
Parents: Kenny and Eileen
Marital status: Single
Family links with cricket: 'Brother Ian played county juniors and was a well-respected local player'
Education: Thornhill Comprehensive School
Qualifications: 7 GCSEs, Level 2 coaching
Career outside cricket: Northern Rock call centre

Off-season: 'Working most of winter; delivering sandwiches is an option'
Overseas tours: England U19 to Bangladesh (U19 World Cup) 2003-04; Durham to India 2004, to South Africa 2005, to Dubai 2005
Career highlights to date: 'Making first-team debut v Essex, and a five-wicket haul for England U19'
Cricket moments to forget: 'Dropping a dolly on Sky for England U19'
Cricket superstitions: 'Three Weetabix on morning of game!'
Cricketers particularly admired: Sachin Tendulkar, Virender Sehwag, Allan Donald, Alec Stewart, Brett Lee
Young players to look out for: Liam Plunkett, Ben Harmison, Luke Anderson
Other sports played: 'Played junior football for Manchester Utd and Sunderland; worst player at Durham now, though – always last picked.' Golf, fishing
Other sports followed: Football (Sunderland AFC)
Injuries: 'First injury-free season, and long may it continue'
Favourite band: Keith Sweat, Dwele, Raheem DeVaughn, Maxwell
Relaxations: 'Golf, iPod, socialising with anyone who's interested, and Pro Evolution 5'
Extras: Represented England U19 2003-04, returning match figures of 9-104 (5-57/4-47) in the second 'Test' v Bangladesh U19 at Taunton 2004
Opinions on cricket: 'Keep giving young English lads a chance. More day/night matches. And new laws to stop it becoming a batsman's game.'
Best batting: 18 Durham v Essex, Riverside 2005
Best bowling: 1-47 Durham v Essex, Riverside 2005

2005 Season

	M	Inns	NO	Runs	HS	Avge	100s	50s	Ct	St	O	M	Runs	Wkts	Avge	Best	5wI	10wM
Test																		
All First	2	2	1	19	18	19.00	-	-	-	-	49	5	166	2	83.00	1-47	-	-
1-Day Int																		
C & G																		
tsL																		
Twenty20	1	0	0	0	0	-	-	-	-	-	2	0	25	0	-		-	-

Career Performances

	M	Inns	NO	Runs	HS	Avge	100s	50s	Ct	St	Balls	Runs	Wkts	Avge	Best	5wI	10wM
Test																	
All First	2	2	1	19	18	19.00	-	-	-	-	294	166	2	83.00	1-47	-	-
1-Day Int																	
C & G																	
tsL																	
Twenty20	1	0	0	0	0	-	-	-	-	-	12	25	0	-		-	-

TURNER, R. J. — Somerset

Name: Robert (<u>Rob</u>) Julian Turner
Role: Right-hand middle-order bat, wicket-keeper
Born: 25 November 1967, Malvern
Height: 6ft 2in **Weight:** 14st
Nickname: Noddy, Turns
County debut: 1991
County cap: 1994
Benefit: 2002
1000 runs in a season: 2
50 dismissals in a season: 9
Place in batting averages: 165th av. 27.70 (2004 194th av. 23.06)
Parents: Derek and Doris
Wife and date of marriage: Lucy, 25 September 1999
Children: Jamie Jonathan Paul, 4 April 2001
Family links with cricket: 'Father and both brothers (Richard and Simon) are closely associated with Weston-super-Mare CC. Simon played for Somerset in 1984, also as a wicket-keeper. My wife, Lucy, plays for MCC Ladies and Somerset Ladies (also as a wicket-keeper!)'
Education: Broadoak Comprehensive, Weston-super-Mare; Millfield School, Street; Magdalene College, Cambridge University

Qualifications: BA (Hons) Engineering, Diploma in Computer Science, NCA coaching award, approved person under the Financial Services Authority
Overseas tours: Millfield School to Barbados 1985; Combined Universities to Barbados 1989; Qantas Airlines Tournament, Kuala Lumpur, Malaysia 1992-93; English Lions to New Zealand (Cricket Max) 1997; MCC to New Zealand 1999, to Canada 2000, to Italy 2004; England A to Bangladesh and New Zealand 1999-2000 (vc)
Overseas teams played for: Claremont-Nedlands, Perth, Western Australia 1991-93
Career highlights to date: 'Winning the C&G Trophy 2001 at Lord's – especially catching a skyer to remove Afridi'
Cricket moments to forget: 'Any dropped catch!'
Cricket superstitions: 'Being last out on to the pitch (but that is just an excuse for being late, really!)'
Cricketers particularly admired: Jack Russell, Ricky Ponting
Other sports played: Golf ('badly, but holed in one at the par three fourth at Oake Manor GC!')
Other sports followed: Football ('The Villa'), hockey (Taunton Vale Ladies)
Relaxations: 'Being entertained by my son; curry club on away trips'
Extras: Captain of Cambridge University (Blue 1988-91) and Combined Universities 1991. Wombwell Cricket Lovers' Society Wicket-keeper of the Year 1999. Highest-placed Englishman in the 1999 batting averages (sixth with 1217 runs at 52.91). Sheffield Cricket Lovers' Society Allrounder of the Year 1999. Was on stand-by for England tours of West Indies 1997-98 and South Africa and Zimbabwe 1999-2000. Shares record for most wicket-keeping dismissals in a match for Somerset (nine) and holds record for most dismissals in an innings for Somerset (seven; all caught) v Northamptonshire at Taunton 2001. Wombwell Cricket Lovers' Society Highlight of the Year 2001 (for catching Shahid Afridi in the C&G final). Released at the end of the 2005 season
Opinions on cricket: 'Twenty20 proved to be a great success once more. It shows that the public enjoy this format of the game and I'm sure we'll see more of it in years to come.'
Best batting: 144 Somerset v Kent, Taunton 1997

2005 Season

	M	Inns	NO	Runs	HS	Avge	100s	50s	Ct	St	O	M	Runs	Wkts	Avge	Best	5wl	10wM
Test																		
All First	9	13	3	277	68 *	27.70	-	1	22	1								
1-Day Int																		
C & G	1	1	0	8	8	8.00	-	-	1	-								
tsL	8	7	4	103	47 *	34.33	-	-	7	1								
Twenty20	1	1	0	1	1	1.00	-	-	-	-								

	M	Inns	NO	Runs	HS	Avge	100s	50s	Ct	St	Balls	Runs	Wkts	Avge	Best	5wI	10wM
Test																	
All First	250	380	70	9519	144	30.70	10	46	703	50	79	58	0	-	-	-	-
1-Day Int																	
C & G	32	26	10	519	52	32.43	-	2	47	3							
tsL	158	137	47	2189	67	24.32	-	6	148	28							
Twenty20	6	5	0	25	11	5.00	-	-	3	-							

UDAL, S. D.   Hampshire

Name: Shaun David Udal
Role: Right-hand bat, off-spin bowler
Born: 18 March 1969, Farnborough, Hants
Height: 6ft 3in **Weight:** 14st
Nickname: Shaggy
County debut: 1989
County cap: 1992
Benefit: 2002
50 wickets in a season: 7
Place in batting averages: 223rd av. 19.60
(2004 113th av. 34.85)
Place in bowling averages: 3rd av. 18.90
(2004 9th av. 22.28)
Strike rate: 37.43 (career 65.48)
Parents: Robin and Mary
Wife and date of marriage: Emma Jane,
5 October 1991
Children: Katherine Mary, 26 August 1992;
Rebecca Jane, 17 November 1995
Family links with cricket: Grandfather (G. F. Udal) played for Leicestershire and
Middlesex. Father played for Camberley CC for over 40 years and also for Surrey
Colts; brother Gary plays for Camberley 1st XI
Education: Cove Comprehensive
Qualifications: 8 CSEs, print finisher, company director
Overseas tours: England to Australia 1994-95, to Pakistan 2005-06, to India 2005-06;
England A to Pakistan 1995-96; England XI to New Zealand (Cricket Max) 1997;
Hampshire to Anguilla 1998, to Cape Town 2001
Overseas teams played for: Hamilton Wickham, Newcastle, NSW 1989-90
Career highlights to date: 'Winning B&H, NatWest and promotion with Hants.
Playing for England'
Cricket moments to forget: 'Getting out twice as nightwatchman hooking'

Cricket superstitions: 'Left side on first'
Cricketers particularly admired: Ian Botham, Shane Warne, Robin Smith
Other sports played: Football, golf (12 handicap)
Other sports followed: Football (West Ham Utd, Aldershot Town)
Favourite band: Blue
Relaxations: 'Going out for a beer and meal; living life to the full; my children'
Extras: Man of the Match on NatWest debut against Berkshire 1991. Hampshire Cricket Association Player of the Year 1993. Vice-captain of Hampshire 1998-2000. Hampshire Players' Player of the Year 2001, 2002
Best batting: 117* Hampshire v Warwickshire, Southampton 1997
Best bowling: 8-50 Hampshire v Sussex, Southampton 1992
Stop press: Made Test debut in the first Test v Pakistan at Multan 2005-06

2005 Season

	M	Inns	NO	Runs	HS	Avge	100s	50s	Ct	St	O	M	Runs	Wkts	Avge	Best	5wI	10wM
Test																		
All First	11	14	4	196	47 *	19.60	-	-	7	-	274.3	54	832	44	18.90	6-44	3	-
1-Day Int																		
C & G	5	2	1	44	44 *	44.00	-	-	-	-	45	1	196	6	32.66	2-33	-	
tsL	15	11	6	94	42	18.80	-	-	8	-	112.5	5	502	25	20.08	4-55	-	
Twenty20	7	5	4	60	34 *	60.00	-	-	1	-	15.3	0	122	7	17.42	2-6	-	

Career Performances

	M	Inns	NO	Runs	HS	Avge	100s	50s	Ct	St	Balls	Runs	Wkts	Avge	Best	5wI	10wM
Test																	
All First	240	341	65	6465	117 *	23.42	1	28	112	-	44985	22156	687	32.25	8-50	33	4
1-Day Int	10	6	4	35	11 *	17.50	-	-	1	-	570	371	8	46.37	2-37	-	
C & G	38	17	8	213	44 *	23.66	-	-	12	-	2073	1273	46	27.67	4-20	-	
tsL	234	159	49	1657	78	15.06	-	8	83	-	10031	7858	271	28.99	5-43	1	
Twenty20	17	14	6	153	37	19.12	-	-	3	-	273	348	17	20.47	2-6	-	

89. Who is Shaun Pollock's 'bunny' in ODIs?

VAAS, W. P. U. J. C.   Worcestershire

Name: Warnakulasuriya Patabendige
Ushantha Joseph <u>Chaminda</u> Vaas
Role: Left-hand bat, left-arm
fast-medium bowler
Born: 27 January 1974, Mattumagala,
Sri Lanka
County debut: 2003 (Hampshire),
2005 (Worcestershire)
County colours: 2005 (Worcestershire)
Test debut: 1994-95
Place in batting averages: 151st av. 30.11
Place in bowling averages: 48th av. 27.82
Strike rate: 61.21 (career 53.53)
Overseas tours: Sri Lanka U19 to England
1992; Sri Lanka to India 1993-94, to
Zimbabwe 1994-95, to South Africa 1994-95,
to New Zealand 1994-95, to Pakistan 1995-
96, to Australia 1995-96, to India and
Pakistan (World Cup) 1995-96, to New Zealand 1996-97, to India 1997-98, to South
Africa 1997-98, to Bangladesh (Wills International Cup) 1998-99, to UK, Ireland and
Holland (World Cup) 1999, to Zimbabwe 1999-2000, to Pakistan 1999-2000, to Kenya
(ICC Knockout Trophy) 2000-01, to South Africa 2000-01, to England 2002, to South
Africa 2002-03, to Africa (World Cup) 2002-03, to West Indies 2003, to Zimbabwe
2004, to Australia 2004, to England (ICC Champions Trophy) 2004, to Pakistan 2004-
05, to New Zealand 2004-05, to India 2005-06, to New Zealand (one-day series) 2005-
06, plus numerous other one-day series and tournaments in Sharjah, Singapore, West
Indies, Kenya, India, Pakistan, Australia, Bangladesh, New Zealand and Morocco; ICC
World XI to Australia (Tsunami Relief) 2004-05; FICA World XI to New Zealand
2004-05
Overseas teams played for: Colts CC, Sri Lanka 1990-91 –
Extras: Man of the Match for his 8-19 v Zimbabwe in the LG Abans Triangular Series
at Colombo 2001-02, a new world's best analysis for ODIs; his figures included a hat-
trick (Carlisle, Wishart, Taibu) as Zimbabwe were bowled out for 38. Took hat-trick
(Hannan Sarkar, Mohammad Ashraful, Ehsanul Haque) with the first three balls of the
match (four wickets in first over) v Bangladesh at Pietermaritzburg in the World Cup
2002-03, finishing with 6-25 and winning Man of the Match award. His other
international awards include Man of the [Test] Series v South Africa 2004 and Man of
the Match (jointly with Brian Lara) in the third Test v West Indies at Colombo 2001-
02 (7-120/7-71). An overseas player with Hampshire in the latter part of the 2003
season; an overseas player with Worcestershire for the early part of the 2005 season
Best batting: 134 Colts v Burgher, Colombo 2004-05
Best bowling: 7-54 Western Province v Southern Province, Colombo 2004-05

2005 Season

	M	Inns	NO	Runs	HS	Avge	100s	50s	Ct	St	O	M	Runs	Wkts	Avge	Best	5wI	10wM
Test																		
All First	7	10	1	271	45	30.11	-	-	3	-	285.4	80	779	28	27.82	3-36	-	-
1-Day Int																		
C & G	2	1	0	5	5	5.00	-	-	-	-	18.5	4	54	5	10.80	3-38	-	
tsL	5	5	1	37	22	9.25	-	-	1	-	44.3	5	180	11	16.36	3-31	-	
Twenty20																		

Career Performances

	M	Inns	NO	Runs	HS	Avge	100s	50s	Ct	St	Balls	Runs	Wkts	Avge	Best	5wI	10wM
Test	88	126	22	2232	74 *	21.46	-	9	27	-	19204	8511	294	28.94	7-71	11	2
All First	154	204	39	3729	134	22.60	3	14	48	-	30159	13692	563	24.31	7-54	25	3
1-Day Int	253	171	56	1627	50 *	14.14	-	1	49	-	12405	8540	326	26.19	8-19	3	
C & G	2	1	0	5	5	5.00	-	-	-	-	113	54	5	10.80	3-38	-	
tsL	13	9	3	72	28 *	12.00	-	-	3	-	666	464	20	23.20	3-31	-	
Twenty20																		

VAN DER WATH, J. J.   Sussex

Name: Johannes Jacobus van der Wath
Role: Right-hand bat, right-arm fast-medium bowler; all-rounder
Born: 10 January 1978, Newcastle, Natal, South Africa
County debut: 2005
Place in bowling averages: 106th av. 39.90
Strike rate: 62.40 (career 58.04)
Education: Ermelo High School
Overseas tours: South Africa A to Sri Lanka 2005-06; South Africa to Australia 2005-06 (VB Series)
Overseas teams played for: Easterns 1995-96 – 1996-97; Free State 1997-98 – 2003-04; Eagles 2004-05 –
Extras: Represented South Africa U19 1996-97 and has represented South Africa A against various touring sides. Scored century (100) and recorded five-wicket innings return (5-30) v Titans at Bloemfontein in the SuperSport Series 2004-05, winning the Man of the Match award. His other match awards include Man of the Match v Dolphins at Durban in the Standard Bank Cup 2004-05 (2-38/91). Was an overseas player with Sussex during the 2005 season as a locum for Naved-ul-Hasan

Best batting: 113* Free State v KwaZulu-Natal, Bloemfontein 2001-02
Best bowling: 6-37 Free State v Boland, Bloemfontein 2001-02
Stop press: Made ODI debut (as super sub) v Australia at Melbourne in the VB Series 2005-06

2005 Season

	M	Inns	NO	Runs	HS	Avge	100s	50s	Ct	St	O	M	Runs	Wkts	Avge	Best	5wI	10wM
Test																		
All First	5	7	2	104	34	20.80	-	-	1	-	104	24	399	10	39.90	3-21	-	-
1-Day Int																		
C & G	2	1	1	14	14 *	-	-	-	-	-	20	4	72	3	24.00	2-39	-	
tsL	6	4	2	161	80 *	80.50	-	2	2	-	40	4	155	4	38.75	2-29	-	
Twenty20	5	3	0	8	6	2.66	-	-	-	-	10	0	86	2	43.00	2-26	-	

Career Performances

	M	Inns	NO	Runs	HS	Avge	100s	50s	Ct	St	Balls	Runs	Wkts	Avge	Best	5wI	10wM
Test																	
All First	49	75	14	1574	113 *	25.80	2	8	20	-	8558	4101	147	27.89	6-37	7	-
1-Day Int																	
C & G	2	1	1	14	14 *	-	-	-	-	-	120	72	3	24.00	2-39	-	
tsL	6	4	2	161	80 *	80.50	-	2	2	-	240	155	4	38.75	2-29	-	
Twenty20	5	3	0	8	6	2.66	-	-	-	-	60	86	2	43.00	2-26	-	

VAN JAARSVELD, M.   Kent

Name: Martin van Jaarsveld
Role: Right-hand top-order bat
Born: 18 June 1974, Klerksdorp, South Africa
Height: 6ft 2in **Weight:** 12st 12lbs
Nickname: Jarre
County debut: 2004 (Northamptonshire), 2005 (Kent)
County cap: 2005 (Kent)
Test debut: 2002-03
1000 runs in a season: 1
1st-Class 200s: 3
Place in batting averages: 56th av. 44.37 (2004 89th av. 37.23)
Strike rate: (career 93.70)
Parents: Leon and Isobel
Marital status: Single

Education: Warmbads High School; University of Pretoria
Qualifications: BComm (Financial Management)
Overseas tours: South Africa A to Sri Lanka 1998, to Zimbabwe 2002-03, to Australia 2002-03; South African Academy to Zimbabwe 1998-99; South Africa to England 2003, to New Zealand 2003-04, to Sri Lanka 2004, to England (ICC Champions Trophy) 2004, to India 2004-05
Overseas teams played for: Northern Transvaal/Northerns Titans 1994-95 – 2003-04; Titans 2004-05 –
Career highlights to date: 'Playing for South Africa. Being chosen as one of the five Cricketers of the Year in South Africa 2002'
Cricket moments to forget: 'Losing the NatWest Series final at Lord's, July 2003'
Cricket superstitions: 'Left pad first when padding up'
Cricketers particularly admired: Michael Atherton, Kepler Wessels
Other sports played: Golf, tennis
Other sports followed: Rugby, 'and most other sports'
Favourite band: Live
Relaxations: 'Having throw-downs; going to the cinema'
Extras: Scored 182* and 158* v Griqualand West at Centurion 2001-02, becoming only the second batsman to record two 150s in the same match in South Africa. Player of the SuperSport Series 2001-02 (934 runs at 84.90); also topped South African first-class averages 2001-02 (1268 runs at 74.58). One of *South African Cricket Annual*'s five Cricketers of the Year 2002. Was an overseas player with Northamptonshire 2004. Scored a century in each innings (118/111) on first-class debut for Kent, v Warwickshire at Canterbury 2005, becoming the first Kent debutant to achieve the feat. Scored 168 v Surrey at Tunbridge Wells 2005, in the process sharing with Robert Key (189) in a new Kent record third-wicket partnership (323). Retired from international cricket in February 2005. Is no longer considered an overseas player
Best batting: 262* Kent v Glamorgan, Cardiff 2005
Best bowling: 1-1 Northerns v Boland, Centurion 1998-99

2005 Season

	M	Inns	NO	Runs	HS	Avge	100s	50s	Ct	St	O	M	Runs	Wkts	Avge	Best	5wI	10wM
Test																		
All First	16	28	1	1198	262 *	44.37	4	4	18	-	35	11	82	3	27.33	1-7	-	-
1-Day Int																		
C & G	3	3	0	44	20	14.66	-	-	1	-	3	0	17	0	-		-	-
tsl.	17	16	2	549	114	39.21	1	4	10	-	6	0	40	0	-		-	-
Twenty20	8	7	1	106	51	17.66	-	1	4	-	5	0	37	2	18.50	2-19	-	

Career Performances

	M	Inns	NO	Runs	HS	Avge	100s	50s	Ct	St	Balls	Runs	Wkts	Avge	Best	5wl	10wM
Test	9	15	2	397	73	30.53	-	3	11	-	42	28	0	-	-	-	-
All First	125	214	20	8617	262 *	44.41	24	36	141	-	1051	540	12	45.00	2-30	-	-
1-Day Int	11	7	1	124	45	20.66	-	-	4	-	31	18	2	9.00	1-0	-	
C & G	7	7	1	271	93 *	45.16	-	2	4	-	79	68	1	68.00	1-1	-	
tsL	24	23	4	795	114	41.84	1	6	14	-	54	58	1	58.00	1-18	-	
Twenty20	13	12	2	280	61 *	28.00	-	3	7	-	42	52	3	17.33	2-19	-	

VAUGHAN, M. P.   Yorkshire

Name: <u>Michael</u> Paul Vaughan
Role: Right-hand bat, off-spin bowler
Born: 29 October 1974, Eccles, Manchester
Height: 6ft 2in **Weight:** 11st 7lbs
Nickname: Frankie, Virgil
County debut: 1993
County cap: 1995
Benefit: 2005
Test debut: 1999-2000
1000 runs in a season: 4
Place in batting averages: 83rd av. 37.60
(2004 54th av. 46.00)
Strike rate: (career 80.78)
Parents: Graham John and Dee
Wife and date of marriage: Nichola,
September 2003
Children: Tallulah Grace, 4 June 2004;
Archie, December 2005
Family links with cricket: Father played league cricket for Worsley CC. Brother plays for Sheffield Collegiate. Mother is related to the famous Tyldesley family (Lancashire and England)
Education: Silverdale Comprehensive, Sheffield
Qualifications: 7 GCSEs
Overseas tours: Yorkshire to West Indies 1994, to South Africa 1995, to Zimbabwe 1996; England U19 to India 1992-93, to Sri Lanka 1993-94 (c); England A to India 1994-95, to Australia 1996-97, to Zimbabwe and South Africa 1998-99 (c); England to South Africa 1999-2000, to Pakistan and Sri Lanka 2000-01, to India and New Zealand 2001-02, to Australia 2002-03, to Africa (World Cup) 2002-03, to Bangladesh and Sri Lanka 2003-04 (c), to West Indies 2003-04 (c), to Zimbabwe (one-day series) 2004-05 (c), to South Africa 2004-05 (c), to Pakistan 2005-06 (c), to India 2005-06 (c)
Cricketers particularly admired: Darren Lehmann, 'all the Yorkshire and England squads'

Other sports played: Football (Baslow FC), golf (10 handicap)
Other sports followed: Football (Sheffield Wednesday), all golf
Relaxations: Most sports. 'Enjoy a good meal with friends'
Extras: Maurice Leyland Batting Award 1990; Cricket Society's Most Promising Young Cricketer 1993; A. A. Thompson Memorial Trophy 1993. Scored 1066 runs in first full season of first-class cricket 1994. Captained England U19. PCA Player of the Year 2002. Highest-scoring batsman in Test cricket for the calendar year 2002 (1481 runs). One of *Wisden*'s Five Cricketers of the Year 2003. Topped Pricewaterhouse Coopers rankings for Test batsmen in early summer 2003. Vodafone Cricketer of the Year 2002-03. Scored century in each innings (103/101*) in the first Test v West Indies at Lord's 2004. His international awards include England's Man of the [Test] Series v India 2002 (615 runs at 102.50) and Man of the [Test] Series v Australia 2002-03 (633 runs at 63.30), as well as Man of the Match v Australia at Edgbaston in the ICC Champions Trophy 2004 (86/2-42 plus run-out). England one-day captain since May 2003 and England Test captain since July 2003; led England to a Test series win over Australia in 2005, their first Ashes success for 18 years. Book *A Year in the Sun* published 2003. Made Twenty20 international debut v Australia at the Rose Bowl 2005
Best batting: 197 England v India, Trent Bridge 2002
Best bowling: 4-39 Yorkshire v Oxford University, The Parks 1994
Stop press: Appointed OBE in 2006 New Year Honours as captain of 2005 Ashes-winning England team. Forced to return home from the England tour to India 2005-06 with a knee injury

2005 Season

	M	Inns	NO	Runs	HS	Avge	100s	50s	Ct	St	O	M	Runs	Wkts	Avge	Best	5wI	10wM
Test	7	12	0	490	166	40.83	2	1	2	-	5	0	21	0	-	-	-	-
All First	9	15	0	564	166	37.60	2	2	2	-	5	0	21	0	-	-	-	-
1-Day Int	8	7	2	132	59 *	26.40	-	2	-	-	7	0	46	0	-	-	-	
C & G	2	2	0	67	58	33.50	-	1	-	-	2	0	6	0	-	-	-	
tsL	2	2	1	147	116 *	147.00	1	-	1	-	11	0	60	2	30.00	2-42	-	
Twenty20																		

Career Performances

	M	Inns	NO	Runs	HS	Avge	100s	50s	Ct	St	Balls	Runs	Wkts	Avge	Best	5wI	10wM
Test	62	111	8	4513	197	43.81	15	13	36	-	936	537	6	89.50	2-71	-	-
All First	224	395	24	14272	197	38.46	39	58	106	-	9210	5142	114	45.10	4-39	-	-
1-Day Int	74	71	10	1730	90 *	28.36	-	15	20	-	664	562	12	46.83	4-22	-	
C & G	29	28	3	889	116 *	35.56	1	6	7	-	354	223	6	37.16	1-4	-	
tsL	99	97	7	2239	116 *	24.87	1	10	32	-	1142	951	33	28.81	4-27	-	
Twenty20																	

VETTORI, D. L.   Warwickshire

Name: <u>Daniel</u> Luca Vettori
Role: Left-hand bat, slow left-arm bowler
Born: 27 January 1979, Auckland,
New Zealand
County debut: 2003 (Nottinghamshire)
County cap: 2003 (Nottinghamshire)
Test debut: 1996-97
Strike rate: (career 71.26)
Family links with cricket: Cousin (J. V.
Hill) and uncle (A. J. Hill) played for Central
Districts in New Zealand
Overseas tours: New Zealand U19 to
England 1996; New Zealand Academy to
South Africa 1997; New Zealand to
Zimbabwe 1997-98, to Australia 1997-98, to
Sri Lanka 1998, to Malaysia (Commonwealth
Games) 1998-99, to Bangladesh (Wills
International Cup) 1998-99, to UK, Ireland

and Holland (World Cup) 1999, to England 1999, to India 1999-2000, to Zimbabwe
2000-01, to Australia 2001-02, to Pakistan 2002, to West Indies 2002, to Sri Lanka
(ICC Champions Trophy) 2002-03, to Africa (World Cup) 2002-03, to Sri Lanka 2003,
to India 2003-04, to England 2004, to England (ICC Champions Trophy) 2004, to
Bangladesh 2004-05, to Australia 2004-05, to Zimbabwe 2005-06, to South Africa
(one-day series) 2005-06, plus other one-day series and tournaments in Singapore, Sri
Lanka, India and Pakistan; ICC World XI to Australia (Tsunami Relief) 2004-05, to
Australia (Super Series) 2005-06
Overseas teams played for: Northern Districts 1996-97 –
Extras: Became youngest player to play Test cricket for New Zealand when he made
his debut in the second Test v England at Wellington 1996-97 aged 18 years 10 days.
One of *New Zealand Cricket Almanack*'s two Cricketers of the Year 2000, 2005. His
awards include Player of the [ODI] Series v Australia 2004-05, Player of the [Test]
Series v Bangladesh 2004-05 (20 wickets; av. 11.20) and Man of the Match in the first
Test v Australia at Auckland 1999-2000 (5-62/7-87). Was an overseas player with
Nottinghamshire during July 2003 as a locum for Stuart MacGill; has joined
Warwickshire as an overseas player for 2006
Best batting: 137* New Zealand v Pakistan, Hamilton 2003-04
Best bowling: 7-87 New Zealand v Australia, Auckland 1999-2000

2005 Season (did not make any first-class or one-day appearances)

Career Performances

	M	Inns	NO	Runs	HS	Avge	100s	50s	Ct	St	Balls	Runs	Wkts	Avge	Best	5wl	10wM
Test	64	92	15	1855	137 *	24.09	2	9	33	-	16055	7136	207	34.47	7-87	12	2
All First	105	144	21	2969	137 *	24.13	3	15	50	-	24873	11159	349	31.97	7-87	22	2
1-Day Int	154	94	30	909	83	14.20	-	1	34	-	6941	4942	146	33.84	5-30	1	
C & G																	
tsL	1	0	0	0	0	-	-	-	-	-	54	36	1	36.00	1-36	-	
Twenty20																	

WAGG, G. G.   Derbyshire

Name: <u>Graham</u> Grant Wagg
Role: Right-hand bat, left-arm fast-medium bowler
Born: 28 April 1983, Rugby
Height: 6ft **Weight:** 12st 10lbs
Nickname: Stiggy, Waggy, Captain Caveman, Wild Card, Ug
County debut: 2002 (Warwickshire)
Strike rate: (career 45.60)
Parents: John and Dawn
Marital status: Single
Family links with cricket: Father is qualified coach
Education: Ashlawn School, Rugby
Qualifications: Level 1 cricket coach
Overseas tours: Warwickshire Development tour to South Africa 1998, to West Indies 2000; England A to Malaysia and India 2003-04
Overseas teams played for: Hams Tech, East London, South Africa 1999
Career highlights to date: 'Four wickets and 50 on first-class debut'
Cricketers particularly admired: Stuart MacGill, John Wagg
Other sports played: Golf, carp fishing
Other sports followed: Football (Man United), cricket (Leamington CC)
Relaxations: 'Fishing, music, clubbing'
Extras: Represented England U16, U17, U18, U19 as well as Development of Excellence (Midlands) XI. Scored 42* from 50 balls, 51 from 57 balls and took 4-43 on first-class debut v Somerset at Edgbaston 2002. ECB National Academy 2003-04. NBC Denis Compton Award for the most promising young Warwickshire player 2003. Released by Warwicks at the end of the 2004 season; has joined Derbyshire for 2006

Best batting: 74 Warwickshire v India A, Edgbaston 2003
Best bowling: 4-43 Warwickshire v Somerset, Edgbaston 2002

2005 Season (did not make any first-class or one-day appearances)

Career Performances

	M	Inns	NO	Runs	HS	Avge	100s	50s	Ct	St	Balls	Runs	Wkts	Avge	Best	5wI	10wM
Test																	
All First	10	15	2	284	74	21.84	-	2	2	-	1049	726	23	31.56	4-43	-	-
1-Day Int																	
C & G	5	4	0	41	21	10.25	-	-	1	-	168	128	4	32.00	3-35	-	
tsL	18	12	1	200	35	18.18	-	-	6	-	402	387	13	29.76	4-50	-	
Twenty20	11	9	1	111	25	13.87	-	-	2	-	102	134	8	16.75	3-33	-	

WAGH, M. A.   Warwickshire

Name: Mark Anant Wagh
Role: Right-hand bat, off-spin bowler
Born: 20 October 1976, Birmingham
Height: 6ft 2in **Weight:** 13st
Nickname: Waggy
County debut: 1997
County cap: 2000
1000 runs in a season: 3
1st-Class 200s: 1
1st-Class 300s: 1
Place in batting averages: (2004 91st av. 36.89)
Place in bowling averages: (2004 145th av. 51.00)
Strike rate: (career 87.27)
Parents: Mohan and Rita
Marital status: Single
Education: King Edward's School, Birmingham; Keble College, Oxford
Qualifications: BA degree, Level 2 coaching award
Overseas tours: Warwickshire U19 to South Africa 1992; ECB National Academy to Australia 2001-02
Career highlights to date: '315 at Lord's 2001'
Cricket moments to forget: 'Too many to mention'
Cricketers particularly admired: Andy Flower
Young players to look out for: Moeen Ali
Favourite band: Dido

Extras: Oxford Blue 1996-98; Oxford University captain 1997. Scored maiden first-class century (116) for Oxford University v Glamorgan at The Parks 1997, following up with another 100 (101) in the second innings. Attended Zimbabwe Cricket Academy 1999. His 315 v Middlesex at Lord's 2001 is the equal second highest individual Championship score made at Lord's (behind Jack Hobbs's 316 in 1926). C&G Man of the Match award for his 102* v Kent at Edgbaston 2004. Included in preliminary England one-day squad of 30 for ICC Champions Trophy 2004
Best batting: 315 Warwickshire v Middlesex, Lord's 2001
Best bowling: 7-222 Warwickshire v Lancashire, Edgbaston 2003

2005 Season

	M	Inns	NO	Runs	HS	Avge	100s	50s	Ct	St	O	M	Runs	Wkts	Avge	Best	5wI	10wM
Test																		
All First	2	2	0	94	66	47.00	-	1	-	-								
1-Day Int																		
C & G																		
tsL																		
Twenty20																		

Career Performances

	M	Inns	NO	Runs	HS	Avge	100s	50s	Ct	St	Balls	Runs	Wkts	Avge	Best	5wI	10wM
Test																	
All First	127	210	18	7429	315	38.69	18	33	69	-	8553	4553	98	46.45	7-222	2	-
1-Day Int																	
C & G	10	10	1	256	102 *	28.44	1	-	1	-	168	142	6	23.66	3-35	-	
tsL	48	44	3	1031	84	25.14	-	8	11	-	754	601	16	37.56	4-35	-	
Twenty20	7	6	0	74	28	12.33	-	-	2	-	75	106	5	21.20	2-16	-	

WAINWRIGHT, D. J. — Yorkshire

Name: David John Wainwright
Role: Left-hand bat, left-arm orthodox spin bowler
Born: 21 March 1985, Pontefract
Height: 5ft 9in **Weight:** 9st 3lbs
Nickname: Wainers
County debut: 2004
Place in bowling averages: 13th av. 23.11
Strike rate: 47.33 (career 48.33)
Parents: Paul and Debbie
Marital status: Single
Family links with cricket: 'Grandfather (Harry Heritage) represented Yorkshire Schoolboys 1950-51'

Education: Hemsworth High School;
Hemsworth Arts and Community College;
Loughborough University
Qualifications: 10 GCSEs, 3 A-levels,
Level 1 coaching
Overseas tours: Yorkshire U15 to South
Africa 2000
Career highlights to date: 'Making
Yorkshire 1st XI debut in 2004 v Somerset'
Cricketers particularly admired: Brian
Lara, Daniel Vettori
Young players to look out for: Tim Bresnan,
Joe Sayers
Other sports played: Football, golf
Other sports followed: Football
(Liverpool FC)
Favourite band: Jackson Five
Relaxations: Listening to music
Extras: Best bowling award at Bunbury Festival for North of England U15. Played for
Loughborough UCCE 2005. Represented British Universities 2005
Opinions on cricket: 'I feel that the game is moving forward, with the introduction of
Twenty20 helping to widen the fan-base. England's success is also helping to promote
the game at grass-roots level.'
Best batting: 62 Yorkshire v Bangladesh A, Headingley 2005
Best bowling: 4-48 LUCCE v Worcestershire, Kidderminster 2005

2005 Season

	M	Inns	NO	Runs	HS	Avge	100s	50s	Ct	St	O	M	Runs	Wkts	Avge	Best	5wI	10wM
Test																		
All First	5	6	2	153	62	38.25	-	1	4	-	142	34	416	18	23.11	4-48	-	-
1-Day Int																		
C & G																		
tsL	2	0	0	0	0	-	-	-	-	-	11	0	59	0	-		-	-
Twenty20																		

Career Performances

	M	Inns	NO	Runs	HS	Avge	100s	50s	Ct	St	Balls	Runs	Wkts	Avge	Best	5wI	10wM
Test																	
All First	6	7	2	158	62	31.60	-	1	4	-	870	421	18	23.38	4-48	-	-
1-Day Int																	
C & G																	
tsL	2	0	0	0	0	-	-	-	-	-	66	59	0	-		-	-
Twenty20																	

WALKER, M. J.   Kent

Name: Matthew (<u>Matt</u>) Jonathan Walker
Role: Left-hand middle-order bat,
right-arm medium-slow bowler
Born: 2 January 1974, Gravesend
Height: 5ft 6½in **Weight:** 14st 7lbs
Nickname: Walks, Pumba
County debut: 1992-93
County cap: 2000
1000 runs in a season: 2
1st-Class 200s: 1
Place in batting averages: 72nd av. 39.72
(2004 23rd av. 55.04)
Strike rate: (career 84.84)
Parents: Richard and June
Wife and date of marriage: Claudia,
25 September 1999
Children: Charlie Jack, 20 November 2002
Family links with cricket: 'Dad played Kent
and Middlesex 2nd XIs and was on Lord's groundstaff. Grandfather kept wicket for
Kent. Mum was women's cricket coach'
Education: King's School, Rochester
Qualifications: 9 GCSEs, 2 A-levels, advanced cricket coaching certificate
Career outside cricket: PE teacher
Off-season: 'Hockey coaching at St Edmund's School'
Overseas tours: Kent U17 to New Zealand 1990-91; England U19 to Pakistan 1991-
92, to India 1992-93 (c); Kent to Zimbabwe 1993
Career highlights to date: 'Captaining England U19. Winning Norwich Union
League 2001'
Cricket moments to forget: 'Losing Lord's B&H final v Surrey 1997'
Cricket superstitions: 'None'
Cricketers particularly admired: Sachin Tendulkar, Muttiah Muralitharan,
Rahul Dravid
Young players to look out for: Chris Piesley, Sam Billings
Other sports played: Hockey (England U14-U21 [captain U15-U17]), rugby
(Kent U18)
Other sports followed: Football (Charlton Athletic), hockey (Gore Court HC)
Favourite band: Pixies, Counting Crows, Coldplay, Jeff Buckley
Relaxations: 'Music and films'
Extras: Captained England U16 cricket and hockey teams in same year. Sir John
Hobbs Silver Jubilee Memorial Prize for outstanding U16 cricketer 1989. Captained
England U19 1993. Woolwich Kent League's Young Cricketer of the Year 1994.

Scored 275* against Somerset in 1996 – the highest ever individual score by a Kent batsman at Canterbury. Scored 151* as Kent reached a county record fourth-innings 429-5 to beat Worcestershire at Canterbury 2004. Ealham Award for Fielding Excellence 2003, 2004, 2005. Cowdrey Award for Kent Player of the Year 2004. Vice-captain of Kent 2005. Became an Eminent Roffensian 1995

Opinions on cricket: 'Should be only one overseas player. Apart from that it's a great game and the sport is in better shape than the press always make it out to be.'

Best batting: 275* Kent v Somerset, Canterbury 1996

Best bowling: 2-21 Kent v Middlesex, Canterbury 2004

2005 Season

	M	Inns	NO	Runs	HS	Avge	100s	50s	Ct	St	O	M	Runs	Wkts	Avge	Best	5wI	10wM
Test																		
All First	16	28	3	993	173	39.72	3	4	8	-	35	1	164	4	41.00	1-6	-	-
1-Day Int																		
C & G	3	3	1	136	56 *	68.00	-	2	2	-	6.5	1	22	4	5.50	2-5	-	
tsL	17	16	1	317	58	21.13	-	3	6	-	23	0	115	3	38.33	2-14	-	
Twenty20	8	8	0	161	36	20.12	-	-	-	-								

Career Performances

	M	Inns	NO	Runs	HS	Avge	100s	50s	Ct	St	Balls	Runs	Wkts	Avge	Best	5wI	10wM
Test																	
All First	149	247	28	7522	275 *	34.34	17	30	106	-	1612	955	19	50.26	2-21	-	-
1-Day Int																	
C & G	21	19	5	504	73	36.00	-	4	9	-	215	145	6	24.16	2-5	-	
tsL	161	150	17	3231	101	24.29	1	18	40	-	629	557	23	24.21	4-24	-	
Twenty20	18	18	2	381	48 *	23.81	-	-	1	-							

90. Which umpire has stood in the most ODIs?

WALKER, N. G. E.   Derbyshire

Name: <u>Nicholas</u> Guy Eades Walker
Role: Right-hand bat, right-arm fast-medium
bowler; all-rounder
Born: 7 August 1984, Enfield
Height: 6ft 2in **Weight:** 13st 6lbs
Nickname: Walks
County debut: 2004
Place in batting averages: 257th av. 14.18
(2004 93rd av. 36.83)
Place in bowling averages: 140th av. 52.47
(2004 99th av. 37.05)
Strike rate: 74.05 (career 61.91)
Parents: Amanda and Martin
Marital status: 'Taken'
Family links with cricket: 'Brother Duncan
plays village cricket on Sundays; brother
Robbie captained Oxford Uni college'
Education: Haileybury Imperial Service
College; 'two terms at Durham Uni'
Qualifications: Level 1 coach
Overseas tours: Haileybury School to South Africa 2000
Overseas teams played for: South Perth, Western Australia 2001-02
Career highlights to date: 'Five-for against Somerset; 80 against Somerset, breaking
Derbyshire record for highest score by number 11'
Cricket moments to forget: 'Missing run-out against Yorkshire to bring in number 11
with two overs to go'
Cricket superstitions: 'Too many'
Cricketers particularly admired: Ian Botham, Kevin Dean, Graeme Welch
Other sports played: Badminton (county), rackets, real tennis, golf
Other sports followed: Rugby (Wasps)
Favourite band: Tracy Chapman
Extras: Struck 57-ball 80 (highest first-class score by a Derbyshire No. 11) in his third
Championship innings, then recorded maiden first-class five-wicket return (5-68), both
v Somerset at Derby 2004. Struck 24-ball fifty (ending with 63*), batting at No. 11 v
Leicestershire at Oakham School 2004. Released by Derbyshire during the 2005-06
off-season
Opinions on cricket: 'Very good game – long days when fielding! A lot of EU players
now coming into the game; not sure if good or bad.'
Best batting: 80 Derbyshire v Somerset, Derby 2004
Best bowling: 5-68 Derbyshire v Somerset, Derby 2004

2005 Season

	M	Inns	NO	Runs	HS	Avge	100s	50s	Ct	St	O	M	Runs	Wkts	Avge	Best	5wI	10wM
Test																		
All First	10	14	3	156	79	14.18	-	1	4	-	209.5	27	892	17	52.47	4-69	-	-
1-Day Int																		
C & G																		
tsL	6	5	1	14	6*	3.50	-	-	3	-	15.4	1	98	1	98.00	1-19	-	
Twenty20	1	1	0	8	8	8.00	-	-	-	-								

Career Performances

	M	Inns	NO	Runs	HS	Avge	100s	50s	Ct	St	Balls	Runs	Wkts	Avge	Best	5wI	10wM
Test																	
All First	18	23	6	377	80	22.17	-	3	7	-	2167	1559	35	44.54	5-68	1	-
1-Day Int																	
C & G	2	2	0	13	12	6.50	-	-	2	-	104	114	4	28.50	3-49	-	
tsL	12	9	1	87	43	10.87	-	-	4	-	130	128	2	64.00	1-19	-	
Twenty20	1	1	0	8	8	8.00	-	-	-	-							

WALLACE, M. A.   Glamorgan

Name: Mark Alexander Wallace
Role: Left-hand bat, wicket-keeper
Born: 19 November 1981, Abergavenny
Height: 5ft 9in   **Weight:** 12st
Nickname: Wally, Grommit, Wash
County debut: 1999
County cap: 2003
50 dismissals in a season: 2
Place in batting averages: 170th av. 26.64
(2004 161st av. 27.71)
Parents: Ryland and Alvine
Marital status: Single
Family links with cricket: 'Father plays for
Abergavenny and Wales Over 50s'
Education: Crickhowell High School
Qualifications: 10 GCSEs, 2 A-levels,
Levels 1 and 2 coaching

Overseas tours: Gwent U15 to South Africa
1996; Wales U16 to Jersey 1996, 1997; England U19 to New Zealand 1998-99, to
Malaysia and (U19 World Cup) Sri Lanka 1999-2000, to India 2000-01; ECB National
Academy to Australia 2001-02, to Australia and Sri Lanka 2002-03
Overseas teams played for: Port Adelaide Magpies, South Australia 2002-03

Career highlights to date: 'NCL titles 2002 and 2004. National Academy selections; captaining National Academy'

Cricket moments to forget: 'With 10 to win off two balls v Kent 2004, getting nutmegged for four byes and seeing Adrian Dale's final ball in county cricket go into the car park for six'

Cricket superstitions: 'More and more every year'

Cricketers particularly admired: Ian Healy, Steve Rhodes, Keith Piper, Warren Hegg, Chris Read, Adam Gilchrist, Alec Stewart, Mike Kasprowicz, Darren Berry

Other sports played: 'Plenty of golf, football, boxing'

Other sports followed: Football (Merthyr FC), rugby (Cardiff Blues), golf

Favourite band: Bon Jovi, Eminem

Extras: Represented England U17. Represented England U19 1998, 1999 and 2000 (captain for second 'Test' 2000). Made first-class debut v Somerset at Taunton 1999 aged 17 years 287 days – youngest ever Glamorgan wicket-keeper. NBC Denis Compton Award 1999. Captained ECB National Academy to innings victory over Commonwealth Bank [Australian] Cricket Academy at Adelaide 2001-02. Byron Denning Glamorgan Clubman of the Year Award 2003

Opinions on cricket: 'EU/Kolpak player situation [*see page 9*] is worrying and is only being fuelled by the increase of foreign coaches. Should get choice of getting extra delivery after a no-ball/wide.'

Best batting: 121 Glamorgan v Durham, Riverside 2003

2005 Season

	M	Inns	NO	Runs	HS	Avge	100s	50s	Ct	St	O	M	Runs	Wkts	Avge	Best	5wI	10wM
Test																		
All First	17	30	2	746	96	26.64	-	6	31	4								
1-Day Int																		
C & G	2	2	0	63	48	31.50	-	-	4	-								
tsL	14	10	5	188	33 *	37.60	-	-	16	4								
Twenty20	7	6	2	46	11	11.50	-	-	4	-								

Career Performances

	M	Inns	NO	Runs	HS	Avge	100s	50s	Ct	St	Balls	Runs	Wkts	Avge	Best	5wI	10wM
Test																	
All First	86	141	12	3542	121	27.45	4	18	230	13							
1-Day Int																	
C & G	8	6	0	104	48	17.33	-	-	10	-							
tsL	68	47	12	532	37 *	15.20	-	-	77	19							
Twenty20	19	16	6	194	32 *	19.40	-	-	8	2							

WALTERS, S. J.　　　　　　　　　　　　　Surrey

Name: <u>Stewart</u> Jonathan Walters
Role: Right-hand bat, right-arm
medium bowler
Born: 25 June 1983, Mornington,
Victoria, Australia
Height: 6ft 1in
Nickname: Forrest
County debut: 2005 (one-day)
Parents: Stewart and Sue
Wife and date of marriage: Jacki,
24 February 2006
Education: Guildford Grammar School,
Perth, Western Australia
Off-season: 'Australia (Midland-
Guildford CC)'
Overseas teams played for: Midland-
Guildford CC, Perth
Career highlights to date: 'First-team
debut 2005'

Cricket moments to forget: 'The ducks!'
Cricket superstitions: 'Right pad first'
Cricketers particularly admired: Steve Waugh
Young players to look out for: Rory Hamilton-Brown
Other sports played: Australian Rules football (AFL)
Other sports followed: Football (Man U)
Favourite band: U2
Relaxations: 'Running; spending time with friends'
Extras: Captain of Western Australia U17 for two years
Opinions on cricket: 'Love the tempo of the one-day game; also the temperament of
the four-day game and seeing players adjust.'

2005 Season

	M	Inns	NO	Runs	HS	Avge	100s	50s	Ct	St	O	M	Runs	Wkts	Avge	Best	5wI	10wM
Test																		
All First																		
1-Day Int																		
C & G																		
tsL	6	6	2	134	32 *	33.50	-	-	4	-								
Twenty20																		

Career Performances

	M	Inns	NO	Runs	HS	Avge	100s	50s	Ct	St	Balls	Runs	Wkts	Avge	Best	5wl	10wM
Test																	
All First																	
1-Day Int																	
C & G																	
tsL	6	6	2	134	32 *	33.50	-	-	4	-							
Twenty20																	

WARD, I. J.   Sussex

Name: Ian James Ward
Role: Left-hand bat
Born: 30 September 1973, Plymouth
Height: 5ft 9in **Weight:** 13st
Nickname: Wardy, Cocker, Son of Baboon,
Dwarf, Stumpy, Pig in a Passage
County debut: 1992 (Surrey), 2004 (Sussex)
County cap: 2000 (Surrey), 2004 (Sussex)
Test debut: 2001
1000 runs in a season: 3
Place in batting averages: 77th av. 38.75
(2004 68th av. 43.00)
Strike rate: (career 106.33)
Parents: Tony and Mary
Wife and date of marriage: Joanne,
15 February 1998
Children: Robert, 21 September;
Lennox, 10 April
Family links with cricket: Grandfather and father played for Devon
Education: Millfield School
Qualifications: 8 GCSEs, 3 A-levels, NCA coaching award
Career outside cricket: 'Sky television/media'
Overseas tours: Surrey U19 to Barbados 1990; Millfield to Jamaica 1991, to
Australia; Malden Wanderers to Jersey 1994; England A to Bangladesh and New
Zealand 1999-2000, to West Indies 2000-01
Overseas teams played for: North Perth CC, Western Australia 1996-97; Perth CC,
Western Australia; Marist Newman Old Boys CC, Perth
Career highlights to date: 'Test debut'
Cricket superstitions: 'None'
Cricketers particularly admired: Alec Stewart, Saqlain Mushtaq, Graham Thorpe
Young players to look out for: Rory Hamilton-Brown

Other sports played: Golf, football, skiing
Other sports followed: Football (Liverpool), Formula One, skiing
Favourite band: 'The Mark Butcher Band!'
Relaxations: Running, walking dog
Extras: Released by Surrey at 18 and missed four years of cricket, returning to the county in 1996. Scored centuries in three successive Busta Cup matches for England A in West Indies 2000-01 and was leading first-class run-scorer on tour (769 av. 64.08). Made Test debut v Pakistan at Lord's 2001 in England's 100th Test at the ground. Scored four centuries in consecutive Championship innings 2002 – including two centuries in match (112/156) v Hampshire at West End – to equal a Surrey record last achieved by Jack Hobbs in 1925. Leading run-scorer in English first-class cricket 2002 with 1759 runs (av. 62.82). Surrey Player of the Year 2002. Retired at the end of the 2005 season to take up broadcasting full-time
Opinions on cricket: 'Leave Twenty20 as it's working. Bring back Benson and Hedges-type one-day competition instead of C&G and totesport but play at right time of year. Practice facilities are not good enough in general in this country. More money to Duncan Fletcher for ECB contracts. It's working.'
Best batting: 168* Surrey v Kent, Canterbury 2002
Best bowling: 1-1 Surrey v Hampshire, West End 2002

2005 Season

	M	Inns	NO	Runs	HS	Avge	100s	50s	Ct	St	O	M	Runs	Wkts	Avge	Best	5wI	10wM
Test																		
All First	10	16	0	620	150	38.75	2	2	3	-	1	1	0	0	-	-	-	-
1-Day Int																		
C & G	3	3	0	68	65	22.66	-	1	1	-								
tsL	9	9	0	313	93	34.77	-	3	3	-								
Twenty20	8	5	0	98	50	19.60	-	1	1	-								

Career Performances

	M	Inns	NO	Runs	HS	Avge	100s	50s	Ct	St	Balls	Runs	Wkts	Avge	Best	5wI	10wM
Test	5	9	1	129	39	16.12	-	-	1	-							
All First	138	230	17	8575	168 *	40.25	23	43	71	-	319	197	3	65.66	1-1	-	-
1-Day Int																	
C & G	24	22	2	735	108	36.75	1	6	3	-	60	49	0	-	-	-	
tsL	113	110	10	2791	136	27.91	1	17	23	-	59	92	0	-	-	-	
Twenty20	18	15	0	351	50	23.40	-	2	4	-							

WARNE, S. K.   Hampshire

Name: <u>Shane</u> Keith Warne
Role: Right-hand bat, leg-spin bowler,
county captain
Born: 13 September 1969, Ferntree Gully,
Victoria, Australia
Height: 6ft **Weight:** 13st 12lbs
Nickname: Warney
County debut: 2000
County cap: 2000
Test debut: 1991-92
50 wickets in a season: 3
Place in batting averages: 137th av. 30.91
(2004 164th av. 27.21)
Place in bowling averages: 10th av. 22.50
(2004 15th av. 24.13)
Strike rate: 44.86 (career 56.98)
Parents: Keith and Brigite
Marital status: Single
Children: Brooke, 8; Jackson, 6; Summer, 4
Education: Mentone Grammar School; Hampton High School
Off-season: Playing for Australia
Overseas tours: Australia YC to West Indies 1990; Australia B to Zimbabwe 1991-92;
Australia to Sri Lanka 1992, to New Zealand 1992-93, to England 1993, to South
Africa 1993-94, to Pakistan 1994-95, to West Indies 1994-95, to India, Pakistan and
Sri Lanka (World Cup) 1995-96, to South Africa 1996-97, to England 1997, to India
1997-98, to West Indies 1998-99, to UK, Ireland and Holland (World Cup) 1999, to Sri
Lanka 1999, to Zimbabwe 1999-2000, to New Zealand 1999-2000, to India 2000-01,
to England 2001, to South Africa 2001-02, to Sri Lanka (ICC Champions Trophy)
2002-03, to Sri Lanka and Sharjah (v Pakistan) 2002-03, to Sri Lanka 2003-04, to
India 2004-05, to New Zealand 2004-05, to England 2005, plus other one-day series
and tournaments in Sharjah, Sri Lanka, Pakistan, New Zealand, India, South Africa
and Kenya; FICA World XI to New Zealand 2004-05
Overseas teams played for: St Kilda, Victoria; Victoria 1990-91 –
Career highlights to date: '1999 World Cup and being selected for Australia'
Cricket moments to forget: 'Losing to the West Indies by one run in 1992-93 season
in Adelaide'
Cricket superstitions: 'I eat pizza the night before I bowl'
Cricketers particularly admired: Sachin Tendulkar, Brian Lara, Ian Chappell, Glenn
McGrath
Young players to look out for: Jimmy Adams, Sean Ervine, Michael Clarke
Other sports played: AFL, golf, tennis

Other sports followed: AFL (St Kilda), football (Chelsea)
Favourite band: Rogue Traders, Bruce Springsteen
Relaxations: 'Yoga and kids'
Extras: One of *Wisden*'s Five Cricketers of the Year 1994, one of *South African Cricket Annual*'s five Cricketers of the Year 1994, and one of *Indian Cricket*'s five Cricketers of the Year 1996; voted one of *Wisden*'s Five Cricketers of the Century 2000. Voted Australia's ODI Player of the Year at the inaugural Allan Border Medal awards January 2000. Took hat-trick (DeFreitas, Gough, Malcolm) in the second Test v England at Melbourne 1994-95. Man of the Match in his 100th Test, v South Africa at Cape Town 2001-02 (2-70/6-161). Has won numerous other Test awards, among them Man of the Series v England 1993 (34 wickets; av. 25.79), v Pakistan in Colombo and Sharjah 2002-03 (27 wickets; av. 12.66 – an Australian three-match-series record) and Australia's Man of the Series v England 2005 (40 wickets; av. 19.92). Has also won numerous ODI awards, including Man of the Match in the 1999 World Cup semi-final v South Africa at Edgbaston (4-29) and final v Pakistan at Lord's (4-33). Has captained Australia in ODIs; has now retired from ODI cricket. Took 1000th first-class wicket in the first Test v New Zealand at Christchurch 2004-05. Was Hampshire's overseas player in 2000; rejoined Hampshire as an overseas player and as captain in 2004. Took 600th Test wicket (Marcus Trescothick) in the third Test v England at Old Trafford 2005. Leading wicket-taker in English first-class cricket 2005 (87; av. 22.50). BBC Overseas Sports Personality of the Year 2005
Opinions on cricket: 'Over rates are appalling.'
Best batting: 107* Hampshire v Kent, Canterbury 2005
Best bowling: 8-71 Australia v England, Brisbane 1994-95
Stop press: Leading Test wicket-taker for the calendar year 2005 (96; av. 22.02). Named Australia's Test Player of the Year at the 2006 Allan Border Medal awards

2005 Season

	M	Inns	NO	Runs	HS	Avge	100s	50s	Ct	St	O	M	Runs	Wkts	Avge	Best	5wI	10wM
Test	5	9	0	249	90	27.66	-	1	5	-	252.5	37	797	40	19.92	6-46	3	2
All First	16	27	3	742	107*	30.91	2	2	18	-	650.3	98	1958	87	22.50	6-46	4	2
1-Day Int																		
C & G	2	1	0	4	4	4.00	-	-	1	-	17	1	52	4	13.00	3-20	-	
tsL	8	7	0	93	27	13.28	-	-	5	-	58	1	276	11	25.09	2-34	-	
Twenty20	1	1	0	12	12	12.00	-	-	-	-	4	0	29	1	29.00	1-29	-	

Career Performances

	M	Inns	NO	Runs	HS	Avge	100s	50s	Ct	St	Balls	Runs	Wkts	Avge	Best	5wI	10wM
Test	128	178	15	2767	99	16.97	-	11	112	-	35954	15675	623	25.16	8-71	32	10
All First	250	341	41	5676	107*	18.92	2	21	212	-	62687	28266	1100	25.69	8-71	53	10
1-Day Int	194	107	29	1018	55	13.05	-	1	79	-	10642	7540	293	25.73	5-33	1	
C & G	7	5	1	25	20	6.25	-	-	1	-	359	183	16	11.43	4-23	-	
tsL	33	30	1	360	48	12.41	-	-	14	-	1644	1164	54	21.55	4-23	-	
Twenty20	2	2	0	12	12	6.00	-	-	-	-	48	51	1	51.00	1-29	-	

WARREN, A. C. Yorkshire

Name: <u>Adam</u> Craig Warren
Role: Right-hand bat, right-arm
medium-fast bowler
Born: 2 July 1975, Hobart, Tasmania
Height: 6ft 3in **Weight:** 15st 5lbs
Nickname: Wazza
County debut: 2005 (one-day)
Parents: Bev and Trevor
Marital status: 'Very much single'
Education: Marcellin College, Randwick,
Sydney; University of Technology, Sydney
('Mechanical Engineering'); Australian
Catholic University ('Sports Science')
Qualifications: 'Trade qualified in joinery'
Career outside cricket: 'Run my own
joinery business in Australia'
Off-season: 'Playing and working
in Australia'
Overseas teams played for: Randwick, Sydney 1990-91 – 2002-03; Prahran,
Melbourne 2003-04; St Kilda, Melbourne 2004-05 – 2005-06
Career highlights to date: 'Getting to actually play an A class [List A] one-day match
last season. Also winning premiership with St Kilda in Melbourne'
Cricket moments to forget: 'Dropping a catch in opening over of one-day final in
Sydney – player went on to make 70 and almost cost us the game'
Cricket superstitions: 'Never have sex for three days before a game or for three days
after a game, and never have sex on game day'
Cricketers particularly admired: Steve Waugh, Richie Richardson, Glenn McGrath
Players to look out for: Usman Khawaja (Australian), John Hitchmough
Other sports played: Baseball ('but not for about five years')
Other sports followed: Football (Liverpool FC), rugby league (Parramatta Eels),
AFL (Sydney Swans)
Injuries: 'Had section of lower leg taken out and skin graft placed over to repair.
Happened prior to 2004-05 Australian season. Time lost: three months'
Favourite band: Pearl Jam
Relaxations: 'Enjoying a quiet drink at friendly establishments to cavort in intelligent
conversation with some members of the opposite sex; or having a few with mates and
seeing what happens – basically the same thing'
Extras: Played for Yorkshire in 2005 as a trialist; not re-engaged for 2006. Is not
considered an overseas player
Opinions on cricket: 'I think 2nd XI cricket is treated too differently by the counties.
Some use it to just play some very young players, while others use it for the players

next in line. I think there should be more importance placed on the U19 programme to look at the young players, rather than playing them against players who are at different levels. The second tier should be practice for players who are ready to come into the first team for injuries or loss of form, yet still many counties seem to play players that they would probably not really consider playing in their first team. I realise experience is also essential, but these games should be played fiercely and give players a small glimpse of what it may be like on the next step up. The difference in standard from first to second teams seems too wide, and that is due to some counties not fielding teams as strong as they could, instead using it to maybe have a look at one or two players and not really worrying about the result. I think this leads to people becoming not as concerned about every match as they should be. I could be wrong, but it's just the impression I've gotten. Other than that, I think English cricket is on the rise and the good players are now playing well more consistently. I think the Kolpak [*see page 9*] and EU players that are in the first teams have probably helped to condense the English talent and maybe have them playing against better opposition more often. While you may not have as many young players at 19 playing in the first teams, it might be good for them to become dominant players at second-team level before playing first-class, rather than getting a game for just experience in the firsts. Other than that I really enjoyed my very brief experience as part of a first-class county.'

2005 Season

	M	Inns	NO	Runs	HS	Avge	100s	50s	Ct	St	O	M	Runs	Wkts	Avge	Best	5wI	10wM
Test																		
All First																		
1-Day Int																		
C & G																		
tsL	1	1	0	3	3	3.00	-	-	-	-	8	0	35	1	35.00	1-35	-	
Twenty20	2	0	0	0	0	-	-	-	-	-	7	0	70	4	17.50	2-32	-	

Career Performances

	M	Inns	NO	Runs	HS	Avge	100s	50s	Ct	St	Balls	Runs	Wkts	Avge	Best	5wI	10wM
Test																	
All First																	
1-Day Int																	
C & G																	
tsL	1	1	0	3	3	3.00	-	-	-	-	48	35	1	35.00	1-35	-	
Twenty20	2	0	0	0	0	-	-	-	-	-	42	70	4	17.50	2-32	-	

WARREN, N. A. Warwickshire

Name: <u>Nick</u> Alexander Warren
Role: Right-hand bat, right-arm
medium-fast bowler
Born: 26 June 1982, Moseley
Height: 5ft 11in **Weight:** 12st 7lbs
Nickname: Wazza
County debut: 2002
Strike rate: (career 66.85)
Parents: Lesley
Marital status: Single
Education: Wheelers Lane Boys School;
Solihull Sixth Form College
Qualifications: 9 GCSEs, BTEC Sports
Science
Overseas tours: Warwickshire U19 to Cape
Town 1998-99; England U17 to Ireland 1999;
England U19 to Malaysia and (U19 World
Cup) Sri Lanka 1999-2000

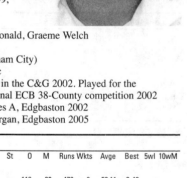

Cricketers particularly admired: Allan Donald, Graeme Welch
Other sports played: Football
Other sports followed: Football (Birmingham City)
Relaxations: Watching films; planes, music
Extras: Played for Warwickshire Board XI in the C&G 2002. Played for the
Warwickshire Board XI side that won the final ECB 38-County competition 2002
Best batting: 11 Warwickshire v West Indies A, Edgbaston 2002
Best bowling: 3-40 Warwickshire v Glamorgan, Edgbaston 2005

2005 Season

	M	Inns	NO	Runs	HS	Avge	100s	50s	Ct	St	O	M	Runs	Wkts	Avge	Best	5wI	10wM
Test																		
All First	6	5	3	11	5 *	5.50	-	-	-	-	119	20	478	9	53.11	3-40	-	-
1-Day Int																		
C & G																		
tsL	1	0	0	0	0	-	-	-	-	-	5	0	39	0	-	-	-	-
Twenty20	2	2	1	1	1 *	1.00	-	-	1	-	6	0	64	4	16.00	3-25	-	

Career Performances

	M	Inns	NO	Runs	HS	Avge	100s	50s	Ct	St	Balls	Runs	Wkts	Avge	Best	5wI	10wM
Test																	
All First	8	8	4	24	11	6.00	-	-	-	-	936	628	14	44.85	3-40	-	-
1-Day Int																	
C & G	1	1	0	0	0	0.00	-	-	2	-	36	29	0	-	-	-	
tsL	3	2	1	2	2	2.00	-	-	-	-	96	115	3	38.33	3-34	-	
Twenty20	2	2	1	1	1 *	1.00	-	-	1	-	36	64	4	16.00	3-25	-	

WARREN, R. J.   Nottinghamshire

Name: <u>Russell</u> John Warren
Role: Right-hand bat, wicket-keeper
Born: 10 September 1971, Northampton
Height: 6ft 2in **Weight:** 13st 4lbs
Nickname: Rab C, Rabbit
County debut: 1992 (Northamptonshire), 2003 (Nottinghamshire)
County cap: 1995 (Northamptonshire), 2004 (Nottinghamshire)
1000 runs in a season: 1
1st-Class 200s: 1
Place in batting averages: 158th av. 29.25 (2004 53rd av. 46.11)
Parents: John and Sally
Wife and date of marriage: Kate, November 2004
Education: Kingsthorpe Middle and Upper Schools

Qualifications: 8 O-levels, 2 A-levels
Overseas tours: England YC to New Zealand 1990-91; Northamptonshire to Cape Town 1993, to Zimbabwe 1996, to Johannesburg 1996, to Grenada 2000; Nottinghamshire to Pretoria 2003
Overseas teams played for: Lancaster Park, Christchurch, and Canterbury B, New Zealand 1991-93; Riverside CC, Lower Hutt, New Zealand 1994-95; Petone CC, Wellington, New Zealand 1995-96; Alma Marist CC, Cape Town, South Africa 1997-98
Cricketers particularly admired: Allan Lamb, Wayne Larkins
Young players to look out for: Samit Patel
Other sports played: Golf, snooker
Other sports followed: Football (Manchester United, Northampton Town, Nottingham Forest), rugby (Northampton Saints), golf, snooker and horse racing

Favourite band: The Thrills

Relaxations: 'Music, watching golf'

Extras: Scored 144 v Somerset at Taunton 2001, in the process sharing with Mike Hussey (208) in a record third-wicket partnership for Northamptonshire in matches against Somerset (287). Scored century in each innings (123/113*) v Middlesex at Lord's 2003

Best batting: 201* Northamptonshire v Glamorgan, Northampton 1996

2005 Season

	M	Inns	NO	Runs	HS		Avge	100s	50s	Ct	St	O	M	Runs	Wkts	Avge	Best	5wl	10wM
Test																			
All First	9	13	1	351	60	*	29.25	-	3	6	-								
1-Day Int																			
C & G	2	2	1	61	48	*	61.00	-	-	1	-								
tsL	6	6	0	42	25		7.00	-	-	1	-								
Twenty20	1	0	0	0	0		-	-	-	-	-								

Career Performances

	M	Inns	NO	Runs	HS		Avge	100s	50s	Ct	St	Balls	Runs	Wkts	Avge	Best	5wl	10wM
Test																		
All First	141	229	25	7636	201	*	37.43	15	40	125	5	6	0	0	-		-	-
1-Day Int																		
C & G	25	23	5	567	100	*	31.50	1	2	23	1							
tsL	123	112	14	2397	93		24.45	-	11	87	10							
Twenty20	2	1	0	26	26		26.00	-	-	-	-							

> 91. Which son of a former Test opener scored over 2500 runs
> and took more than 100 wickets in ODIs for Pakistan?

Name: <u>Huw</u> Thomas Waters
Role: Right-hand bat, right-arm medium bowler
Born: 26 September 1986, Cardiff
Height: 6ft 2in **Weight:** 13st 5lbs
Nickname: Muddy
County debut: 2005
Place in bowling averages: 59th av. 30.18
Strike rate: 54.54 (career 54.54)
Parents: Valerie and Donald
Marital status: Single
Education: Llantarnam CS; Monmouth School
Career outside cricket: 'University in 2006; hoping to study Sports Coaching at Oxford Brookes'
Overseas tours: England U19 to Bangladesh 2005-06, to Sri Lanka (U19 World Cup) 2005-06
Career highlights to date: 'Taking 4-75 on county debut' (*v Notts at Trent Bridge*)
Cricketers particularly admired: Glenn McGrath
Young players to look out for: 'Players from Glamorgan Academy'
Other sports followed: Football (Man United)
Injuries: Out for two weeks with a calf strain
Favourite band: Coldplay
Relaxations: 'Watching movies, listening to music'
Best batting: 34 Glamorgan v Kent, Canterbury 2005
Best bowling: 4-75 Glamorgan v Nottinghamshire, Trent Bridge 2005

2005 Season

	M	Inns	NO	Runs	HS	Avge	100s	50s	Ct	St	O	M	Runs	Wkts	Avge	Best	5wl	10wM
Test																		
All First	7	13	7	41	34	6.83	-	-	-	-	100	15	332	11	30.18	4-75	-	-
1-Day Int																		
C & G	1	1	0	8	8	8.00	-	-	-	-	5	1	13	0	-		-	-
tsL																		
Twenty20																		

Career Performances

	M	Inns	NO	Runs	HS	Avge	100s	50s	Ct	St	Balls	Runs	Wkts	Avge	Best	5wI	10wM
Test																	
All First	7	13	7	41	34	6.83	-	-	-	-	600	332	11	30.18	4-75	-	-
1-Day Int																	
C & G	1	1	0	8	8	8.00	-	-	-	-	30	13	0	-	-	-	
tsL																	
Twenty20																	

WATKINS, R. E.   Glamorgan

Name: Ryan Edward Watkins
Role: Left-hand bat, right-arm
medium bowler
Born: 9 June 1983, Abergavenny,
Monmouthshire
Height: 6ft **Weight:** 14st 5lbs
Nickname: Tets, Bry
County debut: 2003 (one-day),
2005 (first-class)
Place in batting averages: 253rd av. 14.55
Strike rate: (career 74.00)
Parents: Huw and Gaynor
Wife and date of marriage: Lisa,
16 October 2005
Family links with cricket: 'Father and
brother keen club cricketers'
Education: Pontllanfraith Comprehensive
School; Crosskeys College
Qualifications: Level 2 coach, qualified tyre and exhaust fitter
Off-season: 'Training, working on my game'
Overseas teams played for: North Balwyn CC, Victoria, Australia 2003
Career highlights to date: 'First first-class wicket; first-class debut'
Cricket moments to forget: 'Fifth-ball duck on debut live on Sky'
Cricket superstitions: 'Always put right pad on before the left'
Cricketers particularly admired: Matthew Hayden, Brian Lara
Young players to look out for: Willie Bragg, Carwyn James
Other sports played: Football (Ynysddu Crusaders), 'black belt in karaoke'
Other sports followed: Football (Tottenham Hotspur)
Injuries: 'Osteochondrial defect in my knee requiring operation'
Favourite band: Red Hot Chili Peppers
Relaxations: 'Golf; walking my dog, Missy'

Extras: Made 2nd XI Championship debut 2001
Opinions on cricket: 'Tea is too short.'
Best batting: 41 Glamorgan v Hampshire, Cardiff 2005
Best bowling: 2-14 Glamorgan v Sussex, Hove 2005

2005 Season

	M	Inns	NO	Runs	HS	Avge	100s	50s	Ct	St	O	M	Runs	Wkts	Avge	Best	5wl	10wM
Test																		
All First	5	9	0	131	41	14.55	-	-	-	-	37	5	125	3	41.66	2-14	-	-
1-Day Int																		
C & G																		
tsL	3	3	0	52	26	17.33	-	-	-	-	13.2	0	76	3	25.33	2-33	-	
Twenty20																		

Career Performances

	M	Inns	NO	Runs	HS	Avge	100s	50s	Ct	St	Balls	Runs	Wkts	Avge	Best	5wl	10wM
Test																	
All First	5	9	0	131	41	14.55	-	-	-	-	222	125	3	41.66	2-14	-	-
1-Day Int																	
C & G																	
tsL	4	4	0	52	26	13.00	-	-	-	-	110	123	3	41.00	2-33	-	
Twenty20	3	1	1	6	6 *	-	-	-	2	-	30	49	2	24.50	2-8	-	

WATKINSON, M.   Lancashire

Name: Michael Watkinson
Role: Right-hand bat, right-arm medium or
off-spin bowler
Born: 1 August 1961, Westhoughton,
Greater Manchester
Height: 6ft 1½in **Weight:** 13st
Nickname: Winker
County debut: 1982
County cap: 1987
Benefit: 1996 (£209,000)
Test debut: 1995
1000 runs in a season: 1
50 wickets in a season: 7
Strike rate: (career 64.69)
Parents: Albert and Marian
Wife and date of marriage: Susan,
12 April 1986

Children: Charlotte, 24 February 1989; Liam, 27 July 1991
Education: Rivington and Blackrod High School, Horwich
Qualifications: 8 O-levels, HTC Civil Engineering
Career outside cricket: Draughtsman
Overseas tours: England to South Africa 1995-96
Cricketers particularly admired: Clive Lloyd, Imran Khan
Other sports followed: Football
Relaxations: Watching Bolton Wanderers
Extras: Played for Cheshire in Minor Counties Championship and in NatWest Trophy (v Middlesex) 1982. Man of the Match in the first Refuge Assurance Cup final 1988 and for his 50 plus 2-37 in B&H Cup final 1990. Lancashire captain 1994-97, leading the county to one NatWest and two B&H titles. Lancashire Player of the Year 1995. 2nd XI captain and coach 2000-01. Cricket manager since 2002; retired as player but registration retained
Best batting: 161 Lancashire v Essex, Old Trafford 1995
Best bowling: 8-30 Lancashire v Hampshire, Old Trafford 1994

2005 Season (did not make any first-class or one-day appearances)

Career Performances

	M	Inns	NO	Runs	HS	Avge	100s	50s	Ct	St	Balls	Runs	Wkts	Avge	Best	5wl	10wM
Test	4	6	1	167	82 *	33.40	-	1	1	-	672	348	10	34.80	3-64	-	-
All First	308	459	49	10939	161	26.68	11	50	156	-	47806	24960	739	33.77	8-30	27	3
1-Day Int	1	0	0	0	0	-	-	-	-	-	54	43	0	-	-	-	-
C & G	46	40	7	1064	130	32.24	1	7	12	-	2681	1751	46	38.06	3-14	-	
tsL	236	189	38	3262	121	21.60	1	9	59	-	8730	7113	225	31.61	5-46	1	
Twenty20																	

92. To date, which bowler has returned the most
expensive figures for Australia in ODIs?

WATSON, S. R.   Hampshire

Name: <u>Shane</u> Robert Watson
Role: Right-hand bat, right-arm
fast-medium bowler
Born: 17 June 1981, Ipswich,
Queensland, Australia
County debut: 2004
Test debut: 2004-05
1st-Class 200s: 1
Place in batting averages: 1st av. 77.14
Strike rate: (career 50.74)
Overseas tours: Australia U19 to Sri Lanka
(U19 World Cup) 1999-2000; Australia to
South Africa 2001-02, to Kenya (PSO Tri-
Nation Tournament) 2002, to Sri Lanka (ICC
Champions Trophy) 2002-03, to Zimbabwe
(one-day series) 2004, to Holland (Videocon
Cup) 2004, to England (ICC Champions
Trophy) 2004, to India 2004-05, to England

2005 (NatWest Series/Challenge); Australia A to Pakistan 2005-06
Overseas teams played for: Tasmania 2000-01 – 2003-04; Queensland 2004-05 –
Extras: Played for Queensland U17 aged 15. Commonwealth Bank [Australian]
Cricket Academy 2000, 2003. Scored 300* then followed up with 7-29 for Lindisfarne
v North Hobart in Tasmanian grade match at Hobart 2003-04. Tasmania's Player of the
Year 2003-04. His match awards include Man of the Match v Queensland at Hobart in
the Pura Cup 2001-02 (6-32/5-46) and v Victoria at Melbourne in the ING Cup 2003-
04 (2-15/63). Was an overseas player with Hampshire during 2004 as cover for Shane
Warne and Michael Clarke while on international duty; during 2005 as a locum for
Shane Warne. C&G Man of the Match award in the quarter-final v Surrey at The Oval
2005 (115-ball 132)
Best batting: 203* Hampshire v Warwickshire, West End 2005
Best bowling: 6-32 Tasmania v Queensland, Hobart 2001-02
Stop press: Won two ODI Man of the Match awards for Australia v ICC World XI in
the Super Series 2005-06

2005 Season

	M	Inns	NO	Runs	HS	Avge	100s	50s	Ct	St	O	M	Runs	Wkts	Avge	Best	5wI	10wM
Test																		
All First	5	8	1	540	203 *	77.14	1	3	10	-	112	22	372	9	41.33	2-33	-	-
1-Day Int	5	3	1	39	25	19.50	-	-	-	-	34.3	0	166	4	41.50	3-43	-	
C & G	3	3	1	168	132	84.00	1	-	1	-	17	0	63	5	12.60	3-34	-	
tsL	6	6	1	277	106 *	55.40	1	1	2	-	28	2	173	1	173.00	1-30	-	
Twenty20																		

Career Performances

	M	Inns	NO	Runs	HS	Avge	100s	50s	Ct	St	Balls	Runs	Wkts	Avge	Best	5wI	10wM
Test	1	1	0	31	31	31.00	-	-	-	-	114	60	1	60.00	1-32	-	-
All First	45	77	8	3249	203 *	47.08	9	17	30	-	4320	2553	85	30.03	6-32	2	1
1-Day Int	37	23	10	380	77 *	29.23	-	1	10	-	1439	1125	25	45.00	3-27	-	
C & G	3	3	1	168	132	84.00	1	-	1	-	102	63	5	12.60	3-34	-	
tsL	8	8	2	354	106 *	59.00	1	2	3	-	222	212	1	212.00	1-30	-	
Twenty20	5	5	1	122	97 *	30.50	-	1	3	-							

WEDGE, S. A.   Worcestershire

Name: Stuart (<u>Stu</u>) Andrew Wedge
Role: Left-hand bat, left-arm medium bowler
Born: 24 October 1985, Wolverhampton
Height: 5ft 11in   **Weight:** 11st 2lbs
Nickname: Wedgey
County debut: 2005
County colours: 2005
Strike rate: (career 65.20)
Parents: Barrie and Ann
Marital status: Single
Education: Codsall High School;
Rodbaston College
Qualifications: 9 GCSEs, 1 A-level
Off-season: 'Fitness and stamina training'
Career highlights to date: 'Taking five
wickets on my County Championship debut'
Cricket superstitions: 'Have four paces
before I hit my bowling mark'
Cricketers particularly admired: Courtney Walsh, Brian Lara
Other sports played: Golf
Other sports followed: Rugby, football
Injuries: Out for six weeks with an intercostal injury
Favourite band: 'No one in particular'
Relaxations: 'Golf, rugby, music, PlayStation, eating, snooker/pool'
Extras: Took 5-112 in first innings of Championship debut v Essex at Worcester 2005
Opinions on cricket: 'I think that cricket in this country is on the way up, especially
after last summer's Ashes victory. There are a lot of young English cricketers coming
through the ranks, which can only be a positive thing. The majority of our county
teams to be made up of home-grown talent, with the excitement of the overseas
players to give it that extra. In the end the players need to provide entertainment to the
public, without sacrificing the young players who will provide and make up the
England team of the future.'

Best bowling: 5-112 Worcestershire v Essex, Worcester 2005

2005 Season

	M	Inns	NO	Runs	HS	Avge	100s	50s	Ct	St	O	M	Runs	Wkts	Avge	Best	5wI	10wM
Test																		
All First	2	2	2	0	0 *	-	-	-	-	-	-	54.2	8	211	5	42.20	5-112	1	-
1-Day Int																		
C & G																		
tsL																		
Twenty20																		

Career Performances

	M	Inns	NO	Runs	HS	Avge	100s	50s	Ct	St	Balls	Runs	Wkts	Avge	Best	5wI	10wM
Test																	
All First	2	2	2	0	0 *	-	-	-	-	-	326	211	5	42.20	5-112	1	-
1-Day Int																	
C & G																	
tsL																	
Twenty20																	

WEEKES, P. N. Middlesex

Name: Paul Nicholas Weekes
Role: Left-hand bat, right-arm
off-spin bowler; all-rounder
Born: 8 July 1969, Hackney, London
Height: 5ft 10½in **Weight:** 12st 2lbs
Nickname: Twidds, Weekesy
County debut: 1990
County cap: 1993
Benefit: 2002
1000 runs in a season: 2
Place in batting averages: 57th av. 44.31
(2004 63rd av. 43.52)
Place in bowling averages: 142nd av. 54.64
(2004 135th av. 44.84)
Strike rate: 101.92 (career 84.48)
Parents: Robert
Marital status: Single
Children: Cherie, 4 September 1993;
Shyann, 3 May 1998
Family links with cricket: Father played club cricket
Education: Homerton House, Hackney; Hackney College

Qualifications: Level 2 coaching award
Career outside cricket: Cricket coach – Middlesex Youth squads and Hackney Cricket Academy
Overseas tours: England A to India and Bangladesh 1994-95; Middlesex to Johannesburg; three tours with BWIA to the West Indies
Overseas teams played for: Newcastle University, NSW 1988-89; Sunrise CC, Harare 1990-91
Career highlights to date: 'Scoring 171* and 160 in the same match, v Somerset at Uxbridge 1996'
Cricket moments to forget: 'Getting a pair against Essex'
Cricketers particularly admired: Viv Richards, Courtney Walsh, Brian Lara
Favourite band: Burning Flames, Jay-Z
Relaxations: DIY
Extras: Scored 50 in debut innings for both 2nd and 1st teams. Took two catches whilst appearing as 12th man for England in the second Test against West Indies at Lord's in 1995. Middlesex Player of the Year 1999, 2004. First Englishman to score more than 150 in both innings of a first-class game. Has won seven one-day Man of the Match awards (three NatWest/C&G; four B&H). Captained Middlesex to their one-day victory over the Australians at Lord's 2001
Best batting: 171* Middlesex v Somerset, Uxbridge 1996
Best bowling: 8-39 Middlesex v Glamorgan, Lord's 1996

2005 Season

	M	Inns	NO	Runs	HS	Avge	100s	50s	Ct	St	O	M	Runs	Wkts	Avge	Best	5wl	10wM
Test																		
All First	16	26	7	842	128 *	44.31	1	5	7	-	237.5	33	765	14	54.64	3-83	-	-
1-Day Int																		
C & G	2	2	1	211	106 *	211.00	2	-	-	-	19	1	52	1	52.00	1-34	-	
tsL	16	16	1	785	111	52.33	2	7	7	-	79.4	1	386	13	29.69	4-58	-	
Twenty20	6	4	2	28	25 *	14.00	-	-	2	-	18	0	172	2	86.00	1-41	-	

Career Performances

	M	Inns	NO	Runs	HS	Avge	100s	50s	Ct	St	Balls	Runs	Wkts	Avge	Best	5wl	10wM
Test																	
All First	228	357	51	10712	171 *	35.00	19	55	210	-	25260	12421	299	41.54	8-39	5	-
1-Day Int																	
C & G	29	29	6	974	143 *	42.34	4	5	7	-	1456	1015	28	36.25	3-35	-	
tsL	232	205	27	5476	119 *	30.76	5	34	107	-	8009	6747	235	28.71	4-26	-	
Twenty20	15	13	3	341	56	34.10	-	2	4	-	270	352	6	58.66	2-20	-	

WELCH, G.   Derbyshire

Name: Graeme Welch
Role: Right-hand bat, right-arm medium-fast
bowler, county captain
Born: 21 March 1972, Durham
Height: 6ft **Weight:** 13st
Nickname: Pop
County debut: 1992 (one-day,
Warwickshire), 1994 (first-class,
Warwickshire), 2001 (Derbyshire)
County cap: 1997 (Warwickshire),
2001 (Derbyshire)
50 wickets in a season: 4
Place in batting averages: 132nd av. 31.46
(2004 153rd av. 29.00)
Place in bowling averages: 28th av. 25.98
(2004 70th av. 33.88)
Strike rate: 54.95 (career 59.18)
Parents: Jean and Robert
Wife and date of marriage: Emma, 4 October 1997
Children: Ethan, 4 April 2000
Family links with cricket: Brother and father club cricketers in Leeds and
Durham respectively
Education: Hetton Comprehensive
Qualifications: 9 GCSEs, City and Guilds in Sports and Leisure, senior
coaching award
Career outside cricket: Coaching
Overseas tours: Warwickshire to Cape Town 1992-97; England XI to New Zealand
(Cricket Max) 1997
Overseas teams played for: Avendale, Cape Town 1992-94; Wellington Collegians
and Wellington 1996
Career highlights to date: 'Winning the treble with Warwickshire in 1994'
Cricket moments to forget: 'Benson and Hedges game against Lancashire in 1995'
Cricketers particularly admired: Brian Lara, Allan Donald, Sachin Tendulkar
Other sports played: Football
Other sports followed: Football (Newcastle United)
Relaxations: 'A beer at The Brook; spending time with Emma and Ethan'
Extras: Represented England YC. Warwickshire's Most Improved Player 1994. Won
seven trophies with Warwickshire 1994-97. Derbyshire Player of the Year 2005.
Appointed captain of Derbyshire for 2006
Best batting: 115* Derbyshire v Leicestershire, Oakham School 2004
Best bowling: 6-30 Derbyshire v Durham, Riverside 2001

2005 Season

	M	Inns	NO	Runs	HS	Avge	100s	50s	Ct	St	O	M	Runs	Wkts	Avge	Best	5wI	10wM
Test																		
All First	17	29	3	818	112	31.46	1	4	9	-	549.3	139	1559	60	25.98	5-63	3	-
1-Day Int																		
C & G	2	2	0	71	50	35.50	-	1	2	-	20	1	97	0	-		-	-
tsL	15	13	4	254	58 *	28.22	-	1	3	-	111	10	474	12	39.50	2-21	-	
Twenty20	8	7	0	53	20	7.57	-	-	1	-	13	0	145	1	145.00	1-16	-	

Career Performances

	M	Inns	NO	Runs	HS	Avge	100s	50s	Ct	St	Balls	Runs	Wkts	Avge	Best	5wI	10wM
Test																	
All First	156	242	38	4722	115 *	23.14	2	19	65	-	26101	13836	441	31.37	6-30	17	1
1-Day Int																	
C & G	25	19	5	319	50	22.78	-	1	3	-	1312	878	21	41.80	4-26	-	
tsL	150	121	31	1727	82	19.18	-	5	26	-	6315	4633	140	33.09	6-31	3	
Twenty20	16	13	2	113	20	10.27	-	-	3	-	258	393	5	78.60	1-15	-	

WESSELS, M. H.   Northamptonshire

Name: Mattheus Hendrik (<u>Riki</u>) Wessels
Role: Right-hand bat, wicket-keeper
Born: 12 November 1985, Nambour, Australia
Height: 5ft 11in **Weight:** 10st 10lbs
Nickname: Blood, Moose
County debut: 2005
Place in batting averages: 141st av. 30.65
Parents: Kepler and Sally
Marital status: Single
Family links with cricket: 'My dad played a little bit' (*Kepler Wessels played Test and ODI cricket for Australia and South Africa between 1982-83 and 1994-95*)
Education: Woodridge College, Port Elizabeth; University College of Northampton
Qualifications: Coach
Cricket moments to forget: 'Losing in the 2nd XI [Trophy] semi-final by nine wickets [2004]'
Cricket superstitions: 'Lucky shirt'
Cricketers particularly admired: 'My dad and Justin Langer'

Young players to look out for: Alex Wakely
Other sports played: Hockey
Other sports followed: Rugby (Queensland Reds)
Favourite band: Linkin Park
Relaxations: 'Reading autobiographies'
Extras: Northamptonshire Academy Players' Player of the Year 2004. Northamptonshire Young Player of the Year (Frank Rudd Trophy) 2004. Made first-class debut for MCC v West Indians at Arundel 2004. Scored maiden first-class century (102) v Somerset at Northampton 2005 after coming to the wicket on a hat-trick ball
Opinions on cricket: 'Always growing and changing to better the game.'
Best batting: 107 Northamptonshire v Durham, Riverside 2005

2005 Season

	M	Inns	NO	Runs	HS	Avge	100s	50s	Ct	St	O	M	Runs	Wkts	Avge	Best	5wl	10wM
Test																		
All First	14	23	3	613	107	30.65	3	2	23	4								
1-Day Int																		
C & G	3	2	0	18	10	9.00	-	-	5	-								
tsL	13	10	3	233	80	33.28	-	1	12	-								
Twenty20	7	7	2	91	49 *	18.20	-	-	3	1								

Career Performances

	M	Inns	NO	Runs	HS	Avge	100s	50s	Ct	St	Balls	Runs	Wkts	Avge	Best	5wl	10wM
Test																	
All First	15	25	3	648	107	29.45	3	2	27	5							
1-Day Int																	
C & G	3	2	0	18	10	9.00	-	-	5	-							
tsL	13	10	3	233	80	33.28	-	1	12	-							
Twenty20	7	7	2	91	49 *	18.20	-	-	3	1							

93. Which Newhaven brothers played three ODIs between them in the 1980s and 1990s?

WESTFIELD, M. S.   Essex

Name: <u>Mervyn</u> Simon Westfield
Role: Right-hand bat, right-arm fast bowler; all-rounder
Born: 5 May 1988, Romford
Height: 6ft **Weight:** 12st 2lbs
Nickname: Swerve
County debut: 2005
Strike rate: (career 108.00)
Parents: Pam and Mervyn
Marital status: Single
Family links with cricket: 'Began playing cricket at the age of seven and have been coached, influenced and guided by my father'
Education: The Chafford; Barking College
Qualifications: 8 GCSEs, Level 1 coaching
Career outside cricket: 'Full-time student'
Overseas tours: ECB U16 to Cape Town 2004
Cricket moments to forget: 'None'
Cricket superstitions: 'None'
Cricketers particularly admired: Courtney Walsh, Viv Richards
Young players to look out for: Maurice Chambers, Tom Westley (Essex), Michael O'Shea
Other sports followed: Football (Manchester United)
Favourite band: G-Unit
Relaxations: 'Socialising with friends, listening to music'
Extras: Wanstead U11 Young Player of the Year 1997. Wanstead U11 All-Rounder of 1998. Havering District U13 Best Innings 2000. MCC Cricketer of the Year 2003, 2004. *Daily Telegraph* Bunbury Scholar (Best Fast Bowler) 2003
Opinions on cricket: 'Too much sledging is spoiling the spirit of the game. The introduction of Twenty20 cricket has added a fast, furious and fun element to the game.'
Best bowling: 1-90 Essex v Durham, Riverside 2005

2005 Season

	M	Inns	NO	Runs	HS	Avge	100s	50s	Ct	St	O	M	Runs	Wkts	Avge	Best	5wI	10wM
Test																		
All First	1	2	0	0	0	0.00	-	-	-	-	18	0	90	1	90.00	1-90	-	-
1-Day Int																		
C & G																		
tsL																		
Twenty20																		

Career Performances

	M	Inns	NO	Runs	HS	Avge	100s	50s	Ct	St	Balls	Runs	Wkts	Avge	Best	5wI	10wM
Test																	
All First	1	2	0	0	0	0.00	-	-	-	-	108	90	1	90.00	1-90	-	-
1-Day Int																	
C & G																	
tsL																	
Twenty20																	

WESTON, W. P. C.   Gloucestershire

Name: William Philip Christopher Weston
Role: Left-hand bat, left-arm medium bowler
Born: 16 June 1973, Durham City
Height: 6ft 4in **Weight:** 14st
Nickname: Tickle, Weso
County debut: 1991 (Worcestershire), 2003 (Gloucestershire)
County cap: 1995; colours, 2002 (both Worcestershire), 2004 (Gloucestershire)
1000 runs in a season: 4
1st-Class 200s: 1
Place in batting averages: 155th av. 29.58 (2004 105th av. 35.59)
Strike rate: (career 200.20)
Parents: Michael and Kate (deceased)
Wife and date of marriage: Sarah, 30 September 2000
Family links with cricket: Brother Robin played for Durham, Derbyshire and Middlesex. Father played Minor Counties cricket for Durham (and rugby union for England)
Education: Durham School
Qualifications: 9 GCSEs, 4 A-levels, Diploma in Business and Management
Career outside cricket: 'Hoping to pursue a career in property'
Overseas tours: England U18 to Canada (International Youth Tournament) 1991 (vc); England YC to New Zealand 1990-91; England U19 to Pakistan 1991-92 (c); Worcestershire to Zimbabwe 1996
Overseas teams played for: Melville, Perth 1992-94, 1996-97; Swanbourne, Perth 1995-96
Career highlights to date: '2004 C&G final'
Cricket superstitions: 'Not really'

Cricketers particularly admired: Ian Botham
Other sports played: 'Have a go at most sports'
Other sports followed: Rugby union, football (Sunderland AFC)
Favourite band: U2
Relaxations: 'Spending time with my lovely wife; travelling, films, hanging out with friends'
Extras: Represented England YC 1991 and England U19 1992 (Man of the Series). Cricket Society's Most Promising Young Cricketer 1992. Worcestershire Uncapped Player of the Year 1992. C&G Man of the Match award for his 106 v Holland at Amstelveen 2004. Scored century (110*) in the C&G final v Worcs at Lord's 2004
Opinions on cricket: 'Pitches and practice facilities remain an ongoing issue at county level. Registration and qualification needs to be sorted to avoid certain teams becoming too cosmopolitan in their composition. Pleased to see the England team doing well.'
Best batting: 205 Worcestershire v Northamptonshire, Northampton 1997
Best bowling: 2-39 Worcestershire v Pakistanis, Worcester 1992

2005 Season

	M	Inns	NO	Runs	HS	Avge	100s	50s	Ct	St	O	M	Runs	Wkts	Avge	Best	5wI	10wM
Test																		
All First	13	24	0	710	103	29.58	1	5	4	-								
1-Day Int																		
C & G	2	2	0	115	80	57.50	-	1	-	-								
tsL	10	10	0	304	72	30.40	-	4	4	-								
Twenty20	7	5	2	167	73 *	55.66	-	1	3	-								

Career Performances

	M	Inns	NO	Runs	HS	Avge	100s	50s	Ct	St	Balls	Runs	Wkts	Avge	Best	5wI	10wM
Test																	
All First	215	378	33	11680	205	33.85	22	58	122	-	1001	658	5	131.60	2-39	-	-
1-Day Int																	
C & G	23	23	2	760	110 *	36.19	2	3	4	-							
tsL	130	116	8	2798	134	25.90	2	15	28	-	6	2	1	2.00	1-2		
Twenty20	7	5	2	167	73 *	55.66	-	1	3	-							

94. Who was the first batsman to be stranded on 99* in an ODI when his side were bowled out?

WESTWOOD, I. J.   Warwickshire

Name: Ian James Westwood
Role: Left-hand opening bat, right-arm off-spinner
Born: 13 July 1982, Birmingham
Height: 5ft 7½in   **Weight:** 11st
Nickname: Westy, Tomato Head, Wezzo, Sammy Lee, Tot
County debut: 2003
Place in batting averages: 106th av. 34.66
Strike rate: (career 66.00)
Parents: Ann and David
Marital status: Single
Family links with cricket: 'Brother represented Warwickshire Schools from 11 to 16'
Education: Wheelers Lane; Solihull Sixth Form College

Qualifications: 8 GCSEs, BTEC Sports Science
Overseas tours: Warwickshire Development squad to Cape Town 1998
Overseas teams played for: Hawkesbury CC, Sydney 2001-02; Subiaco Marist CC, Perth 2002-03
Cricket superstitions: 'Put right pad on first'
Cricketers particularly admired: Brian Lara, Nick Knight
Young players to look out for: Nick Chase, Vanraj Padhaal
Other sports played: Football (Coleshill Town FC 2001; Moseley Mariners FC)
Other sports followed: Football (Birmingham City)
Favourite band: Fleetwood Mac
Relaxations: 'Music, films, fruit machines, socialising'
Extras: Scored 250* v Worcestershire 2nd XI at Barnt Green 2003, sharing with Jonathan Trott (248) in an opening partnership of 429; also took 6-104 in Worcestershire 2nd XI's only innings
Best batting: 106 Warwickshire v Glamorgan, Colwyn Bay 2005
Best bowling: 1-30 Warwickshire v Surrey, Croydon 2005

	M	Inns	NO	Runs	HS	Avge	100s	50s	Ct	St	O	M	Runs	Wkts	Avge	Best	5wl	10wM
Test																		
All First	11	22	4	624	106	34.66	1	3	6	-	3	0	30	1	30.00	1-30	-	-
1-Day Int																		
C & G																		
tsL	6	3	3	34	17 *	-	-	-	-	1	-							
Twenty20	2	2	2	5	4 *	-	-	-	-	-	-							

Career Performances

	M	Inns	NO	Runs	HS	Avge	100s	50s	Ct	St	Balls	Runs	Wkts	Avge	Best	5wl	10wM
Test																	
All First	13	25	4	684	106	32.57	1	3	6	-	66	87	1	87.00	1-30	-	-
1-Day Int																	
C & G	4	4	0	78	55	19.50	-	1	1	-	180	139	2	69.50	1-28	-	
tsL	6	3	3	34	17 *	-	-	-	-	1	-						
Twenty20	2	2	2	5	4 *	-	-	-	-	-	-						

WHARF, A. G. B.   Glamorgan

Name: Alexander (<u>Alex</u>) George Busfield Wharf
Role: Right-hand bat, right-arm fast-medium bowler; all-rounder
Born: 4 June 1975, Bradford
Height: 6ft 4in **Weight:** 15st
Nickname: Gangster
County debut: 1994 (Yorks), 1998 (Notts), 2000 (Glamorgan)
County cap: 2000 (Glamorgan)
50 wickets in a season: 1
Place in batting averages: 218th av. 20.47 (2004 204th av. 21.92)
Place in bowling averages: 121st av. 44.46 (2004 101st av. 37.44)
Strike rate: 63.71 (career 55.39)
Parents: Jane and Derek
Wife and date of marriage: Shelley Jane, 1 December 2001
Children: Tristan Jack Busfield Wharf, 15 November 1997; Alf Alexander Busfield Wharf, 30 June 2001
Family links with cricket: Father played local cricket and brother Simon plays local cricket

Education: Buttershaw Upper School; Thomas Danby College
Qualifications: 6 GCSEs, City and Guilds in Sports Management, NCA coaching award, junior football coaching award
Overseas tours: England to Zimbabwe (one-day series) 2004-05, to South Africa 2004-05 (one-day series); England VI to Hong Kong 2005; England A to West Indies 2005-06; various pre-season tours with Yorkshire, Nottinghamshire and Glamorgan
Overseas teams played for: Somerset West, Cape Town 1993-95; Johnsonville CC, Wellington, New Zealand 1996-97; Universities, Wellington 1998-99
Cricket moments to forget: 'Too many to mention'
Cricket superstitions: 'None'
Cricketers particularly admired: Ian Botham
Other sports played: Football
Other sports followed: Football (Manchester United, Bradford City)
Relaxations: 'Spending time with family and friends, movies, PlayStation 2, eating (too much), TV, gym, football'
Extras: Took hat-trick (Wagg, Knight, Pretorius) v Warwickshire at Edgbaston in the totesport League 2004. Had figures of 6-5 v Kent at Cardiff in the totesport League 2004 (match reduced to 25 overs a side). Made ODI debut v India at Trent Bridge in the NatWest Challenge 2004, taking a wicket in each of his first three overs, finishing with 3-30 and winning Man of the Match award
Best batting: 113 Glamorgan v Nottinghamshire, Cardiff 2005
Best bowling: 6-59 Glamorgan v Gloucestershire, Bristol 2005

2005 Season

	M	Inns	NO	Runs	HS	Avge	100s	50s	Ct	St	O	M	Runs	Wkts	Avge	Best	5wI	10wM
Test																		
All First	12	21	0	430	113	20.47	1	1	10	-	297.2	40	1245	28	44.46	6-59	2	1
1-Day Int																		
C & G	1	0	0	0	0	-	-	-	2	-	3	0	11	1	11.00	1-11	-	
tsL	11	10	1	286	42	31.77	-	-	4	-	83	3	495	17	29.11	3-71	-	
Twenty20	3	3	0	19	11	6.33	-	-	1	-	11	0	112	5	22.40	3-38	-	

Career Performances

	M	Inns	NO	Runs	HS	Avge	100s	50s	Ct	St	Balls	Runs	Wkts	Avge	Best	5wI	10wM
Test																	
All First	84	125	18	2126	113	19.86	3	9	43	-	11965	7647	216	35.40	6-59	5	1
1-Day Int	13	5	3	19	9	9.50	-	-	1	-	584	428	18	23.77	4-24	-	
C & G	11	7	1	74	24 *	12.33	-	-	2	-	520	320	10	32.00	3-18	-	
tsL	78	54	13	816	72	19.90	-	1	25	-	3164	2712	96	28.25	6-5	1	
Twenty20	10	7	1	55	16	9.16	-	-	2	-	217	314	16	19.62	3-23	-	

WHELAN, C. D.   Middlesex

Name: <u>Christopher</u> David Whelan
Role: Right-hand bat, right-arm fast bowler
Born: 8 May 1986, Liverpool
Height: 6ft 2in   **Weight:** 13st
Nickname: Wheelo, Scouse
County debut: 2004 (one-day), 2005 (first-class)
Strike rate: (career 35.71)
Parents: Sue and Dave
Marital status: Single
Family links with cricket: 'Dad was an accomplished left-hand opening bat'
Education: St Margaret's High School
Qualifications: 11 GCSEs, 3 A-levels, Level 1 coaching
Off-season: 'Winter in Australia playing grade cricket'

Overseas tours: Middlesex to Mumbai 2004-05, 2005-06
Overseas teams played for: Randwick-Petersham, Sydney 2005-06
Career highlights to date: 'First-class debut at the Rose Bowl'
Cricket superstitions: 'None'
Cricketers particularly admired: Brett Lee
Young players to look out for: Paul Horton, Steven Finn, Arun Harinath
Other sports played: Football, golf
Other sports followed: Football (Everton)
Injuries: Out for 12 weeks with a grade three thigh tear
Favourite band: Goo Goo Dolls
Relaxations: 'Internet poker; DVDs'
Extras: Merseyside Young Sports Personality of the Year 2004-05
Opinions on cricket: 'It should be one overseas player per team and one Kolpak player [*see page 9*] per team.'
Best batting: 9* Middlesex v Hampshire, West End 2005
Best bowling: 2-34 Middlesex v CUCCE, Fenner's 2005

2005 Season

	M	Inns	NO	Runs	HS	Avge	100s	50s	Ct	St	O	M	Runs	Wkts	Avge	Best	5wI	10wM
Test																		
All First	2	2	1	10	9 *	10.00	-	-	-	-	41.4	8	182	7	26.00	2-34	-	-
1-Day Int																		
C & G																			
tsL																			
Twenty20																			

Career Performances

	M	Inns	NO	Runs	HS	Avge	100s	50s	Ct	St	Balls	Runs	Wkts	Avge	Best	5wI	10wM
Test																	
All First	2	2	1	10	9 *	10.00	-	-	-	-	250	182	7	26.00	2-34	-	-
1-Day Int																	
C & G																		
tsL	1	1	0	6	6	6.00	-	-	-	-	42	40	0	-		-	-
Twenty20																	

WHITE, A. R. Northamptonshire

Name: <u>Andrew</u> Rowland White
Role: Right-hand bat, right-arm off-spin bowler; all-rounder
Born: 3 July 1980, Newtownards, Northern Ireland
Height: 6ft **Weight:** 12st
Nickname: Whitey, Spud
County debut: 2004
Strike rate: (career 103.50)
Parents: Rowland and Elizabeth
Marital status: Single
Family links with cricket: 'Brother Richard and cousins play league cricket in Ulster. Uncle Andrew and sons, Ben and Rory, play for Cookham Dean, Berkshire'
Education: Regent House Grammar School; University of Ulster
Qualifications: 9 GCSEs, 2 A-levels, honours degree in Sport, Exercise and Leisure, Level 2 cricket coach
Career outside cricket: PE teacher
Off-season: 'Completing PGCE in Physical Education. Training'
Overseas tours: Ireland U19 to Sri Lanka (U19 World Cup) 1999-2000; Ireland to

South Africa 2001, to Toronto (ICC Trophy) 2001, to Namibia (ICC Inter-Continental Cup) 2005

Overseas teams played for: UPE International Cricket Academy, South Africa 2002
Career highlights to date: 'Qualifying for the 2007 World Cup and winning the ICC Inter-Continental Cup with Ireland in 2005. Scoring the winning runs for Ireland in their famous victory over the West Indies in 2004'
Cricket moments to forget: 'Losing the ICC Trophy final in 2005 to Scotland'
Cricket superstitions: 'None'
Cricketers particularly admired: Jonty Rhodes, Steve Waugh
Young players to look out for: Eoin Morgan
Other sports played: Football, golf
Other sports followed: Rugby (Ulster), football (Northern Ireland – '"Our Wee Country" 1-0 v England: what a night!')
Injuries: Out for the entire pre-season with a split spinning finger
Favourite band: U2
Relaxations: 'Snooker; eating out'
Extras: Man of the Match v Surrey at Clontarf in the C&G 2004. Scored 152* on first-class debut for Ireland v Holland at Deventer in the ICC Inter-Continental Cup 2004. Youngest player to pass 1000 runs in history of Irish cricket. Ireland Player of the Year 2004. Northamptonshire Young Player of the Year 2005
Opinions on cricket: 'Real shame to lose cricket from free-to-view television. There is a possibility of a young generation missing out on the game.'
Best batting: 152* Ireland v Holland, Deventer 2004-05
Best bowling: 2-19 Northamptonshire v Warwickshire, Northampton 2004
Stop press: Man of the Match (jointly with Kyle McCallan) in the final of the ICC Inter-Continental Cup v Kenya at Windhoek 2005

2005 Season

	M	Inns	NO	Runs	HS	Avge	100s	50s	Ct	St	O	M	Runs	Wkts	Avge	Best	5wI	10wM
Test																		
All First	2	3	1	36	30*	18.00	-	-	1	-	15	1	82	0	-		-	-	-
1-Day Int																		
C & G	1	0	0	0	0	-	-	-	1	-								
tsL	1	1	0	4	4	4.00	-	-	-	-								
Twenty20																		

Career Performances

	M	Inns	NO	Runs	HS	Avge	100s	50s	Ct	St	Balls	Runs	Wkts	Avge	Best	5wI	10wM
Test																	
All First	6	8	2	288	152*	48.00	1	1	2	-	414	241	4	60.25	2-19	-	-
1-Day Int																	
C & G	6	4	1	69	44	23.00	-	-	2	-	180	137	3	45.66	3-43	-	
tsL	1	1	0	4	4	4.00	-	-	-	-							
Twenty20																	

WHITE, C.   Yorkshire

Name: Craig White
Role: Right-hand bat, right-arm
fast-medium bowler, county captain
Born: 16 December 1969, Morley, Yorkshire
Height: 6ft 1in **Weight:** 11st 11lbs
Nickname: Chalky, Bassey
County debut: 1990
County cap: 1993
Benefit: 2002
Test debut: 1994
Place in batting averages: 40th av. 48.50
(2004 188th av. 24.09)
Place in bowling averages: (2004 22nd
av. 25.63)
Strike rate: (career 53.85)
Parents: Fred Emsley and Cynthia Anne
Wife and date of marriage: Elizabeth Anne,
19 September 1992
Family links with cricket: Father played for Pudsey St Lawrence
Education: Flora Hill High School; Bendigo Senior High School (both
Victoria, Australia)
Overseas tours: Australia YC to West Indies 1989-90; England A to Pakistan
1995-96, to Australia 1996-97; England to Australia 1994-95, to India and Pakistan
(World Cup) 1995-96, to Zimbabwe and New Zealand 1996-97, to South Africa and
Zimbabwe 1999-2000 (one-day series), to Kenya (ICC Knockout Trophy) 2000-01,
to Pakistan and Sri Lanka 2000-01, to India and New Zealand 2001-02, to Australia
2002-03, to Africa (World Cup) 2002-03
Overseas teams played for: Victoria, Australia 1990-91; Central Districts,
New Zealand 1999-2000
Cricketers particularly admired: Graeme Hick, Mark Waugh, Brian Lara
Other sports followed: Leeds RFC, motocross, golf, tennis
Relaxations: Playing guitar, reading, gardening and socialising
Extras: Man of the Match in the second ODI v Zimbabwe at Bulawayo 1999-2000
(5-21/26). Took National League hat-trick (Fleming, Patel, Masters) v Kent at
Headingley 2000. Scored 93 in the first Test at Lahore 2000-01, in the process sharing
with Graham Thorpe (118) in a new record sixth-wicket partnership for England in
Tests v Pakistan (166). Scored maiden Test century (121) in the second Test v India at
Ahmedabad 2001-02, winning Man of the Match award. C&G Man of the Match
award for his 4-35 and 78-ball 100* in the semi-final v Surrey at Headingley 2002.
Captain of Yorkshire since 2004
Best batting: 186 Yorkshire v Lancashire, Old Trafford 2001
Best bowling: 8-55 Yorkshire v Gloucestershire, Gloucester 1998

2005 Season

	M	Inns	NO	Runs	HS	Avge	100s	50s	Ct	St	O	M	Runs	Wkts	Avge	Best	5wl	10wM
Test																		
All First	16	26	8	873	110 *	48.50	1	8	10	-	17	2	71	1	71.00	1-21	-	-
1-Day Int																		
C & G	3	2	1	67	40 *	67.00	-	-	-	-	20	1	93	7	13.28	4-43	-	
tsL	12	12	1	143	39	13.00	-	-	1	-	26	0	140	13	10.76	4-14	-	
Twenty20	8	7	0	111	55	15.85	-	1	3	-	11.4	0	132	1	132.00	1-22	-	

Career Performances

	M	Inns	NO	Runs	HS	Avge	100s	50s	Ct	St	Balls	Runs	Wkts	Avge	Best	5wl	10wM
Test	30	50	7	1052	121	24.46	1	5	14	-	3959	2220	59	37.62	5-32	3	-
All First	250	397	56	11090	186	32.52	17	57	158	-	21056	11174	391	28.57	8-55	11	-
1-Day Int	51	41	5	568	57 *	15.77	-	1	12	-	2364	1727	65	26.56	5-21	1	
C & G	37	33	8	1181	113	47.24	2	7	12	-	1572	1060	40	26.50	4-35	-	
tsL	173	157	17	3367	148	24.05	1	10	48	-	4784	3479	159	21.88	5-19	1	
Twenty20	14	12	0	178	55	14.83	-	1	3	-	70	132	1	132.00	1-22	-	

WHITE, C. L. Somerset

Name: Cameron Leon White
Role: Right-hand bat, leg-spin bowler
Born: 18 August 1983, Bairnsdale, Victoria, Australia
Height: 6ft 1½in **Weight:** 14st 2lbs
Nickname: Whitey
County debut: No first-team appearance
Strike rate: (career 60.45)
Overseas teams played for: Victoria 2000-01 –
Overseas tours: Australia U19 to New Zealand (U19 World Cup) 2001-02; Australia A to Pakistan 2005-06; Australia to Zimbabwe (one-day series) 2003-04, to India 2004-05, to New Zealand (one-day series) 2005-06
Extras: Appointed captain of Victoria one-day side 2003-04 (and deputy in Pura Cup) at age 20, becoming the youngest captain in the state's cricket history; overall captain of Victoria since 2004-05. Has won several match awards, including Man of the Match v Queensland at Brisbane in the Pura Cup 2003-04 and v Tasmania at Devonport in the ING Cup 2003-04

Best batting: 119 Victoria v Queensland, Brisbane 2004-05
Best bowling: 6-66 Victoria v Western Australia, Melbourne 2002-03
Stop press: Made ODI debut (as super sub) v ICC World XI at Melbourne in the Super Series 2005-06

2005 Season (did not make any first-class or one-day appearances)

Career Performances

	M	Inns	NO	Runs	HS	Avge	100s	50s	Ct	St	Balls	Runs	Wkts	Avge	Best	5wI	10wM
Test																	
All First	39	61	7	1514	119	28.03	1	8	45	-	5562	3198	92	34.76	6-66	1	1
1-Day Int																	
C & G																		
tsL																		
Twenty20																		

WHITE, G. G.   Northamptonshire

Name: Graeme Geoffrey White
Role: Right-hand bat, slow left-arm bowler; all-rounder
Born: 18 April 1987, Milton Keynes
Height: 5ft 11in **Weight:** 10st
Nickname: Whitey, Chalky, Pony
County debut: No first-team appearance
Parents: David and Sophie
Marital status: Single
Family links with cricket: 'Sister Rachel played England Women U17. Dad played good standard club cricket and is also a Level 2 coach. Brother Russell plays county U11'
Education: Stowe School; further education 'on hold'
Qualifications: 9 GCSEs, 1 AS-level, 3 A-levels, 'currently doing coaching Level 2'
Overseas tours: Stowe School to India 2004;

England U19 to Sri Lanka (U19 World Cup) 2005-06
Career highlights to date: 'Representing my country at the U19 World Cup in Sri Lanka in 2006 and reaching the semi-finals'
Cricket moments to forget: 'Getting hit for five sixes in one over playing for Stowe School (they kept going further!)'
Cricket superstitions: 'Putting pads on from the top down'
Cricketers particularly admired: Bishen Bedi, Phil Tufnell, Daniel Vettori

Young players to look out for: Russell White, Moeen Ali, Andy Miller
Other sports played: Badminton, hockey, football
Other sports followed: Football ('big Manchester United fan')
Favourite band: Kings of Leon, Bloc Party
Relaxations: 'Like listening to music. Playing PS2'
Extras: Represented England U15, U17 and U19. Dorothy Radd Shield (Northamptonshire) 2003. Colin Shillington Award (Stowe School) 2005

WHITE, R. A.   Northamptonshire

Name: Robert (<u>Rob</u>) Allan White
Role: Right-hand bat, leg-spin bowler
Born: 15 October 1979, Chelmsford, Essex
Height: 5ft 11in   **Weight:** 11st 7lbs
Nickname: Chalky, Toff, Zorro, Whitey, Lamb
County debut: 2000
1st-Class 200s: 1
Place in batting averages: 157th av. 29.27 (2004 234th av. 17.55)
Strike rate: (career 66.44)
Parents: Dennis and Ann
Marital status: Single
Family links with cricket: 'Grandfather on Essex committee for many years. Dad flailed the willow and brother travels the local leagues high and low'
Education: Stowe School; St John's College, Durham University; Loughborough University
Qualifications: 9 GCSEs, 3 A-levels
Cricket moments to forget: 'Franklyn Rose telling me my mates had bet £10 that he couldn't injure me, as I walked out to play Lashings'
Cricketers particularly admired: Ian Botham, Viv Richards, Steve Waugh
Young players to look out for: Monty Panesar
Other sports played: Badminton, squash, golf, kabaddi
Other sports followed: Football (West Ham), rugby (Northampton Saints)
Extras: Northamptonshire League Young Player of the Year and Youth Cricketer of the Year 1999. Northamptonshire Young Player of the Year (Frank Rudd Trophy) 2001. Played for Loughborough UCCE 2001, 2002 and 2003. Recorded the highest maiden century in the history of English first-class cricket (277, including a hundred before lunch on the first day), v Gloucestershire at Northampton 2002 in his fifth first-class match. NBC Denis Compton Award for the most promising young Northamptonshire player 2002. Represented British Universities 2003

Best batting: 277 Northamptonshire v Gloucestershire, Northampton 2002
Best bowling: 2-30 Northamptonshire v Gloucestershire, Northampton 2002

2005 Season

	M	Inns	NO	Runs	HS	Avge	100s	50s	Ct	St	O	M	Runs	Wkts	Avge	Best	5wl	10wM
Test																		
All First	15	24	2	644	95	29.27	-	2	10	-	20	3	66	0	-	-	-	-
1-Day Int																		
C & G	1	1	1	36	36*	-	-	-	-	-								
tsL	11	9	0	198	57	22.00	-	1	2	-								
Twenty20																		

Career Performances

	M	Inns	NO	Runs	HS	Avge	100s	50s	Ct	St	Balls	Runs	Wkts	Avge	Best	5wl	10wM
Test																	
All First	33	58*	3	1656	277	30.10	1	8	20	-	598	385	9	42.77	2-30	-	-
1-Day Int																	
C & G	1	1	1	36	36*	-	-	-	-	-							
tsL	27	25	0	460	101	18.40	1	1	6	-	48	46	2	23.00	2-18	-	
Twenty20	7	7	0	81	28	11.57	-	-	2	-							

WHITE, W. A. — Derbyshire

Name: <u>Wayne</u> Andrew White
Role: Right-hand bat, right-arm fast-medium bowler
Born: 22 April 1985, Derby
Height: 6ft 2in **Weight:** 12st 2lbs
Nickname: Chalky, Player
County debut: 2005
Strike rate: (career 70.60)
Parents: John and Sharon
Marital status: 'Long-term relationship – Elaina Parker'
Family links with cricket: 'Brother plays in Derbyshire age groups and same club side – Swarkestone CC'
Education: John Port School; Nottingham University
Qualifications: 11 GCSEs, 4 A-levels, BA Politics
Career outside cricket: 'Semi-professional footballer; home improvements business with Jake Needham'

Off-season: 'Club cricket in Melbourne'
Career highlights to date: 'First wicket for Derbyshire – Anthony McGrath'
Cricket moments to forget: '0-107 in the first innings of my debut against Yorkshire'
Cricketers particularly admired: Graeme Welch, Mike Hendrick
Young players to look out for: Jake Needham, Dan Redfearn, Harry White
Other sports played: Football (Gresley Rovers, Burton Albion, Mickleover Sports, Derby County), golf; 'darts and pool at The Bridge'
Other sports followed: Football (Derby County)
Injuries: 'Lots of niggles; no days lost'
Favourite band: Faithless, Prodigy, Texas
Relaxations: 'Round of golf; night in with the "missus"; PlayStation/PC; funky house in Susumi'
Extras: Scored 76 and took 7-18 on club cricket debut for Swarkestone
Opinions on cricket: 'More four-day cricket in 2nd XI.'
Best batting: 6 Derbyshire v Yorkshire, Derby 2005
Best bowling: 4-77 Derbyshire v Somerset, Taunton 2005

2005 Season

	M	Inns	NO	Runs	HS	Avge	100s	50s	Ct	St	O	M	Runs	Wkts	Avge	Best	5wI	10wM
Test																		
All First	2	2	0	8	6	4.00	-	-	-	-	58.5	8	280	5	56.00	4-77	-	-
1-Day Int																		
C & G																		
tsL																		
Twenty20																		

Career Performances

	M	Inns	NO	Runs	HS	Avge	100s	50s	Ct	St	Balls	Runs	Wkts	Avge	Best	5wI	10wM
Test																	
All First	2	2	0	8	6	4.00	-	-	-	-	353	280	5	56.00	4-77	-	-
1-Day Int																	
C & G																	
tsL																	
Twenty20																	

95. Who made an Ashes hundred on Test debut,
played 17 ODIs and was the first cricketer to
captain three Australian states?

Name: <u>David</u> Harry Wigley
Role: Right-hand bat, right-arm
fast-medium bowler
Born: 26 October 1981, Bradford, Yorkshire
Height: 6ft 3in **Weight:** 14st
Nickname: Wiggers, Wigs
County debut: 2002 (Yorkshire),
2003 (Worcestershire)
County colours: 2003 (Worcestershire)
Place in bowling averages: 56th av. 29.23
Strike rate: 44.84 (career 58.28)
Parents: Max and Judith
Marital status: Single
Family links with cricket: Father played
league cricket in Liverpool Competition,
Bradford League and Durham Senior League
Education: St Mary's RC Comprehensive,
Menston; Loughborough University
Qualifications: 9 GCSEs, 3 A-levels, degree in Sport and Exercise Science,
ECB Level I coaching
Off-season: 'Training in UK. Possible trip to India'
Overseas tours: British Universities to Cape Town 2004
Overseas teams played for: Gormandale CC, Victoria 2001; Mount Lawley CC,
Perth 2004-05
Career highlights to date: 'Career best bowling in NCL for Worcs (4-37). Winning
Uni final at Lord's 2002'
Cricket moments to forget: 'Losing Uni final at Lord's 2004 in last over'
Cricket superstitions: 'Must turn to left to run in and bowl'
Cricketers particularly admired: Darren Gough, Andrew Flintoff
Young players to look out for: Monty Panesar, Steve Davies, Alastair Cook
Other sports played: Golf, rugby ('used to play to decent standard; gave up at 16')
Other sports followed: Football (Leeds United), rugby (Llanelli Scarlets)
Injuries: Out for six weeks with a broken knuckle on first finger of right hand
Relaxations: 'Music, films, golf'
Extras: Played for ECB Schools v Sri Lanka U19 2000. Yorkshire U19 Bowling
Award 2000. Played for LUCCE 2002-04 (captain 2004), taking 5-71 v Hampshire at
West End and 5-52 v Oxford in the UCCE One-Day Challenge at Lord's 2002.
Represented British Universities 2003-04 (captain 2004). Released by Worcestershire
at the end of the 2005 season and has joined Northamptonshire for 2006
Opinions on cricket: 'Of course system is now perfect now we have won the Ashes.
But probably play too much county cricket, not allowing enough time for recovery and
practice.'

Best batting: 23* LUCCE v Somerset, Taunton 2004
Best bowling: 4-68 Worcestershire v Derbyshire, Derby 2005

2005 Season

	M	Inns	NO	Runs	HS	Avge	100s	50s	Ct	St	O	M	Runs	Wkts	Avge	Best	5wI	10wM
Test																		
All First	4	4	3	11	7 *	11.00	-	-	2	-	97.1	17	380	13	29.23	4-68	-	-
1-Day Int																		
C & G																		
tsL	2	1	0	0	0	0.00	-	-	1	-	7	0	41	2	20.50	1-14	-	
Twenty20																		

Career Performances

	M	Inns	NO	Runs	HS	Avge	100s	50s	Ct	St	Balls	Runs	Wkts	Avge	Best	5wI	10wM
Test																	
All First	11	13	5	102	23 *	12.75	-	-	4	-	1632	1126	28	40.21	4-68	-	-
1-Day Int																	
C & G																	
tsL	6	3	0	3	2	1.00	-	-	1	-	240	199	9	22.11	4-37	-	
Twenty20	2	1	0	1	1	1.00	-	-	-	-	30	33	1	33.00	1-8	-	

WILLIAMS, B. A.   Durham

Name: <u>Brad</u> Andrew Williams
Role: Right-hand bat, right-arm fast bowler
Born: 20 November 1974, Frankston,
Victoria, Australia
Height: 6ft
County debut: 2005
Test debut: 2003-04
Strike rate: (career 60.67)
Overseas tours: Australia U19 to New
Zealand 1992-93; Young Australia (Australia
A) to England and Netherlands 1995;
Australia A to South Africa (one-day series)
2002-03; Australia to West Indies 2002-03, to
India (TVS Cup) 2003-04, to Sri Lanka 2003-
04, to Zimbabwe 2004
Overseas teams played for: Victoria 1994-
95 – 1998-99; Western Australia 1999-2000 –
Extras: Has won several match awards,

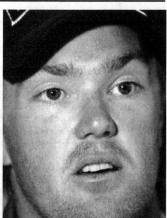

including Man of the Match v New Zealand at Pune in the TVS Cup 2003-04 (5-53)
and v Zimbabwe at Sydney in the VB Series 2003-04 (5-22). Was an overseas player
with Durham towards the end of the 2005 season, replacing Mick Lewis

Best batting: 41* Victoria v Western Australia, Perth 1995-96
Best bowling: 6-74 Western Australia v Victoria, Perth 1999-2000

2005 Season

	M	Inns	NO	Runs	HS	Avge	100s	50s	Ct	St	O	M	Runs	Wkts	Avge	Best	5wl	10wM
Test																		
All First	3	4	3	51	22 *	51.00	-	-	1	-	83.2	12	335	7	47.85	3-73	-	-
1-Day Int																		
C & G																			
tsL	6	0	0	0	0	-	-	-	-	2	-	49.2	4	221	11	20.09	3-52	-
Twenty20																		

Career Performances

	M	Inns	NO	Runs	HS	Avge	100s	50s	Ct	St	Balls	Runs	Wkts	Avge	Best	5wl	10wM
Test	4	6	3	23	10 *	7.66	-	-	4	-	852	406	9	45.11	4-53	-	-
All First	66	83	24	793	41 *	13.44	-	-	25	-	13339	7119	222	32.06	6-74	10	-
1-Day Int	25	6	4	27	13 *	13.50	-	-	4	-	1203	814	35	23.25	5-22	2	
C & G																	
tsL	6	0	0	0	0	-	-	-	2	-	296	221	11	20.09	3-52	-	
Twenty20																	

WILLIAMS, R. E. M. Middlesex

Name: Robert (<u>Robbie</u>) Edward
Morgan Williams
Role: Right-hand bat, right-arm
fast-medium bowler
Born: 19 January 1987, Pembury, Kent
Height: 6ft **Weight:** 13st 2lbs
County debut: No first-team appearance
Parents: Gail and Tim
Marital status: Single
Education: Marlborough College; 'starting at
Durham University in October 2006'
Qualifications: 3 A-levels
Overseas tours: Marlborough College to
South Africa 2003
Overseas teams played for: Corrimal,
Wollongong 2005-06
Career highlights to date: 'Being signed by
Middlesex'

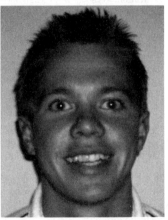

Cricket moments to forget: 'Leaving a ball and getting stumped at the Bunbury
Festival when nine down and three balls from a draw'

Cricket superstitions: 'Batsmen can be jinxed'
Cricketers particularly admired: Brett Lee
Other sports played: Rugby (Marlborough College 1st XV), hockey (Marlborough College 1st XI)
Other sports followed: Rugby union (Leicester Tigers)
Injuries: Out for two weeks with torn abdominals
Favourite band: The Killers, Coldplay, Tenacious D
Relaxations: Sudoku
Extras: Made 2nd XI Championship debut 2005

WILLOUGHBY, C. M. Somerset

Name: <u>Charl</u> Myles Willoughby
Role: Left-hand bat, left-arm fast-medium bowler
Born: 3 December 1974, Cape Town, South Africa
County debut: 2005 (Leicestershire)
County cap: 2005 (Leicestershire)
Test debut: 2003
Place in bowling averages: 111th av. 41.96
Strike rate: 78.15 (career 57.03)
Education: Wynberg Boys' High School; Stellenbosch University
Overseas tours: South African Academy to Zimbabwe 1998-99; South Africa A to West Indies 2000, to Zimbabwe 2004; South Africa to Sharjah (Coca-Cola Sharjah Cup) 1999-2000, to Bangladesh 2003, to England 2003
Overseas teams played for: Boland 1994-95 – 1999-2000; Western Province 2000-01 – 2003-04; Western Province Boland 2004-05; Cape Cobras 2005-06 –
Extras: Played for Berkshire in the NatWest 2000. Has won several match awards, including Man of the Match for South Africa A v Barbados at Bridgetown 2000 (6-24) and for Leicestershire v Somerset at Leicester in the C&G 2005 (6-16; the best one-day return by a Leicestershire bowler). An overseas player with Leicestershire 2005. Has joined Somerset for 2006; is no longer considered an overseas player
Best batting: 17* Boland v North West, Paarl 1999-2000
Best bowling: 7-56 Western Province v Northerns, Centurion 2003-04

2005 Season

	M	Inns	NO	Runs	HS	Avge	100s	50s	Ct	St	O	M	Runs	Wkts	Avge	Best	5wI	10wM
Test																		
All First	14	17	5	68	16 *	5.66	-	-	2	-	429.5	97	1385	33	41.96	4-92	-	-
1-Day Int																		
C & G	2	1	0	0	0	0.00	-	-	-	-	16	3	47	7	6.71	6-16	1	
tsL	16	3	1	7	5	3.50	-	-	2	-	115.5	18	412	13	31.69	2-12	-	
Twenty20	9	2	2	1	1 *	-	-	-	3	-	31.5	1	192	11	17.45	3-11	-	

Career Performances

	M	Inns	NO	Runs	HS	Avge	100s	50s	Ct	St	Balls	Runs	Wkts	Avge	Best	5wI	10wM
Test	2	0	0	0	0	-	-	-	-	-	300	125	1	125.00	1-47	-	-
All First	111	125	51	330	17 *	4.45	-	-	29	-	22987	10192	403	25.29	7-56	13	3
1-Day Int	3	2	2	4	3 *	-	-	-	-	-	168	148	2	74.00	2-39	-	
C & G	4	2	0	0	0	0.00	-	-	1	-	216	101	9	11.22	6-16	1	
tsL	16	3	1	7	5	3.50	-	-	2	-	695	412	13	31.69	2-12	-	
Twenty20	9	2	2	1	1 *	-	-	-	3	-	191	192	11	17.45	3-11	-	

WINDOWS, M. G. N.   Gloucestershire

Name: <u>Matthew</u> Guy Newman Windows
Role: Right-hand bat, left-arm medium bowler
Born: 5 April 1973, Bristol
Height: 5ft 7in **Weight:** 11st 7lbs
Nickname: Steamy, Bedos, Boat
County debut: 1992
County cap: 1998
Benefit: 2006
1000 runs in a season: 3
Place in batting averages: 200th av. 22.80 (2004 197th av. 22.63)
Strike rate: (career 68.50)
Parents: Tony and Carolyn
Wife and date of marriage: Emma, 12 October 2002
Family links with cricket: 'Father (A.R.) played for Gloucestershire (1960-69) and was Cambridge cricket Blue'
Education: Clifton College; Durham University
Qualifications: 9 GCSEs, 3 A-levels, BA (Hons) Sociology (Dunelm), SFA securities representative of the London Stock Exchange

Overseas tours: Clifton College to Barbados 1991; England U19 to Pakistan 1991-92; Durham University to South Africa 1992-93; England A to Zimbabwe and South Africa 1998-99; Gloucestershire's annual pre-season tour to South Africa
Overseas teams played for: Gold Coast Dolphins, Queensland 1996-97
Career highlights to date: 'Winning all the Lord's finals, but [especially] being not out against Glamorgan in the 2000 [B&H] final'
Cricketers particularly admired: David Boon, Courtney Walsh
Young players to look out for: Monty Panesar, Alex Gidman
Other sports played: Rackets (British Open runner-up 1997)
Relaxations: 'Travelling and understanding financial jargon'
Extras: Represented England U19. Gloucestershire Young Player of the Year 1994. Scored 218* for Durham University v Hull University in the BUSA Championships 1995. Gloucestershire Player of the Year 1998
Best batting: 184 Gloucestershire v Warwickshire, Cheltenham 1996
Best bowling: 1-6 Combined Universities v West Indians, The Parks 1995

2005 Season

	M	Inns	NO	Runs	HS	Avge	100s	50s	Ct	St	O	M	Runs	Wkts	Avge	Best	5wI	10wM
Test																		
All First	11	22	1	479	65*	22.80	-	2	2	-								
1-Day Int																		
C & G	1	1	0	0	0	0.00	-	-	-	-								
tsL	14	14	1	354	87	27.23	-	4	-	-								
Twenty20	3	2	0	3	3	1.50	-	-	3	-								

Career Performances

	M	Inns	NO	Runs	HS	Avge	100s	50s	Ct	St	Balls	Runs	Wkts	Avge	Best	5wI	10wM
Test																	
All First	165	293	20	8976	184	32.87	16	47	90	-	137	131	2	65.50	1-6	-	-
1-Day Int																	
C & G	28	25	4	533	82	25.38	-	3	11	-							
tsL	150	143	15	3404	117	26.59	2	19	43	-	48	49	0	-			
Twenty20	8	5	0	39	27	7.80	-	-	6	-							

---

96. Which spinner, whose grandfather opened
the bowling for both Leicestershire and Middlesex, had a 10½-year gap
between his tenth and eleventh ODI appearances?

WOLSTENHOLME, J. P.　　Northamptonshire

Name: <u>John</u> Paul Wolstenholme
Role: Right-hand bat, right-arm medium-fast bowler
Born: 7 May 1982, Northampton
Height: 6ft 10in **Weight:** 17st
Nickname: 'Big Fella, Big Lad … etc'
County debut: 2005
Parents: Patricia and Paul
Marital status: Single
Family links with cricket: 'Father and brother both played second-class cricket for Northants'
Education: Northampton School for Boys; University of Northampton
Qualifications: 10 GCSEs, 3 A-levels, Higher Diploma in Human Biology
Career outside cricket: Family orthotic supplies company
Overseas tours: Northamptonshire U19 to South Africa 2000
Overseas teams played for: Wanneroo District Cricket Club, Perth 2004-05
Career highlights: 'Debut against Bangladesh for Northamptonshire'
Cricket moments to forget: 'Every time I've been hit on the helmet, which became a regular occurrence. It doesn't hurt that much but it's so embarrassing!'
Cricket superstitions: 'None'
Cricketers particularly admired: Alan Hodgson
Young players to look out for: Mark Nelson, Graeme White
Other sports played: Rugby, athletics (400 metres)
Other sports followed: Football (Sheffield Wednesday), rugby (Northampton Saints)
Injuries: Back injury – finished career
Favourite band: Kasabian
Interests/relaxations: 'A good film always chills me out. Females'
Extras: Played for Northamptonshire Board XI in the NatWest 2000
Opinions on cricket: 'A regional system would be a decent idea, but hardly feasible. Having played in grade cricket in Australia, I thought the organisation was superb. It gave any player any opportunity to play at the highest level they could attain. However, this is also not feasible in England (but a nice thought all the same!).'

2005 Season

	M	Inns	NO	Runs	HS	Avge	100s	50s	Ct	St	O	M	Runs	Wkts	Avge	Best	5wI	10wM
Test																		
All First	1	0	0	0	0	-	-	-	2	-	9	3	14	0	-	-	-	-
1-Day Int																		
C & G																		
tsL																		
Twenty20																		

Career Performances

	M	Inns	NO	Runs	HS	Avge	100s	50s	Ct	St	Balls	Runs	Wkts	Avge	Best	5wI	10wM
Test																		
All First	1	0	0	0	0	-	-	-	2	-	54	14	0	-	-	-	-	
1-Day Int																		
C & G	1	1	0	10	10	10.00	-	-	-	-								
tsL																		
Twenty20																		

WOOD, M. J.　　　　　　　　Somerset

Name: <u>Matthew</u> James Wood
Role: Right-hand bat, right-arm off-spin bowler, county vice-captain
Born: 30 September 1980, Exeter
Height: 5ft 11in **Weight:** 12st 6lbs
Nickname: Woody, Gran, Moo
County debut: 2001
County cap: 2005
1000 runs in a season: 1
1st-Class 200s: 1
Place in batting averages: 43rd av. 48.09 (2004 40th av. 50.33)
Parents: James and Trina
Marital status: Single
Family links with cricket: Father is chairman of Devon Cricket Board
Education: Exmouth College; Exeter University
Qualifications: 10 GCSEs, 2 A-levels, ECB Level 3 coach
Career outside cricket: Coach
Overseas tours: West of England U15 to West Indies 1995
Overseas teams played for: Doubleview CC, Perth 2001, 2002

Career highlights to date: 'Winning the Twenty20 Cup and scoring 297 v Yorkshire'
Cricket moments to forget: 'Getting a pair v Essex 2005'
Cricket superstitions: 'None'
Cricketers particularly admired: Marcus Trescothick
Young players to look out for: James Hildreth, Arul Suppiah, John Francis
Other sports followed: Football (Liverpool FC), horse racing
Relaxations: Golf
Extras: NBC Denis Compton Award for the most promising young Somerset player 2001. Scored century in each innings (106/131) v Surrey at Taunton 2002. Somerset Player of the Year 2002. Scored 297 v Yorkshire at Taunton 2005, the fifth highest individual score in Somerset's history. Vice-captain of Somerset since July 2005
Opinions on cricket: 'There should be a minimum number of English-qualified players per county.'
Best batting: 297 Somerset v Yorkshire, Taunton 2005

2005 Season

	M	Inns	NO	Runs	HS	Avge	100s	50s	Ct	St	O	M	Runs	Wkts	Avge	Best	5wl	10wM
Test																		
All First	13	23	1	1058	297	48.09	2	7	4	-								
1-Day Int																		
C & G																		
tsL	14	14	0	442	129	31.57	1	2	2	-								
Twenty20	11	11	0	366	94	33.27	-	3	1	-								

Career Performances

	M	Inns	NO	Runs	HS	Avge	100s	50s	Ct	St	Balls	Runs	Wkts	Avge	Best	5wl	10wM
Test																	
All First	58	102	6	3698	297	38.52	9	22	17	-	85	68	0	-	-	-	-
1-Day Int																	
C & G	4	3	0	38	19	12.66	-	-	1	-							
tsL	45	43	3	1137	129	28.42	1	7	8	-							
Twenty20	13	13	0	431	94	33.15	-	4	1	-							

97. Which rugby international faced Trevor Chappell's underarm ball in the third final of the Benson and Hedges World Series Cup in 1981?

WOOD, M. J. Yorkshire

Name: <u>Matthew</u> James Wood
Role: Right-hand opening bat,
off-spin bowler
Born: 6 April 1977, Huddersfield
Height: 5ft 9in **Weight:** 12st
Nickname: Ronnie, Chuddy
County debut: 1997
County cap: 2001
1000 runs in a season: 4
1st-Class 200s: 3
Place in batting averages: 97th av. 35.89
(2004 85th av. 38.20)
Strike rate: (career 36.00)
Parents: Roger and Kathryn
Marital status: Single
Family links with cricket: 'Father played for
local team Emley. Mum made the teas and
sister Caroline scored'
Education: Shelley High School and Sixth Form Centre
Qualifications: 9 GCSEs, 2 A-levels, NCA coaching award
Overseas tours: England U19 to Zimbabwe 1995-96; Yorkshire CCC to West Indies
1996-97, to Cape Town 1997, 1998; MCC to Kenya 1999, to Bangladesh 1999-2000;
ECB National Academy to Australia 2001-02
Overseas teams played for: Somerset West CC, Cape Town 1994-95; Upper Hutt
United CC, New Zealand 1997-98; Mosman Park, Western Australia 2000-01;
Mosman CC, Sydney 2004-05
Career highlights to date: 'Being on the pitch as fielding 12th man for England
series win v South Africa at Headingley [1998]. Winning the Championship in 2001
and winning the C&G 2002 at Lord's'
Cricket moments to forget: 'Most of the 2002 season'
Cricket superstitions: 'Not any more'
Cricketers particularly admired: Darren Lehmann, Matthew Maynard,
Stephen Fleming, Michael Vaughan
Other sports played: Football (Kirkburton FC)
Other sports followed: Football (Liverpool FC)
Favourite band: Atomic Kitten
Relaxations: 'Socialising, eating out, golf, DIY'
Extras: Represented England U17. Attended Yorkshire Academy. Scored 1000 first-
class runs in first full season 1998. Yorkshire Coach's Player of the Year, Yorkshire
Club Player of the Year and Yorkshire Players' Player of the Year 2003. Set a new
Yorkshire record individual score in the NatWest/C&G (160 from 124 balls) v Devon
at Exmouth 2004, winning Man of the Match award. Vice-captain of Yorks 2003-04

Opinions on cricket: 'Away team captains should have choice to bat/bowl. This would eradicate pitch doctoring. Twenty20 is very good. Should be played on Friday nights, home and away; teams would develop their own support following like Superleague/soccer.'

Best batting: 207 Yorkshire v Somerset, Taunton 2003
Best bowling: 1-4 Yorkshire v Somerset, Headingley 2003

2005 Season

	M	Inns	NO	Runs	HS	Avge	100s	50s	Ct	St	O	M	Runs	Wkts	Avge	Best	5wI	10wM
Test																		
All First	17	30	2	1005	202 *	35.89	1	6	20	-								
1-Day Int																		
C & G	4	4	1	51	36	17.00	-	-	-	-								
tsL	17	17	0	451	111	26.52	1	2	10	-	1	0	10	0	-		-	-
Twenty20	5	5	0	69	30	13.80	-	-	4	-	3	0	32	2	16.00	1-11	-

Career Performances

	M	Inns	NO	Runs	HS	Avge	100s	50s	Ct	St	Balls	Runs	Wkts	Avge	Best	5wI	10wM
Test																	
All First	122	213	20	6620	207	34.30	16	29	106	-	72	39	2	19.50	1-4	-	-
1-Day Int																	
C & G	20	20	5	781	160	52.06	2	3	7	-	36	45	3	15.00	3-45	-
tsL	101	92	6	2048	111	23.81	2	10	39	-	24	26	0	-	-	-
Twenty20	14	14	2	322	96 *	26.83	-	2	11	-	18	32	2	16.00	1-11	-

---

98. Born Leonard Stephen Durtanovich,
this cricketer took 53 ODI wickets in 27 matches.
By what name is he better known?

WOODMAN, R. J. Somerset

Name: <u>Robert</u> James Woodman
Role: Left-hand bat, left-arm medium bowler
Born: 12 October 1986, Taunton
Height: 5ft 11in
Nickname: Woody
County debut: 2005
Strike rate: (career 198.00)
Parents: Janet and Keith
Marital status: Single
Family links with cricket: 'Dad runs youth
section at local club (Taunton Deane CC)'
Education: The Castle School; Richard
Huish College, Taunton
Qualifications: 10 GCSEs, 2 A-levels
Overseas tours: West of England U15 to
West Indies; The Castle School to Barbados
2002; England U19 to Bangladesh 2005-06,
to Sri Lanka (U19 World Cup) 2005-06

Career highlights to date: '46* on debut against Worcestershire. Selection for
England U19 World Cup squad'
Cricket moments to forget: 'Bowling at Neil Carter on Sky Sports and getting hit to
all parts'
Cricket superstitions: 'None'
Cricketers particularly admired: Keith Parsons, Jacques Kallis, Ian Botham,
Wasim Akram, Tony Keitch
Young players to look out for: Moeen Ali, Sam Spurway
Other sports played: Football (Bristol City Academy and Somerset U19), basketball
(Taunton Tigers Academy)
Other sports followed: Football (Tottenham Hotspur)
Favourite band: U2, Kanye West
Relaxations: 'Watching DVDs; meeting up with mates'
Extras: Played for Somerset in the International 20:20 Club Championship 2005
Best batting: 46* Somerset v Worcestershire, Worcester 2005
Best bowling: 1-78 Somerset v Essex, Colchester 2005

2005 Season

	M	Inns	NO	Runs	HS	Avge	100s	50s	Ct	St	O	M	Runs	Wkts	Avge	Best	5wI	10wM
Test																		
All First	3	4	1	54	46 *	18.00	-	-	-	-	66	11	268	2	134.00	1-78	-	-
1-Day Int																		
C & G																		
tsL	4	0	0	0	0	-	-	-	2	-	22	2	136	1	136.00	1-38	-	
Twenty20																		

Career Performances

	M	Inns	NO	Runs	HS	Avge	100s	50s	Ct	St	Balls	Runs	Wkts	Avge	Best	5wI	10wM
Test																	
All First	3	4	1	54	46 *	18.00	-	-	-	-	396	268	2	134.00	1-78	-	-
1-Day Int																	
C & G																	
tsL	4	0	0	0	0	-	-	-	2	-	132	136	1	136.00	1-38	-	
Twenty20																	

WRIGHT, B. J.   Glamorgan

Name: Ben James Wright
Role: Right-hand middle-order bat
Born: 5 December 1987, Fulwood, Preston
Height: 5ft 9in **Weight:** 12st
Nickname: Bej, Rocky
County debut: No first-team appearance
Parents: Julia and Peter
Marital status: Single
Family links with cricket: 'Father played one game of cricket'
Education: Cowbridge Comprehensive
Off-season: England U19 tours
Overseas tours: West of England U15 to West Indies 2003; England U16 to South Africa 2004; England U19 to Bangladesh 2005-06, to Sri Lanka (U19 World Cup) 2005-06
Career highlights to date: 'Playing for England U19 in tri-series v Bangladesh and Sri Lanka'
Cricket superstitions: 'Left pad before right'
Cricketers particularly admired: Matthew Maynard, Michael Clarke
Young players to look out for: Mike O'Shea, Rory Hamilton-Brown, Karl Brown

Other sports played: Rugby (Wales U16 A)
Other sports followed: Rugby (Leicester Tigers), football (Man Utd 'and anyone who beats Crystal Palace')
Favourite band: 'Yogi Bear'
Relaxations: 'Spending time with girlfriend and watching TV'
Extras: Sir John Hobbs Memorial Prize 2003. A.A. Thomson Fielding Prize 2003. BBC *Test Match Special* U15 Young Cricketer of the Year Award 2003
Opinions on cricket: 'Just enjoy watching and playing.'

WRIGHT, C. J. C. Middlesex

Name: Christopher (<u>Chris</u>) Julian Clement Wright
Role: Right-hand bat, right-arm fast-medium bowler
Born: 14 July 1985, Chipping Norton, Oxfordshire
Height: 6ft 3in **Weight:** 12st
Nickname: Wrighty, The Baron
County debut: 2004
Place in batting averages: 169th av. 26.83
Strike rate: (career 111.33)
Parents: Alan and Nikki
Marital status: Single
Family links with cricket: 'Dad captains Hampshire Over 50s'
Education: Eggars Grammar School, Alton; Anglia Polytechnic University
Qualifications: 11 GCSEs, 3 A-levels
Career outside cricket: 'Not sure yet – something involving sports science or travel'
Off-season: 'Am in Sri Lanka until the report-back date playing for Tamil Union Cricket and Athletic Club'
Overseas tours: Cambridge UCCE to Grenada 2004 ('fetching back balls for Craig Buckham')
Overseas teams played for: Tamil Union C&AC 2005-06
Career highlights to date: '76 v Essex at start of 2005 season'
Cricket moments to forget: 'Have batted four times in List A cricket and have the "Audi rings". I know I am better than that!'
Cricket superstitions: 'No superstitions for cricket – they cause more problems than they solve. Have superstitions when at the Ballagio casino in Colombo (Gareth James can never touch my chips!)'
Cricketers particularly admired: Glenn McGrath, Andrew Flintoff, 'Ranjith and all the Middlesex squad (legends)'

Young players to look out for: Billy Godleman, Gareth James, Eoin Morgan, Chris Whelan, Steve Finn, Boyd Rankin
Other sports played: 'Table football to an unbelievable standard and a bit of basketball'
Other sports followed: Football (Arsenal), basketball (Sacramento Kings)
Favourite band: Weezer, Rage Against The Machine, (hed) pe, Guns N' Roses
Relaxations: 'Championship Manager; spending time with girlfriend; eating out and movies'
Extras: Played for Cambridge UCCE 2004-05. Represented British Universities 2005
Opinions on cricket: 'Two up and two down will be an improvement but I like the two division format – and Surrey's "stash vests" are brilliant.'
Best batting: 76 CUCCE v Essex, Fenner's 2005
Best bowling: 2-36 CUCCE v Middlesex, Fenner's 2005

2005 Season

	M	Inns	NO	Runs	HS	Avge	100s	50s	Ct	St	O	M	Runs	Wkts	Avge	Best	5wI	10wM
Test																		
All First	5	6	0	161	76	26.83	-	1	1	-	119.4	14	538	6	89.66	2-36	-	-
1-Day Int																		
C & G																		
tsL	2	2	2	0	0 *	-	-	-	-	-	13	0	99	1	99.00	1-66	-	
Twenty20	1	0	0	0	0	-	-	-	-	-	3	0	29	1	29.00	1-29	-	

Career Performances

	M	Inns	NO	Runs	HS	Avge	100s	50s	Ct	St	Balls	Runs	Wkts	Avge	Best	5wI	10wM
Test																	
All First	9	11	0	257	76	23.36	-	2	4	-	1336	917	12	76.41	2-36	-	-
1-Day Int																	
C & G																	
tsL	5	3	2	0	0 *	0.00	-	-	-	-	186	203	2	101.50	1-34	-	
Twenty20	2	0	0	0	0	-	-	-	-	-	30	44	1	44.00	1-29	-	

99. Which former ODI captain played Minor Counties
cricket for both Shropshire and Herefordshire?

WRIGHT, D. G.   Northamptonshire

Name: <u>Damien</u> Geoffrey Wright
Role: Right-hand bat, right-arm fast-medium bowler, gully fielder
Born: 25 July 1975, Casino, NSW, Australia
County debut: 2003
50 wickets in a season: 1
Place in batting averages: 173rd av. 26.47
Place in bowling averages: 33rd av. 26.37
Strike rate: 54.33 (career 65.66)
Overseas tours: Australia A to South Africa 2002-03
Overseas teams played for: Tasmania 1997-98 –
Extras: Played for Scotland in the C&G 2002, winning two Man of the Match awards. Has also won several domestic awards in Australia, including Man of the Match v Victoria in the ING Cup at Melbourne 2001-

02 (4-23/40). Has represented Australia A. Tasmania's leading wicket-taker in the Pura Cup 2002-03 (31 wickets; av. 27.25) and (jointly with Andrew Downton) 2003-04 (37; 26.49). Tasmanian Player of the Year 2002-03. Named in Australia's initial squad of 30 for the 2002-03 World Cup. Was an overseas player with Northamptonshire in June and July 2003 and in 2005
Best batting: 111 Tasmania v Victoria, Hobart 2004-05
Best bowling: 8-60 Northamptonshire v Yorkshire, Headingley 2005

2005 Season

	M	Inns	NO	Runs	HS	Avge	100s	50s	Ct	St	O	M	Runs	Wkts	Avge	Best	5wI	10wM
Test																		
All First	16	25	2	609	85	26.47	-	4	6	-	480	139	1398	53	26.37	8-60	2	-
1-Day Int																		
C & G	3	2	0	19	10	9.50	-	-	-	-	25.3	6	89	7	12.71	4-38	-	
tsL	16	14	4	223	51 *	22.30	-	1	3	-	120	14	574	26	22.07	5-37	1	
Twenty20	5	5	2	86	38 *	28.66	-	-	-	-	15.1	0	114	4	28.50	3-17	-	

Career Performances

	M	Inns	NO	Runs	HS	Avge	100s	50s	Ct	St	Balls	Runs	Wkts	Avge	Best	5wI	10wM
Test																	
All First	78	119	19	2415	111	24.15	1	12	37	-	16154	7672	246	31.18	8-60	7	-
1-Day Int																	
C & G	5	4	1	127	55	42.33	-	2	2	-	255	140	10	14.00	4-38	-	
tsL	18	16	4	238	51 *	19.83	-	1	4	-	813	659	27	24.40	5-37	1	
Twenty20	5	5	2	86	38 *	28.66	-	-	-	-	91	114	4	28.50	3-17	-	

WRIGHT, L. J. Sussex

Name: <u>Luke</u> James Wright
Role: Right-hand bat, right-arm
medium-fast bowler; all-rounder
Born: 7 March 1985, Grantham
Height: 6ft **Weight:** 13st
Nickname: Wrighty
County debut: 2003 (Leicestershire),
2004 (Sussex)
Place in batting averages: 249th av. 15.75
Place in bowling averages: 24th av. 25.30
Strike rate: 51.23 (career 70.21)
Parents: Keith and Anna
Marital status: Single
Family links with cricket: 'Father very keen
cricketer (Level 2 coach).' Brother Ashley
played for Leicestershire
Education: Belvoir High School, Bottesford;
Ratcliffe College; Loughborough University
Qualifications: 8 GCSEs, National Diploma in Sports Science and Sports Massage,
ECB Level 1 coaching
Off-season: 'England Academy until Christmas, then Cape Town until March'
Overseas tours: Leicestershire U13 to South Africa; Leicestershire U15 to South
Africa; England U19 to Australia 2002-03, to Bangladesh (U19 World Cup) 2003-04;
England A to West Indies 2005-06
Career highlights to date: 'Getting into the England Academy twice. Winning the
totesport division two last year'
Cricket superstitions: 'Too many to name'
Cricketers particularly admired: Andrew Flintoff, Jacques Kallis
Young players to look out for: Stuart Broad, Tim Ambrose, Chris Nash
Other sports played: Football, hockey, squash, tennis
Other sports followed: Football (Newcastle United)

Favourite band: Kelly Clarkson
Relaxations: Music, cinema, going out
Extras: NBC Denis Compton Award for the most promising young Leicestershire player 2002. Took the first ever hat-trick for England U19 in one-day cricket, v South Africa U19 at Hove 2003. Scored maiden first-class century (100) on Sussex debut v LUCCE at Hove 2004. ECB National Academy 2004-05 (part-time), 2005-06
Opinions on cricket: 'Must back home-grown English talent as much as possible.'
Best batting: 100 Sussex v LUCCE, Hove 2004
Best bowling: 3-33 Sussex v Surrey, Hove 2005
Stop press: Called up as a replacement to the England A tour to West Indies 2005-06

2005 Season

	M	Inns	NO	Runs	HS	Avge	100s	50s	Ct	St	O	M	Runs	Wkts	Avge	Best	5wl	10wM
Test																		
All First	7	8	0	126	37	15.75	-	-	5	-	111	23	329	13	25.30	3-33	-	-
1-Day Int																		
C & G	3	1	0	1	1	1.00	-	-	-	-	26	2	96	3	32.00	1-23	-	
tsL	13	8	2	100	35	16.66	-	-	5	-	87	4	362	19	19.05	3-20	-	
Twenty20	8	3	1	4	2	2.00	-	-	1	-	14	0	120	5	24.00	1-6	-	

Career Performances

	M	Inns	NO	Runs	HS	Avge	100s	50s	Ct	St	Balls	Runs	Wkts	Avge	Best	5wl	10wM
Test																	
All First	10	13	1	255	100	21.25	1	-	6	-	983	528	14	37.71	3-33	-	-
1-Day Int																	
C & G	5	3	0	38	21	12.66	-	-	1	-	204	139	3	46.33	1-23	-	
tsL	29	21	5	241	35	15.06	-	-	6	-	1042	788	31	25.41	4-12	-	
Twenty20	12	6	1	23	18	4.60	-	-	2	-	168	231	11	21.00	3-39	-	

YARDY, M. H.   Sussex

Name: Michael (Mike) Howard Yardy
Role: Left-hand bat, left-arm medium/spin bowler
Born: 27 November 1980, Pembury, Kent
Height: 6ft **Weight:** 14st 2lbs
Nickname: Yards, Paolo
County debut: 1999 (one-day), 2000 (first-class)
County cap: 2005
1000 runs in a season: 1
1st-Class 200s: 1
Place in batting averages: 21st av. 56.29 (2004 120th av. 34.14)
Strike rate: (career 111.92)
Parents: Beverly and Howard

Wife and date of marriage: Karin, October 2005

Family links with cricket: 'Brother plays for local team'

Education: William Parker School, Hastings

Qualifications: 5 GCSEs, 2 A-levels, ECB Level 1 coach, Sports Psychology diploma

Overseas tours: Sussex Academy to Barbados 1997; Sussex to Grenada 2001, 2002; England A to West Indies 2005-06

Overseas teams played for: Cape Town CC 1999

Career highlights to date: 'Winning County Championship'

Cricket superstitions: 'Loads – all secret'

Cricketers particularly admired: 'All those who have reached the pinnacle of their careers'

Other sports followed: Football (West Ham)

Favourite band: Bluetones

Relaxations: 'Watching West Ham; relaxing with my wife'

Extras: Played for Sussex U15, U16 and U19. Represented England U17. Attended Sussex Academy. Sussex Most Improved Player 2001. His 257 v Bangladeshis at Hove 2005 is the highest individual score for Sussex against a touring side; also took 5-83 in Bangladeshis' second innings. ECB National Academy 2005-06

Best batting: 257 Sussex v Bangladeshis, Hove 2005

Best bowling: 5-83 Sussex v Bangladeshis, Hove 2005

2005 Season

	M	Inns	NO	Runs	HS	Avge	100s	50s	Ct	St	O	M	Runs	Wkts	Avge	Best	5wI	10wM
Test																		
All First	18	30	3	1520	257	56.29	5	6	16	-	67.2	10	252	9	28.00	5-83	1	-
1-Day Int																		
C & G	3	3	1	61	33 *	30.50	-	-	1	-	10	1	38	0	-		-	-
tsL	18	17	1	244	65	15.25	-	2	9	-	32	0	173	15	11.53	6-27	1	
Twenty20	5	3	2	51	28	51.00	-	-	1	-	7	0	63	0	-		-	-

Career Performances

	M	Inns	NO	Runs	HS	Avge	100s	50s	Ct	St	Balls	Runs	Wkts	Avge	Best	5wI	10wM
Test																	
All First	56	96	11	3245	257	38.17	6	14	43	-	1454	862	13	66.30	5-83	1	-
1-Day Int																	
C & G	13	12	1	190	52	17.27	-	1	5	-	338	304	6	50.66	3-39	-	
tsL	52	48	5	851	88 *	19.79	-	4	22	-	656	589	23	25.60	6-27	1	
Twenty20	9	6	2	83	28	20.75	-	-	5	-	42	63	0	-		-	-

YATES, G.   Lancashire

Name: Gary Yates
Role: Right-hand bat, right-arm
off-spin bowler; 2nd XI captain/coach
Born: 20 September 1967,
Ashton-under-Lyne
Height: 6ft 1in **Weight:** 13st 1lb
Nickname: Sweaty, Yugo, Pearly,
Backyard, Zippy
County debut: 1990
County cap: 1994
Benefit: 2005
Strike rate: (career 74.73)
Parents: Alan and Patricia
Wife and date of marriage: Christine,
20 February 2004
Children: Francis Leonard George,
1 May 1999
Family links with cricket: 'Father played for
Denton St Lawrence and other teams in the Lancashire League'
Education: Manchester Grammar School
Qualifications: 6 O-levels, ECB Level III coach, Australian Cricket Coaching
Council coach
Career outside cricket: 'Sales rep with family business (Digical Ltd), selling diaries,
calendars and business gifts'
Overseas tours: Lancashire to Tasmania and Western Australia 1990, to Western
Australia 1991, to Johannesburg 1992, to Barbados and St Lucia 1992, to Calcutta
1997, to Cape Town 1997-98, to Grenada 2003; MCC to Bangladesh 1999-2000
Overseas teams played for: South Barwon, Geelong, Australia 1987-88; Johnsonville,
Wellington, New Zealand 1989-90; Western Suburbs, Brisbane 1991-92; Old
Selbornian, East London, South Africa 1992-93; Hermanus CC, South Africa 1995-96
Career highlights to date: 'All trophies won while playing with Lancashire'
Cricket moments to forget: 'Not being selected for a 2nd XI Bain Hogg final after
playing all ten round matches and semi-final'
Cricket superstitions: 'They vary'
Cricketers particularly admired: Michael Atherton, Ian Botham, John Emburey
Other sports played: Golf ('represented Lancashire CCC at National *Times* Corporate
Golf Challenge, La Manga, Spain, December 2001')
Other sports followed: 'All sports, especially football (Manchester City), golf,
motor rallying'
Relaxations: 'Playing golf, watching football and good films, eating; spending time
with my son'

Extras: Scored century (106) on Championship debut v Nottinghamshire at Trent Bridge 1990. Rapid Cricketline Player of the Month April/May 1992. Lancashire 2nd XI captain/coach since 2002
Best batting: 134* Lancashire v Northamptonshire, Old Trafford 1993
Best bowling: 6-64 Lancashire v Kent, Old Trafford 1999

2005 Season (did not make any first-class or one-day appearances)

Career Performances

	M	Inns	NO	Runs	HS	Avge	100s	50s	Ct	St	Balls	Runs	Wkts	Avge	Best	5wI	10wM
Test																	
All First	82	107	36	1789	134 *	25.19	3	5	38	-	13751	7025	184	38.17	6-64	5	-
1-Day Int																	
C & G	22	10	5	91	34 *	18.20	-	-	5	-	1266	712	19	37.47	2-15	-	
tsL	115	53	25	435	38	15.53	-	-	28	-	4122	3309	105	31.51	4-34	-	
Twenty20																	

YOUNIS KHAN   Nottinghamshire

Name: Mohammad Younis Khan
Role: Right-hand bat, leg-break bowler, occasional wicket-keeper
Born: 29 November 1977, Mardan, Pakistan
County debut: 2005
Test debut: 1999-2000
1st-Class 200s: 5
Place in batting averages: 204th av. 21.83
Strike rate: (career 85.16)
Overseas tours: Pakistan to Sharjah (Coca-Cola Sharjah Cup) 1999-2000, to West Indies 1999-2000, to Sri Lanka 2000, to New Zealand 2000-01, to England 2001, to Bangladesh 2001-02, to Sharjah (v West Indies) 2001-02, to Sri Lanka (ICC Champions Trophy) 2002-03, to Sri Lanka and Sharjah (v Australia) 2002-03, to Zimbabwe and South Africa 2002-03, to

Africa (World Cup) 2002-03, to New Zealand 2003-04, to Australia 2004-05, to India 2004-05, to West Indies 2004-05, plus other one-day tournaments in Abu Dhabi, Singapore, Sharjah, Australia, Morocco, Kenya, Sri Lanka, England, Holland and India
Overseas teams played for: Peshawar 1998-99 –; Habib Bank 1999-2000 –
Extras: Took a Test innings record for a substitute of four catches v Bangladesh in the Asian Test Championship 2001-02. Has won several match awards, including Man of

the Match v Zimbabwe at Peshawar in the Paktel Cup 2004-05 (77) and in the third Test v India at Bangalore 2004-05 (267/84*). Vice-captain of Pakistan since the tour to India of 2004-05. Was an overseas player with Nottinghamshire during the 2005 season as a locum for Stephen Fleming

Best batting: 267 Pakistan v India, Bangalore 2004-05
Best bowling: 3-24 Habib Bank v Faisalabad, Faisalabad 1999-2000

2005 Season

	M	Inns	NO	Runs	HS	Avge	100s	50s	Ct	St	O	M	Runs	Wkts	Avge	Best	5wI	10wM
Test																		
All First	5	7	1	131	53	21.83	-	1	4	-	37.1	1	151	4	37.75	2-21	-	-
1-Day Int																		
C & G																			
tsL	3	2	1	54	28 *	54.00	-	-	1	-	10.2	1	36	6	6.00	3-5	-	
Twenty20																		

Career Performances

	M	Inns	NO	Runs	HS	Avge	100s	50s	Ct	St	Balls	Runs	Wkts	Avge	Best	5wI	10wM
Test	37	65	3	2765	267	44.59	9	11	41	-	240	164	2	82.00	1-24	-	-
All First	87	138	14	5965	267	48.10	20	24	92	-	1022	651	12	54.25	3-24	-	-
1-Day Int	118	113	14	3091	144	31.22	1	20	66	-	90	99	1	99.00	1-24	-	
C & G																	
tsL	3	2	1	54	28 *	54.00	-	-	1	-	62	36	6	6.00	3-5	-	
Twenty20																	

STOP PRESS

JOHNSON, M. G.   Essex

Name: <u>Mitchell</u> Guy Johnson
Role: Left-hand bat, left-arm fast-medium bowler
Born: 2 November 1981, Townsville, Australia
Extras: Made ODI debut for Australia v New Zealand at Christchurch 2005-06. Has joined Essex as an overseas player for the early part of the 2006 season

---

100. Who were the captains in the first ODI,
which took place on 5 January 1971?

THE UMPIRES

BAILEY, R. J.

Name: Robert (Rob) John Bailey
Born: 28 October 1963, Biddulph,
Stoke-on-Trent
Height: 6ft 3in
Nickname: Bailers
Wife and date of marriage: Rachel,
11 April 1987
Children: Harry, 7 March 1991; Alexandra,
13 November 1993
Family links with cricket: 'Dad Minor
Counties player – Staffordshire; brother plays
in Staffs league'
Education: Biddulph High School
Career outside cricket: Rob Bailey
Ceramics ('promotional mugs etc.')
Off-season: 'Selling pottery'
Other sports played: Badminton (county
schools)
Other sports followed: Football (Stoke City FC)
Appointed to 1st-Class list: 2006
Counties as player: Northamptonshire, Derbyshire
Role: Right-hand bat, off-spin bowler
County debut: 1982 (Northamptonshire), 2000 (Derbyshire)
County cap: 1985 (Northamptonshire), 2000 (Derbyshire)
Benefit: 1993 (Northamptonshire)
Test debut: 1988
Tests: 4
One-Day Internationals: 4
1000 runs in a season: 13
1st-Class 200s: 4
One-Day 100s: 9
One-Day 5 w. in innings: 1
Overseas tours: England to Sharjah 1984-85, 1986-87, to India 1988-89 (cancelled),
to West Indies 1989-90
Overseas teams played for: Rhodes University, Grahamstown, South Africa 1982-83;
Uitenhage CC, South Africa 1983-85; Fitzroy CC, Melbourne 1985-86; Gosnells CC,
Perth 1987-88
Highlights of playing career: 'Loved all of it'
Extras: Won three consecutive NatWest Man of the Match awards 1995 and three
consecutive B&H Gold Awards 1996. Northamptonshire captain 1996-97. In 1999
became sixth player to pass 20,000 first-class runs for Northamptonshire

Best batting: 224* Northamptonshire v Glamorgan, Swansea 1986
Best bowling: 5-54 Northamptonshire v Nottinghamshire, Northampton 1993

First-Class Career Performances

	M	Inns	NO	Runs	HS	Avge	100s	Ct	St	Runs	Wkts	Avge	Best	5wI	10wM
Test	4	8	0	119	43	14.87	-	-	-						
All First	374	628	89	21844	224*	40.52	47	272	-	5144	121	42.51	5-54	2	-

BAINTON, N. L.

Name: Neil Laurence Bainton
Born: 2 October 1970, Romford, Essex
Height: 5ft 8in
Wife and date of marriage: Kay,
25 October 1997
Family links with cricket: Father played and
umpired club cricket
Education: Ilford County High School
Career outside cricket: Postman
Off-season: 'Postman in Braintree, Essex'
Other sports followed: Football (West
Ham), 'most sports'
Appointed to 1st-Class list: 2006
Highlights of umpiring career: 'Being
appointed to first-class list'
Players to watch for the future: Tom
Westley (Essex), Billy Godleman
County as player: Did not play first-class
cricket

Did not play first-class cricket

BENSON, M. R.

Name: <u>Mark</u> Richard Benson
Born: 6 July 1958, Shoreham, Sussex
Height: 5ft 10in
Nickname: Benny
Wife and date of marriage: Sarah Patricia,
20 September 1986
Children: Laurence, 16 October 1987;
Edward, 23 June 1990
Education: Sutton Valence School
Off-season: 'Improving my golf and bridge'
Other sports played: Bridge, golf,
swimming, cycling
Relaxations: Bridge, golf
Appointed to 1st-Class list: 2000
International panel: 2004 –
Tests umpired: 6 (plus 6 as TV umpire)
One-Day Internationals umpired: 24
(plus 9 as TV umpire)
Other umpiring honours: Stood in the C&G Trophy final 2003
County as player: Kent
Role: Left-hand bat
County debut: 1980
County cap: 1981
Benefit: 1991 (£174,619)
Test debut: 1986
Tests: 1
One-Day Internationals: 1
1000 runs in a season: 11
1st-Class 200s: 1
One-Day 100s: 5
Overseas tours: None
Highlights of playing career: '257 v Hampshire. Winning Sunday League as captain
of Kent. Two 90s to win a game against Hampshire with Malcolm Marshall bowling.
One of only four cricketers in the history of Kent to have scored more than 10,000
runs and have an average in excess of 40'
Extras: Scored 1000 runs in first full season. Kent captain 1991-95
Opinions on cricket: 'Teams should be permitted a certain number of appeals against
poor decisions. As an umpire I would be quite happy for a decision to be overturned if
a mistake has been made. If the umpire has been proved to be correct, the team that
has appealed loses one of their appeals. This occurs in American football and works
very well.'

Best batting: 257 Kent v Hampshire, Southampton 1991
Best bowling: 2-55 Kent v Surrey, Dartford 1986

First-Class Career Performances

	M	Inns	NO	Runs	HS	Avge	100s	Ct	St	Runs	Wkts	Avge	Best	5wl	10wM
Test	1	2	0	51	30	25.50	-	-	-						
All First	292	491	34	18387	257	40.23	48	140	-	493	5	98.60	2-55	-	-

BURGESS, G. I.

Name: <u>Graham</u> Iefvion Burgess
Born: 5 May 1943, Glastonbury, Somerset
Education: Millfield School
Appointed to 1st-Class list: 1991
One-Day Internationals umpired: 2 as
TV umpire
County as player: Somerset
Role: Right-hand bat, right-arm
medium bowler
County debut: 1966
County cap: 1968
Testimonial: 1977
One-Day 5 w. in innings: 2
Extras: Played Minor Counties cricket for
Wiltshire 1981-82 and for Cambridgeshire
1983-84
Best batting: 129 Somerset v
Gloucestershire, Taunton 1973

Best bowling: 7-43 Somerset v Oxford University, The Parks 1975

First-Class Career Performances

	M	Inns	NO	Runs	HS	Avge	100s	Ct	St	Runs	Wkts	Avge	Best	5wl	10wM
Test															
All First	252	414	37	7129	129	18.90	2	120	-	13543	474	28.57	7-43	18	2

CONSTANT, D. J.

Name: <u>David</u> John Constant
Born: 9 November 1941,
Bradford-on-Avon, Wiltshire
Height: 5ft 7in
Nickname: Connie
Wife's name: Rosalyn
Children: Lisa, 6 July 1966;
Julie, 21 February 1969
Family links with cricket: Father-in-law,
G.E.E. Lambert, played for Gloucestershire
Education: Grove Park Secondary Modern
Off-season: Bowls
Other sports followed: Football (Millwall)
Interests/relaxations: 'Six grandchildren
and bowls'
Appointed to 1st-Class list: 1969
First appointed to Test panel: 1971
Tests umpired: 36 (plus 5 as TV umpire)
One-Day Internationals umpired: 33 (plus 5 as TV umpire)
Other umpiring honours: Stood in 1975, 1979 and 1983 World Cups
Counties as player: Kent, Leicestershire
Role: Left-hand bat, slow left-arm bowler
County debut: 1961 (Kent), 1965 (Leicestershire)
Extras: County bowls player for Gloucestershire 1984-86 (outdoor). Also represented
Somerset at indoor version of the game in the Liberty Trophy
Best batting: 80 Leicestershire v Gloucestershire, Bristol 1966
Best bowling: 1-28 Leicestershire v Surrey, The Oval 1968

First-Class Career Performances

	M	Inns	NO	Runs	HS	Avge	100s	Ct	St	Runs	Wkts	Avge	Best	5wI	10wM
Test															
All First	61	93	14	1517	80	19.20	-	33	-	36	1	36.00	1-28	-	-

COWLEY, N. G.

Name: <u>Nigel</u> Geoffrey Cowley
Born: 1 March 1953, Shaftesbury, Dorset
Height: 5ft 6½in
Marital status: Divorced
Children: Mark Antony, 14 June 1973;
Darren James, 30 October 1976
Family links with cricket: Darren played
Hampshire Schools U11, U12, U13; Natal
Schools 1993, 1994, 1995; and toured India
with South Africa U19 1996
Education: Duchy Manor, Mere, Wiltshire
Other sports played: Golf (8 handicap)
Other sports followed: Football
(Liverpool FC)
Appointed to 1st-Class list: 2000
Counties as player: Hampshire, Glamorgan
Role: Right-hand bat, off-spin bowler
County debut: 1974 (Hampshire),
1990 (Glamorgan)
County cap: 1978 (Hampshire)
Benefit: 1988 (Hampshire; £88,274)
1000 runs in a season: 1
50 wickets in a season: 2
One-Day 5 w. in innings: 1
Overseas tours: Hampshire to Barbados 1985, 1986, 1987, to Dubai 1989
Overseas teams played for: Paarl CC, 1982-83; Amanzimtoti, 1984-96
(both South Africa)
Extras: Played for Dorset 1972. NatWest Man of the Match award
Best batting: 109* Hampshire v Somerset, Taunton 1977
Best bowling: 6-48 Hampshire v Leicestershire, Southampton 1982

First-Class Career Performances

	M	Inns	NO	Runs	HS	Avge	100s	Ct	St	Runs	Wkts	Avge	Best	5wI	10wM
Test															
All First	271	375	62	7309	109*	23.35	2	105	-	14879	437	34.04	6-48	5	-

DUDLESTON, B.

Name: Barry Dudleston
Born: 16 July 1945, Bebington, Cheshire
Height: 5ft 9in
Nickname: Danny
Wife and date of marriage: Louise Wendy,
19 October 1994
Children: Sharon Louise, 29 October 1968;
Matthew Barry, 12 September 1988;
Jack Nicholas, 29 April 1998
Family links with cricket: 'Dad was a
league cricketer'
Education: Stockport School
Career outside cricket: Managing director
of Sunsport Ltd
Other sports played: Golf
Other sports followed: All sports
Relaxations: Bridge, red wine
Appointed to 1st-Class list: 1984
First appointed to Test panel: 1991

Tests umpired: 2 (plus 4 as TV umpire)
One-Day Internationals umpired: 4 (plus 6 as TV umpire)
Other umpiring honours: Stood in C&G final 2001 and B&H final 2002; also
officiated at the inaugural Twenty20 finals day at Trent Bridge 2003, including
standing in the final
Players to watch for the future: Stuart Broad
Counties as player: Leicestershire, Gloucestershire
Role: Right-hand opening bat, slow left-arm bowler, occasional wicket-keeper
County debut: 1966 (Leicestershire), 1981 (Gloucestershire)
County cap: 1969 (Leicestershire)
Benefit: 1980 (Leicestershire; £25,000)
1000 runs in a season: 8
1st-Class 200s: 1
One-Day 100s: 4
Overseas tours: Kent (as guest player) to West Indies 1972; D.H. Robins' XI
to West Indies 1973; Wisden XI to West Indies 1984; MCC to Kenya 1993
Overseas teams played for: Rhodesia 1976-80
Highlights of playing career: 'Winning County Championship [with Leicestershire]'
Extras: Played for England U25. Holder with John Steele of the highest first-wicket
partnership for Leics, 390 v Derbys at Leicester in 1979. Fastest player in Rhodesian
cricket history to 1000 first-class runs in Currie Cup; second fastest ever in Currie Cup
Opinions on cricket: 'My team-mate Duncan Fletcher is doing a great job.'

Best batting: 202 Leicestershire v Derbyshire, Leicester 1979
Best bowling: 4-6 Leicestershire v Surrey, Leicester 1972

First-Class Career Performances

	M	Inns	NO	Runs	HS	Avge	100s	Ct	St	Runs	Wkts	Avge	Best	5wI	10wM
Test															
All First	295	501	47	14747	202	32.48	32	234	7	1365	47	29.04	4-6	-	-

EVANS, J. H.

Name: Jeffrey (<u>Jeff</u>) Howard Evans
Born: 7 August 1954, Llanelli
Height: 5ft 8in
Education: Llanelli Boys Grammar School;
Dudley College of Education
Career outside cricket: Supply teacher
Off-season: Teaching; coaching
Other sports followed: 'Most sports, rugby
in particular'
Relaxations: Keeping fit, walking,
cycling, skiing
Appointed to 1st-Class list: 2001
Other umpiring honours: Toured Namibia
and Uganda 2004-05 with MCC (as umpire)
Highlights of umpiring career: 'First
Championship match – Yorkshire v Somerset
at Headingley 2001'
Cricket moments to forget: 'Any error of
judgement!'

County as player: Did not play first-class cricket. Played league cricket in South
Wales as a right-hand bat
Extras: Coach to Welsh Schools Cricket Association team on tour to Australia 1993.
Taught in the Gwendraeth Grammar School – 'the old "outside-half factory"'
Opinions on cricket: 'Would like to see more honesty throughout the game!'

Did not play first-class cricket

GOULD, I. J.

Name: Ian James Gould
Born: 19 August 1957, Taplow, Bucks
Height: 5ft 7in
Nickname: Gunner
Wife and date of marriage: Joanne,
27 September 1986
Children: Gemma; Michael; George
Education: Westgate Secondary Modern,
Slough
Career outside cricket: 'Learning to be a
groundsman'
Other sports played: Golf
Other sports followed: Football (Arsenal),
racing
Relaxations: 'Fending off ticket enquiries for
all England cricket in Australia!'
Appointed to 1st-Class list: 2002
Other umpiring honours: Officiated at the
Twenty20 finals days at Edgbaston 2004 and at The Oval 2005, including standing in
both finals. PCA Umpire of the Year 2005
Players to watch for the future: Ollie Rayner
Counties as player: Middlesex, Sussex
Role: Left-hand bat, wicket-keeper
County debut: 1975 (Middlesex), 1981 (Sussex)
County cap: 1977 (Middlesex), 1981 (Sussex)
Benefit: 1990 (Sussex; £87,097)
One-Day Internationals: 18
Overseas tours: England YC to West Indies 1976; D.H. Robins' XI to Canada
1978-79; International XI to Pakistan 1980-81; England to Australia and New Zealand
1982-83; MCC to Namibia
Overseas teams played for: Auckland 1979-80
Highlights of playing career: 'Playing in the World Cup'
Extras: Represented England in the 1983 World Cup. Retired from county cricket
in 1991
Opinions on cricket: 'Cricket seems to be going the right way. People seem more
positive about the game and I feel that they are enjoying playing.'
Best batting: 128 Middlesex v Worcestershire, Worcester 1978
Best bowling: 3-10 Sussex v Surrey, The Oval 1989

First-Class Career Performances

	M	Inns	NO	Runs	HS	Avge	100s	Ct	St	Runs	Wkts	Avge	Best	5wl	10wM
Test															
All First	297	399	63	8756	128	26.06	4	536	67	365	7	52.14	3-10	-	-

HARRIS, M. J.

Name: <u>Michael</u> John Harris
Born: 25 May 1944, St Just-in-Roseland, Cornwall
Height: 6ft 1in
Nickname: Pasty
Wife and date of marriage: Danielle Ruth, 10 September 1969
Children: Jodie; Richard
Education: Gerrans Comprehensive
Career outside cricket: Sports teacher
Other sports followed: Squash, golf
Appointed to 1st-Class list: 1998
Counties as player: Middlesex, Nottinghamshire
Role: Right-hand bat, leg-break bowler, wicket-keeper
County debut: 1964 (Middlesex), 1969 (Nottinghamshire)
County cap: 1967 (Middlesex), 1970 (Nottinghamshire)
1000 runs in a season: 11
1st-Class 200s: 1
One-Day 100s: 3
Overseas teams played for: Eastern Province 1971-72; Wellington 1975-76
Extras: Shared Middlesex then record first-wicket partnership of 312 with Eric Russell v Pakistanis at Lord's 1967. Scored nine centuries in 1971 to equal Nottinghamshire county record for a season, scoring two centuries in a match twice and totalling 2238 runs at an average of 50.86
Best batting: 201* Nottinghamshire v Glamorgan, Trent Bridge 1973
Best bowling: 4-16 Nottinghamshire v Warwickshire, Trent Bridge 1969

First-Class Career Performances

	M	Inns	NO	Runs	HS	Avge	100s	Ct	St	Runs	Wkts	Avge	Best	5wl	10wM
Test															
All First	344	581	58	19196	201*	36.70	41	288	14	3459	79	43.78	4-16	-	-

HARTLEY, P. J.

Name: <u>Peter</u> John Hartley
Born: 18 April 1960, Keighley, Yorkshire
Height: 6ft
Nickname: Jack
Wife and date of marriage: Sharon,
12 March 1988
Children: Megan, 25 April 1992;
Courtney, 25 July 1995
Family links with cricket: Father played
local league cricket
Education: Greenhead Grammar School,
Keighley; Bradford College
Career outside cricket: Sports footwear
agent
Off-season: Development and sales of
footwear within cricket
Other sports played: Golf, skiing
Other sports followed: Football (Chelsea)
Relaxations: 'Gardening, walking the hound'
Appointed to 1st-Class list: 2003
Counties as player: Warwickshire, Yorkshire, Hampshire
Role: Right-hand bat, right-arm fast-medium bowler
County debut: 1982 (Warwickshire), 1985 (Yorkshire), 1998 (Hampshire)
County cap: 1987 (Yorkshire), 1998 (Hampshire)
Benefit: 1996 (Yorkshire)
50 wickets in a season: 7
One-Day 5 w. in innings: 5
Overseas tours: Yorkshire pre-season tours to Barbados 1986-87, to South Africa
1991-92, 1992-93, to Zimbabwe
Overseas teams played for: Melville, New Zealand 1983-84; Adelaide, Australia
1985-86; Harmony and Orange Free State, South Africa 1988-89
Extras: Returned 8-65, his best figures for Hampshire, against Yorkshire, his former
county, at Basingstoke 1999. Recorded his highest B&H score (32*) and best one-day
analysis (5-20) v Sussex at Hove 2000. Retired at the end of the 2000 season
Best batting: 127* Yorkshire v Lancashire, Old Trafford 1988
Best bowling: 9-41 Yorkshire v Derbyshire, Chesterfield 1995

First-Class Career Performances

	M	Inns	NO	Runs	HS	Avge	100s	Ct	St	Runs	Wkts	Avge	Best	5wI	10wM
Test															
All First	232	283	66	4321	127*	19.91	2	68	-	20635	683	30.21	9-41	23	3

HOLDER, J. W.

Name: <u>John</u> Wakefield Holder
Born: 19 March 1945, Barbados
Height: 5ft 11in
Nickname: Benson
Wife's name: Glenda
Children: Christopher, 1968; Nigel, 1970
Education: Combermere High School,
Barbados; Rochdale College
Off-season: 'Relaxing initially, then working
part-time for the European Cricket Council;
keeping fit'
Other sports followed: Football
(Manchester United)
Relaxations: 'Regular visits to the gym
trying to keep fit. Love watching wildlife
programmes on TV and travel'
Appointed to 1st-Class list: 1983
First appointed to Test panel: 1988
Tests umpired: 11 (plus 5 as TV umpire)
One-Day Internationals umpired: 19 (plus 3 as TV umpire)
Other umpiring honours: Umpired in Nehru Cup in India and in Pakistan v India
Test series 1989-90. Umpired in Pepsi Champions Trophy, Sharjah 1993-94 and
Masters Cup, Sharjah 1995-96. MCC tours to Kenya 1999, 2002 and to Greece 2003
(as umpire). Has stood in Refuge Assurance Cup, B&H Cup and NatWest Trophy
finals and in C&G Trophy final 2002. Officiated at the inaugural Twenty20 finals day
at Trent Bridge 2003, including standing in the final, and at finals day at The Oval
2005
Highlights of umpiring career: 'Umpiring Lord's Ashes Test in 2001, when I
met the Queen'
County as player: Hampshire
Role: Right-hand bat, right-arm fast bowler
County debut: 1968
50 wickets in a season: 1
Highlights of playing career: 'Taking 6-7 against International Cavaliers in 1968'
Extras: Championship hat-trick v Kent at Southampton 1972. Retired from county
cricket in 1972
Opinions on cricket: 'A few years ago at Headingley, about two hours before the start
of a National League game, the entire Yorkshire playing staff sat at a row of tables
signing autographs for fans. This is an excellent idea which I believe every county
should copy for two matches every year. This would help foster better relations
between players and the public.'

Best batting: 33 Hampshire v Sussex, Hove 1971
Best bowling: 7-79 Hampshire v Gloucestershire, Gloucester 1972

First-Class Career Performances

	M	Inns	NO	Runs	HS	Avge	100s	Ct	St	Runs	Wkts	Avge	Best	5wI	10wM
Test															
All First	47	49	14	374	33	10.68	-	12	-	3415	139	24.56	7-79	5	1

HOLDER, V. A.

Name: <u>Vanburn</u> Alonza Holder
Born: 8 October 1945, St Michael, Barbados
Height: 6ft 3in
Nickname: Van
Wife's name: Christine
Children: James Vanburn, 2 September 1981
Education: St Leonard's Secondary Modern;
Community High
Other sports followed: Football (Liverpool)
Relaxations: Music, doing crosswords
Appointed to 1st-Class list: 1992
One-Day Internationals umpired: 2 as TV
umpire
County as player: Worcestershire
Role: Right-hand bat, right-arm
fast-medium bowler
County debut: 1968
County cap: 1970
Benefit: 1979
Test debut: 1969
Tests: 40

One-Day Internationals: 12
One-Day 5 w. in innings: 3
Overseas tours: West Indies to England 1969, 1973, 1975 (World Cup), 1976,
to India, Sri Lanka and Pakistan 1974-75, to Australia 1975-76, to India and Sri Lanka
1978-79 (vc); Rest of the World to Pakistan 1973-74
Overseas teams played for: Barbados 1966-78
Extras: Made his debut for Barbados in the Shell Shield competition in 1966-67. Won
John Player League 1973 and County Championship 1974 with Worcestershire. Played
in West Indies 1975 World Cup winning side
Best batting: 122 Barbados v Trinidad, Bridgetown 1973-74
Best bowling: 7-40 Worcestershire v Glamorgan, Cardiff 1974

	M	Inns	NO	Runs	HS	Avge	100s	Ct	St	Runs	Wkts	Avge	Best	5wI	10wM
Test	40	59	11	682	42	14.20	-	16	-	3627	109	33.27	6-28	3	-
All First	311	354	81	3559	122	13.03	1	98	-	23183	948	24.45	7-40	38	3

ILLINGWORTH, R. K.

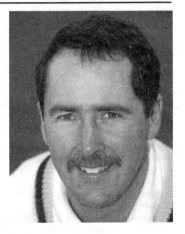

Name: Richard Keith Illingworth
Born: 23 August 1963, Greengates,
near Bradford, Yorkshire
Height: 5ft 11in
Nickname: Harry, Lucy, Illy
Wife and date of marriage: Anne Louise,
20 September 1985
Children: Miles, 28 August 1987; Thomas,
20 April 1989
Family links with cricket: Father played
Bradford League
Education: Salts GS
Off-season: 'Coaching'
Other sports played: Golf
Other sports followed: Football (Leeds),
rugby league (Bradford Bulls), rugby union
(Worcester)
Relaxations: 'Watching my two sons playing
sport; cooking; wine tasting'
Appointed to 1st-Class list: 2006
Counties as player: Worcestershire, Derbyshire
Role: Right-hand bat, left-arm orthodox spin bowler
County debut: 1982 (Worcestershire), 2001 (Derbyshire)
County cap: 1986 (Worcestershire)
Benefit: 1997 (Worcestershire; £271,275)
Test debut: 1991
Tests: 9
One-Day Internationals: 25
50 wickets in a season: 5
One-Day 5 w. in innings: 2
Overseas tours: England A to Kenya and Zimbabwe 1989-90, to Pakistan and Sri
Lanka 1990-91; England to New Zealand and Australia (World Cup) 1991-92, to South
Africa 1995-96, to India and Pakistan (World Cup) 1995-96
Overseas teams played for: Brisbane Colts 1982-83; Zingari, Pietermaritzburg, South
Africa 1984-85, 1988-89; University/St Heliers, New Zealand 1986-88; Natal 1988-
89; Abahani, Bangladesh 1994

Highlights of playing career: 'Playing for England. Being part of many Worcestershire trophy wins. Wicket [Phil Simmons of West Indies] with first ball in Test cricket'

Cricket moments to forget: 'None, apart from getting out for nought or dropping catches (of which there were a few)'

Extras: Scored three centuries batting as a nightwatchman. First Worcestershire bowler to take a one-day hat-trick, v Sussex at Hove in the Sunday League 1993. Retired at the end of the 2001 season

Best batting: 120* Worcestershire v Warwickshire, Worcester 1987

Best bowling: 7-50 Worcestershire v Oxford University, The Parks 1985

First-Class Career Performances

	M	Inns	NO	Runs	HS	Avge	100s	Ct	St	Runs	Wkts	Avge	Best	5wI	10wM
Test	9	14	7	128	28	18.28	-	5	-	615	19	32.36	4-96	-	-
All First	376	435	122	7027	120*	22.45	4	161	-	26213	831	31.54	7-50	27	6

JESTY, T. E.

Name: <u>Trevor</u> Edward Jesty
Born: 2 June 1948, Gosport, Hampshire
Height: 5ft 9in
Nickname: Jets
Wife and date of marriage: Jacqueline, 12 September 1970
Children: Graeme Barry, 27 September 1972; Lorna Samantha, 7 November 1976
Family links with cricket: Daughter played for England XI 2000
Education: Privett County Secondary Modern, Gosport
Off-season: Cricket coaching
Other sports followed: Football (Arsenal)
Relaxations: Gardening, reading
Appointed to 1st-Class list: 1994
One-Day Internationals umpired: 3 as TV umpire

Counties as player: Hampshire, Surrey, Lancashire
Role: Right-hand bat, right-arm medium bowler
County debut: 1966 (Hampshire), 1985 (Surrey), 1988 (Lancashire)
County cap: 1971 (Hampshire), 1985 (Surrey), 1990 (Lancashire)
Benefit: 1982 (Hampshire)
One-Day Internationals: 10
1000 runs in a season: 10

50 wickets in a season: 2
1st-Class 200s: 2
One-Day 100s: 7
Overseas tours: International XI to West Indies 1982; joined England tour to Australia 1982-83; Lancashire to Zimbabwe 1989
Overseas teams played for: Border, South Africa 1973-74; Griqualand West 1974-76, 1980-81; Canterbury, New Zealand 1979-80
Highlights of playing career: 'Winning Championship with Hampshire in 1973. Playing against Australia for England in one-day match on 1982-83 tour'
Extras: One of *Wisden*'s Five Cricketers of the Year 1983
Best batting: 248 Hampshire v Cambridge University, Fenner's 1984
Best bowling: 7-75 Hampshire v Worcestershire, Southampton 1976

First-Class Career Performances

	M	Inns	NO	Runs	HS	Avge	100s	Ct	St	Runs	Wkts	Avge	Best	5wI	10wM
Test															
All First	490	777	107	21916	248	32.71	35	265	1	16075	585	27.47	7-75	19	-

JONES, A. A.

Name: <u>Allan</u> Arthur Jones
Born: 9 December 1947, Horley, Surrey
Height: 6ft 4in
Nickname: Jonah
Wife and date of marriage: Stephanie, 11 December 2004
Education: St John's College, Horsham
Career outside cricket: Sports tours
Off-season: 'Enjoying life'
Other sports played: Golf
Other sports followed: Football (Arsenal)
Relaxations: English history, reading, cooking
Appointed to 1st-Class list: 1985
First appointed to Test panel: 1996
Tests umpired: 3 as TV umpire
One-Day Internationals umpired: 1 (plus 4 as TV umpire)
Other umpiring honours: Has umpired at

Hong Kong Sixes. Stood in the C&G final 2005 at Lord's. Former chairman of the First-Class Umpires' Association
Players to watch for the future: Ed Joyce
Counties as player: Sussex, Somerset, Middlesex, Glamorgan

Role: Right-hand bat, right-arm fast bowler
County debut: 1964 (Sussex), 1970 (Somerset), 1976 (Middlesex), 1980 (Glamorgan)
County cap: 1972 (Somerset), 1976 (Middlesex)
50 wickets in a season: 4
One-Day 5 w. in innings: 5
Overseas teams played for: Northern Transvaal 1971-72; Orange Free State 1976-77; Auckland (Birkenhead)
Highlights of playing career: '9-51 v Sussex 1972'
Extras: Won two Championship medals with Middlesex (1976 and 1977). Was on stand-by for England tour of India 1976-77. Represented MCC v Australians 1977. Was the first person to play for four counties
Best batting: 33 Middlesex v Kent, Canterbury 1978
Best bowling: 9-51 Somerset v Sussex, Hove 1972

First-Class Career Performances

	M	Inns	NO	Runs	HS	Avge	100s	Ct	St	Runs	Wkts	Avge	Best	5wI	10wM
Test															
All First	214	216	68	799	33	5-39	-	50	-	15414	549	28.07	9-51	23	3

KETTLEBOROUGH, R. A.

Name: Richard Allan Kettleborough
Born: 15 March 1973, Sheffield
Height: 5ft 10in
Nickname: Ketts
Marital status: Single
Family links with cricket: 'Dad played for Yorkshire 2nd XI and in league cricket'
Education: Worksop College; Airedale and Wharfdale College
Career outside cricket: Groundsman
Off-season: 'Working on the grounds'
Other sports played: Football
Other sports followed: Football (Sheffield Wednesday FC)
Relaxations: 'Spending time with girlfriend Lucy, and socialising with friends in Sheffield'

Appointed to 1st-Class list: 2006
Highlights of umpiring career: 'All the first-class matches in which I have stood and also the international club 20/20 tournament in 2005'
Players to watch for the future: Alastair Cook, Tom Smith
Counties as player: Yorkshire, Middlesex

Role: Left-hand bat
County debut: 1994 (Yorkshire), 1998 (Middlesex)
Overseas tours: England U18 to Canada 1991; Yorkshire to South Africa 1994, to Zimbabwe 1995, to West Indies 1996; MCC to Hong Kong 2000, to Kenya 2001, to Australia 2002-03, to UAE 2004, to Namibia and Uganda 2005, to India 2006
Overseas teams played for: Somerset West, Cape Town 1993-94; Constantia, Cape Town 2003
Highlights of playing career: 'Yorkshire debut 1994. Maiden first-class hundred v Essex 1996. Winning National Knockout with Sheffield Collegiate CC in 2000'
Cricket moments to forget: 'The years 1998 and 1999 spent in London'
Extras: MCC Young Cricketer of the Year 1988
Opinions on cricket: 'The number of non-English-qualified players needs reducing in order for good young players to break into first-class cricket and not stagnate in county second teams.'
Best batting: 108 Yorkshire v Essex, Headingley 1996
Best bowling: 2-26 Yorkshire v Nottinghamshire, Scarborough 1996

First-Class Career Performances

	M	Inns	NO	Runs	HS	Avge	100s	Ct	St	Runs	Wkts	Avge	Best	5wI	10wM
Test															
All First	33	56	6	1258	108	25.16	1	20	-	243	3	81.00	2-26	-	-

LEADBEATER, B.

Name: Barrie Leadbeater
Born: 14 August 1943, Leeds
Height: 6ft
Nickname: Leady
Marital status: Widower
Wife and date of marriage: Jacqueline, 18 September 1971 (deceased 1997)
Children: Richard Barrie, 23 November 1972; Michael Spencer, 21 March 1976; Daniel Mark Ronnie, 19 June 1981
Education: Harehills County Secondary, Leeds
Career outside cricket: LGV Class 1 driver
Other sports played: Golf, snooker, table tennis
Other sports followed: All sport – football (Leeds United), rugby league (Leeds Rhinos)
Relaxations: 'Reading, going to the pub, running'

Appointed to 1st-Class list: 1981
Tests umpired: 2 as TV umpire
One-Day Internationals umpired: 5 (plus 2 as TV umpire)
Other umpiring honours: Stood in 1983 World Cup. MCC tours to New Zealand 1999 and to Argentina and Chile 2001. Former chairman of the First-Class Umpires' Association
County as player: Yorkshire
Role: Right-hand opening bat, right-arm medium bowler, slip fielder
County debut: 1966
County cap: 1969
Benefit: 1980 (joint benefit with G.A. Cope)
Overseas tours: Duke of Norfolk's XI to West Indies 1970
Overseas teams played for: Johannesburg Municipals 1978-79
Highlights of playing career: 'Man of the Match in Gillette Cup final 1969'
Cricket moments to forget: 'I've forgotten'
Extras: Took part in London Marathon 1997, 1998, 2000. Retired from county cricket in 1979 and played social cricket
Best batting: 140* Yorkshire v Hampshire, Portsmouth 1976
Best bowling: 1-1 Yorkshire v Middlesex, Headingley 1971

First-Class Career Performances

	M	Inns	NO	Runs	HS	Avge	100s	Ct	St	Runs	Wkts	Avge	Best	5wl	10wM
Test															
All First	147	241	29	5373	140*	25.34	1	82	-	5	1	5.00	1-1	-	-

LLONG, N. J.

Name: Nigel James Llong
Born: 11 February 1969, Ashford, Kent
Height: 6ft
Nickname: Nidge
Wife and date of marriage: Melissa, 20 February 1999
Children: Andrew Stuart, 30 August 2002; Matthew James, 14 December 2004
Family links with cricket: Father and brother played local club cricket
Education: North School for Boys, Ashford
Off-season: Coaching – Duke of York School, Dover
Other sports followed: Football (Arsenal), 'generally most sports'
Relaxations: Fishing
Appointed to 1st-Class list: 2002
International panel: 2004 – (as TV umpire)
Tests umpired: 4 as TV umpire
One-Day Internationals umpired: 10 as TV umpire
Other umpiring honours: Officiated at the Twenty20 finals day at Edgbaston 2004,

including standing in the final, and in the
Twenty20 international between England and
Australia at the Rose Bowl 2005
County as player: Kent
Role: Left-hand bat, right-arm
off-spin bowler
County debut: 1991
County cap: 1993
One-Day 100s: 2
Overseas tours: Kent to Zimbabwe 1993
Overseas teams played for: Ashburton,
Melbourne 1988-90, 1996-97; Greenpoint,
Cape Town 1990-95
Highlights of playing career: 'B&H final
1997. Sunday League winners 1995. First
Championship hundred, Lord's 1993'
Cricket moments to forget: 'Sunday League
[1993], last match against Glamorgan
at Canterbury – lost the match and were runners-up. Plus not making the most of
my ability'
Extras: Kent Young Player of the Year 1992. Man of the Match in 2nd XI Trophy
semi-final and final 1999. Retired from county cricket in September 1999 and played
for Norfolk in 2000
Opinions on cricket: 'Good pitches produce good players. One overseas player per
county, especially now with so many Kolpak [*see page 9*] players.'
Best batting: 130 Kent v Hampshire, Canterbury 1996
Best bowling: 5-21 Kent v Middlesex, Canterbury 1996

First-Class Career Performances

	M	Inns	NO	Runs	HS	Avge	100s	Ct	St	Runs	Wkts	Avge	Best	5wI	10wM
Test															
All First	68	108	11	3024	130	31.17	6	59	-	1259	35	35.97	5-21	2	-

LLOYDS, J. W.

Name: <u>Jeremy</u> William Lloyds
Born: 17 November 1954, Penang, Malaya
Height: 5ft 11in
Nickname: Jerry
Wife and date of marriage: Janine,
16 September 1997
Children: Kaeli, 16 November 1991
Family links with cricket: Father played
cricket in Malaya. Brother Chris played for
Somerset 2nd XI
Education: Blundell's School, Tiverton
Career outside cricket: Coaching and setting
up Western Province Youth Programme 1992-
95 in South Africa
Other sports played: Golf (6 handicap)
Other sports followed: Golf, football
(Tottenham Hotspur), American football
(San Francisco 49ers), Formula One and
saloon car racing, rugby (Gloucester)
Relaxations: 'Reading, music and spending time at home with my family'
Appointed to 1st-Class list: 1998
International panel: 2002-2004 as TV umpire; 2004 –
Tests umpired: 5 (plus 10 as TV umpire)
One-Day Internationals umpired: 16 (plus 22 as TV umpire)
Other umpiring honours: Stood in the Twenty20 international between England and
Australia at the Rose Bowl 2005
Counties as player: Somerset, Gloucestershire
Role: Left-hand bat, off-spin bowler
County debut: 1979 (Somerset), 1985 (Gloucestershire)
County cap: 1982 (Somerset), 1985 (Gloucestershire)
1000 runs in a season: 3
Overseas tours: Somerset to Antigua 1982; Gloucestershire to Barbados 1985,
to Sri Lanka 1987
Overseas teams played for: St Stithian's Old Boys, Johannesburg 1978-79; Toombull
DCC, Brisbane 1980-82; North Sydney District 1982-83; Alberton, Johannesburg
1984; Preston CC, Melbourne 1986; Orange Free State 1987; Fish Hoek CC,
Cape Town 1988-92
Highlights of playing career: 'Winning 1983 NatWest final'
Extras: Highest score in Brisbane Premier League 1980-81 (165). Britannic Player of
the Month July 1987. Gloucestershire Player of the Year 1987. Leading run-scorer in
Western Province Cricket League 1988, 1989

Opinions on cricket: 'Too much overseas influence on how to play the game in England. We have more variations in wickets and weather conditions than in most other countries. Yes, take the best of what they have and work it into our game. Also, too much emphasis on all the various levels of coaching certificates. We have been dragged too far away from the *basics* – batting, bowling and fielding. The game hasn't really changed – people's perception of it has! We show people how to play but not the thinking side of it. At times, some players are too robotic. Whatever happened to natural flair?'
Best batting: 132* Somerset v Northamptonshire, Northampton 1982
Best bowling: 7-88 Somerset v Essex, Chelmsford 1982

First-Class Career Performances

	M	Inns	NO	Runs	HS	Avge	100s	Ct	St	Runs	Wkts	Avge	Best	5wl	10wM
Test															
All First	267	408	64	10679	132*	31.04	10	229	-	12943	333	38.86	7-88	13	1

MALLENDER, N. A.

Name: <u>Neil</u> Alan Mallender
Born: 13 August 1961, Kirk Sandall, Doncaster
Height: 6ft
Nickname: Ghostie
Marital status: Divorced
Children: Kirstie, 17; Dominic, 14; Jacob, 9
Education: Beverley Grammar School
Other sports played: Golf (2 handicap)
Other sports followed: 'Most sports'
Relaxations: 'Most sports; music'
Appointed to 1st-Class list: 1999
International panel: 2002-2004
Tests umpired: 3 (plus 5 as TV umpire)
One-Day Internationals umpired: 22
(plus 9 as TV umpire)
Other umpiring honours: Went with MCC
to umpire in Namibia March/April 2001.

PCA Umpire of the Year 2001, 2002, 2003, 2004. Stood in the 2002-03 World Cup. Umpired the 2004 and 2005 C&G Trophy finals
Highlights of umpiring career: 'First ODI at Lord's, England v Pakistan – and game went to the last ball'
Players to watch for the future: James Hildreth, Liam Plunkett, Stuart Broad
Counties as player: Northamptonshire, Somerset
Role: Right-hand bat, right-arm fast-medium bowler

County debut: 1980 (Northamptonshire), 1987 (Somerset)
County cap: 1984 (Northamptonshire), 1987 (Somerset)
Benefit: 1994 (Somerset)
Test debut: 1992
Tests: 2
50 wickets in a season: 6
One-Day 5 w. in innings: 3
Overseas tours: England YC to West Indies 1979-80
Overseas teams played for: Kaikorai, Dunedin, New Zealand; University, Wellington, New Zealand; Otago, New Zealand 1983-84 – 1992-93
Highlights of playing career: 'Test debut at Headingley'
Extras: Represented England YC 1980-81. Took 5-50 on Test debut v Pakistan at Headingley in 1992. Retired from county cricket in 1996
Opinions on cricket: 'In 25 years involved in the game I have never known such interest and enthusiasm for cricket as [in] the summer of 2005. It shows what a great game it is and we are so lucky to be involved!'
Best batting: 100* Otago v Central Districts, Palmerston North 1991-92
Best bowling: 7-27 Otago v Auckland, Auckland 1984-85

First-Class Career Performances

	M	Inns	NO	Runs	HS	Avge	100s	Ct	St	Runs	Wkts	Avge	Best	5wI	10wM
Test	2	3	0	8	4	2.66	-	-	-	215	10	21.50	5-50	1	-
All First	345	396	122	4709	100*	17.18	1	111	-	24654	937	26.31	7-27	36	5

PALMER, R.

Name: Roy Palmer
Born: 12 July 1942, Hampshire
Height: 6ft 3in
Nickname: Arp
Wife and date of marriage: Alyne,
5 November 1983
Children: Nick, 7 October 1968
Family links with cricket: Brother of Ken
Palmer, former Test umpire and Somerset
player; nephew Gary also played for
Somerset
Education: Southbroom Secondary Modern,
Devizes
Off-season: Golf, DIY
Relaxations: Golf
Appointed to 1st-Class list: 1980
First appointed to Test panel: 1992
Tests umpired: 2 (plus 1 as TV umpire)
One-Day Internationals umpired: 8 (plus 2 as TV umpire)
Other umpiring honours: Stood in 1983 World Cup
Players to watch for the future: Ian Bell, Matt Prior
County as player: Somerset
Role: Right-hand bat, right-arm fast-medium bowler
County debut: 1965
50 wickets in a season: 1
One-Day 5 w. in innings: 1
Extras: Won two Man of the Match Awards in the Gillette Cup
Best batting: 84 Somerset v Leicestershire, Taunton 1967
Best bowling: 6-45 Somerset v Middlesex, Lord's 1967

First-Class Career Performances

	M	Inns	NO	Runs	HS	Avge	100s	Ct	St	Runs	Wkts	Avge	Best	5wI	10wM
Test															
All First	74	110	32	1037	84	13.29	-	25	-	5439	172	31.62	6-45	4	-

SHARP, G.

Name: George Sharp
Born: 12 March 1950, West Hartlepool,
County Durham
Height: 5ft 11in
Nickname: Sharpy, Blunt, Razor, Toffee
Wife and date of marriage: Audrey,
14 September 1974
Children: Gareth James, 27 June 1984
Education: Elwick Road Secondary Modern,
Hartlepool
Career outside cricket: Watching all sports
Off-season: Working as joint director of GSB
Loams Ltd for soils and top dressing
Other sports played: Golf (8 handicap)
Other sports followed: Football (Newcastle
Utd and Middlesbrough), rugby
(Northampton Saints)
Relaxations: Golf; 'spend a lot of time in the
gym during the off-season'

Appointed to 1st-Class list: 1992
International panel: 1996-2002
Tests umpired: 15 (plus 1 as TV umpire)
One-Day Internationals umpired: 31 (plus 13 as TV umpire)
Other umpiring honours: Has umpired three B&H finals and one NatWest final and
stood in the inaugural C&G final 2001 and the 2002 final; also officiated at the
inaugural Twenty20 finals day at Trent Bridge 2003 and at finals day 2005 at The
Oval. Has stood in four overseas tournaments, including the Singer Cup (India, Sri
Lanka, Pakistan) in Singapore 1995-96 and the Singer Champions Trophy (Pakistan,
Sri Lanka, New Zealand) in Sharjah 1996-97
County as player: Northamptonshire
Role: Right-hand bat, wicket-keeper
County debut: 1967
County cap: 1973
Benefit: 1982
Overseas tours: England Counties XI to Barbados and Trinidad 1975
Best batting: 98 Northamptonshire v Yorkshire, Northampton 1983
Best bowling: 1-47 Northamptonshire v Yorkshire, Northampton 1980

First-Class Career Performances

	M	Inns	NO	Runs	HS	Avge	100s	Ct	St	Runs	Wkts	Avge	Best	5wI	10wM
Test															
All First	306	396	81	6254	98	19.85	-	565	90	70	1	70.00	1-47	-	-

STEELE, J. F.

Name: <u>John</u> Frederick Steele
Born: 23 July 1946, Stafford
Height: 5ft 10in
Nickname: Steely
Wife and date of marriage: Susan,
17 April 1977
Children: Sarah Jane, 2 April 1982;
Robert Alfred, 10 April 1985
Family links with cricket: Uncle Stan
played for Staffordshire. Brother David
played for Northamptonshire, Derbyshire and
England. Cousin Brian Crump played for
Northamptonshire and Staffordshire
Education: Endon School, Stoke-on-Trent;
Stafford College
Other sports followed: Soccer (Stoke City,
Port Vale), golf
Relaxations: Music and walking
Appointed to 1st-Class list: 1997
Counties as player: Leicestershire, Glamorgan
Role: Right-hand bat, slow left-arm bowler
County debut: 1970 (Leicestershire), 1984 (Glamorgan)
County cap: 1971 (Leicestershire), 1984 (Glamorgan)
Benefit: 1983 (Leicestershire)
1000 runs in a season: 6
One-Day 100s: 1
One-Day 5 w. in innings: 4
Overseas teams played for: Springs HSOB, Northern Transvaal 1971-73;
Pine Town CC, Natal 1973-74, 1982-83; Natal 1975-76, 1978-79
Extras: Played for England U25. Was voted Natal's Best Bowler in 1975-76. First-wicket record partnership for Leicestershire of 390 with Barry Dudleston v Derbyshire
at Leicester 1979. Won two Man of the Match Awards in the Gillette Cup and four in
the Benson and Hedges Cup. Won the award for the most catches in a season in 1984
Best batting: 195 Leicestershire v Derbyshire, Leicester 1971
Best bowling: 7-29 Natal B v Griqualand West, Umzinto 1973-74
7-29 Leicestershire v Gloucestershire, Leicester 1980

First-class career performances

	M	Inns	NO	Runs	HS	Avge	100s	Ct	St	Runs	Wkts	Avge	Best	5wI	10wM
Test															
All First	379	605	85	15053	195	28.94	21	414	-	15793	584	27.04	7-29	16	-

WILLEY, P.

Name: Peter Willey
Born: 6 December 1949, Sedgefield,
County Durham
Height: 6ft 1in
Nickname: Will, 'many unprintable'
Wife and date of marriage: Charmaine,
23 September 1971
Children: Heather Jane, 11 September 1985;
David, 28 February 1990
Family links with cricket: Father played
local club cricket in County Durham
Education: Seaham Secondary School,
County Durham
Other sports followed: All sports
Relaxations: 'Dog-walking, keeping fit (??),
fishing'
Appointed to 1st-Class list: 1993
International panel: 1996-2003
Tests umpired: 25 (plus 7 as TV umpire)
One-Day Internationals umpired: 34 (plus 16 as TV umpire)
Other umpiring honours: Stood in the 1999 and 2002-03 World Cups, in the 1999
Benson and Hedges Super Cup final and in the 2004 C&G Trophy final. Officiated at
Twenty20 finals day at The Oval 2005, including the final. Chairman of the First-Class
Umpires' Association
Counties as player: Northamptonshire, Leicestershire
Role: Right-hand bat, off-break bowler
County debut: 1966 (Northamptonshire), 1984 (Leicestershire)
County cap: 1971 (Northamptonshire), 1984 (Leicestershire)
Benefit: 1981 (Northamptonshire; £31,400)
Test debut: 1976
Tests: 26
One-Day Internationals: 26
1000 runs in a season: 10
50 wickets in a season: 2
1st-Class 200s: 1
One-Day 100s: 9
Overseas tours: England to Australia and India 1979-80, to West Indies 1980-81,
1985-86; unofficial England XI to South Africa 1981-82
Overseas teams played for: Eastern Province, South Africa 1982-85
Extras: Became youngest player ever to play for Northamptonshire, at 16 years 180
days, v Cambridge University in 1966. Leicestershire captain 1987. Played for

Northumberland in 1992. Offered membership of the ICC Elite Panel of umpires in 2002 but declined because of the amount of time the appointment would require away from his family

Opinions on cricket: 'Game is being made too complicated from U9 to first-class at county level. Kids can't enjoy the game. They have too many different coaches giving different opinions so they get confused. Some of the coaches may have passed all the exams, but they frighten me to death with the things they come out with. Keep it simple. Concentrate more on cricket and less on fitness. [Have] no technique and it doesn't matter how fit you are.'

Best batting: 227 Northamptonshire v Somerset, Northampton 1976
Best bowling: 7-37 Northamptonshire v Oxford University, The Parks 1975

First-Class Career Performances

	M	Inns	NO	Runs	HS	Avge	100s	Ct	St	Runs	Wkts	Avge	Best	5wI	10wM
Test	26	50	6	1184	102*	26.90	2	3	-	456	7	65.14	2-73	-	-
All First	559	918	121	24361	227	30.56	44	235	-	23400	756	30.95	7-37	26	3

APPENDICES

Roll of Honour 2005
First-class Averages 2005
Index of Players by County

ROLL OF HONOUR 2005

FRIZZELL COUNTY CHAMPIONSHIP

Division One

		P	W	L	D	T	Bt	Bl	Pts
1	Nottinghamshire (II/1)	16	9	3	4	0	50	44	236
2	Hampshire (II/2)	16	9	3	4	0	46	46	233.5
3	Sussex (I/5)	16	7	3	6	0	57	45	224
4	Warwickshire (I/1)	16	8	5	3	0	42	44	209.5
5	Kent (I/2)	16	6	3	7	0	57	42	202.5
6	Middlesex (I/4)	16	4	5	7	0	56	42	181.5
7	Surrey (I/3)	16	4	3	9	0	53	44	180.5
8	Gloucestershire (I/6)	16	1	10	5	0	26	46	104
9	Glamorgan (II/3)	16	1	14	1	0	33	38	88.5

The bottom three counties were relegated to Division Two for the 2006 season

Division Two

		P	W	L	D	T	Bt	Bl	Pts
1	Lancashire (I/8)	16	7	3	6	0	43	47	212
2	Durham (II/9)	16	6	2	8	0	45	44	205
3	Yorkshire (II/7)	16	5	1	10	0	49	42	200.5
4	Northamptonshire (I/9)	16	5	3	8	0	45	46	193
5	Essex (II/5)	16	5	4	7	0	51	36	185
6	Worcestershire (I/7)	16	5	7	4	0	53	46	179.5
7	Leicestershire (II/6)	16	3	6	7	0	45	45	159.5
8	Somerset (II/4)	16	4	7	5	0	42	37	155
9	Derbyshire (II/8)	16	1	8	7	0	31	43	116

The top three counties were promoted to Division One for the 2006 season

Teams are docked 0.5 points for each over they fail to bowl of the target figure of 16 per hour over the course of a match. The following sides incurred deductions in 2005: Hampshire 0.5, Warwickshire 0.5, Kent 0.5, Middlesex 0.5, Surrey 0.5, Gloucestershire 2, Glamorgan 0.5, Yorkshire 0.5, Worcestershire 5.5, Leicestershire 0.5. In addition on 27 May Surrey were deducted 8 points for ball tampering and on 2 June Kent were docked 8 points for a 'poor' pitch at Maidstone.

TOTESPORT LEAGUE

Division One

		P	W	L	T	NR	Pts
1	Essex (I/6)	16	13	1	0	2	56
2	Middlesex (II/1)	16	10	5	0	1	42
3	Northamptonshire (I/4)	16	7	7	0	2	32
4	Glamorgan (I/1)	16	6	6	0	4	32
5	Nottinghamshire (II/3)	16	6	7	0	3	30
6	Lancashire (I/2)	16	6	9	0	1	26
7	Gloucestershire (I/5)	16	6	9	0	1	26
8	Worcestershire (II/2)	16	5	10	0	1	22
9	Hampshire (I/3)	16	5	10	0	1	22

The bottom three counties were relegated to Division Two for the 2006 season

Division Two

		P	W	L	T	NR	Pts
1	Sussex (II/5)	18	13	4	0	1	54
2	Durham (II/6)	18	12	4	0	2	52
3	Warwickshire (I/7)	18	10	6	0	2	44
4	Leicestershire (II/7)	18	10	7	0	1	42
5	Derbyshire (II/9)	18	9	7	1	1	40
6	Somerset (II/8)	18	9	8	0	1	38
7	Surrey (I/9)	18	7	10	0	1	30
8	Kent (I/8)	18	6	10	0	2	28
9	Yorkshire (II/4)	18	5	13	0	0	20
10	Scotland (II/10)	18	2	14	1	1	12

The top three counties were promoted to Division One for the 2006 season

CHELTENHAM & GLOUCESTER TROPHY

Winners: Hampshire   **Runners-up:** Warwickshire

TWENTY20 CUP

Winners: Somerset   **Runners-up:** Lancashire
Semi-finalists: Leicestershire, Surrey

2005 AVERAGES (all first-class matches)

BATTING AVERAGES – including fielding
Qualifying requirements: 6 completed innings and an average of over 10.00

Name	Matches	Inns	NO	Runs	HS	Avge	100s	50s	Ct	St
S R Watson	5	8	1	540	203*	77.14	1	3	10	-
M E K Hussey	10	18	4	1074	253	76.71	3	5	19	-
M R Ramprakash	14	23	2	1568	252	74.66	6	5	8	-
C J L Rogers	3	6	0	441	209	73.50	1	2	4	-
A Flower	16	25	6	1349	188	71.00	6	4	11	-
D J Hussey	16	21	2	1293	232*	68.05	3	8	30	-
G C Smith	4	8	1	472	311	67.42	1	1	7	-
O A Shah	17	31	5	1728	173*	66.46	7	8	22	-
P A Jaques	13	23	2	1359	219	64.71	4	6	14	-
S C Ganguly	5	9	2	438	142	62.57	1	3	2	-
A Symonds	7	10	0	623	146	62.30	3	1	4	-
E C Joyce	16	29	2	1668	192	61.77	3	13	15	-
S P Fleming	11	16	1	908	238	60.53	4	2	14	-
R W T Key	15	27	1	1556	189	59.84	4	8	8	-
A McGrath	16	28	4	1425	173*	59.37	5	5	20	-
D M Benkenstein	17	25	4	1236	162*	58.85	4	5	12	-
Tushar Imran	5	9	1	467	119	58.37	2	2	-	-
M W Goodwin	15	25	1	1380	158	57.50	4	7	8	-
B F Smith	18	30	3	1546	172	57.25	6	5	20	-
R C Irani	16	23	2	1202	103	57.23	1	10	5	-
M H Yardy	18	30	3	1520	257	56.29	5	6	16	-
M L Love	15	25	1	1345	177	56.04	4	6	36	-
M T G Elliott	7	14	0	746	162	53.28	2	5	6	-
J E R Gallian	17	27	4	1220	199	53.04	3	5	14	-
Azhar Mahmood	9	13	2	582	204*	52.90	1	2	10	-
J M Kemp	8	12	2	527	124	52.70	2	2	8	-
A N Cook	17	30	2	1466	195	52.35	5	6	12	-
I D Blackwell	17	28	4	1256	191	52.33	3	9	5	-
J L Langer	7	13	2	574	115	52.18	2	3	3	-
Javed Omar	4	7	0	365	167	52.14	1	1	1	-
N Pothas	15	24	5	973	139	51.21	3	5	48	3
D J Bicknell	17	27	3	1222	123	50.91	2	10	3	-
P D Collingwood	14	25	3	1120	190	50.90	6	-	16	-
R T Ponting	7	12	1	557	156	50.63	2	2	5	-
J L Sadler	6	10	4	302	82*	50.33	-	3	4	-
M B Loye	16	25	1	1198	200	49.91	4	3	11	-
M J DiVenuto	13	26	2	1193	203	49.70	3	5	12	-

Name	Matches	Inns	NO	Runs	HS	Avge	100s	50s	Ct	St
D I Stevens	16	27	1	1277	208	49.11	4	6	13	-
D A Mascarenhas	11	18	7	540	103*	49.09	2	1	5	-
C White	16	26	8	873	110*	48.50	1	8	10	-
M E Trescothick	11	18	0	872	194	48.44	2	3	13	-
S C Moore	18	33	4	1399	246	48.24	2	6	11	-
M J Wood (So)	13	23	1	1058	297	48.09	2	7	4	-
S A Newman	16	27	0	1286	219	47.62	4	4	14	-
I J Sutcliffe	15	25	3	1046	153	47.54	2	7	15	-
U Afzaal	17	28	3	1187	168 *	47.48	5	1	9	-
D J G Sales	16	27	2	1171	190	46.84	3	6	20	-
J G E Benning	4	7	0	325	124	46.42	1	3	1	-
J P Crawley	16	29	2	1246	311*	46.14	3	4	14	1
A D Brown	16	26	5	958	152*	45.61	3	2	19	-
N V Knight	17	30	3	1222	117	45.25	4	5	9	-
I R Bell	15	26	3	1033	231	44.91	2	6	14	-
K P Pietersen	11	21	1	897	158	44.85	3	4	4	-
K A Parsons	8	12	3	401	94	44.55	-	2	5	-
C M W Read	16	21	4	756	103*	44.47	1	7	62	2
M van Jaarsveld	16	28	1	1198	262*	44.37	4	4	18	-
P N Weekes	16	26	7	842	128*	44.31	1	5	7	-
D L Hemp	16	32	1	1369	171*	44.16	3	8	9	-
J N Batty	16	25	3	961	124	43.68	1	8	50	4
R Clarke	13	22	4	776	127*	43.11	2	3	16	-
M L Hayden	7	12	1	472	138	42.90	1	2	14	-
I J Harvey	13	20	2	772	209*	42.88	2	4	8	-
D D J Robinson	16	27	1	1108	139	42.61	4	4	13	-
C J Adams	17	27	2	1060	120*	42.40	1	9	23	-
I J L Trott	18	30	2	1161	210	41.46	4	2	32	-
Mushfiqur Rahim	4	7	1	248	115*	41.33	1	1	2	-
G P Thorpe	10	14	3	454	95	41.27	-	4	5	-
J D Francis	17	31	5	1062	125*	40.84	4	5	8	-
D Mongia	11	17	0	684	164	40.23	1	5	5	-
S D Stubbings	16	29	1	1126	151	40.21	2	8	9	-
E T Smith	17	32	0	1274	145	39.81	2	7	12	-
M J Walker	16	28	3	993	173	39.72	3	4	8	-
W I Jefferson	15	26	2	938	149	39.08	2	4	11	-
A Flintoff	11	16	1	586	102	39.06	1	5	8	-
S G Law	15	24	2	858	143	39.00	3	2	18	-
P J Horton	6	9	0	350	99	38.88	-	2	2	1
I J Ward	10	16	0	620	150	38.75	2	2	3	-
M P Bicknell	8	11	2	347	76	38.55	-	3	4	-
H D Ackerman	17	29	2	1040	125	38.51	2	7	9	-
A G Botha	17	28	7	808	156*	38.47	1	2	7	-
A J Hall	11	16	2	538	133	38.42	1	2	9	-

Name	Matches	Inns	NO	Runs	HS	Avge	100s	50s	Ct	St
B M Shafayat	17	28	0	1058	161	37.78	2	6	21	-
M P Vaughan	9	15	0	564	166	37.60	2	2	2	-
S M Katich	14	24	1	863	128	37.52	1	6	12	-
A P R Gidman	16	30	3	1012	142	37.48	3	4	14	-
J C Hildreth	16	29	4	937	125*	37.48	2	6	15	-
A Habib	13	21	2	705	153*	37.10	1	3	8	-
D Gough	10	10	2	296	93	37.00	-	2	1	-
T J Murtagh	9	11	3	296	74*	37.00	-	2	4	-
J J Sayers	10	17	1	592	115	37.00	2	2	11	-
D R Martyn	6	10	1	332	154*	36.88	1	1	4	-
W R Smith	7	10	1	332	156	36.88	1	1	4	-
J S Foster	17	25	4	771	107*	36.71	1	5	35	6
L C Parker	9	15	3	440	89	36.66	-	2	5	-
R S Bopara	17	29	5	880	105*	36.66	1	5	7	-
R S C Martin-Jenkins	15	20	4	586	88	36.62	-	2	4	-
M J Wood (Y)	17	30	2	1005	202*	35.89	1	6	20	-
W J Durston	7	11	2	323	146*	35.88	1	-	5	-
M J Chilton	17	28	3	895	130	35.80	3	2	10	-
P A Nixon	16	27	7	708	85	35.40	-	6	40	4
M A Butcher	5	8	0	283	90	35.37	-	2	3	-
C G Taylor	9	17	1	563	176	35.18	1	2	5	-
S M Davies	11	19	1	627	148	34.83	1	2	11	3
B L Hutton	17	31	2	1010	152	34.82	2	4	24	-
M J Powell (Gla)	17	32	2	1044	111	34.80	1	6	10	-
I J Westwood	11	22	4	624	106	34.66	1	3	6	-
G A Hick	16	29	2	932	176	34.51	2	5	36	-
C M Spearman	14	27	0	930	216	34.44	1	3	13	-
M J Lumb	11	21	4	584	130	34.35	2	1	10	-
J W M Dalrymple	13	23	2	721	108	34.33	1	6	3	-
M J Clarke	7	12	0	412	91	34.33	-	3	3	-
N J Astle	5	8	0	273	65	34.12	-	3	3	-
J Moss	17	31	1	1021	109*	34.03	2	7	11	-
Shahriar Nafees	7	13	1	408	63	34.00	-	4	1	-
A R Adams	12	12	1	373	103	33.90	1	-	14	-
J D Middlebrook	16	23	5	609	71	33.83	-	3	9	-
M J Prior	17	27	1	874	109	33.61	2	6	45	1
W K Hegg	15	21	6	502	77*	33.46	-	3	41	5
L D Sutton	17	29	4	833	95	33.32	-	4	52	-
T J New	7	11	1	329	89	32.90	-	2	7	1
G R Breese	17	24	2	715	79*	32.50	-	7	16	-
B J Hodge	8	13	1	390	110*	32.50	1	1	7	-
J O Troughton	12	18	0	583	119	32.38	1	5	6	-
A V Suppiah	7	13	0	419	123	32.23	1	2	1	-
Habibul Bashar	4	7	1	193	75	32.16	-	2	1	-

Name	Matches	Inns	NO	Runs	HS	Avge	100s	50s	Ct	St
A G R Loudon	17	30	4	834	95*	32.07	-	5	12	-
C H Gayle	3	6	0	192	57	32.00	-	2	6	-
B J Phillips	13	20	6	447	58	31.92	-	2	2	-
D G Cork	14	19	2	540	102*	31.76	1	5	12	-
Aftab Ahmed	4	7	1	190	82*	31.66	-	1	-	-
R R Sarwan	7	14	0	442	117	31.57	1	2	9	-
G Welch	17	29	3	818	112	31.46	1	4	9	-
R S Clinton	15	26	0	811	106	31.19	2	5	8	-
Z de Bruyn	11	16	0	498	161	31.12	1	2	10	-
D D Cherry	14	27	0	838	226	31.03	2	1	1	-
J J B Lewis	10	17	1	495	68	30.93	-	3	8	-
S K Warne	16	27	3	742	107*	30.91	2	2	18	-
V S Solanki	13	21	2	585	80	30.78	-	4	9	-
R K J Dawson	14	18	4	430	86	30.71	-	3	8	-
S J Adshead	18	33	3	920	148*	30.66	1	5	40	6
M H Wessels	14	23	3	613	107	30.65	3	2	23	4
C W G Bassano	9	14	0	429	87	30.64	-	2	4	-
G J Muchall	17	29	4	764	123	30.56	1	3	6	-
S M Ervine	16	28	1	821	75	30.40	-	7	8	-
M J Powell (Wa)	13	22	2	608	146	30.40	1	2	8	-
R R Montgomerie	18	30	2	851	184*	30.39	2	3	11	-
M A Ealham	15	19	3	484	72	30.25	-	3	5	-
M Burns	9	17	1	484	87	30.25	-	2	4	-
S B Styris	9	17	1	484	100*	30.25	1	3	4	-
J J McLean	6	9	1	242	68	30.25	-	3	4	-
W P U J C Vaas	7	10	1	271	45	30.11	-	-	3	-
A Singh	7	10	0	301	131	30.10	1	1	2	-
D P Fulton	16	29	1	833	110	29.75	1	5	16	-
A K D Gray	8	13	5	237	77*	29.62	-	1	9	-
W P C Weston	13	24	0	710	103	29.58	1	5	4	-
A J Strauss	11	20	0	588	129	29.40	2	1	12	-
R A White	15	24	2	644	95	29.27	-	2	10	-
R J Warren	9	13	1	351	60*	29.25	-	3	6	-
Hassan Adnan	16	29	1	817	191	29.17	2	3	9	-
Naved-ul-Hasan	9	14	2	346	139	28.83	1	-	5	-
M M Patel	16	21	4	487	87	28.64	-	4	3	-
G J Batty	15	20	4	456	57	28.50	-	3	11	-
J K Maunders	16	27	0	759	148	28.11	1	3	7	-
G M Scott	7	13	2	307	61*	27.90	-	1	2	-
R J Turner	9	13	3	277	68*	27.70	-	1	22	1
Nazimuddin	5	7	0	190	60	27.14	-	2	3	-
T R Ambrose	7	10	1	244	78	27.11	-	1	14	2
M J Saggers	9	13	5	216	45	27.00	-	-	5	-
C J C Wright	5	6	0	161	76	26.83	-	1	1	-

Name	Matches	Inns	NO	Runs	HS	Avge	100s	50s	Ct	St
M A Wallace	17	30	2	746	96	26.64	-	6	31	4
C E W Silverwood	6	7	0	186	80	26.57	-	2	3	-
R D B Croft	17	30	2	743	90	26.53	-	3	5	-
D G Wright	16	25	2	609	85	26.47	-	4	6	-
D L Maddy	15	25	0	660	124	26.40	1	1	17	-
P Mustard	17	23	1	578	80	26.27	-	3	45	3
C D Hopkinson	8	13	0	341	64	26.23	-	3	3	-
P D Trego	7	10	1	234	72	26.00	-	2	2	-
D R Brown	17	26	2	616	122	25.66	1	2	14	-
S T Jayasuriya	7	13	0	327	73	25.15	-	3	2	-
Alok Kapali	5	8	1	175	59	25.00	-	1	1	-
J Lewis	12	19	6	324	55	24.92	-	1	5	-
J N Gillespie	5	8	2	149	53*	24.83	-	1	1	-
B J M Scott	16	23	5	442	64*	24.55	-	3	44	6
N J O'Brien	14	22	4	442	64	24.55	-	3	46	5
D K H Mitchell	6	10	2	196	63*	24.50	-	2	6	-
Khaled Mashud	4	6	0	146	44	24.33	-	-	7	-
C T Tremlett	11	14	5	219	64	24.33	-	1	3	-
C W Henderson	15	21	4	413	55	24.29	-	2	6	-
C D McMillan	4	8	1	169	52	24.14	-	1	-	-
J H K Adams	8	13	0	310	71	23.84	-	3	8	-
C M Gazzard	8	10	2	190	74	23.75	-	1	15	-
G O Jones	10	16	2	330	85	23.57	-	1	41	2
B Lee	6	10	3	164	47	23.42	-	-	2	-
D A Cosker	12	20	7	304	52	23.38	-	1	5	-
M J Brown	13	25	1	560	54	23.33	-	3	13	-
A C Gilchrist	6	10	1	207	49*	23.00	-	-	20	1
A A Noffke	6	8	2	138	65	23.00	-	1	1	-
M J Dennington	4	8	1	161	55	23.00	-	2	3	-
J A Pearson	5	10	1	206	68	22.88	-	2	2	-
M G N Windows	11	22	1	479	65*	22.80	-	2	2	-
J Hughes	13	25	2	511	134*	22.21	2	-	10	-
G Chapple	14	20	1	422	82	22.21	-	3	5	-
G R Napier	8	7	0	153	55	21.85	-	2	2	-
Younis Khan	5	7	1	131	53	21.83	-	1	4	-
I Dawood	12	17	2	326	62*	21.73	-	2	34	1
H H Streak	9	11	2	194	51	21.55	-	1	8	-
A P Davies	7	12	4	172	41*	21.50	-	-	3	-
Kadeer Ali	13	25	2	494	66	21.47	-	4	8	-
G P Swann	16	17	2	322	63	21.46	-	2	7	-
A Khan	14	17	9	170	58*	21.25	-	1	2	-
Mohammad Ashraful	5	9	1	169	102	21.12	1	-	3	-
A F Giles	9	16	3	274	62	21.07	-	2	5	-
V Atri	3	6	0	126	67	21.00	-	1	3	-

Name	Matches	Inns	NO	Runs	HS	Avge	100s	50s	Ct	St
T Frost	16	25	2	482	91	20.95	-	2	42	1
G W Flower	12	19	0	397	115	20.89	1	3	5	-
I D Fisher	9	17	2	310	43	20.66	-	-	8	-
Kabir Ali	13	18	2	328	57	20.50	-	2	9	-
A G B Wharf	12	21	0	430	113	20.47	1	1	10	-
T J Friend	3	6	0	120	82	20.00	-	1	2	-
T T Bresnan	15	20	3	339	74	19.94	-	3	4	-
A R Caddick	11	16	3	256	54	19.69	-	1	3	-
A W Laraman	9	13	1	236	53	19.66	-	2	2	-
S D Udal	11	14	4	196	47*	19.60	-	-	7	-
S D Thomas	7	14	0	274	63	19.57	-	1	-	-
D D Masters	13	16	6	195	36	19.50	-	-	4	-
N M Carter	15	23	3	389	82	19.45	-	1	7	-
R J Kirtley	17	23	13	194	30	19.40	-	-	7	-
G J Kruis	16	18	9	174	37*	19.33	-	-	5	-
D J Pipe	12	19	2	326	80*	19.17	-	1	43	2
O D Gibson	15	24	4	379	91	18.95	-	2	2	-
Mushtaq Ahmed	16	22	3	360	90*	18.94	-	2	4	-
J D C Bryant	4	8	1	132	61	18.85	-	1	2	-
S D Peters	9	16	1	282	88	18.80	-	2	6	-
N Peng	10	15	0	282	87	18.80	-	1	-	-
C T Peploe	7	10	2	147	42	18.37	-	-	2	-
S I Mahmood	8	10	0	177	57	17.70	-	1	-	-
A P Palladino	8	11	5	106	30	17.66	-	-	3	-
T H C Hancock	5	9	1	141	41*	17.62	-	-	11	-
M A Hardinges	13	25	2	404	58*	17.56	-	1	10	-
R T Timms	3	6	0	105	57	17.50	-	1	-	-
R N Grant	4	7	1	103	33	17.16	-	-	1	-
M A Sheikh	5	8	0	137	55	17.12	-	1	-	-
L E Plunkett	14	19	4	256	74*	17.06	-	1	6	-
M M Betts	9	10	2	136	36*	17.00	-	-	-	-
U D U Chandana	6	10	2	136	49*	17.00	-	-	2	-
G A Lamb	9	15	0	250	75	16.66	-	2	13	-
J Louw	15	20	3	277	64	16.29	-	2	2	-
I J Thomas	4	8	0	129	40	16.12	-	-	2	-
L J Wright	7	8	0	126	37	15.75	-	-	5	-
Nafees Iqbal	9	16	0	250	46	15.62	-	-	1	-
I D Hunter	13	20	6	212	40	15.14	-	-	3	-
M S Mason	16	23	5	267	38	14.83	-	-	2	-
R E Watkins	5	9	0	131	41	14.55	-	-	-	-
B J France	7	13	0	189	56	14.53	-	1	3	-
R L Johnson	11	15	0	218	35	14.53	-	-	5	-
J Ormond	9	11	2	129	35	14.33	-	-	2	-
N G E Walker	10	14	3	156	79	14.18	-	1	4	-

Name	Matches	Inns	NO	Runs	HS	Avge	100s	50s	Ct	St
Shoaib Akhtar	4	7	1	84	35	14.00	-	-	1	-
Mohammad Rafique	4	6	0	84	54	14.00	-	1	1	-
M J G Davis	6	6	0	84	50	14.00	-	1	-	-
C M Bandara	8	14	0	194	70	13.85	-	1	6	-
M Davies	12	14	5	120	62	13.33	-	1	2	-
M Muralitharan	6	8	2	78	24*	13.00	-	-	3	-
P S Jones	6	6	0	78	51	13.00	-	1	-	-
J M M Averis	10	16	1	194	33	12.93	-	-	2	-
A Richardson	13	16	5	137	25	12.45	-	-	2	-
M J Hoggard	13	16	3	161	64*	12.38	-	1	4	-
S J Cook	14	18	2	193	38	12.06	-	-	3	-
Rajin Saleh	4	7	1	71	30*	11.83	-	-	2	-
D S Harrison	17	29	2	318	75*	11.77	-	1	9	-
R J Sidebottom	15	15	4	129	31	11.72	-	-	6	-
C C Benham	5	10	0	117	41	11.70	-	-	5	-
Syed Rasel	5	7	0	76	33	10.85	-	-	1	-
S C J Broad	10	12	2	107	31	10.70	-	-	1	-
M Ntini	6	8	1	74	27*	10.57	-	-	1	-
G J Smith	15	16	3	137	26	10.53	-	-	4	-
S P Kirby	13	21	11	105	15*	10.50	-	-	-	-
J M Anderson	16	19	5	145	37*	10.35	-	-	8	-

BOWLING AVERAGES
Qualifying requirements: 10 wickets taken, having bowled in a minimum of 6 innings

Name	Overs	Mdns	Runs	Wkts	Avge	Best	5wI	10wM
M Muralitharan	233.2	69	540	36	15.00	6-50	4	-
M A Davies	296.4	94	810	49	16.53	6-32	2	-
S D Udal	274.3	54	832	44	18.90	6-44	3	-
Naved-ul-Hasan	313.1	53	1076	54	19.92	5-41	2	-
M A Ealham	390.5	90	1165	56	20.80	5-31	1	-
S J Harmison	346.1	54	1142	54	21.14	6-52	4	-
G Chapple	383.1	98	1010	47	21.48	5-22	2	-
J D Lewry	350	80	1044	48	21.75	6-65	4	-
M S Panesar	429.2	106	1146	51	22.47	7-181	4	1
S K Warne	650.3	98	1958	87	22.50	6-46	4	2
R J Sidebottom	433.4	130	1132	50	22.64	5-61	1	-
G Keedy	265.3	67	753	33	22.81	6-33	2	1
D J Wainwright	142	34	416	18	23.11	4-48	-	-
J T A Bruce	91	13	324	14	23.14	3-42	-	-
G D McGrath	134	22	440	19	23.15	5-53	2	-
S B Styris	230.5	44	730	31	23.54	6-73	2	1
D A Mascarenhas	273.4	65	801	34	23.55	5-55	2	-

Name	Overs	Mdns	Runs	Wkts	Avge	Best	5wI	10wM
M L Lewis	169	27	614	26	23.61	5-80	1	-
C M Bandara	352.4	69	1087	45	24.15	5-45	2	-
R J Kirtley	525.1	130	1533	63	24.33	6-80	2	-
S P Jones	230.4	46	808	33	24.48	6-53	2	-
A Flintoff	250.5	43	852	34	25.05	5-78	1	-
A Richardson	471.4	109	1438	57	25.22	7-113	3	-
L J Wright	111	23	329	13	25.30	3-33	-	-
A J Hall	347.5	71	1028	40	25.70	4-32	-	-
G J Smith	393.5	97	1314	51	25.76	5-19	1	-
Harbhajan Singh	187.1	42	517	20	25.85	6-36	1	-
G Welch	549.3	139	1559	60	25.98	5-63	3	-
D G Cork	395.3	98	1118	43	26.00	4-27	-	-
S P Kirby	349.5	79	1170	45	26.00	4-20	-	-
Syed Rasel	136.2	24	520	20	26.00	7-50	1	1
I J Harvey	288.3	83	788	30	26.26	5-40	1	-
D G Wright	480	139	1398	53	26.37	8-60	2	-
A J Harris	325.2	54	1293	49	26.38	6-76	3	-
D D Masters	305.2	85	903	34	26.55	6-74	1	-
Mushtaq Ahmed	600.5	82	2139	80	26.73	6-44	4	1
C T Tremlett	334	57	1232	46	26.78	6-44	2	-
H H Streak	254.2	67	708	26	27.23	6-31	2	-
J K Maunders	105	16	384	14	27.42	4-28	-	-
S R Clark	120.4	22	412	15	27.46	5-61	1	-
M M Patel	598.4	132	1626	59	27.55	6-53	3	-
P J McMahon	137.5	46	332	12	27.66	5-30	1	-
S C J Broad	214.1	37	831	30	27.70	4-64	-	-
M J Hoggard	401.1	83	1386	50	27.72	5-73	1	-
D M Benkenstein	91.4	20	333	12	27.75	4-29	-	-
A R Caddick	443.1	94	1501	54	27.79	6-96	4	1
J Ormond	301	65	1001	36	27.80	7-63	1	-
W P U J C Vaas	285.4	80	779	28	27.82	3-36	-	-
M N Malik	270.3	58	1002	36	27.83	5-71	1	-
M S Mason	496.4	137	1486	53	28.03	5-34	1	-
J F Brown	629.4	184	1551	55	28.20	6-112	6	2
A Khan	415.2	80	1555	55	28.27	6-73	1	-
N Tahir	83	11	313	11	28.45	3-28	-	-
M A Hardinges	259.5	53	915	32	28.59	5-51	1	-
Shoaib Akhtar	86.3	15	405	14	28.92	6-47	2	-
D H Wigley	97.1	17	380	13	29.23	4-68	-	-
A K Suman	158	45	451	15	30.06	4-59	-	-
A F Giles	323.5	44	1023	34	30.08	6-44	3	-
H T Waters	100	15	332	11	30.18	4-75	-	-
J M Anderson	512.4	99	1813	60	30.21	5-79	1	-
A Symonds	177	37	484	16	30.25	3-80	-	-

Name	Overs	Mdns	Runs	Wkts	Avge	Best	5wI	10wM
M P Bicknell	251.5	55	881	29	30.37	6-56	2	-
S J Cook	397.1	103	1247	41	30.41	5-44	2	-
J Lewis	426.3	106	1309	43	30.44	5-57	2	-
A A Noffke	168	45	489	16	30.56	4-19	-	-
G J Kruis	584.3	135	1961	64	30.64	5-59	4	-
D R Brown	495.3	110	1540	50	30.80	5-128	1	-
L E Plunkett	423	80	1573	51	30.84	5-43	2	-
B V Taylor	187.4	34	587	19	30.89	6-45	1	-
Kabir Ali	376.5	59	1578	51	30.94	4-70	-	-
D Gough	291.5	72	839	27	31.07	5-85	1	-
A J Bichel	120.4	25	441	14	31.50	4-122	-	-
R W Price	372.3	90	964	30	32.13	4-64	-	-
J Louw	415.5	94	1424	44	32.36	6-51	2	-
S M Ervine	374.1	79	1360	42	32.38	5-60	3	-
J M Kemp	109.5	14	359	11	32.63	3-53	-	-
P D Collingwood	185.3	28	687	21	32.71	5-52	1	-
M Ntini	192.1	29	721	22	32.77	5-69	1	-
Danish Kaneria	394.4	86	1069	32	33.40	6-74	3	1
T T Bresnan	459	87	1571	47	33.42	5-42	1	-
R A G Cummins	150	38	468	14	33.42	3-32	-	-
N M Carter	410.4	83	1378	41	33.60	4-30	-	-
P A J DeFreitas	111	21	406	12	33.83	4-76	-	-
A R Adams	391.3	111	1218	36	33.83	5-60	1	-
Azhar Mahmood	227.2	44	884	26	34.00	5-72	1	-
B J Phillips	254	73	728	21	34.66	3-42	-	-
G R Breese	332.1	61	1080	31	34.83	5-83	2	-
J E Anyon	105	15	425	12	35.41	4-33	-	-
Mohammad Akram	366.4	54	1542	43	35.86	5-41	2	-
P D Trego	131	21	576	16	36.00	6-59	1	-
W D Rudge	110.1	21	505	14	36.07	3-46	-	-
A G R Loudon	416.2	48	1356	37	36.64	6-66	2	-
Saqlain Mushtaq	189.5	28	593	16	37.06	4-80	-	-
S I Mahmood	141.2	22	521	14	37.21	3-21	-	-
O D Gibson	498.3	84	1682	45	37.37	6-56	1	-
G J Batty	400	74	1240	33	37.57	5-87	1	-
J Moss	326.1	98	944	25	37.76	4-40	-	-
M M Betts	229.1	45	838	22	38.09	4-58	-	-
B Lee	218.1	30	953	25	38.12	4-53	-	-
M A Sheikh	175.5	44	498	13	38.30	4-67	-	-
D I Stevens	199.4	28	655	17	38.52	3-19	-	-
D Pretorius	126.3	13	464	12	38.66	3-88	-	-
A P R Gidman	124.1	11	508	13	39.07	4-47	-	-
R Clarke	152.1	16	708	18	39.33	4-91	-	-
G P Swann	413.2	89	1307	33	39.60	6-57	1	-

Name	Overs	Mdns	Runs	Wkts	Avge	Best	5wI	10wM
J J van der Wath	104	24	399	10	39.90	3-21	-	-
R K J Dawson	325.4	46	1098	27	40.66	4-54	-	-
J W M Dalrymple	248.4	25	940	23	40.86	4-53	-	-
R S C Martin-Jenkins	283.4	71	824	20	41.20	4-31	-	-
M S Kasprowicz	99	15	417	10	41.70	5-67	1	-
C M Willoughby	429.5	97	1385	33	41.96	4-92	-	-
N A M McLean	123	27	507	12	42.25	3-107	-	-
C K Langeveldt	215.1	59	637	15	42.46	3-67	-	-
M J Saggers	258.3	55	854	20	42.70	5-48	1	-
Shahadat Hossain	178.5	16	813	19	42.78	4-33	-	-
C W Henderson	537.2	121	1416	33	42.90	5-63	1	-
J M M Averis	236	50	865	20	43.25	3-11	-	-
D L Maddy	181	36	568	13	43.69	4-65	-	-
J D Middlebrook	467.3	97	1417	32	44.28	5-54	1	-
I D Hunter	382.3	56	1506	34	44.29	5-63	1	-
A G B Wharf	297.2	40	1245	28	44.46	6-59	2	1
C T Peploe	249	57	801	18	44.50	3-77	-	-
I D Fisher	255.4	47	849	19	44.68	4-89	-	-
A P Palladino	162	36	584	13	44.92	4-74	-	-
G R Napier	166.2	32	634	14	45.28	3-25	-	-
A McGrath	231	36	727	16	45.43	3-35	-	-
G M Andrew	104.5	14	500	11	45.45	4-134	-	-
A G Botha	473.4	109	1506	33	45.63	6-104	1	-
U D U Chandana	239.1	38	740	16	46.25	5-117	1	-
A W Laraman	177	21	602	13	46.30	3-68	-	-
Talha Jubair	117.5	11	608	13	46.76	4-99	-	-
T J Murtagh	163.2	30	563	12	46.91	3-71	-	-
A K D Gray	174.4	28	565	12	47.08	3-56	-	-
N D Doshi	294.1	58	1087	23	47.26	3-58	-	-
R S Bopara	214.2	26	959	20	47.95	4-93	-	-
R D B Croft	577.4	77	2134	43	49.62	5-57	2	1
D A Cosker	395.4	60	1405	28	50.17	4-57	-	-
A P Davies	168.1	30	664	13	51.07	3-121	-	-
R L Johnson	287.3	52	1048	20	52.40	4-118	-	-
N G E Walker	209.5	27	892	17	52.47	4-69	-	-
D S Harrison	417.3	71	1649	31	53.19	5-117	1	-
P N Weekes	237.5	33	765	14	54.64	3-83	-	-
I D Blackwell	517.5	107	1569	28	56.03	4-86	-	-
D W Steyn	199.2	38	838	14	59.85	3-69	-	-

Chance to shine

Chance to shine is the Cricket Foundation's campaign to revitalise competitive cricket in our state schools with the focus squarely on the education and well-being of young people. We intend to:

- Restore our summer game to more than a third of state schools within ten years
- Put in high-quality, sustainable cricket programmes that can make a lasting impact

In our pilot scheme in 2005, twelve responsible, well-run cricket clubs worked with 75 schools – primary and secondary. It was a successful start and this summer we're broadening this to 100 clubs and 600 schools.

Over the ten years, we need to raise £25 million and we expect to attract matched funding from government. We've made a good start: more than £8 million has already been secured through individual donors and our first corporate partner, Allianz Cornhill. You can help us give youngsters the chance to shine:

- Make a one-off donation
- Join the Chance to shine club
- Become a volunteer

For details, go to www.chancetoshine.org or contact **Nick Gandon**, Director of the Cricket Foundation, on **020 7432 1259** or **nickgandon.cricketfoundation@ecb.co.uk**

BRINGING CRICKET TO STATE SCHOOLS

INDEX OF PLAYERS BY COUNTY

*denotes not registered for the 2006 season. Where a player is known to have moved in the off-season he is listed under his new county.

DERBYSHIRE

BASSANO, C.W.G.*
BORRINGTON, P.M.
BOTHA, A.G.
BROWNING, R.J.
BRYANT, J.D.C.*
DEAN, K.J.
DIVENUTO, M.J.
FRANCE, B.J.
FRIEND, T.J.*
GRAY, A.K.D.
HASSAN ADNAN
HAVELL, P.M.R.*
HUGHES, L.D.
HUNTER, I.D.
JONES, P.S.
LUNGLEY, T.
MOHAMMAD YOUSUF
MOSS, J.*
NEEDHAM, J.
PAGET, C.D.
PIPE, D.J.
RUDOLPH, J.A.
SHEIKH, M.A.
SMITH, G.M.
SPENDLOVE, B.L.*
STUBBINGS, S.D.
TAYLOR, C.R.
WAGG, G.G.
WALKER, N.G.E.*
WELCH, G.
WHITE, W.A.

DURHAM

ASTLE, N.J.*
BARRICK, D.J.
BENKENSTEIN, D.M.
BREESE, G.R.
BRIDGE, G.D.
COETZER, K.J.
COLLINGWOOD, P.D.
DAVIES, M.A.
GIBSON, O.D.
HAMILTON, G.M.*
HARMISON, B.W.
HARMISON, S.J.
HUSSEY, M.E.K.
KILLEEN, N.
LEWIS, J.J.B.
LEWIS, M.L.
LOWE, J.A.
MAHER, J.P.*
MUCHALL, G.J.
MUSTARD, P.
NOFFKE, A.A.*
ONIONS, G.
PARK, G.T.
PLUNKETT, L.E.
PRATT, G.J.
SCOTT, G.M.
STONEMAN, M.D.
THORP, C.D.
TURNER, M.L.
WILLIAMS, B.A.*

ESSEX

ADAMS, A.R.
AHMED, J.S.
BICHEL, A.J.
BISHOP, J.E.*
BOPARA, R.S.
CHAMBERS, M.A.
CHOPRA, V.
COOK, A.N.
COWAN, A.P.
DANISH KANERIA*
FLOWER, A.
FLOWER, G.W.
FOSTER, J.S.
GOUGH, D.
IRANI, R.C.
JEFFERSON, W.I.
JOHNSON, M.G.
MIDDLEBROOK, J.D.
NAPIER, G.R.
NEL, A.*
PALLADINO, A.P.
PETTINI, M.L.
PHILLIPS, T.J.
STEYN, D.W.*
TEN DOESCHATE, R.N.
TUDOR, A.J.
WESTFIELD, M.S.

GLAMORGAN

CHERRY, D.D.
COSKER, D.A.
CROFT, R.D.B.
DAVIES, A.P.
ELLIOTT, M.T.G.

INDEX OF PLAYERS BY COUNTY

GANGULY, S.C.*
GRANT, R.N.
HARRISON, A.J.
HARRISON, D.S.
HEMP, D.L.
HUGHES, J.*
JONES, S.P.
KASPROWICZ, M.S.
MAYNARD, M.P.*
O'SHEA, M.P.
PENG, N.
POWELL, M.J.
REES, G.P.
SHAW, A.D.
THOMAS, I.J.*
THOMAS, S.D.
WALLACE, M.A.
WATERS, H.T.
WATKINS, R.E.
WHARF, A.G.B.
WRIGHT, B.J.

GLOUCESTERSHIRE

ADSHEAD, S.J.
ALI, KADEER
ALLEYNE, M.W.
AVERIS, J.M.M.
BALL, M.C.J.
BANDARA, C.M.*
BOND, S.E.
BROWN, D.O.
CHANDANA, U.D.U.*
FISHER, I.D.
GIDMAN, A.P.R.
GREENIDGE, C.G.
HANCOCK, T.H.C.*
HARDINGES, M.A.
HODNETT, G.P.

KIRBY, S.P.
LEWIS, J.
MARSHALL, H.J.H.
PEARSON, J.A.*
RUDGE, W.D.
SARWAN, R.R.*
SNELL, S.D.
SPEARMAN, C.M.
TAYLOR, C.G.
WESTON, W.P.C.
WINDOWS, M.G.N.

HAMPSHIRE

ADAMS, J.H.K.
BALCOMBE, D.J.
BENHAM, C.C.
BROWN, M.J.
BRUCE, J.T.A.
BURROWS, T.G.
CARBERRY, M.A.
CRAWLEY, J.P.
ERVINE, S.M.
GRIFFITHS, D.A.
KATICH, S.M.*
KENWAY, D.A.*
LAMB, G.A.
LATOUF, K.J.
LOGAN, R.J.
MASCARENHAS, D.A.
MCLEAN, J.J.
MCMILLAN, C.D.*
MORRIS, R.K.
MULLALLY, A.D.*
PIETERSEN, K.P.
POTHAS, N.
PRITTIPAUL, L.R.*
STOKES, M.S.T.
TAYLOR, B.V.

THORNELY, D.J.
TOMLINSON, J.A.
TREMLETT, C.T.
UDAL, S.D.
WARNE, S.K.
WATSON, S.R.*

KENT

COOK, S.J.
CUSDEN, S.M.J.
DENLY, J.L.
DENNINGTON, M.J.
DEXTER, N.J.
DIXEY, P.G.
FERLEY, R.S.
FULTON, D.P.
HALL, A.J.
JONES, G.O.
JONES, K.J.F.*
JOSEPH, R.H.
KEMP, J.M.
KEY, R.W.T.
KHAN, A.
O'BRIEN, N.J.
PATEL, M.M.
SAGGERS, M.J.
SHERIYAR, A.*
STEVENS, D.I.
STIFF, D.A.
TREDWELL, J.C.
VAN JAARSVELD, M.
WALKER, M.J.

INDEX OF PLAYERS BY COUNTY

LANCASHIRE

ANDERSON, J.M.
BROWN, K.R.
CHAPPLE, G.
CHILTON, M.J.
CORK, D.G.
CROFT, S.J.
CROOK, A.R.
CROSS, G.D.
FLINTOFF, A.
HEGG, W.K.*
HODGE, B.J.
HOGG, K.W.
HORTON, P.J.
KARTIK, M.*
KEEDY, G.
LAW, S.G.
LOYE, M.B.
MAHMOOD, S.I.
MARSHALL, S.J.
MURALITHARAN, M.*
NEWBY, O.J.
NORTH, M.J.*
SMITH, T.C.
SUTCLIFFE, I.J.
SUTTON, L.D.
SYMONDS, A.*
WATKINSON, M.
YATES, G.

LEICESTERSHIRE

ACKERMAN, H.D.
ALLENBY, J.
BOYCE, M.A.G.
BRIGNULL, D.S.*
BROAD, S.C.J.

CUMMINS, R.A.G.
DAGNALL, C.E.*
DEFREITAS, P.A.J.*
HABIB, A.
HARRISON, P.W.
HENDERSON, C.W.
KREJZA, J.J.*
LIDDLE, C.J.
MADDY, D.L.
MASTERS, D.D.
MAUNDERS, J.K.
MOHAMMAD ASIF
MONGIA, D.
NEW, T.J.
NIXON, P.A.
ROBINSON, D.D.J.
SADLER, J.L.
SNAPE, J.N.

MIDDLESEX

BETTS, M.M.
CLARK, S.R.*
COMPTON, N.R.D.
DALRYMPLE, J.W.M.
FINN, S.T.
GODLEMAN, B-A.
GOLWALKAR, Y.A.*
GOUDIE, G.
HAYWARD, M.*
HUTCHISON, P.M.*
HUTTON, B.L.
JONES, C.M.P.*
JOYCE, E.C.
KEEGAN, C.B.
LOUW, J.
MOHAMMAD ALI
MORGAN, E.J.G.
NASH, D.C.

PATHAN, I.K.*
PEPLOE, C.T.
POYNTER, A.D.
RANKIN, W.B.
RICHARDSON, A.
SCOTT, B.J.M.
SHAH, O.A.
SMITH, E.T.
STRAUSS, A.J.
STYRIS, S.B.
WEEKES, P.N.
WHELAN, C.D.
WILLIAMS, R.E.M.
WRIGHT, C.J.C.

NORTHAMPTONSHIRE

AFZAAL, U.
BAKER, T.M.*
BROWN, J.F.
COVERDALE, P.S.
CROOK, S.P.
FRIEDLANDER, M.J.*
HUGGINS, T.B.*
KING, R.E.*
KLUSENER, L.
LOVE, M.L.*
NICHOLSON, M.J.
PANESAR, M.S.
PETERS, S.D.
PHILLIPS, B.J.
PHYTHIAN, M.J.
PIETERSEN, C.
ROBERTS, T.W.*
ROGERS, C.J.L.
SALES, D.J.G.
SHAFAYAT, B.M.
WESSELS, M.H.
WHITE, A.R.

INDEX OF PLAYERS BY COUNTY

INDEX OF PLAYERS BY COUNTY

WARWICKSHIRE

ALI, M.M.
AMBROSE, T.R.
ANYON, J.E.
BELL, I.R.
BROWN, D.R.
CARTER, N.M.
DAGGETT, L.M.
EUSTACE, S.M.*
FROST, T.
GILES, A.F.
GROENEWALD, T.D.
JAMES, N.A.
KNIGHT, N.V.
LOUDON, A.G.R.
MEES, T.*
NTINI, M.*
PARKER, L.C.
PENNEY, T.L.*
PIPER, K.J.*
POONIA, N.S.
POWELL, M.J.
PRETORIUS, D.*
SHANTRY, A.J.
STREAK, H.H.
TAHIR, N.
TROTT, I.J.L.
TROUGHTON, J.O.
VETTORI, D.L.
WAGH, M.A.
WARREN, N.A.
WESTWOOD, I.J.

WORCESTERSHIRE

ALI, KABIR
BATTY, G.J.
BRACKEN, N.W.
DAVIES, S.M.
DE BRUYN, Z.*
FAISAL SHAHID
FOSTER, E.J.
GAYLE, C.H.*
GIFFORD, W.M.
HICK, G.A.
JAQUES, P.A.
JONES, R.A.
KHALID, S.A.
KNAPPETT, J.P.T.
LEATHERDALE, D.A.*
MALIK, M.N.
MASON, M.S.
MCNALLY, J.D.
MITCHELL, D.K.H.
MOORE, S.C.
PRICE, R.W.
SHOAIB AKHTAR*
SILLENCE, R.J.
SMITH, B.F.
SOLANKI, V.S.
VAAS, W.P.U.J.C.*
WEDGE, S.A.

YORKSHIRE

BLAIN, J.A.R.
BLAKEY, R.J.
BRESNAN, T.T.
BROPHY, G.L.
CLAYDON, M.E.
CLEARY, M.F.*
DAWOOD, I.*
DAWSON, R.K.J.
GALE, A.W.
GILBERT, C.R.
GILLESPIE, J.N.
GUY, S.M.
HARVEY, I.J.*
HOGGARD, M.J.
KRUIS, G.J.
LAWSON, M.A.K.
LEHMANN, D.S.
LUCAS, D.S.*
LUMB, M.J.
MCGRATH, A.
PATTERSON, S.A.
PYRAH, R.M.
SAYERS, J.J.
SHAHZAD, A.
SILVERWOOD, C.E.W.
THORNICROFT, N.D.
VAUGHAN, M.P.
WAINWRIGHT, D.J.
WARREN, A.C.*
WHITE, C.
WOOD, M.J.

QUIZ ANSWERS

1. Dennis Amiss
2. Vic Marks
3. Sachin Tendulkar
4. Ian Botham
5. Five (Jonty Rhodes, SA v WI, Mumbai 1993-94)
6. Martin Snedden (2-105, NZ v E, The Oval 1983)
7. Fidel Edwards (6-22, WI v Z, Harare 2003-04)
8. Marcus Trescothick (114*) and Vikram
   Solanki (106), E v SA, The Oval 2003
9. Viv Richards and Michael Holding
10. Paul Reiffel
11. News arrived of the assassination of Mrs Gandhi
12. Zaheer Abbas
13. Jalaluddin (P v A, Hyderabad 1982)
14. Waqar Younis
15. Imran Khan
16. Bill Athey
17. Roger Twose
18. Geoff Humpage
19. Wasim Akram (502)
20. David Bairstow, Richard Blakey and Steve Rhodes
21. Mark Butcher
22. Tony Dodemaide (Australia)
23. Norman Gifford (1985)
24. Colin and Chris Cowdrey; David and
    Graham Lloyd
25. Justin Langer
26. Jeff Wilson
27. Ken MacLeay (Australia)
28. Kepler Wessels (South Africa)
29. Rohan Gavaskar (son of Sunil)
30. Graham McKenzie (Australia)
31. Alan Knott (E v WI, Scarborough 1976)
32. Asif Iqbal
33. Saeed Anwar
34. Ryan Sidebottom (father Arnie played one Test,
    as has Ryan, but no ODIs)
35. Syed Kirmani (126*, I v Z, Tunbridge Wells 1983)
36. Ashantha de Mel (1-97, SL v WI, Karachi 1987)
37. Mike Hendrick
38. West Indies and Australia (Melbourne 1984)
39. Deryck Murray
40. Wasim Bari, Moin Khan and Rashid Latif
41. S. Venkataraghavan
42. Ian and Greg Chappell; Jeff and Martin Crowe;
    Andy and Grant Flower
43. Paul Collingwood (112* and 6-31, E v Bd,
    Trent Bridge 2005)
44. Martin van Jaarsveld (Talha Jubair)
45. Phil Jaques (94, A v SA, Melbourne 2006)
46. Geoff Arnold (1972); Rikki Clarke (2003)
47. Javed Miandad
48. Mahendra Nagamootoo
49. Mohinder Amarnath
50. Marvan Atapattu (40 times)

51. Chris Pringle (46 in 1994)
52. Bob Simpson (Australia)
53. Sharjah Cricket Association Stadium (198 matches)
54. Yuvraj Singh (son of Yograj)
55. Inzamam-ul-Haq
56. Robin Jackman
57. Jehan Mubarak
58. John Emburey
59. Ian Harvey
60. Gordon Greenidge (1988); Chris Gayle (2004)
61. Ricky Ponting
62. Courtney Browne
63. Desmond Haynes (148, WI v A, Antigua 1978)
64. Brian Close (Test debut 1949; ODI debut 1972)
65. Shane Bond (replaced Nathan Astle and took
    6-19, NZ v I, Bulawayo 2005-06)
66. Javed Omar
67. Lou Vincent (172)
68. Mark Bailey
69. M.J. (Mike) Smith
70. Shane Warne
71. Wayne Larkins (Jan 1980-Oct 1989)
72. Alistair Campbell (Zimbabwe)
73. Matthew Fleming
74. Jimmy Cook and Richard Snell
75. Saqlain Mushtaq (69 in 1997)
76. Bruce Reid took Australia's first ODI hat-trick
    – against New Zealand
77. Peter Kirsten
78. C.Z. Harris (father P.G.Z.) and C.L. Cairns
    (father B.L.) of New Zealand
79. Robin Smith (167*, E v A, Edgbaston 1993)
80. England (24)
81. Phil Simmons (10-8-3-4, WI v P, Sydney 1992)
82. Zimbabwe
83. Andy Bichel (7-20, A v E, Port Elizabeth 2003)
84. Brian Strang and Henry Olonga (twice)
85. 27.2 overs (Z 35 all out; SL 40-1, Harare 2004)
86. Geoff Boycott (two matches)
87. Graeme Hick (64)
88. Ewan Chatfield (10)
89. Adam Gilchrist (Pollock has dismissed him on 11
    occasions)
90. David Shepherd (172)
91. Mudassar Nazar (father Nazar Mohammed)
92. Brett Lee (1-85 twice)
93. Colin (2) and Alan (1) Wells
94. Bruce Edgar (NZ v I, Auckland 1980-81)
95. Dirk Wellham, who captained NSW, Tasmania and
    Queensland
96. Shaun Udal (May 1995-Dec 2005)
97. Brian McKechnie (New Zealand)
98. Len Pascoe (Australia)
99. Alvin Kallicharran
100. Raymond Illingworth (E); Bill Lawry (A)